ENCOUNTERING

CULTURES

ENCOUNTERING CULTURES

Reading and Writing in a Changing World

SECOND EDITION

EDITED BY

RICHARD HOLETON

Stanford University

A BLAIR PRESS BOOK

PRENTICE HALL, ENGLEWOOD CLIFFS, NJ 07632

Encountering cultures: reading and writing in a changing world/
    edited by Richard Holeton. —2nd ed.
        p.   cm.
    "A Blair Press book."
    Includes bibliographical references and indexes.
    ISBN 0-13-299827-0
    1. College readers.   2. English language—Rhetoric.   3. Readers—
Intercultural communication.   4. Intercultural communication—
Problems, exercises, etc.   I. Holeton, Richard
PE1417.E46   1995
808'.0427—dc20   94-43412
                                                                                 CIP

Editorial/production supervision
  and interior design: Joanne Lowry, Sally Steele
Cover design: Louise Fili Design
Buyer: Robert Anderson
Cover photo: Jean-Marc Giboux/Gamma Liaison

Acknowledgments appear on pages 611–615, which constitute
a continuation of the copyright page.

A BLAIR PRESS BOOK

 ©1995 by Richard Holeton
Published by Prentice-Hall, Inc.
A Simon & Schuster Company
Englewood Cliffs, New Jersey 07632

Printed in the United States of America
10   9   8   7   6   5   4   3   2   1

ISBN 0-13-299827-0

Prentice-Hall International (UK) Limited, *London*
Prentice-Hall of Australia Pty. Limited, *Sydney*
Prentice-Hall Canada Inc., *Toronto*
Prentice-Hall Hispanoamericana, S.A., *Mexico*
Prentice-Hall of India Private Limited, *New Delhi*
Prentice-Hall of Japan, Inc., *Tokyo*
Simon & Schuster Asia Pte. Ltd., *Singapore*
Editora Prentice-Hall do Brasil, Ltda., *Rio de Janeiro*

FOR MY MOTHER,
WHO TRIED TO TEACH HER CHILDREN
TO EMBRACE DIFFERENCES.

PREFACE

Encountering Cultures: Reading and Writing in a Changing World,
Second Edition, is an anthology of readings addressing issues of cultural diversity and interaction. It is intended for the growing number
of college writing courses in which instructors wish to integrate an exploration of cultural issues with critical reading and writing.

Features Preserved from the First Edition

In revising the book, I have tried to preserve or enhance the following major features of the first edition.

- *Encountering Cultures* is based on the premises that increasing cultural diversity in North America can be best understood in a global
context and with critical attention to the relationship of culture and
language. The three parts of the book—"Encountering Language
and Culture," "Encountering Diversity at Home," and "Encountering Global Diversity"—bring together major approaches to multicultural issues that are usually treated separately.

- The reading selections and editorial apparatus offer a broad view
of cultural identity and cultural groups and facilitate a critical
thinking approach. They emphasize *interactions* across boundaries
based on ethnicity, national origin, language communities, social
class, gender, sexual orientation, and other cultural identities.
Students are encouraged to make connections between each selection they read and their own experience, their own communities, the other essays and short stories in the book, and outside research sources.

- The selections, all contemporary, embrace the widest possible range of difficulty, viewpoints, purposes, audiences, and styles. They include personal, analytical, and argumentative essays; documented academic writing; and some of today's best short fiction. About half of the authors are people of color, and half are women.
- "Brief Encounters"—short, accessible selections—introduce each thematic chapter. They are useful in the classroom as rhetorical models, as the stimulus for discussion, or as the basis for exercises.

Features New to the Second Edition

In addition to preserving the basic approach and enhancing the strengths of the first edition, my goals in revising *Encountering Cultures* were twofold: to extend the cultural and political range of the readings and to make the book easier to use by streamlining the organization and strengthening the editorial apparatus. Many thoughtful instructors and students who used the first edition were invaluable in offering specific suggestions to help me achieve these goals.

Reading Selections

Thirty-one full-length selections and twenty-five "Brief Encounters" are new to this edition. They offer:

- *More attention to language issues.* Readings that focus on language and culture now comprise one-third of the book. These readings explore how gender, stereotypes, social power, and cultural identity are defined and negotiated through language.
- *More attention to issues of class, sexual orientation, and European-American culture.* New thematic chapters are devoted to class issues and sexual orientation, with a wide range of views represented. Diverse reactions to cultural issues from white and/or male members of the majority are represented by writers such as Eugene August, Barbara Ehrenreich, and Arthur Schlesinger.
- *More attention to global cultural and political issues.* More readings address interactions between West and East and between the First World and Third World. The crucial role of the United States in the post-Cold War era is debated by Patrick Glynn and Noam Chomsky.
- *More, and more diverse, fiction.* This edition includes sixteen short stories (five more than the first edition); each thematic chapter includes one or two stories. Users of the first edition reported that fiction selections can open up cultural issues more vividly and

memorably than essays alone. The eight fiction writers new to this edition include R. K. Narayan, B. Traven, Lucia Berlin, and Nicholasa Mohr.

Organization

Twelve thematic chapters, in three parts, make the book's content clear at a glance and easy to use for both instructors and students. The chapters and parts form logical sequences but are completely independent and may be assigned in any order.

- *Part One: Encountering Language and Culture* explores the relationship of both spoken and written language to gender issues ("Language and Gender"), ethnic stereotypes ("Language and Stereotypes"), social power relations ("Language and Social Power"), and bilingual/bicultural identity ("Language and Bicultural Identity"). Many of the selections in Part One also address educational issues and experiences in various contexts including the public school system, private school, college, and adult literacy programs.

- *Part Two: Encountering Diversity at Home* examines four aspects of domestic diversity: immigration and assimilation ("Coming to America"); ethnic identity and ethnic relations ("Ethnicity and Identity"); social class ("Privilege, Poverty, and Mainstream Values"); and sexual orientation ("Sexual Orientation and Diversity"). Together, these four chapters may be seen to form a wide-ranging investigation of the traditional "American Dream"—who defines it, what constitutes it, and for whom it is a reality.

- *Part Three: Encountering Global Diversity* offers a broad perspective on cultural issues and group relations through encounters with diverse international cultures. At the same time, all four chapters— "Leaving Home," "Encountering Stereotypes," "Meeting the Third World," and "Americans in the 'New World Order'"— examine what constitutes a "Western" or North American viewpoint in approaching the rest of the world. They ask: who exactly are "we" and who are "they"?

Apparatus

- *New introductions for students* to Part One, Part Two, and Part Three suggest specific prereading and prewriting activities for each thematic chapter. The introductions also present the major themes in relation to one another, providing a context for students in which to make direct comparisons among the readings.

- *Questions following each selection,* grounded in reader-response theory, ask students to apply their own experience to their reading,
make judgments, and form interpretations. These questions are
useful for individual or collaborative work, group or class discussion, and prewriting or writing activities. Although new to the
second edition, the questions have been classroom-tested and are
often adapted from questions generated by student discussion
leaders in my courses.

- *Questions at the end of each thematic chapter* provide increased emphasis on critical thinking and collaboration. These "Thinking
about [the theme]" questions ask students to make inferences, test
claims, compare texts directly, evaluate evidence from several
sources, and perform other critical thinking activities. Like the
questions following each selection, end-of-chapter questions have
been classroom-tested and are derived from student-generated
questions and student essays.

- *Expanded opportunities for research* appear in a second group of
"Thinking about [the theme]" questions, called "Exploring
Additional Sources." One or more questions suggest comparisons
with selections in other thematic chapters, while the remaining
questions offer research topics or projects with a range of difficulty, scope, and source material. In addition to traditional library
research, every chapter includes practical suggestions for exploring nonlibrary research sources such as student-generated survey
data, information from community organizations, and personal
interviews with peers, professors, and college staff members.

- *Expanded headnotes* provide more contextualization of the selections. The headnotes remain concise and unobtrusive, but now
they offer fuller information about, for example, the purpose or
audience of a selection's original source. When the source is a
magazine or journal unfamiliar to many students—such as
Commentary or *Z Magazine*—the headnote includes a brief description of the publication from the editors or masthead.

- *A revised Rhetorical Index.* This enhanced index organizes the selections according to traditional rhetorical strategies, with full-
length selections easily distinguished from "Brief Encounters,"
and selections that incorporate documented outside sources
marked with an asterisk for easy reference.

I hope that new and veteran users of *Encountering Cultures* alike
will find the second edition a catalyst for engaging students in the important issues of our time and challenging them to think critically about
those issues. In a separately bound Instructor's Manual, I offer brief

summaries of all the reading selections and suggestions for how to use them, along with responses to all the questions in the book. I welcome your comments about both the Instructor's Manual and the book.

Acknowledgments

Thanks to Nancy Perry for her continuing advice, collaboration, and faith in this book. LeeAnn Einert, formerly of Blair Press, supervised innumerable details of the second edition, including putting together the manuscript. Rosanna Rodriguez picked up where LeeAnn left off, taking charge of final details and reformatting the Instructor's Manual. In association with Blair Press, Christine Rutigliano performed difficult permissions work with unfailing efficiency and grace, and Joanne Lowry and the staff at Thompson Steele Production Services did a terrific job designing and producing the book.

The following instructors and colleagues—including experienced users of the first edition—offered invaluable criticism which shaped the revisions described above: Katya Amato, Portland State University; Cathy Birkenstein, Columbia College; Lisa Boyd, University of Tennessee; Glen Brewster, University of Tennessee; Michelle Cheung, Columbia College; Marie E. Foley, Santa Barbara City College; James Gifford, Mohawk Valley Community College; Juan C. Guerra, University of Washington; Angela James, University of Kansas; Barbara Kappler, University of Minnesota; Daniel Lowe, Community College of Allegheny County; Douglas McKinstry, University of Tennessee; Shirley Morahan, Northeast Missouri State University; Carol A. Moyer, Columbia College; Nedra Reynolds, University of Rhode Island; Timothy L. Roach, Rogue Community College; Victoria L. Shannon, Columbia College; Ann Shillinglaw, Columbia College; Linda J. Strom, Youngstown University; Sandra M. Trammell, Kentucky State University; and Linda Wendling, University of Missouri, St. Louis.

I owe a special debt of gratitude to the Stanford freshman students of English 3B-15 and 3B-18, "Encountering Cultures: The Writer as Traveler," winter and spring quarters, 1993–94: Amanda Anbar, Sean Anderson, Alessia Bell, Katie Bryan-Jones, Carrie Casselman, Alice Cathcart, Gallant Chen, Peggy Chen, Jeff Cislini, Jon Cooper, Jeremy Desmon, Bethany Devine, Josh Galanter, Heather Hardwick, Brad Harrington, Matt Hoffman, Hilary Hoover, Michael Hsueh, Wilmer Huang, Kathleen Hughes, Laura Karassik, Albert Lai, Carter Lipton, Jimmy Lu, Jimmy Miyashiro, Elizabeth Nelson, Hans Park, Heidi Schweiker, Anna Sopko, Vivian Sun, Patrick Unemori, Henry Wu, Ben Yang, Rahul Young, Cindy Yu, and

Christian Zupancic. They were my collaborators in preparing this book. In pairs and groups they planned and led discussions, both in class and across the computer network, about all the readings new to this edition. In composing questions, arguing for their interpretations, summarizing their classmates' responses, and incorporating these layers of critical dialogue into their essay drafts, they taught one another—and me—about the readings. I hope their enthusiasm, thoughtfulness, and insight about cultural issues reverberates through these pages.

Richard Holeton

CONTENTS

When they stepped toward him, he made strange noises as in a foreign
language and ran back into the saw grass.

> *which patter and rub across his person with a soft, sandy insistence*
> *unlike both the fumblings of children and the caresses one Caucasian*
> *adult will give another.*

INTRODUCTION:
CROSSING THE LINE

At the residential university where I teach, many first-year students participate each year in a dormitory-based program called "Crossing the Line." The students, who are also fellow residents, gather together on one side of a large room. A facilitator, after introducing the ground rules, calls out a series of descriptions, labels, or categories. For example, "Anyone who is female, please cross the line," "Anyone who is an only child . . ." or "Anyone whose home is a country other than the United States. . . ." People who think a category describes them, and who feel comfortable acknowledging this, then "cross the line" by walking over a line drawn across the middle of the room and turning to face the group they just left. Some people also choose, for certain categories or labels, to straddle the line. After a brief pause, everyone returns to one side and the next category is called out.

Participants report "Crossing the Line" to be a powerful emotional and community-building experience. As the categories get increasingly personal or more controversial—"Anyone who comes from a nontraditional family," "Anyone who has a learning disability," "Anyone who has been sexually abused," "Anyone who feels uncomfortable with homosexuality or bisexuality in others," and so on—people begin to see that "diversity" extends well beyond the common categories of race or ethnicity, social class, gender, and sexual orientation. They find, for example, that a person who fits into the categories female, heterosexual, and African American may also identify herself as Catholic, upper middle class, a Republican, a feminist, someone who once saved another person's life, who is struggling for academic direction, and who has experienced the effects of alcoholism in her family. Participants learn new ways of seeing people they had previously known only as acquaintances; they learn new things about people they thought they knew well. They see, demonstrated concretely, that their fellow students are as difficult to pin down with a label or two as they feel themselves to be. By demonstrating such a multiplicity of ways to divide a community according to different measures and different life experiences, many people see that "cultural diversity" implies a significantly richer and more complex reality than they may have previously imagined.

The discussion that concludes "Crossing the Line" is perhaps the most important part of the program. Here participants compare what they were thinking and feeling during the exercise, exchange reactions to the various categories, and offer explanations for identifying or not identifying themselves with particular categories. When people give entirely different reasons for crossing or straddling the same line, the tapestry of diversity begins to take on depth and texture. At one program a young man from the rural Midwest explained that although his parents were proud of him for being the first in his family to enter college, he felt torn by the academic culture that now pressured him to pull away from his family and community roots. A woman from an affluent Eastern suburb and prep-school background said she felt equally torn, and a conversation ensued about the meaning of "home community."

This third dimension—which engages personal experience and tests it against the experiences of others, which elicits perspectives that may coincide or clash in surprising ways, and which throws open the border between the private and the public—is the beginning of critical thinking. Members of the community have begun to explore, and possibly to reexamine, their shared and divergent values. They have begun to explore how their cultures and the culture of their community are defined through language. They have begun a negotiation with the power or the inadequacy or the persuasiveness of that language.

* * *

I hope that *Encountering Cultures* will provide you with an experience similar to my description of "Crossing the Line." This book brings together a wide variety of essays and stories addressing issues of cultural diversity and interaction. If you browse the table of contents you will see the broad groupings and categories used to organize these readings.

- Part One, "Encountering Language and Culture," explores some of the ways in which spoken and written language relates to your individual and group identities, because, as Alleen Pace Nilsen writes, "Language and society are as intertwined as a chicken and an egg. The language that a culture uses is telltale evidence of the values and beliefs of that culture."

- Part Two, "Encountering Diversity at Home," explores issues arising from the increasing cultural diversity of North America, including immigration and assimilation, ethnicity and social class, mainstream and marginalized values, and sexual orientation. If, as Ishmael Reed suggests, the "exciting destiny" of North America is "to become a place where the cultures of the world crisscross," then how we fulfill that destiny will have a profound impact on the rest of the world.

- Part Three, "Encountering Global Diversity," explores the larger context of our domestic cultural diversity through international encounters between "us" and "them"—Westerners and Easterners, First Worlders and Third Worlders, Christians and Jews, Muslims and practitioners of indigenous native religions, tourists and locals, victims and perpetrators of global political and economic forces, people trying to make the world a better place and those in desperate need of their help.

Here are some features of the book that I hope you will find useful:

Parts One, Two, and Three open with brief introductions highlighting the major themes and offering specific suggestions for informal writing or discussion exercises to do *before* you read the selections that follow. These exercises are intended to help you articulate your own feelings and opinions on the issues that will be explored by the other writers—to help you build a framework of your own experience in which to make judgments about what you read.

Each part is divided into four thematic chapters. These twelve thematic chapters all begin with several short "Brief Encounters" and include four or five complete essays and at least one short story. The individual reading selections, like you and your fellow readers, vary widely in style, viewpoint, basic values, and assumptions about the values of their audience.

The questions that follow each selection and each thematic chapter in *Encountering Cultures* ask you to think critically about your reading. Even if your instructor doesn't assign these questions specifically, trying to answer them—by yourself or in collaboration with others—may help you prepare to discuss or write about the selections. The questions assume that your life experience and your opinions and reactions based on that experience are as valid as another reader's. There are no "right answers" to these questions; rather there is a fairly wide range of judgments that different readers might make based on the same material.

Many of the "Thinking about [the thematic chapter]" questions ask you to make direct comparisons between selections. A second grouping of questions, "Exploring Additional Sources," suggests some comparisons you might make to selections in other chapters and suggests topics for longer research projects. These research suggestions include the use of both library materials and nonlibrary sources such as people in your college, university, or local community.

Another feature of the book you may find useful is the Rhetorical Index at the back, which organizes the readings according to common writing strategies such as description, comparison, and illustration. Even if your instructor does not make writing assignments in the form of such strategies, you may still be asked when you write to describe, compare, illustrate, or make use of other rhetorical strategies indexed here.

*　*　*

If the thematic chapters of *Encountering Cultures* are analogous to the categories and labels of "Crossing the Line," then the individual reading selections—like individual participants in the exercise, and like you as the reader of this book—may not be entirely comfortable within these categories. As you decide in your reading and writing how these lines should be crossed or straddled or perhaps bridged, I hope you will challenge yourself to consider why, and I hope you will begin a dialogue with the other people in your "room" about what matters to you in this process.

It has been said that developing new forms of community is the most urgent challenge facing humanity near the beginning of the twenty-first century. Communities may be described by their culture, which according to anthropologist Renato Rosaldo "refers broadly to the forms through which people make sense of their lives, rather than more narrowly to the opera or art museums." As I suggested in the first edition of *Encountering Cultures*, these forms include everything from the dialect or language people speak to the way they eat their food, build their homes, educate their children, treat strangers, define gender and sexual roles, tell stories, or write essays. You are a participant in shaping our broad culture, and more narrowly, if you are using this book for a writing course, the culture of your classroom. As you test your views, examine your values, and explore the limitations and power of language to articulate these efforts, you are not only "encountering cultures" and "reading and writing in a changing world" but also participating in a kind of re-making of that world: you are helping define a community.

PART ONE

ENCOUNTERING LANGUAGE AND CULTURE

The reading selections in Chapters 1 through 4 address some of the complex ways in which the language you use relates to your identity as an individual and as a member of a cultural group. As new social forces affect the way English is spoken and written near the beginning of the 21st century, how you view the relationship between your language and your culture will increasingly determine the way you talk and write at home, at school, and at work. If the way we use language is, as Alleen Pace Nilsen writes in Chapter 1, "like an x-ray in providing visible evidence of invisible thoughts," then it is also an expression of the values we bring to these occasions. Does our society encourage negative images of female roles with terms like "tomboy" and "sissy," as in one example given by Nilsen? If women are treated in English as "sex objects," as Eugene R. August argues, are men likewise reduced to "success objects"?

To examine our language, then, is also to examine our values, norms, and standards. Even the idea of "standard English" was originally determined by political and social influences, according to Raymond Williams. Recently, during the 1980s and 1990s, our notion of English has been influenced by both global and domestic forces. As

June Jordan points out, hundreds of millions of people worldwide—across several continents besides North America—speak English as a native language, and many more hundreds of millions speak English as a second or additional language. Although its importance as an international language for business and politics has increased, "English is diminishing proportionately" in the 1990s, says Richard Bailey, because of higher birth rates in Third World countries.

Domestically in the United States and Canada, the diversity of English speakers and learners continues to increase rapidly. The 1990s are bringing record numbers of immigrants, both legal and illegal, into the U.S.—the largest such influx since the beginning of the century. Most of these new residents do not come from Europe, as in the past, but from Asia, the Pacific Rim, Central America, and South America. In the face of such changes, it is tempting to reduce the complexity of cross-cultural relations by resorting to stereotypical language and thinking. "Why do people keep saying these things?" laments Amy Tan, in Chapter 2, after reading that Chinese people are "discreet and modest." And Art Carey reminds us that stereotypes are not limited to ethnic minorities, claiming with some humorous exaggeration that "White Guys" are currently vilified as "brutish louts, insensitive, dysfunctional, judgmental, unicultural yahoos and peckerwoods."

But white males, as Carey admits, "still have most of the power . . . have most of the good jobs . . . make most of the money . . . and run the show just about everywhere." Several writers in Chapter 3 examine the way that members of minority groups are negotiating these power relations through language. Barbara Mellix finds "remarkable power" in mastering the "proper English" of academic culture, while Michael Ventura argues that "the university is where language goes to die." People who are brought up speaking more than one language, or those who must learn English after immigrating to the United States, have an especially valuable perspective on the straddling or juggling of two cultural traditions. In Chapter 4, Richard Rodriguez and Gloria Anzaldúa—along with others—offer radically different views of the advantages and disadvantages of such bicultural, bilingual dilemmas.

All of us who wish to improve relations across cultures and groups of people must be concerned with the effects on others of the way we talk and write. To communicate effectively, we must consider the feelings and perspective of the audience we're addressing, just as we hope that audience will consider our own perspective. You can take best advantage of your reading in these chapters if you first ask yourself some tough questions about the way you think, and the way you think about others, through the language you use. Here are some ways you might begin to consider these issues:

Language and Gender (Chapter 1). Write down words and phrases you usually use to refer to the opposite sex, and those you use to refer to members of your own sex. What are the things you like best and least about being male or being female? Generate a group list, male or female, then compare your responses with those of the opposite sex.

Language and Stereotypes (Chapter 2). Make lists of words and phrases specifically associated with your ethnicity, your nationality, your religion, your neighborhood or community or home town, and your school or college. Then make lists of common stereotypes held about each of those groups or places. For each list, consider how the words or terms you listed relate to the stereotypes you wrote down. You might repeat this exercise, but for another ethnic group, a different religion, a different school, and so on. Then compare your lists of terms and stereotypes with those of classmates.

Language and Social Power (Chapter 3). What qualities do you associate with good writing in general? What qualities do you associate with academic writing in particular? Write down these qualities in a notebook or journal, so you can modify or add to them as you do more reading and writing. Who in your life has been responsible for defining your notion of "good English" or standard English? How does your notion of standard English compare with the way you normally speak in less formal contexts?

Language and Bicultural Identity (Chapter 4). How important is your home language—whether American English or another language or dialect—to your identity as an individual and as a member of society? If English is your only language, have you ever felt torn between other kinds of cultural groups with which you identify, such as a peer group and a religious group? If you have studied a second language in school, what concepts have you learned that strike you as belonging to a different cultural tradition than your own?

1

LANGUAGE AND GENDER

Sexist Language

ROSALIE MAGGIO

Sexist language promotes and maintains attitudes that stereotype people according to gender while assuming that the male is the norm—the significant gender. Nonsexist language treats all people equally and either does not refer to a person's sex at all when it is irrelevant or refers to men and women in symmetrical ways.

"A society in which women are taught anything but the management of a family, the care of men, and the creation of the future generation is a society which is on the way out" (L. Ron Hubbard). "Behind every successful man is a woman—with nothing to wear" (L. Grant Glickman). "Nothing makes a man and wife feel closer, these days, than a joint tax return" (Gil Stern). These quotations display various characteristics of sexist writing: (1) stereotyping an entire sex by what might be appropriate for some of it; (2) assuming male superiority; (3) using unparallel terms (*man and wife* should be either *wife and husband/husband and wife* or *woman and man/man and woman*).

The following quotations clearly refer to all people: "It's really hard to be roommates with people if your suitcases are much better than theirs" (J. D. Salinger). "If people don't want to come out to the ball park, nobody's going to stop them" (Yogi Berra). "If men and women of capacity refuse to take part in politics and government, they condemn themselves, as well as the people, to the punishment of living under bad government" (Senator Sam J. Ervin). "I studied the lives of great men and famous women, and I found that the men and women who got to the top were those who did the jobs they had in hand, with everything they had of energy and enthusiasm and hard work" (Harry S. Truman).

—FROM *THE DICTIONARY OF BIAS-FREE USAGE: A GUIDE TO NONDISCRIMINATORY LANGUAGE*, 1991.

In Defense of Gender

CYRA McFADDEN

So pervasive is the neutering of the English language on the progressive West Coast, we no longer have people here, only persons: male persons and female persons, chairpersons and doorpersons, waitpersons, mailpersons—who may be either male or female mailpersons—and refuse-collection persons. In the classified ads, working mothers seek childcare persons, though one wonders how many men (archaic for "male person") take care of child persons as a full-time occupation. One such ad, fusing nonsexist language and the most popular word in the California growth movement, solicits a "nurtureperson."

Dear gents and ladies, as I might have addressed you in less troubled times, this female person knows firsthand the reasons for scourging sexist bias from the language. God knows what damage was done me, at fifteen, when I worked in my first job—as what is now known as a newspaper copyperson—and came running to the voices of men barking, "Boy!"

No aspirant to the job of refuse-collection person myself, I nonetheless take off my hat (a little feathered number, with a veil) to those of my own sex who may want both the job and a genderless title with it. I argue only that there must be a better way, and I wish person or persons unknown would come up with one.

Defend it on any grounds you choose; the neutering of spoken and written English, with its attendant self-consciousness, remains ludicrous. In print, those "person" suffixes and "he/she's" jump out from the page, as distracting as a cloud of gnats, demanding that the reader note the writer's virtue. "Look what a nonsexist writer person I am, voiding the use of masculine forms for the generic."

—FROM "IN DEFENSE OF GENDER," *THE NEW YORK TIMES MAGAZINE*, 1981.

Women's Language and Men's Language

ROBIN LAKOFF

As an experiment, one might present native speakers of standard American English with pairs of sentences, identical syntactically and in terms of referential lexical items, and differing merely in the choice of "meaningless" particle, and ask them which was spoken by a man, which a woman. Consider:

(a)   Oh dear, you've put the peanut butter in the refrigerator again.

(b)   Shit, you've put the peanut butter in the refrigerator again.

It is safe to predict that people would classify the first sentence as part of "women's language," the second as "men's language." It is true that many self-respecting women are becoming able to use sentences like (b) publicly without flinching, but this is a relatively recent development, and while perhaps the majority of Middle America might condone the use of (b) for men, they would still disapprove of its use by women. (It is of interest, by the way, to note that men's language is increasingly being used by women, but women's language is not being adopted by men, apart from those who reject the American masculine image [for example, homosexuals]. This is analogous to the fact that men's jobs are being sought by women, but few men are rushing to become housewives or secretaries. The language of the favored group, the group that holds the power, along with its nonlinguistic behavior, is generally adopted by the other group, not vice versa. In any event, it is a truism to state that the "stronger" expletives are reserved for men, and the "weaker" ones for women.)

—FROM *LANGUAGE AND WOMAN'S PLACE*, 1975

Sexism in English: A 1990s Update

ALLEEN PACE NILSEN

Twenty years ago I embarked on a study of the sexism inherent in 1
American English. I had just returned to Ann Arbor, Michigan, after
living for two years (1967–1969) in Kabul, Afghanistan, where I had
begun to look critically at the role society assigned to women. The
Afghan version of the *chaderi* prescribed for Moslem women was particularly confining. Few women attended the American-built Kabul
University where my husband was teaching linguistics because there
were no women's dormitories, which meant that the only females who
could attend were those whose families happened to live in the capital
city. Afghan jokes and folklore were blatantly sexist; for example, this
proverb: "If you see an old man, sit down and take a lesson; if you see
an old woman, throw a stone."

But it wasn't only the native culture that made me question wom- 2
en's roles; it was also the American community. Nearly 600 Americans
lived in Kabul, mostly supported by U.S. taxpayers. The single women
were career secretaries, school teachers, or nurses. The three women
who had jobs comparable to the American men's jobs were textbook
editors with the assignment of developing reading books in Dari
(Afghan Persian) for young children. They worked at the Ministry of
Education, a large building in the center of the city. There were no
women's restrooms so during their two-year assignment whenever
they needed to go to the bathroom they had to walk across the street
and down the block to the Kabul Hotel.

The rest of the American women were like myself—wives and 3
mothers whose husbands were either career diplomats, employees of
USAID, or college professors teaching at Kabul University. These were
the women who were most influential in changing my way of thinking
because we were suddenly bereft of our traditional roles. Servants
worked for $1.00 a day and our lives revolved around supervising

Alleen Pace Nilsen is a professor of English at Arizona State
University. Her essay originally appeared in *Female Studies VI* as
"Sexism in English: A Feminist View" in 1972, during the height of
the modern feminist movement. Nilsen updated the essay for the
anthology *Language Awareness* (edited by Eschholz, Rosa, and Clark)
in 1990. Her other works include *Literature for Today's Young Adults*
(3rd edition, 1989) and *Language Play: An Introduction to Linguistics*
(1978), cowritten with her husband Don L. F. Nilsen.

these men (women were not allowed to work for foreigners). One woman's husband grew so tired of hearing her stories that he scheduled an hour a week for listening to complaints. The rest of the time he wanted to keep his mind clear to focus on working with his Afghan counterparts and with the president of the University and the Minister of Education. He was going to make a difference in this country, while in the great eternal scheme of things it mattered little that the servant stole the batteries out of the flashlight or put chili powder instead of paprika on the eggs.

I continued to ponder this dramatic contrast between men's and 4 women's work, and when we finished our contract and returned in the fall of 1969 to the University of Michigan in Ann Arbor I was surprised to find that many other women were also questioning the expectations that they had grown up with. I attended a campus women's conference, but I returned home more troubled than ever. Now that I knew housework was worth only a dollar a day, I couldn't take it seriously, but I wasn't angry in the same way these women were. Their militancy frightened me. I wasn't ready for a revolution, so I decided I would have my own feminist movement. I would study the English language and see what it could tell me about sexism. I started reading a desk dictionary and making notecards on every entry that seemed to tell something about male and female. I soon had a dog-eared dictionary, along with a collection of notecards filling two shoe boxes.

Ironically, I started reading the dictionary because I wanted to 5 avoid getting involved in social issues, but what happened was that my notecards brought me right back to looking at society. Language and society are as intertwined as a chicken and an egg. The language that a culture uses is telltale evidence of the values and beliefs of that culture. And because there is a lag in how fast a language changes— new words can easily be introduced, but it takes a long time for old words and usages to disappear—a careful look at English will reveal the attitudes that our ancestors held and that we as a culture are therefore predisposed to hold. My notecards revealed three main points. Friends have offered the opinion that I didn't need to read the dictionary to learn such obvious facts. Nevertheless, it was interesting to have linguistic evidence of sociological observations.

Women Are Sexy; Men Are Successful

First, in American culture a woman is valued for the attractiveness 6 and sexiness of her body, while a man is valued for his physical strength and accomplishments. A woman is sexy. A man is successful.

A persuasive piece of evidence supporting this view are the 7 eponyms—words that have come from someone's name—found in

English. I had a two-and-a-half-inch stack of cards taken from men's names, but less than a half-inch stack from women's names, and most of those came from Greek mythology. In the words that came into American English since we separated from Britain, there are many eponyms based on the names of famous American men: bartlett pear, boysenberry, diesel engine, franklin stove, ferris wheel, gatling gun, mason jar, sideburns, sousaphone, schick test, and winchester rifle. The only common eponyms taken from American women's names are *Alice blue* (after Alice Roosevelt Longworth), bloomers (after Amelia Jenks Bloomer) and *Mae West jacket* (after the buxom actress). Two out of the three feminine eponyms relate closely to a woman's physical anatomy, while the masculine eponyms (except for *sideburns* after General Burnsides) have nothing to do with the namesake's body, but instead honor the man for an accomplishment of some kind.

Although in Greek mythology women played a bigger role than   8 they did in the biblical stories of the Judeo-Christian cultures and so the names of goddesses are accepted parts of the language in such place names as Pomona from the goddess of fruit and Athens from Athena, and in such common words as *cereal* from Ceres, *psychology* from Psyche, and *arachnoid* from Arachne, the same tendency to think of women in relation to sexuality is seen in the eponyms *aphrodisiac* from Aphrodite, the Greek name for the goddess of love and beauty, and *venereal disease*, from Venus, the Roman name for Aphrodite.

Another interesting word from Greek mythology is *Amazon*.   9 According to Greek folk etymology, the *a* means "without" as in *atypical* or *amoral* while *mazon* comes from *mazos* meaning *breast* as still seen in *mastectomy*. In the Greek legend, Amazon women cut off their right breasts so that they could better shoot their bows. Apparently, the storytellers had a feeling that for women to play the active "masculine" role that the Amazons adopted for themselves, they had to trade in part of their femininity.

This preoccupation with women's breasts is not limited to ancient   10 stories. As a volunteer for the University of Wisconsin's *Dictionary of American Regional English (DARE)*, I read a western trapper's diary from the 1830s. I was to make notes of any unusual usages or language patterns. My most interesting finding was that he referred to a range of mountains as *The Teats*, a metaphor based on the similarity between the shapes of the mountains and women's breasts. Because today we use the French wording, *The Grand Tetons*, the metaphor isn't as obvious, but I wrote to mapmakers and found the following listings: *Nippletop* and *Little Nipple Top* near Mt. Marcy in the Adirondacks; *Nipple Mountain* in Archuleta County, Colorado; *Nipple Peak* in Coke County, Texas; *Nipple Butte* in Pennington, South Dakota; *Squaw Peak* in Placer County, California (and many other locations); *Maiden's Peak* and *Squaw Tit* (they're the same mountain) in the Cascade Range in Oregon; *Mary's Nipple* near Salt Lake City, Utah; and *Jane Russell Peaks* near Stark, New Hampshire.

Except for the movie star Jane Russell, the women being referred to are anonymous—it's only a sexual part of their body that is mentioned. When topographical features are named after men, it's probably not going to be to draw attention to a sexual part of their bodies but instead to honor individuals for an accomplishment. For example, no one thinks of a part of the male body when hearing a reference to Pike's Peak, Colorado, or Jackson Hole, Wyoming. 11

Going back to what I learned from my dictionary cards, I was surprised to realize how many pairs of words we have in which the feminine word has acquired sexual connotations while the masculine word retains a serious businesslike aura. For example, a *callboy* is the person who calls actors when it is time for them to go on stage, but a *callgirl* is a prostitute. Compare *sir* and *madam*. *Sir* is a term of respect while *madam* has acquired the specialized meaning of a brothel manager. Something similar has happened to *master* and *mistress*. Would you rather have a painting by *an old master* or *an old mistress*? 12

It's because the word *woman* had sexual connotations as in "She's his woman," that people began avoiding its use, hence such terminology as *ladies room, lady of the house,* and *girl's school* or *school for young ladies*. Feminists, who ask that people use the term *woman* rather than *girl* or *lady,* are rejecting the idea that *woman* is primarily a sexual term. They have been at least partially successful in that today *woman* is commonly used to communicate gender without intending implications about sexuality. 13

I found 200 pairs of words with masculine and feminine forms, for example, *heir/heiress, hero/heroine, steward/stewardess, usher/usherette,* etc. In nearly all such pairs, the masculine word is considered the base with some kind of a feminine suffix being added. The masculine form is the one from which compounds are made; for example, from *king/queen* comes *kingdom* but not *queendom,* from *sportsman/sportslady* comes *sportsmanship* but not *sports/ladyship*. There is one—and only one—semantic area in which the masculine word is not the base or more powerful word. This is in the area dealing with sex and marriage. When someone refers to a *virgin,* a listener will probably think of a female unless the speaker specifies *male* or uses a masculine pronoun. The same is true for *prostitute*. 14

In relation to marriage, there is much linguistic evidence showing that weddings are more important to women than to men. A woman cherishes the wedding and is considered a bride for a whole year, but 15 a man is referred to as a groom only on the day of the wedding. The word *bride* appears in *bridal attendant, bridal gown, bridesmaid, bridal shower,* and even *bridegroom. Groom* comes from the Middle English *grom,* meaning "man," and in this sense is seldom used outside of a wedding. With most pairs of male/female words, people habitually put the masculine word first, *Mr. and Mrs., his and hers, boys and girls, men and women, kings and queens, brothers and sisters, guys and dolls,* and *host and hostess,* but it is the *bride and groom* who are talked about, not the *groom and bride.*

The importance of marriage to a woman is also shown by the fact 16 that when a marriage ends in death, the woman gets the title of *widow.* A man gets the derived title of *widower.* This term is not used in other phrases or contexts, but *widow* is seen in *widowhood, widow's peak,* and *widow's walk.* A *widow* in a card game is an extra hand of cards, while in typesetting it is an extra line of type.

How changing cultural ideas bring changes to language is clearly 17 visible in this semantic area. The feminist movement has caused the differences between the sexes to be downplayed, and since I did my dictionary study two decades ago the word *singles* has largely replaced such sex specific and value-laden terms as *bachelor, old maid, spinster, divorcee, widow,* and *widower.* And in 1970, I wrote that when a man is called *a professional* he is thought to be a doctor or a lawyer, but when people hear a woman referred to as *a professional* they are likely to think of a prostitute. That's not as true today because so many women have become doctors and lawyers that it's no longer incongruous to think of women in those professional roles.

Another change that has taken place is in wedding announce- 18 ments. They used to be sent out from the bride's parents and did not even give the name of the groom's parents. Today, most couples choose to list either all or none of the parents' names. Also, it is now much more likely that both the bride and groom's picture will be in the newspaper, while a decade ago only the bride's picture was published on the "Women's" or the "Society" page. Even the traditional wording of the wedding ceremony is being changed. Many officials now pro- nounce the couple "husband and wife" instead of the old "man and wife," and they ask the bride if she promises "to love, honor, and cher- ish," instead of "to love, honor, and obey."

Women Are Passive; Men Are Active

The wording of the wedding ceremony also relates to the second 19 point that my cards showed, which is that women are expected to play a passive or weak role while men play an active or strong role. In the traditional ceremony, the official asks "Who gives the bride away?"

and the father answers "I do." Some fathers answer "Her mother and I do," but that doesn't solve the problem inherent in the question. The idea that a bride is something to be handed over from one man to another bothers people because it goes back to the days when a man's servants, his children, and his wife were all considered to be his property. They were known by his name because they belonged to him and he was responsible for their actions and their debts.

The grammar used in talking or writing about weddings as well as   20
other sexual relationships shows the expectation of men playing the active role. Men *wed* women while women *become* brides of men. A man *possesses* a woman; he *deflowers* her; he *performs;* he *scores;* he *takes away* her virginity. Although a woman can *seduce* a man, she cannot offer him her virginity. When talking about virginity, the only way to make the woman the actor in the sentence is to say that "She lost her virginity," but people lose things by accident rather than by purposeful actions and so she's only the grammatical, not the real-life, actor.

The reason that women tried to bring the term *Ms.* into the lan-   21
guage to replace *Miss* and *Mrs.* relates to this point. Married women resented being identified only under their husband's names. For example, when Susan Glascoe did something newsworthy she would be identified in the newspaper only as Mrs. John Glascoe. The dictionary cards showed what appeared to be an attitude on the part of editors that it was almost indecent to let a respectable woman's name march unaccompanied across the pages of a dictionary. Women were listed with male names whether or not the male contributed to the woman's reason for being in the dictionary or in his own right was as famous as the woman. For example, Charlotte Brontë was identified as Mrs. Arthur B. Nicholls, Amelia Earhart as Mrs. George Palmer Putnam, Helen Hayes as Mrs. Charles MacArthur, Jenny Lind as Mme. Otto Goldschmit, Cornelia Otis Skinner as the daughter of Otis, Harriet Beecher Stowe as the sister of Henry Ward Beecher, and Edith Sitwell as the sister of Osbert and Sacheverell. A very small number of women got into the dictionary without the benefit of a masculine escort. They were rebels and crusaders: temperance leaders Frances Elizabeth Caroline Willard and Carry Nation, women's rights leaders Carrie Chapman Catt and Elizabeth Cady Stanton, birth control educator Margaret Sanger, religious leader Mary Baker Eddy, and slaves Harriet Tubman and Phillis Wheatley.

Etiquette books used to teach that if a woman had *Mrs.* in front   22
of her name, then the husband's name should follow because *Mrs.* is an abbreviated form of *Mistress* and a woman couldn't be a mistress of herself. As with many arguments about "correct" language usage, this isn't very logical because *Miss* is also an abbreviation of *Mistress.* Feminists hoped to simplify matters by introducing *Ms.* as

an alternative to both *Mrs.* and *Ms.,* but what happened is that *Ms.* largely replaced *Miss* to became a catchall business title for women. Many married women still prefer the title *Mrs.,* and some resent being addressed with the term *Ms.* As one frustrated newspaper reporter complained, "Before I can write about a woman, I have to know not only her marital status but also her political philosophy." The result of such complications may contribute to the demise of titles which are already being ignored by many computer programmers who find it more efficient to simply use names, for example, in a business letter, "Dear Joan Garcia," instead of "Dear Mrs. Joan Garcia," "Dear Ms. Garcia," or "Dear Mrs. Louis Garcia."

The titles given to royalty provide an example of how males can 23 be disadvantaged by the assumption that they are always to play the more powerful role. In British royalty, when a male holds a title, his wife is automatically given the feminine equivalent. But the reverse is not true. For example, a *count* is a high political officer with a *countess* being his wife. The same is true for a *duke* and a *duchess* and a *king* and a *queen.* But when a female holds the royal title, the man she marries does not automatically acquire the matching title. For example, Queen Elizabeth's husband has the title of *prince* rather than *king,* but if Prince Charles should become king while he is still married to Lady or Princess Diana, she will be known as the queen. The reasoning appears to be that since masculine words are stronger, they are reserved for true heirs and withheld from males coming into the royal family by marriage. If Prince Phillip were called *King Phillip,* it would be much easier for British subjects to forget where the true power lies.

The names that people give their children show the hopes and 24 dreams they have for them, and when we look at the differences between male and female names in a culture we can see the cumulative expectations of that culture. In our culture girls often have names taken from small, aesthetically pleasing items, for example, *Ruby, Jewel,* and *Pearl. Esther* and *Stella* mean "star," *Ada* means "ornament," and *Vanessa* means "butterfly." Boys are more likely to be given names with meanings of power and strength; for example, *Neil* means "champion," *Martin* is from Mars, the God of War, *Raymond* means "wise protection," *Harold* means "chief of the army," *Ira* means "vigilant," *Rex* means "king," and *Richard* means "strong king."

We see similar differences in food metaphors. Food is a passive 25 substance just sitting there waiting to be eaten. Many people have recognized this and so no longer feel comfortable describing women as "delectable morsels." However, when I was a teenager, it was considered a compliment to refer to a girl (we didn't call anyone a *woman* until she was middle-aged) as *a cute tomato, a peach, a dish, a cookie, honey, sugar,* or *sweetie-pie.* When being affectionate, women will occasionally call a man *honey* or *sweetie*, but, in general, food metaphors are used much less often with men than with women. If a man is called *a fruit*, his masculinity is being questioned. But it's perfectly acceptable to use a food metaphor if the food is heavier and more substantive than that used for women. For example, pinup pictures of women have long been known as *cheesecake*, but when Burt Reynolds posed for a nude centerfold the picture was immediately dubbed *beefcake*, that is, *a hunk of meat*. That such sexual references to men have come into the general language is another reflection of how society is beginning to lessen the differences between their attitudes toward men and women.

Something similar to the *fruit* metaphor happens with references 26 to plants. We insult a man by calling him *a pansy*, but it wasn't considered particularly insulting to talk about a girl being a *wallflower*, a *clinging vine*, or a *shrinking violet*, or to give girls such names as *Ivy, Rose, Lily, Iris, Daisy, Camellia, Heather*, or *Flora*. A plant metaphor can be used with a man if the plant is big and strong, for example, Andrew Jackson's nickname of *Old Hickory*. Also, the phrases *blooming idiots* and *budding geniuses* can be used with either sex, but notice how they are based on the most active thing a plant can do, which is to bloom or bud.

Animal metaphors also illustrate the different expectations for 27 males and females. Men are referred to as *studs, bucks,* and *wolves* while women are referred to with such metaphors as *kitten, bunny, beaver, bird, chick,* or *lamb*. In the 1950s, we said that boys went *tomcatting*, but today it's just *catting around* and both boys and girls do it. When the term *foxy*, meaning that someone was sexy, first became popular it was used only for girls, but now someone of either sex can be described as *a fox*. Some animal metaphors that are used predominantly with men have negative connotations based on the size and/or strength of the animals, for example, *beast, bullheaded, jackass, rat, loanshark,* and *vulture*. Negative metaphors used with women are based on smaller animals, for example, *social butterfly, mousy, catty,* and *vixen*. The feminine terms connote action, but not the same kind of large-scale action as with the masculine terms.

Women Are Connected with Negative Connotations, Men with Positive Connotations

The final point that my notecards illustrated was how many posi- 28 tive connotations are associated with the concept of masculine, while there are either trivial or negative connotations connected with the corresponding feminine concept. An example from the animal metaphors makes a good illustration. The word *shrew* taken from the name of a small but especially vicious animal was defined in my dictionary as "an ill tempered scolding woman," but the word *shrewd* taken from the same root was defined as "marked by clever, discerning awareness" and was illustrated with the phrase "a shrewd businessman."

Early in life, children are conditioned to the superiority of the   29 masculine role. As child psychologists point out, little girls have much more freedom to experiment with sex roles than do little boys. If a little girl acts like a *tomboy*, most parents have mixed feelings, being at least partially proud. But if their little boy acts like a *sissy* (derived from *sister*), they call a psychologist. It's perfectly acceptable for a little girl to sleep in the crib that was purchased for her brother, to wear his hand-me-down jeans and shirts, and to ride the bicycle that he has outgrown. But few parents would put a boy baby in a white and gold crib decorated with frills and lace, and virtually no parents would have their little boy wear his sister's hand-me-down dresses, nor would they have their son ride a girl's pink bicycle with a flower-bedecked basket. The proper names given to girls and boys show this same attitude. Girls can have "boy" names—*Chris, Craig, Jo, Kelly, Shawn, Teri, Toni,* and *Sam*—but it doesn't work the other way around. A couple of generations ago, *Beverley, Frances, Hazel, Marion,* and *Shirley* were common boys' names. As parents gave these names to more and more girls, they fell into disuse for males, and some older men who have these names prefer to go by their initials or by such abbreviated forms as *Haze* or *Shirl*.

When a little girl is told to *be a lady,* she is being told to sit with her   30 knees together and to be quiet and dainty. But when a little boy is told to *be a man* he is being told to be noble, strong, and virtuous—to have all the qualities that the speaker looks on as desirable. The concept of manliness has such positive connotations that it used to be a compliment to call someone a *he-man,* to say that he was doubly a man. Today, many people are more ambivalent about this term and respond to it much as they do to the word *macho*. But calling someone a *manly man* or a *virile man* is nearly always meant as a compliment. *Virile* comes from the Indo-European *vir* meaning "man," which is also the basis of *virtuous*. Contrast the positive connotations of both *virile* and *virtuous* with the negative connotations of *hysterical*. The Greeks took this latter word from their name for *uterus* (as still seen in *hysterectomy*). They thought that women were the only ones who experienced uncontrolled emotional outbursts and so the condition must have something to do with a part of the body that only women have.

Differences between positive male connotations and negative fe-   31 male connotations can be seen in several pairs of words which differ denotatively only in the matter of sex. *Bachelor* as compared to *spinster* or *old maid* has such positive connotations that women try to adopt them by using the term *bachelor-girl* or *bachelorette*. *Old maid* is so negative that it's the basis for metaphors: pretentious and fussy old men are called *old maids* as are the leftover kernels of unpopped popcorn and the last card in a popular children's game.

   Patron and *matron* (Middle English for *father* and *mother*) have such   32 different levels of prestige that women try to borrow the more positive masculine connotations with the word *patroness,* literally "female father." Such a peculiar term came about because of the high prestige attached to *patron* in such phrases as *a patron of the arts* or *a patron saint*. *Matron* is more apt to be used in talking about a woman in charge of a jail or a public restroom.

   When men are doing jobs that women often do, we apparently try   33 to pay the men extra by giving them fancy titles; for example, a male cook is more likely to be called a *chef* while a male seamstress will get the title of *tailor*. The Armed Forces have a special problem in that they recruit under such slogans as "The Marine Corps builds men!" and "Join the Army! Become a Man." Once the recruits are enlisted, they find themselves doing much of the work that has been traditionally thought of as "women's work." The solution to getting the work done and not insulting anyone's masculinity was to change the titles as shown below:

waitress	orderly
nurse	medic or corpsman
secretary	clerk-typist
assistant	adjutant
dishwasher or kitchen helper	KP (kitchen police)

   Compare *brave* and *squaw*. Early settlers in America truly admired   34 Indian men and hence named them with a word that carried connotations of youth, vigor, and courage. But they used the Algonquin's name for "woman," and over the years it developed almost opposite connotations to those of *brave*. *Wizard* and *witch* contrast almost as much. The masculine *wizard* implies skill and wisdom combined with magic, while the feminine *witch* implies evil intentions combined with magic. Part of the unattractiveness of both *witch* and *squaw* is that they have been used so often to refer to old women, something with which our culture is particularly uncomfortable, just as the Afghans were. Imagine my surprise, when I ran across the phrases *grandfatherly advice* and *old wives' tales* and realized that the underlying implication is the same as the Afghan proverb about old men being worth listening to while old women talk only foolishness.

   Other terms that show how negatively we view old women as   35 compared to young women are *old nag* as compared to *filly, old crow* or *old bat* as compared to *bird,* and being *catty* as compared to being *kittenish.* There is no matching set of metaphors for men. The chicken metaphor tells the whole story of a woman's life. In her youth she is a *chick.* Then she marries and begins *feathering her nest.* Soon she begins feeling *cooped up,* so she goes to *hen parties* where she *cackles* with her friends. Then she has her *brood,* begins to *henpeck* her husband, and finally turns into *an old biddy.*

I embarked on my study of the dictionary not with the intention of   36
prescribing language change but simply to see what the language would tell me about sexism. Nevertheless, I have been both surprised and pleased as I've watched the changes that have occurred over the past two decades. I'm one of those linguists who believes that the new language customs will cause a new generation of speakers to grow up with different expectations. This is why I'm happy about people's efforts to use inclusive language, to say *he or she* or *they* when speaking about individuals whose names they do not know. I'm glad that leading publishers have developed guidelines to help writers use language that is fair to both sexes and I'm glad that most newspapers and magazines list women by their own names instead of only by their husbands' names and that educated and thoughtful people no longer begin their business letters with "Dear Sir" or "Gentlemen" but instead use a memo form or begin with such salutations as "Dear Colleagues," "Dear Reader," or "Dear Committee Members." I'm also glad that such words as *poetess, authoress, conductress,* and *aviatrix* now sound quaint and old fashioned and that *chairman* is giving way to *chair* or *head, mailman* to *mail carrier, clergyman* to *clergy,* and *stewardess* to *flight attendant.* I was also pleased when the National Oceanic and Atmospheric Administration bowed to feminist complaints and in the late seventies began to alternate men's and women's names for hurricanes. However, I wasn't so pleased to discover that the change did not immediately erase sexist thoughts from everyone's mind as shown by a headline about Hurricane David in a 1979 New York tabloid, "David Rapes Virgin Islands." More recently, a similar metaphor appeared in a headline in the *Arizona Republic* about Hurricane Charlie, "Charlie Quits Carolinas, Flirts with Virginia."

What these incidents show is that sexism is not something existing   37
independently in American English or in the particular dictionary that I happened to read. Rather, it exists in people's minds. Language is like an x-ray in providing visible evidence of invisible thoughts. The best thing about people being interested in and discussing sexist language is that as they make conscious decisions about what pronouns they will use, what jokes they will tell or laugh at, how they will write their names, or how they will begin their letters, they are forced to

think about the underlying issue of sexism. This is good because as a problem that begins in people's assumptions and expectations, it's a problem that will be solved only when a great many people have given it a great deal of thought.

QUESTIONS

1. How does Nilsen think that language and culture influence each other?

2. Which of Nilsen's examples do you find most and least persuasive of an English language bias against women? Why? What terms can you add to Nilsen's "update" for the 1990s?

3. How much does Nilsen seem to think that traditional gender roles are changing, and what evidence does she offer for this change? Based on your own experience, to what extent do you agree with her?

Real Men Don't:
Anti-Male Bias in English

EUGENE R. AUGUST

Despite numerous studies of sex bias in language during the past 1
fifteen years, only rarely has anti-male bias been examined. In part, this
neglect occurs because many of these studies have been based upon assumptions which are questionable at best and which at worst exhibit
their own form of sex bias. Whether explicitly or implicitly, many of
these studies reduce human history to a tale of male oppressors and female victims or rebels. In this view of things, all societies become *patriarchal societies*, a familiar term used to suggest that for centuries males
have conspired to exploit and demean females. Accordingly, it is alleged in many of these studies that men control language and that they
use it to define women and women's roles as inferior.

Despite the popularity of such a view, it has received scant support 2
from leading social scientists, including one of the giants of modern anthropology, Margaret Mead. Anticipating current ideology, Mead in
Male and Female firmly rejected the notion of a "male conspiracy to keep
women in their place," arguing instead that

> the historical trend that listed women among the abused minorities
> . . . lingers on to obscure the issue and gives apparent point to the con-
> tention that this is a man-made world in which women have always
> been abused and must always fight for their rights.
>
> It takes considerable effort on the part of both men and women to
> reorient ourselves to thinking—when we think basically—that this is
> a world not made by men alone, in which women are unwilling and
> helpless dupes and fools or else powerful schemers hiding their
> power under their ruffled petticoats, but a world made of mankind
> for human beings of both sexes. (298, 299–300)

The model described by Mead and other social scientists shows a
world in which women and men have lived together throughout

Eugene R. August, professor of English at the University of Dayton
(Ohio), conducts research in the recently developing field of men's
studies and is the author of *Men's Studies: A Selected and Annotated
Interdisciplinary Bibliography* (1985). His other works include critical
studies of Victorian literature and the book *John Stuart Mill* (1975),
about the eighteenth-century British philosopher. The essay that
follows appeared in *The University of Dayton Review,* a journal for
scholarly research in the humanities, where August is assistant editor, in 1987.

history in a symbiotic relationship, often mutually agreeing upon the definition of gender roles and the distribution of various powers and duties.

More importantly for the subject of bias in speech and writing, 3 women—as well as men—have shaped language. As Walter J. Ong reminds us,

> Women talk and think as much as men do, and with few exceptions we all . . . learn to talk and think in the first instance largely from women, usually and predominantly our mothers. Our first tongue is called our "mother tongue" in English and in many other languages. . . . There are no father tongues. . . . (36)

Feminists like Dorothy Dinnerstein agree: "There seems no reason to doubt that the baby-tending sex contributed at least equally with the history-making one to the most fundamental of all human inventions: language" (22). Because gender roles and language are shaped by society in general—that is, by both men and women—anti-male bias in language is as possible as anti-female bias.

To say this, however, is emphatically not to blame women alone, 4 or even primarily, for anti-male usage. If guilt must be assigned, it would have to be placed upon sexist people, both male and female, who use language to manipulate gender role behavior and to create negative social attitudes towards males. But often it is difficult to point a finger of blame: except where prejudiced gender stereotypes are deliberately fostered, most people evidently use sex-biased terminology without clearly understanding its import. In the long run, it is wiser to concentrate not on fixing blame, but on heightening public awareness of anti-male language and on discouraging its use. In particular, teachers and writers need to become aware of and to question language which denigrates or stereotypes males.

In modern English, three kinds of anti-male usage are evident: 5 first, gender-exclusive language which omits males from certain kinds of consideration; second, gender-restrictive language which attempts to restrict males to an accepted gender role, some aspects of which may be outmoded, burdensome, or destructive; and third, negative stereotypes of males which are insulting, dehumanizing, and potentially dangerous.

Although gender-exclusive language which excludes females has 6 often been studied, few students of language have noted usage which excludes males. Those academics, for example, who have protested *alumnus* and *alumni* as gender-exclusive terms to describe a university's male and female graduates have failed to notice that, by the same logic, *alma mater* (nourishing mother) is an equally gender-exclusive term to describe the university itself. Those who have protested *man* and *mankind* as generic terms have not begun to question *mammal* as a term of biological classification, but by categorizing animals according to the female's ability to suckle the young through her mammary glands, *mammal* clearly omits the male of the species. Consequently, it is as suspect as generic *man.*

In general, gender-exclusive usage in English excludes males as ⁊ parents and as victims. Until recently, the equating of *mother* with *parent* in the social sciences was notorious: a major sociological study published in 1958 with the title *The Changing American Parent* was based upon interviews with 582 mothers and no fathers (Roman and Haddad 87). Although no longer prevalent in the social sciences, the interchangeability of *mother* and *parent* is still common, except for *noncustodial parent* which is almost always a synonym for *father.* A recent ad for *Parents* magazine begins: "To be the best mother you can be, you want practical, reliable answers to the questions a mother must face." Despite the large number of men now seen pushing shopping carts, advertisers still insist that "Choosy mothers choose Jif" and "My Mom's a Butternut Mom." Frequently, children are regarded as belonging solely to the mother, as in phrases like *women and their children.* The idea of the mother as primary parent can be glimpsed in such expressions as *mother tongue, mother wit, mother lode, mother of invention,* and *mothering* as a synonym for *parenting.*

The male as victim is ignored in such familiar expressions as *inno-* 8 *cent women and children.* In June 1985, when President Reagan rejected a bombing strike to counter terrorist activities, newspapers reported that the decision had been made to prevent "the deaths of many innocent women and children in strife-torn Lebanon" (Glass). Presumably strife-torn Lebanon contained no innocent men. Likewise, *rape victim* means females only, an assumption made explicit in the opening sentences of this newspaper article on rape: "Crime knows no gender. Yet, there is one offense that only women are prey to: rape" (Mougey). The thousands of males raped annually, in addition to the sexual assaults regularly inflicted upon males in prison, are here entirely overlooked. (That these males have been victimized mostly by other males does not disqualify them as victims of sexual violence, as some people assume.) Similarly, the term *wife and child abuse* conceals the existence of an estimated 282,000 husbands who are battered annually (O'Reilly et al. 23). According to many expressions in English, males are not parents and they are never victimized.

Unlike gender-exclusive language, gender-restrictive language 9 is usually applied to males only, often to keep them within the confines of a socially prescribed gender role. When considering gender-restrictive language, one must keep in mind that—as Ruth E. Hartley has pointed out—the masculine gender role is enforced earlier and more harshly than the feminine role is (235). In addition, because the boy is often raised primarily by females in the virtual absence of close adult males, his grasp of what is required of him to *be a man* is often unsure. Likewise, prescriptions for male behavior are usually given in the negative, leading to the "Real Men Don't" syndrome, a process which further confuses the boy. Such circumstances leave many males extremely vulnerable to language which questions their sense of masculinity.

Furthermore, during the past twenty years an increasing number   10 of men and women have been arguing that aspects of our society's masculine gender role are emotionally constrictive, unnecessarily stressful, and potentially lethal. Rejecting "the myth of masculine priv- ilege," psychologist Herb Goldberg reports in *The Hazards of Being Male* that "every critical statistic in the area of [early death], disease, suicide, crime, accidents, childhood emotional disorders, alcoholism, and drug addiction shows a disproportionately higher male rate" (5). But changes in the masculine role are so disturbing to so many people that the male who attempts to break out of familiar gender patterns often finds himself facing hostile opposition which can be readily and powerfully expressed in a formidable array of sex-biased terms.

To see how the process works, let us begin early in the male life   11 cycle. A boy quickly learns that, while it is usually acceptable for girls to be *tomboys*, God forbid that he should be a *sissy*. In *Sexual Signatures: On Being a Man or a Woman* John Money and Patricia Tucker note:

> The current feminine stereotype in our culture is flexible enough to let a girl behave "boyishly" if she wants to without bringing her fem- ininity into question, but any boy who exhibits "girlish" behavior is promptly suspected of being queer. There isn't even a word corre- sponding to "tomboy" to describe such a boy. "Sissy" perhaps comes closest, or "artistic" and "sensitive," but unlike "tomboy," such terms are burdened with unfavorable connotations. (72)

Lacking a favorable or even neutral term to describe the boy who is quiet, gentle, and emotional, the English language has long had a rich vocabulary to insult and ridicule such boys—*mama's boy, molly- coddle, milksop, muff, twit, softy, creampuff, pantywaist, weenie, Miss Nancy,* and so on. Although sometimes used playfully, the current popular *wimp* can be used to insult males from childhood right into adulthood.

Discussion of words like *sissy* as insults has been often one-sided: 12 most commentators are content to argue that the female, not the male, is being insulted by such usage. "The implicit sexism" in such terms, writes one commentator, "disparages the woman, not the man" (Sorrels 87). Although the female is being slurred indirectly by these terms, a moment's reflection will show that the primary force of the insult is being directed against the male, specifically the male who cannot differentiate himself from the feminine. Ong argues in *Fighting for Life* that most societies place heavy pressure on males to differentiate themselves from females because the prevailing environment of human society is feminine (70–71). In English-speaking societies, terms like *sissy* and *weak sister*, which have been used by both females and males, are usually perceived not as insults to females but as ridicule of males who have allegedly failed to differentiate themselves from the feminine.

Being *all boy* carries penalties, however: for one thing, it means 13 being less lovable. As the nursery rhyme tells children, little girls are made of "sugar and spice and all that's nice," while little boys are made of "frogs and snails and puppy-dogs' tails." Or, as an American version of the rhyme puts it:

> Girls are dandy,
> Made of candy—
> That's what little girls are made of.
> Boys are rotten,
> Made of cotton—
> That's what little boys are made of.
> (*BARING-GOULD* 176–116)

When not enjoined to *be all boy,* our young lad will be urged to *be a big boy, be a brave soldier,* and (the ultimate appeal) *be a man.* These expressions almost invariably mean that the boy is about to suffer something painful or humiliating. The variant—*take it like a man*—provides the clue. As Paul Theroux defines it, *be a man* means: "Be stupid, be unfeeling, obedient and soldierly, and stop thinking."

Following our boy further into the life cycle, we discover that in 14 school he will find himself in a cruel bind: girls his age will be biologically and socially more mature than he is, at least until around age eighteen. Until then, any ineptness in his social role will be castigated by a host of terms which are reserved almost entirely for males. "For all practical purposes," John Gordon remarks, "the word 'turkey' (or whatever the equivalent is now) can be translated as 'a boy spurned by influential girls'" (141). The equivalents of *turkey* are many: *jerk, nerd, clod, klutz, schmuck, dummy, goon, dork, square, dweeb, jackass, meathead, geek, zero, reject, goofball, drip,* and numerous others, including many obscene terms. Recently, a Michigan high school decided to do away with a scheduled "Nerd Day" after a fourteen-year-old male student, who apparently had been so harassed as a nerd by other students, committed suicide ("'Nerd' day"). In this case, the ability of language to devastate the emotionally vulnerable young male is powerfully and pathetically dramatized.

As our boy grows, he faces threats and taunts if he does not take   15 risks or endure pain to prove his manhood. *Coward,* for example, is a word applied almost exclusively to males in our society, as are its numerous variants—*chicken, chickenshit, yellow, yellow-bellied, lily-livered, weak-kneed, spineless, squirrelly, fraidy cat, gutless wonder, weakling, butterfly, jellyfish,* and so on. If our young man walks away from a stupid quarrel or prefers to settle differences more rationally than with a swift jab to the jaw, the English language is richly supplied with these and other expressions to call his masculinity into question.

Chief among the other expressions that question masculinity is a   16 lengthy list of homophobic terms such as *queer, pansy, fag, faggot, queen, queeny, pervert, bugger, deviant, fairy, tinkerbell, puss, priss, flamer, feller, sweet, precious, fruit, sodomite,* and numerous others, many obscene. For many people, *gay* is an all-purpose word of ridicule and condemnation. Once again, although homosexuals are being insulted by these terms, the primary target is more often the heterosexual male who fails or refuses to live up to someone else's idea of masculinity. In "Homophobia Among Men" Gregory Lehne explains, "Homophobia is used as a technique of social control . . . to enforce the norms of male sex-role behavior. . . . [H]omosexuality is not the real threat, the real threat is change in the male sex-role"(77).

Nowhere is this threat more apparent than in challenges to our   17 society's male-only military obligation. When a young man and a young woman reach the age of eighteen, both may register to vote; only the young man is required by law to register for military service. For the next decade at least, he must stand ready to be called into military service and even into combat duty in wars, "police actions," "peace-keeping missions," and "rescue missions," often initiated by legally dubious means. Should he resist this obligation, he may be called a *draft dodger, deserter, peacenik, traitor, shirker, slacker, malingerer,* and similar terms. Should he declare himself a conscientious objector, he may be labeled a *conchy* or any of the variants of *coward.*

In his relationships with women, he will find that the age of   18 equality has not yet arrived. Usually, he will be expected to take the initiative, do the driving, pick up the tab, and in general show a deferential respect for women that is a left-over from the chivalric code. Should he behave in an *ungentlemanly* fashion, a host of words—which are applied almost always to males alone—can be used to tell him so: *louse, rat, creep, sleaze, scum, stain, worm, fink, heel, stinker, animal, savage, bounder, cad, wolf, gigolo, womanizer, Don Juan, pig, rotter, boor,* and so on.

In sexual matters he will usually be expected to take the initiative   19
and to *perform*. If he does not, he will be labeled *impotent*. This word,
writes Goldberg, "is clearly sexist because it implies a standard of
acceptable masculine sexual performance that makes a man abnormal
if he can't live up to it" (*New Male* 248). Metaphorically, *impotent* can
be used to demean any male whose efforts in any area are deemed
unacceptable. Even if our young man succeeds at his sexual performance, the sex manuals are ready to warn him that if he reaches
orgasm before a specified time he is guilty of *premature ejaculation*.

When our young man marries, he will be required by law and   20
social custom to support his wife and children. Should he not succeed
as breadwinner or should he relax in his efforts, the language offers
numerous terms to revile him: *loser, deadbeat, bum, freeloader, leech,
parasite, goldbrick, sponge, mooch, ne'er-do-well, good for nothing*, and so
on. If women in our society have been regarded as sex objects, men
have been regarded as success objects, that is, judged by their ability
to provide a standard of living. The title of a recent book—*How to
Marry a Winner*—reveals immediately that the intended audience is
female (Collier).

When he becomes a father, our young man will discover that he   21
is a second-class parent, as the traditional interchangeability of *mother*
and *parent* indicates. The law has been particularly obtuse in recognizing fathers as parents, as evidenced by the awarding of child custody to mothers in ninety percent of divorce cases. In 1975 a father's
petition for custody of his four-year-old son was denied because, as
the family court judge said, "Fathers don't make good mothers" (qtd.
in Levine 21). The judge apparently never considered whether *fathers*
make good *parents*.

And so it goes throughout our young man's life: if he deviates   22
from society's gender role norm, he will be penalized and he will hear
about it.

The final form of anti-male bias to be considered here is negative   23
stereotyping. Sometimes this stereotyping is indirectly embedded
in the language, sometimes it resides in people's assumptions about
males and shapes their response to seemingly neutral words, and
sometimes it is overtly created for political reasons. It is one thing
to say that some aspects of the traditional masculine gender role
are limiting and hurtful; it is quite another to gratuitously suspect
males in general of being criminal and evil or to denounce them in
wholesale fashion as oppressors, exploiters, and rapists. In *The New
Male* Goldberg writes, "Men may very well be the last remaining sub-
group in our society that can be blatantly, negatively and vilely
stereotyped with little objection or resistance" (103). As our language

demonstrates, such sexist stereotyping, whether unintentional or deliberate, is not only familiar but fashionable.

In English, crime and evil are usually attributed to the male. As [24] an experiment I have compiled lists of nouns which I read to my composition students, asking them to check whether the words suggest "primarily females," "primarily males," or "could be either." Nearly all the words for lawbreakers suggest males rather than females to most students. These words include *murderer, swindler, crook, criminal, burglar, thief, gangster, mobster, hood, hitman, killer, pickpocket, mugger,* and *terrorist.* Accounting for this phenomenon is not always easy. *Hitman* may obviously suggest "primarily males," and the *-er* in *murderer* may do the same, especially if it reminds students of the word's feminine form, *murderess.* Likewise, students may be aware that most murders are committed by males. Other words—like *criminal* and *thief*—are more clearly gender-neutral in form, and it is less clear why they should be so closely linked with "primarily males." Although the dynamics of the association may be unclear, English usage somehow conveys a subtle suggestion that males are to be regarded as guilty in matters of law-breaking.

This hint of male guilt extends to a term like *suspect.* When the [25] person's gender is unknown, the suspect is usually presumed to be a male. For example, even before a definite suspect had been identified, the perpetrator of the 1980–1981 Atlanta child murders was popularly known as *The Man.* When a male and female are suspected of a crime, the male is usually presumed the guilty party. In a recent murder case, when two suspects—Debra Brown and Alton Coleman—were apprehended, police discovered *Brown's* fingerprint in a victim's car and interpreted this as evidence of *Coleman's* guilt. As the Associated Press reported:

> Authorities say for the first time they have evidence linking Alton Coleman with the death of an Indianapolis man.
>
> A fingerprint found in the car of Eugene Scott has been identified as that of Debra Brown, Coleman's traveling companion. . . . ("Police")

Nowhere does the article suggest that Brown's fingerprint found in the victim's car linked Brown with the death: the male suspect was presumed the guilty party, while the female was only a "traveling companion." Even after Brown had been convicted of two murders, the Associated Press was still describing her as "the accused accomplice of convicted killer Alton Coleman" ("Indiana").

In some cases, this presumption of male guilt extends to crimes in [26] which males are not the principal offenders. As noted earlier, a term like *wife and child abuse* ignores battered husbands, but it does more: it suggests that males alone abuse children. In reality most child abuse is committed by mothers (Straus, Gelles, Steinmetz 71). Despite this fact, a 1978 study of child abuse bears the title *Sins of the Fathers* (Inglis).

The term *rape* creates special problems. While the majority of rapes [27] are committed by males and the number of female rape victims out-distances the number of male rape victims, it is widely assumed—as evidenced by the newspaper article cited above—that rape is a crime committed only by males in which only females are victims. Consequently, the word *rape* is often used as a brush to tar all males. In *Against Our Will* Susan Brownmiller writes: "From prehistoric times to the present, I believe, rape ... is nothing more or less than a con-scious process of intimidation by which *all men* keep *all women* in a state of fear" (15; italics in original). Making the point explicitly, Marilyn French states, "All men are rapists and that's all they are" (qtd. in Jennes 33). Given this kind of smear tactic, *rape* can be used metaphorically to indict males alone and to exonerate females, as in this sentence: "The rape of nature—and the ecological disaster it presages—is part and parcel of a dominating masculinity gone out of control" (Hoch 137). The statement neatly blames males alone even when the damage to the environment has been caused in part by fe-males like Anne Gorsuch Burford and Rita Lavelle.

Not only crimes but vices of all sorts have been typically attributed [28] to males. As Muriel R. Schulz points out, "The synonyms for *inebriate* ... seem to be coded primarily 'male': for example, *boozer, drunkard, tippler, toper, swiller, tosspot, guzzler, barfly, drunk, lush, boozehound, souse, tank, stew, rummy,* and *bum*" (126). Likewise, someone may be *drunk as a lord* but never *drunk as a lady*.

Sex bias or sexism itself is widely held to be a male-only fault. [29] When *sexism* is defined as "contempt for women"—as if there were no such thing as contempt for men—the definition of *sexism* is itself sex-ist (Bardwick 34).

Part of the reason for this masculinization of evil may be that in the [30] Western world the source of evil has long been depicted in male terms. In the Bible the Evil One is consistently referred to as *he,* whether the reference is to the serpent in the Garden of Eden, Satan as Adversary in Job, Lucifer and Beelzebub in the gospels, Jesus' tempter in the desert, or the dragon in Revelations. *Beelzebub,* incidentally, is often translated as *lord of the flies,* a term designating the demon as mascu-line. So masculine is the word *devil* that the female prefix is needed, as in *she-devil,* to make a feminine noun of it. The masculinization of evil is so unconsciously accepted that writers often attest to it even while attempting to deny it, as in this passage:

> From the very beginning, the Judeo-Christian tradition has linked
> women and evil. When second-century theologians struggled to
> explain the Devil's origins, they surmised that Satan and his various
> devils had once been angels. (Gerzon 224)

If the Judeo-Christian tradition has linked women and evil so closely, why is the writer using the masculine pronoun *his* to refer to Satan, the source of evil according to that tradition? Critics of sex-bias in religious language seldom notice or mention its masculinization of evil: of those objecting to *God the Father* as sexist, no one—to my knowledge— has suggested that designating Satan as the *Father of Lies* is equally sexist. Few theologians talk about Satan and her legions.

The tendency to blame nearly everything on men has climaxed in 31 recent times with the popularity of such terms as *patriarchy, patriarchal society,* and *male-dominated society.* More political than descriptive, these terms are rapidly becoming meaningless, used as all-purpose smear words to conjure up images of male oppressors and female victims. They are a linguistic sleight of hand which obscures the point that, as Mead has observed (299–300), societies are largely created by both sexes for both sexes. By using a swift reference to *patriarchal structures* or *patriarchal attitudes,* a writer can absolve females of all blame for society's flaws while fixing the onus solely on males. The giveaway of this ploy can be detected when *patriarchy* and its related terms are never used in a positive or neutral context, but are always used to assign blame to males alone.

Wholesale denunciations of males as oppressors, exploiters, 32 rapists, Nazis, and slave-drivers have become all too familiar during the past fifteen years. Too often the academic community, rather than opposing this sexism, has been encouraging it. All too many scholars and teachers have hopped the male-bashing bandwagon to disseminate what John Gordon calls "the myth of the monstrous male." With increasing frequency, this academically fashionable sexism can also be heard echoing from our students. "A white upper-middle-class straight male should seriously consider another college," declares a midwestern college student in *The New York Times Selective Guide to Colleges.* "You [the white male] are the bane of the world. . . . Ten generations of social ills can and will be strapped upon your shoulders" (qtd. in Fiske 12). It would be comforting to dismiss this student's compound of misinformation, sexism, racism, and self-righteousness as an extreme example, but similar yahooisms go unchallenged almost everywhere in modern academia.

Surely it is time for men and women of good will to reject and 33 protest such bigotry. For teachers and writers, the first task is to recognize and condemn forms of anti-male bias in language, whether they are used to exclude males from equal consideration with females, to reinforce restrictive aspects of the masculine gender role, or to stereotype males callously. For whether males are told that *fathers don't make good mothers*, that *real men don't cry*, or that *all men are rapists*, the results are potentially dangerous: like any other group, males can be subtly shaped into what society keeps telling them they are. In *Why Men Are the Way They Are* Warren Farrell puts the matter succinctly: "The more we make men the enemy, the more they will have to behave like the enemy"(357).

Works Cited

Bardwick, Judith. *In Transition: How Feminism, Sexual Liberation, and the Search for Self-Fulfillment Have Altered Our Lives* (New York: Holt, 1979).

Baring-Gould, William S., and Ceil Baring-Gould. *The Annotated Mother Goose Nursery Rhymes Old and New, Arranged and Explained* (New York: Clarkson N. Potter, 1962).

Brownmiller, Susan. *Against Our Will: Men, Women and Rape* (New York: Simon, 1975).

Collier, Phyllis K. *How to Marry a Winner* (Englewood Cliffs, NJ: Prentice, 1982).

Dinnerstein, Dorothy. *The Mermaid and the Minotaur: Sexual Arrangements and Human Malaise* (New York: Harper, 1976).

Farrell, Warren. *Why Men Are the Way They Are: The Male-Female Dynamic* (New York: McGraw-Hill, 1986).

Fiske, Edward B. *The New York Times Selective Guide to Colleges* (New York: Times Books, 1982).

Gerzon, Mark. *A Choice of Heroes: The Changing Faces of American Manhood* (Boston: Houghton, 1982).

Glass, Andrew J. "President wants to unleash military power, but cannot." *Dayton Daily News*, 18 (June 1985), 1.

Goldberg, Herb. *The Hazards of Being Male: Surviving the Myth of Masculine Privilege*. 1976 (New York: NAL, 1977).

———. *The New Male: From Self-Destruction to Self-Care*. 1979 (New York: NAL, 1980).

Gordon, John. *The Myth of the Monstrous Male, and Other Feminist Fables* (New York: Playboy Press, 1982).

Hartley, Ruth E. "Sex-Role Pressures and the Socialization of the Male Child" in *The Forty-Nine Percent Majority: The Male Sex Role*, ed. Deborah S. David and Robert Brannon (Reading, MA: Addison-Wesley, 1976) pp. 235–44.

Hoch, Paul. *White Hero, Black Beast: Racism, Sexism and the Mask of Masculinity*, (London: Pluto Press, 1979).

"Indiana jury finds Brown guilty of murder, molesting." *Dayton Daily News*, 18 (May 1986) 7A.

Inglis, Ruth. *Sins of the Fathers: A Study of the Physical and Emotional Abuse of Children* (New York: St. Martin's, 1978).

Jennes, Gail. "All Men Are Rapists." *People*, 20 (Feb. 1978) 33–34.

Lehne, Gregory. "Homophobia Among Men." *The Forty-Nine Percent Majority: The Male Sex Role*, pp. 66–88.

Levine, James A. *Who Will Raise the Children? New Options for Fathers (and Mothers)* (Philadelphia: Lippincott, 1976).

Mead, Margaret. *Male and Female: A Study of the Sexes in a Changing World* (New York: Morrow, 1949, 1967).

Money, John, and Patricia Tucker. *Sexual Signature: On Being a Man or a Woman* (Boston: Little, 1975).

Mougey, Kate. "An act of confiscation: Rape." *Kettering-Oakwood* [OH] *Times,* 4 (Feb. 1981) 1B.

"'Nerd' day gets a boot after suicide." *Dayton Daily News,* 24 (Jan. 1986) 38.

Ong, Walter J. *Fighting for Life: Contest, Sexuality, and Consciousness* (Ithaca, New York: Cornell Univ. Press, 1981).

O'Reilly, Jane, et al. "Wife-Beating: The Silent Crime." *Time,* 5 (Sept. 1983) 23–4, 26.

"Police: Print links Coleman, death." *Dayton Daily News,* 31 (Aug. 1984) 26.

Roman, Mel, and William Haddad. *The Disposable Parent: The Case for Joint Custody.* (New York: Penguin, 1979).

Schulz, Muriel R. "Is the English Language Anybody's Enemy?" in *Speaking of Words: A Language Reader,* 3rd ed. ed. James MacKillop and Donna Woolfolk Cross (New York: Holt, 1986) pp. 125–27.

Sorrels, Bobbye D. *The Nonsexist Communicator: Solving the Problems of Gender and Awkwardness in Modern English* (Englewood Cliffs, NJ: Prentice, 1983).

Straus, Murray A., Richard J. Gelles, and Suzanne K. Steinmetz. *Behind Closed Doors: Violence in the American Family* (Garden City, New York: Doubleday, 1981).

Theroux, Paul. "The Male Myth." *The New York Times Magazine,* 27 (Nov. 1983) 116.

QUESTIONS

1. According to August, what are the negative effects of anti-male language?

2. August argues that men are unfairly victimized by the language of parenthood (paragraph 7), sexuality and success (paragraphs 19–21). How do you think women are victimized in each of these cases, for example by being more closely associated with parenting roles than men or by men's being "regarded as success objects"? How successfully do you think August anticipates and counters these objections?

Sex, Lies and Conversation:
Why Is It So Hard for Men and
Women to Talk to Each Other?

DEBORAH TANNEN

I was addressing a small gathering in a suburban Virginia living 1
room—a women's group that had invited men to join them. Throughout the evening, one man had been particularly talkative, frequently
offering ideas and anecdotes, while his wife sat silently beside him on
the couch. Toward the end of the evening, I commented that women
frequently complain that their husbands don't talk to them. This man
quickly concurred. He gestured toward his wife and said, "She's the
talker in our family." The room burst into laughter; the man looked
puzzled and hurt. "It's true," he explained. "When I come home from
work I have nothing to say. If she didn't keep the conversation going,
we'd spend the whole evening in silence."

This episode crystallizes the irony that although American men 2
tend to talk more than women in public situations, they often talk less
at home. And this pattern is wreaking havoc with marriage.

The pattern was observed by political scientist Andrew Hacker in 3
the late '70s. Sociologist Catherine Kohler Riessman reports in her new
book *Divorce Talk* that most of the women she interviewed—but only a
few of the men—gave lack of communication as the reason for their di-
vorces. Given the current divorce rate of nearly 50 percent, that
amounts to millions of cases in the United States every year—a virtual
epidemic of failed conversation.

In my own research, complaints from women about their hus- 4
bands most often focused not on tangible inequities such as having
given up the chance for a career to accompany a husband to his, or
doing far more than their share of daily life-support work like cleaning,
cooking, social arrangements and errands. Instead, they focused on

A professor of linguistics at Georgetown University, **Deborah Tannen**
has written numerous articles and several books presenting linguistics
research for a general audience, including *You Just Don't Understand:
Women and Men in Conversation* (1990) and *That's Not What I Meant:
How Conversational Style Makes or Breaks Your Relations with Others*
(1986). Her scholarly works include *Framing in Discourse* (1993) and
Linguistics in Context (1988). The following article, an overview of her
research about male and female conversational patterns, was published in the Sunday *Washington Post* in 1990.

communication: "He doesn't listen to me," "He doesn't talk to me." I found, as Hacker observed years before, that most wives want their husbands to be, first and foremost, conversational partners, but few husbands share this expectation of their wives.

In short, the image that best represents the current crisis is the stereotypical cartoon scene of a man sitting at the breakfast table with a newspaper held up in front of his face, while a woman glares at the back of it, wanting to talk.

Linguistic Battle of the Sexes

How can women and men have such different impressions of communication in marriage? Why the widespread imbalance in their interests and expectations?

In the April [1990] issue of *American Psychologist,* Stanford University's Eleanor Maccoby reports the results of her own and others' research showing that children's development is most influenced by the social structure of peer interactions. Boys and girls tend to play with children of their own gender, and their sex-separate groups have different organizational structures and interactive norms.

I believe these systematic differences in childhood socialization make talk between women and men like cross-cultural communication, heir to all the attraction and pitfalls of that enticing but difficult enterprise. My research on men's and women's conversations uncovered patterns similar to those described for children's groups.

For women, as for girls, intimacy is the fabric of relationships, and talk is the thread from which it is woven. Little girls create and maintain friendships by exchanging secrets; similarly, women regard conversation as the cornerstone of friendship. So a woman expects her husband to be a new and improved version of a best friend. What is important is not the individual subjects that are discussed but the sense of closeness, of a life shared, that emerges when people tell their thoughts, feelings, and impressions.

Bonds between boys can be as intense as girls', but they are based less on talking, more on doing things together. Since they don't assume talk is the cement that binds a relationship, men don't know what kind of talk women want, and they don't miss it when it isn't there.

Boy's groups are larger, more inclusive, and more hierarchical, so boys must struggle to avoid the subordinate position in the group. This may play a role in women's complaints that men don't listen to them. Some men really don't like to listen, because being the listener makes them feel one-down, like a child listening to adults or an employee to a boss.

But often when women tell men, "You aren't listening," and the 12 men protest, "I am," the men are right. The impression of not listening results from misalignments in the mechanics of conversation. The misalignment begins as soon as a man and a woman take physical positions. This became clear when I studied videotapes made by psychologist Bruce Dorval of children and adults talking to their same-sex best friends. I found that at every age, the girls and women faced each other directly, their eyes anchored on each other's faces. At every age, the boys and men sat at angles to each other and looked elsewhere in the room, periodically glancing at each other. They were obviously attuned to each other, often mirroring each other's movements. But the tendency of men to face away can give women the impression they aren't listening even when they are. A young woman in college was frustrated: Whenever she told her boyfriend she wanted to talk to him, he would lie down on the floor, close his eyes, and put his arm over his face. This signaled to her, "He's taking a nap." But he insisted he was listening extra hard. Normally, he looks around the room, so he is easily distracted. Lying down and covering his eyes helped him concentrate on what she was saying.

Analogous to the physical alignment that women and men take in 13 conversation is their topical alignment. The girls in my study tended to talk at length about one topic, but the boys tended to jump from topic to topic. The second-grade girls exchanged stories about people they knew. The second-grade boys teased, told jokes, noticed things in the room and talked about finding games to play. The sixth-grade girls talked about problems with a mutual friend. The sixth-grade boys talked about 55 different topics, none of which extended over more than a few turns.

Listening to Body Language

Switching topics is another habit that gives women the impression 14 men aren't listening, especially if they switch to a topic about themselves. But the evidence of the 10th-grade boys in my study indicates otherwise. The 10th-grade boys sprawled across their chairs with bodies parallel and eyes straight ahead, rarely looking at each other. They looked as if they were riding in a car, staring out the windshield. But they were talking about their feelings. One boy was upset because a girl had told him he had a drinking problem, and the other was feeling alienated from all his friends.

Now, when a girl told a friend about a problem, the friend re- 15 sponded by asking probing questions and expressing agreement and understanding. But the boys dismissed each other's problems. Todd assured Richard that his drinking was "no big problem" because "sometimes you're funny when you're off your butt." And when Todd said he felt left out, Richard responded, "Why should you? You know more people than me."

Women perceived such responses as belittling and unsupportive. 16 But the boys seemed satisfied with them. Whereas women reassure each other by implying, "You shouldn't feel bad because I've had similar experiences," men do so by implying, "You shouldn't feel bad because your problems aren't so bad."

There are even simpler reasons for women's impression that men 17 don't listen. Linguist Lynette Hirschman found that women make more listener-noise, such as "mhm," "uhuh," and "yeah," to show "I'm with you." Men, she found, more often give silent attention. Women who expect a stream of listener-noise interpret silent attention as no attention at all.

Women's conversational habits are as frustrating to men as men's 18 are to women. Men who expect silent attention interpret a stream of listener-noise as overreaction or impatience. Also, when women talk to each other in a close, comfortable setting, they often overlap, finish each other's sentences and anticipate what the other is about to say. This practice, which I call "participatory listenership," is often perceived by men as interruption, intrusion and lack of attention.

A parallel difference caused a man to complain about his wife, 19 "She just wants to talk about her own point of view. If I show her another view, she gets mad at me." When most women talk to each other, they assume a conversationalist's job is to express agreement and support. But many men see their conversational duty as pointing out the other side of an argument. This is heard as disloyalty by women, and refusal to offer the requisite support. It is not that women don't want to see other points of view, but that they prefer them phrased as suggestions and inquiries rather than as direct challenges.

In his book *Fighting for Life,* Walter Ong points out that men use 20 "agonistic" or warlike, oppositional formats to do almost anything; thus discussion becomes debate, and conversation a competitive sport. In contrast, women see conversation as a ritual means of establishing rapport. If Jane tells a problem and June says she has a similar one, they walk away feeling closer to each other. But this attempt at establishing rapport can backfire when used with men. Men take too literally women's ritual "troubles talk," just as women mistake men's ritual challenges for real attack.

The Sounds of Silence

These differences begin to clarify why women and men have such 21 different expectations about communication in marriage. For women, talk creates intimacy. Marriage is an orgy of closeness: you can tell your feelings and thoughts, and still be loved. Their greatest fear is being pushed away. But men live in a hierarchical world, where talk maintains independence and status. They are on guard to protect themselves from being put down and pushed around.

This explains the paradox of the talkative man who said of his 22 silent wife, "She's the talker." In the public setting of a guest lecture, he felt challenged to show his intelligence and display his under-standing of the lecture. But at home, where he has nothing to prove and no one to defend against, he is free to remain silent. For his wife, being home means she is free from the worry that something she says might offend someone, or spark disagreement, or appear to be show-ing off; at home she is free to talk.

The communication problems that endanger marriage can't be 23 fixed by mechanical engineering. They require a new conceptual framework about the role of talk in human relationships. Many of the psychological explanations that have become second nature may not be helpful, because they tend to blame either women (for not being as-sertive enough) or men (for not being in touch with their feelings). A sociolinguistic approach by which male-female conversation is seen as cross-cultural communication allows us to understand the problem and forge solutions without blaming either party.

Once the problem is understood, improvement comes naturally, 24 as it did to the young woman and her boyfriend who seemed to go to sleep when she wanted to talk. Previously, she had accused him of not listening, and he had refused to change his behavior, since that would be admitting fault. But then she learned about and explained to him the differences in women's and men's habitual ways of aligning them-selves in conversation. The next time she told him she wanted to talk, he began, as usual, by lying down and covering his eyes. When the fa-miliar negative reaction bubbled up, she reassured herself that he re-ally was listening. But then he sat up and looked at her. Thrilled she asked why. He said, "You like me to look at you when we talk, so I'll try to do it." Once he saw their differences as cross-cultural rather than right and wrong, he independently altered his behavior.

Women who feel abandoned and deprived when their husbands 25 won't listen to or report daily news may be happy to discover their husbands trying to adapt once they understand the place of small talk in women's relationships. But if their husbands don't adapt, the women may still be comforted that for men, this is not a failure of in-timacy. Accepting the difference, the wives may look to their friends or family for that kind of talk. And husbands who can't provide it shouldn't feel their wives have made unreasonable demands. Some couples will still decide to divorce, but at least their decisions will be based on realistic expectations.

In these times of resurgent ethnic conflicts, the world desperately   26 needs cross-cultural understanding. Like charity, successful cross-cultural communication should begin at home.

QUESTIONS

1. How accurately do the communication patterns observed by Tannen reflect your experience as either a man or a woman? In your experience, how accurately do the patterns represent the opposite sex?

2. How does Tannen think men and women can avoid some of the misunderstandings that arise between the sexes?

When It Changed

JOANNA RUSS

Katy drives like a maniac; we must have been doing over 120 kilo- 1
meters per hour on those turns. She's good, though, extremely good,
and I've seen her take the whole car apart and put it together again in
a day. My birthplace on Whileaway was largely given to farm machinery and I refuse to wrestle with a five-gear shift at unholy speeds, not
having been brought up to it, but even on those turns in the middle of
the night, on a country road as bad as only our district can make them,
Katy's driving didn't scare me. The funny thing about my wife,
though: she will not handle guns. She has even gone hiking in the
forests above the forty-eighth parallel without firearms, for days at a
time. And that *does* scare me.

Katy and I have three children between us, one of hers and two of 2
mine. Yuriko, my eldest, was asleep in the back seat, dreaming twelve-
year-old dreams of love and war: running away to sea, hunting in the
North, dreams of strangely beautiful people in strangely beautiful
places, all the wonderful guff you think up when you're turning twelve
and the glands start going. Some day soon, like all of them, she will disappear for weeks on end to come back grimy and proud, having knifed
her first cougar or shot her first bear, dragging some abominably dangerous dead beastie behind her, which I will never forgive for what it
might have done to my daughter. Yuriko says Katy's driving puts her
to sleep.

For someone who has fought three duels, I am afraid of far, far too 3
much. I'm getting old. I told this to my wife.

"You're thirty-four," she said. Laconic to the point of silence, that 4
one. She flipped the lights on, on the dash—three kilometers to go and
the road getting worse all the time. Far out in the country. Electric-

---

Joanna Russ, an English professor at the University of Washington,
is the author of science fiction novels and stories including *And
Chaos Died* (1970), *The Female Man* (1975), and "Souls," a novella that
won both the Hugo Award from the World Science Fiction
Convention and the Nebula Award from the Science Fiction Writers
of America. Her feminist criticism includes *How to Suppress Women's
Writing* (1983) and *Magic Mommas, Trembling Sisters, Puritans and
Perverts: Feminist Essays* (1985). "When It Changed," which won the
1972 Nebula Award, first appeared in *Again, Dangerous Visions*, an
anthology edited by Harlan Ellison.

green trees rushed into our headlights and around the car. I reached down next to me where we bolt the carrier panel to the door and eased my rifle into my lap. Yuriko stirred in the back. My height but Katy's eyes, Katy's face. The car engine is so quiet, Katy says, that you can hear breathing in the back seat. Yuki had been alone in the car when the message came, enthusiastically decoding her dot-dashes (silly to mount a wide-frequency transceiver near an I. C. engine, but most of Whileaway is on steam). She had thrown herself out of the car, my gangly and gaudy offspring, shouting at the top of her lungs, so of course she had had to come along. We've been intellectually prepared for this ever since the Colony was founded, ever since it was abandoned, but this is different. This is awful.

"Men!" Yuki had screamed, leaping over the car door. "They've 5 come back! Real Earth men!"

We met them in the kitchen of the farmhouse near the place where 6 they had landed; the windows were open, the night air very mild. We had passed all sorts of transportation when we parked outside— steam tractors, trucks, an I. C. flatbed, even a bicycle. Lydia, the district biologist, had come out of her Northern taciturnity long enough to take blood and urine samples and was sitting in a corner of the kitchen shaking her head in astonishment over the results; she even forced herself (very big, very fair, very shy, always painfully blushing) to dig up the old language manuals—though I can talk the old tongues in my sleep. And do. Lydia is uneasy with us; we're Southerners and too flamboyant. I counted twenty people in that kitchen, all the brains of North Continent. Phyllis Spet, I think, had come in by glider. Yuki was the only child there.

Then I saw the four of them. 7

They are bigger than we are. They are bigger and broader. Two 8 were taller than I, and I am extremely tall, one meter eighty centimeters in my bare feet. They are obviously of our species but *off*, indescribably off, and as my eyes could not and still cannot quite comprehend the lines of those alien bodies, I could not, then, bring myself to touch them, though the one who spoke Russian—what voices they have—wanted to "shake hands," a custom from the past, I imagine. I can only say they were apes with human faces. He seemed to mean well, but I found myself shuddering back almost the length of the kitchen—and then I laughed apologetically—and then to set a good example (*intersteller amity*, I thought) did "shake hands" finally. A hard, hard hand. They are heavy as draft horses. Blurred, deep voices. Yuriko had sneaked in between the adults and was gazing at *the men* with her mouth open.

He turned *his* head—those words have not been in our language 9
for six hundred years—and said, in bad Russian:

"Who's that?"   10

"My daughter," I said, and added (with that irrational attention to 11
good manners we sometimes employ in moments of insanity), "My
daughter, Yuriko Janetson. We use the patronymic. You would say
matronymic."

He laughed, involuntarily. Yuki exclaimed, "I thought they would 12
be *good-looking!*" greatly disappointed at this reception of herself.
Phyllis Helgason Spet, whom someday I shall kill, gave me across the
room a cold, level, venomous look, as if to say: *Watch what you say. You
know what I can do.* It's true that I have little formal status, but Madam
President will get herself in serious trouble with both me and her own
staff if she continues to consider industrial espionage good clean fun.
Wars and rumors of wars, as it says in one of our ancestor's books. I
translated Yuki's words into *the man's* dog-Russian, once our *lingua
franca,* and *the man* laughed again.

"Where are all your people?" he said conversationally.   13

I translated again and watched the faces around the room; Lydia 14
embarrassed (as usual), Spet narrowing her eyes with some damned
scheme, Katy very pale.

"This is Whileaway," I said.   15

He continued to look unenlightened.   16

"Whileaway," I said. "Do you remember? Do you have records? 17
There was a plague on Whileaway."

He looked moderately interested. Heads turned in the back of the 18
room, and I caught a glimpse of the local professions-parliament dele-
gate; by morning every town meeting, every district caucus, would be
in full session.

"Plague?" he said. "That's most unfortunate."   19

"Yes," I said. "Most unfortunate. We lost half our population in 20
one generation."

He looked properly impressed.   21

"Whileaway was lucky," I said. "We had a big initial gene pool, 22
we had been chosen for extreme intelligence, we had a high technology and a large remaining population in which every adult was two or
three experts in one. The soil is good. The climate is blessedly easy.
There are thirty millions of us now. Things are beginning to snowball
in industry—do you understand?—give us seventy years and we'll
have more than one real city, more than a few industrial centers, full-
time professions, full-time radio operators, full-time machinists, give
us seventy years and not everyone will have to spend three-quarters of
a lifetime on the farm." And I tried to explain how hard it is when
artists can practice full-time only in old age, when there are so few, so

very few who can be free, like Katy and myself. I tried also to outline our government, the two houses, the one by professions and the geographic one; I told him the district caucuses handled problems too big for the individual towns. And that population control was not a political issue, not yet, though give us time and it would be. This was a delicate point in our history; give us time. There was no need to sacrifice the quality of life for an insane rush into industrialization. Let us go our own pace. Give us time.

"Where are all the people?" said that monomaniac.   23

I realized then that he did not mean people, he meant *men*, and he   24
was giving the word the meaning it had not had on Whileaway for six centuries.

"They died," I said. "Thirty generations ago."   25

I thought we had poleaxed him. He caught his breath. He made as   26
if to get out of the chair he was sitting in; he put his hand to his chest; he looked around at us with the strangest blend of awe and sentimental tenderness. Then he said, solemnly and earnestly:

"A great tragedy."   27

I waited, not quite understanding.   28

"Yes," he said, catching his breath again with the queer smile, that   29
adult-to-child smile that tells you something is being hidden and will be presently produced with cries of encouragement and joy, "a great tragedy. But it's over." And again he looked around at all of us with the strangest deference. As if we were invalids.

"You've adapted amazingly," he said.   30

"To what?" I said. He looked embarrassed. He looked inane.   31
Finally he said, "Where I come from, the women don't dress so plainly."

"Like you?" I said. "Like a bride?" for the men were wearing sil-   32
ver from head to foot. I had never seen anything so gaudy. He made as if to answer and then apparently thought better of it; he laughed at me again. With an odd exhilaration—as if we were something childish and something wonderful, as if he were doing us an enormous favor—he took one shaky breath and said, "Well, we're here."

I looked at Spet, Spet looked at Lydia, Lydia looked at Amalia,   33
who is the head of the local town meeting, Amalia looked at I don't know whom. My throat was raw. I cannot stand local beer, which the farmers swill as if their stomachs had iridium linings, but I took it anyway, from Amalia (it was her bicycle we had seen outside as we parked), and swallowed it all. This was going to take a long time. I said, "Yes, here you are," and smiled (feeling like a fool), and wondered seriously if male-Earth-people's minds worked so very differently from female-Earth-people's minds, but that couldn't be so or the race would have died out long ago. The radio network had got the

news around the planet by now and we had another Russian speaker, flown in from Varna; I decided to cut out when *the man* passed around pictures of his wife, who looked like the priestess of some arcane cult. He proposed to question Yuki, so I barreled her into a back room in spite of her furious protests, and went out on the front porch. As I left, Lydia was explaining the difference between parthenogenesis (which is so easy that anyone can practice it) and what we do, which is the merging of ova. That is why Katy's baby looks like me. Lydia went on to the Ansky Process and Katy Ansky, our one full-polymath genius and the great-great I don't know how many times great-grandmother of my own Katharina.

A dot-dash transmitter in one of the outbuildings chattered faintly 34 to itself: operators flirting and passing jokes down the line.

There was a man on the porch. The other tall man. I watched him 35 for a few minutes—I can move very quietly when I want to—and when I allowed him to see me, he stopped talking into the little machine hung around his neck. Then he said calmly, in excellent Russian, "Did you know that sexual equality has been reestablished on Earth?"

"You're the real one," I said, "aren't you? The other one's 36 for show." It was a great relief to get things cleared up. He nodded affably.

"As a people, we are not very bright," he said. "There's been too 37 much genetic damage in the last few centuries. Radiation. Drugs. We can use Whileaway's genes, Janet." Strangers do not call strangers by the first name.

"You can have cells enough to drown in," I said, "Breed your 38 own."

He smiled. "That's not the way we want to do it." Behind him I 39 saw Katy come into the square of light that was the screened-in door. He went on, low and urbane, not mocking me, I think, but with the self-confidence of someone who has always had money and strength to spare, who doesn't know what it is to be second-class or provincial. Which is very odd, because the day before, I would have said that was an exact description of me.

"I'm talking to you, Janet," he said, "because I suspect you have 40 more popular influence than anyone else here. You know as well as I do that parthenogenetic culture has all sorts of inherent defects, and we do not—if we can help it—mean to use you for anything of the sort. Pardon me; I should not have said 'use.' But surely you can see that this kind of society is unnatural."

"Humanity is unnatural," said Katy. She had my rifle under her 41 left arm. The top of that silky head does not quite come up to my collarbone, but she is as tough as steel; he began to move, again with that queer smiling deference (which his fellow had showed to me but he had not), and the gun slid into Katy's grip as if she had shot with it all her life.

"I agree," said the man. "Humanity is unnatural. I should know. I have metal in my teeth and metal pins here." He touched his shoulder. "Seals are harem animals," he added, "and so are men; apes are promiscuous and so are men; doves are monogamous and so are men; there are even celibate men and homosexual men. There are homosexual cows, I believe. But Whileaway is still missing something." He gave a dry chuckle. I will give him the credit of believing that it had something to do with nerves.

"I miss nothing," said Katy, "except that life isn't endless."

"You are—?" said the man, nodding from me to her.

"Wives," said Katy. "We're married." Again the dry chuckle.

"A good economic arrangement," he said, "for working and taking care of the children. And as good an arrangement as any for randomizing heredity, if your reproduction is made to follow the same pattern. But think, Katharina Michaelason, if there isn't something better that you might secure for your daughters. I believe in instincts, even in Man, and I can't think that the two of you—a machinist, are you? and I gather you are some sort of chief of police—don't feel somehow what even you must miss. You know it intellectually, of course. There is only half a species here. Men must come back to Whileaway."

Katy said nothing.

"I should think, Katharina Michaelason," said the man gently, "that you, of all people, would benefit most from such a change," and he walked past Katy's rifle into the square of light coming from the door. I think it was then that he noticed my scar, which really does not show unless the light is from the side: a fine line that runs from temple to chin. Most people don't even know about it.

"Where did you get that?" he said, and I answered with an involuntary grin. "In my last duel." We stood there bristling at each other for several seconds (this is absurd but true) until he went inside and shut the screen door behind him. Katy said in a brittle voice, "You damned fool, don't you know when we've been insulted?" and swung up the rifle to shoot him through the screen, but I got to her before she could fire and knocked the rifle out of aim; it burned a hole through the porch floor. Katy was shaking. She kept whispering over and over, "That's why I never touched it, because I knew I'd kill someone. I knew I'd kill someone." The first man—the one I'd spoken with first— was still talking inside the house, something about the grand movement to recolonize and rediscover all the Earth had lost. He stressed the advantages to Whileaway: trade, exchange of ideas, education. He, too, said that sexual equality had been reestablished on Earth.

Katy was right, of course; we should have burned them down 50 where they stood. Men are coming to Whileaway. When one culture has the big guns and the other has none, there is a certain predictability about the outcome. Maybe men would have come eventually in any case. I like to think that a hundred years from now my great-grandchildren could have stood them off or fought them to a standstill, but even that's no odds; I will remember all my life those four people I first met who were muscled like bulls and who made me—if only for a moment—feel small. A neurotic reaction, Katy says. I remember everything that happened that night; I remember Yuki's excitement in the car, I remember Katy's sobbing when we got home as if her heart would break, I remember her lovemaking, a little peremptory as always, but wonderfully soothing and comforting. I remember prowling restlessly around the house after Katy fell asleep with one bare arm hung into a patch of light from the hall. The muscles of her forearms are like metal bars from all that driving and testing of her machines. Sometimes I dream about Katy's arms. I remember wandering into the nursery and picking up my wife's baby, dozing for a while with the poignant, amazing warmth of an infant in my lap, and finally returning to the kitchen to find Yuriko fixing herself a late snack. My daughter eats like a Great Dane.

"Yuki," I said, "do you think you could fall in love with a man?" 51 and she whooped derisively. "With a ten-foot toad!" said my tactful child.

But men are coming to Whileaway. Lately I sit up nights and 52 worry about the men who will come to this planet, about my two daughters and Betta Katharinason, about what will happen to Katy, to me, to my life. Our ancestors' journals are one long cry of pain and I suppose I ought to be glad now, but one can't throw away six centuries, or even (as I have lately discovered) thirty-four years. Sometimes I laugh at the question those four men hedged about all evening and never quite dared to ask, looking at the lot of us, hicks in overalls, farmers in canvas pants and plain shirts: *Which of you plays the role of the man?* As if we had to produce a carbon copy of their mistakes! I doubt very much that sexual equality has been reestablished on Earth. I do not like to think of myself mocked, of Katy deferred to as if she were weak, of Yuki made to feel unimportant or silly, of my other children cheated of their full humanity or turned into strangers. And I'm afraid that my own achievements will dwindle from what they were—or what I thought they were—to the not-very-interesting curiosa of the human race, the oddities you read about in the back of the book, things to laugh at sometimes because they are so exotic, quaint but not impressive, charming but not useful. I find this more painful than I can say. You will agree that for a woman who has fought three duels, all of them kills, indulging in such fears is ludicrous. But what's around the corner now is a duel so big that I don't think I have the guts for it; in Faust's words: *Verweile doch, du bist so schoen!* Keep it as it is. Don't change.

Sometimes at night I remember the original name of this planet, 53 changed by the first generation of our ancestors, those curious women for whom, I suppose, the real name was too painful a reminder after the men died. I find it amusing, in a grim way, to see it all so completely turned around. This, too, shall pass. All good things must come to an end.

Take my life but don't take away the meaning of my life.   54

For-A-While.   55

QUESTIONS

1. What traditionally male roles in society do the females on Whileaway perform?

2. Explain why you agree or disagree with the man who says that Whileaway, despite its adjustments to the lack of men, "is still missing something" (paragraph 42).

3. How do the men who arrive reveal their attitude toward the women of Whileaway, and how do the women respond? Why do you think the narrator Janet "doubt[s] very much that sexual equality has been reestablished on Earth" (paragraph 49)?

THINKING ABOUT LANGUAGE AND GENDER

1. "Defend it on any grounds you choose," writes McFadden; "the neutering of spoken and written English, with its attendant self-consciousness, remains ludicrous." On what grounds would Maggio and Lakoff defend the "neutering of English"? What is your own view?

2. Nilsen says that "the whole story of a woman's life" can be told through chicken metaphors (paragraph 35), and August traces the male life cycle through "gender restrictive" language in paragraphs 11 to 22. While growing up, how have you personally been affected by the terminology used to refer to your gender? How have you been affected by the terminology used to refer to the opposite sex?

3. Nilsen and August use similar or identical evidence to support opposite arguments. For example, both discuss the language of sexuality in English, and both examine the contrast between the terms *tomboy* and *sissy*. For one of these examples, compare Nilsen's and August's arguments and use of the same evidence, and explain which you find more persuasive.

4. On what points do you think Nilsen and August could agree? How about August and Tannen? Create a three-way dialogue between Nilsen, August, and Tannen in which each presents solutions for improving relations between men and women. Use this dialogue to generate and support your own solutions.

5. In Russ's story, what evidence do you find on Whileaway for (a) the kinds of anti-female language analyzed by Nilsen; (b) the anti-male language analyzed by August; (c) the communication gaps analyzed by Tannen?

6. Based on the essays and story in this chapter, how inevitable do you feel gender stereotyping in language is? How harmful do you think it is?

Exploring Additional Sources

7. Language and gender issues are also raised in "Two Deserts" by Valerie Matsumoto (page 73), "The Girl Who Wouldn't Sing" by Kit Yuen Quan (page 118), "Suburbia, of Thee I Sing" by Phyllis McGinley (page 268), "Traveling Alone in Mexico" by Mary Morris (page 408), and "A Moroccan Memoir" by Sarah Streed (page 486). Analyze one or more of these selections using criteria from Nilsen, August, or Tannen.

8.   Nilsen and Tannen both develop their arguments from original data they collected themselves, or primary sources—a selection of dictionary words and definitions for Nilsen, and direct observations of communication behaviors for Tannen. Write an essay drawing conclusions based on your own such original or primary research. For example, you might study a selection of gender-biased terms you find in a dictionary of slang; or you could design and conduct a brief survey of classmates, dormmates, or fellow workers about male and female language or communication in the context of their home or job.

9.   Look up in a research library some of the studies cited by August or Tannen (or in the bibliography at the end of Tannen's book *You Just Don't Understand*) to get a feel for the large amount of social science research in gender, language, and communication. Pick a narrow angle that interests you for a research paper, such as the language of parenting or male-female interaction in the classroom.

2

LANGUAGE AND STEREOTYPES

"Redneck" Is Not a Dirty Word

PAUL GREENBERG

It is reported with a straight face that one Harold Smith, president of the local historical society in Smyrna, Ga., will lead an effort to get the National Geographic to apologize for using "redneck" to describe his town.

Can the gentleman from Smyrna be under the impression that "redneck" is a term of opprobrium rather than an estate, like matrimony, to be honored and preserved? If so, he is laboring under an illusion that has grown common even south of Mason-Dixon's Line. To quote Kathryn Jensen, author of the best one-volume guide to redneckin' that I know (*Redneckin,'* Putnam, 1983):

"We know some folks hold that redneck ain't a particular nice name for a body. Well, we don't agree.... Your basic redneck is just common folk livin' common style and tryin' the best he can to get along the best he can. Redneckin' is enjoyin' the simple things in life, workin' hard, not a-lettin' yourself be bothered by a heap a hard questions and worrisome ideas, and raisin' a little hell ever now and then."

Redneck is just another name for no-airs, and if the gentleman from Smyrna would think about which he'd rather see when stranded by the side of the road with a flat tire or a busted fan belt—a yuppie with Perfect Hair Syndrome whizzing past in his BMW, or a good ol' boy chugging along in an old pickup with a gun rack and time to spare for his fellow man. Well, he might come to realize that redneck is an encomium, not an insult.

As usual, the nicefiers of the language would deprive us not only of an honest word but of what it stands for, too. If they are allowed their way, and redneck becomes unmentionable in the National Geographic and other artifacts of polite society, the concept itself may have to go. What a loss that would be, not just to the language but to the region. What would replace the redneck—some neutral, indistinct, colorless species too bland to have a name? A sort of imitation Yankee?

—FROM *THE LOS ANGELES TIMES*, 1988

White Guys

ART CAREY

How did this happen so fast?

Just yesterday, it seems, White Guys were on top of the heap, exercising dominion over Earth and all its creatures. Guardians of civilization, makers of history, wagers of war and leaders of empires. Some people admired White Guys; some people feared them, but everybody (White Guys assumed) wanted to be like them. After all, White Guys were made in the image of God (i.e., Charlton Heston), and were masters of the universe.

Now look at them. They still have most of the power. Still have most of the good jobs. Still make most of the money. Still call the shots and run the show just about everywhere. But nobody "likes" White Guys anymore. In fact, plenty of people "hate" White Guys.

Briefly, the bill of indictment runs like this: White Guys are brutish louts, insensitive, dysfunctional, judgmental, unicultural yahoos and peckerwoods who are poisoned by testosterone and irredeemably guilty of centuries of patriarchal hegemony as well as just about every "ism" in the book, including, but not limited to: racism, sexism, ageism, classism and, last but not least, looks-ism.

It's hard to believe: White Guys as a "targeted group." White Guys as "victims"! But how else to explain the popularity of a "Zeitgeist" movie such as "Falling Down," wherein a bespectacled middle-aged White Guy with an astronaut haircut goes berserk because he's fed up with the manifold insults and indignities of modern life and is tired of taking abuse from the diverse denizens of rainbow-coalition America. "Beleaguered by feminism, multiculturalism, affirmative action and PC zealotry, white males are starting to fray at the seams," asserts a *Newsweek* cover story about "white male paranoia."

White Guys probably had it coming. But do they really deserve so much scorn and contumely? Are they really all that bad? Is there anybody out there who can say anything good about White Guys now that (although not exactly down) they're being so enthusiastically kicked around?

—FROM "10 GOOD THINGS ABOUT WHITE GUYS," *SAN JOSE MERCURY NEWS*, 1993.

Black and White

WILLIAM RASPBERRY

Name one pursuit, aside from athletics, entertainment or sexual performance in which a white practitioner will feel complimented to be told he does it "black." Tell a white broadcaster he talks "black" and he'll sign up for diction lessons. Tell a white reporter he writes "black" and he'll take a writing course. Tell a white lawyer he reasons "black" and he might sue you for slander.

What we have here is a tragically limited definition of blackness, and it isn't only white people who buy it.

Think of all the ways black children can put one another down with charges of "whiteness." For many of these children, hard study and hard work are "white." Trying to please a teacher might be criticized as acting "white." Speaking correct English is "white." Scrimping today in the interest of tomorrow's goals is "white." Educational toys and games are "white."

An incredible array of habits and attitudes that are conducive to success in business, in academia, in the non-entertainment professions are likely to be thought of as somehow "white." Even economic success, unless it involves such "black" undertakings as numbers banking, is defined as "white."

—From "What It Means to Be Black," *The Washington Post*, 1985.

The Dehumanization of the Indian

HAIG A. BOSMAJIAN

While the state and church as institutions have defined the Indian into subjugation, there has been in operation the use of a suppressive language by society at large which has perpetuated the dehumanization of the Indian. Commonly used words and phrases relegate the Indian to an inferior, infantile status: "The only good Indian is a dead Indian"; "Give it back to the Indians"; "drunken Indians"; "dumb Indians"; "Redskins"; "Indian giver." Writings and speeches include references to the "Indian problem" in the same manner that references have been made by whites to "the Negro problem" and by the Nazis to "the Jewish problem." There was no "Jewish problem" in Germany until the Nazis linguistically created the myth; there was no "Negro problem" until white Americans created the myth; similarly, the "Indian problem" has been created in such a way that the oppressed, not the oppressor, evolve as "the problem."

As the list of negative "racial characteristics" of the "Indian race" grew over the years, the redefinition of the individual Indian became easier and easier. He or she was trapped by the racial definitions, stereotypes, and myths. No matter how intelligent, how "civilized" the Indian became, he or she was still an Indian.

—From *The Language of Oppression*, 1974

The Indian Chant and the Tomahawk Chop

WARD CHURCHILL

During the past couple of seasons, there has been an increasing 1
wave of controversy regarding the names of professional sports teams
like the Atlanta "Braves," Cleveland "Indians," Washington
"Redskins," and Kansas City "Chiefs." The issue extends to the names
of college teams like Florida State University "Seminoles," University
of Illinois "Fighting Illini," and so on, right on down to high school out-
fits like the Lamar (Colorado) "Savages." Also involved have been
team adoption of "mascots," replete with feathers, buckskins, beads,
spears and "warpaint" (some fans have opted to adorn themselves in
the same fashion), and nifty little "pep" gestures like the "Indian
Chant" and "Tomahawk Chop."

A substantial number of American Indians have protested that use 2
of native names, images and symbols as sports team mascots and the
like is, by definition, a virulently racist practice. Given the historical relationship between Indians and non-Indians during what has been
called the "Conquest of America," American Indian Movement leader
(and American Indian Anti-Defamation Council founder) Russell
Means has compared the practice to contemporary Germans naming
their soccer teams the "Jews," "Hebrews," and "Yids," while adorning
their uniforms with grotesque caricatures of Jewish faces taken from
the Nazis' anti-Semitic propaganda of the 1930s. Numerous demon-
strations have occurred in conjunction with games—most notably dur-

---

Formerly professor of American Indian Studies at the University
of Colorado, **Ward Churchill** is a writer and active member of
the American Indian Anti-Defamation League. His recent books
include *Fantasies of the Master Race: Literature, Cinema, and the
Colonization of American Indians* (1992) and *Indians Are Us: Culture and
Genocide in Native North America* (1994). "The Indian Chant and the
Tomahawk Chop" is from the longer essay "Crimes Against
Humanity," which appeared in *Z Magazine* (1993). The editors of
Z Magazine describe their journal as "an independent political magazine of critical thinking on political, cultural, social, and economic life
in the United States. It sees the racial, sexual, class, and political
dimensions of personal life as fundamental to understanding and
improving contemporary circumstances; and it aims to assist activist
efforts to attain a better future."

ing the November 15, 1992 match-up between the Chiefs and Redskins in Kansas City—by angry Indians and their supporters.

In response, a number of players—especially African Americans 3 and other minority athletes—have been trotted out by professional team owners like Ted Turner, as well as university and public school officials, to announce that they mean not to insult but to honor native people. They have been joined by the television networks and most major newspapers, all of which have editorialized that Indian discomfort with the situation is "no big deal," insisting that the whole thing is just "good, clean fun." The country needs more such fun, they've argued, and "a few disgruntled Native Americans" have no right to undermine the nation's enjoyment of its leisure time by complaining. This is especially the case, some have argued, "in hard times like these." It has even been contended that Indian outrage at being systematically degraded—rather than the degradation itself—creates "a serious barrier to the sort of intergroup communication so necessary in a multicultural society such as ours."

Okay, let's communicate. We are frankly dubious that those ad- 4 vancing such positions really believe their own rhetoric, but, just for the sake of argument, let's accept the premise that they are sincere. If what they say is true, then isn't it time we spread such "inoffensiveness" and "good cheer" around among *all* groups so that *everybody* can participate *equally* in fostering the round of national laughs they call for? Sure it is—the country can't have too much fun or "intergroup involvement"—so the more, the merrier. Simple consistency demands that anyone who thinks the Tomahawk Chop is a swell pastime must be just as hearty in their endorsement of the following ideas—by the logic used to defend the defamation of American Indians—should help us all really start yukking it up.

First, as a counterpart to the Redskins, we need an NFL team 5 called "Niggers" to honor Afro-Americans. Half-time festivities for fans might include a simulated stewing of the opposing coach in a large pot while players and cheerleaders dance around it, garbed in leopard skins and wearing fake bones in their noses. This concept obviously goes along with the kind of gaiety attending the Chop, but also with the actions of the Kansas City Chiefs, whose team members—prominently including black team members—lately appeared on a poster looking "fierce" and "savage" by way of wearing Indian regalia. Just a bit of harmless "morale boosting," says the Chiefs' front office. You bet.

So that the newly-formed Niggers sports club won't end up too 6 out of sync while expressing the "spirit" and "identity" of Afro-Americans in the above fashion, a baseball franchise—let's call this one the "Sambos"—should be formed. How about a basketball team called the "Spearchuckers"? A hockey team called the "Jungle Bunnies"? Maybe the "essence" of these teams could be depicted by images of tiny black faces adorned with huge pairs of lips. The players could appear on TV every week or so gnawing on chicken legs and spitting watermelon seeds at one another. Catchy, eh? Well, there's "nothing to be upset about," according to those who love wearing "war bonnets" to the Super Bowl or having "Chief Illiniwik" dance around the sports arenas of Urbana, Illinois.

And why stop there? There are plenty of other groups to include. 7 "Hispanics"? They can be "represented" by the Galveston "Greasers" and San Diego "Spics," at least until the Wisconsin "Wetbacks" and Baltimore "Beaners" get off the ground. Asian Americans? How about the "Slopes," "Dinks," "Gooks," and "Zipperheads"? Owners of the latter teams might get their logo ideas from editorial page cartoons printed in the nation's newspapers during World War II: slant-eyes, buck teeth, big glasses, but nothing racially insulting or derogatory, according to the editors and artists involved at the time. Indeed, this Second World War–vintage stuff can be seen as just another barrel of laughs, at least by what current editors say are their "local standards" concerning American Indians.

Let's see. Who's been left out? Teams like the Kansas City "Kikes," 8 Hanover "Honkies," San Leandro "Shylocks," Daytona "Dagos," and Pittsburgh "Polacks" will fill a certain social void among white folk. Have a religious belief? Let's all go for the gusto and gear up the Milwaukee "Mackerel Snappers" and Hollywood "Holy Rollers." The Fighting Irish of Notre Dame can be rechristened the "Drunken Irish" or "Papist Pigs." Issues of gender and sexual preference can be addressed through creation of teams like the St. Louis "Sluts," Boston "Bimbos," Detroit "Dykes," and the Fresno "Fags." How about the Gainesville "Gimps" and Richmond "Retards," so the physically and mentally impaired won't be excluded from our fun and games?

Now, don't go getting "overly sensitive" out there. None of this is 9 demeaning or insulting, at least not when it's being done to Indians. Just ask the folks who are doing it, or their apologists like Andy Rooney in the national media. They'll tell you—as in fact they *have* been telling you—that there's been no harm done, regardless of what their victims think, feel, or say. The situation is exactly the same as when those with precisely the same mentality used to insist that Step 'n' Fetchit was okay, or Rochester on the Jack Benny Show, or Amos and Andy, Charlie Chan, the Frito Bandito, or any of the other cutsey symbols making up the lexicon of American racism. Have we communicated yet?

Let's get just a little bit real here. The notion of "fun" embodied in   10
rituals like the Tomahawk Chop must be understood for what it is.
There's not a single non-Indian example used above which can be considered socially acceptable in even the most marginal sense. The reasons are obvious enough. So why is it different where American
Indians are concerned? One can only conclude that, in contrast to the
other groups at issue, Indians are (falsely) perceived as being too few,
and therefore too weak, to defend themselves effectively against racist
and otherwise offensive behavior.

Fortunately, there are some glimmers of hope. A few teams and   11
their fans have gotten the message and have responded appropriately.
Stanford University, which opted to drop the name "Indians" from
Stanford, has experienced no resulting drop-off in attendance.
Meanwhile, the local newspaper in Portland, Oregon recently decided
its long-standing editorial policy prohibiting use of racial epithets
should include derogatory team names. The Redskins, for instance, are
now referred to as "the Washington team," and will continue to be described in this way until the franchise adopts an inoffensive moniker
(newspaper sales in Portland have suffered no decline as a result).

Such examples are to be applauded and encouraged. They stand   12
as figurative beacons in the night, proving beyond all doubt that it is
quite possible to indulge in the pleasure of athletics without accepting
blatant racism into the bargain.

QUESTIONS

1. At least on the surface, the names "Braves," "Indians," and
"Chiefs" would not seem to be as insulting to Native Americans as the
"Redskins" mascot. Why does Churchill argue that these other mascots, too, are examples of "blatant racism," and to what extent do you
agree with him?

2. How effective do you find the analogies that Churchill draws between Indian mascots and stereotypes of African Americans,
Hispanics, and other ethnic groups? How effective are the analogies
with other kinds of groups (those based on gender, sexuality, etc.)?

The Etymology of the International Insult

CHARLES F. BERLITZ

"What is a kike?" Disraeli once asked a small group of fellow 1
politicians. Then, as his audience shifted nervously, Queen Victoria's
great Jewish Prime Minister supplied the answer himself. "A kike," he
observed, "is a Jewish gentleman who has just left the room."

The word kike is thought to have derived from the ending *-ki* or 2
-ky found in many names borne by the Jews of Eastern Europe. Or, as
Leo Rosten suggests, it may come from *kikel,* Yiddish for a circle, the
preferred mark for name signing by Jewish immigrants who could not
write. This was used instead of an *X*, which resembles a cross. Kikel
was not originally pejorative, but has become so through use.

Yid, another word for Jew, has a distinguished historic origin, com- 3
ing from the German *Jude* (through the Russian *zhid*). *Jude* itself derives
from the tribe of Judah, a most honorable and ancient appellation. The
vulgar and opprobrious word "Sheeny" for Jew is a real inversion,
as it derives from *shaine* (Yiddish) or *schön* (German), meaning "beautiful." How could beautiful be an insult? The answer is that it all
depends on the manner, tone or facial expression or sneer (as our own
Vice President has trenchantly observed) with which something
is said. The opprobrious Mexican word for an American—*gringo,* for
example, is essentially simply a sound echo of a song the American
troops used to sing when the Americans were invading Mexico—
"Green Grow the Lilacs." Therefore the Mexicans began to call
the Americans something equivalent to "los green-grows" which became Hispanized to *gringo.* But from this innocent beginning
to the unfriendly emphasis with which many Mexicans say *gringo*
today there is a world of difference—almost a call to arms, with unfor-
gettable memories of past real or fancied wrongs, including "lost"
Texas and California.

Charles F. Berlitz, born in New York City, is a linguist, the author of
more than one hundred language-teaching books, and the grandson
of the founder of the Berlitz School. Since 1967, Mr. Berlitz has not
been connected with the Berlitz schools in any way. "The Etymology
of the International Insult" was originally published in *Penthouse*
magazine (1970).

The pejorative American word for Mexicans, Puerto Ricans, 4
Cubans and other Spanish-speaking nationals is simply *spik,* excerpted
from the useful expression "No esspick Englitch." Italians, whether in
America or abroad, have been given other more picturesque appellations. *Wop,* an all-time pejorative favorite, is curiously not insulting at
all by origin, as it means, in Neapolitan dialect, "handsome," "strong"
or "good looking." Among the young Italian immigrants some of the
stronger and more active—sometimes to the point of combat—were
called *guappi,* from which the first syllable, "wop," attained an "immediate insult" status for all Italians.

"Guinea" comes from the days of the slave trade and is derived 5
from the African word for West Africa. This "guinea" is the same word
as the British unit of 21 shillings, somehow connected with African
gold profits as well as New Guinea, which resembled Africa to its dis-
coverers. Dark or swarthy Italians and sometimes Portuguese were
called *Guineas* and this apparently spread to Italians of light complexion as well.

One of the epithets for Negroes has a curious and tragic historic 6
origin, the memory of which is still haunting us. The word is *"coons."*
It comes from *baracoes* (the *o* gives a nasal *n* sound in Portuguese), and
refers to the slave pens or barracks (*"baracoons"*) in which the victims
of the slave trade were kept while awaiting transshipment. Their descendants, in their present emphasizing of the term "black" over
"Negro," may be in the process of upgrading the very word "black,"
so often used pejoratively, as in "blackhearted," "black day," "black
arts," "black hand," etc. Even some African languages use "black" in a
negative sense. In Hausa "to have a black stomach" means to be angry
or unhappy.

The sub-Sahara African peoples, incidentally, do not think that 7
they are black (which they are not, anyway). They consider themselves
a healthy and attractive "people color," while whites to them look
rather unhealthy and somewhat frightening. In any case, the efforts of
African Americans to dignify the word "black" may eventually represent a semantic as well as a socio-racial triumph.

A common type of national insult is that of referring to nationali- 8
ties by their food habits. Thus "Frogs" for the French and "Krauts" for
the Germans are easily understandable, reflecting on the French addiction to *cuisses de grenouilles* (literally "thighs of frogs") and that of
the Germans for various kinds of cabbage, hot or cold. The French call
the Italians *"les macaronis"* while the German insult word for Italians is
Katzenfresser (Cat-eaters), an unjust accusation considering the hordes
of cats among the Roman ruins fed by individual cat lovers—unless
they are fattening them up? The insult word for an English person is

"limey," referring to the limes distributed to seafaring Englishmen as an antiscurvy precaution in the days of sailing ships and long periods at sea.

At least one of these food descriptive appellations has attained a 9 permanent status in English. The word "Eskimo" is not an Eskimo word at all but an Algonquin word unit meaning "eaters-of-flesh." The Eskimos naturally do not call themselves this in their own language but, with simple directness, use the word *Inuit*—"the men" or "the people."

Why is it an insult to call Chinese "Chinks"? Chink is most proba- 10 bly a contraction of the first syllables of *Chung-Kuo-Ren*—"Middle Country Person." In Chinese there is no special word for China, as the Chinese, being racially somewhat snobbish themselves (although *not* effete, according to recent reports), have for thousands of years considered their land to be the center or middle of the world. The key character for China is therefore the word *chung* or "middle" which, added to *kuo*, becomes "middle country" or "middle kingdom"—the complete Chinese expression for "China" being *Chung Hwa Min Kuo* ("Middle Flowery People's Country"). No matter how inoffensive the origin of "Chink" is, however, it is no longer advisable for everyday or anyday use now.

Jap, an insulting diminutive that figured in the [1968] national U.S. 11 election (though its use in the expression "fat Jap" was apparently meant to have an endearing quality by our Vice President) is a simple contraction of "Japan," which derives from the Chinese word for "sun." In fact the words "Jap" and "Nip" both mean the same thing. "Jap" comes from Chinese and "Nip" from Japanese in the following fashion: *Jihpen* means "sun origin" in Chinese, while *Ni-hon* (Nippon) gives a like meaning in Japanese, both indicating that Japan was where the sun rose. Europeans were first in contact with China, and so originally chose the Chinese name for Japan instead of the Japanese one.

The Chinese "insult" words for whites are based on the observa- 12 tions that they are too white and therefore look like ghosts or devils, *fan kuei* (ocean ghosts), or that their features are too sharp instead of being pleasantly flat, and that they have enormous noses, hence *tabee-tsu* (great-nosed ones). Differences in facial physiognomy have been fully reciprocated by whites in referring to Asians as "Slants" or "Slopes."

Greeks in ancient times had an insult word for foreigners too, but 13 one based on the sound of their language. This word is still with us, though its original meaning has changed. The ancient Greeks divided the world into Greeks and "Barbarians"—the latter word coming from a description of the ridiculous language the stanger was speaking. To the Greeks it sounded like the "baa-baa" of a sheep—hence "Barbarians"!

The black peoples of South Africa are not today referred to as 14 Negro or Black but as Bantu—not in itself an insult but having somewhat the same effect when you are the lowest man on the totem pole. But the word means simply "the men," *ntu* signifying "man" and *ba* being the plural prefix. This may have come from an early encounter with explorers or missionaries when Central or South Africans on being asked by whites who they were may have replied simply "men"—with the implied though probably unspoken follow-up questions, "And who are you?"

This basic and ancient idea that one's group are the only people— 15 at least the only friendly or nondangerous ones—is found among many tribes throughout the world. The Navajo Indians call themselves *Dine*—"the people"—and qualify other tribes generally as "the enemy." Therefore an Indian tribe to the north would simply be called "the northern enemy," one to the east "the eastern enemy," etc., and that would be the *only* name used for them. These ancient customs, sanctified by time, of considering people who differ in color, customs, physical characteristics and habits—and by enlargement all strangers—as potential enemies is something mankind can no longer afford, even linguistically. Will man ever be able to rise above using insult as a weapon? It may not be possible to love your neighbor, but by understanding him one may be able eventually to tolerate him. Meanwhile, if you stop calling him names, he too may eventually learn to dislike *you* less.

QUESTIONS

1.   What do you think is Berlitz's purpose in explaining the origins of these insulting terms?

2.   Discuss an experience when you used, heard others use, or had used against you one of the racial or ethnic slurs that Berlitz writes about. Consider your feelings at the time and also later, upon reflection. How does Berlitz's explanation of the origin of the slur affect your view of the incident?

Conversational Ballgames

NANCY MASTERSON SAKAMOTO

After I was married and had lived in Japan for a while, my 1
Japanese gradually improved to the point where I could take part in
simple conversations with my husband and his friends and family.
And I began to notice that often, when I joined in, the others would
look startled, and the conversational topic would come to a halt. After
this happened several times, it became clear to me that I was doing
something wrong. But for a long time, I didn't know what it was.

Finally, after listening carefully to many Japanese conversations, I 2
discovered what my problem was. Even though I was speaking
Japanese, I was handling the conversation in a western way.

Japanese-style conversations develop quite differently from west- 3
ern-style conversations. And the difference isn't only in the languages.
I realized that just as I kept trying to hold western-style conversations
even when I was speaking Japanese, so my English students kept trying to hold Japanese-style conversations even when they were speaking English. We were unconsciously playing entirely different conversational ballgames.

A western-style conversation between two people is like a game of 4
tennis. If I introduce a topic, a conversational ball, I expect you to hit it
back. If you agree with me, I don't expect you simply to agree and do
nothing more. I expect you to add something—a reason for agreeing,
another example, or an elaboration to carry the idea further. But I don't
expect you always to agree. I am just as happy if you question me, or
challenge me, or completely disagree with me. Whether you agree or
disagree, your response will return the ball to me.

And then it is my turn again. I don't serve a new ball from my orig- 5
inal starting line. I hit your ball back again from where it has bounced.
I carry your idea further, or answer your questions or objections, or
challenge or question you. And so the ball goes back and forth, with

Nancy Masterson Sakamoto is professor of American Studies at
Shitennoji Gakuen University, Hawaii Institute and coauthor of
Mutual Understanding of Different Cultures (1981). A former English
teacher and teacher trainer in Japan, she cowrote (with Reiko
Naotsuka) a bilingual textbook for Japanese students called *Polite
Fictions: Why Japanese and Americans Seem Rude to Each Other* (1982);
"Conversational Ballgames" is a chapter from *Polite Fictions*.

each of us doing our best to give it a new twist, an original spin, or a powerful smash.

And the more vigorous the action, the more interesting and excit- 6 ing the game. Of course, if one of us gets angry, it spoils the conversation, just as it spoils a tennis game. But getting excited is not at all the same as getting angry. After all, we are not trying to hit each other. We are trying to hit the ball. So long as we attack only each other's opinions, and do not attack each other personally, we don't expect anyone to get hurt. A good conversation is supposed to be interesting and exciting.

If there are more than two people in the conversation, then it is like 7 doubles in tennis, or like volleyball. There's no waiting in line. Whoever is nearest and quickest hits the ball, and if you step back, someone else will hit it. No one stops the game to give you a turn. You're responsible for taking your own turn.

But whether it's two players or a group, everyone does his best to 8 keep the ball going, and no one person has the ball for very long.

A Japanese-style conversation, however, is not at all like tennis or 9 volleyball. It's like bowling. You wait for your turn. And you always know your place in line. It depends on such things as whether you are older or younger, a close friend or a relative stranger to the previous speaker, in a senior or junior position, and so on.

When your turn comes, you step up to the starting line with your 10 bowling ball, and carefully bowl it. Everyone else stands back and watches politely, murmuring encouragement. Everyone waits until the ball has reached the end of the alley, and watches to see if it knocks down all the pins, or only some of them, or none of them. There is a pause, while everyone registers your score.

Then, after everyone is sure that you have completely finished 11 your turn, the next person in line steps up to the same starting line, with a different ball. He doesn't return your ball, and he does not begin from where your ball stopped. There is no back and forth at all. All the balls run parallel. And there is always a suitable pause between turns. There is no rush, no excitement, no scramble for the ball.

No wonder everyone looked startled when I took part in Japanese 12 conversations. I paid no attention to whose turn it was, and kept snatching the ball halfway down the alley and throwing it back at the bowler. Of course the conversation died. I was playing the wrong game.

This explains why it is almost impossible to get a western-style 13 conversation or discussion going with English students in Japan. I used to think that the problem was their lack of English language ability. But I finally came to realize that the biggest problem is that they, too, are playing the wrong game.

Whenever I serve a volleyball, everyone just stands back and 14
watches it fall, with occasional murmurs of encouragement. No one
hits it back. Everyone waits until I call on someone to take a turn. And
when that person speaks, he doesn't hit my ball back. He serves a new
ball. Again, everyone just watches it fall.

So I call on someone else. This person does not refer to what 15
the previous speaker has said. He also serves a new ball. Nobody
seems to have paid any attention to what anyone else has said.
Everyone begins again from the same starting line, and all the balls run
parallel. There is never any back and forth. Everyone is trying to bowl
with a volleyball.

And if I try a simpler conversation, with only two of us, then the 16
other person tries to bowl with my tennis ball. No wonder foreign
English teachers in Japan get discouraged.

Now that you know about the difference in the conversational 17
ballgames, you may think that all your troubles are over. But if you
have been trained all your life to play one game, it is no simple matter
to switch to another, even if you know the rules. Knowing the rules is
not at all the same thing as playing the game.

Even now, during a conversation in Japanese I will notice a star- 18
tled reaction, and belatedly realize that once again I have rudely interrupted by instinctively trying to hit back the other person's bowling
ball. It is no easier for me to "just listen" during a conversation, than it
is for my Japanese students to "just relax" when speaking with foreigners. Now I can truly sympathize with how hard they must find it
to try to carry on a western-style conversation.

If I have not yet learned to do conversational bowling in Japanese, 19
at least I have figured out one thing that puzzled me for a long time.
After his first trip to America, my husband complained that
Americans asked him so many questions and made him talk so much
at the dinner table that he never had a chance to eat. When I asked him
why he couldn't talk and eat at the same time, he said that Japanese do
not customarily think that dinner, especially on fairly formal occasions, is a suitable time for extended conversation.

Since westerners think that conversation is an indispensable part 20
of dining, and indeed would consider it impolite not to converse with
one's dinner partner, I found this Japanese custom rather strange. Still,
I could accept it as a cultural difference even though I didn't really understand it. But when my husband added, in explanation, that
Japanese consider it extremely rude to talk with one's mouth full, I got
confused. Talking with one's mouth full is certainly not an American
custom. We think it very rude, too. Yet we still manage to talk a lot and
eat at the same time. How do we do it?

For a long time, I couldn't explain it, and it bothered me. But after 21
I discovered the conversational ballgames, I finally found the answer.
Of course! In a western-style conversation, you hit the ball, and
while someone else is hitting it back, you take a bite, chew, and swallow. Then you hit the ball again, and then eat some more. The more
people there are in the conversation, the more chances you have to eat.
But even with only two of you talking, you still have plenty of chances
to eat.

Maybe that's why polite conversation at the dinner table has never 22
been a traditional part of Japanese etiquette. Your turn to talk would
last so long without interruption that you'd never get a chance to eat.

QUESTIONS

1. The note about the author explains that this selection is from a
bilingual Japanese-English textbook. In what ways do you think
Sakamoto tries to appeal specifically to her primary audience of
Japanese students learning English? How successfully do you think
her essay appeals to a broader audience?

2. How accurately do you think Sakamoto's tennis analogy represents typical American conversations? What would you add to her
analogy, or how would you modify it, to describe the way members of
your own family or peer group usually communicate? If you are from
or familiar with another cultural tradition, devise your own analogies
to compare typical communication in that tradition with Anglo-
American communication.

The Language of Discretion

AMY TAN

At a recent family dinner in San Francisco, my mother whispered 1
to me: "Sau-sau [Brother's Wife] pretends too hard to be polite! Why
bother? In the end, she always takes everything."

My mother thinks like a *waixiao*, an expatriate, temporarily away 2
from China since 1949, no longer patient with ritual courtesies. As if to
prove her point, she reached across the table to offer my elderly aunt
from Beijing the last scallop from the Happy Family seafood dish.

Sau-sau scowled. "*B'yao, zhen, b'yao!*" (I don't want it, really I 3
don't!) she cried, patting her plump stomach.

"Take it! Take it!" scolded my mother in Chinese. 4

"Full, I'm already full," Sau-sau protested weakly, eyeing the 5
beloved scallop.

"Ai!" exclaimed my mother, completely exasperated. "Nobody 6
else wants it. If you don't take it, it will only rot!"

At this point, Sau-sau sighed, acting as if she were doing my 7
mother a big favor by taking the wretched scrap off her hands.

My mother turned to her brother, a high-ranking communist offi- 8
cial who was visiting her in California for the first time: "In America a
Chinese person could starve to death. If you say you don't want it, they
won't ask you again forever."

My uncle nodded and said he understood fully: Americans take 9
things quickly because they have no time to be polite.

I thought about this misunderstanding again—of social contexts 10
failing in translation—when a friend sent me an article from the *New
York Times Magazine* (24 April 1988). The article, on changes in New
York's Chinatown, made passing reference to the inherent ambivalence of the Chinese language.

Chinese people are so "discreet and modest," the article stated, 11
there aren't even words for "yes" and "no."

Amy Tan, from San Francisco, is the author of short stories, the novels *The Joy Luck Club* (1989) and *The Kitchen God's Wife* (1991), and the
children's book *The Moon Lady* (1992). Her fiction deals with several
generations of Chinese and Chinese American women and the relationships of mothers and daughters. *The Joy Luck Club* was made into
a feature film released in 1993. This essay was written for the anthology *The State of the Language*, edited by Christopher Ricks and
Leonard Michaels (1990).

That's not true, I thought, although I can see why an outsider   12
might think that. I continued reading.

If one is Chinese, the article went on to say, "One compromises,   13
one doesn't hazard a loss of face by an overemphatic response."

My throat seized. Why do people keep saying these things? As if   14
we truly were those little dolls sold in Chinatown tourist shops, heads
bobbing up and down in complacent agreement to anything said!

I worry about the effect of one-dimensional statements on the un-   15
wary and guileless. When they read about this so-called vocabulary
deficit, do they also conclude that Chinese people evolved into a mild-
mannered lot because the language only allowed them to hobble forth
with minced words?

Something enormous is always lost in translation. Something in-   16
sidious seeps into the gaps, especially when amateur linguists continue to compare, one-for-one, language differences and then put forth
notions wide open to misinterpretation: that Chinese people have no
direct linguistic means to make decisions, assert or deny, affirm or
negate, just say no to drug dealers, or behave properly on the witness
stand when told, "Please answer yes or no."

Yet one can argue, with the help of renowned linguists, that the   17
Chinese are indeed up a creek without "yes" and "no." Take any number of variations on the old language-and-reality theory stated years
ago by Edward Sapir: "Human beings . . . are very much at the mercy
of the particular language which has become the medium for their society. . . . The fact of the matter is that the 'real world' is to a large extent built up on the language habits of the group."[1]

This notion was further bolstered by the famous Sapir-Whorf hy-   18
pothesis, which roughly states that one's perception of the world and
how one functions in it depends a great deal on the language used. As
Sapir, Whorf, and new carriers of the banner would have us believe,
language shapes our thinking, channels us along certain patterns embedded in words, syntactic structures, and intonation patterns.
Language has become the peg and the shelf that enables us to sort out
and categorize the world. In English, we see "cats" and "dogs"; what
if the language had also specified *glatz*, meaning "animals that leave
fur on the sofa," and *glotz*, meaning "animals that leave fur and drool
on the sofa"? How would language, the enabler, have changed our
perceptions with slight vocabulary variations?

And if this were the case—of language being the master of des-   19
tined thought—think of the opportunities lost from failure to evolve

---

[1]Edward Sapir, *Selected Writings*, ed. D. G. Mandelbaum (Berkeley and Los Angeles, 1949).

two little words, *yes* and *no,* the simplest of opposites! Ghenghis Khan could have been sent back to Mongolia. Opium wars might have been averted. The Cultural Revolution could have been sidestepped.

There are still many, from serious linguists to pop psychology 20 cultists, who view language and reality as inextricably tied, one being the consequence of the other. We have traversed the range from the Sapir-Whorf hypothesis to est and neurolinguistic programming, which tell us "you are what you say."

I too have been intrigued by the theories. I can summarize, albeit 21 badly, ages-old empirical evidence: of Eskimos and their infinite ways to say "snow," their ability to *see* the differences in snowflake configurations, thanks to the richness of their vocabulary, while non-Eskimo speakers like myself founder in "snow," "more snow," and "lots more where that came from."

I too have experienced dramatic cognitive awakenings via the 22 word. Once I added "mauve" to my vocabulary I began to see it everywhere. When I learned how to pronounce *prix fixe,* I ate French food at prices better than the easier-to-say *à la carte* choices.

But just how seriously are we supposed to take this? 23

Sapir said something else about language and reality. It is the part 24 that often gets left behind in the dot-dot-dots of quotes: ". . . No two languages are ever sufficiently similar to be considered as representing the same social reality. The worlds in which different societies live are distinct worlds, not merely the same world with different labels attached."

When I first read this, I thought, Here at last is validity for the 25 dilemmas I felt growing up in a bicultural, bilingual family! As any child of immigrant parents knows, there's a special kind of double bind attached to knowing two languages. My parents, for example, spoke to me in both Chinese and English; I spoke back to them in English.

"Amy-ah!" they'd call to me. 26

"What?" I'd mumble back. 27

"Do not question us when we call," they scolded me in Chinese. 28 "It is not respectful."

"What do you mean?" 29

"Ai! Didn't we just tell you not to question?" 30

To this day, I wonder which parts of my behavior were shaped by 31 Chinese, which by English. I am tempted to think, for example, that if I am of two minds on some matter it is due to the richness of my linguistic experiences, not to any personal tendencies toward wishy-washiness. But which mind says what?

Was it perhaps patience—developed through years of deciphering 32 my mother's fractured English—that had me listening politely while a woman announced over the phone that I had won one of five valuable prizes? Was it respect—pounded in by the Chinese imperative to accept convoluted explanations—that had me agreeing that I might find it worthwhile to drive seventy-five miles to view a time-share resort? Could I have been at a loss for words when asked, "Wouldn't you like to win a Hawaiian cruise or perhaps a fabulous Star of India designed exclusively by Carter and Van Arpels?"

And when this same woman called back a week later, this time complaining that I had missed my appointment, obviously it was my type A language that kicked into gear and interrupted her. Certainly, my blunt denial—"Frankly I'm not interested"—was as American as apple pie. And when she said, "But it's in Morgan Hill," and I shouted, "Read my lips. I don't care if it's Timbuktu," you can be sure I said it with the precise intonation expressing both cynicism and disgust. 33

It's dangerous business, this sorting out of language and behavior. Which one is English? Which is Chinese? The categories manifest themselves: passive and aggressive, tentative and assertive, indirect and direct. And I realize they are just variations of the same theme: that Chinese people are discreet and modest. 34

Reject them all! 35

If my reaction is overly strident, it is because I cannot come across as too emphatic. I grew up listening to the same lines over and over again, like so many rote expressions repeated in an English phrasebook. And I too almost came to believe them. 36

Yet if I consider my upbringing more carefully, I find there was nothing discreet about the Chinese language I grew up with. My parents made everything abundantly clear. Nothing wishy-washy in their demands, no compromises accepted: "Of course you will become a famous neurosurgeon," they told me. "And yes, a concert pianist on the side." 37

In fact, now that I remember, it seems that the more emphatic outbursts always spilled over into Chinese: "Not that way! You must wash rice so not a single grain spills out." 38

I do not believe that my parents—both immigrants from mainland China—are an exception to the modest-and-discreet rule. I have only to look at the number of Chinese engineering students skewing minority ratios at Berkeley, MIT, and Yale. Certainly they were not raised by passive mothers and fathers who said, "It is up to you, my daughter. Writer, welfare recipient, masseuse, or molecular engineer—you decide." 39

And my American mind says, See, those engineering students weren't able to say no to their parents' demands. But then my Chinese mind remembers: Ah, but those parents all wanted their sons and daughters to be *pre-med*. 40

Having listened to both Chinese and English, I also tend to be sus- 41
picious of any comparisons between the two languages. Typically, one
language—that of the person doing the comparing—is often used as
the standard, the benchmark for a logical form of expression. And so
the language being compared is always in danger of being judged deficient or superfluous, simplistic or unnecessarily complex, melodious
or cacophonous. English speakers point out that Chinese is extremely
difficult because it relies on variations in tone barely discernible to the
human ear. By the same token, Chinese speakers tell me English is extremely difficult because it is inconsistent, a language of too many broken rules, of Mickey Mice and Donald Ducks.

Even more dangerous to my mind is the temptation to compare 42
both language and behavior *in translation*. To listen to my mother
speak English, one might think she has no concept of past or future
tense, that she doesn't see the difference between singular and plural,
that she is gender blind because she calls my husband "she." If one
were not careful, one might also generalize that, based on the way
my mother talks, all Chinese people take a circumlocutory route to
get to the point. It is, in fact, my mother's idiosyncratic behavior to
ramble a bit.

Sapir was right about differences between two languages and their 43
realities. I can illustrate why word-for-word translation is not enough
to translate meaning and intent. I once received a letter from China
which I read to non-Chinese speaking friends. The letter, originally
written in Chinese, had been translated by my brother-in-law in
Beijing. One portion described the time when my uncle at age ten discovered his widowed mother (my grandmother) had remarried—as a
number three concubine, the ultimate disgrace for an honorable family. The translated version of my uncle's letter read in part:

> In 1925, I met my mother in Shanghai. When she came to me, I
> didn't have greeting to her as if seeing nothing. She pull me to a cor-
> ner secretly and asked me why didn't have greeting to her. I couldn't
> control myself and cried, "Ma! Why did you leave us? People told
> me: one day you ate a beancake yourself. Your sister-in-law found it
> and sweared at you, called your names. So . . . is it true?" She clasped
> my hand and answered immediately, "It's not true, don't say what
> like this." After this time, there was a few chance to meet her.

"What!" cried my friends. "Was eating a beancake so terrible?" 44

Of course not. The beancake was simply a euphemism; a ten-year- 45
old boy did not dare question his mother on something as shocking as

concubinage. Eating a beancake was his equivalent for committing this selfish act, something inconsiderate of all family members, hence, my grandmother's despairing response to what seemed like a ludicrous charge of gluttony. And sure enough, she was banished from the family, and my uncle saw her only a few times before her death.

While the above may fuel people's argument that Chinese is indeed a language of extreme discretion, it does not mean that Chinese people speak in secrets and riddles. The contexts are fully understood. It is only those on the *outside* that the language seems cryptic, the behavior inscrutable.   46

I am, evidently, one of the outsiders. My nephew in Shanghai, who recently started taking English lessons, has been writing me letters in English. I had told him I was a fiction writer, and so in one letter he wrote, "Congratulate to you on your writing. Perhaps one day I should like to read it." I took it in the same vein as "Perhaps one day we can get together for lunch." I sent back a cheery note. A month went by and another letter arrived from Shanghai. "Last one perhaps I hadn't writing distinctly," he said. "In the future, you'll send a copy of your works for me."   47

I try to explain to my English-speaking friends that Chinese language use is more *strategic* in manner, whereas English tends to be more direct; an American business executive may say, "Let's make a deal," and the Chinese manager may reply, "Is your son interested in learning about your widget business?" Each to his or her own purpose, each with his or her own linguistic path. But I hesitate to add more to the pile of generalizations, because no matter how many examples I provide and explain, I fear that it appears defensive and only reinforces the image: that Chinese people are "discreet and modest"—and it takes an American to explain what they really mean.   48

Why am I complaining? The description seems harmless enough (after all, the *New York Times Magazine* writer did not say "slippery and evasive"). It is precisely the bland, easy acceptability of the phrase that worries me.   49

I worry that the dominant society may see Chinese people from a limited—and limiting—perspective. I worry that seemingly benign stereotypes may be part of the reason there are few Chinese in top management positions, in mainstream political roles. I worry about the power of language: that if one says anything enough times—in *any* language—it might become true.   50

Could this be why Chinese friends of my parents' generation are 51 willing to accept the generalization?

"Why are you complaining?" one of them said to me. "If people 52 think we are modest and polite, let them think that. Wouldn't Americans be pleased to admit they are thought of as polite?"

And I do believe anyone would take the description as a compli- 53 ment—at first. But after a while, it annoys, as if the only things that people heard one say were phatic remarks: "I'm so pleased to meet you. I've heard many wonderful things about you. For me? You shouldn't have!"

These remarks are not representative of new ideas, honest emo- 54 tions, or considered thought. They are what is said from the polite distance of social contexts: of greetings, farewells, wedding thank-you notes, convenient excuses, and the like.

It makes me wonder though. How many anthropologists, how 55 many sociologists, how many travel journalists have documented so-called "natural interactions" in foreign lands, all observed with spiral notebook in hand? How many other cases are there of the long-lost primitive tribe, people who turned out to be sophisticated enough to put on the stone-age show that ethnologists had come to see?

And how many tourists fresh off the bus have wandered into 56 Chinatown expecting the self-effacing shopkeeper to admit under duress that the goods are not worth the price asked? I have witnessed it.

"I don't know," the tourist said to the shopkeeper, a Cantonese 57 woman in her fifties. "It doesn't look genuine to me. I'll give you three dollars."

"You don't like my price, go somewhere else," said the shop- 58 keeper.

"You are not a nice person," cried the shocked tourist, "not a nice 59 person at all!"

"Who say I have to be nice," snapped the shopkeeper. 60

"So how does one say 'yes' and 'no' in Chinese?" ask my friends a 61 bit warily.

And here I do agree in part with the *New York Times Magazine* ar- 62 ticle. There is no one word for "yes" or "no"—but not out of necessity to be discreet. If anything, I would say the Chinese equivalent of answering "yes" or "no" is dis*crete*, that is, specific to what is asked.

Ask a Chinese person if he or she has eaten, and he or she might 63 say *chrle* (eaten already) or perhaps *meiyou* (have not).

Ask, "So you had insurance at the time of the accident?" and the 64 response would be *dwei* (correct) or *meiyou* (did not have).

Ask, "Have you stopped beating your wife?" and the answer   65
refers directly to the proposition being asserted or denied: stopped already, still have not, never beat, have no wife.

What could be clearer?   66

As for those who are still wondering how to translate the language   67
of discretion, I offer this personal example.

My aunt and uncle were about to return to Beijing after a three-   68
month visit to the United States. On their last night I announced I
wanted to take them out to dinner.

"Are you hungry?" I asked in Chinese.   69

"Not hungry," said my uncle promptly, the same response he once   70
gave me ten minutes before he suffered a low-blood-sugar attack.

"Not too hungry," said my aunt. "Perhaps you're hungry?"   71

"A little," I admitted.   72

"We can eat, we can eat," they both consented.   73

"What kind of food?" I asked.   74

"Oh, doesn't matter. Anything will do. Nothing fancy, just some   75
simple food is fine."

"Do you like Japanese food? We haven't had that yet," I sug-   76
gested.

They looked at each other.   77

"We can eat it," said my uncle bravely, this survivor of the Long   78
March.

"We have eaten it before," added my aunt. "Raw fish."   79

"Oh, you don't like it?" I said. "Don't be polite. We can go some-   80
where else."

"We are not being polite. We can eat it," my aunt insisted.   81

So I drove them to Japantown and we walked past several restau-   82
rants featuring colorful plastic displays of sushi.

"Not this one, not this one either," I continued to say, as if search-   83
ing for a Japanese restaurant similar to the last. "Here it is," I finally
said, turning into a restaurant famous for its Chinese fish dishes from
Shandong.

"Oh, Chinese food!" cried my aunt, obviously relieved.   84

My uncle patted my arm. "You think Chinese."   85

"It's your last night here in America," I said. "So don't be polite.   86
Act like an American."

And that night we ate a banquet.   87

QUESTIONS

1. What bothers Tan about the "seemingly benign" stereotyping of Chinese people as "discreet and modest"? Do you think her concerns are justified?

2. Discuss some of the complexities Tan reveals about attempts to translate between the Chinese and English languages and cultures, such as the difficulty of comparing "yes" and "no" in the two languages. To what extent are you persuaded that the "discreet and modest" stereotype of Chinese people is inaccurate or misleading?

3. "To this day," writes Tan, "I wonder which parts of my behavior were shaped by Chinese, which by English" (paragraph 31). If you grew up in a bicultural or bilingual family, discuss how your different cultural traditions have influenced you.

Two Deserts

VALERIE MATSUMOTO

Emiko Oyama thought the Imperial Valley of California was the loneliest place she had ever seen. It was just like the Topaz Relocation Camp, she told her husband, Kiyo, but without the barbed wire fence and crowded barracks. Miles of bleached desert, punctuated sparsely by creosote bush and debris, faced her from almost every window in their small house. Only the living room had a view of the dirt road which ended in front of their home, and across it, a row of squat, faded houses where other farmers' families lived. They waved to her and Kiyo in passing, and Jenny played with the Garcia children, but Emiko's Spanish and their English were too limited for more than casual greetings. 1

Emiko felt a tug of anticipation on the day the moving van pulled up to the Ishikawa's place across the road—the house which in her mind had become inextricably linked with friendship. She had felt its emptiness as her own when Sats, Yuki, and their three children gave up farming and departed for a life which later came to her in delicious fragments in Yuki's hastily scrawled letters. Yuki made the best sushi rice in the world and had given her the recipe. She could draw shy Kiyo into happy banter. And her loud warm laugh made the desert seem less drab, less engulfing. 2

The morning of moving day Emiko had been thinking about Yuki as she weeded the yard and vegetable plot in preparation for planting. Sats and Yuki had advised her to plant marigolds around the vegetables to keep away nematodes, and she liked the idea of a bold orange border. Emiko liked bright colors, especially the flaming scarlet of the bougainvillea which rose above the front door, where Kiki their cat lay sunning himself. There was a proud look in those amber eyes, for Kiki the hunter had slain three scorpions and laid them in a row on the porch, their backs crushed and deadly stingers limp, winning extravagant praise from Jenny and Emiko. The scorpions still lay there, at Jenny's insistence, awaiting Kiyo's return that evening. Emiko 3

Valerie Matsumoto, professor of history at the University of California, Los Angeles, studied Japanese Americans in California in her Ph.D. thesis, *The Cortez Colony: Family, Farm, and Community among Japanese Americans, 1919–1982* (1985). Her short story "Two Deserts" was first published in *Making Waves: An Anthology by and about Asian American Women* (1989), edited by Asian Women United of California.

73

shuddered every time she entered the house, glancing at the curved stingers and thinking of Jenny's sandaled feet.

Emiko had finished weeding the front border and was about to go 4 inside to escape the heat, when she saw the new neighbor woman plodding across the sand toward her. A cotton shift could not conceal her thinness, nor a straw hat her tousled gray curls. Her eyes were fragile lilac glass above a wide smile.

"Hello, I'm Mattie Barnes. I just thought I'd come over and intro- 5 duce myself while Roy is finishing up with the movers. Your bougainvillea caught my eye first thing, and I thought, 'Those are some folks who know what will grow in the desert.' I hope you'll give me some advice about what to plant in my yard once we get settled in."

They talked about adjusting to desert life and Emiko learned that 6 Mattie's husband Roy had recently retired. "We decided to move here because the doctor said it would be better for my lungs," Mattie explained, wiping her brow.

"Would you like a glass of lemonade?" Emiko offered. "Or maybe 7 later, after you've finished moving."

"Oh, I'd love something cold," Mattie said, adding vaguely, "Roy 8 will take care of everything—he's more particular about those things than I am."

Emiko led Mattie into the house, hoping that Jenny was not lying 9 on the cool linoleum, stripped to her underwear. As she crossed the threshold, Mattie gave a shriek and stopped abruptly, eyeing the scorpions lined up neatly on the porch.

"What on earth are these things doing here?" 10

"Our cat killed them," Emiko said, feeling too foolish to admit her 11 pride in Kiki's prowess. "Jenny wants me to leave them to show her father when he comes home from the field."

"Awful creatures," Mattie shuddered. "Roy can't stand them, but 12 then he can't abide insects. He said to me this morning, 'Of all the places we could have moved to, we had to choose the buggiest.'"

There was no buggier place than the Imperial Valley, Emiko 13 agreed, especially in the summer when the evening air was thick with mosquitoes, gnats, and moths, and cicadas buzzed in deafening chorus from every tree. They danced in frenzied legions around the porch light and did kamikaze dives into the bath water, and all of them came in dusty gray hordes, as though the desert had sapped their color, but not their energy. And late at night, long after Kiyo had fallen into exhausted sleep, Emiko would lie awake, perspiring, listening to the tinny scrabble of insects trapped between the window glass and screen.

". . . but I like the desert," Mattie was saying, dreamily clinking the 14 ice cubes in her glass. "It's so open and peaceful. As long as I can have a garden, I'll be happy."

Within a few weeks after their arrival, the Barneses had settled 15 into a routine: Roy made daily trips to the local store and the Roadside Cafe; Mattie tended her garden and walked to church once a week with Emiko and Jenny. By the end of June, Mattie had been enlisted with Emiko to make crepe paper flowers for the church bazaar.

"My, your flowers turned out beautifully," Mattie exclaimed one 16 morning, looking wistfully at the cardboard box filled with pink, yellow, scarlet, and lavender blossoms set on wire stems. "They'll make lovely corsages." She sighed. "I seem to be all thumbs—my flowers hardly look like flowers. I don't know how you do it. You Japanese are just very artistic people."

Emiko smiled and shook her head, making a polite disclaimer. But 17 the bright blur of flowers suddenly dissolved into another mass of paper blooms, carrying her more than a decade into the past. She was a teenager in a flannel shirt and denim pants with rolled cuffs, seated on a cot in a cramped barrack room, helping her mother fashion flowers from paper. Her own hands had been clumsy at first, though she strived to imitate her mother's precise fingers which gave each fragile petal lifelike curves, the look of artless grace. The only flowers for elderly Mr. Wasaka, shot by a guard in Topaz, were those which bloomed from the fingertips of *issei* and *nisei* women, working late into the night to complete the exquisite wreaths for his funeral. Each flower was a silent voice crying with color, each flower a tear.

"I did a little flower making as a teenager," Emiko said. 18

"Will you come over and show me how?" Mattie asked. "I'm too 19 embarrassed to take these awful things, and I've still got lots of crepe paper spread all over the kitchen."

"Sure," Emiko nodded. "I'll help you get started and you'll be a 20 whiz in no time. It isn't too hard; it just takes patience."

Mattie smiled, a slight wheeze in her voice when she said, "I've 21 got plenty of that, too."

They were seated at the Barneses' small table, surrounded by 22 bright masses of petals like fallen butterflies, their fingers sticky from the florist tape, when Roy returned from shopping. When he saw Emiko, he straightened and pulled his belt up over his paunch.

"A sight for sore eyes!" he boomed, giving her a broad wink. 23 "What mischief are you ladies up to?"

"Emi's teaching me how to make flowers," Mattie explained, hold- 24 ing up a wobbly rose.

"Always flowers! I tell you," he leaned over Emiko's chair and said 25 in a mock conspiratorial voice, "all my wife thinks about is flowers."

I keep telling her there are other things in life. Gardening is for old folks."

"And what's wrong with that?" Mattie protested, waving her 26 flower at him. "We are old folks."

"Speak for yourself," he winked at Emiko again. "What's so great 27 about gardens, anyway?"

"I hold with the poem that says you're closest to God's heart in a 28 garden," said Mattie.

"Well, I'm not ready to get that close to God's heart, yet." There 29 was defiance in Roy's voice. "What do you think about that, Emi?"

"I like working in the yard before it gets too hot," she said care- 30 fully. Her words felt tight and deliberate, like the unfurled petals on the yellow rose in her hands. "I don't have Mattie's talent with real flowers, though—aside from the bougainvillea and Jenny's petunias, nothing ever seems to bloom. The soil is too dry and saline for the things I used to grow. Now I've got my hopes pinned on the vegetable garden."

"Vegetables—hmph!" Roy snorted, stomping off to read the 31 paper.

"Oh, that Roy is just like a boy sometimes," Mattie said. "I tell you, 32 don't ever let your husband retire or you'll find him underfoot all day long."

"Doesn't Roy have any hobbies?" Emiko thought of her father and 33 his books, his Japanese brush painting, his meetings.

"He used to play golf," Mattie said, "but there's no golf course 34 here. He says this town is one giant sand trap."

"There have been times when I felt that way, too," Emiko admit- 35 ted lightly.

"Well, don't let Roy hear you say that or you'll never get him off 36 the topic," Mattie chuckled. "The fact is, Roy doesn't much know how to be by himself. I've had forty years to learn, and I've gotten to like it. And I suppose maybe he will, too."

Her voice trailed off, and Emiko suddenly realized that Mattie 37 didn't much care whether he did or not.

One day while Emiko was engrossed in pinning a dress pattern for 38 Jenny, she suddenly heard a tapping on the screen, like the scrabbling of a large beetle. She half turned and felt a jolt of alarm at the sight of a grinning gargoyle hunched before the window. It was Roy, his nose pushed up against the glass, hands splayed open on either side of his face, the caricature of a boy peering covetously into a toystore.

"Hey there! I caught you daydreaming!" he chortled. "Looks to 39 me like you need some company to wake you up."

"I'm not daydreaming; I'm trying to figure out how to make a 40 two-and-a-half yard dress out of two yards," she said. "Jenny is growing so fast, I can hardly keep up with her."

Roy walked into the house unbidden, confident of a welcome, and 41
drew a chair up to the table. He fingered the bright cotton print spread over the table and gazed at Emiko, his head cocked to one side.

"You must get pretty lonesome here by yourself all day. No won- 42
der you're sitting here dreaming."

"No," she said, her fingers moving the pattern pieces. "There's so 43
much to do, I don't have time to be lonesome. Besides, Jenny is here, and Kiyo comes home for lunch."

"But still—cooped up with a kiddie all day." Roy shook his head. 44
He chose to disregard Kiyo, who had no place in his imagined scenarios, and was hard at work miles away.

Emiko delicately edged the cotton fabric away from Roy's damp, 45
restless fingers. "I'll be darned if I offer him something to drink," she thought, as he mopped his brow and cast an impatient glance at the kitchen. "I haven't seen Mattie outside this week. How is she feeling?"

"Oh, 'bout the same, 'bout the same," he said, his irritation sub- 46
siding into brave resignation. "She has her good days and her bad days. The doctor told her to stay in bed for awhile and take it easy."

"It must be hard on Mattie, having to stay indoors," Emiko said, 47
thinking of her peering out through the pale curtains at the wilting zinnias and the new weeds in the back yard.

"I suppose so—usually you can't tear Mattie away from her gar- 48
den." Roy shook his head. "Mattie and me are real different. Now, I like people—I've always been the sociable type—but Mattie! All she cares about are plants."

"Well, Kiyo and I have different interests," Emiko said, "but it 49
works out well that way. Maybe you could learn a few things from Mattie about plants."

Even as the suggestion passed her lips, she regretted saying it. Roy 50
viewed the garden as the site of onerous labor. To Mattie, it was the true world of the heart, with no room for ungentle or impatient hands. It was a place of deeply sown hopes, lovingly nurtured, and its colors were the colors of unspoken dreams.

"Plants!" Roy threw up his hands. "Give me people any time. I 51
always liked people and had a knack for working with them—that's how I moved up in the business."

"Why don't you look into some of the clubs here?" Emiko tried 52
again. "The Elks always need people with experience and time."

"Sweetheart, I'm going to spend my time the way I want. I'm fin- 53
ished with work—it's time to enjoy life! Besides, how much fun can I have with a bunch of old geezers? That's not for me, Emily, my dear."

She stiffened as he repeated the name, savoring the syllables. "Emily . . . Emily . . . Yes, I like the sound of that—Emily."

"My name is Emiko," she said quietly, her eyes as hard as agate.   54
"I was named after my grandmother." That unfaltering voice had spoken the same words in first, second, third, fourth, fifth, and sixth grades. All the grammar school teachers had sought to change her name, to make her into an Emily: "Emily is so much easier to pronounce, dear, and it's a nice American name." She was such a well-mannered child, the teachers were always amazed at her stubbornness on this one point. Sometimes she was tempted to relent, to give in, but something inside her resisted. "My name is Emiko," she would insist politely. I am an American named Emiko. I was named for my grandmother who was beautiful and loved to swim. When she emerged from the sea, her long black hair would glitter white with salt. I never met her, but she was beautiful and she would laugh when she rose from the waves. "My name is Emiko; Emi for short."

"But Emily is such a pretty name," Roy protested. "It fits you."   55

"It's not my name," she said, swallowing a hard knot of anger.   56
"I don't like to be called Emily!"

"Temper, temper!" He shook his finger at her, gleeful at having   57
provoked her.

"Well, I guess I'll be in a better temper when I can get some work   58
done," she said, folding up the cloth with tense, deliberate hands. She raised her voice. "Jenny! Let's go out and water the vegetable garden now."

If Jenny thought this a strange task in the heat of the afternoon, it   59
did not show in her face when she skipped out of her room, swinging her straw hat. It still sported a flimsy, rainbow-hued scarf which had been the subject of much pleading in an El Centro dime store. At that moment, Emiko found it an oddly reassuring sight. She smiled and felt her composure return.

"Tell Mattie to let me know if there's anything I can do to help,"   60
she told Roy, as he unwillingly followed them out of the house and trudged away across the sand. After they went back inside, Emiko, for the first time, locked the door behind them. When Kiyo returned home, his face taut with fatigue, she told him it was because of the hoboes who came around.

Emiko went to see Mattie less and less frequently, preferring in-   61
stead to call her on the phone, even though they lived so close. Roy, however, continued to drop by, despite Emiko's aloofness. His unseemly yearning tugged at her with undignified hands, but what he craved most was beyond her power to give. She took to darning and mending in the bedroom with the curtains drawn, ignoring his insistent knock; she tried to do her gardening in the evening after dinner

when her husband was home, but it was hard to weed in the dusk. She was beginning to feel caged, pent up, restless. Jenny and Kiyo trod quietly, puzzled by her edginess, but their solicitude only made her feel worse.

Finally one morning Emiko decided to weed the vegetables, 62 sprouting new and tender. Surely the midmorning heat would discourage any interference. Although perspiration soon trickled down her face, she began to enjoy the satisfying rhythm of the work. She was so engrossed she did not notice when Roy Barnes unlatched the gate and stepped into the yard, a determined twinkle in his faded eye.

"Howdy, Emi! I saw you working away out here by your lone- 63 some and thought maybe you could use some help."

"Thanks, but I'm doing all right," she said, wrenching a clump of 64 puncture vine from the soil and laying it in the weed box, careful to avoid scattering the sharp stickers. Jenny was close by, digging at her petunias and marigolds, ignoring Mr. Barnes, who had no place in the colorful jungle she was imagining.

"If I had a pretty little wife, I sure wouldn't let her burn up out 65 here, no sir." His voice nudged at her as she squatted on the border of the vegetable plot. If Mattie looked out of the window, she would see only a pleasant tableau: Roy nodding in neighborly fashion as Emiko pointed out young rows of zucchini and yellow squash, watermelon, cantaloupe, eggplant, and tomatoes. Mattie would not see the strain on Emiko's face, which she turned away when Roy leaned over and mumbled, "Say, you know what I like best in this garden?"

Emiko grabbed the handle of the shovel and stood up before he 66 could tell her, moving away from him to pluck a weed. "I know Mattie likes cantaloupe," she said. "So do I. Kiyo prefers Crenshaws, but I couldn't find any seeds this year. What do you and Mattie have in your garden?"

"Just grass," he said, undeterred. "Mattie's always fussing over 67 her flowers—you know what she's like," he chuckled indulgently. "But I'd rather spend my time doing other things than slaving in the yard."

Emiko hacked away at the stubborn clumps of grass roots and the 68 persistent runners with myriad finer roots, thread-thin, but tough as wire. She worked with desperate energy, flustered, her gloved hands sweating on the shovel handle, forehead damp. She was groping for the language to make him understand, to make him leave her in peace, but he was bent on not understanding, not seeing, not leaving until he got what he wanted.

"You know what, Emi?" He moistened his dry lips, beginning to 69 grin reminiscently. "You remind me of somebody I met in Tokyo. Have you ever been to Tokyo?"

"No," she said, digging hard. "Never."   70

"You'd like it; it's a wonderful place, so clean and neat, and the   71
people so friendly. When I was in Tokyo, I met up with the cutest
geisha girl you ever saw—just like a little doll. She'd never seen anybody with blue eyes before, and couldn't get over it." He chuckled. "I
couldn't think who you reminded me of at first, and then it just hit me
that you are the spitting image of her."

"Did Mattie like Tokyo, too?" Emiko said, continuing to spade   72
vigorously, as his eyes slid over her, imagining a doll in exotic robes.

"She didn't go—it was a business trip," he said impatiently. Then   73
his voice relaxed into a drawl, heavy with insinuation. "After all, I like
to do some things on my own." He was moving closer again.

Then she saw it. Emiko had just turned over a rock, and as she   74
raised the shovel, it darted from its refuge, pincers up, the deadly tail
curved menacingly over the carapaced back. It moved a little to the left
and then the right, beginning the poison dance. Emiko glanced to see
where Jenny was and saw Roy jump back hastily; the scorpion, startled by his movement, scuttled sideways toward Jenny, who lay on her
stomach, still dreaming of her jungle.

The blood pounded in Emiko's head. She brought down the   75
shovel hard with one quick breath, all her rage shooting down the
thick handle into the heavy crushing iron. She wielded the shovel like
a samurai in battle, swinging it down with all her force, battering her
enemy to dust. Once had been enough, but she struck again and again,
until her anger was spent, and she leaned on the rough handle, breathing hard.

"Mommy! What did you do?" Jenny had scrambled to Emiko's   76
side. There was fear in her eyes as she gazed at the unrecognizable
fragments in the dirt.

"I killed a scorpion," Emiko said. She scornfully tossed the re-   77
mains into the weed box, and wiped her brow on her arm, like a
farmer, or a warrior. "I don't like to kill anything," she said aloud, "but
sometimes you have to."

Roy Barnes recoiled from the pitiless knowledge in her eyes. He   78
saw her clearly now, but it was too late. His mouth opened and closed,
but the gush of words had gone dry. He seemed to age before her eyes,
like Urashima-taro who opened the precious box of youth and was instantly wrinkled and broken by the unleashed tide of years.

"You'll have to leave now, Mr. Barnes. I'm going in to fix lunch."   79
Emiko's smile was quiet as unsheathed steel. "Tell Mattie I hope she's
feeling better."

She watched him pick his way across the dirt, avoiding the punc-   80
ture vine and rusted tin cans, and looking as gray as the rags that

bleached beneath the fierce sun. Jenny stared past him and the small houses of their neighborhood, to the desert sand beyond, glittering like an ocean with shards of mica.

"Do you think we might ever find gold?" she asked.   81

They gazed together over the desert, full of unknown perils and   82 ancient secrets, the dust of dreams and battles.

"Maybe." Emiko stood tall, shading her eyes from the deceptive   83 shimmer. "Maybe."

QUESTIONS

1.   What do you think the scorpion that she kills with the shovel represents to Emiko? To Jenny? To Roy?

2.   Discuss the ways in which Roy Barnes seems to view Emiko in categorical, stereotypical terms. Why do you think he prefers the name "Emily" to "Emiko"? Would you describe Roy as racist? Sexist? Why or why not?

3.   To what extent do you think Matsumoto portrays Roy Barnes in stereotypical terms? How necessary or effective is this portrayal, according to your interpretation of Matsumoto's purposes in the story?

THINKING ABOUT LANGUAGE
AND STEREOTYPES

1. To what extent do you agree with Carey that "nobody 'likes' White Guys anymore"? Test out Carey's "bill of indictment" against White Guys in other selections in this chapter, such as those by Greenberg, Churchill, and Matsumoto.

2. Based on Churchill's essay about the negative stereotyping of Native Americans by means of sports team mascots, how would you answer Berlitz's question in paragraph 15, "Will man ever be able to rise above using insult as a weapon?"

3. The *American Heritage College Dictionary* defines a stereotype as "a conventional, formulaic, and oversimplified conception or image." How does Sakamoto use stereotypes in a different way than Churchill or Berlitz?

4. Using Tan's idea of "social contexts failing in translation" (paragraph 10), compare her analysis of Chinese and English communication with Sakamoto's analysis of Japanese and western communication styles.

5. Use Sakamoto's criteria for Japanese and western-style conversations to analyze the "conversational ballgames" played by the main characters in Matsumoto's "Two Deserts," Emiko and Roy. How might you change Sakamoto's tennis and bowling analogies to better reflect Emiko's and Roy's communication styles?

6. Do you think that some stereotyping (defined as the use of formulaic or oversimplified images) is necessary or desirable in order, ironically, to *combat* stereotyping? Support your views with evidence from the essays by Churchill or Sakamoto and the short story by Matsumoto.

Exploring Additional Sources

7. Language and gender stereotypes are explored in "Sexism in English: A 1990s Update" by Alleen Pace Nilsen (page 8), "Real Men Don't: Anti-Male Bias in English" (page 20), and "Sex, Lies, and Conversation: Why Is It So Hard for Men and Women to Talk to Each Other?" by Deborah Tannen (page 32). Using evidence from one or more of these essays, discuss how the issue of gender stereotyping affects your view of Matsumoto's story or Sakamoto's or Tan's essay.

8. Research a particular mascot controversy about a school or professional sports team. Consider all sides of the controversy, and argue for what you believe to be the best solution.

9. Research the etymology and historical uses of another insulting slang term not discussed by Berlitz, such as one of those discussed by Churchill in his essay. Consult etymological dictionaries, dictionaries of slang, the *Oxford English Dictionary*, and the historical sources referred to in these books.

10. Look up some of the writings of Edward Sapir and Benjamin Whorf referred to by Tan and study the original version of the "Sapir-Whorf hypothesis" she discusses. Read what some current researchers have to say about this linguistic controversy, and test the hypothesis with your own experience or by interviewing some bilingual or multilingual people. To what extent do you believe that people think differently in different languages?

3

LANGUAGE AND SOCIAL POWER

Good English

JOHN SIMON

You are going to be judged, whether you like it or not, by the correctness of your English as much as by the correctness of your thinking; there are some people to whose ear bad English is as offensive as gibberish, or as your picking your nose in public would be to their eyes and stomachs. The fact that people of linguistic sensibilities may be a dying breed does not mean that they are wholly extinct, and it is best not to take any unnecessary chances.

To be sure, if you are a member of a currently favored minority, many of your linguistic failings may be forgiven you—whether rightly or wrongly is not my concern here. But if you cannot change your sex or color to the one that is getting preferential treatment . . . you might as well learn good English and profit by it in your career, your social relations, perhaps even in your basic self-confidence. That, if you will, is the ultimate practical application of good English.

—FROM *PARADIGMS LOST: REFLECTIONS ON LITERACY AND ITS DECLINE*, 1980

No Reggae Spoken Here

MICHELLE CLIFF

One of the effects of assimilation, indoctrination, passing into the anglocentrism of British West Indian culture is that you believe absolutely in the hegemony of the King's English and in the form in which it is meant to be expressed. Or else your writing is not literature; it is folklore, and folklore can never be art. Read some poetry by West Indian writers—some, not all—and you will see what I mean. You have to dissect stanza after extraordinarily anglican stanza for Afro-Caribbean truth; you may never find the latter. But this has been our education. The anglican ideal—Milton, Wordsworth, Keats—was held before us with an assurance that we were unable, and would never be enabled, to compose a work of similar correctness. No reggae spoken here.

To write as a complete Caribbean woman, or man for that matter, demands of us retracing the African part of ourselves, reclaiming as our own, and as our subject, a history sunk under the sea, or scattered as potash in the canefields, or gone to bush, or trapped in a class system notable for its rigidity and absolute dependence on color stratification. On a past bleached from our minds. It means finding the art forms of these of our ancestors and speaking in the *patois* forbidden us. It means realizing our knowledge will always be wanting. It means also, I think, mixing in the forms taught us by the oppressor, undermining his language and co-opting his style, and turning it to our purpose. In my current work-in-progress, a novel, I alternate the King's English with *patois,* not only to show the class background of characters, but to show how Jamaicans operate within a split consciousness. It would be as dishonest to write the novel entirely in *patois* as to write entirely in the King's English.

—FROM "A JOURNEY INTO SPEECH," *THE LAND OF LOOK BEHIND,* 1985

Dialect

RAYMOND WILLIAMS

Dialect came into English in 1C16, from fw *dialecte,* F, rw *dialektos,* Gk. The original Greek meaning of "discourse" or "conversation" had already widened to indicate also a way of speaking or the language of

---

Abbreviations

The following abbreviations are used here and in the other selections by Raymond Williams in Chapters 6, 11, & 12.

fw:	immediate forerunner of a word, in the same or another language.	F:	French.
		mF:	Medieval French.
rw:	ultimate traceable word, from which 'root' meanings are derived.	oF:	Old French.
		G:	German.
q.v.:	see entry under word noted.	Gk:	Classical Greek.
C:	followed by numeral, century (C19: nineteenth century).	It:	Italian.
		L:	Latin.
eC:	first period (third) of a century.	lL:	late Latin.
mC:	middle period (third) of a century.	mL:	Medieval Latin.
lC:	last period (third) of a century.	vL:	Vulgar Latin.
c:	(before a date) approximately.	Rom:	Romanic.
AN:	Anglo-Norman.	Sp:	Spanish.
mE:	Middle English (c. 1100-1500).	OED:	*New English Dictionary on Historical*
oE:	Old English (to c. 1100).		*Principles* (Oxford).

a country or district. In English, except in occasional uses, it became specialized from C17 and especially C18 to its dominant modern sense, which is not only that of the language of a district but, as OED defines it, "one of the subordinate forms or varieties of a language arising from local peculiarities of vocabulary, pronunciation and idiom." The key word here is "subordinate," which has to be understood in the context of the further OED definition: "a variety of speech differing from the standard or literary 'language.' "

Putting quotation marks on *language*, in that last definition, can be seen as a prudent afterthought. What is at issue in the history is not the evident fact that ways of speaking differ in different parts of a country or other language area, but the confidence of that designation as "subordinate." This is closely related to the development of the idea of a STANDARD (q.v.) English or other language, in which a selected (in English, class-based) usage becomes authoritative and dominant ("correct"). The alternative reference to "literary language" is not primarily a reference to the language of LITERATURE (q.v.), in the modern sense of imaginative writing, but to the older sense of the language appropriate in "polite learning" and above all in that kind of writing.

The confusions are then obvious. Earlier uses do not carry the sense of "subordinate." They designate a place to indicate a variation. Indeed there is a use from 1635 in which the **dialects** would now be called *languages:* "the Slavon tongue is of great extent: of it there be many Dialects, as the Russe, the Polish, the Bohemick, the Illyrian . . .," where we would now speak of a "family" of "national languages." It is indeed in the stabilization of a "national" language, and then within that centralizing process of a "standard," that wholly NATIVE (q.v.), authentic and longstanding variations become designated as culturally subordinate. The language, seen neutrally, exists as this body of variations. But within the process of cultural domination, what is projected is not only a selected authoritative version, from which all other variations can be judged to be inferior or actually incorrect, but also a virtually metaphysical notion of the language as existing in other than its actual variations. There is not only *standard English* and then **dialects;** there is also, by this projection, a singular *English* and then *dialects of English.*

It is interesting to observe adjustments in this kind of dominating description, as other social relationships change. A good example is the transition from "Yankee dialect" to "American English," only completed (on this side of the Atlantic) in mC20. The case is similar in the common phrase "minority languages," which carries the implication of "less important," in its usual pairing with "major languages." This is also a form of dominance. There are indeed languages of minorities; often of minorities who are in that social situation because their country or place has been annexed or incorporated into a larger political unit. This does not make them "minority languages," except in the perspective of dominance. In their own place (if they can resist what are often formidable pressures) it is their own language—a specific language like any other. In comparable ways, a dialect is simply the way of speaking in a particular place.

—FROM *KEYWORDS: A VOCABULARY OF CULTURE AND SOCIETY* REVISED EDITION, 1985

The Primary Function of Writing

CLAUDE LÉVI-STRAUSS

Between the invention of writing and the birth of modern science, the western world has lived through some five thousand years, during which time the sum of its knowledge has rather gone up and down than known a steady increase. It has often been remarked that there was no great difference between the life of a Greek or Roman citizen and that of a member of the well-to-do European classes in the eighteenth century. In the neolithic age, humanity made immense strides forward without any help from writing; and writing did not save the civilizations of the western world from long periods of stagnation. Doubtless the scientific expansion of the nineteenth and twentieth centuries could hardly have occurred, had writing not existed. But this condition, however necessary, cannot in itself explain that expansion.

If we want to correlate the appearance of writing with certain other characteristics of civilization, we must look elsewhere. The one phenomenon which has invariably accompanied it is the formation of cities and empires: the integration into a political system, that is to say, of a considerable number of individuals, and the distribution of those individuals into a hierarchy of castes and classes. Such is, at any rate, the type of development which we find, from Egypt right across to China, at the moment when writing makes its debuts; it seems to favor rather the exploitation than the enlightenment of mankind. This exploitation made it possible to assemble workpeople by the thousand and set them tasks that taxed them to the limits of their strength: to this, surely, we must attribute the beginnings of architecture as we know it. If my hypothesis is correct, the primary function of writing, as a means of communication, is to facilitate the enslavement of other human beings.

—FROM "A WRITING LESSON," *TRISTES TROPIQUES*, 1955

From Outside, In

BARBARA MELLIX

Two years ago, when I started writing this paper, trying to bring order out of chaos, my ten-year-old daughter was suffering from an acute attack of boredom. She drifted in and out of the room complaining that she had nothing to do, no one to "be with" because none of her friends were at home. Patiently I explained that I was working on something special and needed peace and quiet, and I suggested that she paint, read, or work with her computer. None of these interested her. Finally, she pulled up a chair to my desk and watched me, now and then heaving long, loud sighs. After two or three minutes (nine or ten sighs), I lost my patience. "Looka here, Allie," I said, "you too old for this kinda carryin' on. I done told you this is important. You wronger than dirt to be in here haggin' me like this and you know it. Now git on outta here and leave me off before I put my foot all the way down."

I was at home, alone with my family, and my daughter understood that this way of speaking was appropriate in that context. She knew, as a matter of fact, that it was almost inevitable; when I get angry at home, I speak some of my finest, most cherished black English. Had I been speaking to my daughter in this manner in certain other environments, she would have been shocked and probably worried that I had taken leave of my sense of propriety.

Like my children, I grew up speaking what I considered two distinctly different languages—black English and standard English (or as I thought of them then, the ordinary everyday speech of "country" coloreds and "proper" English)—and in the process of acquiring these languages, I developed an understanding of when, where, and how to use them. But unlike my children, I grew up in a world that was primarily black. My friends, neighbors, minister, teachers—almost everybody I associated with every day—were black. And we spoke to one another in our own special language: *That sho is a pretty dress you got on. If she don' soon leave me off I'm gon tell her head a mess. I was so mad I could'a pissed a blue nail. He all the time trying to low-rate somebody. Ain't that just about the nastiest thing you ever set ears on?*

Barbara Mellix teaches composition and fiction writing at the University of Pittsburgh, Greensburg. She grew up in Greeleyville, South Carolina, and went to college after working and starting a family in Pittsburgh, eventually earning a Master of Fine Arts in creative writing. Her essay first appeared in *The Georgia Review,* which publishes fiction, poetry, and essays, in 1987.

Then there were the "others," the "proper" blacks, transplanted   4
relatives and one-time friends who came home from the city for weddings, funerals, and vacations. And the whites. To these we spoke
standard English. "Ain't?" my mother would yell at me when I used
the term in the presence of "others." "You *know* better than that." And
I would hang my head in shame and say the "proper" word.

I remember one summer sitting in my grandmother's house in   5
Greeleyville, South Carolina, when it was full of the chatter of city relatives who were home on vacation. My parents sat quietly, only now
and then volunteering a comment or answering a question. My mother's face took on a strained expression when she spoke. I could see
that she was being careful to say just the right words in just the right
way. Her voice sounded thick, muffled. And when she finished speaking, she would lapse into silence, her proper smile on her face. My father was more articulate, more aggressive. He spoke quickly, his
words sharp and clear. But he held his proud head higher, a signal
that he, too, was uncomfortable. My sisters and brothers and I stared
at our aunts, uncles, and cousins, speaking only when prompted.
Even then, we hesitated, formed our sentences in our minds, then
spoke softly, shyly.

My parents looked small and anxious during those occasions, and   6
I waited impatiently for our leave-taking when we would mock our
relatives the moment we were out of their hearing. "Reeely," we
would say to one another, flexing our wrists and rolling our eyes,
"how dooo you stan' this heat? Chile, it just tooo hy*ooo*-mid for
words." Our relatives had made us feel "country," and this was our
way of regaining pride in ourselves while getting a little revenge in the
bargain. The words bubbled in our throats and rolled across our
tongues, a balming.

As a child I felt this same doubleness in uptown Greeleyville   7
where the whites lived. "Ain't that a pretty dress you're wearing!"
Toby, the town policeman, said to me one day when I was fifteen.
"Thank you very much," I replied, my voice barely audible in my own
ears. The words felt wrong in my mouth, rigid, foreign. It was not that
I had never spoken that phrase before—it was common in black
English, too—but I was extremely conscious that this was an occasion
for proper English. I had taken out my English and put it on as I did
my church clothes, and I felt as if I were wearing my Sunday best in
the middle of the week. It did not matter that Toby had not spoken
grammatically correct English. He was white and could speak as he
wished. I had something to prove. Toby did not.

Speaking standard English to whites was our way of demonstrat-   8
ing that we knew their language and could use it. Speaking it to stan-

dard-English-speaking blacks was our way of showing them that we, as well as they, could "put on airs." But when we spoke standard English, we acknowledged (to ourselves and to others—but primarily to ourselves) that our customary way of speaking was inferior. We felt foolish, embarrassed, somehow diminished because we were ashamed to be our real selves. We were reserved, shy in the presence of those who owned and/or spoke *the* language.

My parents never set aside time to drill us in standard English. 9 Their forms of instruction were less formal. When my father was feeling particularly expansive, he would regale us with tales of his exploits in the outside world. In almost flawless English, complete with dialogue and flavored with gestures and embellishment, he told us about his attempt to get a haircut at a white barbershop; his refusal to acknowledge one of the town merchants until the man addressed him as "Mister"; the time he refused to step off the sidewalk uptown to let some whites pass; his airplane trip to New York City (to visit a sick relative) during which the stewardesses and porters—recognizing that he was a "gentleman"—addressed him as "Sir." I did not realize then—nor, I think, did my father—that he was teaching us, among other things, standard English and the relationship between language and power.

My mother's approach was different. Often, when one of us said, 10 "I'm gon wash off my feet," she would say, "And what will you walk on if you wash them off!" Everyone would laugh at the victim of my mother's "proper" mood. But it was different when one of us children was in a proper mood. "You think you are so superior," I said to my oldest sister one day when we were arguing and she was winning. "Superior!" my sister mocked. "You mean I am acting 'biggidy'?" My sisters and brothers sniggered, then joined in teasing me. Finally, my mother said, "Leave your sister alone. There's nothing wrong with using proper English." There was a half-smile on her face. I had gotten "uppity," had "put on airs" for no good reason. I was at home, alone with the family, and I hadn't been prompted by one of my mother's proper moods. But there was also a proud light in my mother's eyes; her children were learning English very well.

Not until years later, as a college student, did I begin to under- 11 stand our ambivalence toward English, our scorn of it, our need to master it, to own and be owned by it—an ambivalence that extended to the public-school classroom. In our school, where there were no whites, my teachers taught standard English but used black English to do it. When my grammar-school teachers wanted us to write, for example, they usually said something like, "I want y'all to write five sentences that make a statement. Anybody git done before the rest can color." It was probably almost those exact words that led me to write these sentences in 1953 when I was in the second grade:

> The white clouds are pretty.
> There are only 15 people in our room.
> We will go to gym.
> We have a new poster.
> We may go out doors.

Second grade came after "Little First" and "Big First," so by then I knew the implied rules that accompanied all writing assignments. Writing was an occasion for proper English. I was not to write in the way we spoke to one another: The white clouds pretty; There ain't but 15 people in our room; We going to gym; We got a new poster; We can go out in the yard. Rather I was to use the language of "other": clouds *are*, there *are*, we *will*, we *have*, we *may*.

My sentences were short, rigid, perfunctory, like the letters my   12
mother wrote to relatives:

Dear Papa,

How are you? How is Mattie? Fine I hope. We are fine. We will come to see you Sunday. Cousin Ned will give us a ride.

Love,

Daughter

The language was not ours. It was something from outside us, something we used for special occasions.

But my coloring on the other side of that second-grade paper is   13
different. I drew three hearts and a sun. The sun has a smiling face that radiates and envelops everything it touches. And although the sun and its world are enclosed in a circle, the colors I used—red, blue, green, purple, orange, yellow, black—indicate that I was less restricted with drawing and coloring than I was with writing standard English. My valentines were not just red. My sun was not just a yellow ball in the sky.

By the time I reached the twelfth grade, speaking and writing stan-   14
dard English had taken on new importance. Each year, about half of the newly graduated seniors of our school moved to large cities—particularly in the North—to live with relatives and find work. Our English teacher constantly corrected our grammar: "Not 'ain't,' but 'isn't.'" We seldom wrote papers, and even those few were usually plot summaries of short stories. When our teacher returned the papers, she usually lectured on the importance of using standard English: "I

am; you *are;* he, she, or it *is,"* she would say, writing on the chalkboard as she spoke. "How you gon git a job talking about 'I is,' or 'I isn't' or 'I ain't'?"

In Pittsburgh, where I moved after graduation, I watched my aunt   15
and uncle—who had always spoken standard English when in Greeleyville—switch from black English to standard English to a mixture of the two, according to where they were or who they were with. At home and with certain close relatives, friends, and neighbors, they spoke black English. With those less close, they spoke a mixture. In public and with strangers, they generally spoke standard English.

In time, I learned to speak standard English with ease and to   16
switch smoothly from black to standard or a mixture, and back again. But no matter where I was, no matter what the situation or occasion, I continued to write as I had in school:

> Dear Mommie,
>
> How are you? How is everybody else? Fine I hope. I am fine. So are Aunt and Uncle. Tell everyone I said hello. I will write again soon.
>
> > Love,
> >
> > Barbara

At work, at a health insurance company, I learned to write letters to customers. I studied form letters and letters written by co-workers, memorizing the phrases and the ways in which they were used. I dictated:

> Thank you for your letter of January 5. We have made the changes in your coverage you requested. Your new premium will be $150 every three months. We are pleased to have been of service to you.

In a sense, I was proud of the letters I wrote for the company: they were proof of my ability to survive in the city, the outside world—an indication of my growing mastery of English. But they also indicate that writing was still mechanical for me, something that didn't require much thought.

Reading also became a more significant part of my life during   17
those early years in Pittsburgh. I had always liked reading, but now I devoted more and more of my spare time to it. I read romances, mysteries, popular novels. Looking back, I realize that the books I liked best were simple, unambiguous: good versus bad and right versus wrong with right rewarded and wrong punished, mysteries unraveled and all set right in the end. It was how I remembered life in Greeleyville.

Of course I was romanticizing. Life in Greeleyville had not been so   18
very uncomplicated. Back there I had been—first as a child, then as a

young woman with limited experience in the outside world—living in a relatively closed-in society. But there were implicit and explicit principles that guided our way of life and shaped our relationships with one another and the people outside—principles that a newcomer would find elusive and baffling. In Pittsburgh, I had matured, become more experienced: I had worked at three different jobs, associated with a wider range of people, married, had children. This new environment with different prescripts for living required that I speak standard English much of the time, and slowly, imperceptibly, I had ceased seeing a sharp distinction between myself and "others." Reading romances and mysteries, characterized by dichotomy, was a way of shying away from change, from the person I was becoming.

But that other part of me—that part which took great pride in my   19
ability to hold a job writing business letters—was increasingly drawn to the new developments in my life and the attending possibilities, opportunities for even greater change. If I could write letters for a nationally known business, could I not also do something better, more challenging, more important? Could I not, perhaps, go to college and become a school teacher? For years, afraid and a little embarrassed, I did no more than imagine this different me, this possible me. But sixteen years after coming north, when my younger daughter entered kindergarten, I found myself unable—or unwilling—to resist the lure of possibility. I enrolled in my first college course: Basic Writing, at the University of Pittsburgh.

For the first time in my life, I was required to write extensively   20
about myself. Using the most formal English at my command, I wrote these sentences near the beginning of the term:

> One of my duties as a homemaker is simply picking up after others. A day seldom passes that I don't search for a mislaid toy, book, or gym shoe, etc. I change the Ty-D-Bol, fight "ring around the collar," and keep our laundry smelling "April fresh." Occasionally, I settle arguments between my children and suggest things to do when they're bored. Taking telephone messages for my oldest daughter is my newest (and sometimes most aggravating) chore. Hanging the toilet paper roll is my most insignificant.

My concern was to use "appropriate" language, to sound as if I belonged in a college classroom. But I felt separate from the language—as if it did not and could not belong to me. I couldn't think and feel genuinely in that language, couldn't make it express what I thought and felt about being a housewife. A part of me resented, among other things, being judged by such things as the appearance of my family's laundry and toilet bowl, but in that language I could only imagine and write about a conventional housewife.

For the most part, the remainder of the term was a period of ad-   21
justment, a time of trying to find my bearing as a student in college
composition class, to learn to shut out my black English whenever I
composed, and to prevent it from creeping into my formulations; a
time for trying to grasp the language of the classroom and reproduce
it in my prose; for trying to talk about myself in that language, reach
others through it. Each experience of writing was like standing naked
and revealing my imperfection, my "otherness." And each new assignment was another chance to make myself over in language, re-
shape myself, make myself "better" in my rapidly changing image of
a student in a college composition class.

But writing became increasingly unmanageable as the term pro-   22
gressed, and by the end of the semester, my sentences sounded like this:

> My excitement was soon dampened, however, by what seemed like
> a small voice in the back of my head saying that I should be careful
> with my long awaited opportunity. I felt frustrated and this seemed
> to make it difficult to concentrate.

There is a poverty of language in these sentences. By this point, I knew
that the clichéd language of my Housewife essay was unacceptable,
and I generally recognized trite expressions. At the same time, I had-
n't yet mastered the language of the classroom, hadn't yet come to see
it as belonging to me. Most notable is the lifelessness of the prose, the
apparent absence of a person behind the words. I wanted those sentences—and the rest of the essay—to convey the anguish of yearning
to, at once, become something more and yet remain the same. I had the
sensation of being split in two, part of me going into a future the other
part didn't believe possible. As that person, the student writer at that
moment, I was essentially mute. I could not—in the process of composing—use the language of the old me, yet I couldn't imagine myself
in the language of "others."

I found this particularly discouraging because at midsemester I   23
had been writing in a much different way. Note the language of this introduction to an essay I had written then, near the middle of the term:

> Pain is a constant companion to the people in "Footwork." Their
> jobs are physically damaging. Employers are insensitive to their
> feelings and in many cases add to their problems. The general pub-
> lic wounds them further by treating them with disgrace because of
> what they do for a living. Although the workers are as diverse as
> they are similar, there is a definite link between them. They suffer a
> great deal of abuse.

The voice here is stronger, more confident, appropriating terms
like "physically damaging," "wounds them further," "insensitive,"

"diverse"—terms I couldn't have imagined using when writing about my own experience—and shaping them into sentences like "Although the workers are as diverse as they are similar, there is a definite link between them." And there is the sense of a personality behind the prose, someone who sympathizes with the workers. "The general public wounds them further by treating them with disgrace because of what they do for a living."

What caused these differences? I was, I believed, explaining other people's thoughts and feelings, and I was free to move about in the language of "others" so long as I was speaking *of* others. I was unaware that I was transforming into my best classroom language my own thoughts and feelings about people whose experiences and ways of speaking were in many ways similar to mine. **24**

The following year, unable to turn back or to let go of what had become something of an obsession with language (and hoping to catch and hold the sense of control that had eluded me in Basic Writing), I enrolled in a research writing course. I spent most of the term learning how to prepare for and write a research paper. I chose sex education as my subject and spent hours in libraries, searching for information, reading, taking notes. Then (not without messiness and often-demoralizing frustration) I organized my information into categories, wrote a thesis statement, and composed my paper—a series of paraphrases and quotations spaced between carefully constructed transitions. The process and results felt artificial, but as I would later come to realize I was passing through a necessary stage. My sentences sounded like this: **25**

> This reserve becomes understandable with examination of who the abusers are. In an overwhelming number of cases, they are people the victims know and trust. Family members, relatives, neighbors and close family friends commit seventy-five percent of all reported sex crimes against children, and parents, parent substitutes and relatives are the offenders in thirty to eighty percent of all reported cases.[12] While assault by strangers does occur, it is less common, and is usually a single episode.[13] But abuse by family members, relatives and acquaintances may continue for an extended period of time. In cases of incest, for example, children are abused repeatedly for an average of eight years.[14] In such cases, "the use of physical force is rarely necessary because of the child's trusting, dependent relationship with the offender. The child's cooperation is often facilitated by the adult's position of dominance, an offer of material goods, a threat of physical violence, or a misrepresentation of moral standards."[15]

The completed paper gave me a sense of profound satisfaction, and I read it often after my professor returned it. I know now that what I was pleased with was the language I used and the professional voice it helped me maintain. "Use better words," my teacher had snapped at me one day after reading the notes I'd begun accumulating **26** from my research, and slowly I began taking on the language of my sources. In my next set of notes, I used the word "vacillating"; my professor applauded. And by the time I composed the final draft, I felt at ease with terms like "overwhelming number of cases," "single episode," and "reserve," and I shaped them into sentences similar to those of my "expert" sources.

If I were writing the paper today, I would of course do some 27 things differently. Rather than open with an anecdote—as my teacher suggested—I would begin simply with a quotation that caught my interest as I was researching my paper (and which I scribbled, without its source, in the margin of my notebook): "Truth does not do so much good in the world as the semblance of truth does evil." The quotation felt right because it captured what was for me the central idea of my paper—and expressed it in a way I would like to have said it. The anecdote, a hypothetical situation I invented to conform to the information in the paper, felt forced and insincere because it represented—to a great degree—my teacher's understanding of the essay, her idea of what in it was most significant. Improving upon my previous experiences with writing, I was beginning to think and feel in the language I used, to find my own voice in it, to sense that how one speaks influences how one means. But I was not yet secure enough, comfortable enough with the language to trust my intuition.

Now that I know that to seek knowledge, freedom, and autonomy 28 means always to be in the concentrated process of becoming—always to be venturing into new territory, feeling one's way at first, then getting one's balance, negotiating, accommodating, discovering one's self in ways that previously defined "others"—I sometimes get tired. And I ask myself why I keep on participating in this highbrow form of violence, this slamming against perplexity. But there is no real futility in the question, no hint of that part of the old me who stood outside standard English, hugging to herself a disabling mistrust of language she thought could not represent a person with her history and experience. Rather, the question represents a person who feels the consequence of her education, the weight of her possibilities as a teacher and writer and human being, a voice in society. And I would not change that person, would not give back the good burden that accompanies my growing expertise, my increasing power to shape myself in language and share that self with "others."

"To speak," says Frantz Fanon, "means to be in a position to use a 29 certain syntax, to grasp the morphology of this or that language, but it means above all to assume a culture, to support the weight of a civilization."[1] To write means to do the same, but in a more profound

[1]*Black Skin, White Masks* (1952; rpt. New York: Grove Press, 1967), pp. 17–18.

sense. However, Fanon also says that to achieve mastery means to "get" in a position of power, to "grasp," to "assume." This, I have learned both as a student and subsequently as a teacher, can involve tremendous emotional and psychological conflict for those attempting to master academic discourse. Although as a beginning student writer I had a fairly good grasp of ordinary spoken English and was proficient at what Labov calls "code-switching" (and what John Baugh in *Black Street Speech* terms "style shifting"), when I came face to face with the demands of academic writing, I grew increasingly self-conscious, constantly aware of my status as a black and a speaker of one of the many black English vernaculars—a traditional outsider. For the first time, I experienced my sense of doubleness as something menacing, a built-in enemy. Whenever I turned inward for salvation, the balm so available during my childhood, I found instead this new fragmentation which spoke to me in many voices. It was the voice of my desire to prosper, but at the same time it spoke of what I had relinquished and could not regain: a safe way of being, a state of powerlessness which exempted me from responsibility for who I was and might be. And it accused me of betrayal, of turning away from blackness. To recover balance, I had to take on the language of the academy, the language of "others." And to do that, I had to learn to imagine myself a part of the culture of that language, and therefore someone free to manage that language, to take liberties with it. Writing and rewriting, practicing, experimenting, I came to comprehend more fully the generative power of language. I discovered—with the help of some especially sensitive teachers—that through writing one can continually bring new selves into being, each with new responsibilities and difficulties, but also with new possibilities. Remarkable power, indeed. I write and continually give birth to myself.

QUESTIONS

1. Mellix says her father helped teach her "the relationship between language and power" (paragraph 9). What does that relationship seem to consist of, according to Mellix? Based on her essay, exactly what kinds of power do you think she means?

2. Reread the samples Mellix offers from her student essays. How do you judge her assessment of her writing at each stage?

3. To what extent do you agree with Mellix that increasing one's fluency in academic writing helps to "continually bring new selves into being" (paragraph 29)?

Nobody Mean More to Me Than You and the Future Life of Willie Jordan

JUNE JORDAN

Black English is not exactly a linguistic buffalo; as children, most 1
of the thirty-five million Afro-Americans living here depend on this
language for our discovery of the world. But then we approach our
maturity inside a larger social body that will not support our efforts to
become anything other than the clones of those who are neither our
mothers nor our fathers. We begin to grow up in a house where every
true mirror shows us the face of somebody who does not belong there,
whose walk and whose talk will never look or sound "right," because
that house was meant to shelter a family that is alien and hostile to us.
As we learn our way around this environment, either we hide our original word habits, or we completely surrender our own voice, hoping to
please those who will never respect anyone different from themselves:
Black English is not exactly a linguistic buffalo, but we should understand its status as an endangered species, as a perishing, irreplaceable
system of community intelligence, or we should expect its extinction,
and, along with that, the extinguishing of much that constitutes our
own proud, and singular identity.

What we casually call "English" less and less defers to England 2
and its "gentlemen." "English" is no longer a specific matter of geography or an element of class privilege; more than thirty-three countries
use this tool as a means of "intranational communication." Countries
as disparate as Zimbabwe and Malaysia, or Israel and Uganda, use it
as their non-native currency of convenience. Obviously, this tool, this
"English," cannot function inside thirty-three discrete societies on the
basis of rules and values absolutely determined somewhere else, in a
thirty-fourth other country, for example.

June Jordan is professor of African American Studies at the
University of California, Berkeley, where she also teaches freshman
composition courses. She has written juvenile fiction, biography,
essays, and several volumes of poetry including *Naming Our Destiny:
New and Selected Poems* (1989). Jordan was born in Harlem and raised
in Brooklyn. Her social and political commentary, focusing on her
impassioned concern for social justice, has been collected in *Civil
Wars* (1981), *Technical Difficulties: African-American Notes on the State
of the Union* (1992), and *On Call: Political Essays* (1985), where this
essay appeared.

In addition to that staggering congeries of non-native users of [3] English, there are five countries, or 333,746,000 people, for whom this thing called "English" serves as a native tongue. Approximately 10% of these native speakers of "English" are Afro-American citizens of the U.S.A. I cite these numbers and varieties of human beings dependent on "English" in order, quickly, to suggest how strange and how tenuous is any concept of "Standard English." Obviously, numerous forms of English now operate inside a natural, an uncontrollable, continuum of development. I would suppose "the standard" for English in Malaysia is not the same as "the standard" in Zimbabwe. I know that standard forms of English for Black people in this country do not copy those of whites. And, in fact, the structural differences between these two kinds of English have intensified, becoming more Black, or less white, despite the expected homogenizing effects of television and other mass media.

Nonetheless, white standards of English persist, supreme and un- [4] questioned, in these United States. Despite our multi-lingual population, and despite the deepening Black and white cleavage within that conglomerate, white standards control our official and popular judgements of verbal proficiency and correct, or incorrect, language skills, including speech. In contrast to India, where at least fourteen languages co-exist as legitimate Indian languages, in contrast to Nicaragua, where all citizens are legally entitled to formal school instruction in their regional or tribal languages, compulsory education in America compels accommodation to exclusively white forms of "English." White English, in America, is "Standard English."

This story begins two years ago. I was teaching a new course, "In [5] Search of the Invisible Black Woman," and my rather large class seemed evenly divided between young Black women and men. Five or six white students also sat in attendance. With unexpected speed and enthusiasm we had moved through historical narratives of the 19th century to literature by and about Black women, in the 20th. I had assigned the first forty pages of Alice Walker's *The Color Purple*, and I came, eagerly, to class that morning:

"So!" I exclaimed, aloud. "What did you think? How did you [6] like it?"

The students studied their hands, or the floor. There was no re- [7] sponse. The tense, resistant feeling in the room fairly astounded me.

At last, one student, a young woman still not meeting my eyes, [8] muttered something in my direction:

"What did you say?" I prompted her. [9]

"Why she have them talk so funny. It don't sound right." [10]

"You mean the language?" [11]

Another student lifted his head: "It don't look right, neither. I   12
couldn't hardly read it."

At this, several students dumped on the book. Just about unani-   13
mously, their criticisms targeted the language. I listened to what they
wanted to say and silently marvelled at the similarities between their casual speech patterns and Alice Walker's written version of Black English.

But I decided against pointing to these identical traits of syntax; I   14
wanted not to make them self-conscious about their own spoken language—not while they clearly felt it was "wrong." Instead I decided to
swallow my astonishment. Here was a negative Black reaction to a
prize-winning accomplishment of Black literature that white readers
across the country had selected as a best seller. Black rejection was
aimed at the one irreducibly Black element of Walker's work: the language—Celie's Black English. I wrote the opening lines of *The Color
Purple* on the blackboard and asked the students to help me translate
these sentences into Standard English:

> *You better not never tell nobody but God. It'd kill your mammy.*
> Dear God,
>   I am fourteen years old. I have always been a good girl. Maybe you
> can give me a sign letting me know what is happening to me.
>   Last spring after Little Lucious come I heard them fussing. He was
> pulling on her arm. She say it too soon, Fonso. I ain't well. Finally he
> leave her alone. A week go by, he pulling on her arm again. She say,
> Naw, I ain't gonna. Can't you see I'm already half dead, an all of
> the children.

Our process of translation exploded with hilarity and even hysterical,
shocked laughter: The Black writer, Alice Walker, knew what she was
doing! If rudimentary criteria for good fiction includes the manipula-
tion of language so that the syntax and diction of sentences will tell
you the identity of speakers, the probable age and sex and class of
speakers, and even the locale—urban/rural/southern/western—then
Walker had written, perfectly. This is the translation into Standard
English that our class produced:

> *Absolutely, one should never confide in anybody besides God. Your secrets
> could prove devastating to your mother.*
> Dear God,
>   I am fourteen years old. I have always been good. But now, could
> you help me to understand what is happening to me?
>   Last spring, after my little brother, Lucious, was born, I heard my par-
> ents fighting. My father kept pulling at my mother's arm. But she told
> him, "It's too soon for sex, Alfonso. I am still not feeling well." Finally,
> my father left her alone. A week went by, and then he began bother-
> ing my mother again: pulling her arm. She told him, "No, I won't!
> Can't you see I'm already exhausted from all of these children?"

(Our favorite line was "It's too soon for sex, Alphonso.")   15

Once we could stop laughing, once we could stop our exponen- 16
tially wild improvisations on the theme of Translated Black English,
the students pushed me to explain their own negative first reactions to
their spoken language on the printed page. I thought it was probably
akin to the shock of seeing yourself in a photograph for the first time.
Most of the students had never before seen a written facsimile of the
way they talk. None of the students had ever learned how to read and
write their own verbal system of communication: Black English.
Alternatively, this fact began to baffle or else bemuse and then infuri-
ate my students. Why not? Was it too late? Could they learn how to do
it, now? And, ultimately, the final test question, the one testing my sincerity: Could I teach them? Because I had never taught anyone Black
English and, as far as I knew, no one, anywhere in the United States,
had ever offered such a course, the best I could say was "I'll try."

He looked like a wrestler.   17

He sat dead center in the packed room and, every time our eyes 18
met, he quickly nodded his head as though anxious to reassure and encourage, me.

Short, with strikingly broad shoulders and long arms, he spoke 19
with a surprisingly high, soft voice that matched the soft bright movement of his eyes. His name was Willie Jordan. He would have seemed
even more unlikely in the context of Contemporary Women's Poetry,
except that ten or twelve other Black men were taking the course, as
well. Still, Willie was conspicuous. His extreme fitness, the muscular
density of his presence underscored the riveted, gentle attention that
he gave to anything anyone said. Generally, he did not join the loud
and rowdy dialogue flying back and forth, but there could be no doubt
about his interest in our discussions. And, when he stood to present an
argument he'd prepared, overnight, that nervous smile of his vanished
and an irregular stammering replaced it, as he spoke with visceral sincerity, word by word.

That was how I met Willie Jordan. It was in between "In Search of 20
the Invisible Black Women" and "The Art of Black English." I was
waiting for Departmental approval and I supposed that Willie might
be, so to speak, killing time until he, too, could study Black English. But
Willie really did want to explore Contemporary Women's Poetry and,
to that end, volunteered for extra research and never missed a class.

Towards the end of that semester, Willie approached me for an 21
independent study project on South Africa. It would commence the
next semester. I thought Willie's writing needed the kind of improvement only intense practice will yield. I knew his intelligence was

outstanding. But he'd wholeheartedly opted for "Standard English" at a rather late age, and the results were stilted and frequently polysyllabic, simply for the sake of having more syllables. Willie's unnatural formality of language seemed to me consistent with the formality of his research into South African apartheid. As he projected his studies, he would have little time, indeed, for newspapers. Instead, more than 90% of his research would mean saturation in strictly historical, if not archival, material. I was certainly interested. It would be tricky to guide him into a more confident and spontaneous relationship with both language and apartheid. It was going to be wonderful to see what happened when he could catch up with himself, entirely, and talk back to the world.

September, 1984: Breezy fall weather and much excitement! My 22 class, "The Art of Black English," was full to the limit of the fire laws. And, in Independent Study, Willie Jordan showed up, weekly, fifteen minutes early for each of our sessions. I was pretty happy to be teaching, altogether!

I remember an early class when a young brother, replete with his 23 ever-present pork-pie hat, raised his hand and then told us that most of what he'd heard was "all right" except it was "too clean." "The brothers on the street," he continued, "they mix it up more. Like 'fuck' and 'motherfuck.' Or like 'shit.' " He waited. I waited. Then all of us laughed a good while, and we got into a brawl about "correct" and "realistic" Black English that led to Rule 1.

Rule 1: *Black English is about a whole lot more than mothafuckin.*   24

As a criterion, we decided, "realistic" could take you anywhere 25 you want to go. Artful places. Angry places. Eloquent and sweetalkin places. Polemical places. Church. And the local Bar & Grill. We were checking out a language, not a mood or a scene or one guy's forgettable mouthing off.

It was hard. For most of the students, learning Black English re- 26 quired a fallback to patterns and rhythms of speech that many of their parents had beaten out of them. I mean *beaten.* And, in a majority of cases, correct Black English could be achieved only by striving for *incorrect* Standard English, something they were still pushing at, quite uncertainly. This state of affairs led to Rule 2.

Rule 2: *If it's wrong in Standard English it's probably right in Black* 27 *English, or, at least, you're hot.*

It was hard. Roommates and family members ridiculed their stud- 28 ies, or remained incredulous. "You *studying* that shit? At school?" But we were beginning to feel the companionship of pioneers. And we decided that we needed another rule that would establish each one of us as equally important to our success. This was Rule 3.

Rule 3: *If it don't sound like something that come out somebody mouth* 29
then it don't sound right. If it don't sound right then it ain't hardly right.
Period.

This rule produced two weeks of compositions in which the stu- 30
dents agonizingly tried to spell the sound of the Black English sentence they wanted to convey. But Black English is, preeminently, an
oral/spoken means of communication. *And spelling don't talk.* So we
needed Rule 4.

Rule 4: *Forget about the spelling. Let the syntax carry you.* 31

Once we arrived at Rule 4 we started to fly because syntax, the 32
structure of an idea, leads you to the world view of the speaker and reveals her values. The syntax of a sentence equals the structure of your
consciousness. If we insisted that the language of Black English ad-
heres to a distinctive Black syntax, then we were postulating a profound difference between white and Black people, *per se.* Was it a difference to prize or to obliterate?

There are three qualities of Black English—the presence of life, 33
voice, and clarity—that testify to a distinctive Black value system that
we became excited about and self-consciously tried to maintain.

1. Black English has been produced by a pre-technocratic, if not 34
anti-technological, culture. More, our culture has been constantly
threatened by annihilation or, at least, the swallowed blurring of assimilation. Therefore, our language is a system constructed by people
constantly needing to insist that we exist, that we are present. Our
language devolves from a culture that abhors all abstraction, or anything tending to obscure or delete the fact of the human being who is
here and now/the truth of the person who is speaking or listening.
Consequently, *there is no passive voice construction possible in Black
English.* For example, you cannot say, "Black English is being eliminated." You must say, instead, "White people eliminating Black
English." The assumption of the presence of life governs all of Black
English. Therefore, overwhelmingly, *all action takes place in the language of the present indicative.* And every sentence assumes the living
and active participation of at least two human beings, the speaker and
the listener.

2. A primary consequence of the person-centered values of Black 35
English is the delivery of voice. If you speak or write Black English, your
ideas will necessarily possess that otherwise elusive attribute, *voice.*

3. One main benefit following from the person-centered values of 36
Black English is that of *clarity.* If your idea, your sentence, assumes the
presence of at least two living and active people, you will make it understandable because the motivation behind every sentence is the wish
to say something real to somebody real.

As the weeks piled up, translation from Standard English into 37
Black English or vice versa occupied a hefty part of our course work.

> Standard English (hereafter S.E.): "In considering the idea of study-
> ing Black English those questioned suggested—"
>   (What's the subject? Where's the person? Is anybody alive in
> there, in that idea?)
>   Black English (hereafter B.E.): "I been asking people what you
> think about somebody studying Black English and they answer me
> like this:"

But there were interesting limits. You cannot "translate" instances of
Standard English preoccupied with abstraction or with nothing/no-
body evidently alive, into Black English. That would warp the language into uses antithetical to the guiding perspective of its community of users. Rather you must first change those Standard English
sentences, themselves, into ideas consistent with the person-centered
assumptions of Black English.

Guidelines For Black English

1. Minimal number of words for every idea: This is the source for the 38
   aphoristic and/or poetic force of the language; eliminate every
   possible word.
2. Clarity: If the sentence is not clear it's not Black English.   39
3. Eliminate use of the verb *to be* whenever possible. This leads to the 40
   deployment of more descriptive and therefore more precise verbs.
4. Use *be* or *been* only when you want to describe a chronic, ongoing 41
   state of things.
   He *be* at the office, by 9. (He is always at the office by 9.)
   He *been* with her since forever.
5. Zero copula: Always eliminate the verb *to be* whenever it would 42
   combine with another verb, in Standard English.
   S.E.: She is going out with him.
   B.E.: She going out with him.
6. Eliminate *do* as in: 43
   S.E.: What do you think? What do you want?
   B.E.: What you think? What you want?

Rules number 3, 4, 5, and 6 provide for the use of the minimal 44
number of verbs per idea and, therefore, greater accuracy in the choice
of verb.

7. In general, if you wish to say something really positive, try to   45
   formulate the idea using emphatic negative structure.
   S.E.: He's fabulous.
   B.E.: He bad.

8. Use double or triple negatives for dramatic emphasis.   46
   S.E.: Tina Turner sings out of this world.
   B.E.: Ain nobody sing like Tina.

9. Never use the *-ed* suffix to indicate the past tense of a verb.   47
   S.E.: She closed the door.
   B.E.: She close the door. Or, she have close the door.

10. Regardless of intentional verb time, only use the third person   48
    singular, present indicative, for use of the verb *to have,* as an aux-
    iliary.
    S.E.: He had his wallet then he lost it.
    B.E.: He have him wallet then he lose it.
    S.E.: We had seen that movie.
    B.E.: We seen that movie. Or, we have see that movie.

11. Observe a minimal inflection of verbs. Particularly, never change   49
    from the first person singular forms to the third person singular.
    S.E.: Present Tense Forms: He goes to the store.
    B.E.: He go to the store.
    S.E.: Past Tense Forms: He went to the store.
    B.E.: He go to the store. Or, he gone to the store. Or, he been to
    the store.

12. The possessive case scarcely ever appears in Black English. Never   50
    use an apostrophe ('s) construction. If you wander into a posses-
    sive case component of an idea, then keep logically consistent:
    ours, his, theirs, mines. But, most likely, if you bump into such a
    component, you have wandered outside the underlying world-
    view of Black English.
    S.E.: He will take their car tomorrow.
    B.E.: He taking they car tomorrow.

13. Plurality: Logical consistency, continued: If the modifier indicates   51
    plurality, then the noun remains in the singular case.
    S.E.: He ate twelve doughnuts.
    B.E.: He eat twelve doughnut.
    S.E.: She has many books.
    B.E.: She have many book.

14. Listen for, or invent, special Black English forms of the past   52
    tense, such as: "He losted it. That what she felted." If they are
    clear and readily understood, then use them.

Do not hesitate to play with words, sometimes inventing them; 53
e.g., "astropotomous" means huge like a hippo plus astronomical and,
therefore, signifies real big.

15. In Black English, unless you keenly want to underscore the past 54
    tense nature of an action, stay in the present tense and rely on
    the overall context of your ideas for the conveyance of time and
    sequence.

16. Never use the suffix *-ly* form of an adverb in Black English. 55
    S.E.: The rain came down rather quickly.
    B.E.: The rain come down pretty quick.

17. Never use the indefinite article *an* in Black English. 56
    S.E.: He wanted to ride an elephant.
    B.E.: He want to ride him a elephant.

18. In variant syntax: In correct Black English it is possible to formu- 57
    late an imperative, an interrogative, and a simple declarative idea
    with the same syntax:
    B.E.: You going to the store?
          You going to the store.
          You going to the store!

Where was Willie Jordan? We'd reached the mid-term of the 58
semester. Students had formulated Black English guidelines, by consensus, and they were now writing with remarkable beauty, purpose,
and enjoyment:

I ain hardly speakin for everybody but myself so understan that.

—KIM PARKS

Samples from student writings:

"Janie have a great big ole hole inside her. Tea Cake the only thing 59
that fit that hole. . . .

"That pear tree beautiful to Janie, especial when bees fiddlin with 60
the blossomin pear there growin large and lovely. But personal
speakin, the love she get from starin at that tree ain the love what
starin back at her in them relationship." (Monica Morris)

"Love is a big theme in *They Eye Was Watching God*. Love show 61
people new corners inside theyself. It pull out good stuff and stuff
back bad stuff. . . . Joe worship the doing uh his own hand and need
other people to worship him too. But he ain't think about Janie that she
a person and ought to live like anybody common do. Queen life not for
Janie." (Monica Morris)

"In both life and writin, Black womens have varietous experience 62
of love that be cold like a iceberg or fiery like a inferno. Passion got for
the other partner involve, man or woman, seem as shallow, ankle-deep
water or the most profoundest abyss." (Constance Evans)

"Family love another bond that ain't never break under no pres- 63
sure." (Constance Evans)

"You know it really cold/When the friend you/Always get out 64
the fire/Act like they don't know you/When you in the heat."
(Constance Evans)

"Big classroom discussion bout love at this time. I never take no 65
class where us have any long arguin for and against for two or three
day. New to me and great. I find the class time talkin a million time
more interestin than detail bout the book." (Kathy Esseks)

As these examples suggest, Black English no longer limited the 66
students, in any way. In fact, one of them, Philip Garfield, would
shortly "translate" a pivotal scene from Ibsen's *Doll House,* as his final
term paper:

Nora: I didn't gived no shit. I thinked you a asshole back then, too, you
make it so hard for me save mines husband life.

Krogstad: Girl, it clear you ain't any idea what you done. You done exact
what once done, and I losed my reputation over it.

Nora: You asks me believe you once act brave save you wife life?

Krogstad: Law care less why you done it.

Nora: Law must suck.

Krogstad: Suck or no, if I wants, judge screw you wid dis paper.

Nora: No way, man. (Philip Garfield)

But where was Willie? Compulsively punctual, and always thor- 67
oughly prepared with neatly typed compositions, he had disappeared.
He failed to show up for our regularly scheduled conference, and I received neither a note nor a phone call of explanation. A whole week
went by. I wondered if Willie had finally been captured by the extremely current happenings in South Africa: passage of a new constitution that did not enfranchise the Black majority, and militant Black
South African reaction to that affront. I wondered if he'd been hurt,
somewhere. I wondered if the serious workload of weekly readings
and writings had overwhelmed him and changed his mind about independent study. Where was Willie Jordan?

One week after the first conference that Willie missed, he called: 68
"Hello, Professor Jordan? This is Willie. I'm sorry I wasn't there last
week. But something has come up and I'm pretty upset. I'm sorry but
I really can't deal right now."

I asked Willie to drop by my office and just let me see that he was   69
okay: He agreed to do that. When I saw him I knew something hideous
had happened. Something had hurt him and scared him to the mar-
row. He was all agitated and stammering and terse and incoherent. At
last, his sadly jumbled account let me surmise as follows: Brooklyn police had murdered his unarmed, twenty-five-year-old brother, Reggie
Jordan. Neither Willie nor his elderly parents knew what to do about
it. Nobody from the press was interested. His folks had no money.
Police ran his family around and around, to no point. And Reggie was
really dead. And Willie wanted to fight, but he felt helpless.

With Willie's permission I began to try to secure legal counsel for   70
the Jordan family. Unfortunately Black victims of police violence are
truly numerous while the resources available to prosecute their killers
are truly scarce. A friend of mine at the Center for Constitutional
Rights estimated that just the preparatory costs for bringing the cops
into court normally approaches $180,000. Unless the execution of
Reggie Jordan became a major community cause for organizing and
protest, his murder would simply become a statistical item.

Again with Willie's permission, I contacted every newspaper and   71
media person I could think of. But the William Bastone feature article
in *The Village Voice* was the only result from that canvassing.

Again with Willie's permission, I presented the case to my class in   72
Black English. We had talked about the politics of language. We had
talked about love and sex and child abuse and men and women. But
the murder of Reggie Jordan broke like a hurricane across the room.

There are few "issues" as endemic to Black life as police violence.   73
Most of the students knew and respected and liked Jordan. Many of
them came from the very neighborhood where the murder had occurred. All of the students had known somebody close to them who
had been killed by police, or had known frightening moments of gra-
tuitous confrontation with the cops. They wanted to do everything at
once to avenge death. Number One: They decided to compose personal statements of condolence to Willie Jordan and his family, written in Black English. Number Two: They decided to compose individual messages to the police, in Black English. These should be
prefaced by an explanatory paragraph composed by the entire group.
Number Three: These individual messages, with their lead paragraph, should be sent to *Newsday*.

The morning after we agreed on these objectives, one of the young   74
women students appeared with an unidentified visitor, who sat
through the class, smiling in a peculiar, comfortable way.

Now we had to make more tactical decisions. Because we wanted   75
the messages published, and because we thought it imperative that

our outrage be known by the police, the tactical question was this: Should the opening, group paragraph be written in Black English or Standard English?

I have seldom been privy to a discussion with so much heart at the 76 dead heat of it. I will never forget the eloquence, the sudden haltings of speech, the fierce struggle against tears, the furious throwaways and useless explosions that this question elicited.

That one question contained several others, each of them extraor- 77 dinarily painful to even contemplate. How best to serve the memory of Reggie Jordan? Should we use the language of the killers—Standard English—in order to make our ideas acceptable to those controlling the killers? But wouldn't what we had to say be rejected, summarily, if we said it in our own language, the language of the victim, Reggie Jordan? But if we sought to express ourselves by abandoning our language, wouldn't that mean our suicide on top of Reggie's murder? But if we expressed ourselves in our own language, wouldn't that be suicidal to the wish to communicate with those who, evidently, did not give a damn about us/Reggie/police violence in the Black community?

At the end of one of the longest, most difficult hours of my own 78 life, the students voted, unanimously, to preface their individual messages with a paragraph composed in the language of Reggie Jordan. *"At least we don't give up nothing else. At least we stick to the truth: Be who we been. And stay all the way with Reggie."*

It was heartbreaking to proceed, from that point. Everyone in the 79 room realized that our decision in favor of Black English had doomed our writings, even as the distinctive reality of our Black lives always has doomed our efforts to "be who we been" in this country.

I went to the blackboard and took down this paragraph, dictated 80 by the class:

> . . . You Cops!
> We the brother and sister of Willie Jordan, a fellow stony brook student who the brother of the dead Reggie Jordan. Reggie, like many brother and sister, he a victim of brutal racist police, October 25, 1984. Us appall, fed up, because that another senseless death what occur in our community. This what we feel, this, from our heart, for we ain't stayin' silent no more.

With the completion of this introduction, nobody said anything. I 81 asked for comments. At this invitation, the unidentified visitor, a young Black man, ceaselessly smiling, raised his hand. He was, it so happens, a rookie cop. He had just joined the force in September and, he said, he thought he should clarify a few things. So he came forward and sprawled easily into a posture of barroom, or fireside, nostalgia:

"See," Officer Charles enlightened us, "most times when you out 82 on the street and something come down you do one of two things.

Over-react or under-react. Now, if you under-react then you can get yourself kilt. And if you over-react then maybe you kill somebody. Fortunately it's about nine times out of ten and you will over-react. So the brother got kilt. And I'm sorry about that, believe me. But what you have to understand is what kilt him: over-reaction. That's all. Now you talk about Black people and white police but see, now, I'm a cop myself. And [big smile] I'm Black. And just a couple months ago I was on the other side. But see it's the same for me. You a cop, you the ulti-mate authority: the Ultimate Authority. And you on the street, most of the time you can only do one of two things: over-react or under-react. That's all it is with the brother. Over-reaction. Didn't have nothing to do with race."

That morning Officer Charles had the good fortune to escape with- 83 out being boiled alive. But barely. And I remember the pride of his smile when I read about the fate of Black policemen and other collab-orators in South Africa. I remember him, and I remember the shock and palpable feeling of shame that filled the room. It was as though that foolish, and deadly, young man had just relieved himself of his foolish, and deadly, explanation, face to face with the grief of Reggie Jordan's father and Reggie Jordan's mother. Class ended quietly. I copied the paragraph from the blackboard, collected the individual messages, and left to type them up.

Newsday rejected the piece.   84

The Village Voice could not find room in their "Letters" section to 85 print the individual messages from the students to the police.

None of the tv news reporters picked up the story.   86

Nobody raised $180,000 to prosecute the murder of Reggie Jordan. 87

Reggie Jordan is really dead.   88

I asked Willie Jordan to write an essay pulling together everything 89 important to him from that semester. He was still deeply beside him-self with frustration and amazement and loss. This is what he wrote, un-edited, and in its entirety:

> Throughout the course of this semester I have been researching the effects of oppression and exploitation along racial lines in South Africa and its neighboring countries. I have become aware of South African police brutalization of native Africans beyond the extent of the law, even though the laws themselves are catalyst affliction upon Black men, women and children. Many Africans die each year as a result of the deliberate use of police force to protect the white power structure.
>
> Social control agents in South Africa, such as policemen, are also used to force compliance among citizens through both overt and covert tactics. It is not uncommon to find bold-faced coercion and cold-blooded killings of Blacks by South African police for undetermined and/or inadequate reasons. Perhaps the truth is that

the only reason for this heinous treatment of Blacks rests in racial differences. We should also understand that what is conveyed through the media is not always accurate and may sometimes be construed as the tip of the iceberg at best.

I recently received a painful reminder that racism, poverty, and the abuse of power are global problems which are by no means unique to South Africa. On October 25, 1984 at approximately 3:00 p.m. my brother, Mr. Reginald Jordan, was shot and killed by two New York City policemen from the 75th precinct in the East New York section of Brooklyn. His life ended at the age of twenty-five. Even up to this current point in time the Police Department has failed to provide my family, which consists of five brothers, eight sisters, and two parents, with a plausible reason for Reggie's death. Out of the many stories that were given to my family by the Police Department, not one of them seems to hold water. In fact, I honestly believe that the Police Department's assessment of my brother's murder is nothing short of absolute bullshit, and thus far no evidence had been produced to alter this perception of the situation.

Furthermore, I believe that one of three cases may have occurred in this incident. First, Reggie's death may have been the desired outcome of the police officer's action, in which case the killing was premeditated. Or, it was a case of mistaken identity, which clarifies the fact that the two officers who killed my brother and their commanding parties are all grossly incompetent. Or, both of the above cases are correct, i.e., Reggie's murderers intended to kill him and the Police Department behaved insubordinately.

Part of the argument of the officers who shot Reggie was that he had attacked one of them and took his gun. This was their major claim. They also said that only one of them had actually shot Reggie. The facts, however, speak for themselves. According to the Death Certificate and autopsy report, Reggie was shot eight times from point-blank range. The Doctor who performed the autopsy told me himself that two bullets entered the side of my brother's head, four bullets were sprayed into his back, and two bullets struck him in the back of his legs. It is obvious that unnecessary force was used by the police and that it is extremely difficult to shoot someone in his back when he is attacking or approaching you.

After experiencing a situation like this and researching South Africa I believe that to a large degree, justice may only exist as rhetoric. I find it difficult to talk of true justice when the oppression of my people both at home and abroad attests to the fact that inequality and injustice are serious problems whereby Blacks and Third World people are perpetually short-changed by society. Something has to be done about the way in which this world is set up. Although it is a difficult task, we do have the power to make a change.

—WILLIE J. JORDAN JR.
EGL 487, SECTION 58, NOVEMBER 14, 1984

It is my privilege to dedicate this book to the future life of Willie J. Jordan Jr.

August 8, 1985

QUESTIONS

1. Why does Jordan say that the concept of "Standard English" is "strange and tenuous" (paragraph 3)? Do you agree with her that, in America, standard English is "White English"?

2. Discuss what Jordan's students had to gain, and what they had to lose, in their decision to write the introduction to their group messages in Black English. Do you think they made a good decision? Why or why not?

3. If the community or neighborhood you come from has its own language or dialect, compose a set of rules and guidelines governing its usage, like those created by Jordan and her class.

Talkin' American 2

MICHAEL VENTURA

Flannery O'Connor wrote American with the cut and grace of a 1 master. She said this once about the sort of language encouraged on our campuses: "Everywhere I go I'm asked if I think the university stifles writers. My opinion is that they don't stifle enough of them."

The university is where language goes to die—and where young 2 people, expecting to be taught, ingest corruption as education. For it is corrupt to analyze art with words that intimidate people less moneyed or lucky than you; it's a way of keeping them out of the galleries and museums, a way of keeping culture all to yourself and your kind. And it is corrupt to teach literature (which would not exist except for passion) in terms that deny or mock passion; what's really being taught is that all behavior beyond the repartee of a faculty dinner party is ridiculous or unclean. And finally, it is corrupt to express theories about the psyche or society in words that conceal the consequences of your thought—words beyond reach of those who must bear the burden of whatever bright ideas will excuse the next excesses of power.

This corruption hides in plain sight, in something as obvious and 3 as overlooked as vocabulary. There's a jargon to be learned for every study now—usually a multisyllable mishmash guaranteed to drain the life out of any sentence and strain the attention of any listener. But it doesn't take a lot of syllables to be pernicious. Literature students, for instance, no longer delve into novels and poems, they study "texts." Same stuff, but with very different assumptions about it. See, the word "poem" still holds just enough residue of intensity that one approaches it as something at least strange, something with secrets to tell. And presences as disturbing as Dostoevski's follow the word "novel" into your mind. But "text" is barren, a cold word, clinical and belittling. The intent in calling, say, *As I Lay Dying* a "text" is to make the book passive, short out its charge, control it before it gets *to* you. Don't let Faulkner's spirit take over the classroom—that would show up the prof. Such language allows professors to appear more important, more in command, than mere texts and the fragile, driven people who compose them.

Michael Ventura is a writer and social critic. During the 1980s he wrote a column for the *L.A. Weekly,* an independent, non-mainstream newspaper published in Los Angeles, where this essay appeared in 1990. Ventura is the author of the novel *Night Time Losing Time* (1989), and his essays have been collected in *Shadow Dancing in the U.S.A.* (1985).

How different this is from what Rilke says: "Works of art are of an 4
infinite loneliness and with nothing so little to be reached as with criticism. Only love can grasp and hold and be just toward them." But
what does Rilke know? He didn't have anything better to do with his
life than make up texts.

If the student senses that to parrot these technical vocabularies 5
would do violence to something within, and senses this so strongly
that he or she can't or won't learn the stuff—that student fails.
Consider: what may well be a victory of the student's heart over a
chilly system is framed instead as a lack, and the student is lessened in
the eyes of the world. All of which works nicely to weed out the spirited: not only won't they get the credentials that carry such weight in
our society, but they'll be looked down on and their confidence will
have been shaken, so it's less likely they'll be a threat. As for those who
stay in the university system, spirited or not, their jargons make them
separate. They can talk only to each other. They can't go most places
and discuss their knowledge and be understood. There grows a wall
of language between these "educated" people and the rest of society.
They've been ghettoized, trapped by the very terms in which they've
been trained to think. It's a good way to keep knowledgeable people
from causing trouble.

Crueler yet, most of these students are diving deep into debt for 6
the privilege of having their minds crippled. They're going to have to
behave, and behave very well, as soon as they get out of college, to
handle this debt. Then they *really* won't be a threat. They've been had,
coming and going. And did I say their minds are crippled? Does "crippled" seem too strong a word? Make no mistake: hobble someone's
language and they'll never be what they might have been. At least, not
without putting in hard time to undo the damage—an effort most
don't attempt, because most don't know they've been hurt. Not consciously, anyway. They *think* they've been educated. It says so on the
diploma. The diminishment they feel, the sense of being littler inside
than they once were—what could *that* possibly have to do with their
education? It must be their own fault. Or their parents'. Or God's. And,
thinking like this, they feel yet *more* diminished, more ineffectual.

That's some racket. Whether it was intended or whether, as they 7
say in the South, it "jes grew," it's vicious: teach a bunch of innocents
just enough to run your technological society, but teach them in such
a way that they'll feel lousy about themselves and cut off from the rest
of their people. And yes, there are *some* inspiring teachers, *some* inspired students; there are always a few tough and canny enough to
break the bounds. But once we spoke a united language up and down
the culture, and now we don't; fragmentation has been instituted in
our mouths, it is a social disaster, and it happened in the very places

that are supposed to protect against such things. (Interesting that this insidious usage didn't exist or hadn't dug in during the student wildness of the '60s. Universities have become more passive the deeper such vocabularies have taken hold.)

And what about the professors? They must really believe they're 8 instructing, not enslaving. Yet, whatever the field, most can't see beyond the medium of the jargons that pay their rent. You can only think as flexibly as your language. So they, too, are trapped inside the matrix of their words, a style learned when they were as impressionable as their students. Their very vocabulary walls them off from the freshness they need.

These are the brutal prices paid for giving up the common tongue, 9 for concocting specialized speech that people must pay to learn. Understand it's not that the American language won't carry the weight of our time. It's still Shakespeare's child. Or grandchild. True, it speaks in mostly one- and two-syllable words, but so did he. ("To be or not to be, that is the question.") The enormous vocabulary our American language has picked up from all over the world—and its flair for turning verbs and adjectives into nouns, and nouns, adjectives and even names into verbs—make it a language where, as Robert Bly says, "hairy words sit down next to shiny words, scholarly words next to groovy words," with an agility that can handle just about anything. (Bly adds, defending big words too, "Language is the greatest gift of our ancestors, and we need to keep words like 'transfiguration' as well as 'bread' and 'yeast.' ") So these new synthesized jargons on sale at your nearby campus don't exist because they're needed *as language;* rather, they exist because it profits people to control and sell syntax that befuddles and discourages anyone outside the managing class.

But some don't befuddle easy: 10

> I have the wall against my back . . .
> I can't run nor fly nor hide so I ATTACK!

That's Earl the Poet, in a rap video on MTV. The great thing is that 11 language doesn't need the campuses of the middle class to keep it alive, nor can it be destroyed by their evasions. The liveliest American speech is rising back up from the street, as always. Writing about rap in 1984, I said, "While the media and the government have written off [urban blacks] as functional illiterates, they themselves have developed rapping . . . an incredible, instinctual fight to preserve the integrity of [their] language," and hence the vitality of their minds. Rap had been the major medium in black neighborhoods for a while by then, but in 1984 you still couldn't see it on TV, hear it on the radio or buy it at chain record stores. All that's changed. Rap is everywhere now, and the reason was summed up well by a member of the group N.W.A: "You can turn on some rap music and hear everything that's goin' on."

We hunger for vivid language with an almost physical need to "hear everything that's goin' on," to speak and be spoken to with words that beat like hearts. Our need can be messed with, but the words it draws forth can't be crushed. In an age when a new management class with vast resources is trying to impose a stupefying lingo so we can't question its management—a young man like Vernon Reid, of the group Living Colour, breaks through and describes how the 20th century *feels* with more accuracy than any poet, sociologist, scientist, critic or novelist. And he does it in seven words that anyone can understand, and millions hear: "Everything is possible, but nothing is real."

That's 1990. While the sense that everything is possible sparks energy, the feeling that nothing is real weakens and sabotages that energy. Stating both in one line of forceful music gives strength to what might be possible and helps break through the unreality. When the song is over we're in a different place.

No one can overestimate how valuable it is that someone said this to and for everyone. People hear it and a hardness in them unknots. "Ah, that's right, that's how these crazy days make *me* feel. What will I do with that feeling, now that these words help me touch it?" the psyche wonders deep below the level of thought. And some change starts to happen, way down, juiced by the clarity of the line. A rebellion rises, questions our confusion, begins to pierce it: the knowledge that some things *are* real and it's our job to search them out, name them all over again if we have to, share the names, make the stand. That's what vivid language makes possible. You can't do the work until you do the words.

QUESTIONS

1. Ventura does not offer many examples of either the specialized academic jargon he objects to or the vivid language of the street or rap music he prefers. What other examples in either category can you provide?

2. Although education is more commonly thought to be a broadening experience, Ventura says that students are paying instead "for the privilege of having their minds crippled" (paragraph 6). Have you ever felt "diminished" rather than enriched by your educational experiences?

3. Why does Ventura feel that the language of academia is "corrupt"? What purposes does Ventura suggest or imply are being served by the educational system?

The Girl Who Wouldn't Sing

KIT YUEN QUAN

It was really hard deciding how to talk about language because I 1 had to go through my blocks with language. I stumble upon these blocks whenever I have to write, speak in public or voice my opinions in a group of native English speakers with academic backgrounds. All of a sudden as I scramble for words, I freeze and am unable to think clearly. Minutes pass as I struggle to retrieve my thoughts until I finally manage to say something. But it never comes close to expressing what I mean. I think it's because I'm afraid to show who I really am. I cannot bear the thought of the humiliation and ridicule. And I dread having to use a language that has often betrayed my meaning. Saying what I need to say using my own words usually threatens the status quo.

People assume that I don't have a language problem because I can 2 speak English, even when I ask them to take into account that English is my second language. This is the usual reaction I have gotten while working in the feminist movement. It's true that my language problems are different from those of a recent immigrant who cannot work outside of Chinatown because she or he doesn't speak enough English. Unlike my parents, I don't speak with a heavy accent. After twenty years of living in this country, watching American television and going through its school system, I have acquired adequate English skills to function fairly well. I can pass as long as I don't have to write anything or say what I really think around those whom I see as being more educated and articulate than I am. I can spend the rest of my life avoiding jobs that require extensive reading and writing skills. I can join the segment of the population that reads only out of necessity rather than for information, appreciation or enlightenment.

It's difficult for people to accept that I believe I have a literacy 3 problem because they do not understand the nature of my blocks with language. Learning anything new terrifies me, especially if it involves words or writing. I get this overwhelming fear, this heart-stopping panic that I won't understand it. I won't know how to do it. My body tenses up and I forget to breathe if there is a word in a sentence that I don't know or several sentences in a paragraph containing unfamiliar

---

Kit Yuen Quan was born in Hong Kong and is currently on the staff of a publishing house in San Francisco, where she also works on literacy issues. Her essay was originally published in the anthology *Making Face, Making Soul/Haciendo Caras: Creative and Critical Perspectives by Women of Color* (1990), edited by Gloria Anzaldua.

118

words. My confidence dwindles and I start to feel the ground falling from under me. In my frustration I feel like crying, running out or smashing something, but that would give me away, expose my defect. So I tune out or nod my head as if there is nothing wrong. I've had to cover it up in order to survive, get jobs, pass classes and at times to work and live with people who do not care to understand my reality.

Living with this fear leaves me exhausted. I feel backed against a   4
wall of self-doubt, pushed into a corner, defeated, unable to stretch or take advantage of opportunities. Beyond just being able to read and write well enough to get by, I need to be able to learn, understand, communicate, to articulate my thoughts and feelings, and participate fully without feeling ashamed of who I am and where I come from.

When I first arrived in San Francisco from Hong Kong at age   5
seven and a half, the only English I knew was the alphabet and a few simple words: cat, dog, table, chair. I sat in classrooms for two to three years without understanding what was being said, and cried while the girl next to me filled in my spelling book for me. In music class when other kids volunteered to go up in front of the class to play musical instruments, I'd never raise my hand. I wouldn't sing. The teacher probably wondered why there were always three Chinese girls in one row who wouldn't sing. In art class, I was so traumatized that I couldn't be creative. While other kids moved about freely in school, seeming to flow from one activity to the next, I was disoriented, out of step, feeling hopelessly behind. I went into a "survivor mode" and couldn't participate in activities.

I remember one incident in particular in the fourth grade during   6
a kickball game. I had just missed the ball when Kevin, the class jock, came running across the yard and kicked me in the butt. Had I been able to speak English, I might have screamed my head off or called for the teacher, but I just stood there trying to numb out the pain, feeling everyone's eyes on me. I wasn't sure it wasn't all part of the game.

At home I spoke the sam yup dialect of Cantonese with my par-   7
ents, who were completely unaware of the severity of my problems at school. In their eyes I was very lucky to be going to school in America. My father had had only a high school education before he had to start working. And we children would not have had any chance to go to college had we stayed in Hong Kong. We had flown over the Pacific Ocean three times between the time I was seven and a half and eight and a half because they were so torn about leaving their home to resettle in a foreign country and culture. At the dinner table after a day of toiling at their jobs and struggling with English, they aired their frustrations about the racism and discrimination they were feeling everywhere: at their jobs, on the bus, at the supermarket. Although they didn't feel very hopeful about their own lives, they

were comforted by the fact that my brother and I were getting a good education. Both my parents had made incredible sacrifices for my education. Life would be easier for us, with more opportunities and options, because we would know the language. We would be able to talk back or fight back if need be. All we had to do was study hard and apply ourselves. So every day after school I would load my bag full of textbooks and walk up two hills to where we lived the first few years after we landed here. I remember opening each book and reading out loud a paragraph or two, skipping over words I didn't know until I gave up in frustration.

My parents thought that by mastering the English language, I   8 would be able to attain the Chinese American dream: a college education, a good-paying job, a house in the suburbs, a Chinese husband and children. They felt intimidated and powerless in American society and so clung tightly to me to fulfill their hopes and dreams. When I objected to these expectations using my limited Chinese, I received endless lectures. I felt smothered by their traditional values of how a Chinese girl should behave and this was reason enough not to learn more Chinese. Gradually language came to represent our two or more opposing sets of values. If I asserted my individuality, wanted to go out with my friends, had opinions of my own, or disagreed with their plans for me, I was accused of becoming too smart for my own good now that I had grown wings. "*Cheun neuih,* stupid girl. Don't think you're better than your parents just because you know more English. You don't know anything! We've eaten more salt than you've eaten rice." Everything I heard in Chinese was a dictate. It was always one more thing I wasn't supposed to do or be, one more way I wasn't supposed to think. At school I felt stupid for not knowing the language. At home I was under attack for my rebellious views. The situation became intolerable after I came out to my parents as a lesbian.

When I ran away from home at sixteen, I sought refuge in the   9 women's community working part-time at a feminist bookstore. I felt like I had no family, no home, no identity or culture I could claim. In between hiding from my parents and crashing at various women's houses, I hung out in the Mission playing pool with other young dykes, got high, or took to the streets when I felt like I was going to explode. Sometimes at night I found myself sitting at the counter of some greasy spoon Chinese restaurant longing for a home-cooked meal. I was lonely for someone to talk to who could understand how I felt, but I didn't even have the words to communicate what I felt.

At the bookstore, I was discovering a whole other world: women,   10 dykes, feminists, authors, political activists, artists—people who read and talked about what they were reading. As exciting as it all was, I didn't understand what people were talking about. What was political theory? What was literary criticism? Words flew over my head like planes over a runway. In order to communicate with other feminists, most of whom were white or middle class or both, educated, and at least ten years older than me, I had to learn feminist rhetoric.

Given my uprooted and transplanted state, I have a difficult time 11 explaining to other people how I feel about language. Usually they don't understand or will even dispute what I'm saying. A lot of times I'll think it's because I don't have the right words, I haven't read enough books, or I don't know the language. That's how I felt all the time while working at a feminist bookstore. It wasn't only white, educated people who didn't understand how I felt. Women of color or Third World women who had class privilege and came from literary backgrounds thought the problem was more my age and my lack of political development. I often felt beaten down by these kinds of attitudes while still thinking that my not being understood was the result of my inability to communicate rather than an unreceptive environment.

Even though feminist rhetoric does give me words to describe 12 how I'm being oppressed, it still reflects the same racist, classist standards of the dominant society and of colleges and universities. I get frustrated because I constantly feel I'm being put down for what I'm saying or how I talk. For example, in a collective meeting with other women, I spoke about how I felt as a working class person and why I felt different from them. I told them they felt "middle class" to me because of the way they behaved and because of the values they had, that their "political vision" didn't include people with my experience and concerns. I tried to say all of this using feminist rhetoric, but when I used the term "working class," someone would argue. "You can't use that term. . . ." Because they were educated they thought they owned the language and so could say, "You can't use 'middle class,' you can't use 'working class,' because nowadays everybody is working class and it's just a matter of whether you're poor or comfortable." They did not listen to the point I was trying to make. They didn't care that I was sitting there in the circle stumbling along, struggling to explain how I felt oppressed by them and the structure and policies of the organization. Instead of listening to why I felt that way, they invalidated me for the way I used language and excluded me by defending themselves and their positions and claiming that my issues and feelings were "personal" and that I should just get over them.

Another example of my feeling excluded is when people in a room 13 make all sorts of literary allusions. They make me feel like I should have read those books. They throw around metaphors that leave me feeling lost and confused. I don't get to throw in my metaphors. Instead of acknowledging our different backgrounds and trying to include me in the discussion, they choose to ignore my feelings of isolation. I find that among feminists, white and colored, especially those who pride themselves on being progressive political activists with credentials, there's an assumption that if a person just read more, studied more, she would find the right words, the right way to use them, and even the right thoughts. A lot of times my language and the language of other working class, non-academic people become the target of scrutiny and criticism when others don't want to hear what we have to say. They convince themselves we're using the wrong words: "What definition are you using?" "What do you mean by that?" And then we get into debate about what was meant, we get lost in semantics and then we really don't know what we're saying.

Why should I try to use all of these different words when I'm being manipulated and suppressed by those whose rhetoric is more developed, whether it's feminist, academic, or leftist? 14

Those of us who feel invisible or misunderstood when we try to name what is oppressing us within supposedly feminist or progressive groups need to realize that our language is legitimate and valid. It comes from our families, our cultures, our class backgrounds, our experiences of different and conflicting realities. And we don't need to read another book to justify it. If I want to say *I'm working class,* I should be able to *say* I'm working class without having to read or quote Marx. But just saying that I'm working class never gives me enough of the understanding that I want. Because our experiences and feelings are far too complex to be capsulized in abstractions like "oppression," "sexism," "racism," etc., there is no right combination of these terms which can express why we feel oppressed. 15

I knew that I needed to go some place where some of my experiences with language would be mirrored. Through the Refugee Women's Program in the Tenderloin district of San Francisco, I started to tutor two Cambodian refugee girls. The Buth family had been in the U.S. for one and a half years. They lived, twelve people to a room, in an apartment building on Eddy Street half a block from the porno theaters. I went to their home one evening a week and on Sundays took the girls to the children's library. The doorbells in the building were out of order, so visitors had to wait to be let in by someone on their way out. Often I stood on their doorsteps watching the street life. The fragrant smell of jasmine rice wafting from the windows of the apartment building mixed with the smell of booze and piss on the street. Newspapers, candy wrappers and all kinds of garbage swept up by the wind colored the sidewalks. Cars honked and sped past while Asian, Black and white kids played up and down the street. Mothers carrying their babies weaved through loose gatherings of drunk men and prostitutes near the corner store. Around me I heard a medley of languages: Vietnamese, Chinese, Cambodian, English, Black English, Laotian. 16

Sometimes, I arrived to find Yan and Eng sitting on the steps be- 17
hind the security gate waiting to let me in. Some days they wore their
school clothes, while on other days they were barefooted and wore
their traditional sarongs. As we climbed the stairs up to their apartment, we inhaled fish sauce and curry and rice. Six-year-old Eng
would chatter and giggle but Yan was quieter and more reserved.
Although she was only eight years old, I couldn't help but feel like
I was in the company of a serious adult. I immediately identified
with her. I noticed how, whenever I gave them something to do, they
didn't want to do it on their own. For example, they often got excited
when I brought them books, but they wouldn't want to read by themselves. They became quiet and withdrawn when I asked them questions. Their answer was always a timid "I don't know," and they
never asked a question or made a request. So I read with them. We did
everything together. I didn't want them to feel like they were supposed to automatically know what to do, because I remembered how
badly that used to make me feel.

Play time was the best part of our time together. All the little kids 18
joined in and sometimes even their older brothers. Everybody was so
excited that they forgot they were learning English. As we played jig-
saw sentences and word concentration and chickens and whales, I became a little kid again, except this time I wasn't alone and unhappy.
When they made Mother's Day cards, I made a Mother's Day card.
When they drew pictures of our field trip to the beach, I sketched pictures of us at the beach. When we made origami frogs and jumped
them all over the floor, I went home and made dinosaurs, kangaroos,
spiders, crabs and lobsters. Week after week, I added to my repertoire
until I could feel that little kid who used to sit like the piece of un-
molded clay in front of her in art class turn into a wide-eyed origami
enthusiast.

As we studied and played in the middle of the room surrounded 19
by the rest of the family who were sleeping, nursing, doing homework, playing cards, talking, laughing or crying, Yan would frequently interrupt our lesson to answer her mother. Sometimes it was
a long conversation, but I didn't mind because English was their second language. They spoke only Cambodian with their family. If they
laughed at something on television, it was usually at the picture and
not at the dialogue. English was used for schoolwork and to talk to me.
They did not try to express their thoughts and feelings in English.
When they spoke to each other, they were not alone or isolated.
Whether they were living in a refugee camp in the Philippines or in
Thailand or in a one-room apartment on Eddy Street, they were connected to each other through their language and their culture. They
had survived war, losing family members, their country and their

home, but in speaking their language, they were able to love and comfort each other. Sitting there on the bamboo mat next to the little girls, Eng and her younger sister Oeun, listening to their sweet little voices talking and singing, I understood for the first time what it was like to be a child with a voice and it made me remember my first love, the Chinese language.

While searching for an address, I came across a postcard of the San   20 Francisco-Oakland Bay Bridge. I immediately recognized it as the postcard I had sent to my schoolmate in Hong Kong when I first got here. On the back was my eight-and-a-half-year-old handwriting.

In English it says: 21

> Dear Kam Yee, I received your letter. You asked if I've been to school yet. Yes, I've already found a school. My family has decided to stay in America. My living surroundings are very nice. Please don't worry about me. I'm sorry it has taken so long for me to return your letter. Okay lets talk some more next time. Please give my regards to your parents and your family. I wish you happiness. Signed: Your classmate, Yuen Kit, August 30th.

The card, stamped "Return to Sender," is postmarked 1970.   22 Although I have sketchy memories of my early school days in Hong Kong, I still remember the day when Kam Yee and I found each other. The bell rang signaling the end of class. Sitting up straight in our chairs, we had recited "Goodbye, teacher" in a chorus. While the others were rushing out the door to their next class, I rose from my desk and slowly put away my books. Over my left shoulder I saw Kam Yee watching me. We smiled at each other as I walked over to her desk. I had finally made a friend. Soon after that my family left Hong Kong and I wrote my last Chinese letter.

All the time that I was feeling stupid and overwhelmed by lan-   23 guage, could I have been having the Chinese blues? By the time I was seven, I was reading the Chinese newspaper. I remember because there were a lot of reports of raped and mutilated women's bodies found in plastic bags on the side of quiet roads. It was a thrill when my father would send me to the newsstand on the corner to get his newspaper. Passing street vendors peddling sweets and fruit, I would run as quickly as I could. From a block away I could smell the stinky odor of *dauh fuh fa*, my favorite snack of slippery, warm, soft tofu in sweet syrup.

Up until a year ago, I could only recognize some of the Chinese   24 characters on store signs, restaurant menus and Chinese newspapers on Stockton and Powell Streets, but I always felt a tingle of excitement whenever I recognized a word or knew its sound, like oil sizzling in a wok just waiting for something to fry.

On Saturdays I sit with my Chinese language teacher on one of the   25
stone benches lining the overpass where the financial district meets
Chinatown and links Portsmouth Square to the Holiday Inn Hotel. We
have been meeting once a week for me to practice speaking, reading
and writing Chinese using whatever material we can find. Sometimes
I read a bilingual Chinese American weekly newspaper called the *East
West Journal,* other times Chinese folk tales for young readers from the
Chinatown Children's Library, or bilingual brochures describing free
services offered by non-profit Chinatown community agencies, and
sometimes even Chinese translations of Pacific Bell Telephone inserts.
I look forward to these sessions where I reach inward to recover all
those lost sounds that once were the roots of my childhood imagination. This exercise in trying to use my eight-year-old vocabulary to
verbalize my thoughts as an adult is as scary as it is exhilarating. At
one time Chinese was poetry to me. Words, their sounds and their
rhythms, conjured up images that pulled me in and gave me a physical sense of their meanings. The Chinese characters that I wrote and
practiced were pictographs of water, grass, birds, fire, heart and
mouth. With my calligraphy brush made of pig's hair, I made the rain
fall and the wind blow.

Now, speaking Chinese with my father is the closest I have felt to   26
coming home. In a thin but sage-like voice, he reflects on a life-time of
hard work and broken dreams and we slowly reconnect as father and
daughter. As we sit across the kitchen table from one another, his old
and tattered Chinese dictionary by his side, he tells me of the loving
relationship he had with his mother, who encouraged him in his interest in writing and the movies. Although our immigrant experiences
are generations apart and have been impacted differently by
American culture, in his words I see the core of who I am. I cannot express my feelings fully in either Chinese or English or make him understand my choices. Though I am still grappling with accepting the
enormous love behind the sacrifices he has made to give me a better
life, I realize that with my ability to move in two different worlds I am
the fruit of his labor.

For 85 cents, I can have unlimited refills of tea and a *gai mei baau*   27
at The Sweet Fragrance Cafe on Broadway across from the World
Theatre. After the first bite, the coconut sugar and butter ooze down
my palm. Behind the pastry counter, my favorite clerk is consolidating
trays of walnut cupcakes. Pointing to some round fried bread covered
with sesame seeds, she urges the customer with "Four for a dollar,
very fresh!"

Whole families from grandparents to babies sleeping soundly   28
on mothers' backs some here for porridge, pastries and coffee. Mothers
stroll in to get sweets for little ones waiting at home. Old women

carrying their own mugs from home come in to chat with their buddies. Workers wearing aprons smeared with pig's blood or fresh fish scales drop in for a bite during their break. Chinese husbands sit for hours complaining and gossiping not unlike the old women in the park.

A waitress brings bowls of beef stew noodles and pork liver porridge. Smokers snub out their cigarettes as they pick up their chopsticks. The man across from me is counting sons and daughters on the fingers of his left hand: one son, another son, my wife, one daughter. He must have family in China waiting to immigrate. 29

The regulars congregate at the back tables, shouting opinions from one end of the long table to the other. The Chinese are notorious for their loud conversations at close range that can easily be mistaken for arguments and fights until someone breaks into laughter or gives his companion a friendly punch. Here the drama of life is always unfolding in all different dialects. I may not understand a lot of it, but the chuckling, the hand gestures, the raising of voices in protest and in accusation, and the laughter all flow like music, like a Cantonese opera. 30

Twenty years seems like a long time, but it has taken all twenty years for me to understand my language blocks and to find ways to help myself learn. I have had to create my own literacy program. I had to recognize that the school system failed to meet my needs as an immigrant and that this society and its institutions doesn't reflect or validate my experiences. I have to let myself grieve over the loss of my native language and all the years wasted in classrooms staring into space or dozing off when I was feeling depressed and hopeless. My various activities now help to remind me that my relationship with language is more complex than just speaking enough English to get by. In creative activity and in anything that requires words, I'm still eight years old. Sometimes I open a book and I still feel I can't read. It may take days or weeks for me to work up the nerve to open that book again. But I do open it and it gets a little easier each time that I work through the fear. As long as there are bakeries in Chinatown and as long as I have 85 cents, I know I have a way back to myself. 31

QUESTIONS

1.   Because "the school system failed to meet my needs as an immigrant," Quan says, "I have had to create my own literacy program" (paragraph 31). What does this program consist of for her? How successful was each component for her, in your opinion?

2.   What effect did it have on you when Quan revealed, at the end of paragraph 8, her lesbian sexual orientation? How important do you think her sexual orientation is in her struggles to overcome language blocks?

3.   Discuss Quan's encounter with the language of feminists and college-educated people. What are her specific complaints about this "unreceptive environment"? What does Quan seem to feel is missing from political and academic rhetoric?

The Loudest Voice

GRACE PALEY

There is a certain place where dumb-waiters boom, doors slam, 1
dishes crash; every window is a mother's mouth bidding the street
shut up, go skate somewhere else, come home. My voice is the loudest.

There, my own mother is still as full of breathing as me and the 2
grocer stands up to speak to her. "Mrs. Abramowitz," he says, "people
should not be afraid of their children."

"Ah, Mr. Bialik," my mother replies, "if you say to her or her father 3
'Ssh,' they say, 'In the grave it will be quiet.' "

"From Coney Island to the cemetery," says my papa. "It's the same 4
subway; it's the same fare."

I am right next to the pickle barrel. My pinky is making tiny whirl- 5
pools in the brine. I stop a moment to announce: "Campbell's Tomato
Soup. Campbell's Vegetable Beef Soup. Campbell's S-c-otch Broth . . ."

"Be quiet," the grocer says, "the labels are coming off." 6

"Please, Shirley, be a little quiet," my mother begs me. 7

In that place the whole street groans: Be quiet! Be quiet! but steals 8
from the happy chorus of my inside self not a tittle or a jot.

There, too, but just around the corner, is a red brick building that 9
has been old for many years. Every morning the children stand before
it in double lines which must be straight. They are not insulted. They
are waiting anyway.

I am usually among them. I am, in fact, the first, since I begin 10
with "A."

One cold morning the monitor tapped me on the shoulder. "Go to 11
Room 409, Shirley Abramowitz," he said. I did as I was told. I went in
a hurry up a down staircase to Room 409, which contained sixth-
graders. I had to wait at the desk without wiggling until Mr. Hilton,
their teacher, had time to speak.

After five minutes he said, "Shirley?" 12

"What?" I whispered. 13

Grace Paley's short stories have been collected in *The Little
Disturbances of Man: Stories of Women and Men at Love* (1959)—from
which this selection comes—*Enormous Changes at the Last Minute*
(1974), and *Later the Same Day* (1985); her poems are collected in
Leaning Forward (1985) and *Long Walks and Intimate Talks* (1991). She
grew up in the Bronx, has taught writing at colleges and workshops,
and has been a political activist for peace issues. Her stories are often
set in New York and portray diverse groups of people and their particular ways of talking.

He said, "My! My! Shirley Abramowitz! They told me you had a   14
particularly loud, clear voice and read with lots of expression. Could
that be true?"

"Oh yes," I whispered.   15

"In that case, don't be silly; I might very well be your teacher   16
someday. Speak up; speak up."

"Yes," I shouted.   17

"More like it," he said. "Now, Shirley, can you put a ribbon in   18
your hair or a bobby pin? It's too messy."

"Yes!" I bawled.   19

"Now, now, calm down." He turned to the class. "Children, not a   20
sound. Open at page 39. Read till 52. When you finish, start again." He
looked me over once more. "Now, Shirley, you know, I suppose, that
Christmas is coming. We are preparing a beautiful play. Most of the
parts have been given out. But I still need a child with a strong voice,
lots of stamina. Do you know what stamina is? You do? Smart kid. You
know, I heard you read 'The Lord is my shepherd' in Assembly yesterday. I was very impressed. Wonderful delivery. Mrs. Jordan, your
teacher, speaks highly of you. Now listen to me, Shirley Abramowitz,
if you want to take the part and be in the play, repeat after me, 'I swear
to work harder than I ever did before.' "

I looked to heaven and said at once, "Oh, I swear." I kissed my   21
pinky and looked at God.

"That is an actor's life, my dear," he explained. "Like a soldier's,   22
never tardy or disobedient to his general, the director. Everything," he
said, "absolutely everything will depend on you."

That afternoon, all over the building, children scraped and   23
scrubbed the turkeys and the sheaves of corn off the schoolroom windows. Goodbye Thanksgiving. The next morning a monitor brought
red paper and green paper from the office. We made new shapes and
hung them on the walls and glued them to the doors.

The teachers became happier and happier. Their heads were ring-   24
ing like the bells of childhood. My best friend Evie was prone to evil,
but she did not get a single demerit for whispering. We learned "Holy
Night" without an error. "How wonderful!" said Miss Glacé, the student teacher. "To think that some of you don't even speak the language!" We learned "Deck the Halls" and "Hark! The Herald
Angels". . . . They weren't ashamed and we weren't embarrassed.

Oh, but when my mother heard about it all, she said to my father: 25
"Misha, you don't know what's going on there. Cramer is the head of
the Tickets Committee."

"Who?" asked my father. "Cramer? Oh yes, an active woman."   26

"Active? Active has to have a reason. Listen," she said sadly, "I'm   27
surprised to see my neighbors making tra-la-la for Christmas."

My father couldn't think of what to say to that. Then he decided: 28 "You're in America! Clara, you wanted to come here. In Palestine the Arabs would be eating you alive. Europe you had pogroms. Argentina is full of Indians. Here you got Christmas. . . . Some joke, ha?"

"Very funny, Misha. What is becoming of you? If we came to a 29 new country a long time ago to run away from tyrants, and instead we fall into a creeping pogrom, that our children learn a lot of lies, so what's the joke? Ach, Misha, your idealism is going away."

"So is your sense of humor." 30

"That I never had, but idealism you had a lot of." 31

"I'm the same Misha Abramovitch, I didn't change an iota. Ask 32 anyone."

"Only ask me," says my mama, may she rest in peace. "I got the 33 answer."

Meanwhile the neighbors had to think of what to say too. 34

Marty's father said: "You know, he has a very important part, my 35 boy."

"Mine also," said Mr. Sauerfeld. 36

"Not my boy!" said Mrs. Klieg. "I said to him no. The answer is no. 37 When I say no! I mean no!"

The rabbi's wife said, "It's disgusting!" But no one listened to her. 38 Under the narrow sky of God's great wisdom she wore a strawberry-blond wig.

Every day was noisy and full of experience. I was Right-hand 39 Man. Mr. Hilton said: "How could I get along without you, Shirley?"

He said: "Your mother and father ought to get down on their 40 knees every night and thank God for giving them a child like you."

He also said: "You're absolutely a pleasure to work with, my dear, 41 dear child."

Sometimes he said: "For God's sakes, what did I do with the 42 script? Shirley! Shirley! Find it."

Then I answered quietly: "Here it is, Mr. Hilton." 43

Once in a while, when he was very tired, he would cry out: 44 "Shirley, I'm just tired of screaming at those kids. Will you tell Ira Pushkov not to come in till Lester points to that star the second time?"

Then I roared: "Ira Pushkov, what's the matter with you? Dope! 45 Mr. Hilton told you five times already, don't come in till Lester points to that star the second time."

"Ach, Clara," my father asked, "what does she do there till six 46 o'clock she can't even put the plates on the table?"

"Christmas," said my mother coldly. 47

"Ho! Ho!" my father said. "Christmas. What's the harm? After all, 48 history teaches everyone. We learn from reading this is a holiday from pagan times also, candles, lights, even Chanukah. So we learn it's not altogether Christian. So if they think it's a private holiday, they're only ignorant, not patriotic. What belongs to history, belongs to all men. You want to go back to the Middle Ages? Is it better to shave your head with a secondhand razor? Does it hurt Shirley to learn to speak up? It does not. So maybe someday she won't live between the kitchen and the shop. She's not a fool."

I thank you, Papa, for your kindness. It is true about me to this 49 day. I am foolish but I am not a fool.

That night my father kissed me and said with great interest in my 50 career, "Shirley, tomorrow's your big day. Congrats."

"Save it," my mother said. Then she shut all the windows in order 51 to prevent tonsillitis.

In the morning it snowed. On the street corner a tree had been dec- 52 orated for us by a kind city administration. In order to miss its chilly shadow our neighbors walked three blocks east to buy a loaf of bread. The butcher pulled down black window shades to keep the colored lights from shining on his chickens. Oh, not me. On the way to school, with both my hands I tossed it a kiss of tolerance. Poor thing, it was a stranger in Egypt.

I walked straight into the auditorium past the staring children. 53 "Go ahead, Shirley!" said the monitors. Four boys, big for their age, had already started work as propmen and stagehands.

Mr. Hilton was very nervous. He was not even happy. Whatever 54 he started to say ended in a sideward look of sadness. He sat slumped in the middle of the first row and asked me to help Miss Glacé. I did this, although she thought my voice too resonant and said, "Show-off!"

Parents began to arrive long before we were ready. They wanted 55 to make a good impression. From among the yards of drapes I peeked out at the audience. I saw my embarrassed mother.

Ira, Lester, and Meyer were pasted to their beards by Miss Glacé. 56 She almost forgot to thread the star on its wire, but I reminded her. I coughed a few times to clear my throat. Miss Glacé looked around and saw that everyone was in costume and on line waiting to play his part. She whispered, "All right . . ." Then:

Jackie Sauerfeld, the prettiest boy in first grade, parted the curtains 57 with his skinny elbow and in a high voice sang out:

> Parents dear
> We are here
> To make a Christmas play in time.
> It we give
> In narrative
> And illustrate with pantomine.

He disappeared. 58

My voice burst immediately from the wings to the great shock of   59
Ira, Lester, and Meyer, who were waiting for it but were surprised all
the same.

"I remember, I remember, the house where I was born . . ."   60

Miss Glacé yanked the curtain open and there it was, the house—   61
an old hayloft, where Celia Kornbluh lay in the straw with Cindy Lou,
her favorite doll. Ira, Lester, and Meyer moved slowly from the wings
toward her, sometimes pointing to a moving star and sometimes
ahead to Cindy Lou.

It was a long story and it was a sad story. I carefully pronounced   62
all the words about my lonesome childhood, while little Eddie
Braunstein wandered upstage and down with his shepherd's stick,
looking for sheep. I brought up lonesomeness again, and not being understood at all except by some women everybody hated. Eddie was
too small for that and Marty Groff took his place, wearing his father's
prayer shawl. I announced twelve friends, and half the boys in the
fourth grade gathered round Marty, who stood on an orange crate
while my voice harangued. Sorrowful and loud, I declaimed about
love and God and Man, but because of the terrible deceit of Abie Stock
we came suddenly to a famous moment. Marty, whose remembering
tongue I was, waited at the foot of the cross. He stared desperately at
the audience. I groaned, "My God, my God, why hast thou forsaken
me?" The soldiers who were sheiks grabbed poor Marty to pin him up
to die, but he wrenched free, turned again to the audience, and spread
his arms aloft to show despair and the end. I murmured at the top of
my voice, "The rest is silence, but as everyone in this room, in this
city—in this world—now knows, I shall have life eternal."

That night Mrs. Kornbluh visited our kitchen for a glass of tea.   63

"How's the virgin?" asked my father with a look of concern.   64

"For a man with a daughter, you got a fresh mouth,   65
Abramovitch."

"Here," said my father kindly, "have some lemon, it'll sweeten   66
your disposition."

They debated a little in Yiddish, then fell in a puddle of Russian   67
and Polish. What I understood next was my father, who said, "Still
and all, it was certainly a beautiful affair, you have to admit, introducing us to the beliefs of a different culture."

"Well, yes," said Mrs. Kornbluh. "The only thing . . . you know   68
Charlie Turner—that cute boy in Celia's class—a couple others? They
got very small parts or no part at all. In very bad taste, it seemed to me.
After all, it's their religion."

"Ach," explained my mother, "what could Mr. Hilton do? They   69
got very small voices; after all, why should they holler? The English

language they know from the beginning by heart. They're blond like angels. You think it's so important they should get in the play? Christmas . . . the whole piece of goods . . . they own it."

I listened and listened until I couldn't listen any more. Too sleepy, 70 I climbed out of bed and kneeled. I made a little church of my hands and said, "Hear, O Israel . . ." Then I called out in Yiddish, "Please, good night, good night. Ssh." My father said, "Ssh yourself," and slammed the kitchen door.

I was happy. I fell asleep at once. I had prayed for everybody: my 71 talking family, cousins far away, passersby, and all the lonesome Christians. I expected to be heard. My voice was certainly the loudest.

QUESTIONS

1. What part of the Christmas story does Shirley play? In what ways do you think her part in the play reflects her part in the larger story, "The Loudest Voice"?

2. Contrast the ways that Shirley's mother and father react to the Christmas play. What seems to be Shirley's own attitude towards the play?

3. Discuss experiences you or classmates have had participating in an unfamiliar religious or cultural observance, and compare your feelings with those of characters in Paley's story.

THINKING ABOUT LANGUAGE
AND SOCIAL POWER

1.   How do you suppose Cliff would explain what Simon calls "linguistic failings"? How would you apply Williams's definition of "dialect" to Simon's advice about learning "good English"?

2.   Based on the views she expresses about Black English, standard English, and academic language, how do you think Mellix might respond to the "three qualities of Black English—the presence of life, voice, and clarity" discussed by Jordan in paragraphs 33 to 36? How might Mellix have fit into Jordan's class as a student?

3.   Compare Mellix's and Quan's experiences with what Quan calls "my blocks with language," being "afraid to show who I really am" (paragraph 1), and the ways "language came to represent . . . two or more opposing sets of values" (paragraph 8).

4.   Make a list of the qualities you associate with academic language. Jordan, Quan, and Ventura all criticize standard English and the conventional language of the academy. How would you describe their own writing styles in each case? Which writer has the most in common, and which the least, with the qualities you listed?

5.   Based on your own experience and evidence from the essays by Mellix, Jordan, and Quan, to what extent do you agree with Ventura that "the university is where language goes to die" (paragraph 2)?

6.   Quan explains that she ran away from home at age 16. Could you imagine Shirley Abramowitz, in Paley's story, doing likewise? Why or why not? To support your response, compare or contrast Shirley's and Quan's experiences with parents and school.

7.   Language, written or spoken, helps people gain status or social power in all the selections in this chapter. Choose two or three of these selections and compare how and for whom this power is gained. You might use your comparison to evaluate the criteria suggested by Simon ("good English" versus "linguistic failings") or Williams (a dominant majority language versus a subordinate "minority language").

Exploring Additional Sources

8.   Many selections in Chapters 1, 2, and 4 address other aspects of the relationship between language and social power. Analyze one of the selections in Chapter 3 in terms of gender language bias (using

Nilsen's "Sexism in English: A 1990s Update" or August's "Real Men Don't: Anti-Male Bias in English"), stereotypes (using Tan's "The Language of Discretion" or Matsumoto's "Two Deserts"), or bicultural identity (using Rodriguez's "Public and Private Language" or Anzaldua's "How to Tame a Wild Tongue").

9.   Mellix says that her "teachers taught standard English but used black English to do it." Find out to what extent this method is used today and what linguistic researchers say about the most effective ways to combine Black English and standard English in the classroom.

10.   Research a literacy program in your community and evaluate its success. If possible, conduct interviews with administrators, volunteers, and participants and integrate their views and experiences, along with social science studies, into your paper.

11.   Study lyrics from rap or another form of music in which you're interested. To what extent do you agree with Ventura that this language "describes how the 20th century *feels* with more accuracy than any poet, sociologist, scientist, critic or novelist"? Using magazines such as *Rolling Stone,* integrate the views of music critics and the musicians themselves into your own argument about social power and rap or other music lyrics.

12.   Read two or more volumes of Paley's short stories and decide on a thematic or stylistic angle for a literary research paper, such as Paley's view of love or use of dialogue. After formulating a tentative thesis, test your ideas against those in critical essays about Paley found in the MLA Bibliography. Alternatively, if your media library has the film *Enormous Changes* (directed by Mirra Bank and Ellen Hovde, 1987), compare the film version with the three Paley stories from *Enormous Changes at the Last Minute* on which it's based.

4

LANGUAGE AND
BICULTURAL IDENTITY

English in the Next Decade

RICHARD W. BAILEY

I invite readers to reflect on three political and cultural developments that will shape the use of English in the next decade.

The first is the remarkable rise in multilingualism. (More people
than ever before, both numerically and proportionately, now routinely
use two or more languages.) As Peter Strevens has pointed out, those
who command only one language are at a distinct disadvantage, especially those monolinguals (including English-speaking monolinguals)
who seek consent and commerce from language communities richer or
more powerful than their own.[1]

A second trend will have even greater impact: far from approaching the status of a universal language, English is diminishing proportionately as explosive birthrates shift the balance of the world's
population toward other language communities. No doubt English is
the most frequently chosen *additional* language, and it is likely to
continue to enjoy that popularity. But even the major centers of the
anglophone world (Britain, Canada, the United States, and Australia)
are becoming more and more diverse in languages and language varieties. These demographic facts have implications for the future of
English and for the kinds of languages we will use in the future.

A third issue that merits our present consideration derives from
research in second-language instruction: the attitude of those acquiring a new language is the most influential of the variables that predict
the rate and success of learning—more important than aptitude, age,
or teaching method.

—FROM "ENGLISH AT ITS TWILIGHT," IN *THE STATE OF THE LANGUAGE*, 1990

---

[1]See Peter Strevens, "Language Teaching Contributes to and Is Influenced by the Spread of
Languages," in *Language Spread and Language Policy: Issues, Implications, and Case Studies,* ed. Peter H.
Lowenberg (Washington, D.C., 1988), pp. 320–330.

Bilingual Advantages

JANE MILLER

Where a child grows up speaking more than one language or dialect, and those languages or dialects have equivalent status in his own and in other people's eyes, and where the connections between those languages and their differences are made explicit, multilingualism can be an unqualified good. Mr. Orme's pupil, Andreas, is in that rare position. He still visits Cyprus. English people know about Greek, even hear it spoken on their holidays. Andreas speaks Greek for most of the time at home, but other members of his family speak English too; and he is not aware of making conscious decisions about which language to speak to whom, about what or where. He could read and write in Greek before he arrived in England, and he learned English in a school where it was assumed, rightly, that he was competent linguistically even if he didn't know English, and where they have come to rely on and to admire his success. He was lucky too to embark on the second of his languages before he was too old to do so easily and to learn it principally through using it with children of his own age. As an example of bilingual advantages he is ideal, though hardly typical.

It is a characteristic irony that while the learning of languages can be an expensive business, nearly all those people in the world who grow up bilingual do so because their mother tongue or dialect has associations with poverty which make it likely to be thought inappropriate for education and some kinds of employment.

—FROM "HOW DO YOU SPELL GUJARATI, SIR?" IN *THE STATE OF THE LANGUAGE*, 1980

Acoma and English

SIMON J. ORTIZ

In my childhood, the language we all spoke was Acoma, and it was a struggle to maintain it against the outright threats of corporal punishment, ostracism, and the invocation that it would impede our progress towards Americanization. Children in school were punished and looked upon with disdain if they did not speak and learn English quickly and smoothly, and so I learned it. It has occurred to me that I learned English simply because I was forced to, as so many other Indian children were. But I know, also, there was another reason, and this was that I loved language, the sound, meaning, and magic of language. Language opened up vistas of the world around me, and it allowed me to discover knowledge that would not be possible for me to know without the use of language. Later, when I began to experiment with and explore language in poetry and fiction, I allowed that a portion of that impetus was because I had come to know English through forceful acculturation. Nevertheless, the underlying force was the beauty and poetic power of language in its many forms that instilled in me the desire to become a user of language as a writer, singer, and storyteller. Significantly, it was the Acoma language, which I don't use enough of today, that inspired me to become a writer. The concepts, values, and philosophy contained in my original language and the struggle it has faced have determined my life and vision as a writer.

—FROM "THE LANGUAGE WE KNOW," *I TELL YOU NOW:*
AUTOBIOGRAPHICAL ESSAYS BY NATIVE AMERICAN WRITERS, 1984

My Name

SANDRA CISNEROS

In English my name means hope. In Spanish it means too many letters. It means sadness, it means waiting. It is like the number nine. A muddy color. It is the Mexican records my father plays on Sunday mornings when he is shaving, songs like sobbing.

It was my great-grandmother's name and now it is mine. She was a horse woman too, born like me in the Chinese year of the horse—which is supposed to be bad luck if you're born female—but I think this is a Chinese lie because the Chinese, like the Mexicans, don't like their women strong.

My great-grandmother. I would've liked to have known her, a wild horse of a woman, so wild she wouldn't marry until my great-grandfather threw a sack over her head and carried her off. Just like that, as if she were a fancy chandelier. That's the way he did it.

And the story goes she never forgave him. She looked out the window all her life, the way so many women sit their sadness on an elbow. I wonder if she made the best with what she got or was she sorry because she couldn't be all the things she wanted to be. Esperanza. I have inherited her name, but I don't want to inherit her place by the window.

At school they say my name funny as if the syllables were made out of tin and hurt the roof of your mouth. But in Spanish my name is made out of a softer something, like silver, not quite as thick as sister's name Magdalena which is uglier than mine. Magdalena who at least can come home and become Nenny. But I am always Esperanza.

I would like to baptize myself under a new name, a name more like the real me, the one nobody sees. Esperanza as Lisandra or Maritza or Zeze the X. Yes. Something like Zeze the X will do.

—FROM *THE HOUSE ON MANGO STREET*, 1984

Chief Wachuseh

JOSE ANTONIO BURCIAGA

I first heard the word *wachuseh* before I started school and learned 1
English. For me, the word had always been Spanish. "This is better than
wachuseh," my father would say in Spanish and I would be impressed
because he reserved the word for only the best. He never told me what
it meant, but I knew. Wachuseh was a mythical Indian chief, perhaps
an Aztec emperor, or at least the Indian chief on the red covers of
school writing tablets. I could visualize him, tall, muscular, toasted
brown with an Aztec feathered head dress, the epitome of perfection.

Eventually, I came to decode and recognize that wachuseh came 2
from the question "What did you say?" But by then the four-word
question had become so engraved in my mind that to this day, an
Indian chief comes to mind when I hear it. Wachuseh became a word
meaning something that was better than anything anyone could say.

Wachuseh has been a common and popular phrase among immi- 3
grants to this country. It's often used as a question when someone
doesn't understand English or the concept of what is being said in
English. The phrase may have originated from English speakers who
could not understand the accented speech of an immigrant. It's also
popular among many Afro-Americans and effectively expressed as
"whachusay?" when questioning or disbelieving a statement.

I love words such as wachuseh as much as the people who use 4
them. The significance of such compressed words goes beyond their
original meaning to say even more. Born into a bicultural and bilingual
world, I have experienced the birth of new words, new worlds, ideas
that came from two languages and two cultures, words that changed
meanings and power. So many other cultures and languages from
Black English to Yiddish have contributed to the evolution and enrich-
ment of the English language. These words enriched because they gave
birth to a new world of ideas from a combination of cultures, ideas that
were lacking a name until then.

Raised in El Paso, Texas, **Jose Antonio Burciaga** is a writer, artist,
muralist, and Resident Fellow at Casa Zapata, a Mexican American
theme residence at Stanford University. Burciaga was also a founding
member of the comedy group "Culture Clash." He has written
*Undocumented Love—Amor Indocumentado: A Personal Anthology of
Poetry*, which won a Before Columbus American Book Award in 1981,
and *Weedee Peepo: A Collection of Essays—Una Coleccion de Ensayos*
(1988). "Chief *Wachuseh*" is the introductory essay in *Drink Cultura:
Chicanismo* (1993), his latest collection of essays.

Chutzpah filled a void in the English language; there was nothing 5 in our slang like it. The introduction of *macho* into the English language was another such idea, even though the English definition has a more negative connotation than the Spanish, where the term can be as innocent as its basic literal definition of "male." In Mexican Spanish it's *huevos,* in peninsular Spanish it's *cojones* for "balls." Some Mexican or Chicano ideas have no English words. To call someone a *pendejo* in Spanish is not the same as calling him or her stupid or even *estúpido* or *estúpida.*

My father had a vocabulary of Spanish words that to this day are 6 not found in popular Spanish language dictionaries. He was born into a poor, migrant farm working family in a community of people that still used ancient words that some found improper and backwards but are to be found in Miguel Cervantez's classic *Don Quixote.* My father commonly used words such as *minjurne* for mixture, or *cachibaches* for junk. I would hear them without knowing their definition but I knew exactly what he meant when talking within a specific context. Some words were archaic, others were a combination of English and Spanish. And though he knew the "standard" Spanish of "educated" people, he also worked, lived, laughed and cried with words that were more expressive and indigenous to the border than standard Spanish.

Drink Cultura is a collection of stories and commentaries about 7 what you say, about what they said, about what my father said, about what I say, about what I've heard said—going beyond the question and shooting it back as wachuseh. The ironies in the experience of living within, between and sometimes outside of two cultures; the damnation and the salvation, the celebration of it all.

QUESTIONS

1. Why does Burciaga "love words such as wachuseh as much as the people who use them" (paragraph 4)?

2. Based on this introductory essay, what would you expect to read about in the rest of the book *Drink Cultura?*

Public and Private Language

RICHARD RODRIGUEZ

I remember to start with that day in Sacramento—a California now 1
nearly thirty years past—when I first entered a classroom, able to understand some fifty stray English words.

The third of four children, I had been preceded to a neighborhood 2
Roman Catholic school by an older brother and sister. But neither of
them had revealed very much about their classroom experiences. Each
afternoon they returned, as they left in the morning, always together,
speaking in Spanish as they climbed the five steps of the porch. And
their mysterious books, wrapped in shopping-bag paper, remained on
the table next to the door, closed firmly behind them.

An accident of geography sent me to a school where all my class- 3
mates were white, many the children of doctors and lawyers and business executives. All my classmates certainly must have been uneasy on
that first day of school—as most children are uneasy—to find themselves apart from their families in the first institution of their lives. But
I was astonished.

The nun said, in a friendly but oddly impersonal voice, "Boys and 4
girls, this is Richard Rodriguez." (I heard her sound out: *Rich-heard
Road-ree-guess.*) It was the first time I had heard anyone name me in
English. "Richard," the nun repeated more slowly, writing my name
down in her black leather book. Quickly I turned to see my mother's
face dissolve in a watery blur behind the pebbled glass door.

Many years later there is something called bilingual education—a 5
scheme proposed in the late 1960s by Hispanic-American social
activists, later endorsed by a congressional vote. It is a program that
seeks to permit non-English-speaking children, many from lower-
class homes, to use their family language as the language of school.
(Such is the goal its supporters announce.) I hear them and am forced
to say no: It is not possible for a child—any child—ever to use his

---

Richard Rodriguez is a writer, editor for Pacific News Service in San
Francisco, and a contributing editor for *Harper's* magazine and the
Sunday "Opinion" section of the *Los Angeles Times*. Selections from
his memoir *Hunger of Memory: The Education of Richard Rodriguez*
(1982)—such as the essay that appears here—have been widely
anthologized in composition readers. In 1992 Rodriguez published
the collection of essays *Days of Obligation: An Argument with My
Mexican Father.*

family's language in school. Not to understand this is to misunderstand the public uses of schooling and to trivialize the nature of intimate life—a family's "language."

Memory teaches me what I know of these matters; the boy 6 reminds the adult. I was a bilingual child, a certain kind—socially disadvantaged—the son of working-class parents, both Mexican immigrants.

In the early years of my boyhood, my parents coped very well in 7 America. My father had steady work. My mother managed at home. They were nobody's victims. Optimism and ambition led them to a house (our home) many blocks from the Mexican south side of town. We lived among *gringos* and only a block from the biggest, whitest houses. It never occurred to my parents that they couldn't live wherever they chose. Nor was the Sacramento of the fifties bent on teaching them a contrary lesson. My mother and father were more annoyed than intimidated by those two or three neighbors who tried initially to make us unwelcome. ("Keep your brats away from my sidewalk!") But despite all they achieved, perhaps because they had so much to achieve, any deep feeling of ease, the confidence of "belonging" in public was withheld from them both. They regarded the people at work, the faces in crowds, as very distant from us. They were the others, *los gringos*. That term was interchangeable in their speech with another, even more telling, *los americanos*.

I grew up in a house where the only regular guests were my rela- 8 tions. For one day, enormous families of relatives would visit and there would be so many people that the noise and the bodies would spill out to the backyard and front porch. Then, for weeks, no one came by. (It was usually a salesman who rang the doorbell.) Our house stood apart. A gaudy yellow in a row of white bungalows. We were the people with the noisy dog. The people who raised pigeons and chickens. We were the foreigners on the block. A few neighbors smiled and waved. We waved back. But no one in the family knew the names of the old couple who lived next door; until I was seven years old, I did not know the names of the kids who lived across the street.

In public, my father and mother spoke a hesitant, accented, not al- 9 ways grammatical English. And they would have to strain—their bodies tense—to catch the sense of what was rapidly said by *los gringos*. At home they spoke Spanish. The language of their Mexican past sounded in counterpoint to the English of public society. The words would come quickly, with ease. Conveyed through those sounds was the pleasing, soothing, consoling reminder of being at home.

During those years when I was first conscious of hearing, my 10 mother and father addressed me only in Spanish; in Spanish I learned to reply. By contrast, English (*inglés*), rarely heard in the house, was the language I came to associate with *gringos*. I learned my first words of English overhearing my parents speak to strangers. At five years age, I knew just enough English for my mother to trust me on errands to stores one block away. No more.

I was a listening child, careful to hear the very different sounds of 11 Spanish and English. Wide-eyed with hearing, I'd listen to sounds more than words. First, there were English (*gringo*) sounds. So many words were still unknown that when the butcher or the lady at the drugstore said something to me, exotic polysyllabic sounds would bloom in the midst of their sentences. Often, the speech of people in public seemed to me very loud, booming with confidence. The man behind the counter would literally ask, "What can I do for you?" But by being so firm and so clear, the sound of his voice said that he was a *gringo;* he belonged in public society.

I would also hear then the high nasal notes of middle-class 12 American speech. The air stirred with sound. Sometimes, even now, when I have been traveling abroad for several weeks, I will hear what I heard as a boy. In hotel lobbies or airports, in Turkey or Brazil, some Americans will pass, and suddenly I will hear it again—the high sound of American voices. For a few seconds I will hear it with pleasure, for it is now the sound of *my* society—a reminder of home. But inevitably—already on the flight headed for home—the sound fades with repetition. I will be unable to hear it anymore.

When I was a boy, things were different. The accent of *los gringos* 13 was never pleasing nor was it hard to hear. Crowds at Safeway or at bus stops would be noisy with sound. And I would be forced to edge away from the chirping chatter above me.

I was unable to hear my own sounds, but I knew very well that I 14 spoke English poorly. My words could not stretch far enough to form complete thoughts. And the words I did speak I didn't know well enough to make into distinct sounds. (Listeners would usually lower their heads, better to hear what I was trying to say.) But it was one thing for *me* to speak English with difficulty. It was more troubling for me to hear my parents speak in public: their high-whining vowels and guttural consonants; their sentences that got stuck with "ch" and "ah" sounds; the confused syntax; the hesitant rhythm of sounds so different from the way *gringos* spoke. I'd notice, moreover, that my parents' voices were softer than those of *gringos* we'd meet.

I am tempted now to say that none of this mattered. In adulthood 15 I am embarrassed by childhood fears. And, in a way, it didn't matter very much that my parents could not speak English with ease. Their linguistic difficulties had no serious consequences. My mother and father made themselves understood at the county hospital clinic and at

government offices. And yet, in another way, it mattered very much—
it was unsettling to hear my parents struggle with English. Hearing
them, I'd grow nervous, my clutching trust in their protection and
power weakened.

There were many times like the night at a brightly lit gasoline sta-   16
tion (a blaring white memory) when I stood uneasily, hearing my father. He was talking to a teenaged attendant. I do not recall what they
were saying, but I cannot forget the sounds my father made as he
spoke. At one point his words slid together to form one word—sounds
as confused as the threads of blue and green oil in the puddle next to
my shoes. His voice rushed through what he had left to say. And, toward the end, reached falsetto notes, appealing to his listener's understanding. I looked away to the lights of passing automobiles. I tried not
to hear anymore. But I heard only too well the calm, easy tones in the
attendant's reply. Shortly afterward, walking toward home with my
father, I shivered when he put his hand on my shoulder. The very first
chance that I got, I evaded his grasp and ran on ahead into the dark,
skipping with feigned boyish exuberance.

But then there was Spanish. *Español:* my family's language.   17
Español: the language that seemed to me a private language. I'd hear
strangers on the radio and in the Mexican Catholic church across town
speaking in Spanish, but I couldn't really believe that Spanish was a
public language, like English. Spanish speakers, rather, seemed related
to me, for I sensed that we shared—through our language—the experience of feeling apart from *los gringos.* It was thus a ghetto Spanish
that I heard and I spoke. Like those whose lives are bound by a barrio,
I was reminded by Spanish of my separateness from *los otros, los gringos* in power. But more intensely than for most barrio children—because I did not live in a barrio—Spanish seemed to me the language of
home. (Most days it was only at home that I'd hear it.) It became the
language of joyful return.

A family member would say something to me and I would feel   18
myself specially recognized. My parents would say something to me
and I would feel embraced by the sounds of their words. Those sounds
said: *I am speaking with ease in Spanish. I am addressing you in words I
never use with* los gringos. *I recognize you as someone special, close, like no
one outside. You belong with us. In the family.*

(*Ricardo.*)   19

At the age of five, six, well past the time when most other children   20
no longer easily notice the difference between sounds uttered at home
and words spoken in public, I had a different experience. I lived in a
world magically compounded of sounds. I remained a child longer
than most; I lingered too long, poised at the edge of language—often

frightened by the sounds of *los gringos,* delighted by the sounds of Spanish at home. I shared with my family a language that was startlingly different from that used in the great city around us.

For me there were none of the gradations between public and private society so normal to a maturing child. Outside the house was public society; inside the house was private. Just opening or closing the screen door behind me was an important experience. I'd rarely leave home all alone or without reluctance. Walking down the sidewalk, under the canopy of tall trees, I'd warily notice the—suddenly—silent neighborhood kids who stood warily watching me. Nervously, I'd arrive at the grocery store to hear there the sounds of the *gringo*—foreign to me—reminding me that in this world so big, I was a foreigner. But then I'd return. Walking back toward our house, climbing the steps from the sidewalk, when the front door was open in summer, I'd hear voices beyond the screen door talking in Spanish. For a second or two, I'd stay, linger there, listening. Smiling, I'd hear my mother call out, saying in Spanish (words): "Is that you, Richard?" All the while her sounds would assure me: *You are home now; come closer; inside. With us.* 21

"Si," I'd reply. 22

Once more inside the house I would resume (assume) my place in the family. The sounds would dim, grow harder to hear. Once more at home, I would grow less aware of that fact. It required, however, no more than the blurt of the doorbell to alert me to listen to sounds all over again. The house would turn instantly still while my mother went to the door. I'd hear her hard English sounds. I'd wait to hear her voice return to soft-sounding Spanish, which assured me, as surely as did the clicking tongue of the lock on the door, that the stranger was gone. 23

Plainly, it is not healthy to hear such sounds so often. It is not healthy to distinguish public words from private sounds so easily. I remained cloistered by sounds, timid and shy in public, too dependent on voices at home. And yet it needs to be emphasized: I was an extremely happy child at home. I remember many nights when my father would come back from work, and I'd hear him call out to my mother in Spanish, sounding relieved. In Spanish, he'd sound light and free notes he never could manage in English. Some nights I'd jump up just at hearing his voice. With *mis hermanos* I would come running into the room where he was with my mother. Our laughing (so deep was the pleasure!) became screaming. Like others who know the pain of public alienation, we transformed the knowledge of our public separateness and made it consoling—the reminder of intimacy. *We are speaking now the way we never speak out in public. We are alone—together,* voices sounded, surrounded to tell me. Some nights, no one seemed willing to loosen the hold sounds had on us. At dinner, we invented 24 new words. (Ours sounded Spanish, but made sense only to us.) We pieced together new words by taking, say, an English verb and giving it Spanish endings. My mother's instructions at bedtime would be lacquered with mock-urgent tones. Or a word like *si* would become, in several notes, able to convey added measures of feeling. Tongues explored the edges of words, especially the fat vowels. And we happily sounded that military drum roll, the twirling roar of the Spanish *r*. Family language: my family's sounds. The voices of my parents and sisters and brother. Their voices insisting: *You belong here. We are family members. Related. Special to one another. Listen!* Voices singing and sighing, rising, straining, then surging, teeming with pleasure that burst syllables into fragments of laughter. At times it seemed there was steady quiet only when, from another room, the rustling whispers of my parents faded and I moved closer to sleep.

Supporters of bilingual education today imply that students like 25 me miss a great deal by not being taught in their family's language. What they seem not to recognize is that, as a socially disadvantaged child, I considered Spanish to be a private language. What I needed to learn in school was that I had the right—and the obligation—to speak the public language of *los gringos*. The odd truth is that my first-grade classmates could have become bilingual, in the conventional sense of that word, more easily than I. Had they been taught (as upper-middle-class children are often taught early) a second language like Spanish or French, they could have regarded it simply as that: another public language. In my case such bilingualism could not have been so quickly achieved. What I did not believe was that I could speak a single public language.

Without question, it would have pleased me to hear my teachers 26 address me in Spanish when I entered the classroom. I would have felt much less afraid. I would have trusted them and responded with ease. But I would have delayed—for how long postponed?—having to learn the language of public society. I would have evaded—and for how long could I have afforded to delay?—learning the great lesson of school, that I had a public identity.

Fortunately, my teachers were unsentimental about their respon- 27 sibility. What they understood was that I needed to speak a public language. So their voices would search me out, asking me questions. Each time I'd hear them, I'd look up in surprise to see a nun's face frowning at me. I'd mumble, not really meaning to answer. The nun would persist, "Richard, stand up. Don't look at the floor. Speak up. Speak to the entire class, not just to me!" But I couldn't believe that the English language was mine to use. (In part, I did not want to believe it.) I continued to mumble. I resisted the teacher's demands. (Did I somehow suspect that once I learned public language my pleasing family life would be changed?) Silent, waiting for the bell to sound, I remained dazed, diffident, afraid.

Because I wrongly imagined that English was intrinsically a pub-   28
lic language and Spanish an intrinsically private one, I easily noted the difference between classroom language and the language of home. At school, words were directed to a general audience of listeners. ("Boys and girls.") Words were meaningfully ordered. And the point was not self-expression alone but to make oneself understood by many others. The teacher quizzed: "Boys and girls, why do we use that word in this sentence? Could we think of a better word to use there? Would the sentence change its meaning if the words were differently arranged? And wasn't there a better way of saying much the same thing?" (I couldn't say. I wouldn't try to say.)

Three months. Five. Half a year passed. Unsmiling, ever watchful,   29
my teachers noted my silence. They began to connect my behavior with the difficult progress my older sister and brother were making. Until one Saturday morning three nuns arrived at the house to talk to our parents. Stiffly, they sat on the blue living room sofa. From the doorway of another room, spying the visitors, I noted the incongruity—the clash of two worlds, the faces and voices of school intruding upon the familiar setting of home. I overheard one voice gently wondering, "Do your children speak only Spanish at home, Mrs. Rodriguez?" While another voice added, "That Richard especially seems so timid and shy."

That Rich-heard!   30

With great tact the visitors continued, "Is it possible for you and   31
your husband to encourage your children to practice their English when they are home?" Of course, my parents complied. What would they not do for their children's well-being? And how could they have questioned the Church's authority which those women represented? In an instant, they agreed to give up the language (the sounds) that had revealed and accentuated our family's closeness. The moment after the visitors left, the change was observed. "*Ahora,* speak to us *en inglés,*" my father and mother united to tell us.

At first, it seemed a kind of game. After dinner each night, the   32
family gathered to practice "our" English. (It was still then *inglés,* a language foreign to us, so we felt drawn as strangers to it.) Laughing, we would try to define words we could not pronounce. We played with strange English sounds, often overanglicizing our pronunciations. And we filled the smiling gaps of our sentences with familiar Spanish sounds. But that was cheating, somebody shouted. Everyone laughed. In school, meanwhile, like my brother and sister, I was required to at-

tend a daily tutoring session. I needed a full year of special attention. I also needed my teachers to keep my attention from straying in class by calling out, *Rich-heard*—their English voices slowly prying loose my ties to my other name, its three notes, *Ri-car-do*. Most of all I needed to hear my mother and father speak to me in a moment of seriousness in broken—suddenly heartbreaking—English. The scene was inevitable: One Saturday morning I entered the kitchen where my parents were talking in Spanish. I did not realize that they were talking in Spanish however until, at the moment they saw me, I heard their voices change to speak English. Those *gringo* sounds they uttered startled me. Pushed me away. In that moment of trivial misunderstanding and profound insight, I felt my throat twisted by unsounded grief. I turned quickly and left the room. But I had no place to escape to with Spanish. (The spell was broken.) My brother and sisters were speaking English in another part of the house.

Again and again in the days following, increasingly angry, I was 33 obliged to hear my mother and father: "Speak to us *en inglés. (Speak.)*" Only then did I determine to learn classroom English. Weeks after, it happened: One day in school I raised my hand to volunteer an answer. I spoke out in a loud voice. And I did not think it remarkable when the entire class understood. That day, I moved very far from the disadvantaged child I had been only days earlier. The belief, the calming assurance that I belonged in public, had at last taken hold.

Shortly after, I stopped hearing the high and loud sounds of *los* 34 *gringos*. A more and more confident speaker of English, I didn't trouble to listen to *how* strangers sounded, speaking to me. And there simply were too many English-speaking people in my day for me to hear American accents anymore. Conversations quickened. Listening to persons who sounded eccentrically pitched voices, I usually noted their sounds for an initial few seconds before I concentrated on *what* they were saying. Conversations became content-full. Transparent. Hearing someone's *tone* of voice—angry or questioning or sarcastic or happy or sad—I didn't distinguish it from the words it expressed. Sound and word were thus tightly wedded. At the end of a day, I was often bemused, always relieved to realize how "silent," though crowded with words, my day in public had been. (This public silence measured and quickened the change in my life.)

At last, seven years old, I came to believe what had been techni- 35 cally true since my birth: I was an American citizen.

But the special feeling of closeness at home was diminished by 36 then. Gone was the desperate, urgent, intense feeling of being at home; rare was the experience of feeling myself individualized by family intimates. We remained a loving family, but one greatly changed. No longer so close; no longer bound tight by the pleasing and troubling knowledge of our public separateness. Neither my older brother nor sister rushed home after school anymore. Nor did I. When I arrived home there would often be neighborhood kids in the house. Or the house would be empty of sounds.

The silence at home, however, was finally more than a literal si- 37 lence. Fewer words passed between parent and child, but more profound was the silence that resulted from my inattention to sounds. At about the time I no longer bothered to listen with care to the sounds of English in public, I grew careless about listening to the sounds family members made when they spoke. Most of the time I heard someone speaking at home and didn't distinguish his sounds from the words people uttered in public. I didn't even pay much attention to my parents' accented and ungrammatical speech. At least not at home. Only when I was with them in public would I grow alert to their accents. Though, even then, their sounds caused me less and less concern. For I was increasingly confident of my own public identity.

I would have been happier about my public success had I not 38 sometimes recalled what it had been like earlier, when my family had conveyed its intimacy through a set of conveniently private sounds. Sometimes in public, hearing a stranger, I'd hark back to my past. A Mexican farmworker approached me downtown to ask directions to somewhere. "¿Hijito . . .?" he said. And his voice summoned deep longing. Another time, standing beside my mother in the visiting room of a Carmelite convent, before the dense screen which rendered the nuns shadowy figures, I heard several Spanish-speaking nuns—their busy, singsong overlapping voices—assure us that yes, yes, we were remembered, all our family was remembered in their prayers. (Their voices echoed faraway family sounds.) Another day, a dark-faced old woman—her hand light on my shoulder—steadied herself against me as she boarded a bus. She murmured something I couldn't quite comprehend. Her Spanish voice came near, like the face of a never-before-seen relative in the instant before I was kissed. Her voice, like so many of the Spanish voices I'd hear in public, recalled the golden age of my youth. Hearing Spanish then, I continued to be a careful, if sad, listener to sounds. Hearing a Spanish-speaking family walking behind me, I turned to look. I smiled for an instant, before my glance found the Hispanic-looking faces of strangers in the crowd going by.

Today I hear bilingual educators say that children lose a degree 39 of "individuality" by becoming assimilated into public society. (Bilingual schooling was popularized in the seventies, that decade when middle-class ethnics began to resist the process of assimilation

—the American melting pot.) But the bilingualists simplistically scorn the value and necessity of assimilation. They do not seem to realize that there are *two ways* a person is individualized. So they do not realize that while one suffers a diminished sense of *private* individuality by becoming assimilated into public society, such assimilation makes possible the achievement of *public* individuality.

The bilingualists insist that a student should be reminded of his 40 difference from others in mass society, his heritage. But they equate mere separateness with individuality. The fact is that only in private— with intimates—is separateness from the crowd a prerequisite for individuality. (An intimate draws me apart, tells me that I am unique, unlike all others.) In public, by contrast, full individuality is achieved, paradoxically, by those who are able to consider themselves members of the crowd. Thus it happened for me: Only when I was able to think of myself as an American, no longer an alien in *gringo* society, could I seek the rights and opportunities necessary for full public individuality. The social and political advantages I enjoy as a man result from the day that I came to believe that my name, indeed, is *Rich-heard Road-ree-guess.* It is true that my public society today is often impersonal. (My public society is usually mass society.) Yet despite the anonymity of the crowd and despite the fact that the individuality I achieve in public is often tenuous—because it depends on my being one in a crowd—I celebrate the day I acquired my new name. Those middle-class ethnics who scorn assimilation seem to me filled with decadent self-pity, obsessed by the burden of public life. Dangerously, they romanticize public separateness and they trivialize the dilemma of the socially disadvantaged.

QUESTIONS

1. Discuss the distinctions Rodriguez draws between private or family language and public language. What memories does he associate with each type of language?

2. How do you think Rodriguez would define "American" or "American citizen"?

3. Rodriguez argues against bilingual education by distinguishing between what he calls "*private* individuality" and the "*public* individuality" made possible by assimilation. How heavy a price does Rodriguez think he paid for gaining a sense of "public individuality"? How heavy a price do *you* think he paid?

How to Tame a Wild Tongue

GLORIA ANZALDÚA

"We're going to have to control your tongue," the dentist says, 1
pulling out all the metal from my mouth. Silver bits plop and tinkle
into the basin. My mouth is a motherlode.

The dentist is cleaning out my roots. I get a whiff of the stench 2
when I gasp. "I can't cap that tooth yet, you're still draining," he says.

"We're going to have to do something about your tongue," I hear 3
the anger rising in his voice. My tongue keeps pushing out the wads of
cotton, pushing back the drills, the long thin needles. "I've never seen
anything as strong or as stubborn," he says. And I think, how do you
tame a wild tongue, train it to be quiet, how do you bridle and saddle
it? How do you make it lie down?

> *Who is to say that robbing a people of its language is less
> violent than war?*
>
> —RAY GWYN SMITH[1]

I remember being caught speaking Spanish at recess—that was 4
good for three licks on the knuckles with a sharp ruler. I remember
being sent to the corner of the classroom for "talking back" to the
Anglo teacher when all I was trying to do was tell her how to pronounce my name. "If you want to be American, speak 'American.' If
you don't like it, go back to Mexico where you belong."

"I want you to speak English. *Pa' hallar buen trabajo tienes que saber* 5
hablar el inglés bien. Qué vale toda tu educación si todavía hablas inglés con
un 'accent,' " my mother would say, mortified that I spoke English like

---

[1]Ray Gwyn Smith, *Moorland is Cold Country,* unpublished book.

Gloria Anzaldúa is a poet, fiction writer, and feminist cultural critic
from south Texas now living in Santa Cruz, California. She has taught
creative writing, feminist studies, and Chicano Studies at several colleges and universities. She is the author of a bilingual children's book
and a collection of prose and poetry, *Borderlands/La Frontera: The New
Mestiza* (1987), where this essay first appeared. Anzaldua also edited
the anthology *Making Face, Making Soul/Haciendo Caras: Creative and
Critical Perspectives by Women of Color* (1990) and co-edited (with
Cherrie Moraga) *This Bridge Called My Back: Writings by Radical Women
of Color* (1983), which won a Before Columbus Foundation American
Book Award.

a Mexican. At Pan American University, I, and all Chicano students were required to take two speech classes. Their purpose: to get rid of our accents.

Attacks on one's form of expression with the intent to censor are a   6 violation of the First Amendment. *El Anglo con cara de inocente nos arrancó la lengua.* Wild tongues can't be tamed, they can only be cut out.

Overcoming the Tradition of Silence

> *Ahogadas, escupimos el oscuro.*
> *Peleando con nuestra propia sombra*
> *el silencio nos sepulta.*

En boca cerrada no entran moscas. "Flies don't enter a closed mouth"   7 is a saying I kept hearing when I was a child. *Ser habladora* was to be a gossip and a liar, to talk too much. *Muchachitas bien criadas,* well-bred girls don't answer back. *Es una falta de respeto* to talk back to one's mother or father. I remember one of the sins I'd recite to the priest in the confession box the few times I went to confession: talking back to my mother, *hablar pa' 'tras, repelar. Hocicona, repelona, chismosa,* having a big mouth, questioning, carrying tales are all signs of being *mal criada.* In my culture they are all words that are derogatory if applied to women—I've never heard them applied to men.

The first time I heard two women, a Puerto Rican and a Cuban, say   8 the word "*nosotras,*" I was shocked. I had not known the word existed. Chicanas use *nosotros* whether we're male or female. We are robbed of our female being by the masculine plural. Language is a male discourse.

> *And our tongues have become*
> *dry   the wilderness has*
> *dried out our tongues   and*
> *we have forgotten speech.*
>
> —IRENA KLEPFISZ[2]

Even our own people, other Spanish speakers *nos quieren poner*   9 *candados en la boca.* They would hold us back with their bag of *reglas de academia.*

Oyé como ladra: el lenguaje de la frontera

> *Quien tiene boca se equivoca.*
>
> —MEXICAN SAYING

---

[2]Irena Klepfisz, "*Di rayze aheym*/The Journey Home," in *The Tribe of Dina: A Jewish Women's Anthology,* eds. Melanie Kaye/Kantrowitz, and Irena Klepfisz (Montpelier, VT: Sinister Wisdom Books, 1986), p. 49.

"*Pocho,* cultural traitor, you're speaking the oppressor's language   10
by speaking English, you're ruining the Spanish language," I have
been accused by various Latinos and Latinas. Chicano Spanish is considered by the purist and by most Latinos deficient, a mutilation of
Spanish.

But Chicano Spanish is a border tongue which developed natu-   11
rally. Change, *evolución, enriquecimiento de palabras nuevas por invención
o adopción* have created variants of Chicano Spanish, *un nuevo lenguaje.
Un lenguaje que corresponde a un modo de vivir.* Chicano Spanish is not
incorrect, it is a living language.

For a people who are neither Spanish nor live in a country in   12
which Spanish is the first language; for a people who live in a country
in which English is the reigning tongue but who are not Anglo; for a
people who cannot entirely identify with either standard (formal,
Castillian) Spanish nor standard English, what recourse is left to them
but to create their own language? A language which they can connect
their identity to, one capable of communicating the realities and values true to themselves—a language with terms that are neither *español
ni inglés,* but both. We speak a patois, a forked tongue, a variation of
two languages.

Chicano Spanish sprang out of the Chicanos' need to identify our-   13
selves as a distinct people. We needed a language with which we
could communicate with ourselves, a secret language. For some of us,
language is a homeland closer than the Southwest—for many
Chicanos today live in the Midwest and the East. And because we are
a complex, heterogeneous people, we speak many languages. Some of
the languages we speak are:

1. Standard English
2. Working class and slang English
3. Standard Spanish
4. Standard Mexican Spanish
5. North Mexican Spanish dialect
6. Chicano Spanish (Texas, New Mexico, Arizona and
   California have regional variations)
7. Tex-Mex
8. *Pachuco* (called caló)

My "home" tongues are the languages I speak with my sister and   14
brothers, with my friends. They are the last five listed, with 6 and 7
being closest to my heart. From school, the media and job situations,
I've picked up standard and working class English. From Mama-
grande Locha and from reading Spanish and Mexican literature, I've

picked up Standard Spanish and Standard Mexican Spanish. From *los recién llegados,* Mexican immigrants, and *braceros,* I learned the North Mexican dialect. With Mexicans I'll try to speak either Standard Mexican Spanish or the North Mexican dialect. From my parents and Chicanos living in the Valley, I picked up Chicano Texas Spanish, and I speak it with my mom, younger brother (who married a Mexican and who rarely mixes Spanish with English), aunts and older relatives.

With Chicanas from *Nuevo México* or *Arizona* I will speak Chicano   15
Spanish a little, but often they don't understand what I'm saying. With most California Chicanas I speak entirely in English (unless I forget). When I first moved to San Francisco, I'd rattle off something in Spanish, unintentionally embarrassing them. Often it is only with another Chicana *tejana* that I can talk freely.

Words distorted by English are known as anglicisms or *pochismos.*   16
The *pocho* is an anglicized Mexican or American of Mexican origin who speaks Spanish with an accent characteristic of North Americans and who distorts and reconstructs the language according to the influence of English.[3] Tex-Mex, or Spanglish, comes most naturally to me. I may switch back and forth from English to Spanish in the same sentence or in the same word. With my sister and my brother Nune and with Chicano *tejano* contemporaries I speak Tex-Mex.

From kids and people my own age I picked up *Pachuco. Pachuco*   17
(the language of the zoot suiters) is a language of rebellion, both against Standard Spanish and Standard English. It is a secret language. Adults of the culture and outsiders cannot understand it. It is made up of slang words from both English and Spanish. *Ruca* means girl or woman, *vato* means guy or dude, *chale* means no, *simón* means yes, *churro* is sure, talk is *periquiar, pigionear* means petting, *que gacho* means how nerdy, *ponte águila* means watch out, death is called *la pelona.* Through lack of practice and not having others who can speak it, I've lost most of the *Pachuco* tongue.

Chicanos, after 250 years of Spanish/Anglo colonization, have de-   18
veloped significant differences in the Spanish we speak. We collapse two adjacent vowels into a single syllable and sometimes shift the stress in certain words such as *maíz/maiz, cohete/cuete.* We leave out certain consonants when they appear between vowels: *lado/lao, mojado/mojao.* Chicanos from South Texas pronounce *f* as *j* as in *jue (fue).* Chicanos use "archaisms," words that are no longer in the Spanish language, words that have been evolved out. We say *semos, truje, haiga, ansina,* and *naiden.* We retain the "archaic" *j,* as in *jalar,* that derives from an earlier *h* (the French *halar* or the Germanic *halon* which

---

[3]R. C. Ortega, *Dialectologia Del Barrio,* trans. Hortencia S. Alwan (Los Angeles: R. C. Ortega Publisher & Bookseller, 1977), p. 132.

was lost to standard Spanish in the 16th century), but which is still found in several regional dialects such as the one spoken in South Texas. (Due to geography, Chicanos from the Valley of South Texas were cut off linguistically from other Spanish speakers. We tend to use words that the Spaniards brought over from Medieval Spain. The majority of the Spanish colonizers in Mexico and the Southwest came from Extremadura—Hernán Cortés was one of them—and Andalucía. Andalucians pronounce *ll* like a *y*, and their *d*'s tend to be absorbed by adjacent vowels: *tirado* becomes *tirao*. They brought *el lenguaje popular, dialectos y regionalismos.*)[4]

Chicanos and other Spanish speakers also shift *ll* to *y* and *z* to *s*.[5] We   19
leave out initial syllables, saying *tar* for *estar, toy* for *estoy, hora* for *ahora* (*cubanos* and *puertorriqueños* also leave out initial letters of some words.) We also leave out the final syllable such as *pa* for *para*. The intervocalic *y*, the *ll* as in *tortilla, ella, botella* gets replaced by *tortia* or *tortiya, ea, botea*. We add an additional syllable at the beginning of certain words: *atocar* for *tocar, agastar* for *gastar*. Sometimes we'll say *lavaste las vacijas*, other times *lavates* (substituting the *ates* verb endings for the *aste*).

We use anglicims, words borrowed from English: *bola* from ball,   20
carpeta from carpet, *máchina de lavar* (instead of *lavadora*) from washing machine. Tex-Mex argot, created by adding a Spanish sound at the beginning or end of an English word such as *cookiar* for cook, *watchar* for watch, *parkiar* for park, and *rapiar* for rape, is the result of the pressures on Spanish speakers to adapt to English.

We don't use the word *vosotros/as* or its accompanying verb form.   21
We don't say *claro* (to mean yes), *imagínate*, or *me emociona*, unless we picked up Spanish from Latinas, out of a book, or in a classroom. Other Spanish-speaking groups are going through the same, or similar, development in their Spanish.

Linguistic Terrorism

> Deslenguadas. Somos los del español deficiente. *We are your linguistic nightmare, your linguistic aberration, your linguistic mestisaje, the subject of your burla. Because we speak with tongues of fire we are culturally crucified. Racially, culturally and linguistically somos* huérfanos—*we speak an orphan tongue.*

---

[4]Eduardo Hernandéz-Chávez, Anderew D. Cohen, and Anthony F. Beltramo, *El Lenguaje de los Chicanos: Regional and Social Characteristics of Language Used by Mexican Americanas* (Arlington, VA: Center for Applied Linguistics, 1975), p. 39.

[5]Ibid., p. xvii.

Chicanas who grew up speaking Chicano Spanish have internal-   22
ized the belief that we speak poor Spanish. It is illegitimate, a bastard
language. And because we internalize how our language has been
used against us by the dominant culture, we use our language differences against each other.

Chicana feminists often skirt around each other with suspicion   23
and hesitation. For the longest time I couldn't figure it out. Then it
dawned on me. To be close to another Chicana is like looking into the
mirror. We are afraid of what we'll see there. *Pena.* Shame. Low estimation of self. In childhood we are told that our language is wrong.
Repeated attacks on our native tongue diminish our sense of self. The
attacks continue throughout our lives.

Chicanas feel uncomfortable talking in Spanish to Latinas, afraid   24
of their censure. Their language was not outlawed in their countries.
They had a whole lifetime of being immersed in their native tongue;
generations, centuries in which Spanish was a first language, taught in
school, heard on radio and TV, and read in the newspaper.

If a person, Chicana or Latina, has a low estimation of my native   25
tongue, she also has a low estimation of me. Often with *mexicanas y
latinas* we'll speak English as a neutral language. Even among
Chicanas we tend to speak English at parties or conferences. Yet, at the
same time, we're afraid the other will think we're *agringadas* because
we don't speak Chicano Spanish. We oppress each other trying to out-
Chicano each other, vying to be the "real" Chicanas, to speak like
Chicanos. There is no one Chicano language just as there is no one
Chicano experience. A monolingual Chicana whose first language is
English or Spanish is just as much a Chicana as one who speaks sev-
eral variants of Spanish. A Chicana from Michigan or Chicago or
Detroit is just as much a Chicana as one from the Southwest. Chicano
Spanish is as diverse linguistically as it is regionally.

By the end of this century, Spanish speakers will comprise the   26
biggest minority group in the U.S., a country where students in high
schools and colleges are encouraged to take French classes because
French is considered more "cultured." But for a language to remain
alive it must be used.[6] By the end of this century English, and not
Spanish, will be the mother tongue of most Chicanos and Latinos.

So, if you want to really hurt me, talk badly about my language.   27
Ethnic identity is twin skin to linguistic identity—I am my language.
Until I can take pride in my language, I cannot take pride in myself.
Until I can accept as legitimate Chicano Texas Spanish, Tex-Mex and

---

[6]Irena Klepfisz, "Secular Jewish Identity: Yidishkayt in America," in *The Tribe of Dina*, eds.
Kaye/Kantrowitz and Klepfisz, p. 43.

all the other languages I speak, I cannot accept the legitimacy of myself. Until I am free to write bilingually and to switch codes without having always to translate, while I still have to speak English or Spanish when I would rather speak Spanglish, and as long as I have to accommodate the English speakers rather than having them accommodate me, my tongue will be illegitimate.

I will no longer be made to feel ashamed of existing. I will have my 28 voice: Indian, Spanish, white. I will have my serpent's tongue—my woman's voice, my sexual voice, my poet's voice. I will overcome the tradition of silence.

> My fingers
> move sly against your palm
> Like women everywhere, we speak in code . . .
>
> —MELANIE KAYE/KANTROWITZ[7]

"Vistas," corridos, y comida: My Native Tongue

In the 1960s, I read my first Chicano novel. It was *City of Night* by 29 John Rechy, a gay Texan, son of a Scottish father and a Mexican mother. For days I walked around in stunned amazement that a Chicano could write and could get published. When I read *I Am Joaquín*[8] I was surprised to see a bilingual book by a Chicano in print. When I saw poetry written in Tex-Mex for the first time, a feeling of pure joy flashed through me. I felt like we really existed as a people. In 1971, when I started teaching High School English to Chicano students, I tried to supplement the required texts with works by Chicanos, only to be reprimanded and forbidden to do so by the principal. He claimed that I was supposed to teach "American" and English literature. At the risk of being fired, I swore my students to secrecy and slipped in Chicano short stories, poems, a play. In graduate school, while working toward a Ph.D., I had to "argue" with one advisor after the other, semester after semester, before I was allowed to make Chicano literature an area of focus.

Even before I read books by Chicanos or Mexicans, it was the 30 Mexican movies I saw at the drive-in—the Thursday night special of $1.00 a carload—that gave me a sense of belonging. "*Vámonos a las vistas*," my mother would call out and we'd all—grandmother, brothers, sister and cousins—squeeze into the car. We'd wolf down cheese and bologna white bread sandwiches while watching Pedro Infante in melodramatic tearjerkers like *Nosotros los pobres*, the first "real"

---

[7]Melanie Kaye/Kantrowitz, "Sign," in *We Speak in Code: Poems and Other Writings* (Pittsburgh: Motheroot Publications, 1980), p. 85.

[8]Rodolfo Gonzales, *I Am Joaquín/Yo Soy Joaquín* (New York: Bantam Books, 1972). It was first published in 1967.

Mexican movie (that was not an imitation of European movies). I remember seeing *Cuando los hijos se van* and surmising that all Mexican movies played up the love a mother has for her children and what ungrateful sons and daughters suffer when they are not devoted to their mothers. I remember the singing-type "westerns" of Jorge Negrete and Miquel Aceves Mejía. When watching Mexican movies, I felt a sense of homecoming as well as alienation. People who were to amount to something didn't go to Mexican movies, or *bailes,* or tune their radios to *bolero, rancherita,* and *corrido* music.

The whole time I was growing up, there was *norteño* music, some-   31 times called North Mexican border music, or Tex-Mex music, or Chicano music, or *cantina* (bar) music. I grew up listening to *conjuntos,* three- or four-piece bands made up of folk musicians playing guitar, *bajo sexto,* drums and button accordion, which Chicanos had borrowed from the German immigrants who had come to Central Texas and Mexico to farm and build breweries. In the Rio Grande Valley, Steve Jordan and Little Joe Hernández were popular, and Flaco Jiménez was the accordion king. The rhythms of Tex-Mex music are those of the polka, also adapted from the Germans, who in turn had borrowed the polka from the Czechs and Bohemians.

I remember the hot, sultry evenings when *corridos*—songs of love   32 and death on the Texas-Mexican borderlands—reverberated out of cheap amplifiers from the local *cantinas* and wafted in through my bedroom window.

Corridos first became widely used along the South Texas/Mexican   33 border during the early conflict between Chicanos and Anglos. The *corridos* are usually about Mexican heroes who do valiant deeds against the Anglo oppressors. Pancho Villa's song, *"La cucaracha,"* is the most famous one. *Corridos* of John F. Kennedy and his death are still very popular in the Valley. Older Chicanos remember Lydia Mendoza, one of the great border *corrido* singers who was called *la Gloria de Tejas.* Her *"El tango negro,"* sung during the Great Depression, made her a singer of the people. The everpresent *corridos* narrated one hundred years of border history, bringing news of events as well as entertaining. These folk musicians and folk songs are our chief cultural mythmakers, and they made our hard lives seem bearable.

I grew up feeling ambivalent about our music. Country-western   34 and rock-and-roll had more status. In the 50s and 60s, for the slightly educated and *agringado* Chicanos, there existed a sense of shame at being caught listening to our music. Yet I couldn't stop my feet from thumping to the music, could not stop humming the words, nor hide from myself the exhilaration I felt when I heard it.

There are more subtle ways that we internalize identification, es-   35 pecially in the forms of images and emotions. For me food and certain smells are tied to my identity, to my homeland. Woodsmoke curling up to an immense blue sky; woodsmoke perfuming my grandmother's clothes, her skin. The stench of cow manure and the yellow patches on the ground; the crack of a .22 rifle and the reek of cordite. Homemade white cheese sizzling in a pan, melting inside a folded *tortilla*. My sister Hilda's hot, spicy *menudo, chile colorado* making it deep red, pieces of *panza* and hominy floating on top. My brother Carito barbecuing *fajitas* in the backyard. Even now and 3,000 miles away, I can see my mother spicing the ground beef, pork and venison with *chile*. My mouth salivates at the thought of the hot steaming *tamales* I would be eating if I were home.

Si le preguntas a mi mamá, "¿Qué eres?"

> *"Identity is the essential core of who we are as individuals, the conscious experience of the self inside."*
>
> —KAUFMAN[9]

Nosotros los Chicanos straddle the borderlands. On one side of us, 36 we are constantly exposed to the Spanish of the Mexicans, on the other side we hear the Anglos' incessant clamoring so that we forget our language. Among ourselves we don't say *nosotros los americanos, o nosotros los españoles, o nosotros los hispanos. We say nosotros los mexicanos* (by *mexicanos* we do not mean citizens of Mexico; we do not mean a national identity, but a racial one). We distinguish between *mexicanos del otro lado* and *mexicanos de este lado.* Deep in our hearts we believe that being Mexican has nothing to do with which country one lives in. Being Mexican is a state of soul—not one of mind, not one of citizenship. Neither eagle nor serpent, but both. And like the ocean, neither animal respects borders.

> *Dime con quien andas y te diré quien eres.*
> *(Tell me who your friends are and I'll tell you who you are.)*
>
> —MEXICAN SAYING

Si le preguntas a mi mamá, "¿Qué eres?" te dirá, "Soy mexicana." My 37 brothers and sister say the same. I sometimes will answer *"soy mexicana"* and at others will say *"soy Chicana" o "soy tejana."* But I identified as *"Raza"* before I ever identified as *"mexicana"* or "Chicana."

As a culture, we call ourselves Spanish when referring to ourselves as a linguistic group and when copping out. It is then that we 38

---

[9]Gershen Kaufman, *Shame: the Power of Caring* (Cambridge: Schenkman Books, 1980), p. 68.

forget our predominant Indian genes. We are 70–80% Indian.[10] We call ourselves Hispanic[11] or Spanish-American or Latin American or Latin when linking ourselves to other Spanish-speaking peoples of the Western hemisphere and when copping out. We call ourselves Mexican-American[12] to signify we are neither Mexican nor American, but more the noun "American" than the adjective "Mexican" (and when copping out).

Chicanos and other people of color suffer economically for not ac- 39
culturating. This voluntary (yet forced) alienation makes for psychological conflict, a kind of dual identity—we don't identify with the Anglo-American cultural values and we don't totally identify with the Mexican cultural values. We are a synergy of two cultures with various degrees of Mexicanness or Angloness. I have so internalized the borderland conflict that sometimes I feel like one cancels out the other and we are zero, nothing, no one. *A veces no soy nada ni nadie. Pero hasta cuando no lo soy, lo soy.*

When not copping out, when we know we are more than nothing, 40
we call ourselves Mexican, referring to race and ancestry; *mestizo* when affirming both our Indian and Spanish (but we hardly ever own our Black) ancestry; Chicano when referring to a politically aware people born and/or raised in the U.S.; *Raza* when referring to Chicanos; *tejanos* when we are Chicanos from Texas.

Chicanos did not know we were a people until 1965 when Cesar 41
Chavez and the farmworkers united and *I Am Joaquín* was published and *La Raza Unida* party was formed in Texas. With that recognition, we became a distinct people. Something momentous happened to the Chicano soul—we became aware of our reality and acquired a name and a language (Chicano Spanish) that reflected that reality. Now that we had a name, some of the fragmented pieces began to fall together—who we were, what we were, how we had evolved. We began to get glimpses of what we might eventually become.

Yet the struggle of identities continues, the struggle of borders is 42
our reality still. One day the inner struggle will cease and a true integration take place. In the meantime, *tenémos que hacer la lucha. ¿Quién está protegiendo los ranchos de mi gente? ¿Quién está tratando de cerrar la fisura entre la india y el blanco en nuestra sangre? El Chicano, si, el Chicano que anda como un ladrón en su propia casa.*

---

[10]Hernandéz-Chávez, *El Lenguaje de los Chicanos,* pp. 88–90.

[11]"Hispanic" is derived from *Hispanis* (*España,* a name given to the Iberian Peninsula in ancient times when it was a part of the Roman Empire) and is a term designated by the U.S. government to make it easier to handle us on paper.

[12]The Treaty of Guadalupe Hidalgo created the Mexican-American in 1848.

Los Chicanos, how patient we seem, how very patient. There is the 43
quiet of the Indian about us.[13] We know how to survive. When other
races have given up their tongue, we've kept ours. We know what it is
to live under the hammer blow of the dominant *norteamericano* culture.
But more than we count the blows, we count the days the weeks the
years the centuries the eons until the white laws and commerce and
customs will rot in the deserts they've created, lie bleached. *Humildes*
yet proud, *quietos* yet wild, *nosotros los mexicanos-Chicanos* will walk by
the crumbling ashes as we go about our business. Stubborn, persevering, impenetrable as stone, yet possessing a malleability that renders
us unbreakable, we, the *mestizas* and *mestizos,* will remain.

QUESTIONS

1.   What does the "wild tongue" of the title refer to, besides the literal
tongue in the opening dentist's-chair anecdote? What forces does
Anzaldúa suggest are trying to "tame" it, or "train it to be quiet"?

2.   Anzaldúa writes that "ethnic identity is twin skin to linguistic
identity" (paragraph 27). On the basis of her essay, how would you
describe her ethnic and linguistic identities? Are your own cultural
identities easier or more difficult to pin down than Anzaldúa's?

3.   If you don't read Spanish, how many of the untranslated passages
in Spanish (and Chicano Spanish, etc.) can you understand from the
context in which they're used? Why do you think Anzaldúa decided to
mix languages in her essay, and what is the effect for you?

---

[13]Anglos, in order to alleviate their guilt for dispossessing the Chicano, stressed the Spanish
part of us and perpetrated the myth of the Spanish Southwest. We have accepted the fiction that we
are Hispanic, that is Spanish, in order to accommodate ourselves to the dominant culture and its
abhorrence of Indians. Hernandéz-Chávez, pp. 88–91.

The English Lesson

NICHOLASA MOHR

"Remember our assignment for today everybody! I'm so confident that you will all do exceptionally well!" Mrs. Susan Hamma smiled enthusiastically at her students. "Everyone is to get up and make a brief statement as to why he or she is taking this course in Basic English. You must state your name, where you originally came from, how long you have been here, and . . . uh . . . a little something about yourself, if you wish. Keep it brief, not too long; remember, there are twenty-eight of us. We have a full class, and everyone must have a chance." Mrs. Hamma waved a forefinger at her students. "This is, after all, a democracy, and we have a democratic class; fairness for all!" 1

Lali grinned and looked at William, who sat directly next to her. He winked and rolled his eyes toward Mrs. Hamma. This was the third class they had attended together. It had not been easy to persuade Rudi that Lali should learn better English. 2

"Why is it necessary, eh?" Rudi had protested. "She works here in the store with me. She don't have to talk to nobody. Besides, everybody that comes in speaks Spanish—practically everybody, anyway." 3

But once William had put the idea to Lali and explained how much easier things would be for her, she kept insisting until Rudi finally agreed. "Go on, you're both driving me nuts. But it can't interfere with business or work—I'm warning you!" 4

Adult Education offered Basic English, Tuesday evenings from 6:30 to 8:00, at a local public school. Night customers did not usually come into Rudi's Luncheonette until after eight. William and Lali promised that they would leave everything prepared and make up for any inconvenience by working harder and longer than usual, if necessary. 5

The class admitted twenty-eight students, and because there were only twenty-seven registered, Lali was allowed to take the course even after missing the first two classes. William had assured Mrs. Hamma 6

Nicholasa Mohr is a writer from New York City. Her fiction for both young readers and adults often features Puerto Rican characters in urban settings, like the El Barrio section of New York where Mohr was born. She won a 1981 American Book Award from the Before Columbus Foundation for *Felita* (1979); her other books include *El Bronx Remembered: A Novella and Stories* (2nd edition, 1986), *Rituals of Survival: A Woman's Portfolio* (1985), and *Nilda: A Novel* (2nd edition, 1986). This short story appeared in her collection *In Nueva York,* first published in 1977 and reissued in 1986.

that he would help Lali catch up; she was glad to have another student to make up the full registration.

Most of the students were Spanish-speaking. The majority were   7
American citizens—Puerto Ricans who had migrated to New York and spoke very little English. The rest were immigrants admitted to the United States as legal aliens. There were several Chinese, two Dominicans, one Sicilian, and one Pole.

Every Tuesday Mrs. Hamma traveled to the Lower East Side from   8
Bayside, Queens, where she lived and was employed as a history teacher in the local junior high school. She was convinced that this small group of people desperately needed her services. Mrs. Hamma reiterated her feelings frequently to just about anyone who would listen. "Why, if these people can make it to class after working all day at those miserable, dreary, uninteresting, and often revolting jobs, well, the least I can do is be there to serve them, making every lesson count toward improving their conditions! My grandparents came here from Germany as poor immigrants, working their way up. I'm not one to forget a thing like that!"

By the time class started most of the students were quite tired.   9
And after the lesson was over, many had to go on to part-time jobs, some even without time for supper. As a result there was always sluggishness and yawning among the students. This never discouraged Mrs. Hamma, whose drive and enthusiasm not only amused the class but often kept everyone awake.

"Now this is the moment we have all been preparing for." Mrs.   10
Hamma stood up, nodded, and blinked knowingly at her students. "Five lessons, I think, are enough to prepare us for our oral statements. You may read from prepared notes, as I said before, but please try not to read every word. We want to hear you speak; conversation is what we're after. When someone asks you about yourself, you cannot take a piece of paper and start reading the answers, now can you? That would be foolish. So . . ."

Standing in front of her desk, she put her hands on her hips and   11
spread her feet, giving the impression that she was going to demonstrate calisthenics.

"Shall we begin?"   12

Mrs. Hamma was a very tall, angular woman with large extremi-   13
ties. She was the tallest person in the room. Her eyes roamed from student to student until they met William's.

"Mr. Colón, will you please begin?"   14

Nervously William looked around him, hesitating.   15

"Come on now, we must get the ball rolling. All right now . . . did   16
you hear what I said? Listen, 'getting the ball rolling' means getting

started. Getting things going, such as—" Mrs. Hamma swiftly lifted her right hand over her head, making a fist, then swung her arm around like a pitcher and, with an underhand curve, forcefully threw an imaginary ball out at her students. Trying to maintain her balance, Mrs. Hamma hopped from one leg to the other. Startled, the students looked at one another. In spite of their efforts to restrain themselves, several people in back began to giggle. Lali and William looked away, avoiding each other's eyes and trying not to laugh out loud. With assured countenance, Mrs. Hamma continued.

"An idiom!" she exclaimed, pleased. "You have just seen me 17 demonstrate the meaning of an idiom. Now I want everyone to jot down this information in his notebook." Going to the blackboard, Mrs. Hamma explained, "It's something which literally says one thing, but actually means another. Idiom . . . idiomatic." Quickly and obediently, everyone began to copy what she wrote. "Has everyone got it? OK, let's GET THE BALL ROLLING, Mr. Colón!"

Uneasily William stood up; he was almost the same height stand- 18 ing as sitting. When speaking to others, especially in a new situation, he always preferred to sit alongside those listening; it gave him a sense of equality with other people. He looked around and cleared his throat; at least everyone else was sitting. Taking a deep breath, William felt better.

"My name is William Horacio Colón," he read from a prepared 19 statement. "I have been here in New York City for five months. I coming from Puerto Rico. My town is located in the mountains in the central part of the island. The name of my town is Aibonito, which means in Spanish 'oh how pretty.' It is name like this because when the Spaniards first seen that place they was very impressed with the beauty of the section and—"

"Make it brief, Mr. Colón," Mrs. Hamma interrupted, "there are 20 others, you know."

William looked at her, unable to continue. 21

"Go on, go on, Mr. Colón, please!" 22

"I am working here now, living with my mother and family in 23 Lower East Side of New York City," William spoke rapidly. "I study Basic English por que . . . because my ambition is to learn to speak and read English very good. To get a better job. Y—y también, to help my mother y familia." He shrugged. "Y do better, that's all."

"That's all? Why, that's wonderful! Wonderful! Didn't he do well, 24 class?" Mrs. Hamma bowed slightly toward William and applauded him. The students watched her and slowly each one began to imitate her. Pleased, Mrs. Hamma looked around her; all together they gave William a healthy round of applause.

Next, Mrs. Hamma turned to a Chinese man seated at the other 25 side of the room.

"Mr. Fong, you may go next." 26

Mr. Fong stood up; he was a man in his late thirties, of medium 27 height and slight build. Cautiously he looked at Mrs. Hamma, and waited.

"Go on, Mr. Fong. Get the ball rolling, remember?" 28

"All right. Get a ball rolling . . . is idiot!" Mr. Fong smiled. 29

"No, Mr. Fong, idio*mmmmmm!*" Mrs. Hamma hummed her *m*'s, 30 shaking her head. "Not an—It's idiomatic!"

"What I said!" Mr. Fong responded with self-assurance, looking 31 directly at Mrs. Hamma. "Get a ball rolling, idiomit."

"Never mind." She cleared her throat. "Just go on." 32

"I said OK?" Mr. Fong waited for an answer. 33

"Go on, please." 34

Mr. Fong sighed, "My name is Joseph Fong. I been here in this 35 country United States New York City for most one year." He too read from a prepared statement. "I come from Hong Kong but original born in city of Canton, China. I working delivery food business and live with my brother and his family in Chinatown. I taking the course in Basic English to speak good and improve my position better in this country. Also to be eligible to become American citizen."

Mrs. Hamma selected each student who was to speak from a dif- 36 ferent part of the room, rather than in the more conventional orderly fashion of row by row, or front to back, or even alphabetical order. This way, she reasoned, no one will know who's next; it will be more spontaneous. Mrs. Hamma enjoyed catching the uncertain looks on the faces of her students. A feeling of control over the situation gave her a pleasing thrill, and she made the most of these moments by look-ing at several people more than once before making her final choice.

There were more men than women, and Mrs. Hamma called two 37 or three men for each woman. It was her way of maintaining a balance. To her distress, most read from prepared notes, despite her efforts to discourage this. She would interrupt them when she felt they went on too long, then praise them when they finished. Each statement was fol-lowed by applause from everyone.

All had similar statements. They had migrated here in search of a 38 better future, were living with relatives, and worked as unskilled la-borers. With the exception of Lali, who was childless, every woman gave the ages and sex of her children; most men referred only to their "family." And, among the legal aliens, there was only one who did not want to become an American citizen, Diego Torres, a young man from the Dominican Republic, and he gave his reasons.

"... and to improve my economic situation." Diego Torres hesi-   39
tated, looking around the room. "But is one thing I no want, and is to
become American citizen"—he pointed to an older man with a dark
complexion, seated a few seats away—"like my fellow countryman
over there!" The man shook his head disapprovingly at Diego Torres,
trying to hide his annoyance. "I no give up my country, Santo
Domingo, for nothing," he went on, "nothing in the whole world. OK,
man? I come here, pero I cannot help. I got no work at home. There, is
political. The United States control most the industry which is sugar
and tourismo. Y—you have to know somebody. I tell you, is political
to get a job, man! You don't know nobody and you no work, eh? So I
come here from necessity, pero this no my country—"

"Mr. Torres," Mrs. Hamma interrupted, "we must be brief, please,   40
there are—"

"I no finish lady!" he snapped. "You wait a minute when I finish!"   41

There was complete silence as Diego Torres glared at Susan   42
Hamma. No one had ever spoken to her like that, and her confusion
was greater than her embarrassment. Without speaking, she lowered
her eyes and nodded.

"OK, I prefer live feeling happy in my country, man. Even I don't   43
got too much. I live simple but in my own country I be contento. Pero
this is no possible in the situation of Santo Domingo now. Someday we
gonna run our own country and be jobs for everybody. My reasons to
be here is to make money, man, and go back home buy my house and
property. I no be American citizen, no way. I'm Dominican and proud!
That's it. That's all I got to say." Abruptly, Diego Torres sat down.

"All right." Mrs. Hamma had composed herself. "Very good; you   44
can come here and state your views. That is what America is all about!
We may not agree with you, but we defend your right to an opinion.
And as long as you are in this classroom, Mr. Torres, you are in
America. Now, everyone, let us give Mr. Torres the same courtesy as
everyone else in this class." Mrs. Hamma applauded with a polite light
clap, then turned to find the next speaker.

"Bullshit," whispered Diego Torres.   45

Practically everyone had spoken. Lali and the two European im-   46
migrants were the only ones left. Mrs. Hamma called upon Lali.

"My name is Rogelia Dolores Padillo. I come from Canovanas   47
in Puerto Rico. Is a small village in the mountains near El Yunque Rain
Forest. My family is still living there. I marry and live here with my
husband working in his business of restaurant. Call Rudi's
Luncheonette. I been here New York City Lower East Side since
I marry, which is now about one year. I study Basic English to improve my vocabulario and learn more about here. This way I help my

husband in his business and I do more also for myself, including to be able to read better in English. Thank you."

Aldo Fabrizi, the Sicilian, spoke next. He was a very short man, 48 barely five feet tall. Usually he was self-conscious about his height, but William's presence relieved him of these feelings. Looking at William, he thought being short was no big thing; he was, after all, normal. He told the class that he was originally from Palermo, the capital of Sicily, and had gone to Milano, in the north of Italy, looking for work. After three years in Milano, he immigrated here six months ago and now lived with his sister. He had a good steady job, he said, working in a copper wire factory with his brother-in-law in Brooklyn. Aldo Fabrizi wanted to become an American citizen and spoke passionately about it, without reading from his notes.

"I be proud to be American citizen. I no come here find work live 49 good and no have responsibility or no be grateful." He turned and looked threateningly at Diego Torres. "Hey? I tell you all one thing, I got my nephew right now fighting in Vietnam for this country!" Diego Torres stretched his hands over his head, yawning, folded his hands, and lowered his eyelids. "I wish I could be citizen to fight for this country. My whole family is citizens—we all Americans and we love America!" His voice was quite loud. "That's how I feel."

"Very good," Mrs. Hamma called, distracting Aldo Fabrizi. "That 50 was well stated. I'm sure you will not only become a citizen, but you will also be a credit to this country."

The last person to be called on was the Pole. He was always neatly 51 dressed in a business suit, with a shirt and tie, and carried a briefcase. His manner was reserved but friendly.

"Good evening fellow students and Madame Teacher." He nodded 52 politely to Mrs. Hamma. "My name is Stephan Paczkowski. I am originally from Poland about four months ago. My background is I was born in capital city of Poland, Warsaw. Being educated in capital and also graduating from the University with degree of professor of music with specialty in the history of music."

Stephan Paczkowski read from his notes carefully, articulating 53 every word. "I was given appointment of professor of history of music at University of Krakow. I work there for ten years until about year and half ago. At this time the political situation in Poland was so that all Jewish people were requested by the government to leave Poland. My wife who also is being a professor of economics at University of Krakow is of Jewish parents. My wife was told she could not remain in position at University or remain over there. We made arrangements for my wife and daughter who is seven years of age and myself to come here with my wife's cousin who is to be helping us.

"Since four months I am working in large hospital as position of 54
porter in maintenance department. The thing of it is, I wish to take
Basic English to improve my knowledge of English language, and be
able to return to my position of professor of history of music. Finally, I
wish to become a citizen of United States. That is my reasons. I thank
you all."

After Stephan Paczkowski sat down, there was a long awkward si- 55
lence and everyone turned to look at Mrs. Hamma. Even after the confrontation with Diego Torres, she had applauded without hesitation.
Now she seemed unable to move.

"Well," she said, almost breathless, "that's admirable! I'm sure, sir, 56
that you will do very well . . . a person of your . . . like yourself, I mean
. . . a professor, after all, it's really just admirable." Everyone was listening intently to what she said. "That was well done, class. Now, we
have to get to next week's assignment." Mrs. Hamma realized that no
one had applauded Stephan Paczkowski. With a slightly pained expression, she began to applaud. "Mustn't forget Mr. Paczkowski;
everybody here must be treated equally. This is America!" The class
joined her in a round of applause.

As Mrs. Hamma began to write the next week's assignment on the 57
board, some students looked anxiously at their watches and others
asked about the time. Then they all quickly copied the information into
their notebooks. It was almost eight o'clock. Those who had to get to
second jobs did not want to be late; some even hoped to have time for
a bite to eat first. Others were just tired and wanted to get home.

Lali looked at William, sighing impatiently. They both hoped Mrs. 58
Hamma would finish quickly. There would be hell to pay with Rudi if
the night customers were already at the luncheonette.

"There, that's next week's work, which is very important, by the 59
way. We will be looking at the history of New York City and the different ethnic groups that lived here as far back as the Dutch. I can't tell
you how proud I am of the way you all spoke. All of you—I have no
favorites, you know."

Mrs. Hamma was interrupted by the long, loud buzzing sound, 60
bringing the lesson to an end. Quickly everyone began to exit.

"Good night, see you all next Tuesday!" Mrs. Hamma called out. 61
"By the way, if any of you here wants extra help, I have a few minutes
this evening." Several people bolted past her, excusing themselves. In
less than thirty seconds, Mrs. Hamma was standing in an empty classroom.

William and Lali hurried along, struggling against the cold, sharp 62
March wind that whipped across Houston Street, stinging their faces
and making their eyes tear.

In a few minutes they would be at Rudi's. So far, they had not 63
been late once.

"You read very well—better than anybody in class. I told you 64
there was nothing to worry about. You caught up in no time."

"Go on. I was so nervous, honestly! But, I'm glad she left me for 65
one of the last. If I had to go first, like you, I don't think I could open
my mouth. You were so calm. You started the thing off very well."

"You go on now, I was nervous myself!" He laughed, pleased. 66

"Mira, Chiquitín," Lali giggled, "I didn't know your name was 67
Horacio. William Horacio. Ave María, so imposing!"

"That's right, because you see, my mother was expecting a 68
valiant warrior! Instead, well"—he threw up his hands—"no one
warned me either. And what a name for a Chiquitín like me."

Lali smiled, saying nothing. At first she had been very aware of 69
William's dwarfishness. Now it no longer mattered. It was only when
she saw others reacting to him for the first time that she was once
more momentarily struck with William's physical difference.

"We should really try to speak in English, Lali. It would be good 70
practice for us."

"Dios mío . . . I feel so foolish, and my accent is terrible!" 71

"But look, we all have to start some place. Besides, what about 72
the Americanos? When they speak Spanish, they sound pretty awful,
but we accept it. You know I'm right. And that's how people get
ahead, by not being afraid to try."

They walked in silence for a few moments. Since William had 73
begun to work at Rudi's, Lali's life had become less lonely. Lali was
shy by nature; making friends was difficult for her. She had grown
up in the sheltered environment of a large family living in a tiny
mountain village. She was considered quite plain. Until Rudi had
asked her parents for permission to court her, she had only gone out
with two local boys. She had accepted his marriage proposal expecting great changes in her life. But the age difference between her
and Rudi, being in a strange country without friends or relatives,
and the long hours of work at the luncheonette confined Lali to a
way of life she could not have imagined. Every evening she found
herself waiting for William to come in to work, looking forward to
his presence.

Lali glanced over at him as they started across the wide busy 74
street. His grip on her elbow was firm but gentle as he led her to the
sidewalk.

"There you are, Miss Lali, please to watch your step!" he spoke in 75
English.

His thick golden-blond hair was slightly mussed and fell softly, 76
partially covering his forehead. His wide smile, white teeth, and large

shoulders made him appear quite handsome. Lali found herself staring at William. At that moment she wished he could be just like everybody else.

"Lali?" William asked, confused by her silent stare. "Is something 77 wrong?"

"No." Quickly Lali turned her face. She felt herself blushing. "I . . . 78 I was just thinking how to answer in English, that's all."

"But that's it . . . don't think! What I mean is, don't go worrying 79 about what to say. Just talk natural. Get used to simple phrases and the rest will come, you'll see."

"All right," Lali said, glad the strange feeling of involvement had 80 passed, and William had taken no notice of it. "It's an interesting class, don't you think so? I mean—like that man, the professor. Bendito! Imagine, they had to leave because they were Jewish. What a terrible thing!"

"I don't believe he's Jewish; it's his wife who is Jewish. She was a 81 professor too. But I guess they don't wanna be separated . . . and they have a child."

"Tsk, tsk, los pobres! But, can you imagine, then? A professor from 82 a university doing the job of a porter? My goodness!" Lali sighed. "I never heard of such a thing!"

"But you gotta remember, it's like Mrs. Hamma said, this is 83 America, right? So . . . everybody got a chance to clean toilets! Equality, didn't she say that?"

They both laughed loudly, stepping up their pace until they 84 reached Rudi's Luncheonette.

The small luncheonette was almost empty. One customer sat at the 85 counter.

"Just in time," Rudi called out. "Let's get going. People gonna 86 be coming in hungry any minute. I was beginning to worry about you two!"

William ran in the back to change into his workshirt.   87

Lali slipped into her uniform and soon was busy at the grill.   88

"Well, did you learn anything tonight?" Rudi asked her.   89

"Yes."   90

"What?"   91

"I don't know," she answered, without interrupting her work. 92 "We just talked a little bit in English."

"A little bit in English—about what?"   93

Lali busied herself, ignoring him. Rudi waited, then tried once 94 more.

"You remember what you talked about?" He watched her as she 95 moved, working quickly, not looking in his direction.

"No." Her response was barely audible.   96

Lately Rudi had begun to reflect on his decision to marry such a 97
young woman. Especially a country girl like Lali, who was shy and
timid. He had never had children with his first wife and wondered if
he lacked the patience needed for the young. They had little in common and certainly seldom spoke about anything but the business.
Certainly he could not fault her for being lazy; she was always working without being asked. People would accuse him in jest of over-
working his young wife. He assured them there was no need, because
she had the endurance of a country mule. After almost one year of marriage, he felt he hardly knew Lali or what he might do to please her.

William began to stack clean glasses behind the counter. 98

"Chiquitín! How about you and Lali having something to eat? We 99
gotta few minutes yet. There's some fresh rice pudding."

"Later . . . I'll have mine a little later, thanks." 100

"Ask her if she wants some," Rudi whispered, gesturing toward 101
Lali.

William moved close to Lali and spoke softly to her. 102

"She said no." William continued his work. 103

"Listen, Chiquitín, I already spoke to Raquel Martinez who lives 104
next door. You know, she's got all them kids? In case you people are
late, she can cover for you and Lali. She said it was OK."

"Thanks, Rudi, I appreciate it. But we'll get back on time." 105

"She's good, you know. She helps me out during the day when- 106
ever I need extra help. Off the books, I give her a few bucks. But, mira,
I cannot pay you and Raquel both. So if she comes in, you don't get
paid. You know that then, OK?"

"Of course. Thanks, Rudi." 107

"Sure, well, it's a good thing after all. You and Lali improving 108
yourselves. Not that she really needs it, you know. I provide for her.
As I said, she's my wife, so she don't gotta worry. If she wants something, I'll buy it for her. I made it clear she didn't have to bother with
none of that, but"—Rudi shrugged—"if that's what she wants, I'm not
one to interfere."

The door opened. Several men walked in. 109

"Here they come, kids!" 110

Orders were taken and quickly filled. Customers came and went 111
steadily until about eleven o'clock, when Rudi announced that it was
closing time.

The weeks passed, then the months, and this evening, William and 112
Lali sat with the other students listening to Mrs. Hamma as she taught
the last lesson of the Basic English course.

"It's been fifteen long hard weeks for all of you. And I want you to 113
know how proud I am of each and every one here."

William glanced at Lali; he knew she was upset. He felt it too, 114
wishing that this was not the end of the course. It was the only time he
and Lali had free to themselves together. Tuesday had become their
evening.

Lali had been especially irritable that week, dreading this last ses- 115
sion. For her, Tuesday meant leaving the world of Rudi, the luncheonette, that street, everything that she felt imprisoned her. She was
accomplishing something all by herself, and without the help of the
man she was dependent upon.

Mrs. Hamma finally felt that she had spent enough time assuring 116
her students of her sincere appreciation.

"I hope some of you will stay and have a cup of coffee or tea, and 117
cookies. There's plenty over there." She pointed to a side table where
a large electric coffeepot filled with hot water was steaming. The table
was set for instant coffee and tea, complete with several boxes of assorted cookies. "I do this every semester for my classes. I think it's nice
to have a little informal chat with one another; perhaps discuss our
plans for the future and so on. But it must be in English! Especially
those of you who are Spanish-speaking. Just because you outnumber
the rest of us, don't you think you can get away with it!" Mrs. Hamma
lifted her forefinger threateningly but smiled. "Now, it's still early, so
there's plenty of time left. Please turn in your books."

Some of the people said good-bye quickly and left, but the major- 118
ity waited, helping themselves to coffee or tea and cookies. Small clusters formed as people began to chat with one another.

Diego Torres and Aldo Fabrizi were engaged in a friendly but 119
heated debate on the merits of citizenship.

"Hey, you come here a minute, please," Aldo Fabrizi called out to 120
William, who was standing with a few people by the table, helping
himself to coffee. William walked over to the two men.

"What's the matter?" 121

"What do you think of your paisano. He don't wanna be citizen. I 122
say—my opinion—he don't appreciate what he got in this country.
This a great country! You the same like him, what do you think?"

"Mira, please tell him we no the same," Diego Torres said with ex- 123
asperation. "You a citizen, pero not me. Este tipo no comprende, man!"

"Listen, you comprendo . . . yo capito! I know what you say. He be 124
born in Puerto Rico. But you see, we got the same thing. I be born in
Sicily—that is another part of the country, separate. But I still Italiano,
capito?"

"Dios mío!" Diego Torres smacked his forehead with an open 125
palm. "Mira"—he turned to William—"explain to him, por favor."

William swallowed a mouthful of cookies. "He's right. Puerto Rico 126
is part of the United States. And Sicily is part of Italy. But not the

Dominican Republic where he been born. There it is not the United States. I was born a citizen, do you see?"

"Sure!" Aldo Fabrizi nodded. "Capito. Hey, but you still no can vote, right?"   127

"Sure I can vote; I got all the rights. I am a citizen, just like any-body else," William assured him.   128

"You some lucky guy then. You got it made! You don't gotta worry like the rest of—"   129

"Bullshit," Diego Torres interrupted. "Why he got it made, man? He force to leave his country. Pendejo, you no capito nothing, man . . ."   130

As the two men continued to argue, William waited for the right moment to slip away and join Lali.   131

She was with some of the women, who were discussing how sincere and devoted Mrs. Hamma was.   132

"She's hardworking . . ."   133

"And she's good people . . ." an older woman agreed.   134

Mr. Fong joined them, and they spoke about the weather and how nice and warm the days were.   135

Slowly people began to leave, shaking hands with their fellow students and Mrs. Hamma, wishing each other luck.   136

Mrs. Hamma had been hoping to speak to Stephan Paczkowski privately this evening, but he was always with a group. Now he offered his hand.   137

"I thank you very much for your good teaching. It was a fine semester."   138

"Oh, do you think so? Oh, I'm so glad to hear you say that. You don't know how much it means. Especially coming from a person of your caliber. I am confident, yes, indeed, that you will soon be back to your profession, which, after all, is your true calling. If there is anything I can do, please . . ."   139

"Thank you, miss. This time I am registering in Hunter College, which is in Manhattan on Sixty-eighth Street in Lexington Avenue, with a course of English Literature for beginners." After a slight bow, he left.   140

"Good-bye." Mrs. Hamma sighed after him.   141

Lali, William, and several of the women picked up the paper cups and napkins and tossed them into the trash basket.   142

"Thank you so much, that's just fine. Luis the porter will do the rest. He takes care of these things. He's a lovely person and very helpful. Thank you."   143

William shook hands with Mrs. Hamma, then waited for Lali to say good-bye. They were the last ones to leave.   144

"Both of you have been such good students. What are your plans? I hope you will continue with your English."   145

"Next term we're taking another course," Lali said, looking at   146
William.

"Yes," William responded, "it's more advance. Over at the   147
Washington Irving High School around Fourteenth Street."   148

"Wonderful." Mrs. Hamma hesitated. "May I ask you a question   149
before you leave? It's only that I'm a little curious about something."

"Sure, of course." They both nodded.   150

"Are you two related? I mean, you are always together and yet
have different last names, so I was just . . . wondering."

"Oh, we are just friends," Lali answered, blushing.   151

"I work over in the luncheonette at night, part-time."   152

"Of course." Mrs. Hamma looked at Lali. "Mrs. Padillo, your hus-   153
band's place of business. My, that's wonderful, just wonderful! You
are all just so ambitious. Very good . . ."

They exchanged farewells.   154

Outside, the warm June night was sprinkled with the sweetness of   155
the new buds sprouting on the scrawny trees and hedges planted
along the sidewalks and in the housing project grounds. A brisk
breeze swept over the East River on to Houston Street, providing a
freshness in the air.

This time they were early, and Lali and William strolled at a re-   156
laxed pace.

"Well," Lali shrugged, "that's that. It's over!"   157

"Only for a couple of months. In September we'll be taking a more   158
advanced course at the high school."

"I'll probably forget everything I learned by then."   159

"Come on, Lali, the summer will be over before you know it. Just   160
you wait and see. Besides, we can practice so we don't forget what
Mrs. Hamma taught us."

"Sure, what do you like to speak about?" Lali said in English.   161

William smiled, and clasping his hands, said, "I would like to say   162
to you how wonderful you are, and how you gonna have the most fabulous future . . . after all, you so ambitious!"

When she realized he sounded just like Mrs. Hamma, Lali began   163
to laugh.

"Are you"—Lali tried to keep from giggling, tried to pretend to   164
speak in earnest—"sure there is some hope for me?"

"Oh, heavens, yes! You have shown such ability this"—William   165
was beginning to lose control, laughing loudly—"semester!"

"But I want"—Lali was holding her sides with laughter—"some   166
guarantee of this. I got to know."

"Please, Miss Lali." William was laughing so hard tears were com-   167
ing to his eyes. "After . . . after all, you now a member in good standing . . . of the promised future!"

William and Lali broke into uncontrollable laughter, swaying and limping, oblivious to the scene they created for the people who stared and pointed at them as they continued on their way to Rudi's. 168

QUESTIONS

1. Besides being their English teacher, what does Mrs. Hamma seem to represent to Lali and William? Why do you think they break out in "uncontrollable laughter" while imitating her at the end of the story?

2. How would you compare Lali's relationships with William and Rudi? How supportive is Rudi of Lali's English lessons?

3. If you have taken a Basic English or English as a Second Language course, compare your experiences with those of Mrs. Hamma's students. Which character do you most identify with, and why?

THINKING ABOUT LANGUAGE AND BICULTURAL IDENTITY

1. How do you think Burciaga's attitude towards "wachuseh" compares with that of Cisneros's narrator towards the name "Esperanza"? Whether or not you're bilingual, you should be able to recall a word or name that meant a great deal to you when you were a child. Try exploring that meaning in a short essay or story like Burciaga's or Cisneros's.

2. Miller relates the experience of Andreas as an "ideal, though hardly typical . . . example of bilingual advantages." How would you compare the experiences related by Ortiz and Cisneros to this ideal? Rodriguez and Anzaldúa describe their learning of English and Spanish in some detail; how do you think their experiences measure up to Miller's ideal?

3. How might Anzaldúa respond to Rodriguez's argument against bilingual education and for "the value and necessity of assimilation" (paragraph 39)? Would she accuse him of what she calls "linguistic terrorism" (paragraph 22)? If Anzaldúa suggested that Rodriguez's "wild tongue" had been "tamed," how might Rodriguez reply? Which argument do you find more persuasive?

4. Whose views about Chicano language would Burciaga seem to agree with more, Rodriguez's or Anzaldúa's? Why?

5. Based on his distinction between "public language" and "private language" and criteria such as those he suggests in paragraphs 26 to 29, how do you think Rodriguez would evaluate the teaching performance of Mrs. Hamma in "The English Lesson"?

6. Rodriguez, Anzaldúa, and Mohr describe experiences from three different educational contexts: private parochial school, the public school system, and "Adult Education Basic English." How do you think these different contexts affect each writer's portrayal of the dominant Anglo culture and of his or her bicultural dilemma?

Exploring Additional Sources

7. Issues relevant to this chapter are also raised in "The Language of Discretion" by Amy Tan (page 64), "From Outside, In" by Barbara Mellix (page 89), "Nobody Mean More to Me than You and the Future Life of Willie Jordan" by June Jordan (page 99), "The Girl Who Wouldn't Sing" by Kit Yuen Quan (page 118), "It's My Country Too"

by Juan Cadena (page 199), and "The Trip Back" by Robert Olen Butler (page 214). Analyze an aspect of bicultural identity raised in one or two of these selections in conjunction with the essays in this chapter by Rodriguez and/or Anzaldúa.

8. During the 1980s and 1990s, at least eleven U.S. states have adopted some version of a law establishing English as an official language. Investigate the debate surrounding one of these laws and evaluate how well it has functioned in practice.

9. Rodriguez suggests that bilingual education would have delayed his learning of English. Find the most recent studies you can of bilingual education efforts in the United States and evaluate Rodriguez's speculative claim, narrowing your research to a particular group such as Mexican Americans or Vietnamese Americans. Which programs and approaches have addressed this group's educational needs most effectively?

10. Research and write about a basic literacy or English as a second language program in your own community or school. Interview teachers, administrators, and students in the program, and ask them to suggest books and journal articles for you to read. You might evaluate the program's basis in current theory or research, try to measure its success, and/or recommend specific changes in the program that you address to the department or committee in charge.

PART TWO

ENCOUNTERING DIVERSITY AT HOME

We tend to think of diversity as referring primarily to racial or immigration issues, and indeed the racial diversity of North America is increasing rapidly as many people come here from all over the world. But from a larger historical perspective, this diversity is more the rule than the exception. The very first "Americans" were from Asia, Mongol peoples who journeyed across the Bering Strait in present-day Alaska and migrated south. These original Americans developed such widely diverse cultures and civilizations that some experts estimate they spoke over 2000 distinct languages when Christopher Columbus arrived in 1492.

The European conquest that followed Columbus all but eliminated this range of native cultures, then provided new sources of ethnic diversity by bringing to the Americas large groups of English, Scottish, Irish, and German immigrants as well as West Africans imported as slaves. Alexis de Tocqueville, Henry David Thoreau, and Ishmael Reed offer, in Chapter 5, widely divergent views of the Puritans who settled New England in the seventeenth century. In the eighteenth century, the future United States had a largely rural population of English Protestants, Black slaves, and native Indians. As the Indians were decimated by war and disease, according to Kevin Mullen in "The Irish

179

Cop," Europeans turned nineteenth-century America into "a long, violent struggle between successive waves of immigrants who were fighting for their livelihood." De Tocqueville, by contrast, observed in his travels that "Americans become assimilated. . . . They all get closer to one type"—the "melting pot" image coined by Hector St. John de Crecevoeur, another Frenchman, during the previous century.

As mentioned in the introduction to Part One, the latest waves of U.S. immigrants are coming primarily from Latin America and—in what might be seen as a case of history repeating itself—Asia. Like their European predecessors, many of these new Americans are adapting rapidly. Mr. Khanh, the Vietnamese American narrator of Robert Olen Butler's story "The Trip Back," says that he "was no longer comfortable with the old ways. Like the extended family. Like other things, too. The Vietnamese indirectness, for instance. The superstition. I was a good American now. . . ." But Alexandra Tantranon-Saur suggests, in Chapter 6, that European Americans and Asian/Pacific people have much to learn about how to respect each other's cultures and how to communicate through "a layer of seemingly innocuous assumptions."

Some people are uncomfortable with what they see as a contemporary overemphasis, in schools and popular media, on cultural background. Arthur Schlesinger, Jr., calls this trend "the cult of ethnicity," which he says threatens the "historic American goals of assimilation" and unity. The whole notion of dividing people by "race" or "ethnicity," like the issue of immigration, is greatly complicated by politics and values. According to Raymond Williams, the word "ethnic" was used a century ago to mean "heathen" or "pagan," and today people still use "ethnicity" to refer to "*native* and *subordinate* tradition[s]." These connotations may help explain why Barbara Ehrenreich, a white American of Scottish-Irish-English background, answers "None" to her friend's question, "What is your ethnic background?" Ehrenreich goes on to explore a different kind of family cultural tradition, involving skepticism and tolerance, which she identifies with more strongly than the clans and kilts of her Scottish ancestors.

Like Ehrenreich, most people identify closely with their family, just as the majority of Americans can be lumped together as belonging to the "middle class." The selections in Chapter 7 constitute a critical dialogue about middle class or mainstream values in the United States, the proverbial "American Dream." The responses range from Phyllis McGinley's idyllic suburban vision of trimmed-hedge, picket-fence "Spruce Manor" to the urban anarchism of Julia Gilden's self-styled "garbage people," and from Shelby Steele's defense of upwardly-mobile middle-class blacks to James Baldwin's angry warning about white America's indifference to the inner-city ghetto.

"Family values," strongly associated with the American mainstream, have been the subject of much public discourse of the 1990s. President Clinton's attempt to lift the U.S. military ban on gay people, partially enacted in a new policy in 1993, sparked a sometimes rancorous debate about homosexuality. In Chapter 8, gay and lesbian writers such as Edmund White, Jan Clausen, and David Leavitt explore diverse sexuality in significantly greater depth and complexity than you may have encountered previously in considering this subject. "For instance," says White, "there are gay men who prefer the feel of women's bodies to men's, who are even more comfortable sexually with women, but whose emotions crave contact with other men." Jan Clausen rhetorically asks, "Am I some sort of weirdo, or is it just that most people are a lot more complicated than the common wisdom of either gay or straight society encourages us to think?"

Even if we take great pride in our sexual orientation, or in our ethnic or class background, most of us would agree that our complexity as individual human beings cannot be reduced to any simple categories. What are the advantages and disadvantages of identifying ourselves with particular cultural groups, or of using these categories to analyze the experiences of people as groups? You might keep this overriding question in mind as you read the following chapters. If the experiences and ideas explored by these writers raise more questions for you than they answer, they will serve a valuable purpose. Before you read, try giving some thought to your own experiences, attitudes, and values about cultural diversity. You might respond in a journal to questions such as the following, and then discuss your responses with friends, family, or classmates:

Coming to America (Chapter 5). Where did your own ancestors come from? When, where, and how did they arrive in North America? Why did they choose this destination, and why did they leave their previous home?

Ethnicity and Identity (Chapter 6). How do you identify your own ethnicity? What do you call yourself, and why? How important a part of your personal identity is your ethnicity? How does your ethnicity affect your relationships with other people?

Privilege, Poverty, and Mainstream Values (Chapter 7). What values do you associate with the mainstream middle class in North America? To what extent do you share these values? How would you define "the American Dream"? How attainable and desirable is this dream for you?

Sexual Orientation and Diversity (Chapter 8). How does your own family experience compare to the traditional model of the nuclear family? What do you think of when you hear the phrase "family values"?

What is your attitude towards homosexuality? If any of your family members or acquaintances is gay or lesbian, how were you affected by learning this? Have you ever felt ambivalent about your role as a man or woman, or about your own sexuality?

5

COMING TO AMERICA

Turtle Island

GARY SNYDER

Turtle Island—the old/new name for the continent, based on many creation myths of the people who have been living here for millenia, and reapplied by some of them to "North America" in recent years. Also, an idea found world-wide, of the earth, or cosmos even, sustained by a great turtle or serpent-of-eternity.

A name: that we may see ourselves more accurately on this continent of watersheds and life-communities—plant zones, physiographic provinces, culture areas; following natural boundaries. The "U.S.A." and its states and counties are arbitrary and inaccurate impositions on what is really here.

The poems speak of place, and the energy-pathways that sustain life. Each living being is a swirl in the flow, a formal turbulence, a "song." The land, the planet itself, is also a living being—at another pace. Anglos, Black people, Chicanos, and others beached up on these shores all share such views at the deepest levels of their old cultural traditions—African, Asian, or European. Hark again to those roots, to see our ancient solidarity, and then to the work of being together on Turtle Island.

—FROM INTRODUCTORY NOTE TO *TURTLE ISLAND* (POEMS), 1974

The Founding of New England

ALEXIS DE TOCQUEVILLE

The foundation of New England was something new in the world, all the attendant circumstances being both peculiar and original.

In almost all other colonies the first inhabitants have been men without wealth or education, driven from their native land by poverty or misconduct, or else greedy speculators and industrial entrepreneurs. Some colonies cannot claim even such an origin as this; San

183

Domingo was founded by pirates, and in our day the English courts of justice are busy populating Australia.

But all the immigrants who came to settle on the shores of New England belonged to the well-to-do classes at home. From the start, when they came together on American soil, they presented the unusual phenomenon of a society in which there were no great lords, no common people, and, one may almost say, no rich or poor. In proportion to their numbers, these men had a greater share of accomplishments than could be found in any European nation now. All, perhaps without a single exception, had received a fairly advanced education, and several had made a European reputation by their talents and their knowledge. The other colonies had been founded by unattached adventurers, whereas the immigrants to New England brought with them wonderful elements of order and morality; they came with their wives and children to the wilds. But what most distinguished them from all others was the very aim of their enterprise. No necessity forced them to leave their country; they gave up a desirable social position and assured means of livelihood; nor was their object in going to the New World to better their position or accumulate wealth; they tore themselves away from home comforts in obedience to a purely intellectual craving; in facing the inevitable sufferings of exile they hoped for the triumph of *an idea*.

The immigrants, or as they so well named themselves, the Pilgrims, belonged to that English sect whose austere principles had led them to be called Puritans. Puritanism was not just a religious doctrine; in many respects it shared the most absolute democratic and republican theories. That was the element which had aroused its most dangerous adversaries. Persecuted by the home government, and with their strict principles offended by the everyday ways of the society in which they lived, the Puritans sought a land so barbarous and neglected by the world that there at last they might be able to live in their own way and pray to God in freedom.

—FROM *DEMOCRACY IN AMERICA*, 1835

The Yankee and the Red Man

HENRY DAVID THOREAU

Some spring the white man came, built him a house, and made a clearing here, letting in the sun, dried up a farm, piled up the old gray stones in fences, cut down the pines around his dwelling, planted orchard seeds brought from the old country, and persuaded the civil apple tree to blossom next to the wild pine and the juniper, shedding its perfume in the wilderness. Their old stocks still remain. He culled the graceful elm from out the woods and from the riverside, and so refined and smoothed his village plot. And thus he plants a town. He rudely bridged the stream, and drove his team afield into the river meadows, cut the wild grass, and laid bare the homes of beaver, otter, muskrat, and with the whetting of his scythe scared off the deer and bear. He set up a mill, and fields of English grain sprang in the virgin soil. And with his grain he scattered the seeds of the dandelion and the wild trefoil over the meadows, mingling his English flowers with the wild native ones. The bristling burdock, the sweet scented catnip, and the humble yarrow, planted themselves along his woodland road, they too seeking "freedom to worship God" in their way. The white man's mullein soon reigned in Indian corn-fields, and sweet scented English grasses clothed the new soil. Where, then, could the red man set his foot? The honey bee hummed through the Massachusetts woods, and sipped the wild flowers round the Indian's wigwam, perchance unnoticed, when, with prophetic warning, it stung the red child's hand, forerunner of that industrious tribe that was to come and pluck the wild flower of his race up by the root.

The white man comes, pale as the dawn, with a load of thought, with a slumbering intelligence as a fire raked up, knowing well what he knows, not guessing but calculating; strong in community, yielding obedience to authority; of experienced race; of wonderful, wonderful common sense; dull but capable, slow but persevering, severe but just, of little humor but genuine; a laboring man, despising game and sport; building a house that endures, a framed house. He buys the Indian's moccasins and baskets, then buys his hunting grounds, and at length forgets where he is buried, and plows up his bones. And here town records, old, tattered, time-worn, weather-stained chronicles, contain the Indian sachem's mark, perchance an arrow or a beaver, and the few fatal words by which he deeded his hunting grounds away. He comes with a list of ancient Saxon, Norman, and Celtic names, and strews them up and down this river,—Framingham, Sudbury, Bedford, Carlisle, Billerica, Chelmsford—and this is New Angle-land, and these are the new West Saxons, whom the red men call, not Angle-ish or English, but Yengeese, and so at last they are known for Yankees.

—FROM *A WEEK ON THE CONCORD AND MERRIMACK RIVERS*, 1849

Different Drummers

CHARLES KURALT

I love to read about the travels of those who wandered the country before me, de Tocqueville, Mark Twain, John Steinbeck, and all the rest. Each of them caught a little bit of the truth about America and wrote it down. Even the best of them never got it all into one book, because the country is too rich and full of contradictions. Newspaper columnists, on slow days, write columns about "the mood of America." That takes a lot of nerve, I think. The mood of America is infinitely complex and always changing and highly dependent on locale and circumstance. The mood of Tribune, Kansas, depends on whether that black cloud to the west becomes a hailstorm that flattens the wheat crop or passes harmlessly. The mood of Haines, Alaska, depends on whether the lumber mill is hiring. The mood of Altoona rises and falls with the fortunes of the high school football team. The mood of New York City is much affected by heat and rain and the percentage of taxis with their off-duty signs lighted at any given time. You can't get your thumb on America's mood. I never try.

Even the clearest-eyed observers of the country, like Alexis de Tocqueville, got into trouble by overgeneralizing. "As they mingle," de Tocqueville wrote, "the Americans become assimilated. . . . They all get closer to one type." Right there, the great de Tocqueville stubbed his toe. The assimilation never came to pass; the "Melting Pot," so much written about, never succeeded in melting us. Americans are made of some alloy that won't be melted. To this day we retain a dread of conformity.

Henry Thoreau, who never traveled at all (except, as he said, "a good deal in Concord"), composed us a credo in 1854: "If a man does not keep pace with his companions, perhaps it is because he hears a different drummer. Let him step to the music which he hears. . . ."

We admire de Tocqueville, but it was Thoreau we listened to.

—FROM *ON THE ROAD WITH CHARLES KURALT*, 1985

America: The Multinational Society

ISHMAEL REED

*At the annual Lower East Side Jewish Festival yesterday, a Chinese woman
ate a pizza slice in front of Ty Thuan Duc's Vietnamese grocery store. Beside
her a Spanish-speaking family patronized a cart with two signs: "Italian
Ices" and "Kosher by Rabbi Alper." And after the pastrami ran out, everybody ate knishes.*

—NEW YORK TIMES, JUNE 23, 1983

On the day before Memorial Day, 1983, a poet called me to describe   1
a city he had just visited. He said that one section included mosques,
built by the Islamic people who dwelled there. Attending his reading,
he said, were large numbers of Hispanic people, forty thousand of
whom lived in the same city. He was not talking about a fabled city located in some mysterious region of the world. The city he'd visited was
Detroit.

A few months before, as I was leaving Houston, Texas, I heard it   2
announced on the radio that Texas's largest minority was Mexican-
American, and though a foundation recently issued a report critical of
bilingual education, the taped voice used to guide the passengers on
the air trams connecting terminals in Dallas Airport is in both Spanish
and English. If the trend continues, a day will come when it will be difficult to travel through some sections of the country without hearing
commands in both English and Spanish; after all, for some Western
states, Spanish was the first written language and the Spanish style
lives on in the Western way of life.

Shortly after my Texas trip, I sat in an auditorium located on the   3
campus of the University of Wisconsin at Milwaukee as a Yale professor—whose original work on the influence of African cultures upon

---

Ishmael Reed, born in Chattanooga, Tennessee, is a poet, fiction
writer, and essayist. His books include *Poems: New and Collected Poems*
(1988) and the novels *Mumbo Jumbo* (1972, 1978), *The Last Days of
Louisiana Red* (1974), and *Reckless Eyeballing* (1986). In 1976, Reed co-
founded (with Victor Hernandez Cruz) the Before Columbus
Foundation, which promotes the American multicultural literary tradition through avenues such as its annual American Book Awards.
Reed's essays and articles about social and political issues have been
collected in *God Made Alaska for the Indians: Selected Essays* (1982) and
Airing Dirty Laundry (1993) as well as *Writin' Is Fightin': Thirty-Seven
Years of Boxing on Paper* (1988), where this selection appeared.

those of the Americas has led to his ostracism from some monocul-
tural intellectual circles—walked up and down the aisle, like an old-
time Southern evangelist, dancing and drumming the top of the
lectern, illustrating his points before some serious Afro-American intellectuals and artists who cheered and applauded his performance
and his mastery of information. The professor was "white." After his
lecture, he joined a group of Milwaukeeans in a conversation. All of
the participants spoke Yoruban, though only the professor had ever
traveled to Africa.

One of the artists told me that his paintings, which included 4
African and Afro-American mythological symbols and imagery, were
hanging in the local McDonald's restaurant. The next day I went to
McDonald's and snapped pictures of smiling youngsters eating ham-
burgers below paintings that could grace the walls of any of the country's leading museums. The manager of the local McDonald's said, "I
don't know what you boys are doing, but I like it," as he commissioned the local painters to exhibit in his restaurant.

Such blurring of cultural styles occurs in everyday life in the 5
United States to a greater extent than anyone can imagine and is probably more prevalent than the sensational conflict between people
of different backgrounds that is played up and often encouraged by
the media. The result is what the Yale professor, Robert Thompson,
referred to as a cultural bouillabaisse, yet members of the nation's
present educational and cultural Elect still cling to the notion that the
United States belongs to some vaguely defined entity they refer to as
"Western civilization," by which they mean, presumably, a civilization created by the people of Europe, as if Europe can be viewed in
monolithic terms. Is Beethoven's Ninth Symphony, which includes
Turkish marches, a part of Western civilization, or the late nineteenth-
and twentieth-century French paintings, whose creators were influenced by Japanese art? And what of the cubists, through whom the influence of African art changed modern painting, or the surrealists,
who were so impressed with the art of the Pacific Northwest Indians
that, in their map of North America, Alaska dwarfs the lower forty-
eight in size?

Are the Russians, who are often criticized for their adoption of 6
"Western" ways by Tsarist dissidents in exile, members of Western
civilization? And what of the millions of Europeans who have black
African and Asian ancestry, black Africans having occupied several
countries for hundreds of years? Are these "Europeans" members of
Western civilization, or the Hungarians, who originated across the
Urals in a place called Greater Hungary, or the Irish, who came from
the Iberian Peninsula?

Even the notion that North America is part of Western civilization 7
because our "system of government" is derived from Europe is being
challenged by Native American historians who say that the founding
fathers, Benjamin Franklin especially, were actually influenced by the
system of government that had been adopted by the Iroquois hundreds of years prior to the arrival of large numbers of Europeans.

Western civilization, then, becomes another confusing category 8
like Third World, or Judeo-Christian culture, as man attempts to impose his small-screen view of political and cultural reality upon a complex world. Our most publicized novelist[1] recently said that Western
civilization was the greatest achievement of mankind, an attitude that
flourishes on the street level as scribbles in public restrooms: "White
Power," "Niggers and Spics Suck," or "Hitler was a prophet," the latter being the most telling, for wasn't Adolph Hitler the archetypal
monoculturalist who, in his pigheaded arrogance, believed that one
way and one blood was so pure that it had to be protected from alien
strains at all costs? Where did such an attitude, which has caused so
much misery and depression in our national life, which has tainted
even our noblest achievements, begin? An attitude that caused the in-
carceration of Japanese-American citizens during World War II, the
persecution of Chicanos and Chinese-Americans, the near-extermina-
tion of the Indians, and the murder and lynchings of thousands of
Afro-Americans.

Virtuous, hardworking, pious, even though they occasionally 9
would wander off after some fancy clothes, or rendezvous in the
woods with the town prostitute, the Puritans are idealized in our
schoolbooks as "a hardy band" of no-nonsense patriarchs whose discipline razed the forest and brought order to the New World (a term
that annoys Native American historians). Industrious, responsible, it
was their "Yankee ingenuity" and practicality that created the work
ethic. They were simple folk who produced a number of good poets,
and they set the tone for the American writing style, of lean and spare
lines, long before Hemingway. They worshiped in churches whose
colors blended in with the New England snow, churches with simple
structures and ornate lecterns.

The Puritans were a daring lot, but they had a mean streak. They 10
hated the theater and banned Christmas. They punished people in a
cruel and inhuman manner. They killed children who disobeyed their
parents. When they came in contact with those whom they considered
heathens or aliens, they behaved in such a bizarre and irrational manner that this chapter in the American history comes down to us as a

---

[1]A reference to Saul Bellow (1915–), American novelist born in Canada. (Ed.)

late-movie horror film. They exterminated the Indians, who taught them how to survive in a world unknown to them, and their encounter with the calypso culture of Barbados resulted in what the tourist guide in Salem's Witches' House refers to as the Witchcraft Hysteria.

The Puritan legacy of hard work and meticulous accounting led to   11
the establishment of a great industrial society; it is no wonder that the American industrial revolution began in Lowell, Massachusetts, but there was the other side, the strange and paranoid attitudes toward those different from the Elect.

The cultural attitudes of that early Elect continue to be voiced in   12
everyday life in the United States: the president of a distinguished university, writing a letter to the *Times,* belittling the study of African civilizations; the television network that promoted its show on the Vatican art with the boast that this art represented "the finest achievements of the human spirit." A modern up-tempo state of complex rhythms that depends upon contacts with an international community can no longer behave as if it dwelled in a "Zion Wilderness" surrounded by beasts and pagans.

When I heard a schoolteacher warn the other night about the in-   13
vasion of the American educational system by foreign curriculums, I wanted to yell at the television set, "Lady, they're already here." It has already begun because the world is here. The world has been arriving at these shores for at least ten thousand years from Europe, Africa, and Asia. In the late nineteenth and early twentieth centuries, large numbers of Europeans arrived, adding their cultures to those of the European, African, and Asian settlers who were already here, and recently millions have been entering the country from South America and the Caribbean, making Yale Professor Bob Thompson's bouillabaisse richer and thicker.

One of our most visionary politicians said that he envisioned a   14
time when the United States could become the brain of the world, by which he meant the repository of all of the latest advanced information systems. I thought of that remark when an enterprising poet friend of mine called to say that he had just sold a poem to a computer magazine and that the editors were delighted to get it because they didn't carry fiction or poetry. Is that the kind of world we desire? A humdrum homogeneous world of all brains and no heart, no fiction, no poetry; a world of robots with human attendants bereft of imagination, of culture? Or does North America deserve a more exciting destiny? To become a place where the cultures of the world crisscross. This is possible because the United States is unique in the world: The world is here.

QUESTIONS

1.   Why does Reed find the term "Western civilization" inadequate to describe North American culture?

2.   Discuss your own experiences with what Reed calls the "blurring of cultural styles" (paragraph 5). Do you agree with Reed that (a) this blurring is "more prevalent than the sensational conflict between people of different backgrounds," and (b) inter-group conflicts are "played up and often encouraged by the media"? Support your views with specific examples from current events and media coverage.

The Wild Man of the Green Swamp

MAXINE HONG KINGSTON

For eight months in 1975, residents on the edge of Green Swamp, 1
Florida, had been reporting to the police that they had seen a Wild
Man. When they stepped toward him, he made strange noises as in a
foreign language and ran back into the saw grass. At first, authorities
said the Wild Man was a mass hallucination. Man-eating animals
lived in the swamp, and a human being could hardly find a place to
rest without sinking. Perhaps it was some kind of a bear the children
had seen.

In October, a game officer saw a man crouched over a small fire, 2
but as he approached, the figure ran away. It couldn't have been a
bear because the Wild Man dragged a burlap bag after him. Also, the
fire was obviously man-made.

The fish-and-game wardens and the sheriff's deputies entered the 3
swamp with dogs but did not search for long; no one could live in the
swamp. The mosquitoes alone would drive him out.

The Wild Man made forays out of the swamp. Farmers encoun- 4
tered him taking fruit and corn from the turkeys. He broke into a
house trailer, but the occupant came back, and the Wild Man escaped
out a window. The occupant said that a bad smell came off the Wild
Man. Usually, the only evidence of him were his abandoned camp-
sites. At one he left the remains of a four-foot-long alligator, of which
he had eaten the feet and tail.

In May a posse made an air and land search; the plane signaled 5
down to the hunters on the ground, who circled the Wild Man. A fish-
and-game warden "brought him down with a tackle," according to the
news. The Wild Man fought, but they took him to jail. He looked
Chinese, so they found a Chinese in town to come translate.

The Wild Man talked a lot to the translator. He told him his name. 6
He said he was thirty-nine years old, the father of seven children, who
were in Taiwan. To support them, he had shipped out on a Liberian

---

Maxine Hong Kingston, currently from Hawaii, was born in
Stockton, California. She is the author of *The Woman Warrior: Memoirs
of a Girlhood among Ghosts* (1976), about growing up in the U.S. with
Chinese immigrant parents, which has been frequently excerpted for
composition anthologies. Her 1989 novel *The Tripmaster Monkey: His
Fake Book* concerns a charismatic Chinese American activist. *China
Men* (1980), where this selection appeared, is a series of essays and
stories about Chinese and Chinese American men.

freighter. He had gotten very homesick and asked everyone if he could leave the ship and go home. But the officers would not let him off. They sent messages to China to find out about him. When the ship landed, they took him to the airport and tried to put him on an airplane to some foreign place. Then, he said, the white demons took him to Tampa Hospital, which is for insane people, but he escaped, just walked out and went into the swamp.

The interpreter asked how he lived in the swamp. He said he ate 7 snakes, turtles, armadillos, and alligators. The captors could tell how he lived when they opened up his bag, which was not burlap but a pair of pants with the legs knotted. Inside, he had carried a pot, a piece of sharpened tin, and a small club, which he had made by sticking a railroad spike into a section of aluminum tubing.

The sheriff found the Liberian freighter that the Wild Man had 8 been on. The ship's officers said that they had not tried to stop him from going home. His shipmates had decided that there was something wrong with his mind. They had bought him a plane ticket and arranged his passport to send him back to China. They had driven him to the airport, but there he began screaming and weeping and would not get on the plane. So they found him a doctor, who sent him to Tampa Hospital.

Now the doctors at the jail gave him medicine for the mosquito 9 bites, which covered his entire body, and medicine for his stomachache. He was getting better, but after he'd been in jail for three days, the U.S. Border Patrol told him they were sending him back. He became hysterical. That night, he fastened his belt to the bars, wrapped it around his neck, and hung himself.

In the newspaper picture he did not look very wild, being led by 10 the posse out of the swamp. He did not look dirty, either. He wore a checkered shirt unbuttoned at the neck, where his white undershirt showed; his shirt was tucked into his pants; his hair was short. He was surrounded by men in cowboy hats. His fingers stretching open, his wrists pulling apart to the extent of the handcuffs, he lifted his head, his eyes screwed shut, and cried out.

11

There was a Wild Man in our slough too, only he was a black man. He wore a shirt and no pants, and some mornings when we walked to school, we saw him asleep under the bridge. The police came and took him away. The newspaper said he was crazy; it said the police had been on the lookout for him for a long time, but we had seen him every day.

QUESTIONS

1. Discuss some of the instances of miscommunication or misinterpretation of facts in the Wild Man incident, and try to trace their causes. Whose account of the freighter trip do you believe more, the Wild Man's or the Liberians'? Could both be true?

2. Kingston offers little interpretation of this incident, mostly reporting the known facts in straightforward, journalistic fashion, until paragraphs 10 and 11. How do you think Kingston wishes us to see the Wild Man? Why do you think she ends the piece by introducing another Wild Man, the black man?

3. Try re-telling the entire Wild Man incident from the viewpoint of a particular character, such as the residents of Green Swamp, the police or sheriff's deputies, the game officer or wardens, the occupant of the house trailer, the translator, the Liberian officers, the doctors, the Border Patrol, the reporters, or the Wild Man himself. You might divide these perspectives with other readers, and then compare your different versions of the story.

The Irish Cop

KEVIN MULLEN

Today the city of San Francisco is governed by the Irish vote.

—RUDYARD KIPLING, 1889

At the swearing-in ceremony for his newly appointed Irish 1
American police commissioner in the 1970s, New York Mayor Edward
Koch was asked by a reporter whether the appointment wasn't "just a
continuation of the old Irish Mafia syndrome."

The mayor, feigning shock, turned to Robert McGuire and cried, 2
"You told me you were Jewish!"

"No, I didn't, Mr. Mayor," replied the new commissioner. "I just 3
told you I *looked* Jewish."

In these days of acrimonious debates about affirmative action, it 4
seems that an Irish surname can be a disadvantage for anyone seeking
a career in American law enforcement. The recent selection of a police
chief in San Francisco ended with the appointment of an Irish-named
candidate, Willis Casey—but only, it is said, after the search period
was extended while the mayor and the police commission tried to find
a suitable non-white candidate who would take the job.

The irony is that, not so long ago, the Irish cop was a stereotypical 5
American image, from the caricatured police chiefs in "Batman" and
"Dick Tracy" comic strips all the way back to the ham-fisted Irish beat
cop of the horse-and-buggy era.

Until the early decades of the 19th century, the United States was 6
largely a rural society, peopled mainly by white Protestants (most of
English extraction), blacks and Indians. Then began the great European
immigration that would change the demographic face of American
cities—and the Irish were among the first to come. By 1850, of the
United States' 23 million people, a million were foreign-born Irish.

Like later unskilled arrivals, Irish immigrants tended to huddle 7
together in cities, working at low-paid jobs. Soon, middle- and upperclass Protestants began moving out, leaving behind lower-income

Kevin Mullen was a police officer for 26 years and former deputy
police chief in the San Francisco Police Department. His book *Let
Justice Be Done: Crime and Politics in Early San Francisco* (1989) is a
study of the criminal justice system from the founding of San
Francisco as an American city until the mid-nineteenth century. This
article appeared in the *San Francisco Chronicle* Sunday magazine, *This
World*, in 1992.

residents to greet the hordes of arriving Irish. One view of 19th century America, in fact, is that of a long, violent struggle between successive waves of immigrants who were fighting for their livelihood.
The first round of that fight was between native-born Protestant
Americans and Irish Catholic newcomers.

The modern municipal police force evolved out of this strife. Large 8
departments were first formed in the 1830s to do combat on an equal
footing with street gangs. At first, the immigrant Irish were kept out of
police jobs by earlier arrivals, who dominated the election machinery
and thus controlled the supply of public jobs. But as more and more
Irish became naturalized American citizens, they began to make their
weight felt at the polls. Like many later immigrants, they saw public
employment as a way out of dead-end jobs in the slums.

From the start, the Irish had a better time of it in the West. When 9
San Francisco exploded into cityhood during the Gold Rush, immigrants flocked in. In a town with no tradition of exclusionary employment practices, almost anyone could go as far as his talent allowed.

The Irish quickly made a place for themselves in the city's wide- 10
open politics. David Broderick, an immigrant Irish stonemason's son,
fled the Protestant-controlled Tammany politics of New York City and
came West to build a political career. As the head of the "New Ireland"
faction of the Democratic party, he became a leader of California politics in the 1850s.

And when the San Francisco Police Department was formed in 11
August 1849, the man appointed as first chief was Democratic politician Malachi Fallon, a native of Athlone, Ireland. Like Broderick, he
had been raised in New York City, where he had served as a keeper of
the Tombs Prison. Among the first 30 officers he appointed were men
named Casserly, Cassidy, Claughley, Mullen, McGlaughin, McIntire,
McRay and Sweeney.

For the next 140 years, the Irish played a major role in the San 12
Francisco police. Once entrenched, son followed father into the "business," as they often do even now.

As recently as the 1940s, Chief of Police Michael Riordan, a native 13
of County Kerry, allowed that 40 percent of the department was na-
tive-born Irish, another 40 percent Irish and 20 percent "other."
Perhaps he overstated the case, but not by much. Former Mayor
Joseph Alioto remembers a time when "the chief of police in San
Francisco not only had to be Irish, he had to be born in Ireland."

Meanwhile, other ethnic groups were working hard to get the Irish 14
into a different line of work.

First it was the WASPs. When native-born Protestants came to the 15
realization, in the mid-1850s, that they were losing control of municipal affairs, they moved the discussion to the statehouses, which were

then dominated by rural, largely Protestant and Republican voters. New laws placed city police departments under state control, thus diluting Irish influence over who got the jobs. It happened in New York in 1857, Baltimore in 1860, Chicago in 1861, Detroit in 1865, Cleveland in 1866 and Boston in 1885.

San Franciscans had similar concerns. But because San Francisco 16 voters also dominated the state legislature, more direct methods were called for. In the summer of 1856, a group of San Francisco citizens, claiming outrage at crime and civic corruption, formed a Committee of Vigilance, hanged four of its adversaries and banished a number more under penalty of death. Historians still debate the vigilante movement, but one thing is certain: Irish Catholic Democrats were as noticeable by their absence on the committee as they were by their strong representation among those hanged or banished.

County Supervisor James Casey was the first to be hanged. Yankee 17 Sullivan, an Irish-born former heavyweight contender, died under mysterious circumstances in vigilante confinement. Those banished, like Charles Duane, Billy Mulligan, Martin Gallagher and Billy Carr, had served as political operatives for David Broderick. Broderick himself left San Francisco during the vigilante period; when it was over, his "Young Ireland" faction was in disarray.

For the next decade or so, San Francisco was run by the Peoples 18 Party, the political arm of the Vigilance Committee, and while Irish names could still be found on the rolls of the police department, they were not present in their former numbers. It was only after the Civil War, during which Irish immigrants swelled the population of San Francisco and California, that they again made their presence felt in local politics.

The final decade of the 19th century marked the beginning of 19 the Progressive movement. The WASPs were horrified at the vice and corruption in American cities; the newcomers, to whom public jobs promised an entree to the better things in American life, were less concerned. In city after city, noisy investigations into civic graft and corruption, usually focusing on the police, occupied the next several decades.

One reform was the introduction of civil service merit systems, re- 20 placing political influence with written entrance and promotion examinations. Though the reforms were intended in many cities to break the Irish stranglehold on city jobs, the Irish seem to have mastered the new process, for their numbers did not decline appreciably. Ironically, generations later their descendants would be accused of using the merit system to exclude others from the job.

The world has turned a few times since Irish police first trod 21 the streets of San Francisco, and the city has changed greatly.

Demographic reality suggests that in the future the Irish will not dominate the force as they did in the past. More recent arrivals are knocking at the door; minority police chiefs and large cadres of minority officers are appearing in major American cities, and not just in those with non-Anglo voting majorities.

The ethnic shift in police staffing is being accompanied by as much 22 sound, if not as much fury, as attended the emergence of the Irish police officer in the last century.

It's argued by some that a disproportionate number of police jobs 23 must go to nonwhites to redress past inequalities and to provide role models. Others argue that police departments should reflect the composition of the communities they serve. Still others say that the selection and promotion process should be strictly based on merit, that the sins of the father should not be visited on the son, and that hard-won professional excellence should not be sacrificed to political or social goals.

And, inevitably, the Irish have been singled out for special criti- 24 cism in the discussion.

Cast as it is in moral terms, the whole argument misses the point. 25 The simple fact is that today's newcomers, like the immigrants of a past century, want the jobs and have the political horsepower to get them. Perhaps, someday, urban Americans will wonder what all the fuss was about.

Who today remembers, after all, that in 1851 in Boston—that typ- 26 ical Irish American city of the recent past—the first Irish police officer, Barney McGinnity, was placed on the job under court order? When he showed up for work, the chief of police and the entire night watch resigned in protest.

QUESTIONS

1.   According to Mullen, what was the purpose of laws placing police departments under state control and the introduction of civil service merit systems?

2.   Mullen says that "today's newcomers, like the immigrants of a past century, want the jobs and have the political horsepower to get them" (paragraph 25). What examples can you think of to support Mullen's comparison? In what ways might the nineteenth-century struggles of Irish Americans to find jobs and earn respect be different from the experiences of minority immigrant groups in the twentieth century?

It's My Country Too

JUAN CADENA

I work for the Muscatine Migrant Committee. We're a govern-   1
ment-funded organization that's been in existence for over twenty
years. We provide medical help for migrants and seasonal farm workers. I've been the director of the program since 1971.

"Migrant" and "immigrant" are not synonymous. Our definition   2
of a migrant is someone who has earned half of their income within a
twelve-consecutive-month period in the past twenty-four months. And
the fact that they're from Mexico or any other country or are white or
speak Spanish or don't speak Spanish is really not relevant. On the
other hand, 99 percent of the migrants are Mexican-Americans and
mexicanos. With seasonal farm workers it's just the opposite, 90 percent
are white, European-Americans from Iowa. I don't know what percentage of the migrants are Mexican citizens. Fifteen years ago, a great
percentage of our migrants were from Texas and were American citizens by birth. In the last three or four years we have had a higher proportion of Mexican citizens than before.

I grew up in the Midwest. I was born in Texas, but we moved to   3
Saginaw, Michigan, when I was ten years old. When we first moved to
Carleton, just across the Saginaw River, there was a little—what we call
colonia. It didn't amount to much, there were only eight migrant
houses, and we lived right down the tracks in another little house near
the sugar beet company. We made friends with everybody in the *colonia.* We all went to the same school. Well, a couple of years later my father bought a house about three or four miles from there, in the Buena
Vista neighborhood. We were only half a block from Saginaw, but I
kept in contact with the people from the *colonia.*

We used to have Mexican dances. First in a real small hall, then we   4
graduated to the auditorium, then to the armory. By the 1960s, "Los
Relámpagos del Norte" came and there were two thousand people at
the dance. It just grew and grew. After I left Saginaw in the seventies,

---

Juan Cadena is outreach coordinator for the Muscatine (Iowa) School
District and former director of the Muscatine Migrant Committee, an
experience he discusses in this selection. "It's My Country Too" comes
from *Mexican Voices/American Dreams: An Oral History of Mexican
Immigration to the United States* (1990), edited by Marilyn P. Davis. An
oral history is usually collected from interviews on audio tape, then
transcribed and edited, so its written form is purposefully informal
and conversational.

Vincente Fernández came to the Civic Center and they had a real turnout.

So there is a substantial number of Hispanics in Saginaw. The 5 community college, when we left, had over 200 Mexicans enrolled. A few years ago, I went back and they had 400 in the community college.

When I was a community organizer we had clubs in each of the 6 high schools for Mexican kids, to encourage them to go to college. One school had over 250 kids. The Graduation Club was started back in the forties for all the Mexicans who are going to graduate from high school. They have their own prom and bring speakers such as Senator Chavez and Senator Montoya, to give a special commencement. The kids still go to graduation with their respective schools, but they also have a separate one just for Mexicans.

I don't know if they still do, but in Saginaw they used to celebrate 7 the *diez de septiembre* and *cinco de mayo*. I don't think half of them know what the heck's being celebrated. That's the truth. I was in San Antonio and these Mexicans, my wife, Martha's cousins, live in an affluent, nice neighborhood on the north side. They were all excited because they were going to this Festival San Jacinto and Martha says, "Well what is the celebration about?" And they didn't know. *¿Verdad, Martha?* They didn't know. I knew, but I didn't say nothing. They said, *"No sabemos lo que es,* but we have a lot of fun." But this whole holiday is about when the *mexicanos* got whipped by the whites here in San Jacinto and they don't even know. They're going out there to celebrate. So you know they don't even care. Even the whites don't know what the San Jacinto's about anymore, and nobody gives a hoot.

In Saginaw I had no real close friends that were not Mexicans. I 8 wasn't unfriendly with anyone, but I really never got associated with whites very much until I went in the army. Actually in those years I never paid any attention to who was from Mexico and who was from Texas, who was from Saginaw, who was from out of town, no attention whatsoever. I never even thought about it until I came here.

And here, when we first came to Muscatine it was like I was wear- 9 ing a sign on my forehead, "I'm Mexican." It wasn't just my perception, because when my relations would come down from Saginaw to visit, they would say, "What's wrong with the people in Muscatine? They stare at you." Well, that's not true anymore, but that was the situation when we first came here in '71. It was like a little cultural shock for me too, because I was confronted with this, "You're a Mexican." I knew I was a Mexican, but I didn't want people to be looking at me like, "Hey, Mexican!" They didn't say it, but that's the feeling you got. In Saginaw it wasn't that way at all—the relationship between whites and Mexicans is real good. There's really not that obvious discrimination. There was a little bit in the forties but not after that. Now there's even a lot of intermarriage.

See here, it was pretty bad. I was standing in line at the bank one 10 day—this is one example—and this guy says, "This is the way Mexicans line up for food stamps," and everybody was ha-ha-ha. Well I didn't laugh. I felt like grabbing the guy and throwing him through the window. But I was going to a church council meeting, I was president. Now how would I be getting into a fight? I was getting a little more religious, so I started thinking and acting different. A few years before I probably would have tried to throw him through the window.

Another time I called this number for a house to rent. I guess he 11 was busy and didn't notice that I had an accent. So when we got there he said, "Stop right there, I'm not renting to no Mexicans!" You know it was kind of comical.

I said, "Did I hear what you said?"   12

He said, "That's right, I don't rent to Mexicans."   13

I said, "Oh Christ!" So I called the civil rights commission, I was 14 going to do something, but I never followed up on it.

A couple, Anglo friends, did a consumers' report here. We would 15 send a Mexican couple, or pretend-to-be couple, to rent an apartment, and the landlord would say there wasn't any place to rent. Then our Anglo friends would come right behind them an hour later and, like magic, they would have a vacancy. After about twenty cases, they wrote a report. Those landlords were mad! But see we started exposing all that foolishness. Then in the schools there was also a lot of discrimination. I'm sure there still is, to some extent, but it has changed a lot. ¿Verdad, Martha? There's a lot of good Anglos in this community.

I was considered real militant in Saginaw, and when I came here I 16 was in the mood that I could do anything. That's the way I was. I sort of enjoyed it, you know. I was thirty-four, so I was no young kid. But nothing scared me, nothing.

I don't know. We had this old Mexican guy that was being ripped 17 off in West Liberty. This was a long time ago, but this justice of the peace had rented a place to the Mexican. In the first place it was small, a real shack. But beyond that there's no way that any thinking person could have expected the old guy to pay this kind of rent for the amount of money he was earning. So a friend and I, he was a law student, we went over there. Out comes this justice of the peace, and this guy looks like he's from *Petticoat Junction*, had his striped coveralls with this little hat and the whole bit. He said, "We don't want all those Mexicans coming into town. They park their cars and half of the time they're leaking oil and they leave all those oil spots all over and all that." My friend was saying, "Write that down, Juan." And I was writing notes, writing notes.

The justice of the peace would tell his lawyer, "They're gonna get 18 me. They're gonna get us, Ernie."

"Ah, don't worry about it." But you could see he was all worried. 19 So finally the lawyer said, "Juan, I'll talk to you, I don't want to talk to your friend. I'll talk to you, just you and I."

See, we were playing the good cop, bad cop. I went in but told my 20 friend, "You stay out of here." Then I told the justice's lawyer, "Well, I'll keep this lawyer away from here if you cut the rent in half and . . ." And this is exactly what the man had wanted. He agreed to everything.

"You're not going to take it any further than this?" 21

I said, "No, we'll forget the whole thing." 22

So we went back for the old goat to sign the papers and he said, 23 "Well, I'm sorry what I said about Mexicans, it's not only Mexicans that do that, niggers and Puerto Ricans do the same."

Can you believe that? He was serious. God, I'll never forget that. 24 How can you get angry with somebody like that? You can't, these people are crazy. He was apologizing and insulting us at the same time. I've noticed that people are like that. If you really look at them, they're hilarious. The only time I'm really worried about a racist person is if they're in a position to determine someone's economic or social future.

Before I came here I was a coordinator for the grape boycott, for 25 Cesar Chavez in the Saginaw area. We confronted a lot of people, people who would spit on us and say, "Go back to Mexico, you wetbacks!" And we were all from the United States. A lot of Anglos were helping us out, but in a way I was a racist. I wanted Mexicans to be doing something for Mexicans, but we were all American citizens. When I joined the grape boycott movement it was being led by some seventeen-year-old Anglo girl, and 99 percent of the people doing the marching were Anglos, nuns, and priests. I took it over and chased them all out. I didn't tell them directly to leave, but in a month or so they were all gone except the real hard-nosed. I would have 100 or 150 and they were all Mexicans. ¿Verdad, Martha? The Anglos didn't want me because I was coming across too hard. They wanted to make waves but not BIG waves, and I was making REAL BIG waves.

But here in Muscatine it was a different ballgame than Saginaw. 26 If you're really trying to do something useful and to really help or change conditions, you have to adapt to the conditions that you're dealing with. You can't just sing the same songs.

In Saginaw there really wasn't that many poor people. Now I'm 27 used to it, but when we came here, we went riding around to the southside. We saw Anglos, blue-eyed, blond kids with stringy hair and dirty faces, scroungy looking, and I said, "Well wait a minute, I thought I would have to go to the Ozarks to see this. Not Iowa, the breadbasket of America." I thought everybody would be like you know, *Ozzie and Harriet*. But you see a lot of poor people, and really I don't know how you would say it, riff-raff maybe.

We don't have that in Saginaw. There's a large middle class, and 28 everybody works in the plants, and they all make a lot of money. There I could say, "Look at the way the poor Mexicans live here." Because there were a few poor Mexicans. But here, I can't say that because we have as many poor whites.

Another difference, in Saginaw everybody works side by side 29 there at the plants, and it doesn't matter whether you're white, yellow, or blue. You earn the same kind of money, the same kind of education and everything else.

People wanted me to get involved with the union here too, like 30 the grape boycott. But I said, "It isn't going to work. In Saginaw we used to go to a supermarket. I would take six people and we would turn away 50 percent of the people. Here you can take 200 people and you aren't going to turn 5 percent of the people away. They don't identify with the union. In Saginaw everybody was union." I don't care if they were Polish or Mexican or black, they were all union people. So it was real easy to close down a store. Here it wouldn't work. People are not union oriented. Cesar Chavez came and people said, "Let's get him down to organize." It isn't going to work. The whole thing was a different world, and I found that out real quick.

I've read a lot of books. The bible has influenced me. I've 31 read Espinoza, Jung, Marx, Ché Guevara, Fidel Castro, Mao Tse-tung, Gandhi, and Franz Fanon. Spicer, an anthropologist, influenced me too.

In school when I was growing up in Texas, the history books were 32 always lying. My dad would correct the history like Pancho Villa and the Alamo, and say, "This is a bunch of lies. These *gringos* are telling you a bunch of lies." So I started thinking for myself. I remember once the nuns wanted us to sign some papers they were going to drop over China and I didn't sign them. My sister Lupe didn't sign it either. She was the only one in her class and I was the only one in mine. I said, "How do I know communism is wrong? How do I know that they're not right and I'm wrong?" White people have been lying to us all these years, and they have discriminated against us in Texas, so how come they're supposed to be so good? They broke all those treaties with the Indians and treated them like dogs, and now they're going to tell me that they're good and the Chinese are bad. I said, "No. I hope the Chinese come and take this country over." That's what I told them.

And the nuns would say, "We're going to have Father come and talk to you because you're a communist." I said, "How can I be a communist? You don't even know what a communist is." I didn't completely buy that little trick of the land of the free and the home of the brave. The United States, I do agree, is probably the best country in the world. And I'm glad I'm an American citizen and was born in this country. But the point is, you can't just swallow everything that they try to tell us, especially when it comes to minorities. I always saw the United States as an extension of Europe, and if you were not of European ancestry somehow you weren't American. What the heck, I was born here, but if I said anything against the United States they would say, "Why don't you go back to Mexico." Well, why don't you go back to Europe. Why should you be trying to send me to Mexico. What's the difference? 33

Like one guy—we were at a school board hearing where I was pushing for bilingual education—he told the superintendent of schools, "You mean to tell me this man"—talking about me, I was sitting right in front of him—"expects us to teach his kids Spanish in school?" 34

And then I told the superintendent, "You mean to tell me that this man here expects me to teach his kid English in school?" 35

He said, "What do you mean, you speak Spanish at home, don't you?" 36

I said, "Well what do you speak at home, Chinese? If you expect me to teach my kid Spanish at home, then you teach your kid English at home." 37

He said, "Well I don't mind, maybe you people already living here have the right to speak Spanish, but I'm talking about the other people coming in." 38

"Fine, I'm okay if you speak English, but all new people coming in should speak Spanish. What makes you right and me wrong?" 39

He said, "Well because we're the majority." 40

I said, "No, no, no, what about Zimbabwe? You white Europeans want to push your culture and your language everywhere. In Zimbabwe you're the minority." I wanted to make the same argument. If he would say my argument wasn't right, it would be because he thought I was a second-class citizen, but why should he be more of a citizen than me? I'm a taxpayer. It's my money too. It's my country too. It's my school system too. It's a matter of perceiving what we're all about here in the United States. 41

QUESTIONS

1. Based on Cadena's recollections, compare and contrast Saginaw and Muscatine. Which place does Cadena seem to prefer, and why?

2. Think about an experience you or someone you know has had with racism or prejudice. How do you feel about Cadena's reaction, in paragraph 24, to the racist justice of the peace? Do you agree that you should only be "worried about a racist person . . . if they're in a position to determine someone's economic or social future"?

Thank God for the Jews

TAHIRA NAQVI

On a morning like any other August morning with its promising 1
bright sunshine, its late summer aura of capricious warmth so unlike
the faithful, torrid heat of August mornings in Lahore, Ali said, "Kamal
is bringing his mother over for dinner."

"Aunt Sakina? When?" Fatima asked, forgetting how many 2
teabags she had dropped into the small white Corningware teapot.
Five would be too many and three not enough. Peering into the pot she
counted: three bags were clearly visible, the fourth could be an illusion.
She tore off a Tetley tag and threw an extra one in. The water gurgled
with a familiar sound as she poured it into the pot and steam rose to
embrace her face warmly. "But she said she was going to be in New
Jersey for another week."

"She must have changed her mind. Anyway, Kamal called me at 3
the hospital and I told him Sunday would be fine." Ali was speaking
from the bedroom. He had this knack of starting a serious conversation
with Fatima when he was not in the same room with her.

Fatima wasn't sure whether she should be glad at the prospect of 4
seeing her cousin who got along well with Ali, excited at the thought
of meeting Aunt Sakina who would have more gossip about the relatives from Lahore, or upset that Ali hadn't checked with her before giving Kamal the okay for dinner. After all, preparations had to be made.

The unwashed plates in the sink and the two Farberware pots 5
crusty with over-cooked spices from last night's supper fed her aggra-
vation. The disarray on the cramped kitchen counters—bottles of the
baby's food, assorted Beech-Nut juices, and cans of formula huddling
together as if seeking safety in numbers—didn't help either. After Ali
had left for the hospital around eleven to attend to an emergency, she
had settled comfortably on the sofa in the living room to watch the
Eleven o'Clock Movie on channel 9. *The Snows of Kilimanjaro*. Gregory
Peck. The man who had invaded her daydreams many an afternoon
when she was a teenager. Even now he smiled and she wished she

Tahira Naqvi was born in Pakistan and lives in Connecticut. She has
completed a collection of stories entitled *Journeys* and has edited two
anthologies of Urdu short fiction in translation. This story first
appeared in *Imagining America: Stories from the Promised Land* (1991), a
multicultural anthology of American fiction edited by Wesley Brown
and Amy Ling.

were Ava Gardner. Nobody's going to come and inspect my kitchen at this hour of night. She had waved the dishes away.

Leaving the tea to steep under the only tea cozy she possessed, 6
Fatima walked into the bedroom determined to have it out with her husband. She found him thrashing through a drawer, looking for clean underwear.

"But that's the day after tomorrow," she said, picking up his white 7
cotton pajama and kurta from the bedroom floor with one hand, his discarded socks with the other.

"Yes," Ali replied. Now he was rummaging for socks.   8

He's already beside a patient, no doubt. Taking a pulse. The round 9
ends of the stethoscope snug into the little cavities of his ears. Playing God with such a casual air, nonchalantly. A face she does not know, does not understand. She turned to straighten the bedsheets and he was gone from there.

"And she'll eat only halal meat!" Fatima ran after him. In the 10
kitchen now, he was pouring himself a cup of tea.

"We don't have any in the freezer?" he asked, seemingly unmoved 11
by the panic in her voice. Uf! Gulping tea again. It's not mango squash. Sip it, slowly, savor it. He was pouring a second cup already. His long, dark brows formed short uneven waves over his nose as he picked up a piece of toast and crunched it noisily.

"Of course we don't. We bought a couple of pounds from Halal 12
Meats in Queens when we were there last month to see *Mughal-e-Azam*. Remember? It's all gone."

Sometimes Fatima and Ali bought halal meat, meat prepared the 13
Islamic way, from one of the many Pakistani shops that ubiquitously lined Jackson Boulevard in Queens. Every once in a while they also ventured into the small, busy place called Halal Meats on Lexington in Manhattan. But for the most part it was beef, chicken, and lamb from Grand Union for them. Packed in shiny, neat packages that led Fatima to believe that someone had gone through a great deal of trouble to give the shoppers only the best, the meat always had a fresh, clean color, and the packages were so easy to pick up and throw into the shopping cart. Whenever Fatima remembered to, she recited, "There is no God but Allah and Muhammad is His Prophet" while she rinsed the meat with cold water. Remembering to undertake that little ritual made her feel pious and wise beyond her years.

"It's not like we're giving her pork," she protested. "Once we've 14
said the kalima while washing the meat, it's okay, isn't it? Aba said that's all the Quran requires us to do. That's all I do. All this nonsense about bleeding the animal, or pronouncing the name of Allah at the time the poor animal is put to the knife—it's ridiculous!" Frustration

hung in her head like the beginnings of a migraine and she realized she hadn't had any tea yet; also, this wasn't a good time to engage her husband in a discussion about rational approaches to the preparation of halal meat.

He finished his second cup of tea and vigorously rubbed down 15 the corners of his moustache with a paper napkin. "Your father's a rationalist, Fatima. But we both know there's more to Islam than what's in the Quran. Anyway, that's not the point. In Pakistan you ate only halal, didn't you?"

"Yes, but this is different . . ." Why, he might ask. She knew why, 16 but there wasn't enough time to explain.

He was saying, "Well, some people are more conservative; they 17 don't want to compromise. They'll eat halal wherever they go."

"I know," Fatima said glumly. 18

"Anyway, what about fish?" he asked. They were standing in the 19 foyer now, his hand reaching for the door knob. Was he going to kiss her or was he going to forget?

"Fish?" She leaned over to brush a tiny crumb that dangled invit- 20 ingly from his dark, thick moustache.

True, fish was not subject to the same stringent laws as other types 21 of meat. It had probably been spared because there was no blood to contend with; what else could it be? But Fatima had such bad luck with fish, always. Whenever she tried to fry fillets dipped in gram flour batter, invariably the fish and the batter separated as soon as the piece was dropped into hot oil. Curried fish suffered a worse fate: no sooner had she turned the cubed chunks over than the chunks disintegrated, becoming mush. Usually she just threw everything into the trash and started all over again with something else. If her mother saw her, she would cringe at her wastefulness.

"Fish?" She looked at Ali to make sure he wasn't teasing. "In the 22 first place I don't make very good fish, and in the second place how many kinds of fish are we going to serve? Who knows, maybe Aunt Sakina hates fish."

"Maybe not. Try the fish. It's never that bad." Surely he is desper- 23 ate. He doesn't want to upset Aunt Sakina. And what tales she might take back home. They've already forgotten their ways. Imagine not eating halal. What will it be next, pork?

"Okay," Fatima said, "I'll try the fish. But don't blame me if it's a 24 disaster. I hope they have some bluefish at Grand Union, that's the only kind that works well in a curry. I'm not going to try the frying recipe."

"All right, all right. And don't forget to use some oregano." He 25 glanced at the clock on the living room wall, tweaked her cheek and was out of the door with a smile and a "Bye," before she could ask, "But what do you know about oregano?" It probably reminded him of something his mother used in her fish recipe, perhaps ajwain. He had forgotten to kiss her.

Left alone, Fatima dawdled in the foyer as if she were a guest in   26 her own home. Looking down at her feet she observed the scuff marks made by Haider's walker on the yellow and beige linoleum; looking above she glanced upon the throng of cobwebs that looped with silken finesse in two corners of the white ceiling. She must do some cleaning this afternoon. Her son, Haider, impervious to the trivialities and banalities of custom and habit gone awry in Westchester County, was still asleep. From the kitchen, tea beckoned as a deliverer's promise would. All else must wait and be taken care of after this one cup of Tetley tea, Tetley which had become their choice after a protracted dalliance with the likes of Earl Grey and other "Indian" teas; the Americans had done something right with tea after all.

With the cup cradled in her palm, she came into the living room,   27 pulled down the shades from force of habit to shut out the bright morning sun, turned on the TV, and sat down on the settee. The warmth from the first gulp slunk down her throat and made her feel good, sure of herself. She took another sip and crossed her legs. The *Eight o'Clock News* had just begun. The Jews and the Muslims were fighting again in the Middle East. A tall, handsome reporter, who, with his upturned coat collar and straw-colored, wind-swept hair, seemed to belong in an ad for Burberrys in the *New Yorker*, was saying something about "recent acts of terrorism" in a faraway voice. An Israeli school bus had been bombed. Its carcass sat forlornly on a hill; some children had been killed, some injured; a girl, who was perhaps four years older than Haider, ran away wildly from the soldier who scrambled after her to hold her. The camera moved abruptly to another scene before he caught up with her. An Arab village in ruins. Nearly all the houses had been demolished, the survivors of the attack moving in slow motion like zombies. An old woman whose face looked familiar squatted before a crumbled, hollowed-out dwelling and cried without restraint, her mouth hanging open in a grotesque caricature of a smile.

During a commercial break Fatima decided to make a list so she   28 wouldn't forget anything when Ali took her to Grand Union this evening. She wrote down "oregano." Now I know, the old woman in the news. Crying in despair. She resembled Aunt Sakina. All old women look the same at some point, I suppose.

Aunt Sakina was Fatima's father's cousin. Last summer, when   29 Fatima visited her in Pakistan, Aunt Sakina confessed secretively that she missed Kamal terribly, especially now that she had lost her husband and her daughter was also married. "A daughter-in-law will make this house come to life again," she said in a quavering voice. She confessed Kamal had been begging her to come to America for a visit. Her eyes, set far into their sockets and glazed over with age, filled quickly with tears. "But don't say anything to him," she entreated, wiping with a corner of her white dupatta the moisture that had trickled thickly over her grooved, leathery cheeks. "You must come then, Auntie," Fatima had said. "Why are you so reluctant to come?" Fatima knew Aunt Sakina was biding her time, waiting until Kamal begged. Her mother would do the same. Mothers like their grown sons to beg, to fawn over them. That's because they usually ignore them altogether. Stay away.

Still feeling uncomfortable about fish, Fatima put an oversized question mark after "Boston Blue" on the grocery list. A segment about Jerusalem was on the air. The handsome, roving reporter, unchanged in his appearance, disconnected still from his surroundings, was speaking in a crisp accent that wasn't anything like what she heard on the streets in New York or Westville: "Jerusalem, named Yeroshalayim by the Jews and Bayt al Mugaddas by the Muslims, is a city which the Muslims want as much as the Jews and Christians do." Jewish pilgrims stood in grave postures at the Wailing Wall, called the Wall of Suleiman by the Arabs, she remembered from her high school history book. Suddenly she felt guilty for not having offered prayers or read the Quran in what was surely a very long time. If Aunt Sakina found out she had been so lazy, she'd certainly tell her a thing or two. Just then the muezzin's call to prayer, the azan, arose and rang like a siren song, insinuating its way into the murmurings of Hebrew prayer and the hubbub of the bazaars. Poor King Hussein. So debonair, so patient. An unhappy monarch who had let Jerusalem slip from his hands. 30

"O Fab, we're glad/There's lemon-freshened borax in you!" Remembering she was out of laundry detergent, she jotted down "detergent—Fab" on her list. But why not consult the Quran anyway? That was the spring of Islamic law. The source. 31

She leafed through the Pickthall translation. "*The Cow: 2:168.* Believers, eat of the wholesome things with which we have provided you. . . . He has forbidden you carrion, blood, and the flesh of the swine; also any flesh that is consecrated other than in the name of Allah." 32

So, the issue was no issue at all. The commandment clear-cut. But will Aunt Sakina accede to such argument? No. We're all creatures of custom and habit. 33

At that moment Fatima envied the women in Lahore who didn't have to torment themselves with such absurd doubts when they were 34 planning a feast for a husband's friend's mother. Their concern would be with the menu, with having enough sugar and milk for kheer, with getting to the market early so that the best portions of mutton or beef could be had, with finding a plump chicken for a reasonable price, and with securing enough ice for drinking water. How her cousin Zenab would laugh if she were to see her now. How she would snicker if she knew that Fatima's dinner party was preceded by scholarly research on the matter of halal meat. Fatima blushed at her own foolishness. But Zenab wasn't around to see her in her moment of weakness. She was alone, and Haider was too young to know anything.

She riffled through the paperback Quran. On page 357 she read: 35 "Women shall have rights similar to those exercised against men, although men have a status above women. Allah is mighty and wise." Adeeba, she thought. Why hadn't she thought of Adeeba before?

Adeeba knew most things there were to know. She and her hus- 36 band, a second year resident, had been in the U.S. a little longer than Fatima and Ali and many of the others. Often Fatima had heard Samina, or one of the other Pakistani wives say in a tone of absolute trust, "Ask Adeeba, she'll know." As a matter of fact Samina was getting to be rather good herself. Already adept at keeping a close watch on sales and where to buy the best 220-volt appliances for taking back to Pakistan as gifts, she was also developing an eye for eligible young women who might be suitable for the Pakistani bachelors at Westville Hospital.

However, Adeeba wasn't home, which didn't surprise Fatima at 37 all; Adeeba was rarely to be found at home. After all, how could she know so much if she didn't window-shop and hunt for bargains early in the day, before shoppers crowded the stores looking for discounts? Fatima decided to try Samina instead and dialed her number. After a few rings Samina's sluggish "Hallo" greeted her. Since Samina didn't have any children, there was a silent agreement among the women that she be allowed to sleep late. Fatima apologized for having woken her.

"Don't be silly," Samina said sleepily, "I was awake, just lying 38 down." For a whole minute she and Fatima chatted energetically about the fabric sale at Singer's. "Don't forget to look over the dollar-a-yard table at the far end of the shop," Samina advised.

"No, I won't," Fatima acceded hastily. Who cares about that, and 39 anyway, I've already done my fabric shopping for the month. Now, how to do this. "By the way Samina, is there any halal meat available around here?" Fatima finally asked. She knew by asking this she had condemned herself; surely her ignorance would now be evident to all.

"Halal? Are you joking? We always get ours from Queens. Are 40 you out?"

"Yes," Fatima said, playing with her wedding band. "And I need 41
some desperately. We're having company on Sunday and there's no
time to go to New York." Will she offer me some of hers? I don't think
so, unless I ask. I wish she had offered. One packet would make all the
difference.

"What about kosher?" Samina's voice rang with authority. 42

"Kosher?" Fatima queried inanely. The word had a familiar ring, 43
like the name of an acquaintance whose face one can't place. Oh my
God! Yes! I've seen it on hot dog labels at Grand Union. Jewish, surely.
But what does Samina mean? Afraid of exposing her ignorance further
and fully, Fatima didn't elaborate her question. Samina loved to talk,
so she let her.

"Yes, kosher chicken," Samina was saying, seemingly undisturbed 44
by Fatima's perplexity on the matter of kosher. "There's kosher hot
dogs too, and all the meat's prepared just like ours. They recite God's
name before slaughtering the animal and bleed the animal afterward."

They? Fatima winced at her own stupidity. 45

"Anyway, what's kosher is okay for us." Samina spoke with 46
greater authority than before. Fatima could picture her at the other
end, her small, beady eyes shining, her face flushed, the expression on
it triumphant with the knowledge that she had offered valuable advice, that she could now move closer to Adeeba's league.

"Does Adeeba use kosher too?" I have to be sure. Know every- 47
thing. What if Aunt Sakina decides to quiz me.

"Of course. We all do." 48

All? Ohhhh. . . . 49

"Especially in the winter. It's difficult to make frequent trips to 50
New York when the weather's so bad, you know. Thank God for the
Jews."

"Yes." Fatima's voice floundered. 51

"Pathmark always has a good supply." Samina volunteered more 52
information quickly.

Should I put my trust wholly in Samina's word? After all, she's 53
only a fledgling disciple. And isn't a Jewish prayer different from a
Muslim prayer?

Chamber's Twentieth Century Dictionary had traveled with her 54
from Pakistan, one of the few books Fatima had brought along with
her. Inside, on the first blank page, was her brother's name, below
hers, while her sister's girlish flourish lurched precariously immediately under his. The pages of the dictionary were sere, curling at
the edges, and brittle. Gingerly she worked on the top right corner of
each page until she had it secure between her forefinger and thumb.
Then she lifted it slowly, with care. Twice she went through J and

twice, arriving at L, missed K. Finally she wet a finger, slowly leafed this time, found "junk" and, running a finger down, came to "kosher" in the column at the left. Right under "Koran." It said: "pure, clean according to the Jewish ordinances—as of meat killed and prepared by Jews. [Hebrew, from *yashar*, to be right]."

Fatima crossed out "Boston Blue" on her grocery list and put 55 down "kosher chicken—Pathmark" instead. The segment on fighting in the Middle East was winding down. A mist had settled over Jerusalem. The prayer shawls and *abas* appeared like dabs of white paint on a dark canvas. The handsome roving reporter was nowhere in sight. Fatima switched the channel to PBS so that Haider, who was now awake and whimpering, could watch "Sesame Street."

The rest of the day dragged. At eleven she watched Hitchcock's *To* 56 *Catch a Thief* on channel 9. When Haider dozed off around two, she also took a nap during which she dreamt she and Aunt Sakina were roaming around in an Arab village looking for oregano. In the dream she led her aunt by her arm through a maze of dust-ridden streets bright with torrid sunshine, encountering on her way her son who ran from her as if she were a stranger. When she woke up she was sweating and her throat was dry. Just as she was about to get up from the bed to get a drink of water she heard Ali's key turn in the front door.

Breathless with excitement, she left her bed and ran to the door. 57 No sooner had Ali stepped into the foyer than she said, "Ali, our troubles are over. Thank God for the Jews!"

QUESTIONS

1.   Discuss how assimilation to life in the United States—"the trivialities and banalities of custom and habit gone awry in Westchester County" (paragraph 26)—is portrayed for Fatima and her family. To what extent do you think Fatima is more concerned with the forms than the substance of her religious and cultural background?

2.   Fatima's dilemma about the dinner menu is played out against a background of fighting between Jews and Muslims portrayed on the television news. What do you think Naqvi is trying to say in this story about ethnic and religious divisions? How satisfactory do you find Fatima's solution to use kosher meat as a substitute for halal?

3.   Fatima is apparently reminded of her friend Adeeba by reading a passage from the Quran about the rights and status of women and men (paragraph 35). How do you see those gender roles being manifested in the story?

The Trip Back

ROBERT OLEN BUTLER

I am just a businessman, not a poet. It is the poet who is supposed 1
to see things so clearly and to remember. Perhaps it is only the poets
who can die well. Not the rest of us. I drove from my home in Lake
Charles, Louisiana, to the airport in Houston, Texas, to pick up my
wife's grandfather. And what is it that I experienced on that trip? What
is it that struck me as I got off the interstate highway in Beaumont,
knowing the quick route to the airport as I do? I was driving through
real towns in Texas. One was named China, another Nome. One was
Liberty. If I were a man who believed in symbols and omens, I would
have smiled at this. I was passing through Liberty to pick up my wife's
grandfather whose own liberty my wife and I and the man's nephew
in San Francisco had finally won, after many years of trying. He was
arriving this very day from the West Coast after living thirteen years
under Communist rule in our home country of Vietnam. Perhaps a
poet would think of those things—about Liberty, Texas, and my wife's
grandfather—and write a memorable poem. Though maybe not. I am
ignorant of these matters. Maybe it is only the bird taking flight or the
frog jumping into the pond that the poet is interested in.

All I know is that for me I drove the two-lane highway across 2
Texas and I just noticed the businesses—the little ones that seemed so
Vietnamese to me in the way the people always looked for some new
angle, some empty corner in the marketplace. I noticed the signs for
stump grinding and for house leveling and for mud pumping, the different stands along the way—fireworks, fruit and vegetables, hubcaps,
and antiques. The Paradise Club had a miniskirt contest, the Bait Barn
had a nightcrawler special, and Texas Winners had a baseball trophy
sale. There was a Donut Delight and a Future Star Twirling Academy
and a handpainted sign on a post saying that the finest porch swings

---

Robert Olen Butler, who served with the U.S. Army as a linguist and
translator during the Vietnam War, teaches creative writing at
McNeese State University in Lake Charles, Louisiana. His novels
include *The Alleys of Eden* (1981), *Sun Dogs* (1982), *The Deuce* (1989),
and *They Whisper* (1994). "The Trip Back" was originally published in
the literary journal *The Southern Review*, was reprinted in *The Best
American Short Stories, 1991* (edited by Alice Adams and Katrina
Kenison), and was part of his 1992 collection of stories, *A Good Scent
from a Strange Mountain*, about the experiences of Vietnamese people
living in the United States.

214

were a mile down this dusty road. The Mattress Man said on his sign, right underneath his business name, "Jesus Is Lord."

I am a Catholic and I must say that this made me smile. The Lord of the Universe, the Man of Sorrows, turned into the Lord of the Mattress, the Mattress Man. But even so, I understood what this owner was trying to do, appealing specially to those of his own kind. This is good business practice, when you know your sales area. I have done very well for myself in Lake Charles in the laundry and dry cleaning business. It is very simple. People sweat a lot in the climate of southern Louisiana, and there was a place for a very good laundry and dry cleaner. I have two locations in Lake Charles, and I will soon open one in Sulphur. So it was this that interested me as I drove through Texas, as it always does. I am a businessman. It is my way.

And if I were a man who believed in symbols and omens, I would have been very interested toward the end of my journey when I came to a low highway bridge that took me across the wide converging of two rivers, for as I entered the bridge, the sign said, "Lost and Old Rivers." These two rivers were full of little islands and submerged trees, and it was hard to see how the two ran together, for they looked more like one sprawling thing, like perhaps a large lake, something that was bound in and not moving, not flowing. Lost and old.

I had not given much serious thought to Mr. Chinh, my wife's grandfather. I knew this: my wife loved him very much. We are all like that in Vietnam. We honor our families. My four children honor me very much, and I honor them. My wife is devoted to me, and I am devoted to her. I love her. We were very lucky in that our parents allowed us to marry for love. That is to say, my mother and father and my wife's mother allowed it. Her father was dead. We still have a little shrine in our house and pray for him, which is the way of all Vietnamese, even if they are Catholic. As Catholics we understand this as the communion of saints. But my wife has no clear memory of her father. He died when she was very young. He drowned swimming in the South China Sea. And after that, Mr. Chinh became like a father for my wife.

She wept the night before my trip to the airport. She was very happy to have her grandfather again and very sorry that she missed all those years with him. I heard her muffling the sound of her crying in the pillow, and I touched her on the shoulder and felt her shaking, and then I switched on the light by the bed. She turned her face sharply away from me, as if I would reproach her for her tears, as if there was some shame in it. I said to her, "Mai, it is all right. I understand your feeling."

"I know," she said, but she did not turn back to me. So I switched the light off once more, and in the dark she came to me and I held her.

You must wait to understand why it is important, but at this point 8
I must confess one thing. My wife came to me in the dark and I held
her, and her crying slowed and stopped, and of course I was happy for
that. I was happy to hold my wife in the dark in this moment of strong
feeling for her and to be of help, but as I lay there, my mind could not
focus on this woman that I love. My mind understood that she was
feeling these things for a man of her own blood who had been very important to her and who then disappeared from her life for more than a
decade and now was coming back into it. But these are merely blood-
less words, things of the mind. And that was all they were to me even
lying there in the dark. I made those words run in my head, but what
was preoccupying me at that moment was an itching on my heel that
I could not scratch and the prices of two different types of paint for the
outer shop of the new dry cleaning store. My wife was a certain pressure, a warmth against me, but there was also a buzz in the electric
alarm clock that I was just as conscious of.

Do not misjudge me. I am not a cold man. I drew my wife closer 9
as she grew quieter, but it was a conscious decision, and even saying
that, I have to work hard to remember the moment, and the memory
that I have is more like a thought than a memory of my senses. And
it's not as if the itching on my heel, the buzz of the clock, are any more
vivid. I have to work extremely hard to reconstruct this very recent
night so that I can even tell you with assurance that there was a clock
in the room or that there was a foot at the end of my leg.

But you will see that it is Mr. Chinh who has put me in this 10
present state of agitation. After a time, as I held her in the bed, my
wife said, "My tears are mostly happy. Don't worry for me, Khanh. I
only wish I was small enough and his back was strong enough that
I could ride upon it again."

At the airport gate I looked at the people filing through the door 11
from the jetway. The faces were all white or Spanish, and they filed
briskly through the door and rushed away, and then there were a long
few moments when no one appeared. I began to think that Mr. Chinh
had missed the plane. I thought of the meal that my wife was preparing at home. She and my children and our best friends in Lake Charles
had been working since dawn on the house and on the food for this
wonderful reuniting, and when the door to the jetway gaped there
with no one coming through, that is the only thought I had, that the
food would be ruined. I did not worry about Mr. Chinh or wonder
what the matter could really be.

I looked over to the airline agents working behind their comput- 12
ers, checking in the passengers for the next flight. I was ready to seek
their help when I glanced back to the door and there was Mr. Chinh.
He was dressed in a red-and-black plaid sport shirt and chino pants,

and he was hunched a little bit over a cane, but what surprised me was that he was not alone. A Vietnamese man about my age was holding him up on the side without the cane and bending close and talking into his ear. Then the younger man looked up and saw me, and I recognized a cousin of my wife, the son of Mr. Chinh's nephew. He smiled at me and nodded a hello, and he jiggled the old man into looking at me as well. Mr. Chinh raised his head, and an overhead light flashed in his glasses, making his eyes disappear. He too smiled, so I felt that it was all right.

They approached me, and I shook Mr. Chinh's hand first. "I am so   13
happy you have come to visit us," I said.

I would have said more—I had a little speech in my head about   14
my wife's love for him, and how she is so sorry she is not at the airport, and how much his great-grandchildren want to see him. But my wife's cousin cut in before I had a chance. "This is Mr. Khanh," he said to the old man. "The one I told you about who would meet you."

Mr. Chinh nodded and looked at me and repeated my name. He   15
spoke no more, and I looked to the cousin, who said, "I'm Huong," and he bowed to me very formally.

"I remember you," I said, and I offered my hand. He took it read-   16
ily, but I knew from his formality that there could be things I did not know about Mr. Chinh. It is the custom of Vietnamese, especially of the old school of manners, not to tell you things that are unpleasant to hear. The world need not be made worse than it is by embracing the difficult things. It is assumed that you wish to hear that all is well, and many people will tell you this no matter what the situation really is. Huong struck me as being of this tradition—as surely his father must, too, for this is how an otherwise practical people learns an attitude such as this.

But I am a blunt man. Business has made me that way, particularly   17
business in America. So I said to Mr. Huong, "Is there something wrong with Mr. Chinh?"

He smiled at me as if I were a child asking about the thunder.   18
"I came with our dear uncle to make sure he traveled safely. He is very old."

I suddenly felt a little uncomfortable talking about the man as if he   19
wasn't there, so I looked at him. He was leaning contentedly on his cane, gazing around the circle of gates. I bent nearer to him and said, "Mr. Chinh, do you like the airport?"

He turned to me at once and said, "This is a fine airport. The best   20
I have seen."

The man's voice was strong, and this reassured me. I liked his ap-   21
preciation of the airport, which I too admired, so I said to Mr. Huong, "Is he a little frail, physically?"

"Yes," said Mr. Huong, happy, I suppose, to have words put in his 22 mouth sufficient to answer my blunt question. I did not like this cousin Huong.

But I was compelled to ask, "Will you be coming to Lake Charles 23 to join us?"

"No. I must decline your gracious invitation. I return by a flight 24 later this day."

I was blunt again. "You came all this way never to leave the air- 25 port? Just to return at once?"

Mr. Huong shrugged. "It is my pleasure to make sure our beloved 26 uncle arrives safely. My father said that if you should wish to discuss Uncle Chinh's permanent home after perhaps a week or so, he will await your call."

I didn't know the details of all that, except that I was prepared for 27 my wife's sake and the sake of our country's family tradition to make him part of our household. So I just nodded and took Mr. Chinh by the arm and said a brief goodbye to Mr. Huong, and the old man and I started off for the baggage check.

Mr. Chinh was enchanted with the airport, gawking about as we 28 moved, and his interest was so intense and his pleasure so evident from the little clucks and nods he made that I did not try to speak with him. Twice he asked me a question, once about where they would take the luggage, answered by our arrival at the carousel, which caused him to laugh loudly when the bell rang and the silver metal track began to run. Mr. Chinh stood at the opening, and he watched each bag emerging through the plastic flaps as closely as a customs inspector. The second question was if I had a car. And when I said yes, he seemed very pleased, lifting his cane before him and tapping it down hard. "Good," he said. "Don't tell me what kind. I will see for myself."

But in the parking garage, he was baffled. He circled the car and 29 touched it gently with the rubber tip of his cane, touched it several places, on a taillight, a hubcap, the front bumper, the name on the grille. "I don't know this car," he said. "I don't know it at all."

"It's an Acura," I said. 30

He shook the name off as if a mosquito had just buzzed his ear. "I 31 thought you would own a French car. A Citröen, I had predicted. A 15CV sedan."

"No, Mr. Chinh. It's an Acura. It's a very good car," and I stopped 32 myself from telling him it was from Japan.

Mr. Chinh lifted his shoulders and let them drop heavily, like he 33 was greatly disappointed and perhaps even a little scornful. I put his bags in the trunk and opened the door for him, and we made it out of the airport and back onto the two-lane highway before any more words were spoken. I was holding my eyes on the road, trying to think of small talk, something I'm not very good at, when Mr. Chinh finally said, "The inside is very nice."

I didn't understand. I glanced over to him, and he was running his hand along the dashboard, and I realized that he'd been thinking about the car all this time. "Good," I said. "I'm glad you like it." 34

"Not as nice as many others," he said. "But nice." 35

There's no car interior short of a Rolls that is nicer than my Acura, but I nodded at the old man, and I told myself that there was no need to debate with him or entertain him but just to be cordial to him. Let him carry the conversation, if he wished one. But the trip looked very long ahead of me. We hadn't even gotten out into the country of stump grinders and fruit stands. It was still franchised fast food and clusters of gas stations and minimalls and car dealerships. There were many miles to go. 36

Then up ahead I saw the work of a clever man, a car dealer who had dangled a big luxury car from the top of what looked like at least a seventy-foot crane. I said to Mr. Chinh, "There's something the Citröens don't do," and I motioned the man's attention to the car in the sky. He bent down and angled his head up to look, and his mouth gaped open. He said nothing but quickly shifted to the side window as we passed the car dealership, and then he turned around to watch out the back window until the car on the crane was out of sight. 37

I expected Mr. Chinh to remark on this. Perhaps a word on how no one would ever do such a thing to a French car. There would be no need. Something like that. But he said nothing, and after a time, I decided to appreciate the silence. I just concentrated on covering these miles before the old man would be reunited with the granddaughter he loved. I found that I myself was no longer comfortable with the old ways. Like the extended family. Like other things, too. The Vietnamese indirectness, for instance. The superstition. I was a good American now, and though I wished I could do more for this old man next to me, at least for my wife's sake, it was not an unpleasant thought that I had finally left Vietnam behind. 38

And I'd left behind more than the customs. I don't suppose that struck me as I was driving home from the airport. But it is clear to me now. I grew up, as did my wife, in Vung Tau. Both our families were pretty well off and we lived year-round in this seaside resort on the South China Sea. The French had called it Cap St. Jacques. The sand was white and the sea was the color of jade. But I say these things not from any vivid recollection, but from a thought in my head, as real only as lines from a travel brochure. I'd left behind me the city on the coast and the sea as well. 39

But you must understand that ultimately this doesn't have any- 40
thing to do with being a refugee in the United States. When I got to the
two rivers again, Old and Lost, I could recognize the look of them, like
a lake, but it was only my mind working.

Perhaps that is a bad example. What are those two rivers to me? I 41
mention them now only to delay speaking of the rest of my ride with
Mr. Chinh. When we crossed the rivers, I suppose I was reminded of
him somehow. Probably because of the earlier thoughts of the rivers as
an omen. But now I tried once more to think of small talk. I saw a large
curl of rubber on the shoulder of the road and then another a little later
on, and I said to Mr. Chinh, "Those are retreads from trucks. In
Vietnam some enterprising man would have already collected those to
make some use of them. Here no one cares."

The old man did not speak, but after a few moments I sensed 42
something beside me, and I glanced and found him staring at me. "Do
we have far to go?" he asked.

"Perhaps an hour and a half," I said.   43

"May I roll down the window?"   44

"Of course," I said. I turned off the air conditioning, and as he 45
made faint grabbing motions at the door, I pressed the power button
and lowered his window. Mr. Chinh turned his face to me with eyes
slightly widened in what looked to me like alarm. "They're power
windows," I said. "No handle."

His face did not change. I thought to explain further, but before I 46
could, he turned to the window and leaned slightly forward so that the
wind rushed into his face, and his hair—still more black than gray—
rose and danced, and he was just a little bit scary to me for some reason. So I concentrated again on the road, and I was happy to let him
stay silent, watching the Texas highway, and this was a terrible mistake.

If I'd forced him into conversation earlier, I would've had more 47
time to prepare for our arrival in Lake Charles. Not that I could have
done much, though. As it was, we were only fifteen minutes or so from
home. We'd already crossed the Sabine River into Louisiana and I'd
pointed it out to Mr. Chinh, the first words spoken in the car for an
hour. Even that didn't start the conversation. Some time later the wandering of his own mind finally made him speak. He said, "The air feels
good here. It's good when you can feel it on your face as you drive."

I naturally thought he was talking to me, but when I said, "Yes, 48
that's right," he snapped his head around as if he'd forgotten that I
was there.

What could I have said to such a reaction? I should have spoken of 49
it to him right away. But I treated it as I would treat Mai waking from
a dream and not knowing where she is. I said, "We're less than twenty
miles from Lake Charles, Mr. Chinh."

He did not reply, but his face softened, as if he were awake now.   50

I said, "Mai can't wait to see you. And our children are very   51
excited."

He did not acknowledge this, which I thought was rude for the   52
grandfather who was becoming the elder of our household. Instead,
he looked out the window again, and he said, "My favorite car of all
was a Hotchkiss. I had a 1934 Hotchkiss. An AM80 tourer. It was a
wonderful car. I would drive it from Saigon to Hanoi. A fine car. Just
like the car that won the Monte Carlo rally in 1932. I drove many cars
to Hanoi over the years. Citröen, Peugeot, Ford, DeSoto, Simca. But
the Hotchkiss was the best. I would drive to Hanoi at the end of the
year and spend ten days and return. It was eighteen hundred kilometers. I drove it in two days. I'd drive in the day, and my driver would
drive at night. At night it was very nice. We had the top down, and the
moon was shining, and we drove along the beach. Then we'd stop and
turn the lights on, and rabbits would come out, and we'd catch them.
Very simple. I can see their eyes shining in the lights. Then we'd make
a fire on the beach. The sparks would fly up, and we'd sit and eat and
listen to the sea. It was very nice, driving. Very nice."

Mr. Chinh stopped speaking. He kept his face to the wind, and I   53
was conscious of the hum of my Acura's engine, and I felt very
strange. This man beside me was rushing along the South China Sea.
Right now. He had felt something so strong that he could summon it
up and place himself within it, and the moment would not fade, the
eyes of the rabbits still shone, and the sparks still climbed into the sky,
and he was a happy man.

Then we were passing the oil refineries west of the lake, and we   54
rose on the I-10 bridge, and Lake Charles was before us, and I said to
Mr. Chinh, "We are almost home now."

And the old man turned to me and said, "Where is it that we are   55
going?"

"Where?"   56

"You're the friend of my nephew?"   57

"I'm the husband of Mai, your granddaughter," I said, and I tried   58
to tell myself he was still caught on some beach on the way to Hanoi.

"Granddaughter?" he said.   59

"Mai. The daughter of your daughter Diem." I was trying to hold   60
off the feeling in my chest that moved like the old man's hair was moving in the wind.

Mr. Chinh slowly cocked his head, and he narrowed his eyes, and   61
he thought for a long moment and said, "Diem lost her husband in
the sea."

"Yes," I said, and I drew a breath in relief.   62

But then the old man said, "She had no daughter."   63

"What do you mean? Of course she had a daughter."   64

"I think she was childless."   65

"She had a daughter and a son." I found that I was shouting.   66
Perhaps I should have pulled off to the side of the road at that moment. I should have pulled off and tried to get through to Mr. Chinh.
But it would have been futile, and then I would still have been forced
to take him to my wife. I couldn't very well just walk him into the lake
and drive away. As it was, I had five more minutes as I drove to our
house, and I spent every second trying carefully to explain who Mai
was. But Mr. Chinh could not remember. Worse than that. He was certain I was wrong.

I stopped at the final stop sign before our house, and I tried once   67
more. "Mai is the daughter of Nho and Diem. Nho died in the sea, just
as you said. Then you were like a father to Mai. . . . You carried her on
your back."

"My daughter Diem had no children. She lived in Nha Trang."   68

"Not in Nha Trang. She never lived in Nha Trang."   69

Mr. Chinh shook his head no, refuting me with the gentleness of   70
absolute conviction. "She lived on the beach of Nha Trang, a very
beautiful beach. And she had no children. She was just a little girl herself. How could she have children?"

I felt weak now. I could barely speak the words, but I said, "She   71
had a daughter. My wife. You love her."

The old man finally just turned his face away from me. He sat with   72
his head in the window as if he were patiently waiting for the wind to
start up again.

I felt very bad for my wife. But it wasn't that simple. I've become   73
a blunt man. Not like a Vietnamese at all. It's the way I do business. So
I will say this bluntly. I felt bad for Mai, but I was even more concerned for myself. The old man frightened me. And it wasn't in the
way you might think, with my saying to myself, Oh that could be me
over there sitting with my head out the window and forgetting who
my closest relatives are. It was different from that, I knew.

I drove the last two blocks to our house on the corner. The long   74
house with the steep roof and the massively gnarled live oak in the
front yard. My family heard my car as I turned onto the side street and
then into our driveway. They came to the side door and poured out,
and I got out of the car quickly, intercepting the children. I told my
oldest son to take the others into the house and wait, to give their
mother some time alone with her grandfather whom she hadn't seen
in so many years. I have good children, obedient children, and they
disappeared again even as I heard my wife opening the car door for
Mr. Chinh.

I turned and looked, and the old man was standing beside the 75
car. My wife embraced him, and his head was perched on her shoulder, and there was nothing on his face at all, no feeling except perhaps the faintest wrinkling of puzzlement. Perhaps I should have
stayed at my wife's side as the old man went on to explain to her that
she didn't exist. But I could not. I wished to walk briskly away, far
from this house, far from the old man and his granddaughter. I
wished to walk as fast as I could, to run. But at least I fought that desire. I simply turned away and moved off, along the side of the house
to the front yard.

I stopped near the live oak and looked about, trying to see things. 76
Trying to see this tree, for instance. This tree as black as a charcoal
cricket and with great lower limbs, as massive themselves as the main
trunks of most other trees, shooting straight out and then sagging and
rooting again in the ground. A monstrous tree. I leaned against it, and
as I looked away, the tree faded within me. It was gone, and I envied
the old man, I knew. I envied him driving his Hotchkiss along the
beach half a century ago. Envied him his sparks flying into the air. But
my very envy frightened me. Look at the man, I thought. He remembered his car, but he can't remember his granddaughter.

And I demanded of myself: Could I? Even as I stood there? Could 77
I remember this woman whom I loved? I'd seen her just moments ago.
I'd lived with her for more than twenty years. And certainly if she was
standing there beside me, if she spoke, she would have been intensely
familiar. But separated from her, I could not picture her clearly. I
could construct her face accurately in my mind. But the image did not
burn there, did not rush upon me and fill me up with the feelings that
I genuinely held for her. I could not put my face into the wind and see
her eyes as clearly as Mr. Chinh saw the eyes of the rabbits in his
headlights.

Not the eyes of my wife and not my country either. I'd lost a whole 78
country, and I didn't give it a thought. Vung Tau was a beautiful city,
and if I put my face into the wind I could see nothing of it clearly, not
its shaded streets or its white sand beaches, not the South China Sea
lying there beside it. I can speak these words, and perhaps you can see
these things clearly because you are using your imagination. But I cannot imagine these things because I lived them, and to remember them
with the vividness I know they should have is impossible. They are
lost to me.

Until perhaps when I am as old as Mr. Chinh. Perhaps he, too, 79
moved through his life as distracted as me. Perhaps only after he forgot his granddaughter did he remember his Hotchkiss. And perhaps
that was necessary. Perhaps he had to forget the one to remember the

other. Not that I think he'd made that conscious choice. Something deep inside him was sorting out his life as it was about to end. And that is what frightens me the most. I am afraid that deep down I am built on a much smaller scale than the surface of my mind aspires to. When something finally comes back to me with real force, perhaps it will be a luxury car hanging on a crane or the freshly painted wall of a new dry cleaning store or the faint buzz of the alarm clock beside my bed. Deep down, secretly, I may be prepared to betray all that I think I love the most.

This is what brought me to the slump of grief against the live oak   80
in my front yard. I leaned there, and the time passed, and then my wife crept up beside me. I turned to her, and she was crying quietly, her head bowed and her hand covering her eyes.

"I'm sorry," I said.   81

"I put him in the guest room," she said. "He thanked me as he   82
would an innkeeper." She sobbed faintly, and I wanted to touch her, but my arm was very heavy, as if I was standing at the bottom of the sea. It rose only a few inches from my side. Then she said, "I thought he might remember after he slept."

I could neither reassure her with a lie nor make her face the truth.   83
But I had to do something. I had thought too much about this already. A good businessman knows when to stop thinking and to act instead. I drew close to my wife, but only briefly did my arm rise and hold her. That was the same as all the other forgotten gestures of my life. Suddenly I surprised myself and my wife, too. I stepped in front of her and crouched down, and before either of us could think to feel foolish, I had taken Mai onto my back and straightened up, and I began to move about the yard, walking at first, down the long drooping lower branch of the oak tree and then faster along the sidewalk and then up the other side of the house, and I was going faster, and she only protested for a moment before she was laughing and holding on tighter, clinging with her legs about my waist and her arms around my neck, and I ran with her, ran as fast as I could so that she laughed harder, and I felt her clinging against me, pressing against me, and I felt her breath on the side of my face as warm and moist as a breeze off the South China Sea.

QUESTIONS

1.   Khanh, the narrator of the story, tells us he's become "a good American now" (paragraph 38), "not like a Vietnamese at all" (73). To what extent do you agree that he has assimilated into American culture? Has he "lost a whole country" (78), as he fears?

2.   From the beginning Khanh claims to be "just a businessman, not a poet." Judging by the criteria that he offers—the poet's ability to see things clearly and to remember and the businessman's lack of belief in symbols and omens, and so on—to what extent do you agree with or dispute his claim?

3.   Why do you think Khanh picks up his wife and runs around the yard with her at the end of the story?

THINKING ABOUT COMING TO AMERICA

1.   Share the impressions you have held, from previous school classes or other sources, about the Puritans who founded the New England colony in America. How do De Tocqueville's, Thoreau's, and Reed's views of the Puritans differ? Whose view comes closest to your previous impression?

2.   To what extent do you think the selections by Kingston, Mullen, and Cadena provide evidence for Reed's claim that "the sensational conflict between people of different backgrounds . . . is played up and often encouraged by the media" (paragraph 5)?

3.   To what extent do you think the short stories by Naqvi and Butler provide evidence of Reed's "blurring of cultural styles" (paragraph 5)? Compare the ways cultural styles are "blurred" in the two stories with some of Reed's examples.

4.   Mullen likens the struggles of Irish Americans in the nineteenth century to the struggles of other minority groups in the twentieth century (see question 2, page 198). How might Kingston or Cadena respond to this analogy? Based on Cadena's oral history, how would you compare or contrast the experiences—in finding jobs, facing discrimination, and so on—of Mexican Americans with those of Irish Americans, as described by Mullen?

5.   Compare the ways in which, and the extent to which, you think Fatima in "Thank God for the Jews" and Khanh in "The Trip Back" sacrifice their home cultures in the process of assimilation to American culture.

6.   Reed contrasts the visions of "a humdrum homogeneous world of all brains and no heart . . . a world of robots with human attendants bereft of imagination, of culture" with the "more exciting destiny . . . [of] a place where the cultures of the world crisscross" (paragraph 14). Based on your experience and your reading in this chapter, which vision do you think is closer to reality?

Exploring Additional Sources

7.   Other perspectives on coming to America are offered in a number of selections in Chapter 4 and Chapter 6, such as "The English Lesson" by Nicholasa Mohr (page 163), "Thanksgiving Border Crossing" by Arturo Islas (page 233), "Cultural Baggage" by Barbara Ehrenreich (page 255), and "The Cult of Ethnicity" by Arthur M.

Schlesinger, Jr. (page 259). Analyze one or two of these selections together with an essay or story in this chapter, comparing how language or ethnicity affects the immigrant experience.

8.   Test in a research library some of the competing claims made about the Puritans by De Tocqueville, Thoreau, and Reed, such as De Tocqueville's claim that they were all affluent and well educated or Reed's claim that they killed children who misbehaved. Include primary materials in your research, such as newspaper articles or personal memoirs from the seventeenth century, if these sources are available in your library.

9.   Cadena mentions the existence of separate high school proms and graduation ceremonies for Mexican high school students in Saginaw. For a particular ethnic group in a particular school or school district, research the controversy surrounding these practices and write an essay taking a position about their relative advantages and disadvantages.

10.   Investigate the current socioeconomic status and political concerns of a particular immigrant group in North America, such as those from China, Ireland, Mexico, Pakistan, or Vietnam. Use your research to help design questions for fellow students, fellow workers, or other members of this group from your community. Your questions might take the form of a brief written survey and/or taped interviews which you transcribe and edit into oral histories like Juan Cadena's. How do the particular experiences of these people from your community reflect the status and concerns of this immigrant group more generally?

11.   Interview family members to determine when and under what conditions your own ancestors first came to the United States. Conduct research, finding primary sources such as newspaper accounts from the time, about the historical context and social conditions that your ancestors left in another country or encountered in this country when they arrived. Use your research as a basis to evaluate your family members' decision to migrate or immigrate.

6

ETHNICITY AND IDENTITY

Melting Pot in Lewellen, Nebraska

MALGORZATA NIEZABITOWSKA

We met a lot of people and heard many stories. All of them compose that extraordinary mosaic called America, but now as I get ready for my trip back to Poland, one memory keeps returning particularly often. One night during a sudden storm we stopped over in a small town in Nebraska. The motel was the only one in town, and we were the only guests. In the morning we discovered that the town had one paved street and about 300 inhabitants. It was called Lewellen.

For breakfast we went to the only cafe in town. The manager, three days' growth on his face, stood behind the counter. The customers, all men, were seated around the tables. In the middle stood a round, large and empty table. And that was where we sat to have our cinnamon rolls. Our entrance caused a sensation. All conversations died down, and everybody stared at us in silence. Finally a tall, red-bearded man brought over the coffeepot from the counter and offered to refill our cups, which were still full.

In a moment our table was teeming with people, all of them asking us questions and talking about themselves. It turned out that among these 15 or so Lewellen citizens there were a Greek, an Italian, an Irishman, a Hungarian, a German, and a Pole—if not in the first, then in the second or third generation. They teased each other good-humoredly about the supposed foibles of different nationalities, and we quickly joined in the fun.

Obviously life in Lewellen is no idyll, and everybody isn't always joking. Yet the image of this big table and the people gathered around it, whose ancestors came to a lost-in-the-prairie town from different parts of the world, has for me great charm and importance.

—FROM "DISCOVERING AMERICA," IN *NATIONAL GEOGRAPHIC*, 1988

Colonia Mexicana

ERNESTO GALARZA

In the hotels and rooming houses scattered about the barrio the Filipino farm workers, riverboat stewards, and houseboys made their homes. Like the Mexicans they had their own poolhalls, which they called clubs. Hindus from the rice and fruit country north of the city stayed in the rooming houses when they were in town, keeping to themselves. The Portuguese and Italian families gathered in their own neighborhoods along Fourth and Fifth Streets southward toward the Y-street levee. The Poles, Yugo-Slavs, and Koreans, too few to take over any particular part of it, were scattered throughout the barrio. Black men drifted in and out of town, working the waterfront. It was a kaleidoscope of colors and languages and customs that surprised and absorbed me at every turn. . . .

For the Mexicans the *barrio* was a colony of refugees. We came to know families from Chihuahua, Sonora, Jalisco, and Durango. Some had come to the United States even before the revolution, living in Texas before migrating to California. Like ourselves, our Mexican neighbors had come this far moving step by step, working and waiting, as if they were feeling their way up a ladder. They talked of relatives who had been left behind in Mexico, or in some far-off city like Los Angeles or San Diego. From whatever place they had come, and however short or long the time they had lived in the United States, together they formed the *colonia mexicana*. In the years between our arrival and the First World War, the *colonia* grew and spilled out from the lower part of town. Some families moved into the alley shacks east of the Southern Pacific tracks, close to the canneries and warehouses and across the river among the orchards and rice mills.

The *colonia* was like a sponge that was beginning to leak along the edges, squeezed between the levee, the railroad tracks, and the river front. But it wasn't squeezed dry, because it kept filling with newcomers who found families who took in boarders: basements, alleys, shanties, run-down rooming houses and flop joints where they could live.

—FROM *BARRIO BOY*, 1971

The WASP Stereotype

ROBERT CLAIBORNE

I come of a long line of WASPs; if you disregard my French great-great-grandmother and a couple of putatively Irish ancestors of the same vintage, a rather pure line. My mother has long been one of the

Colonial Dames, an organization some of whose members consider the Daughters of the American Revolution rather parvenu. My umpty-umpth WASP great-grandfather, William Claiborne, founded the first European settlement in what is now Maryland (his farm and trading post were later ripped off by the Catholic Lord Baltimore, Maryland politics being much the same then as now).

As a WASP, the mildest thing I can say about the stereotype emerging from the current wave of anti-WASP chic is that I don't recognize myself. As regards emotional uptightness and sexual inhibition, modesty forbids comment—though I dare say various friends and lovers of mine could testify on these points if they cared to. I will admit to enjoying work—because I am lucky enough to be able to work at what I enjoy—but not, I think, to the point of compulsiveness. And so far as ruling America, or even New York, is concerned, I can say flatly that (a) it's a damn lie because (b) if I *did* rule them, both would be in better shape than they are. Indeed I and all my WASP relatives, taken in a lump, have far less clout with the powers that run this country than any one of the Buckleys or Kennedys (Irish Catholic), the Sulzbergers or Guggenheims (Jewish), or the late A. P. Giannini (Italian) of the Bank of America.

Admittedly, both corporate and (to a lesser extent) political America are dominated by WASPs—just as (let us say) the garment industry is dominated by Jews, and organized crime by Italians. But to conclude from this that The WASPs are the American elite is as silly as to say that The Jews are cloak-and-suiters or The Italians are gangsters. WASPs, like other ethnics, come in all varieties, including criminals—political, corporate, and otherwise.

—FROM "A WASP STINGS BACK," IN *NEWSWEEK*, 1974

Ethnic[1]

RAYMOND WILLIAMS

Ethnic has been in English since mC14. It is from fw *ethnikos*, Gk—heathen (there are possible but unproved connections between *ethnic* and *heathen*, fw *haethen*, oE). It was widely used in the senses of heathen, pagan or Gentile, until C19, when this sense was generally superseded by the sense of a RACIAL (q.v.) characteristic. **Ethnics** came to be used in the United States as what was described in 1961 as "a polite term for Jews, Italians and other lesser breeds." **Ethnology, ethnography**, and various associated words, date from the 1830s and 1840s,

---

[1]See page 86 for a key to the abbreviations used in this selection. (Ed.)

probably from German influence, and the early relations with AN-THROPOLOGY (q.v.) are complex. The scientific uses are now specialized areas within anthropology, typically **enthnography** for descriptive studies of customs and ethnology for theories of cultural development.

Meanwhile in mC20 **ethnic** reappeared, probably with effect from the earlier American use of **ethnics**, in a sense close to FOLK (q.v.), as an available contemporary style, most commonly in dress, music and food. The use ranges from serious affiliation to a (NATIVE (q.v.) and *subordinate*) tradition, as among some social groups in USA, to a term of fashion in metropolitan commerce.

—FROM *Keywords: A Vocabulary of Culture and Society,* Revised Edition, 1985.

Thanksgiving Border Crossing

ARTURO ISLAS

For Thanksgiving in 1947, Eduviges, in a fit of guilt, decided to 1
bake a turkey with all the trimmings. She had memorized the recipes
in the glossy American magazines while waiting her turn at the
Safeway checkout counter.

Because the girls were in public school and learning about North 2
American holidays and customs, Eduviges thought her plan would
please them. It did and even Josie allowed her mother to embrace her
in that quick, embarrassed way she had of touching them. As usual,
Sancho had no idea why she was going to such lengths preparing for a
ritual that meant nothing to him.

"I don't see why we can't have the enchiladas you always make," 3
he said. "I don't even like turkey. Why don't you let me bring you a
nice, fat pheasant from the Chihuahua mountains? At least it'll taste
like something. Eating turkey is going to turn my girls into little
gringas. Is that what you want?"

"Oh, Daddy, please! Everybody else is going to have turkey." The 4
girls, wearing colored paper headdresses they had made in art class,
were acting out the Pocahontas story and reciting from "Hiawatha" in
a hodgepodge of Indian sentiment that forced Sancho to agree in order
to keep them quiet.

"All right, all right," he said. "Just stop all the racket, please. And 5
Serena, *querida,* don't wear that stuff outside the house or they'll pick
you up and send you to a reservation. That would be okay with me, but
your mother wouldn't like it."

Serena and Josie gave each other knowing glances. "They" were 6
the *migra,* who drove around in their green vans, sneaked up on innocent dark-skinned people, and deported them. Their neighbor down
the block—Benito Cruz, who was lighter-skinned than Serena and did
not look at all like an Indian—had been picked up three times already,
detained at the border for hours, and then released with the warning

---

Arturo Islas (1938–1991), from El Paso, Texas, was a professor of
English at Stanford University. He is author of the novels *The Rain
God* (1984) and *Migrant Souls* (1990), which examine the lives of the
Angel family along the Texas-Mexico border. Before his death Islas
completed a third novel set in the same border region, *La Mollie and
the King of Tears* (1994), posthumously edited by Paul Skenazy of the
University of California, Santa Cruz. "Thanksgiving Border
Crossing" is excerpted from *Migrant Souls.*

that he was to carry his identification papers at all times. That he was an American citizen did not seem to matter to the immigration officers.

The Angel children were brought up on as many deportation sto- 7 ries as fairy tales and family legends. The latest border incident had been the discovery of twenty-one young Mexican males who had been left to asphyxiate in an airtight boxcar on their way to pick cotton in the lower Rio Grande Valley.

When they read the newspaper articles about how the men died, 8 both Josie and Serena thought of the fluttering noises made by the pigeons their mother first strangled and then put under a heavy cardboard box for minutes that seemed eternal to the girls. They covered their ears to protect their souls from the thumping and scratching noises of the doomed birds.

Even their mother had shown sympathy for the Mexican youths, 9 especially when it was learned that they were not from the poorest class. "I feel very bad for their families," she said. "Their mothers must be in agony."

What about their fathers? Josie felt like asking but did not. Because 10 of the horror she imagined they went through, Josie did not want to turn her own feelings for the young men into yet another argument with her mother about "wetbacks" or about who did and did not "deserve" to be in the United States.

In the first semester of seventh grade, Josie had begun to wonder 11 why being make-believe North American Indians seemed to be all right with their mother. "Maybe it was because those Indians spoke English," Josie said to Serena. Mexican Indians were too close to home and the truth, and the way Eduviges looked at Serena in her art class getup convinced Josie she was on the right track.

That year on the Saturday before Thanksgiving, their mother and 12 father took them across the river in search of the perfect turkey. Sancho borrowed his friend Tacho Morales' pickup and they drove down the valley to the Zaragoza crossing. It was closer to the ranch where Eduviges had been told the turkeys were raised and sold for practically nothing. Josie and Serena sat in the front seat of the pickup with their father. Eduviges and Ofelia followed them in the Chevy in case anything went wrong.

Sancho was a slower, more patient driver than their mother, who 13 turned into a speed demon with a sharp tongue behind the wheel. More refined than her younger sisters, Ofelia was scandalized by every phrase that came out of Eduviges' mouth when some sorry driver from Chihuahua or New Mexico got in her way.

"Why don't they teach those imbecilic cretins how to drive?" she 14 said loudly in Spanish, window down and honking. Or, "May all your teeth fall out but one and may that ache until the day you die" to the man who pulled out in front of her without a signal.

Grateful that her mother was being good for once and following 15
slowly and at a safe distance behind the pickup, Ofelia dozed, barely
aware of the clear day so warm for November. Only the bright yellow
leaves of the cottonwood trees reminded her that it was autumn. They
clung to the branches and vibrated in the breeze, which smelled of
burning mesquite and Mexican alders. As they followed her father
away from the mountains and into the valley, Ofelia began to dream
they were inside one of Mama Chona's Mexican blue clay bowls, suspended in midair while the sky revolved around them.

To Josie and Serena, it seemed their father was taking forever to 16
get to where they were going. "Are we there yet?" they asked him
until he told them that if they asked again, he would leave them in the
middle of nowhere and not let their mother rescue them. The threat
only made them laugh more and they started asking him where the
middle of nowhere was until he, too, laughed with them.

"The middle of nowhere, smart alecks, is at the bottom of the sea 17
and so deep not even the fish go there," Sancho said, getting serious
about it.

"No, no," Serena said. "It's in the space between two stars and no 18
planets around."

"I already said the middle of nowhere is in Del Sapo, Texas," Josie 19
said, not wanting to get serious.

"I know, I know. It's in the Sahara Desert where not even the tum- 20
bleweeds will grow," their father said.

"No, Daddy. It's at the top of Mount Everest." Serena was proud 21
of the B she had gotten for her report on the highest mountain in the
world. They fell silent and waited for Josie to take her turn.

"It's here," Josie said quietly and pointed to her heart.   22

"Oh, for heaven's sake, Josie, don't be so dramatic. You don't even 23
know what you are saying," Serena said. Their father changed the
subject.

When they arrived at the ranch, he told Eduviges and the girls 24
that the worst that could happen on their return was that the turkey
would be taken away from them. But the girls, especially, must do and
say exactly as he instructed them.

Their mother was not satisfied with Sancho's simple directions 25
and once again told them about the humiliating body search her
friend from New Mexico, la señora Moulton, had been subjected to at
the Santa Fe Street bridge. She had just treated her daughter Ethel and
her granddaughters, Amy and Mary Ann, to lunch at the old Central
Cafe in Juarez. When la señora had been asked her citizenship, she had
replied in a jovial way, "Well, what do I look like, sir?"

They made her get out of the car, led her to a special examining 26
cell, ordered her to undress, and made her suffer unspeakable morti-
fications while her relatives waited at least four hours in terror,

wondering if they would ever see her again or be allowed to return to the country of their birth. Then, right on cue, Josie and Serena said along with Eduviges, "And they were Anglos and blond!"

While their parents were bargaining for the bird, the girls looked   27
with awe upon the hundreds of adult turkeys kept inside four large corrals. As they walked by each enclosure, one of the birds gobbled and the rest echoed its call until the racket was unbearable. Serena was struck by an attack of giggles.

"They sure are stupid," Josie said in Spanish to their Mexican   28
guide.

"They really are," he said with a smile. "When it rains, we have to   29
cover the coops of the younger ones so they won't drown." He was a dark red color and very shy. Josie liked him instantly.

"How can they drown?" Serena asked him. "The river is nowhere   30
near here. Does it flood?"

"No," the young man said, looking away from them. "Not from   31
the Rio Bravo. From the rain itself. They stretch their necks, open their beaks wide, and let it pour in until they drown. They keel over all bloated. That's how stupid they are." He bent his head back and showed them as they walked by an enclosure. "Gobble, gobble," the guide called and the turkeys answered hysterically.

Josie and Serena laughed all the way back to the pickup. Ofelia had   32
not been allowed to join them because of the way their mother thought the guide was looking at her. She was dreaming away in the backseat of the Chevy while their father struggled to get the newly bought and nervous turkey into a slatted crate. Eduviges was criticizing every move he made. At last, the creature was in the box and eerily silent.

"Now remember, girls," Sancho said, wiping his face, "I'll do all   33
the talking at the bridge. You just say 'American' when the time comes. Not another word, you hear? Think about Mrs. Moulton, Josie." He gave her a wink.

The turkey remained frozen inside the crate. Sancho lifted it onto   34
the pickup, covered it with a yellow plastic tablecloth they used on picnics, and told Serena to sit on top of it with her back against the rear window.

"Serena," he said, "I'd hate to lose you because of this stupid bird,   35
but if you open your mouth except to say 'American,' I won't be responsible for what happens. Okay?" He kissed her on the cheek as if in farewell forever, Josie thought, looking at them from the front seat. She was beginning to wish they had not begged so successfully for a traditional North American ceremony. Nothing would happen to Ofelia, of course. She was protected in their mother's car and nowhere near the turkey. Josie felt that Serena was in great peril and made up her mind to do anything to keep her from harm.

On the way to the bridge, Josie made the mistake of asking her fa- 36
ther if they were aliens. Sancho put his foot on the brake so hard that
Eduviges almost rear-ended the truck. He looked at Josie very hard
and said, "I do not ever want to hear you use that word in my presence again. About anybody. We are not aliens. We are American citizens of Mexican heritage. We are proud of both countries and have
never and will never be that word you just said to me."

"Well," Josie said. Sancho knew she was not afraid of him. He 37
pulled the truck away from the shoulder and signaled for his wife to
continue following them. "That's what they call Mexican people in all
the newspapers. And Kathy Jarvis at school told me real snotty at recess yesterday that we were nothing but a bunch of resident aliens."

After making sure Eduviges was right behind them, Sancho said 38
in a calmer, serious tone, "Josie, I'm warning you. I do not want to hear
those words again. Do you understand me?"

"I'm only telling you what Kathy told me. What did she mean? Is 39
she right?"

"Kathy Jarvis is an ignorant little brat. The next time she tells you 40
that, you tell her that Mexican and Indian people were in this part of
the country long before any *gringos,* Europeans (he said
'Yurrupbeans') or anyone else decided it was theirs. That should shut
her up. If it doesn't, tell her those words are used by people who think
Mexicans are not human beings. That goes for the newspapers, too.
They don't think anyone is human." She watched him look straight
ahead, then in the rearview mirror, then at her as he spoke.

"Don't you see, Josie. When people call Mexicans those words, it 41
makes it easier for them to deport or kill them. Aliens come from outer
space." He paused. "Sort of like your mother's family, the blessed
Angels, who think they come from heaven. Don't tell her I said that."

Before he made that last comment, Josie was impressed by her fa- 42
ther's tone. Sancho seldom became that passionate in their presence
about any issue. He laughed at the serious and the pompous and especially at religious fanatics.

During their aunt Jesus Maria's visits, the girls and their cousins 43
were sent out of the house in the summer or to the farthest room away
from the kitchen in the winter so that they would not be able to hear
her and Sancho arguing about God and the Church. Unnoticed, the
children sneaked around the house and crouched in the honeysuckle
under the kitchen window, wide open to the heat of July. In horror and
amusement, they listened to Jesus Maria tell Sancho that he would
burn in hell for all eternity because he did not believe in an afterlife
and dared to criticize the infallibility of the Pope.

"It's because they're afraid of dying that people make up an after- 44
life to believe in," Sancho said.

"That's not true. God created Heaven, Hell, and Purgatory before   45
He created man. And you are going to end up in Hell if you don't start
believing what the Church teaches us." Jesus Maria was in her glory
defending the teachings of Roman Catholicism purged by the fires of
the Spanish Inquisition.

"Oh, Jessie—" he began.   46

"Don't call me that. My name is Jesus Maria and I am proud of it."   47
She knew the children were listening.

"Excuse me, Jesus Maria," he said with a flourish. "I just want to   48
point out to you that it's hotter here in Del Sapo right now than in
hell." He saw her bristle but went on anyway. "Haven't you figured it
out yet? This is hell and heaven and purgatory right here. How much
worse, better, or boring can the afterlife be?" Sancho was laughing at
his own insight.

"If you are going to start joking about life-and-death matters, I   49
simply won't talk about anything serious with you again," their aunt
said. They knew she meant it. "I, like the Pope, am fighting for your
everlasting soul, Sancho. If I did not love you because you are my sister's husband, I would not be telling you these things."

"Thank you, Jessie. I appreciate your efforts and love. But the pope   50
is only a man. He is not Christ. Don't you read history? All most popes
have cared about is money and keeping the poor in rags so that they
can mince about in gold lamé dresses."

"Apostate!" their aunt cried.   51

"What's that?" Serena whispered to Josie.   52

"I don't know but it sounds terrible. We'll look it up in the dictio-   53
nary as soon as they stop." They knew the arguing was almost over
when their aunt began calling their father names. Overwhelmed by the
smell of the honeysuckle, the children ran off to play kick the can.
Later, when Josie looked up the word "apostate," she kept its meaning
to herself because she knew that Serena believed in an afterlife and
would be afraid for her father.

That one word affected her father more than another was a mys-   54
tery to Josie. She loved words and believed them to be more real than
whatever they described. In her mind, she, too, suspected that she was
an apostate but, like her father, she did not want to be an alien.

"All right, Daddy. I promise I won't say that word again. And I   55
won't tell Mother what you said about the Angels."

They were now driving through the main streets of Juarez, and   56
Sancho was fighting to stay in his lane. "God, these Mexicans drive
like your mother," he said with affection.

At every intersection, young Indian women with babies at their   57
breast stretched out their hands. Josie was filled with dread and pity.
One of the women knocked on her window while they waited for the

light to change. She held up her baby and said, "*Señorita, por favor. Dinero para el niño.*" Her hair was black and shiny and her eyes as dark as Josie's. The words came through the glass in a muted, dreamlike way. Silent and unblinking, the infant stared at Josie. She had a quarter in her pocket.

"Don't roll down the window or your mother will have a fit," 58 Sancho said. He turned the corner and headed toward the river. The woman and child disappeared. Behind them, Eduviges kept honking almost all the way to the bridge.

"I think it was blind," Josie said. Her father did not answer and 59 looked straight ahead.

The traffic leading to the declaration points was backed up several 60 blocks, and the stop-and-go movement as they inched their way to the American side was more than Josie could bear. She kept looking back at Serena, who sat like a *Virgen de Guadalupe* statue on her yellow plastic-covered throne.

Knowing her sister, Josie was certain that Serena was going to free 61 the turkey, jump out of the truck with it, gather up the beggarly women and children, and disappear forever into the sidestreets and alleys of Juarez. They drove past an old Indian woman, her long braids silver gray in the sun, begging in front of Curley's Club. And that is how Josie imagined Serena years from that day—an ancient and withered creature, bare feet crusted with clay, too old to recognize her little sister. The vision made her believe that the middle of nowhere was exactly where she felt it was. She covered her chest with her arms.

"What's the matter? Don't tell me you're going to be sick," her fa- 62 ther said.

"No. I'm fine. Can't you hurry?" 63

Seeing the fear in her face, Sancho told her gently that he had not 64 yet figured out how to drive through cars without banging them up. Josie smiled and kept her hands over her heart.

When they approached the border patrolman's station, the turkey 65 began gobbling away. "Oh, no," Josie cried and shut her eyes in terror for her sister.

"Oh, shit," her father said. "I hate this goddamned bridge." At that 66 moment, the officer stuck his head into the pickup and asked for their citizenship.

"American," said Sancho. 67

"American," said Josie. 68

"Anything to declare? Any liquor or food?" he asked in an accus- 69 ing way. While Sancho was assuring him that there was nothing to declare, the turkey gobbled again in a long stream of high-pitched gurgles that sent shivers up and down Josie's spine. She vowed to go into the cell with Serena when the search was ordered.

"What's that noise?" the patrolman wanted to know. Sancho 70
shrugged and gave Josie and then the officer a look filled with the ignorance of the world.

Behind them, Serena began gobbling along with the bird and it 71
was hard for them to tell one gobble from another. Their mother
pressed down on the horn of the Chevy and made it stick. Eduviges
was ready to jump out of the car and save her daughter from a fate
worse than death. In the middle of the racket, the officer's frown was
turning into anger and he started yelling at Serena.

"American!" she yelled back and gobbled. 72

"What have you got there?" The officer pointed to the plastic-cov- 73
ered crate.

"It's a turkey," Serena shouted. "It's American, too." She kept 74
gobbling along with the noise of the horn. Other drivers had begun
honking with impatience.

The patrolman looked at her and yelled, "Sure it is! Don't move," 75
he shouted toward Sancho.

Eduviges had opened the hood and was pretending not to know 76
what to do. Rushing toward the officer, she grabbed him by the sleeve
and pulled him away from the pickup. Confused by the din, he made
gestures that Sancho took as permission to drive away. "Relax, *señora*.
Please let go of my arm."

In the truck, Sancho was laughing like a maniac and wiping the 77
tears and his nose on his sleeve. "Look at that, Josie. The guy is twice
as big as your mother."

She was too scared to laugh and did not want to look. Several 78
blocks into South Del Sapo, she was still trembling. Serena kept on gobbling in case they were being followed by the *migra* in unmarked cars.

Fifteen minutes later, Eduviges and Ofelia caught up with them on 79
Alameda Street. Sancho signaled his wife to follow him into the vacant
lot next to Don Luis Leal's Famous Tex-Mex Diner. They left the
turkey unattended and silent once more.

"Dumb bird," Sancho said. With great ceremony, he treated them 80
to *menudo* and *gorditas* washed down with as much Coca-Cola as they
could drink.

QUESTIONS

1.   Right after Sancho tells the girls that "the worst that could happen on their return was that the turkey would be taken away from them," Eduviges tells the story of Mrs. Moulton being strip-searched at the border (paragraphs 5–26). In your opinion, what roles does the fear of the *migra* or border police play in this story?

2.   How do Josie, Serena, Eduviges, and Sancho react similarly and differently to Anglo culture?

3.   How do the main characters identify to different degrees and in different ways with their ethnic Mexican culture?

What We Can Learn from Hawaii

HAL GLATZER

Race relations in America need improvement, and the best place to 1
look for inspiration is Hawaii. The "Aloha spirit" there is more than a
slogan. Granted, Hawaiian history is benign compared to that of the
U.S. as a whole, but there *have* been interracial conflicts. What is different is that—at times of crisis—the people in the islands have found it
economically, politically or socially unprofitable to be racist.

Native Hawaiians descended from Polynesian voyagers; they re- 2
spected people who could cross the enormous ocean. Many of the
Caucasians who settled in Hawaii in the 19th century were anti-colonial,
either from religious convictions or because they believed that their self-
interests would be better served by a local monarchy. They respected
the Hawaiian royalty and encouraged them to proclaim sovereignty.

Those Caucasians who became sugar planters were paternalistic; 3
that's not considered enlightened today, but then, it was forward-
thinking and benevolent. The planters neither enslaved the native islanders nor drove them into reservations. When the Hawaiians suc-
cumbed to foreign diseases (measles was the worst), the planters and
the royal families—together—decided to encourage immigrants.

Foreign workers came voluntarily; they were generally well-paid 4
and well treated. After their contracts were fulfilled, many Chinese
joined the emerging middle class as entrepreneurs and shopkeepers,
while many Japanese stayed on the sugar plantations, organizing
themselves into a labor union.

A powerful clique of North Americans, however, lobbied 5
Washington for annexation, and when it came in 1898, Hawaiians
staged an armed rebellion. With a gunboat in Honolulu harbor, U.S.
forces quickly overwhelmed the nationalists, and the new rulers placed
the last Hawaiian queen under house arrest.

The Americans discouraged but did not actively suppress or oblit- 6
erate the native culture; if anything, they simplified, packaged and
promoted it to tourists. Gaining an audience, Hawaiians integrated

---

Hal Glatzer is a journalist who spent eleven years working in Hawaii.
He has written a novel set in Hawaii called *Kamehameha County* and is
the author of several books about computers and telecommunica-
tions, including *The Birds of Babel: Satellites for a Human World* (1983)
and *Who Owns the Rainbow? Conserving the Radio Spectrum* (1984). In
the condensed version of this essay that appeared in the Sunday *San
Francisco Chronicle* in 1991, Glatzer identifies himself as a "Jewish
Haole" (see his essay for a definition of "Haole").

Caucasian artistic and musical styles with their own; the Portuguese *braguinha* became the ukulele in Hawaiian hands.

Conflicts have occasionally erupted since Annexation. Unproven 7
allegations of interracial rape in the 1930s led to the blatantly unjust Massey trials, which provoked violence in the streets. In the 1960s and '70s, young thugs calling themselves "Primo Warriors" tried to purge Hawaii of newcomers. Some labor victories in a century of union activism were tainted by racial hatreds. And there were attempts in the 1980s to pass laws restricting foreign ownership of Island property in the wake of multi-million-dollar investments by Japanese and Chinese nationals.

Mainland U.S. history is far more stained with blood, and some 8
vocal Americans still continue to provoke ethnic hatreds. Yet most Americans believe we have a comfortably polycultural nation. We gasp to see Serbs "cleansing" Yugoslavia of Muslims, and German skinheads firebombing Turkish "guest workers." We wonder how Castillian Peruvians can look down their noses at Incan Peruvians, or why Melanesian Fijians should want to oust Indian Fijians from the country they both call home. But the rest of the world looks at America and sees . . . what? Crown Heights, Brooklyn, and South Central Los Angeles.

If the U.S. cannot lead the way in showing the world how to live 9
together, no one else will. It especially behooves states like California and New York—which set so many American trends—to start the ball rolling: soon after the turn of the century, for the first time, America's "minorities" there will be in the majority.

But Americans all must aspire, as the people of Hawaii do, to the 10
Aloha spirit: welcoming strangers and sharing what we have. In Hawaii, no one is an island. After two centuries of living together in close quarters, people in Hawaii do not make war on one another. They know how to relax around people who are different, and very few are overtly prejudiced.

How do the Islanders avoid xenophobia and bigotry? What can 11
the rest of us learn from them?

Know who you are. I was asked by a young woman, "What kind 12
of Haole are you?" In Hawaii, every white Caucasian is called "Haole" (a Hawaiian word, literally "foreigner"). What she wanted to know was: am I Polish, Italian, Jewish, or what? She was a former Miss Hawaii who described herself as "Filipino-Scottish-Hawaiian-Portuguese."

It is not a faux pas in Hawaii to ask straightforwardly about some- 13
one's race. At a party, I heard a Haole ask an Asian who had just said his name, "Are you a Chinese 'L-e-e' or a Korean 'L-i'?" In North

America we have been warned against asking questions like that, for fear the other person may take offense and demand, "Why? Do we all look alike to you?"

Even more poignantly, I have heard this question asked too: "You 14 have Polynesian features; are you part Hawaiian?" Imagine the silence that would fall on a gathering of California Haoles in which someone said, "You're rather dark; is one of your parents Black?"

In Hawaii you are expected to be proud of your ancestry, and to 15 share the pride of others in theirs.

Laugh at your stereotype—everyone else does. Stereotypes are 16 not inherently derogatory. They are a starting point for the getting-to-know-you process. Every Islander knows his own: Haoles are rich, Chinese are stingy, Japanese are bureaucratic, Hawaiians are lazy, Portuguese are dense, and Samoans are fierce. Yet everyone also knows or has heard of Haole paupers, Chinese philanthropists, Japanese artists, Hawaiian entrepreneurs, Portuguese professors, or Samoan therapists.

Stand-up comedy in Hawaii draws heavily on ethnic jokes, both 17 in-group and out-group. Rather than conditioning people to accept stereotypes, humor forces them to question underlying assumptions. And there is nothing wrong with making assumptions about people, so long as you are flexible. A sixth-grader, after visiting the Mainland U.S. for the first time, told me his greatest amazement came from seeing the rubbish collectors: they were Haoles!

Americans sometimes forget that they do not call attention to a 18 person's ethnicity if it matches their own. And there are limits to what people can say with ethnic references, even in Hawaii. It is permissible to use an ethnic description to identify someone ("That Haole guy can run!"), but it is not acceptable to slur an entire group on the basis of some individual's behavior.

In Hawaii you can still hear older Filipino Americans complain 19 about "the Japanese" when they mean local government workers, partly because so many Japanese Americans are represented in the civil service but mainly because, historically, the Philippines suffered under Imperial Japan. But that is increasingly rare; younger generations have grown up without perpetuating racial epithets. That's not to say they never heard them, but rather that those slurs were not hurled in anger.

During World War II, when they volunteered for the U.S. Army, 20 many Japanese Americans from the Mainland met for the first time Japanese Americans from Hawaii. The Mainlanders called the Islanders "bobura" ("pumpkin-head," implying "country bumpkin"). The Islanders, who were generally huskier, wrestled down the Mainlanders and called them "kotonk" which, they said, was the sound a Mainlander's head made when it hit the ground. Such intramural name-calling did not stop these Japanese Americans from fighting side-by-side against European Fascists.

In Hawaii, ethnic humor is a safety valve that keeps tension from 21 building up. The common wisdom in the Islands is: anticipate how other people expect you to behave, then allow them to be pleasantly surprised. If the mood gets rough, laugh it off or (by behaving differently) head it off—preferably both.

Share one another's cultures. Possibly the greatest contribution 22 the U.S. military has made to Hawaii is that a hitch in the service is the Islanders' chance to see the world beyond the reef. They return with a tolerance for—or at least a healthy curiosity about—other people's lifestyles.

Some children in Hawaii study ballet, but practically every kid 23 learns hula. Most people play sports, but quite a few pursue the Asian martial arts as well. There are as many Haoles or others as there are Japanese in a summertime Bon dance. Since the 1970s, when a movement for ethnic pride arose around the world, there has been a renaissance of true Hawaiiana. At annual festivals, thousands of people from all races now applaud the men who perform the athletic dances, and the chanters who have mastered the ancient language.

Everyday conversations are filled with words borrowed from 24 other people's tongues. Traffic reporters use the Hawaiian directions: "mauka"—uphill—and "makai"—toward the sea. A group effort is a "hui" (Chinese). Your sphere of influence isn't your "bailiwick" (Irish), it's your "kuleana" (Hawaiian). You dismiss exaggerated promises not as "B.S." (English) but as "shibai" (Japanese).

Eat one another's food. The typical family picnic in Hawaii in- 25 cludes potato or macaroni salad, teriyaki beef or chicken, and rice— none of which is indigenous. At the annual opening-day parties at the state legislature, everyone eats Hawaiian poi (taro paste), Filipino lumpia (spring rolls), Chinese dim sum (dumplings), and Japanese sashimi (raw fish). A single streetside lunch wagon may sell Hawaiian pipikaula (beef jerky), Portuguese loko-moko (hamburger with fried egg), and Chinese stir-fried vegetables. McDonalds there offers saimin (noodle soup). One Honolulu drive-in sells Korean pickled cabbage under a big sign that says, "Kim Chee To Go."

Respect one another's traditions. Most people in Hawaii remove 26 their shoes before entering a house. The Asian custom is to keep outdoor footwear out of doors. Haoles adopted the custom, probably as an overt gesture of politeness, and now practically everybody does it. Watch visitors from Hawaii when they're on the Mainland: as they approach a front door, they instinctively begin to slip off their shoes.

Acknowledge your minority. The population in the Islands today 27
is approximately one-third Haole, one-third Japanese, and one-third
all the rest. Everyone in Hawaii knows that his or her ethnic group is
outnumbered by others. Some Mainland Haoles who move to Hawaii
find this fact very hard to accept. Most of them grew up in states where
they were members of a clear majority, and they return "home" in dismay because they could not adjust to being a minority in a multicultural, pluralistic society. Yet that is the fact worldwide, and that is the
inexorable trend in the U.S. It will be realized in California and New
York in a few years, and the sooner all American Haoles get used to it
the better.

Make political alliances. No one's politics, anywhere, is color 28
blind. Race is always an issue; in Hawaii, they don't pretend it isn't.
Since no ethnic group there is a majority, none can rule alone. Tickets
are always balanced.

Appointments are made with one eye on ethnicity: the racial 29
heritage of people who serve on boards of directors, commissions and
other deliberative bodies has often been a public issue. Obstructionists
might label it a quota system, but it's perceived in Hawaii as common
sense and fairness. Local pundits are up-front about the impact of
various ethnic voting blocs.

Politicians advance by making friends, not enemies. Right after 30
Pearl Harbor, the Honolulu chief of police (an Irish Haole) stood up
against the U.S. government and a lot of other Haoles on behalf of
Hawaii's Japanese Americans. They were not spies, Jack Burns insisted, and should not be shipped away to camps. So they were permitted to stay in the Islands during the war, and when Hawaii became
a state, they turned out in force to elect Burns governor.

Burns chose George Ariyoshi (Japanese) to be his Lieutenant 31
Governor; when Ariyoshi succeeded Burns, John Waihee (Hawaiian)
was Ariyoshi's running mate. Now Waihee is Governor, and
Lieutenant Governor Ben Cayetano (Filipino) is next in line.

Share your children. Extended families and multigenerational 32
households are the norm in Hawaii. If a brother or sister falls on hard
times, the rest of the family will take in their children, adopting them
if necessary, to keep everyone together.

Many youngsters grow up with "calabash cousins": kids who are 33
raised as siblings though they are more distantly (or not at all) related,
and are sometimes not even of the same race, but who all eat from the
same bowl (calabash). All are equally loved by the elders. Parents who
have no fear teach no fear.

Every child in Hawaii has friends from other ethnic groups. 34
Neighborhoods are divided mainly by income, not by race. Kids learn

to cope with strangers quickly; some get into a fight or two, but they all grow up together. The shared experience of being a "local" boy or girl is not based on your ethnicity but on where you went to school.

Do business the Asian way. Haoles working in Japan have 35 learned to accept an alternative business style, but many Haoles who come to Hawaii think that—because it's an American state—they can operate in Haole fashion: confronting opponents and making unilateral decisions. In Hawaii the prevailing business climate is Asian: taking time to make friends, entering negotiations slowly, and then working toward a consensus.

This has paid real dividends. Attorneys and insurance agents are 36 well-represented among Hawaii's legislators, and—as everywhere—are traditional antagonists. Yet they cooperated to develop a plan for statewide medical insurance that made everybody happy. All employers of six or more people must insure their employees. With such a large rate base guaranteed, the insurance companies accept individuals at comparatively low rates. Patients—knowing they are well covered—seek medical attention easily and quickly. Providers can reach the entire population, making it easy to encourage prevention and early treatment, while amortizing the cost of sophisticated care over the whole state.

While other factors are surely involved (including the relative lack 37 of interracial stress), the upshot of this political miracle is that the life span of the average person in Hawaii is statistically longer than that of any other American citizen.

QUESTIONS

1.   What experiences have you had with Glatzer's specific suggestions for improving relations between ethnic and racial groups? Compare your experiences and their relative success with those of classmates or other readers.

2.   Do you agree with Glatzer's implication that, on the mainland, it's more taboo to identify straightforwardly with one's ethnicity? How do you feel about his suggestion to use humor and even ethnic jokes for poking fun at stereotypes?

3.   What major differences from the mainland does Glatzer suggest make Hawaii more conducive to harmony among its various ethnic groups? What historical or other differences can you think of that Glatzer doesn't mention? Given these differences, how difficult do you think it will be for the mainland to follow the example of Hawaii, as Glatzer recommends?

What's behind the "Asian Mask"?

ALEXANDRA TANTRANON-SAUR

First the "yellow peril," now the "model minority"—most of you 1 know enough to scoff at these racist stereotypes. Some are beginning to know the violence and sorrow visited upon the Asian and Pacific peoples in this country by ordinary white people blinded by stereotypes, and mourn and rage with us as we demand justice.

But there is yet another layer to penetrate, a layer of seemingly in- 2 nocuous assumptions, that clouds your vision of us, and confuses your attempts to find, work with, experience us. You see us wearing masks; we see you imagining we should prefer your cultures to ours! Let's take a look at this "Asian mask."

Asian/Pacific people are quiet. Asian/Pacific people are not quiet! 3 Certainly in this area[1] most of us have had a chance to visit one Chinatown or another; is it quiet? Lots of Chinese, especially the older immigrants, walking on the streets having loud and musical conversations with each other. Chinese working-class women waiting tables and shouting to each other and the cooks. Pushing their carts of dim sum through the aisles, tempting the weekend brunch crowd with *"Ha gow! Shui mei! Cha-shu bow!"* For the Chinese, as for many other peoples, the issue of speaking quietly versus loudly is a class issue.

And as for the volume of spoken words—no one can tell me 4 Asian/Pacific people don't say much. My mother, sister and I outtalk my non-Asian father hands down. My Asian/Pacific friends can outtalk me. Go into the Thai Buddhist temple during service. The monks have to chant over the microphone; everyone else is talking. In language class, the children talk and the teachers talk louder.

Don't get me wrong; I'm sure there are some quiet Asian/Pacific 5 people. I've heard there are. (Even I occasionally like to be quiet.) I just don't know any.

So why does it appear to non-Asian/Pacific people (and in fact to 6 many Asian/Pacific Americans as well) that we are quiet? A closer

---

[1]The San Francisco Bay area.

Alexandra Tantranon-Saur was born in New York City of Thai and English-Swedish parents. A computer consultant and luthier, or builder of stringed musical instruments, she also works with counseling and support groups and workshops focusing on cross-cultural communication. She wrote this article in 1986 for *Our Asian Inheritance,* a journal for lay counselors.

look at some common Asian/Pacific-American conversational habits may surprise you.

The *pause.* I learned the proper way to speak was to leave pauses 7 in between thoughts and even sentences. We sculpt the flow of our words with silences; spaces for thinking, reflecting, relaxing. Get together with people who talk like this, hold your tongue, and you'll see how comfortably a conversation goes. You can think with pauses! You can see that, from a purely mechanical point of view, most people who speak without pauses will be constantly interrupting us; and while we wait for the longer pause which signals that the speaker has finished a thought and that the next speaker may start, the non-Asian/Pacific people will talk on and on, marveling that they have found such a good listener who seems to have nothing to say.

But this is more than just a mechanical speech pattern. I was 8 taught, and I observe this in other Asian/Pacific Americans, to be constantly aware of the attention level of my listener, in fact to monitor and nurture it. The *pause* is part of this. If someone else immediately grabs the moment of silence, then that person must not have been listening with much attention, right? In fact, they may have been waiting desperately to get a chance to unload. So of course they should get the attention if they're that desperate.

The pause is also often lengthened into the *question pause.* That is: 9 from time to time it is good to stop in the middle and see if a listener asks, "What else? Say more!" This is a useful check to see if they are listening and interested. If they don't ask, why continue to talk?

In addition to monitoring the attention level in our listener, the 10 *start-off question* is the most clear example of actively building our listener's attention level. You all know this one. I want to tell you what I think about the World Bank (we have been talking about canoeing), so I ask you what *you* think about the World Bank. Why don't I just start out on the World Bank? Well, why should I assume that you'll be able to listen to that? First I check, and I listen to you, and by the time you have gotten whatever you need to off your chest, you will probably realize that you want to know what *I* think about the World Bank.

You may notice another attention-maintaining technique we use in 11 conversations. It is the frequent *sorry*'s you hear. If you find this irritating, it's no wonder—you probably think we are apologizing! Many people were apparently raised to think that "I'm sorry" is an admission of guilt or statement of contriteness or self-denigration. I'm sorry, it's not true. It simply means, "no offense intended by what I have to say to you." It means, "listen to me knowing that you are not being personally attacked"; it means, "listen attentively with an open mind."

You will notice that my behavior is based on the assumption that 12 I pay better attention to others than do non-Asian/Pacific people. Can this be true? In the sense of having the habit of thinking about others in uncomfortable situations, it is true. How can this happen, that we pay better attention?

Part of this is a survival technique, not unique to Asian/Pacific   13 Americans: the experience of an oppressed people is that we have to pay more attention to the feelings of our oppressors than vice versa. Everyone knows this one—how much time do we spend talking about the boss? We know the boss's habits, preferences, moods, irrationalities—we have to! But the boss is unlikely to know ours. The same thing happens between people of color and white people.

But the primary reason that Asian/Pacific people pay more atten-   14 tion to others has to do with the principles of cooperation and exchange, which form the basis of our societies and cultures. Consider typical Asian/Pacific group behavior:

Asian/Pacific people have a pattern of going last ("invisibility"). If you   15 could be a fly on my shoulder in an Asian/Pacific group, you would notice the conversational customs I mentioned above. If you look also at how the group attention flows from subject to subject, you would see that our number one priority is to take care of the group as a whole. You will notice us attending to business matters first. We will rarely risk the integrity of the group by presenting "personal" needs or demands before all the group needs are taken care of. This cooperative behavior functions quite well in the Asian/Pacific context.

Let me tell you a story illustrating what often happens in the   16 mixed context. In a group dealing with issues of internalized racism, we first separated into our "racial" groups (Asian/Pacific, African, European, Latino/a[2,3]) with a list of questions to answer and two lists to make and present to the larger group. The schedule allowed forty-five minutes total for presentations. Back in the larger group, we Asians made our presentation first, and for the most part simply read through the two lists. That took about five minutes. The African group was next. They had decided not to do the assigned questions and lists, and instead made up four different lists, and presented them, each member of the group speaking several times. That took about twenty minutes. It was important for the African group to make the exercise useful by changing it as needed, and to express to the group the feelings that had come up for them. The schedule would just have to give. It was important to us to make sure things moved along as planned (i.e., time-wise and assignment-wise); instead of changing the assignment and schedule, we would wait with our feelings.

---

[2]We unfortunately had no Native American group.

[3]These terms are not inclusive or descriptive enough. African Americans, Latinos, and Latinas are working hard to find names that define themselves accurately and respectfully.

Both fine approaches. But again, simply the mechanics of mixing 17
the two approaches means that, without thoughtful intervention, our
personal needs will come last, if at all. If others are unaware of our approach, and are carrying around "quiet/unemotional Asian" stereotypes of us, it may never occur to them to ask us, after everything else
is done, "Well, what about *your* feelings?"

Asian/Pacific people are "nice" and "polite." These so-called Asian 18
traits are praised by those who would like to keep us in line (teachers
and employers, for example) and damned by our loving supporters
who wish we would assimilate to Western-style bumper-car social interactions. I'm sorry, folks (see above), but I just have to complain
about labeling being "nice" and "polite" as a problem. Why don't we
use the right words? Gracious and hospitable. Cultural strengths
which help us maintain the functioning and integrity of our families
and groups. It sure never stopped us from making war on each other,
exploiting each other, defending ourselves, or making revolution! The
problem is not the behavior itself; it is the inability to choose another
behavior when more appropriate. Obviously *that* has nothing to do
with being Asian or Pacific, but rather with the experience of being immigrant minorities and being murdered in large numbers.

A variation on this is *Asian/Pacific people don't show their feelings.* 19
Just like anyone else, we will laugh, cry, rage, shiver, and melt with
love, as soon as we get enough loving attention. And, just like anyone
else, our feelings are written all over our faces and bodies. Not seeing
how we express it is part of the "they all look the same to me" syndrome. "But what if someone always has the same look on their face?"
you say. Put on your thinking cap! What does it mean if your friend
has the same feelings frozen into her face all the time she's around
you? That's a rather eloquent message, I would say. "But she
can't/won't tell me what she's feeling!" Nope, we sure do resist translating for you, don't we?

Asian/Pacific people need assertiveness training. It sure might look like 20
that to someone accustomed to bumper-car social interactions. But
welcome, ye weary bumper cars, to another cultural setting.
Interactions between Asian/Pacific people are based to a great extent
upon cooperation and exchange. Consider the group behavior—cooperation before individualism. Consider the *start-off question*—I give
you attention first, then you offer it back to me. Exchange is an important cultural principle. A non-Asian/Pacific American was counseling
an Indian woman on a decision she needed to make. The conversation
went something like this:

"After all, who's the most important?" 21
"My mother." 22
"Wrong!" 23

"My father?"   24
"No!"   25
"My sister??"   26
"*You* are!"   27
"???"   28

In the Indian social system, you make someone else the most im-   29
portant; watch out for their welfare, make decisions based on their
needs. *You* get to be the most important for someone else; you have
someone thinking about *your* needs. You give and you get, and it all
evens out.

Several Japanese and Japanese-American customs also illustrate   30
this exchange principle. You don't split up the bill at a restaurant; you
treat your friends, knowing that the next time they will treat you back.
People pay attention to each other through *exchange of appreciations.*
The woman who has spent three days preparing a feast offers it to her
guests with "This isn't much, but please help yourselves." This is a signal for the guests to express their appreciation of her. They respond
without rancor, because they, too, will get validated by the same
mechanism. This extends to speaking about the children—"My daughter, she isn't very good at that." "But she's so good at these other
things. You have a fine daughter!" Of course, sometimes it is important that you let someone know what you can do. In that case, your
friend speaks for you. You never have to toot your own horn.

This is not to say that people don't get squished by these rules. The   31
Japanese have a saying, "The nail that stands above the others will get
hammered down to the same level." The historical lack of natural resources required cooperation and discouraged individualism, there
having been no excess to cover the risks of individual mistakes. Now
the Japanese are far beyond survival level, and the cultural survival
techniques have not been discarded. But within the cultural context,
the exchange principle functions well.

What's a friend to do? How can you put your new-found insights   32
into action? These suggestions and exercises will not only bring you
closer to us, but will also challenge you to act clearly and decisively in
groups and one-to-one relationships.

1. Take responsibility for equal time-sharing, especially in mixed   33
   groups.

2. Notice and deal with the feelings that come up for you when   34
   there is silence in a conversation. There is often desperation behind the habit of filling every second with words. An appreciation of silence will allow you to awarely encourage us to break the
   silence when we choose.

3. Notice when Asian/Pacific people are not talking. Assume that 35 when we are not talking, you are interrupting us. It will become obvious what to do. Also, don't assume we are finished when we stop talking. It may be a *thinking pause* or a *question pause,* instead of an *end-of-thought pause.* It is perfectly acceptable to simply ask if we are finished.

4. Don't try to assist us by taking the perspective that we should 36 change our behavior, but rather that we need to have more choices. Remember the exchange principle. We need to deal with the hurt we experience when other people don't come through on the exchange, but instead simply take from us. Encourage us to have the highest expectations of our allies, to require your attention, in fact to demand it, instead of always giving it first and waiting for it to be offered back.

5. Talk and listen Asian/Pacific-style with us. Practice recognizing 37 and using the various *pauses.*

6. Remember that our "politeness," "apologies," et cetera, are not 38 necessarily forms of self-invalidation. In European-American culture, these habits are often also considered to be signs of the weakness of the female. In this way, acting out sexism/internalized sexism by wishing us to give up our "weak" habits can turn out to be racist. Don't buy it! These are women's cultural strengths as well as Asian/Pacific cultural strengths.

7. Remember that, just like anyone else, we will express and release 39 the full range of emotions as soon as we get enough caring attention. And, just like anyone else, our feelings are written all over our faces and bodies. We will do you the favor of not translating. Trust your thinking, make lots of mistakes, and pretty soon you'll be able not only to translate, but to think and see Asian/Pacific-style, too.

QUESTIONS

1. If you are not Asian or Asian American, which of the "seemingly innocuous assumptions" (paragraph 2) about Asian/Pacific people analyzed by Tantranon-Saur did you share before reading this essay? If you identify your own ethnicity as Asian/Pacific or Asian American, to what extent do you agree with Tantranon-Saur's response to stereotypes about this group?

2. Make a list of common stereotypes about your own ethnic group (or your nationality, religion, regional identification, gender, or sexual orientation). Analyze or refute these stereotypes, as Tantranon-Saur does, then address a list of suggestions or exercises to sympathetic members of another ethnic (or religious, etc.) group.

3. To what extent do you think Tantranon-Saur tries to address a broader audience than the lay (non-professional) counselors for whom she wrote this article? How successful is she in appealing to this larger audience?

Cultural Baggage

BARBARA EHRENREICH

An acquaintance was telling me about the joys of rediscovering 1
her ethnic and religious heritage. "I know exactly what my ancestors
were doing 2,000 years ago," she said, eyes gleaming with enthusiasm,
"and I can do the same things now." Then she leaned forward and in-
quired politely, "And what is your ethnic background, if I may ask?"

"None," I said, that being the first word in line to get out of my 2
mouth. Well, not "none," I backtracked. Scottish, English, Irish—that
was something, I supposed. Too much Irish to qualify as a WASP; too
much of the hated English to warrant a "Kiss Me, I'm Irish" button;
plus there are a number of dead ends in the family tree due to adop-
tions, missing records, failing memories and the like. I was blushing by
this time. Did "none" mean I was rejecting my heritage out of Anglo-
Celtic self-hate? Or was I revealing a hidden ethnic chauvinism in
which the Britannically derived serve as a kind of neutral standard
compared with the ethnic "others"?

Throughout the 1960s and '70s I watched one group after another 3
—African Americans, Latinos, Native Americans—stand up and
proudly reclaim their roots while I just sank back ever deeper
into my seat. All this excitement over ethnicity stemmed, I uneasily
sensed, from a past in which their ancestors had been trampled upon
by my ancestors, or at least by people who looked very much like
them. In addition, it had begun to seem almost un-American not to
have some sort of hyphen at hand, linking one to more venerable times
and locales.

But the truth is, I was raised with none. We'd eaten ethnic foods in 4
my childhood home, but these were all borrowed, like the pasties, or
Cornish meat pies, my father had picked up from his fellow miners in
Butte, Montana. If my mother had one rule, it was militant ecumenism
in all matters of food and experience. "Try new things," she would

Barbara Ehrenreich writes about social and political issues as a regular columnist for *Time* and contributor to other magazines such as *The
Nation* and *Mother Jones*. Her books include *Witches, Midwives, and
Nurses: A History of Women Healers* (co-authored with Deirdre English,
1973), *The Hearts of Men: American Dreams and the Flight from
Commitment* (1983), *Fear of Falling: The Inner Life of the Middle Class*
(1989), and *The Worst Years of Our Lives: Irreverent Notes from a Decade
of Greed* (1990), about the 1980s. This essay appeared in *The New York
Times Magazine* in 1992.

say, meaning anything from sweet-breads to clams, with an emphasis on the "new."

As a child, I briefly nourished a craving for tradition and roots. I 5 immersed myself in the works of Sir Walter Scott. I pretended to believe that the bagpipe was a musical instrument. I was fascinated to learn from a grandmother that we were descended from certain Highland clans and longed for a pleated skirt in one of their distinctive tartans.

But in *Ivanhoe,* it was the dark-eyed "Jewess" Rebecca I identified 6 with, not the flaxen-haired bimbo Rowena. As for clans: Why not call them tribes—those bands of half-clad peasants and warriors whose idea of cuisine was stuffed sheep gut washed down with whisky? And then there was the sting of Disraeli's remark—which I came across in my early teens—to the effect that his ancestors had been leading orderly, literate lives when my ancestors were still rampaging through the Highlands daubing themselves with blue paint.

Motherhood put the screws on me, ethnicity-wise. I had hoped 7 that by marrying a man of Eastern European Jewish ancestry I would acquire for my descendants the ethnic genes that my own forebears so sadly lacked. At one point I even subjected the children to a seder of my own design, including a little talk about the flight from Egypt and its relevance to modern social issues. But the kids insisted on buttering their matzos and snickering through my talk. "Give me a break, Mom," the older one said. "You don't even believe in God."

After the tiny pagans had been put to bed, I sat down to brood 8 over Elijah's wine. What had I been thinking? The kids knew that their Jewish grandparents were secular folks who didn't hold seders themselves. And if ethnicity eluded me, how could I expect it to take root in my children, who are not only Scottish English Irish, but Hungarian Polish Russian to boot?

But, then, on the fumes of Manischewitz, a great insight took form 9 in my mind. It was true, as the kids said, that I didn't "believe in God." But this could be taken as something very different from an accusation—a reminder of a genuine heritage. My parents had not believed in God either, nor had my grandparents or any other progenitors going back to the great-great level. They had become disillusioned with Christianity generations ago—just as, on the in-law side, my children's other ancestors had shaken off their Orthodox Judaism. This insight did not exactly furnish me with an "identity," but it was at least something to work with: We are the kind of people, I realized—whatever our distant ancestors' religions—who do not believe, who do not carry on traditions, who do not do things just because someone has done them before.

The epiphany went on: I recalled that my mother never introduced 10 a procedure for cooking or cleaning by telling me, "Grandma did it this way." What did Grandma know, living in the days before vacuum cleaners and disposable toilet mops? In my parents' general view, new things were better than old and the very fact that some ritual had been performed in the past was a good reason for abandoning it now. Because what was the past, as our forebears knew it? Nothing but poverty, superstition and grief. "Think for yourself," Dad used to say. "Always ask why."

In fact, this may have been the ideal cultural heritage for my par- 11 ticular ethnic strain—bounced as it was from the Highlands of Scotland across the sea, out to the Rockies, down into the mines and finally spewed out into high-tech, suburban America. What better philosophy, for a race of migrants, than "think for yourself"? What better maxim, for a people whose whole world was rudely inverted every 30 years or so, than "try new things"?

The more tradition-minded, the newly enthusiastic celebrants 12 of Purim and Kwanzaa and Solstice, may see little point to survival if the survivors carry no cultural freight—religion, for example, or ethnic tradition. To which I would say that skepticism, curiosity and wide-eyed ecumenical tolerance are also worthy elements of the human tradition and are at least as old as such notions as "Serbian" or "Croatian," "Scottish" or "Jewish." I make no claims for my personal line of progenitors except that they remained loyal to the values that may have induced all of our ancestors, long, long ago, to climb down from the trees and make their way into the open plains.

A few weeks ago I cleared my throat and asked the children, now 13 mostly grown and fearsomely smart, whether they felt any stirrings of ethnic or religious identity, which might have been, ahem, insufficiently nourished at home. "None," they said, adding firmly, "and the world would be a better place if nobody else did, either." My chest swelled with pride, as would my mother's, to know that the race of "none" marches on.

QUESTIONS

1. How sympathetic are you with Ehrenreich's suspicion that "all this excitement over ethnicity" by African Americans, Native Americans, and other groups "stemmed . . . from a past in which their ancestors had been trampled upon by my ancestors" (paragraph 3)? If you are Caucasian, do you also identify your ethnic background as "none," as Ehrenreich does in this essay? Why or why not?

2. Discuss the nature of the identity that Ehrenreich seems to discover in lieu of an ethnic identity. How satisfied does she seem with this identity? How satisfactory do you consider her solution to finding a group identity?

The Cult of Ethnicity

ARTHUR M. SCHLESINGER JR.

The history of the world has been in great part the history of the 1
mixing of peoples. Modern communication and transport accelerate
mass migrations from one continent to another. Ethnic and racial diversity is more than ever a salient fact of the age.

But what happens when people of different origins, speaking dif- 2
ferent languages and professing different religions, inhabit the same
locality and live under the same political sovereignty? Ethnic and
racial conflict—far more than ideological conflict—is the explosive
problem of our times.

On every side today ethnicity is breaking up nations. The Soviet 3
Union, India, Yugoslavia, Ethiopia, are all in crisis. Ethnic tensions
disturb and divide Sri Lanka, Burma, Indonesia, Iraq, Cyprus,
Nigeria, Angola, Lebanon, Guyana, Trinidad—you name it. Even nations as stable and civilized as Britain and France, Belgium and Spain,
face growing ethnic troubles. Is there any large multiethnic state that
can be made to work?

The answer to that question has been, until recently, the United 4
States. "No other nation," Margaret Thatcher has said, "has so successfully combined people of different races and nations within a single culture." How have Americans succeeded in pulling off this almost unprecedented trick?

We have always been a multiethnic country. Hector St. John 5
de Crevecoeur, who came from France in the 18th century, marveled at
the astonishing diversity of the settlers—"a mixture of English, Scotch,
Irish, French, Dutch, Germans and Swedes . . . this promiscuous breed."
He propounded a famous question: "What then is the American, this
new man?" And he gave a famous answer: "Here individuals of all
nations are melted into a new race of men." *E pluribus unum.*

Arthur M. Schlesinger, Jr., is a historian and professor of humanities
at City University of New York. He served as a special assistant to
Presidents Kennedy and Johnson in 1961–1964. His books on presidential history include *The Age of Jackson* (1945, winner of the Pulitzer
Prize for History), *The Age of Roosevelt* (1957, 1959, 1960), and *A
Thousand Days: John F. Kennedy in the White House* (1965, winner of the
Pulitzer Prize for Biography and a National Book Award); *Robert
Kennedy and His Times* (1978) also won a National Book Award. His
most recent book, *The Disuniting of America* (1992), explores ethnic
relations in the United States. This essay appeared in *Time* magazine
in 1991.

The U.S. escaped the divisiveness of a multiethnic society by a bril-   6
liant solution: the creation of a brand-new national identity. The point
of America was not to preserve old cultures but to forge a new,
American culture. "By an intermixture with our people," President
George Washington told Vice President John Adams, immigrants will
"get assimilated to our customs, measures and laws: in a word, soon
become one people." This was the ideal that a century later Israel
Zangwill crystallized in the title of his popular 1908 play *The Melting
Pot*. And no institution was more potent in molding Crevecoeur's
"promiscuous breed" into Washington's "one people" than the
American public school.

The new American nationality was inescapably English in lan-   7
guage, ideas and institutions. The pot did not melt everybody, not
even all the white immigrants; deeply bred racism put black
Americans, yellow Americans, red Americans and brown Americans
well outside the pale. Still, the infusion of other stocks, even of non-
white stocks, and the experience of the New World reconfigured the
British legacy and made the U.S., as we all know, a very different
country from Britain.

In the 20th century, new immigration laws altered the composition   8
of the American people, and a cult of ethnicity erupted both among
non-Anglo whites and among nonwhite minorities. This had many
healthy consequences. The American culture at last began to give
shamefully overdue recognition to the achievements of groups subor-
dinated and spurned during the high noon of Anglo dominance, and
it began to acknowledge the great swirling world beyond Europe.
Americans acquired a more complex and invigorating sense of their
world—and of themselves.

But, pressed too far, the cult of ethnicity has unhealthy conse-   9
quences. It gives rise, for example, to the conception of the U.S. as a nation composed not of individuals making their own choices but of in-
violable ethnic and racial groups. It rejects the historic American goals
of assimilation and integration.

And, in an excess of zeal, well-intentioned people seek to trans-   10
form our system of education from a means of creating "one people"
into a means of promoting, celebrating and perpetuating separate ethnic origins and identities. The balance is shifting from *unum* to *pluribus*.

That is the issue that lies behind the hullabaloo over "multicultur-   11
alism" and "political correctness," the attack on the "Eurocentric" curriculum and the rise of the notion that history and literature should be
taught not as disciplines but as therapies whose function is to raise minority self-esteem. Group separatism crystallizes the differences, mag-
nifies tensions, intensifies hostilities. Europe—the unique source of the

liberating ideas of democracy, civil liberties and human rights—is portrayed as the root of all evil, and non-European cultures, their own many crimes deleted, are presented as the means of redemption.

I don't want to sound apocalyptic about these developments. 12 Education is always in ferment, and a good thing too. The situation in our universities, I am confident, will soon right itself. But the impact of separatist pressures on our public schools is more troubling. If a Kleagle of the Ku Klux Klan wanted to use the schools to disable and handicap black Americans, he could hardly come up with anything more effective than the "Afrocentric" curriculum. And if separatist tendencies go unchecked, the result can only be the fragmentation, resegregation and tribalization of American life.

I remain optimistic. My impression is that the historic forces 13 driving toward "one people" have not lost their power. The eruption of ethnicity is, I believe, a rather superficial enthusiasm stirred by romantic ideologues on the one hand and by unscrupulous con men on the other: self-appointed spokesmen whose claim to represent their minority groups is carelessly accepted by the media. Most American-born members of minority groups, white or nonwhite, see themselves primarily as Americans rather than primarily as members of one or another ethnic group. A notable indicator today is the rate of intermarriage across ethnic lines, across religious lines, even (increasingly) across racial lines. "We Americans," said Theodore Roosevelt, "are children of the crucible."

The growing diversity of the American population makes the 14 quest for unifying ideals and a common culture all the more urgent. In a world savagely rent by ethnic and racial antagonisms, the U.S. must continue as an example of how a highly differentiated society holds itself together.

QUESTIONS

1. Write a brief definition of "the cult of ethnicity" based on Schlesinger's argument. Of the definitions given for "cult" in the dictionary, which do you think comes closest to Schlesinger's use of the word?

2. Discuss the healthy and unhealthy consequences that Schlesinger claims have followed from "the cult of ethnicity." Schlesinger seems especially concerned with the educational system. What specific experiences have you had in school that support or don't support Schlesinger's claims?

3. Schlesinger presents his analysis of ethnicity as a debate or conflict between a unified "American nationality [that] was inescapably English in language, ideas and institutions" (paragraph 7) and "group separatism" leading to "fragmentation, resegregation and tribalization of American life" (paragraph 12). What alternatives, if any, do you see to these two conditions?

THINKING ABOUT ETHNICITY AND IDENTITY

1. Which of Glatzer's specific suggestions for improving race relations in America do you think are embodied in Islas's story? How so? How might you modify or add to Glatzer's suggestions based on Islas's story? You might consider relations *among* the diverse Mexican Americans in the story as well as relations between Mexican Americans and the Anglo majority. Who could benefit the most from Glatzer's advice?

2. How are Glatzer's and Tantranon-Saur's suggestions for improving relations across ethnic groups similar and how are they different? Whose advice do you find more useful, and why?

3. To what extent do you think that Schlesinger means the same thing by "the cult of ethnicity" that Ehrenreich means by "cultural baggage"? How compatible are their reactions to the increased emphasis on ethnicity in North America?

4. Glatzer's essay originally appeared in a newspaper, Ehrenreich's in a Sunday magazine supplement, and Schlesinger's in the news magazine *Time*. What stylistic features do these pieces of journalism have in common? What distinguishes their styles from one another?

5. Tantranon-Saur says that "the experience of an oppressed people is that we have to pay more attention to the feelings of our oppressors than vice versa" (paragraph 13). How do you think she would apply this analysis to dispute Schlesinger's argument about the dangers of a "cult of ethnicity"?

6. Schlesinger says that those who encourage "the eruption of ethnicity" are "self-appointed spokesmen," "romantic ideologues," or "unscrupulous con men" (paragraph 13). To whom do you think he is referring? Using Schlesinger's criteria, would you classify Islas, Glatzer, or Tantranon-Saur as a "separatist"? How might these writers respond to such a charge, and what is your own view?

7. Compare how members of the white majority are portrayed in two or more of the selections by Niezabitowska, Claiborne, Islas, Tantranon-Saur, and Ehrenreich.

Exploring Additional Sources

8. Issues of ethnicity and identity are addressed in many other selections in *Encountering Cultures*. Here are several promising comparisons to write about or discuss:

(a) Analyze Islas's story in conjunction with "Public and Private Language" by Richard Rodriguez (page 142) or "How to Tame a Wild Tongue" by Gloria Anzaldua (page 152).

(b) Analyze Tantranon-Saur's essay in conjunction with "The Language of Discretion" by Amy Tan (page 64) or "Two Deserts" by Valerie Matsumoto (page 73);

(c) Analyze Schlesinger's essay in conjunction with "America: The Multinational Society" by Ishmael Reed (page 187) or "The Age of Balkanization" by Patrick Glynn (page 587).

9. Research an aspect of Hawaiian history referred to by Glatzer, such as the American annexation, the Massey trials, the Primo Warriors of the 1960s and 1970s, or Japanese and Chinese investments of the past two decades. Construct an argument about how this history has affected relations between ethnic groups.

10. Test Tantranon-Saur's claims about the way Asian/Pacific people communicate with scholarly studies of cross-cultural communication. What evidence have social scientists found for the "pause," the "question pause," the "start-off question," and so on? Based on your research, how do you evaluate Tantranon-Saur's list of suggestions and exercises? Alternatively, research interethnic communication between two other ethnic groups you're interested in, and take a position about how to improve this communication.

11. Schlesinger says that "the U.S. escaped the divisiveness of a multiethnic society by a brilliant solution: the creation of a brand-new national identity," while Kevin Mullen, in Chapter 5, portrays nineteenth-century America as "a long, violent struggle between successive waves of immigrants who were fighting for their livelihood." Test these contrary claims in the particular case of one immigrant group, as Mullen does with Irish Americans.

7

PRIVILEGE, POVERTY, AND MAINSTREAM VALUES

Workers' Utopia, The Bronx

KATE SIMON

For a time I enjoyed the "coops," as the new houses were called. Our apartment was light and fresh and the atmosphere as impassioned in its own way as that of Lafontaine Avenue, my childhood street. This was to be Utopia, a workers' Utopia, run justly and lovingly, truly democratically. It was culturally avid, education of all sorts organized before the last toilets were placed in the bathrooms. There were dance classes, classes in Russian, in English, in political science, in crafts. There was a cafeteria that served huge Jewish-kitchen portions with generous slabs of bread and side orders of pickles and beet salad. There was a large food shop, run cooperatively, to which I refused to go after a comrade clerk laughed at me when I asked for Oscar Wilde sardines. I should have asked for King Oscar but hated him for correcting me, although my error proved the superior quality of my thoughts. In time the food store failed, partially as a result of excessive democracy: a committee of cutters, bookkeepers, and Yiddish journalists, in spite of—or because of—their lengthy discussions, failed to catch the freshest crates of spinach at the most advantageous prices, were bilked by capitalist canned soup suppliers, and blamed each other for costly errors. The cafeteria closed; too many disputes among the cooking comrades, the serving comrades, the cleaning-up comrades, and prices didn't stay idealistically low.

In spite of difficulties and disappointments, spirits stayed high and hot. Rent strikes in the neighborhood were signaled by a banging on apartment doors. "Come! Out! Run! Leave everything, the cossacks [cops] are here!" Whether they wanted to or not, many ran; not always sure they knew where or why, especially the unenlightened housewives caught elbow-deep in washtubs or frying the delicate, perishable crepes or blintzes. Others, always at the ready, dashed with revolutionary fervor. My mother never responded. She said the women who did were *mishigoyim*[1] looking for excitement, anything to get away from their sinks and kids. She might have been somewhat right. The children of the most vigorous rent-strike militants, the most insistent shouters and bangers on doors, were the shabbiest, most neglected children, free of bourgeois traits like socks that matched and regular meals. They were often renamed, to their bewilderment, from Solly, Benny, Davy, to Lenin, Marx, Trotsky, which, with the addition of the inescapable diminutive, became Leninel, Marxele, Trotskele. Their mothers, married to the same passive husbands for twenty years, redesigned their lives as well; now members of a new world, they discarded the word "husband" and spoke of their bland men as "mein comrade"—a stormer of barricades, the bearer of the reddest banner.

—FROM *A WIDER WORLD: PORTRAITS IN AN ADOLESCENCE*, 1986

The Western Code

GRETEL EHRLICH

Wyoming tips down as you head northeast; the highest ground— the Laramie Plains—is on the Colorado border. Up where I live, the Big Horn River leaks into difficult, arid terrain. In the basin where it's dammed, sandhill cranes gather and, with delicate legwork, slice through the stilled water. I was driving by with a rancher one morning when he commented that cranes are "old-fashioned." When I asked why, he said, "Because they mate for life." Then he looked at me with a twinkle in his eyes, as if to say he really did believe in such things but also understood why we break our own rules.

In all this open space, values crystallize quickly. People are strong on scruples but tenderhearted about quirky behavior. A friend and I found one ranch hand, who's "not quite right in the head," sitting in front of the badly decayed carcass of a cow, shaking his finger and saying, "Now, I don't want you to do this ever again!" When I asked what was wrong with him, I was told, "He's goofier than hell, just like the rest of us." Perhaps because the West is historically new, conventional morality is still felt to be less important than rock-bottom truths. Though there's always a lot of teasing and sparring around, people are blunt with each other, sometimes even cruel, believing honesty is stronger medicine than sympathy, which may console but often conceals.

---

[1]Crazy people; *goyim* is a Yiddish term for Gentiles (non-Jews). (Ed.)

The formality that goes hand in hand with the rowdiness is known as "the Western Code." It's a list of practical dos and don'ts, faithfully observed. A friend, Cliff, who runs a trapline in the winter, cut off half his foot while axing a hole in the ice. Alone, he dragged himself to his pickup and headed for town, stopping to open the ranch gate as he left, and getting out to close it again, thus losing, in his observance of rules, precious time and blood. Later, he commented, "How would it look, them having to come to the hospital to tell me their cows had gotten out?". . . .

The roominess of the state has affected political attitudes as well. Ranchers keep up with world politics and the convulsions of the economy but are basically isolationists. Being used to running their own small empires of land and livestock, they're suspicious of big government. It's a "don't fence me in" holdover from a century ago. They still want the elbow room their grandfathers had, so they're strongly conservative, but with a populist twist.

—FROM "WYOMING: THE SOLACE OF OPEN SPACES," *THE SOLACE OF OPEN SPACES*, 1985.

Huppies

ROSE DEL CASTILLO GUILBAULT

We hear a lot about the growing number of Hispanics in this country—mostly about high poverty rates and low educational levels. But few stories discuss the sizable and increasing Hispanic middle class. Here in the Bay Area, a third of the Hispanic population is middle-class, with some of the highest average incomes in the country.

Although the demographics of the Hispanic middle class make us attractive to businesses and politicians, we're not well understood. We don't fit the accepted "poor" and "illiterate" Hispanic stereotype. We're professors, executives, politicians, lawyers and doctors— not janitors, seasonal workers, busboys or cleaning ladies. To outsiders, we're made of baffling incongruities. To poor Hispanics, we appear Anglo, and to Anglos we're Hispanics, sure—but not "like the others."

The Hispanic middle class has assimilated well, but the upstream migration has left many in a state of suspended cultural animation— a state of privileged limbo.

—FROM THE *SAN FRANCISCO CHRONICLE*, 1990

Suburbia, of Thee I Sing

PHYLLIS MCGINLEY

Twenty miles east of New York City as the New Haven Railroad   1
flies sits a village I shall call Spruce Manor. The Boston Post Road,
there, for the length of two blocks, becomes Main Street, and on one
side of that thundering thoroughfare are the grocery stores and the
drug stores and the Village Spa where teen-agers gather of an afternoon to drink their cokes and speak their curious confidences. There
one finds the shoe repairers and the dry cleaners and the secondhand
stores which sell "antiques" and the stationery stores which dispense
comic books to ten-year-olds and greeting cards and lending library
masterpieces to their mothers. On the opposite side stand the bank, the
fire house, the public library. The rest of this town of perhaps four or
five thousand people lies to the south and is bounded largely by Long
Island Sound, curving protectively on three borders. The movie theater
(dedicated to the showing of second-run, single-feature pictures) and
the grade schools lie north, beyond the Post Road, and that is a source
of worry to Spruce Manorites. They are always a little uneasy about the
children, crossing, perhaps, before the lights are safely green.
However, two excellent policemen—Mr. Crowley and Mr. Lang—station themselves at the intersections four times a day, and so far there
have been no accidents.

Spruce Manor in the spring and summer and fall is a pretty town,   2
full of gardens and old elms. (There are few spruces, but the village
Council is considering planting a few on the station plaza, out of sheer
patriotism.) In the winter, the houses reveal themselves as comfortable,
well-kept, architecturally insignificant. Then one can see the town for
what it is and has been since it left off being farm and woodland some

---

Phyllis McGinley (1905–1978) was a writer of light verse, children's
books, and essays. Her poetry books include *One More Manhattan*
(1937), *A Pocketful of Wry* (1959), and *Times Three: Selected Verse from
Three Decades, with Seventy New Poems* (1961), which won the 1961
Pulitzer Prize for poetry; her essay collections include *Sixpence in Her
Shoe* (1964) and *Saint-Watching* (1969). McGinley's poems and essays,
published in magazines such as *The New Yorker*, *The Atlantic Monthly*,
Good Housekeeping, and *Ladies' Home Journal*, deal with family themes,
religion, women's roles, and her suburban life in New Rochelle and
Larchmont, New York, and Weston, Connecticut. "Suburbia, of Thee
I Sing" was originally published in *Harper's* magazine in 1949 and
was collected in *The Province of the Heart* (1959).

sixty years ago—the epitome of Suburbia, not the country and certainly not the city. It is a commuter's town, the living center of a web which unrolls each morning as the men swing aboard the locals, and contracts again in the evening when they return. By day, with even the children pent in schools, it is a village of women. They trundle mobile baskets at the A&P, they sit under driers at the hairdressers, they sweep their porches and set out bulbs and stitch up slip covers. Only on weekends does it become heterogeneous and lively, the parking places difficult to find.

Spruce Manor has no country club of its own, though devoted 3 golfers have their choice of two or three not far away. It does have a small yacht club and a beach which can be used by anyone who rents or owns a house here. The village supports a little park with playground equipment and a counselor, where children, unattended by parents, can spend summer days if they have no more pressing engagements.

It is a town not wholly without traditions. Residents will point out 4 the two-hundred-year-old manor house, now a minor museum; and in the autumn they line the streets on a scheduled evening to watch the Volunteer Firemen parade. That is a fine occasion, with so many heads of households marching in their red blouses and white gloves, some with flaming helmets, some swinging lanterns, most of them genially out of step. There is a bigger parade on Memorial Day with more marchers than watchers and with the Catholic priest, the rabbi, and the Protestant ministers each delivering a short prayer when the paraders gather near the War Memorial. On the whole, however, outside of contributing generously to the Community Chest, Manorites are not addicted to municipal get-togethers.

No one is very poor here and not many families rich enough to be 5 awesome. In fact, there is not much to distinguish Spruce Manor from any other of a thousand suburbs outside of New York City or San Francisco or Detroit or Chicago or even Stockholm, for that matter. Except for one thing. For some reason, Spruce Manor has become a sort of symbol to writers and reporters familiar only with its name or trivial aspects. It has become a symbol of all that is middle-class in the worst sense, of settled-downness or rootlessness, according to what the writer is trying to prove; of smug and prosperous mediocrity—or even, in more lurid novels, of lechery at the country club and Sunday morning hangovers.

To condemn Suburbia has long been a literary cliché, anyhow. I 6 have yet to read a book in which the suburban life was pictured as the good life or the commuter as a sympathetic figure. He is nearly as much a stock character as the old stage Irishman: the man who "spends his life riding to and from his wife," the eternal Babbitt[1] who knows all about Buicks and nothing about Picasso, whose sanctuary is the club locker room, whose ideas spring readymade from the illiberal newspapers. His wife plays politics at the P.T.A. and keeps up with the Joneses. Or—if the scene is more gilded and less respectable—the commuter is the high-powered advertising executive with a station wagon and an eye for the ladies, his wife a restless baggage given to too many cocktails in the afternoon.

These clichés I challenge. I have lived in the country, I have lived in the city. I have lived in an average Middle Western small town. But for the best eleven years of my life I have lived in Suburbia and I like it. 7

"Compromise!" cried our friends when we came here from an expensive, inconvenient, moderately fashionable tenement in Manhattan. It was the period in our lives when everyone was moving somewhere. Farther uptown, farther downtown, across town to Sutton Place, to a half-dozen rural acres in Connecticut or New Jersey or even Vermont. But no one in our rather rarefied little group was thinking of moving to the suburbs except us. They were aghast that we could find anything appealing in the thought of a middle-class house on a middle-class street in a middle-class village full of middle-class people. That we were tired of town and hoped for children, that we couldn't afford both a city apartment and a farm, they put down as feeble excuses. To this day they cannot understand us. You see, they read the books. They even write them. 8

Compromise? Of course we compromise. But compromise, if not the spice of life, is its solidity. It is what makes nations great and marriages happy and Spruce Manor the pleasant place it is. As for its being middle-class, what is wrong with acknowledging one's roots? And how free we are! Free of the city's noise, of its ubiquitous doormen, of the soot on the windowsill and the radio in the next apartment. We have released ourselves from the seasonal hegira to the mountains or the seashore. We have only one address, one house to keep supplied with paring knives and blankets. We are free from the snows that block the countryman's roads in winter and his electricity which always goes off in a thunderstorm. I do not insist that we are typical. There is nothing really typical about any of our friends and neighbors here, and therein lies my point. The true suburbanite needs to conform less than anyone else; much less than the gentleman farmer with his remodeled salt-box or than the determined cliff dweller with his necessity for living at the right address. In Spruce Manor all addresses are right. And since we are fairly numerous here, we need not fall back on the people 9

---

[1]Middle-class protagonist in Sinclair Lewis's 1922 novel *Babbitt*. (Ed.)

nearest us for total companionship. There is not here, as in a small city away from truly urban centers, some particular family whose codes must be ours. And we could not keep up with the Joneses even if we wanted to, for we know many Joneses and they are all quite different people leading the most various lives.

The Albert Joneses spend their weekends sailing, the Bertram 10
Joneses cultivate their delphinium, the Clarence Joneses—Clarence being a handy man with a cello—are enthusiastic about amateur chamber music. The David Joneses dote on bridge, but neither of the Ernest Joneses understands it, and they prefer staying home of an evening so that Ernest Jones can carve his witty caricatures out of pieces of old fruit wood. We admire each other's gardens, applaud each other's sailing records; we are too busy to compete. So long as our clapboards are painted and our hedges decently trimmed, we have fulfilled our community obligations. We can live as anonymously as in a city or we can call half the village by their first names.

On our half-acre or three-quarters, we can raise enough tomatoes 11
for our salads and assassinate enough beetles to satisfy the gardening urge. Or we can buy our vegetables at the store and put the whole place to lawn without feeling that we are neglecting our property. We can have privacy and shade and the changing of the seasons and also the Joneses next door from whom to borrow a cup of sugar or a stepladder. Despite the novelists, the shadow of the country club rests lightly on us. Half of us wouldn't be found dead with a golf stick in our hands, and loathe Saturday dances. Few of us expect to be deliriously wealthy or world-famous or divorced. What we do expect is to pay off the mortgage and send our healthy children to good colleges.

For when I refer to life here, I think, of course, of living with chil- 12
dren. Spruce Manor without children would be a paradox. The summer waters are full of them, gamboling like dolphins. The lanes are alive with them, the yards overflow with them, they possess the tennis courts and the skating pond and the vacant lots. Their roller skates wear down the asphalt, and their bicycles make necessary the twenty-five-mile speed limit. They converse interminably on the telephones and make rich the dentist and the pediatrician. Who claims that a child and a half is the American middle-class average? A nice medium Spruce Manor family runs to four or five, and we count proudly, but not with amazement, the many solid households running to six, seven, eight, even up to twelve. Our houses here are big and not new, most of them, and there is a temptation to fill them up, let the décor fall where it may.

Besides, Spruce Manor seems designed by providence and town 13
planning for the happiness of children. Better designed than the city; better, I say defiantly, than the country. Country mothers must be

constantly arranging and contriving for their children's leisure time.
There is no neighbor child next door for playmate, no school within
walking distance. The ponds are dangerous to young swimmers, the
woods full of poison ivy, the romantic dirt roads unsuitable for bicycles. An extra acre or two gives a fine sense of possession to an adult;
it does not compensate children for the give-and-take of our village,
where there is always a contemporary to help swing the skipping
rope or put on the catcher's mitt. Where in the country is the Friday
evening dancing class or the Saturday morning movie (approved by
the P.T.A.)? It is the greatest fallacy of all time that children love the
country as a year-around plan. Children would take a dusty corner of
Washington Square or a city sidewalk, even, in preference to the
lonely sermons in stones and books in running brooks which their
contemporaries cannot share.

As for the horrors of bringing up progeny in the city, for all its mu-   14
seums and other cultural advantages (so perfectly within reach of suburban families if they feel strongly about it), they were summed up for
me one day last winter. The harried mother of one, speaking to me on
the telephone just after Christmas, sighed and said, "It's been a really
wonderful time for me, as vacations go. Barbara has had an engagement with a child in our apartment house every afternoon this week. I
have had to take her almost nowhere." Barbara is eleven. For six of
those eleven years, I realized, her mother must have dreaded
Christmas vacation, not to mention spring, as a time when Barbara had
to be entertained. I thought thankfully of my own daughters whom I
had scarcely seen since school closed, out with their skis and their
sleds and their friends, sliding down the roped-off hill half a block
away, coming in hungrily for lunch and disappearing again, hearty,
amused, and safe—at least as safe as any sled-borne child can be.

Spruce Manor is not Eden, of course. Our taxes are higher than we   15
like, and there is always that eight-eleven in the morning to be caught,
and we sometimes resent the necessity of rushing from a theater to a
train on a weekday evening. But the taxes pay for our really excellent
schools and for our garbage collections (so that the pails of orange
peels need not stand in the halls overnight as ours did in the city) and
for our water supply which does not give out every dry summer as it
frequently does in the country. As for the theaters—they are twenty
miles away and we don't get to them more than twice a month. But
neither, I think, do many of our friends in town. The eight-eleven is
rather a pleasant train, too, say the husbands; it gets them to work in
thirty-four minutes and they read the papers restfully on the way.

"But the suburban mind!" cry our die-hard friends in Manhattan   16
and Connecticut. "The suburban conversation! The monotony!" They
imply that they and I must scintillate or we perish. Let me anatomize

Spruce Manor, for them and for the others who envision Suburbia as a congregation of mindless housewives and amoral go-getters.

From my window, now, on a June morning, I have a view. It contains neither solitary hills nor dramatic skyscrapers. But I can see my roses in bloom, and my foxglove, and an arch of trees over the lane. I think comfortably of my friends whose houses line this and other streets rather like it. Not one of them is, so far as I know, doing any of the things that suburban ladies are popularly supposed to be doing. One of them, I happen to know, has gone bowling for her health and figure, but she had already tidied up her house and arranged to be home before the boys return from school. Some, undoubtedly, are ferociously busy in the garden. One lady is on her way to Ellis Island, bearing comfort and gifts to a Polish boy—a seventeen-year-old stowaway who did slave labor in Germany and was liberated by a cousin of hers during the war—who is being held for attempting to attain the land of which her cousin told him. The boy has been on the Island for three months. Twice a week she takes this tedious journey, meanwhile besieging courts and immigration authorities on his behalf. This lady has a large house, a part-time maid, and five children.

My friend around the corner is finishing her third novel. She writes daily from nine-thirty until two. After that her son comes back from school and she plunges into maternity; at six, she combs her pretty hair, refreshes her lipstick, and is charming to her doctor husband. The village dancing school is run by another neighbor, as it has been for twenty years. She has sent a number of ballerinas on to the theatrical world as well as having shepherded for many a successful season the white-gloved little boys and full-skirted little girls through their first social tasks.

Some of the ladies are no doubt painting their kitchens or a nursery; one of them is painting the portrait, on assignment, of a very distinguished personage. Some of them are nurses' aides and Red Cross workers and supporters of good causes. But all find time to be friends with their families and to meet the 5:32 five nights a week. They read something besides the newest historical novel, Braque is not unidentifiable to most of them, and their conversation is for the most part as agreeable as the tables they set. The tireless bridge players, the gossips, the women bored by their husbands live perhaps in our suburb, too. Let them. Our orbits need not cross.

And what of the husbands, industriously selling bonds or practicing law or editing magazines or looking through microscopes or managing offices in the city? Do they spend their evenings and their weekends in the gaudy bars of Fifty-second Street? Or are they the perennial householders, their lives a dreary round of taking down screens and mending drains? Well, screens they have always with them, and a man who is good around the house can spend happy hours with the plumbing even on a South Sea island. Some of them cut their own lawns and some of them try to break par and some of them sail their little boats all summer with their families for crew. Some of them are village trustees for nothing a year and some listen to symphonies and some think Milton Berle ought to be President. There is a scientist who plays wonderful bebop, and an insurance salesman who has bought a big old house nearby and with his own hands is gradually tearing it apart and reshaping it nearer to his heart's desire. Some of them are passionate hedge-clippers and some read Plutarch for fun. But I do not know many—though there may be such—who either kiss their neighbor's wives behind doors or whose idea of sprightly talk is to tell you the plot of an old movie.

It is June, now, as I have said. This afternoon my daughters will 21 come home from school with a crowd of their peers at their heels. They will eat up the cookies and drink up the ginger ale and go down for a swim at the beach if the water is warm enough, that beach which is only three blocks away and open to all Spruce Manor. They will go unattended by me, since they have been swimming since they were four, and besides there are lifeguards and no big waves. (Even our piece of ocean is a compromise.) Presently it will be time for us to climb into our very old Studebaker—we are not car-proud in Spruce Manor— and meet the 5:32. That evening expedition is not vitally necessary, for a bus runs straight down our principal avenue from the station to the shore, and it meets all trains. But it is an event we enjoy. There is something delightfully ritualistic about the moment when the train pulls in and the men swing off, with the less sophisticated children running squealing to meet them. The women move over from the driver's seat, surrender the keys, and receive an absent-minded kiss. It is the sort of picture that wakes John Marquand[2] screaming from his sleep. But, deluded people that we are, we do not realize how mediocre it all seems. We will eat our undistinguished meal, probably without even a cocktail to enliven it. We will drink our coffee at the table, not carry it into the living room; if a husband changes for dinner here it is into old and spotty trousers and more comfortable shoes. The children will then go through the regular childhood routine—complain about their homework, grumble about going to bed, and finally accomplish both ordeals. Perhaps later the Gerard Joneses will drop in. We will talk a great deal of unimportant chatter and compare notes on food prices;

---

[2]American novelist (1893–1960). (Ed.)

we will also discuss the headlines and disagree. (Some of us in the Manor are Republicans, some are Democrats, a few lean plainly leftward. There are probably anti-Semites and anti-Catholics and even anti-Americans. Most of us are merely anti-antis.) We will all have one highball, and the Joneses will leave early. Tomorrow and tomorrow and tomorrow the pattern will be repeated. This is Suburbia.

But I think that some day people will look back on our little inter-   22
val here, on our Spruce Manor way of life, as we now look back on the Currier and Ives kind of living, with nostalgia and respect. In a world of terrible extremes, it will stand out as the safe, important medium.

Suburbia, of thee I sing!   23

QUESTIONS

1.   Why is Spruce Manor such a nice place for children, according to McGinley? To what extent do you agree?

2.   McGinley defends suburbia from accusations of "monotony" by outlining the interests of the women and men of Spruce Manor (paragraphs 16 to 20). How varied do you find their interests to be? How would you compare their lifestyles to those of other groups of people not living in suburbia?

3.   In challenging the clichés and stereotypes about 1950s-era suburbia, what values does McGinley assert? What other values are implied in, for example, the social roles played by men and women in Spruce Manor or McGinley's emphasis on children?

4.   How much do you think mainstream values have changed in the "Spruce Manors" of the 1990s?

Warehouse Tribes: Living in the Cracks of Civilization

JULIA GILDEN

On a nippy evening in a warehouse in San Francisco, urban sur- 1
vivors gather around candles and a space heater. Like tired warriors,
they swap stories of their days at get-by jobs. Lupe cleans; Patrick
paints houses. Bubba, the family dog, and Sir Lawrence, a six-toed cat
that insisted on joining the tribe in Seattle, join the circle.

This scene is replicated in big cities all over the country. Young 2
refugees from middle-class America have left their comfortable
homes and predictable futures to forge lives that closely resemble
homelessness. They scavenge in curbside dumpsters and free boxes
to create temporary homes in warehouses or abandoned buildings.
Some groups just sneak in and "squat"; most pay rent to absentee
landlords. The impermanence of their groupings makes their numbers difficult to estimate. They live for the short term.

At the same time, they mean to forge new societal bonds, and 3
find a new kind of family closeness, through living by their wits.

For them, living in the shadows of the city is guerrilla training 4
for surviving in a brittle society, soon to be shattered. "We are making ourselves tough," says Laurie Spencer, a member of an ad hoc collective who call themselves the Killgood Gang or, generically,
"garbage people."

The Killgood Gang's living room is on the second floor of a di- 5
lapidated warehouse that has been sectioned off into sleeping lofts, a
bathroom and a kitchen area, leaving a large center space with several used sofas for frequently staged performance art pieces. On the
ground-floor level are elaborate skateboard ramps, a soundproofed
room with two full drum sets facing each other, and an assortment of
bottles and boxes labeled "Stuff" and "Junk."

Julia Gilden, from San Francisco, is a freelance reporter who has
written for such newspapers as *The New York Times* and the *San
Francisco Examiner*. She is co-author, with Mark Friedman, of *Woman
to Woman: Entertaining and Enlightening Quotes by Women about Women*
(1994) and is developing a book on the politics of shelter. This article,
a shorter version of which was written for Pacific News Service,
appeared in the *San Francisco Chronicle* Sunday magazine supplement, *This World*, in 1989.

People live in these collectives or "squats" for different reasons. 6
For Laurie, the life is a dynamic experiment in sharing—sometimes
food, sometimes space—with a goal of "personal empowerment."
Others in this and similar warehouses feel they are waging a political
struggle. Jeff Curtis, who lives in Project Artaud, wishes to battle
"systemic forces that deprive communities of organic life." Project
Artaud, a housing collective owned by the artists who live and work
there, was originally a squat.

A collective, for garbage people, means "doing it without 7
money." "Garbage people" implies being dirty, even being human
refuse, but it's really just lower-end economics—using up what is
considered waste.

"We put on three plays with no budget. Free," says Patrick Shade, 8
who studied theater arts at the University of Arizona. "We got the-
ater-quality lights. People didn't have to pay. They could bring
dumpster food, or whatever they wanted.

"We went to a garbage performance in Tucson where all the pa- 9
trons were in their 40s. The artist lay in chopped glass and passed out
dumpster fruit. No one knew where it came from. It was delicious."

For a while, "garbage was the only thing that was free," says 10
Andrew Vermont, a Cornell University dropout who now studies
English literature at San Francisco State University and works in a
community thrift shop to augment an education stipend from his parents. "But now garbage is less and less free. People drive around at
night and collect boxes and cans. In fact, when I drink a can of Coke
now, I leave the can on the street where it will be easy to pick up."

Andrew compares his life to that of an extraterrestrial: He might 11
not know the monetary value of things, but would evaluate each object by how it could be used. "Everything here came from the streets.
We brought little and stole nothing—well, maybe a few planks of
wood. We wanted to build our own bathroom from scratch. We
wanted to decide where the walls of each bedroom would be."

Freedom from imposed boundaries is part of the garbage peo- 12
ple's self-definition. "Our dog is a garbage dog, not on a leash like
other people's dogs," says Andrew. "People walking their dogs on
leashes are on leashes themselves. You just can't see them."

Warehouse people build their survival skills by dropping out of 13
comfortable life-styles, becoming invisible in the urban tapestry, and
then finding the creative forces they believe were deadened during
their formative years in an overprotective environment. At the same
time, they are reluctant to speak unkindly of their parents' middle-
class, goal-oriented lives, which they see as parents' misguided attempts to provide the best for their children.

Laurie, Patrick, and Andrew are all in their mid-twenties. Patrick   14
first lived in a warehouse in Tucson. He and Laurie have a new daughter named Rogue. His performance art is a statement against, in his
words, "the consumer mentality, the wholesale acceptance of some de-
veloper's greed—a way of life that is not about discovery, that is insu-
lated from the difficulties of life."

"We lived in a cocoon," said Andrew, originally from   15
Philadelphia. "I had to get out and find real life."

What they seek seems the antithesis of the American Dream.   16
Instead of staking their own turf, they purposely move frequently
from one abandoned industrial property to another. Instead of collecting inventories of household goods, they choose to salvage cast-offs,
which they often destroy in acts of performance art.

Although each warehouse tribe develops its own subtle philo-   17
sophical variations, it is generally understood that they are not skinheads, not heavy metal rockers, and not hippies. "Hippies were the
last big alternative movement. But they were unrealistic," says
Andrew's sister, Lupe. "They used a lot of drugs, did a lot of experimenting, and lost their momentum."

Two common denominators among warehouse tribes—transient   18
living and rejection of social control—are reminiscent of ideas found in
the 1987 TV series *Max Headroom,* which portrayed survival society
after The Bomb. In the series, "Fringers" exist on the edges of society
in any kind of dwelling they can scrape together; "Blanks" are intentional outlaws who have avoided the computerized number identities
mandated by the system, and who live by their own code of honor.
Warehouse tribes seem to be acting out these Orwellian fantasies, except that the system they try to escape is not a totalitarian government
but the benign devouring marshmallow of The Good Life.

But the most seminal ideas of warehouse life and art come from   19
punk rock, whose lyrics discourage most forms of permanence and
hero worship. "One of the most important things about punk rock is
not to immortalize stars," says Andrew. "Most groups that are famous
don't even have records." Andrew says he listened as a teenager to
Minor Threat and The Bad Brains, both East Coast groups, and to Stiff
Little Fingers, of Ireland.

In Europe, in a parallel movement, industrial sites and abandoned   20
warehouses attract a cross-section of disaffected young people. But
there are differences. The movement is more overtly political, and at
the same time the European squats are better tolerated by mainstream
society. People are sometimes even paid by landlords to refurbish old
buildings, or they may set up rent-free households in abandoned
buildings whose owners look the other way. The only city known for

tolerating squatters in America is New York, according to underground travelers.

Bernd Gruenwald lives in a squat in Cologne, Germany, where he says the motivations for warehouse living are similar to those in America, but more formalized. "The movement is old and quite established; the groups are drawn together from all walks of life for radical political purposes," Bernd says. "There is a historical perspective. In America, people are not so involved in larger movements. They are on more individual trips."   21

Bruce Momich, a twenty-eight-year-old former Navy sailor, house painter, and veteran of warehouse life in Philadelphia and San Francisco, agrees. "Here, each person can have his own rendition of how he wants to live. Some warehouses are drugs, art, noise. In others, everybody works and goes to bed early."   22

Lupe Vermont, who has spent years in European and American warehouses and squats, says the problem here is that everything is so spread out. "In Europe people don't give up so easily; they're more persistent. They fight for low-rent or no-rent housing as a basic human right. In the United States there's more financial necessity"—fewer "safety net" benefits—"and it's harder to piece together a movement because we're so spaced out geographically."   23

In his book *Lipstick Traces,* music critic Greil Marcus has compared the punk rock movement to earlier European nihilism and Dadaism, which aimed to destroy everything, including oneself, and start over. People now in their twenties grew up with predictions of global nuclear holocaust and environmental collapse, giving some of them a kind of cheerful hopelessness. Punk is anarchic and anti-egocentric, striving to tear down Western civilization's self-centered structures and build more organic communities in their place. These are strong themes in European and American warehouse collectives. Squats and warehouses often house organizers for the new environmental Green political parties in Europe and America. And in San Francisco, Food Not Bombs—a collective that sets up mobile soup kitchens for the homeless in Golden Gate Park—has used the Killgood Gang's warehouse kitchen to prepare meals.   24

Like most tribes, warehouse dwellers revel in their distinctive costume. Most often they can be seen weaving their way through cities on skateboards like urban jackrabbits, wearing ragged layers of sweats and '50s-era print shirts and dresses, all of which become unisex clothing. They sport tattoos and nose rings, personalized high-top sneakers, and an amazing variety of Mohawks.   25

Though everyone might not agree that such an outrageous style lends itself to camouflage, there is a conspiratorial feeling among   26 warehouse tribes that they succeed in being invisible to most outsiders. "We are surrounded by people who don't know what's going on here," says Andrew. "I never knew about warehouse life in Philly until I left. I was living in the middle of it and never saw it."

Bruce says, "You can find [us] in every town in America, but espe- 27 cially in the Rust Belt, where there is so much industry. I can go to any town and within two hours find my people just by standing on the corner in the right part of town."

"We recognize that a number of people are using industrial build- 28 ings for residential purposes," says Paul Lord of the San Francisco City Planning Department, but neither his department nor other city agencies nationwide know how large the number is. Margie O'Driscoll of Art House, a nonprofit organization created three years ago as a joint project of the San Francisco Arts Commission and California Lawyers for the Arts to help artists find living space, estimates that there are two hundred legal live-work spaces and five hundred illegal spaces in the city. The Killgood Gang estimates there are fifteen hundred.

Laurie, a twenty-six-year-old Purdue University dropout who has 29 supported herself as a masseuse, recalls a visit to Anchorage, Alaska, where she found a local variation of a warehouse tribe. "After a few hours in town, we went to a bar, and there they were—Mohawks, colored hair, very friendly. They lived in a garbage house. It was full of trash, the walls and windows were trashed, and they had found a 'Model Home' sign to put out in front. They were out of there within two weeks, but it was totally cool while it lasted."

American warehouse people do not aspire to be identified with 30 residents of formalized live-work lofts—long-established domiciles on the East Coast that are considered upwardly mobile, refined "artist" spaces, controlled by individuals and passed along through friends. Instead, warehouse collectives are amorphous and unpredictable. "There's no long-term potential," says Laurie.

Recently Art House presented a seminar on "How to Legalize 31 Your Living Space." A bunch of tribe members walked out before it was over.

On the other side of the city, in the abandoned Plaza West public 32 housing project at Divisadero and Eddy streets, warehouse tribe ideas are being acted out by a performance art group called Contraband. For several weekends the artists have re-created a piece originally staged in the former Gartland Pit, a vacant lot at 16th and Valencia streets whose deep walls were covered for years with angry neighborhood graffiti. The Gartland Pit was what remained after a seedy hotel for transients

was destroyed by arson thirteen years ago. The pit itself is now gone, 33
too, filled in by the foundations of a new apartment building.

Contraband chose the Plaza West site, in the shadow of St.
Ignatius Church, because it has, according to member Keith Hennessy,
"a history of community rights violations." The piece, called
"Religare," explores the helplessness of people deprived of dwelling
space due to social forces beyond their control, and the inherent tendencies of humans to bind together for protection and definition. The
piece comments on the displacement of indigenous peoples by San
Francisco settlers, the forced evacuation of Japanese to concentration
camps during World War II, the eviction of blacks in the 1960s from
the Western Addition and, finally, the ongoing routing of transient 34
"homesteaders" from the abandoned project itself.

The Latin word *religare* means "to bind back together"—in this
case to reconstruct the tribe and find its home. Contraband's flyer an-
nounces: "Admission by sliding scale. No one turned away for lack of 35
funds."

Contraband has performed in the Killgood Gang's warehouse,
bringing more formalized politics to their amiable anarchy. Many of
the performers themselves live in warehouses and feel at the mercy of
the implacable forces of modern society. Director Sara Shelton Mann
lives in Project Artaud. Even though her home is relatively "respectable" and her company has received grants to perform here and
abroad, living space is as much an issue for her and her group as it is
for the transient warehouse tribes. "Contraband is obsessed with
housing and real estate," Mann says.   36

It is an open question whether warehouse people will someday return to the mainstream, making the same kinds of compromises earlier 37
radicals have frequently made.

Laurie says she has been thinking a lot about her life, and the
kinds of controls her daughter will face as she grows up. "I don't know
what will happen to me, and I don't know how much this way of life
will affect Rogue, but I expect to keep finding creative ways to live.
Being able to define my space, to change it if I want to—that's very important to me."

*The warehouse tribe interviewed for this story no longer exists. All the
Killgood Gang have regrouped, and several new tribes have been born.*

QUESTIONS

1.   How are Gilden's "warehouse tribes" similar to and different from other urban street people you have encountered, either in your own experience or as you have seen them portrayed in the media?

2.   Based on the reasons people give to join warehouse tribes, their lifestyles, and Gilden's analysis of their philosophies, how would you describe the value system of what Gilden calls "the antithesis of the American Dream" (paragraph 16)?

3.   Do you agree with Andrew Vermont that "people walking their dogs on leashes are on leashes themselves" (paragraph 12)? Why or why not? What is "the benign devouring marshmallow of The Good Life" (paragraph 18), and how appropriate do you find this image for modern society?

Fifth Avenue, Uptown: A Letter from Harlem

JAMES BALDWIN

There is a housing project standing now where the house in which 1
we grew up once stood, and one of those stunted city trees is snarling
where our doorway used to be. This is on the rehabilitated side of the
avenue. The other side of the avenue—for progress takes time—has not
been rehabilitated yet and it looks exactly as it looked in the days when
we sat with our noses pressed against the windowpane, longing to be
allowed to go "across the street." The grocery store which gave us
credit is still there, and there can be no doubt that it is still giving credit.
The people in the project certainly need it—far more, indeed, than they
ever needed the project. The last time I passed by, the Jewish proprietor was still standing among his shelves, looking sadder and heavier
but scarcely any older. Farther down the block stands the shoe-repair
store in which our shoes were repaired until reparation became impossible and in which, then, we bought all our "new" ones. The Negro
proprietor is still in the window, head down, working at the leather.

These two, I imagine, could tell a long tale if they would (perhaps 2
they would be glad to if they could), having watched so many, for so
long, struggling in the fishhooks, the barbed wire, of this avenue.

The avenue is elsewhere the renowned and elegant Fifth. The area 3
I am describing, which, in today's gang parlance, would be called "the
turf," is bounded by Lenox Avenue on the west, the Harlem River on
the east, 135th Street on the north, and 130th Street on the south. We
never lived beyond these boundaries; this is where we grew up.
Walking along 145th Street—for example—familiar as it is, and similar,

---

A celebrated and controversial African American writer, **James
Baldwin** (1924–1987) was born in New York and later moved to
France. He wrote poetry, plays, and novels including *Go Tell It on the
Mountain* (1953), *Giovanni's Room* (1956), and *Another Country* (1962).
Baldwin's social criticism and essays about race relations and the
experiences of Black Americans include *Notes of a Native Son* (1955),
The Fire Next Time (1963), and *The Price of the Ticket: Collected Nonfiction
1948–1985* (1985). "Fifth Avenue, Uptown: A Letter from Harlem"
was collected in *Nobody Knows My Name: More Notes of a Native Son*
(1961) and originally appeared in *Esquire* in 1960, a few years before
the civil rights movement received widespread national attention and
race riots broke out in cities like Detroit and Los Angeles.

does not have the same impact because I did not know any of the people on the block. But when I turn east on 131st Street and Lenox Avenue, there is first a soda-pop joint, then a shoeshine "parlor," then a grocery store, then a dry cleaners', then the houses. All along the street there are people who watched me grow up, people who grew up with me, people I watched grow up along with my brothers and sisters; and, sometimes in my arms, sometimes underfoot, sometimes at my shoulder—or on it—their children, a riot, a forest of children, who include my nieces and nephews.

When we reach the end of this long block, we find ourselves on   4 wide, filthy, hostile Fifth Avenue, facing that project which hangs over the avenue like a monument to the folly, and the cowardice, of good intentions. All along the block, for anyone who knows it, are immense human gaps, like craters. These gaps are not created merely by those who have moved away, inevitably into some other ghetto; or by those who have risen, almost always into a greater capacity for self-loathing and self-delusion; or yet by those who, by whatever means—War II, the Korean war, a policeman's gun or billy, a gang war, a brawl, madness, an overdose of heroin, or, simply, unnatural exhaustion—are dead. I am talking about those who are left, and I am talking principally about the young. What are they doing? Well, some, a minority, are fanatical churchgoers, members of the more extreme of the Holy Roller sects. Many, many more are "moslems," by affiliation or sympathy, that is to say that they are united by nothing more—and nothing less—than a hatred of the white world and all its works. They are present, for example, at every Buy Black street-corner meeting—meetings in which the speaker urges his hearers to cease trading with white men and establish a separate economy. Neither the speaker nor his hearers can possibly do this, of course, since Negroes do not own General Motors or RCA or the A&P, nor, indeed, do they own more than a wholly insufficient fraction of anything else in Harlem (those who *do* own anything are more interested in their profits than in their fellows). But these meetings nevertheless keep alive in the participators a certain pride of bitterness without which, however futile this bitterness may be, they could scarcely remain alive at all. Many have given up. They stay home and watch the TV screen, living on the earnings of their parents, cousins, brothers, or uncles, and only leave the house to go to the movies or to the nearest bar. "How're you making it?" one may ask, running into them along the block, or in the bar. "Oh, I'm TV-ing it"; with the saddest, sweetest, most shame-faced of smiles, and from a great distance. This distance one is compelled to respect; anyone who has traveled so far will not easily be dragged again into the world. There are further retreats, of course, than the TV screen or the bar. There are those who are simply sitting on their stoops, "stoned," animated for a moment only, and hideously, by the approach of someone who may lend them the money for a "fix." Or by the approach of someone from whom they can purchase it, one of the shrewd ones, on the way to prison or just coming out.

And the others, who have avoided all of these deaths, get up in the morning and go downtown to meet "the man." They work in the white man's world all day and come home in the evening to this fetid block. They struggle to instill in their children some private sense of honor or dignity which will help the child survive. This means, of course, that they must struggle, stolidly, incessantly, to keep this sense alive in themselves, in spite of the insults, the indifference, and the cruelty they are certain to encounter in their working day. They patiently browbeat the landlord into fixing the heat, the plaster, the plumbing; this demands prodigious patience; nor is patience usually enough. In trying to make their hovels habitable, they are perpetually throwing good money after bad. Such frustration, so long endured, is driving many strong, admirable men and women whose only crime is color to the very gates of paranoia.

One remembers them from another time—playing handball in the playground, going to church, wondering if they were going to be promoted at school. One remembers them going off to war—gladly, to escape this block. One remembers their return. Perhaps one remembers their wedding day. And one sees where the girl is now—vainly looking for salvation from some other embittered, trussed, and struggling boy—and sees the all-but-abandoned children in the streets.

Now I am perfectly aware that there are other slums in which white men are fighting for their lives, and mainly losing. I know that blood is also flowing through those streets and that the human damage there is incalculable. People are continually pointing out to me the wretchedness of white people in order to console me for the wretchedness of blacks. But an itemized account of the American failure does not console me and it should not console anyone else. That hundreds of thousands of white people are living, in effect, no better than the "niggers" is not a fact to be regarded with complacency. The social and moral bankruptcy suggested by this fact is of the bitterest, most terrifying kind.

The people, however, who believe that this democratic anguish has some consoling value are always pointing out that So-and-So, white, and So-and-So, black, rose from the slums into the big time. The existence—the public existence—of, say, Frank Sinatra and Sammy Davis, Jr. proves to them that America is still the land of opportunity and that inequalities vanish before the determined will. It proves nothing of the sort. The determined will is rare—at the moment, in this country, it is unspeakably rare—and the inequalities suffered by the many are in no way justified by the rise of a few. A few have always risen—in every country, every era, and in the teeth of regimes which can by no stretch of the imagination be thought of as free. Not all of these people, it is worth remembering, left the world better than they found it. The determined will is rare, but it is not invariably benevolent. Furthermore, the American equation of success with the big times reveals an awful disrespect for human life and human achievement. This equation has placed our cities among the most dangerous in the world and has placed our youth among the most empty and most bewildered. The situation of our youth is not mysterious. Children have never been very good at listening to their elders, but they have never failed to imitate them. They must, they have no other models. That is exactly what our children are doing. They are imitating our immorality, our disrespect for the pain of others.

All other slum dwellers, when the bank account permits it, can   9 move out of the slum and vanish altogether from the eye of persecution. No Negro in this country has ever made that much money and it will be a long time before any Negro does. The Negroes in Harlem, who have no money, spend what they have on such gimcracks as they are sold. These include "wider" TV screens, more "faithful" hi-fi sets, more "powerful" cars, all of which, of course, are obsolete long before they are paid for. Anyone who has ever struggled with poverty knows how extremely expensive it is to be poor; and if one is a member of a captive population, economically speaking, one's feet have simply been placed on the treadmill forever. One is victimized, economically, in a thousand ways—rent, for example, or car insurance. Go shopping one day in Harlem—for anything—and compare Harlem prices and quality with those downtown.

The people who have managed to get off this block have only got   10 as far as a more respectable ghetto. This respectable ghetto does not even have the advantages of the disreputable one—friends, neighbors, a familiar church, and friendly tradesmen; and it is not, moreover, in the nature of any ghetto to remain respectable long. Every Sunday, people who have left the block take the lonely ride back, dragging their increasingly discontented children with them. They spend the day talking, not always with words, about the trouble they've seen and the trouble—one must watch their eyes as they watch their children—they are only too likely to see. For children do not like ghettos. It takes them nearly no time to discover exactly why they are there.

The projects in Harlem are hated. They are hated almost as much   11 as policemen, and this is saying a great deal. And they are hated for the same reason: both reveal, unbearably, the real attitude of the white world, no matter how many liberal speeches are made, no matter how many lofty editorials are written, no matter how many civil-rights commissions are set up.

The projects are hideous, of course, there being a law, apparently 12 respected throughout the world, that popular housing shall be as cheerless as a prison. They are lumped all over Harlem, colorless, bleak, high, and revolting. The wide windows look out on Harlem's invincible and indescribable squalor: the Park Avenue railroad tracks, around which, about forty years ago, the present dark community began; the unrehabilitated houses, bowed down, it would seem, under the great weight of frustration and bitterness they contain; the dark, the ominous schoolhouses from which the child may emerge maimed, blinded, hooked, or enraged for life; and the churches, churches, block upon block of churches, niched in the walls like cannon in the walls of a fortress. Even if the administration of the projects were not so insanely humiliating (for example: one must report raises in salary to the management, which will then eat up the profit by raising one's rent; the management has the right to know who is staying in your apartment; the management can ask you to leave, at their discretion), the projects would still be hated because they are an insult to the meanest intelligence.

Harlem got its first private project, Riverton[1]—which is now, nat- 13 urally, a slum—about twelve years ago because at that time Negroes were not allowed to live in Stuyvesant Town. Harlem watched Riverton go up, therefore, in the most violent bitterness of spirit, and hated it long before the builders arrived. They began hating it at about the time people began moving out of their condemned houses to make room for this additional proof of how thoroughly the white world despised them. And they had scarcely moved in, naturally, before they began smashing windows, defacing walls, urinating in the elevators, and fornicating in the playgrounds. Liberals, both white and black, were appalled at the spectacle. I was appalled by the liberal innocence—or cynicism, which comes out in practice as much the same thing. Other people were delighted to be able to point to proof positive that nothing could be done to better the lot of the colored people. They were, and are, right in one respect: that nothing can be done as long as

---

[1]The inhabitants of Riverton were much embittered by this description; they have, apparently, forgotten how their project came into being; and have repeatedly informed me that I cannot possibly be referring to Riverton, but to another housing project which is directly across the street. It is quite clear, I think, that I have no interest in accusing any individuals or families of the depredations herein described: but neither can I deny the evidence of my own eyes. Nor do I blame anyone in Harlem for making the best of a dreadful bargain. But anyone who lives in Harlem and imagines that he has *not* struck this bargain, or that what he takes to be his status (in whose eyes?) protects him against the common pain, demoralization, and danger, is simply self-deluded.

they are treated like colored people. The people in Harlem know they are living there because white people do not think they are good enough to live anywhere else. No amount of "improvement" can sweeten this fact. Whatever money is now being earmarked to improve this, or any other ghetto, might as well be burnt. A ghetto can be improved in one way only: out of existence.

Similarly, the only way to police a ghetto is to be oppressive. 14 None of the Police Commissioner's men, even with the best will in the world, have any way of understanding the lives led by the people they swagger about in twos and threes controlling. Their very presence is an insult, and it would be, even if they spent their entire day feeding gumdrops to children. They represent the force of the white world, and the world's real intentions are, simply, for the world's criminal profit and ease, to keep the black man corraled up here, in his place. The badge, the gun in the holster, and the swinging club make vivid what will happen should his rebellion become overt. Rare, indeed, is the Harlem citizen, from the most circumspect church member to the most shiftless adolescent, who does not have a long tale to tell of police incompetence, injustice, or brutality. I myself have witnessed and endured it more than once. The businessmen and racketeers also have a story. And so do the prostitutes. (And this is not, perhaps, the place to discuss Harlem's very complex attitude toward black policemen, nor the reasons, according to Harlem, that they are nearly all downtown.)

It is hard, on the other hand, to blame the policeman, blank, good- 15 natured, thoughtless, and insuperably innocent, for being such a perfect representative of the people he serves. He, too, believes in good intentions and is astounded and offended when they are not taken for the deed. He has never, himself, done anything for which to be hated—which of us has?—and yet he is facing, daily and nightly, people who would gladly see him dead, and he knows it. There is no way for him not to know it: there are few things under heaven more unnerving than the silent, accumulating contempt and hatred of a people. He moves through Harlem, therefore, like an occupying soldier in a bitterly hostile country; which is precisely what, and where, he is, and is the reason he walks in twos and threes. And he is not the only one who knows why he is always in company: the people who are watching him know why, too. Any street meeting, sacred or secular, which he and his colleagues uneasily cover has as its explicit or implicit burden the cruelty and injustice of the white domination. And these days, of course, in terms increasingly vivid and jubilant, it speaks of the end of that domination. The white policeman standing on a Harlem street corner finds himself at the very center of the revolution now occurring in the world. He is not prepared for it—

naturally, nobody is—and, what is possibly much more to the point, he is exposed, as few white people are, to the anguish of the black people around him. Even if he is gifted with the merest mustard grain of imagination, something must seep in. He cannot avoid observing that some of the children, in spite of their color, remind him of children he has known and loved, perhaps even of his own children. He knows that he certainly does not want *his* children living this way. He can retreat from his uneasiness in only one direction: into a callousness which very shortly becomes second nature. He becomes more callous, the population becomes more hostile, the situation grows more tense, and the police force is increased. One day, to everyone's astonishment, someone drops a match in the powder keg and everything blows up. Before the dust has settled or the blood congealed, editorials, speeches, and civil-rights commissions are loud in the land, demanding to know what happened. What happened is that Negroes want to be treated like men.

Negroes want to be treated like men: a perfectly straightforward state- 16
ment, containing only seven words. People who have mastered Kant, Hegel, Shakespeare, Marx, Freud, and the Bible find this statement utterly impenetrable. The idea seems to threaten profound, barely conscious assumptions. A kind of panic paralyzes their features, as though they found themselves trapped on the edge of a steep place. I once tried to describe to a very well-known American intellectual the conditions among Negroes in the South. My recital disturbed him and made him indignant; and he asked me in perfect innocence, "Why don't all the Negroes in the South move North?" I tried to explain what *has* happened, unfailingly, whenever a significant body of Negroes move North. They do not escape Jim Crow: they merely encounter another, not-less-deadly variety. They do not move to Chicago, they move to the South Side; they do not move to New York, they move to Harlem. The pressure within the ghetto causes the ghetto walls to expand, and this expansion is always violent. White people hold the line as long as they can, and in as many ways as they can, from verbal intimidation to physical violence. But inevitably the border which has divided the ghetto from the rest of the world falls into the hands of the ghetto. The white people fall back bitterly before the black horde; the landlords make a tidy profit by raising the rent, chopping up the rooms, and all but dispensing with the upkeep; and what has once been a neighborhood turns into a "turf." This is precisely what happened when the Puerto Ricans arrived in their thousands— and the bitterness thus caused is, as I write, being fought out all up and down those streets.

Northerners indulge in an extremely dangerous luxury. They 17
seem to feel that because they fought on the right side during the Civil

War, and won, they have earned the right merely to deplore what is going on in the South, without taking any responsibility for it; and that they can ignore what is happening in Northern cities because what is happening in Little Rock or Birmingham is worse. Well, in the first place, it is not possible for anyone who has not endured both to know which is "worse." I know Negroes who prefer the South and white Southerners, because "At least there, you haven't got to play any guessing games!" The guessing games referred to have driven more than one Negro into the narcotics ward, the madhouse, or the river. I know another Negro, a man very dear to me, who says with conviction and with truth, "The spirit of the South is the spirit of America." He was born in the North and did his military training in the South. He did not, as far as I can gather, find the South "worse"; he found it, if anything, all too familiar. In the second place, though, even if Birmingham *is* worse, no doubt Johannesburg, South Africa, beats it by several miles, and Buchenwald was one of the worst things that ever happened in the entire history of the world. The world has never lacked for horrifying examples; but I do not believe that these examples are meant to be used as justification for our own crimes. This perpetual justification empties the heart of all human feeling. The emptier our hearts become, the greater will be our crimes. Thirdly, the South is not merely an embarrassingly backward region, but a part of this country, and what happens there concerns every one of us.

As far as the color problem is concerned, there is but one differ-   18
ence between the Southern white and the Northerner: the Southerner remembers, historically and in his own psyche, a kind of Eden in which he loved black people and they loved him. Historically, the flaming sword laid across this Eden is the Civil War. Personally, it is the Southerner's sexual coming of age, when, without any warning, unbreakable taboos are set up between himself and his past. Everything, thereafter, is permitted him except the love he remembers and has never ceased to need. The resulting, indescribable torment affects every Southern mind and is the basis of the Southern hysteria.

None of this is true for the Northerner. Negroes represent nothing   19
to him personally, except, perhaps, the dangers of carnality. He never sees Negroes. Southerners see them all the time, Northerners never think about them whereas Southerners are never really thinking of anything else. Negroes are, therefore, ignored in the North and are under surveillance in the South, and suffer hideously in both places. Neither the Southerner nor the Northerner is able to look on the Negro simply as a man. It seems to be indispensable to the national self-esteem that the Negro be considered either as a kind of ward (in which case we are told how many Negroes, comparatively, bought Cadillacs

last year and how few, comparatively, were lynched), or as a victim (in which case we are promised that he will never vote in our assemblies or go to school with our kids). They are two sides of the same coin and the South will not change—*cannot* change—until the North changes. The country will not change until it reexamines itself and discovers what it really means by freedom. In the meantime, generations keep being born, bitterness is increased by incompetence, pride, and folly, and the world shrinks around us.

It is terrible, an inexorable, law that one cannot deny the humanity 20 of another without diminishing one's own: in the face of one's victim, one sees oneself. Walk through the streets of Harlem and see what we, this nation, have become.

QUESTIONS

1. To whom do you think Baldwin is addressing his "letter"? Put another way, who is he asking to "walk through the streets of Harlem and see what we, this nation, have become" (paragraph 20)? How would you describe his tone in addressing this audience?

2. What objections to his argument does Baldwin anticipate and respond to? How persuasive do you find his rebuttals?

3. As noted in the biographical footnote, Baldwin published this essay originally in 1960. How relevant do you think his argument still is for the 1990s?

On Being Black and Middle Class

SHELBY STEELE

Not long ago a friend of mine, black like myself, said to me that the 1
term "black middle class" was actually a contradiction in terms. Race,
he insisted, blurred class distinctions among blacks. If you were black,
you were just black and that was that. When I argued, he let his eyes
roll at my naiveté. Then he went on. For us, as black professionals, it
was an exercise in self-flattery, a pathetic pretension, to give meaning
to such a distinction. Worse, the very idea of class threatened the unity
that was vital to the black community as a whole. After all, since when
had white America taken note of anything but color when it came to
blacks? He then reminded me of an old Malcolm X line that had been
popular in the sixties. Question: What is a black man with a Ph.D.?
Answer: A nigger.

For many years I had been on my friend's side of this argument. 2
Much of my conscious thinking on the old conundrum of race and
class was shaped during my high school and college years in the race-
charged sixties, when the fact of my race took on an almost religious
significance. Progressively, from the mid-sixties on, more and more aspects of my life found their explanation, their justification, and their
motivation in race. My youthful concerns about career, romance,
money, values, and even styles of dress became subject to consultation
with various oracular sources of racial wisdom. And these ranged
from a figure as ennobling as Martin Luther King, Jr., to the under-
world elegance of dress I found in jazz clubs on the South Side of
Chicago. Everywhere there were signals, and in those days I considered myself so blessed with clarity and direction that I pitied my white
classmates who found more embarrassment than guidance in the fact
of *their* race. In 1968, inflated by my new power, I took a mischievous
delight in calling them culturally disadvantaged.

Shelby Steele, born in Chicago, is a professor of English at San Jose
State University. He is the author of *The Content of Our Character: A
New Vision of Race in America* (1990), and he has written about the
African American experience and race relations in magazines and
journals. This essay was selected for *The Best American Essays 1989*
(edited by Geoffrey Wolff); it first appeared in *Commentary*, a politically conservative journal addressing contemporary issues published
by the American Jewish Committee.

But now, hearing my friend's comment was like hearing a priest   3
from a church I'd grown disenchanted with. I understood him, but my
faith was weak. What had sustained me in the sixties sounded monotonous and off the mark in the eighties. For me, race had lost much of
its juju, its singular capacity to conjure meaning. And today, when I
honestly look at my life and the lives of many other middle-class blacks
I know, I can see that race never fully explained our situation in
American society. Black though I may be, it is impossible for me to sit
in my single-family house with two cars in the driveway and a swing
set in the back yard and *not* see the role class has played in my life. And
how can my friend, similarly raised and similarly situated, not see it?

Yet despite my certainty I felt a sharp tug of guilt as I tried to   4
explain myself over my friend's skepticism. He is a man of many
comedic facial expressions and, as I spoke, his brow lifted in extreme
moral alarm as if I were uttering the unspeakable. His clear implication was that I was being elitist and possibly (dare he suggest?) anti-
black—crimes for which there might well be no redemption. He pretended to fear for me. I chuckled along with him, but inwardly I did
wonder at myself. Though I never doubted the validity of what I was
saying, I felt guilty saying it. Why?

After he left (to retrieve his daughter from a dance lesson) I real-   5
ized that the trap I felt myself in had a tiresome familiarity and, in a
sort of slow-motion epiphany, I began to see its outline. It was like the
suddenly sharp vision one has at the end of a burdensome marriage
when all the long-repressed incompatibilities come undeniably to light.

What became clear to me is that people like myself, my friend, and
middle-class blacks generally are caught in a very specific double bind   6
that keeps two equally powerful elements of our identity at odds with
each other. The middle-class values by which we were raised—the
work ethic, the importance of education, the value of property ownership, of respectability, of "getting ahead," of stable family life, of initiative, of self-reliance—are, in themselves, raceless and even assimi-
lationist. They urge us toward participation in the American
mainstream, toward integration, toward a strong identification with
the society—and toward the entire constellation of qualities that are
implied in the word "individualism." These values are almost rules
for how to prosper in a democratic, free-enterprise society that ad-
mires and rewards individual effort. They tell us to work hard for ourselves and our families and to seek our opportunities whenever they
appear, inside or outside the confines of whatever ethnic group we
may belong to.

But the particular pattern of racial identification that emerged in   7
the sixties and that still prevails today urges middle-class blacks (and

all blacks) in the opposite direction. This pattern asks us to see ourselves as an embattled minority, and it urges an adversarial stance toward the mainstream, an emphasis on ethnic consciousness over individualism. It is organized around an implied separatism.

The opposing thrust of these two parts of our identity results in the double bind of middle-class blacks. There is no forward movement on either plane that does not constitute backward movement on the other. This was the familiar trap I felt myself in while talking with my friend. As I spoke about class, his eyes reminded me that I was betraying race. Clearly, the two indispensable parts of my identity were a threat to each other. 8

Of course when you think about it, class and race are both similar in some ways and also naturally opposed. They are two forms of collective identity with boundaries that intersect. But whether they clash or peacefully coexist has much to do with how they are defined. Being both black and middle class becomes a double bind when class and race are defined in sharply antagonistic terms, so that one must be repressed to appease the other. 9

But what is the "substance" of these two identities, and how does each establish itself in an individual's overall identity? It seems to me that when we identify with any collective we are basically identifying with images that tell us what it means to be a member of that collective. Identity is not the same thing as the fact of membership in a collective; it is, rather, a form of self-definition, facilitated by images of what we wish our membership in the collective to mean. In this sense, the images we identify with may reflect the aspirations of the collective more than they reflect reality, and their content can vary with shifts in those aspirations. 10

But the process of identification is usually dialectical. It is just as necessary to say what we are *not* as it is to say what we are—so that finally identification comes about by embracing a polarity of positive and negative images. To identify as middle class, for example, I must have both positive and negative images of what being middle class entails; then I will know what I should and should not be doing in order to be middle class. The same goes for racial identity. 11

In the racially turbulent sixties the polarity of images that came to define racial identification was very antagonistic to the polarity that defined middle-class identification. One might say that the positive images of one lined up with the negative images of the other, so that to identify with both required either a contortionist's flexibility or a dangerous splitting of the self. The double bind of the black middle class was in place. 12

* * *

The black middle class has always defined its class identity by 13
means of positive images gleaned from middle- and upper-class white
society, and by means of negative images of lower-class blacks. This
habit goes back to the institution of slavery itself, when "house" slaves
both mimicked the whites they served and held themselves above the
"field" slaves. But in the sixties the old bourgeois impulse to dissoci-
ate from the lower classes (the "we-they" distinction) backfired when
racial identity suddenly called for the celebration of this same black
lower class. One of the qualities of a double bind is that one feels it
more than sees it, and I distinctly remember the tension and strange
sense of dishonesty I felt in those days as I moved back and forth like
a bigamist between the demands of class and race.

Though my father was born poor, he achieved middle-class stand- 14
ing through much hard work and sacrifice (one of his favorite words)
and by identifying fully with solid middle-class values—mainly hard
work, family life, property ownership, and education for his children
(all four of whom have advanced degrees). In his mind these were not
so much values as laws of nature. People who embodied them made
up the positive images in his class polarity. The negative images came
largely from the blacks he had left behind because they were "going
nowhere."

No one in my family remembers how it happened, but as time 15
went on, the negative images congealed into an imaginary character
named Sam, who, from the extensive service we put him to, quickly
grew to mythic proportions. In our family lore he was sometimes a
trickster, sometimes a boob, but always possessed of a catalogue of sly
faults that gave up graphic images of everything we should not be. On
sacrifice: "Sam never thinks about tomorrow. He wants it now or he
doesn't care about it." On work: "Sam doesn't favor it too much." On
children: "Sam likes to have them but not to raise them." On money:
"Sam drinks it up and pisses it out." On fidelity: "Sam has to have two
or three women." On clothes: "Sam features loud clothes. He likes to
see and be seen." And so on. Sam's persona amounted to a negative instruction manual in class identity.

I don't think that any of us believed Sam's faults were accurate 16
representations of lower-class black life. He was an instrument of self-
definition, not of sociological accuracy. It never occurred to us that he
looked very much like the white racist stereotype of blacks, or that he
might have been a manifestation of our own racial self-hatred. He
simply gave us a counterpoint against which to express our aspirations. If self-hatred was a factor, it was not, for us, a matter of hating
lower-class blacks but of hating what we did not want to be.

Still, hate or love aside, it is fundamentally true that my middle- 17
class identity involved a dissociation from images of lower-class black

life and a corresponding identification with values and patterns of responsibility that are common to the middle class everywhere. These
values sent me a clear message: be both an individual and a responsible citizen; understand that the quality of your life will approximately
reflect the quality of effort you put into it; know that individual responsibility is the basis of freedom and that the limitations imposed by
fate (whether fair or unfair) are no excuse for passivity.

Whether I live up to these values or not, I know that my accep-   18
tance of them is the result of lifelong conditioning. I know also that I
share this conditioning with middle-class people of all races and that I
can no more easily be free of it than I can be free of my race. Whether
all this got started because the black middle class modeled itself on the
white middle class is no longer relevant. For the middle-class black,
conditioned by these values from birth, the sense of meaning they provide is as immutable as the color of his skin.

I started the sixties in high school feeling that my class-condition-   19
ing was the surest way to overcome racial barriers. My racial identity
was pretty much taken for granted. After all, it was obvious to the
world that I was black. Yet I ended the sixties in graduate school a little embarrassed by my class background and with an almost desperate need to be "black." The tables had turned. I knew very clearly
(though I struggled to repress it) that my aspirations and my sense of
how to operate in the world came from my class background, yet
"being black" required certain attitudes and stances that made me feel
secretly a little duplicitous. The inner compatibility of class and race I
had known in 1960 was gone.

For blacks, the decade between 1960 and 1969 saw racial identifi-   20
cation undergo the same sort of transformation that national identity
undergoes in times of war. It became more self-conscious, more narrowly focused, more prescribed, less tolerant of opposition. It
spawned an implicit party line, which tended to disallow competing
forms of identity. Race-as-identity was lifted from the relative slumber
it knew in the fifties and pressed into service in a social and political
war against oppression. It was redefined along sharp adversarial lines
and directed toward the goal of mobilizing the great mass of black
Americans in this warlike effort. It was imbued with a strong moral
authority, useful for denouncing those who opposed it and for celebrating those who honored it as a positive achievement rather than as
a mere birthright.

The form of racial identification that quickly evolved to meet this   21
challenge presented blacks as a racial monolith, a singular people with
a common experience of oppression. Differences within the race, no
matter how ineradicable, had to be minimized. Class distinctions were

one of the first such differences to be sacrificed, since they not only threatened racial unity but also seemed to stand in contradiction to the principle of equality which was the announced goal of the movement for racial progress. The discomfort I felt in 1969, the vague but relentless sense of duplicity, was the result of a historical necessity that put my race and class at odds, that was asking me to cast aside the distinction of my class and identify with a monolithic view of my race.

If the form of this racial identity was the monolith, its substance 22 was victimization. The civil rights movement and the more radical splinter groups of the late sixties were all dedicated to ending racial victimization, and the form of black identity that emerged to facilitate this goal made blackness and victimization virtually synonymous. Since it was our victimization more than any other variable that identified and unified us, moreover, it followed logically that the purest black was the poor black. It was images of him that clustered around the positive pole of the race polarity; all other blacks were, in effect, required to identify with him in order to confirm their own blackness.

Certainly there were more dimensions to the black experience 23 than victimization, but no other had the same capacity to fire the indignation needed for war. So, again out of historical necessity, victimization became the overriding focus of racial identity. But this only deepened the double bind for middle-class blacks like me. When it came to class we were accustomed to defining ourselves against lower-class blacks and identifying with at least the values of middle-class whites; when it came to race we were now being asked to identify with images of lower-class blacks and to see whites, middle class or otherwise, as victimizers. Negative lining up with positive, we were called upon to reject what we had previously embraced and to embrace what we had previously rejected. To put it still more personally, the Sam figure I had been raised to define myself against had now become the "real" black I was expected to identify with.

The fact that the poor black's new status was only passively 24 earned by the condition of his victimization, not by assertive, positive action, made little difference. Status was status apart from the means by which it was achieved, and along with it came a certain power—the power to define the terms of access to that status, to say who was black and who was not. If a lower-class black said you were not really "black"—a sellout, an Uncle Tom—the judgment was all the more devastating because it carried the authority of his status. And this judgment soon enough came to be accepted by many whites as well.

In graduate school I was once told by a white professor, "Well, 25 but . . . you're not really black. I mean, you're not disadvantaged." In his mind my lack of victim status disqualified me from the race itself. More recently I was complimented by a black student for speaking reasonably correct English, "proper" English as he put it. "But I don't know if I really want to talk like that," he went on. "Why not?" I asked. "Because then I wouldn't be black no more," he replied without a pause.

To overcome his marginal status, the middle-class black had to 26 identify with a degree of victimization that was beyond his actual experience. In college (and well beyond) we used to play a game called "nap matching." It was a game of one-upmanship, in which we sat around outdoing each other with stories of racial victimization, symbolically measured by the naps of our hair. Most of us were middle class and so had few personal stories to relate, but if we could not match naps with our own biographies, we would move on to those legendary tales of victimization that came to us from the public domain.

The single story that sat atop the pinnacle of racial victimization 27 for us was that of Emmett Till, the Northern black teenager who, on a visit to the South in 1955, was killed and grotesquely mutilated for supposedly looking at or whistling at (we were never sure which, though we argued the point endlessly) a white woman. Oh, how we probed his story, finding in his youth and Northern upbringing the quintessential embodiment of black innocence, brought down by a white evil so portentous and apocalyptic, so gnarled and hideous, that it left us with a feeling not far from awe. By telling his story and others like it, we came to *feel* the immutability of our victimization, its utter indigenousness, as a thing on this earth like dirt or sand or water.

Of course, these sessions were a ritual of group identification, a 28 means by which we, as middle-class blacks, could be at one with our race. But why were we, who had only a moderate experience of victimization (and that offset by opportunities our parents never had), so intent on assimilating or appropriating an identity that in so many ways contradicted our own? Because, I think, the sense of innocence that is always entailed in feeling victimized filled us with a corresponding feeling of entitlement, or even license, that helped us endure our vulnerability on a largely white college campus.

In my junior year in college I rode to a debate tournament with 29 three white students and our faculty coach, an elderly English professor. The experience of being the lone black in a group of whites was so familiar to me that I thought nothing of it as our trip began. But then halfway through the trip the professor casually turned to me and, in an isn't-the-world-funny sort of tone, said that he had just refused to rent an apartment in a house he owned to a "very nice" black couple because their color would "offend" the white couple who lived downstairs. His eyebrows lifted helplessly over his hawkish nose, suggesting that he too, like me, was a victim of America's racial farce. His look

assumed a kind of comradeship: he and I were above this grimy business of race, though for expediency we had occasionally to concede the
world its madness.

My vulnerability in this situation came not so much from the pro-   30
fessor's blindness to his own racism as from his assumption that I
would participate in it, that I would conspire with him against my
own race so that he might remain comfortably blind. Why did he think
I would be amenable to this? I can only guess that he assumed my
middle-class identity was so complete and all-encompassing that I
would see his action as nothing more than a trifling concession to the
folkways of our land, that I would in fact applaud his decision not to
disturb propriety. Blind to both his own racism and to me—one blindness serving the other—he could not recognize that he was asking me
to betray my race in the name of my class.

His blindness made me feel vulnerable because it threatened to ex-   31
pose my own repressed ambivalence. His comment pressured me to
choose between my class identification, which had contributed to my
being a college student and a member of the debating team, and my
desperate desire to be "black." I could have one but not both; I was
double-bound.

Because double binds are repressed there is always an element of   32
terror in them: the terror of bringing to the conscious mind the buried
duplicity, self-deception, and pretense involved in serving two masters. This terror is the stuff of vulnerability, and since vulnerability is
one of the least tolerable of all human feelings, we usually transform
it into an emotion that seems to restore the control of which it has
robbed us; most often, that emotion is anger. And so, before the professor had even finished his little story, I had become a furnace of rage.
The year was 1967, and I had been primed by endless hours of nap-
matching to feel, at least consciously, completely at one with the victim-focused black identity. This identity gave me the license, and the
impunity, to unleash upon this professor one of those volcanic erup-
tions of racial indignation familiar to us from the novels of Richard
Wright. Like Cross Damon in *Outsider*, who kills in perfectly righteous
anger, I tried to annihilate the man. I punished him not according to
the measure of his crime but according to the measure of my vulnerability, a measure set by the cumulative tension of years of repressed
terror. Soon I saw that terror in *his* face, as he stared hollow-eyed at the
road ahead. My white friends in the back seat, knowing no conflict between their own class and race, were astonished that someone they
had taken to be so much like themselves could harbor a rage that for
all the world looked murderous.

Though my rage was triggered by the professor's comment, it was   33
deepened and sustained by a complex of need, conflict, and repression

in myself of which I had been wholly unaware. Out of my racial vulnerability I had developed the strong need of an identity with which to defend myself. The only such identity available was that of me as victim, him as victimizer. Once in the grip of this paradigm, I began to do far more damage to myself than he had done.

Seeing myself as a victim meant that I clung all the harder to my   34
racial identity, which, in turn, meant that I suppressed my class identity. This cut me off from all the resources my class values might have offered me. In those values, for instance, I might have found the means to a more dispassionate response, the response less of a victim attacked by a victimizer than of an individual offended by a foolish old man. As an individual I might have reported this professor to the college dean. Or I might have calmly tried to reveal his blindness to him, and possibly won a convert. (The flagrancy of his remark suggested a hidden guilt and even self-recognition on which I might have capitalized. Doesn't confession usually signal a willingness to face oneself?) Or I might have simply chuckled and then let my silence serve as an answer to his provocation. Would not my composure, in any form it might take, deflect into his own heart the arrow he'd shot at me?

Instead, my anger, itself the hair-trigger expression of a long-re-   35
pressed double bind, not only cut me off from the best of my own resources, it also distorted the nature of my true racial problem. The righteousness of this anger and the easy catharsis it brought buoyed the delusion of my victimization and left me as blind as the professor himself.

As a middle-class black I have often felt myself *contriving* to be   36
"black." And I have noticed this same contrivance in others—a certain stretching away from the natural flow of one's life to align oneself with a victim-focused black identity. Our particular needs are out of sync with the form of identity available to meet those needs. Middle-class blacks need to identify racially; it is better to think of ourselves as black and victimized than not black at all; so we contrive (more unconsciously than consciously) to fit ourselves into an identity that denies our class and fails to address the true source of our vulnerability.

For me this once meant spending inordinate amounts of time at   37
black faculty meetings, though these meetings had little to do with my real racial anxieties or my professional life. I was new to the university, one of two blacks in an English department of over seventy, and I felt a little isolated and vulnerable, though I did not admit it to myself. But at these meetings we discussed the problems of black faculty and students within a framework of victimization. The real vulnerability we felt was covered over by all the adversarial drama the victim/victimized polarity inspired, and hence went unseen and unassuaged. And this, I think, explains our rather chronic ineffectiveness as a group.

Since victimization was not our primary problem—the university had long ago opened its doors to us—we had to contrive to make it so, and there is not much energy in contrivance. What I got at these meetings was ultimately an object lesson in how fruitless struggle can be when it is not grounded in actual need.

At our black faculty meetings, the old equation of blackness with 38 victimization was ever present—to be black was to be a victim; therefore, not to be a victim was not to be black. As we contrived to meet the terms of this formula there was an inevitable distortion of both ourselves and the larger university. Through the prism of victimization the university seemed more impenetrable than it actually was, and we more limited in our powers. We fell prey to the victim's myopia, making the university an institution from which we could seek redress but which we could never fully join. And this mind-set often led us to look more for compensations for our supposed victimization than for opportunities we could pursue as individuals.

The discomfort and vulnerability felt by middle-class blacks in the 39 sixties, it could be argued, was a worthwhile price to pay considering the progress achieved during that time of racial confrontation. But what may have been tolerable then is intolerable now. Though changes in American society have made it an anachronism, the monolithic form of racial identification that came out of the sixties is still very much with us. It may be more loosely held, and its power to punish heretics has probably diminished, but it continues to catch middle-class blacks in a double bind, thus impeding not only their own advancement but even, I would contend, that of blacks as a group.

The victim-focused black identity encourages the individual to 40 feel that his advancement depends almost entirely on that of the group. Thus he loses sight not only of his own possibilities but of the inextricable connection between individual effort and individual advancement. This is a profound encumbrance today, when there is more opportunity for blacks than ever before, for it reimposes limitations that can have the same oppressive effect as those the society has only recently begun to remove.

It was the emphasis on mass action in the sixties that made the 41 victim-focused black identity a necessity. But in the eighties and beyond, when racial advancement will come only through a multitude of individual advancements, this form of identity inadvertently adds itself to the forces that hold us back. Hard work, education, individual initiative, stable family life, property ownership—these have always been the means by which ethnic groups have moved ahead in America. Regardless of past or present victimization, these "laws" of advancement apply absolutely to black Americans also. There is no getting around this. What we need is a form of racial identity that energizes the individual by putting him in touch with both his possibilities and his responsibilities.

It has always annoyed me to hear from the mouths of certain 42 arbiters of blackness that middle-class blacks should "reach back" and pull up those blacks less fortunate than they—as though middle-class status were an unearned and essentially passive condition in which one needed a large measure of noblesse oblige to occupy one's time. My own image is of reaching back from a moving train to lift on board those who have no tickets. A noble enough sentiment—but might it not be wiser to show them the entire structure of principles, effort, and sacrifice that puts one in a position to buy a ticket any time one likes? This, I think, is something members of the black middle class can realistically offer to other blacks. Their example is not only a testament to possibility but also a lesson in method. But they cannot lead by example until they are released from a black identity that regards that example as suspect, that sees them as "marginally" black, indeed that holds *them* back by catching them in a double bind.

To move beyond the victim-focused black identity we must learn 43 to make a difficult but crucial distinction: between actual victimization, which we must resist with every resource, and identification with the victim's status. Until we do this we will continue to wrestle more with ourselves than with the new opportunities which so many paid so dearly to win.

QUESTIONS

1. What values does Steele associate with the middle class and American mainstream? How is it that black Americans, according to Steele, are caught in a "double bind"?

2. Instead of what he calls "the victim-focused black identity" of the 1960s, Steele argues for a new "form of racial identity that energizes the individual by putting him in touch with both his possibilities and his responsibilities" (paragraph 41). From Steele's essay, how would you elaborate these possibilities and responsibilities? How differently does Steele seem to envision the possibilities and responsibilities for middle-class blacks as opposed to lower-class blacks?

3. If you have a heritage other than African American or identify with a socioeconomic group other than the "middle class," write an essay called "On Being [your ethnicity] and Middle Class [or Working Class, Upper Middle or Upper Class, etc.]" in which you address the ways that your ethnic identity and your class identity coincide or conflict.

The Upperclass and
Mothers N the Hood

HOLLY SKLAR

The reality is that most poor Americans are white, many married   1
couples are poor, and even if there were no nonwhite children and no
single mother families, the United States would have one of the highest child poverty rates among the capitalist powers. But that doesn't
stop liberals and conservatives alike from blaming poverty on single
mothers, especially Black single mothers, and accusing them of breeding a pathological underclass culture of poverty, drug abuse, sloth,
and savagery.

In a 1992 speech to Yale University, slandering single mothers and   2
affirmative action, neoliberal Massachusetts Senator John Kerry recy-
cled the refuted, racist Black matriarchy myth popularized by neoconservative Daniel Patrick Moynihan in a 1965 report released by the
White House shortly after the Watts riots: "Twenty-seven years ago,
my Senate colleague Daniel Patrick Moynihan warned that: 'from the
wild Irish slums of the 19th century eastern seaboard, to the riot-torn
suburbs of Los Angeles, there is one unmistakable lesson in American
history: A society that allows a large number of young men to grow up
in broken families . . . never acquiring any stable relationship to . . . authority, never acquiring any rational expectations about the future—
that society asks for and gets chaos. Crime, violence, unrest, disorder—more particularly, the furious, unrestrained lashing out at the
whole social structure—that is not only to be expected; it is very near
inevitable.'" [ellipses Kerry's] (See Z, May/June 1992.)

As films like *Boyz N the Hood* show, you don't have to be a neo-   3
conservative (Black or white) to equate Black female-headed families

---

Holly Sklar is a writer and lecturer on political, socioeconomic, and
international issues. She is the author, with Peter Medoff, of *Streets of
Hope: The Fall and Rise of an Urban Neighborhood* (1994), which explores
successful strategies for inner city revitalization. She is also the author
of *Washington's War on Nicaragua* (1988), the editor of *Trilateralism: The
Trilateral Commission and Elite Planning for World Management* (1980),
and co-author, with Karin Stallard and Barbara Ehrenreich, of *Poverty
in the American Dream: Women and Children First* (1983). "The
Upperclass and Mothers N the Hood" was written for *Z Magazine* in
1993; for a description of *Z Magazine*'s progressive social agenda, see
the author's note for Ward Churchill on page 52.

with disorder, savagery, and death and male-headed families with discipline, salvation, and success. Once again, children are stigmatized from birth as the pathological bastards of their mother's presence and their father's absence. Once again, misogynist myths are used to perpetuate racial, gender, and class discrimination.

Mammys, Matriarchs, and Patriarchy

Culture of poverty theories are neither new nor true, but back they 4 come to mask cultures of greed, racism, and sexism. "It's clear women have been viewed as the breeders of poverty, juvenile delinquency, criminality, and other social problems," says Mimi Abramovitz, professor of Social Work at Hunter College, "from the 'tenement class' of the mid 1800s and the 'dangerous classes' of the 1880s, to Social Darwinism and eugenics, to Freudian theories of motherhood, to today's 'underclass.'"

Stereotypes reflect power relations, as some past generations of 5 poor white European immigrants could attest. As Oscar Handlin writes in *Boston's Immigrants,* "the Irish were the largest components of the state poorhouse population and a great majority of all paupers . . . after 1845." They were economically exploited and socially stereotyped as immoral, drunkards, and criminals (recall the term "Paddy wagon" for police wagon). Alcoholism was once recorded as a cause of death for Irish immigrants in the Massachusetts registry, not for Protestant Anglo-Saxons. A century later, Oscar Lewis coined the phrase "culture of poverty," first for Mexicans in 1959, then Puerto Ricans and African-Americans.

Imagine labeling married-couple families as pathological breeding 6 grounds of patriarchal domestic violence, or suggesting that women should never marry, because they are more likely to be beaten and killed by a spouse than a stranger. In Massachusetts during the first half of 1992, nearly three out of four women whose murderers are known were killed by husbands, boyfriends, or ex-partners. Misogynist domestic violence is so rampant that over 50,000 Massachusetts women have taken out restraining orders against former mates. Violence is the leading cause of injuries to women ages 15 to 44, "more common than automobile accidents, muggings, and cancer deaths combined." It is estimated that a woman has between a one in five and a one in three chance of being physically assaulted by a partner or ex-partner during her lifetime. More than 90 women were murdered every week in 1991. In the words of an October 1992 Senate Judiciary Committee report, "Every week is a week of terror for at least 21,000 American women" of all races, regions, educational, and economic backgrounds, whose "domestic assaults, rapes and murders were reported to the police." As many as three million more domestic violence crimes may go unreported.

Stephanie Coontz writes in her myth-busting study of families, 7 *The Way We Never Were*, "families whose members are police officers or who serve in the military have much higher rates of divorce, family violence, and substance abuse than do other families, but we seldom accuse them of constituting an 'underclass' with a dysfunctional culture."

In *The Negro Family*, published the year following the 1964 Civil 8 Rights Act, Moynihan embellished sociologist E. Franklin Frazier's thesis of the Black matriarch in whom "neither economic necessity nor tradition had instilled the spirit of subordination to masculine authority." Moynihan's notion that matriarchal families are at the core of a Black "tangle of pathology" was the perfect divisive response to the Black liberation movement, feminism, and the welfare rights movement.

African-American women have been stereotyped since slavery as 9 "mammies, matriarchs, and other controlling images," explains Patricia Hill Collins in *Black Feminist Thought*. The mammy was "the faithful, obedient domestic servant. Created to justify the economic exploitation of house slaves and sustained to explain Black women's long-standing restriction to domestic service, the mammy represents the normative yardstick to evaluate all Black women's behavior. By loving, nurturing, and caring for her white children and 'family' better than her own, the mammy symbolizes the dominant group's perceptions of the ideal Black female relationship to elite white male power. . . . She has accepted her subordination." While "the mammy represents the 'good' Black mother, the matriarch symbolizes the 'bad' Black mother. . . . Spending too much time away from home, these working mothers ostensibly cannot properly supervise their children and are a major contributing factor to their children's school failure. As overly aggressive, unfeminine women, Black matriarchs allegedly emasculate their lovers and husbands."

Collins notes that the image of the Black matriarch in the post- 10 World War II era was "a powerful symbol for both Black and white women of what can go wrong if white patriarchal power is challenged. Aggressive, assertive women are penalized—they are abandoned by their men, end up impoverished, and are stigmatized as being unfeminine."

During World War II, societal images of women changed to re- 11 inforce their role in wartime industry. As Susan Faludi writes in *Backlash:* "Rosie the Riveter was revered and, in 1941, Wonder Woman was introduced." Women protested for equal pay and expanded day care and overwhelmingly voiced their intention to keep their jobs in peacetime. When the war ended, so did the supportive images of women workers. Women were abruptly purged from higher-paid industrial jobs and the government shut down its wartime day care services. "Employers who had applauded women's work during the war," says Faludi, "now accused working women of incompetence or 'bad attitudes'—and laid them off at rates that were 75 percent higher than men's. . . . The rise in female autonomy and aggressiveness, scholars and government officials agreed, was causing a rise in juvenile delinquency and divorce rates—and would only lead to the collapse of the family. Child-care authorities, most notably Dr. Benjamin Spock, demanded that wives stay home."

"The backlash of the feminine-mystique years did not return 12 working women to the home," continues Faludi. "Rather, the culture derided them; employers discriminated against them; government promoted new [discriminatory] employment policies . . . the proportion of [women] who were relegated to low-paying jobs rose, their pay gap climbed, and occupational segregation increased as their numbers in the higher-paying professions declined from one-half in 1930 to about one-third by 1960." Faludi observes, "Women's contradictory circumstances in the '50s—rising economic participation coupled with an embattled and diminished cultural stature—is the central paradox of women under a backlash." And backlashes hit women of color the hardest.

"Welfare Queens" and Worker Bees

The third controlling image of Black women, explains Patricia Hill 13 Collins, is the welfare mother. "Essentially an updated version of the breeder woman image created during slavery, this image provides an ideological justification for efforts to harness Black women's fertility to the needs of a changing political economy. . . . Slaveowners wanted enslaved Africans to 'breed' because every slave child born represented a valuable unit of property, another unit of labor, and, if female, the prospects for more slaves." The welfare mother is labeled a bad mother, like the matriarch, but "while the matriarch's unavailability contributed to her children's poor socialization, the welfare mother's accessibility is deemed the problem." Blacks made up a higher percentage of the U.S. population in 1850 than in 1950 or any time in the twentieth century.

In the postwar period, as the percentage of births to unmarried 14 women rose, especially among white women, and Aid to Dependent Children was opened to their offspring, both Black and white women were viewed as breeders, observes Ricki Solinger in *Wake Up Little Susie: Single Pregnancy and Race Before Roe v. Wade*. But white unwed mothers "were viewed as socially productive breeders whose babies" if given up for adoption "could offer infertile couples their only chance to construct proper families." Black women "were viewed as socially unproductive breeders, constrainable only by punitive, legal sanctions. Proponents of school segregation, restrictive public housing, exclusionary welfare policies, and enforced sterilization or birth control all used the issue of relatively high rates of black illegitimacy to support their campaigns." White unwed mothers could be redeemed from their state of "shame" through racially-biased government supported maternity homes, adoption, and subsequent homemaker mom/breadwinner dad marriage—which, though rare for most American history, was enshrined as traditional with the help of postwar television.

Black women, explains Solinger, were "simply blamed" for the 15 "population bomb," escalating welfare costs, and giving birth "to Black America, with all its 'defects.' " For Black women, "there was no redemption . . . only the retribution of sterilization, harassment by welfare officials, and public policies that threatened to starve them and their babies." As Solinger puts it, "the bodies of black women became political terrain on which some proponents of white supremacy mounted their campaigns" and "the black illegitimate baby became the child white politicians and taxpayers loved to hate."

Aid to Families with Dependent Children (AFDC) expanded for 16 many reasons, among them the inclusion of mothers (and not just their children) as recipients after 1950, higher rates of female-headed households due to divorce and unmarried births, and later the mobilization of poor people in the National Welfare Rights Organization. Black women were "blamed" though only about 16 percent of nonwhite unwed mothers received welfare grants while 30 percent of the unwed white mothers who did not give their children up for adoption received grants in 1959. (In 1960, about 94 percent of Black and 29 percent of white "illegitimate" babies lived with natural parents or relatives.) As Piven and Cloward point out in *Regulating the Poor*, the proportion of Blacks on AFDC rose after 1948 because of two often-neglected factors: the displacement of Blacks from southern agriculture by mechanization and their migration to northern cities (where jobs and low-cost housing became scarcer) and the lessening of eligibility discrimination. While the proportion of AFDC parents who are white (non-Hispanic) was the same in 1973 (38 percent) as 1990, the proportion who are Black declined from 45.8 percent to 39.7 percent in the same period.

The stereotype "welfare queen" lazily collects government checks 17 and reproduces poverty by passing on her pathologies to her many children. Two decades ago, Senator Russell Long of Louisiana referred to welfare mothers as "brood mares." The slaveowners' control of fertility is mirrored again in the present economy which wants Black women's reproduction further reduced because Black workers and therefore Black children are increasingly seen as surplus. Norplant contraceptive implants, which can cause bleeding and other side effects, have become a eugenics weapon for judges and politicians.

The myth of an intergenerational matriarchy of "welfare queens" [18] is particularly disgusting since Black women were enslaved workers for over two centuries and have always had a high labor force participation rate and a disproportionate share of low wages and poverty. In 1900, Black women's labor force participation rate was 40.7 percent, white women's 16 percent. The 1960 rates were 42.2 percent for Black women and 33.6 percent for whites; in 1970, 49.5 percent and 42.6 percent; in 1980, 53.2 percent and 51.2 percent; and in 1991 they converged at 57 percent.

Rosemary Bray, a former editor of the *New York Times Book Review*, [19] wrote a moving account of her own experience as an African-American child on welfare beginning in 1960 (*New York Times Magazine*, November 8, 1992). "What fueled our dreams and fired our belief that our lives could change for the better was the promise of the civil rights movement and the war on poverty," she recalls. "Had I been born a few years earlier, or a decade later, I might now be living on welfare in the Robert Taylor Homes or working as a hospital nurse's aide for $6.67 an hour." The demonization of the welfare mother allows "for denial about the depth and intransigence of racism" and reinforcement of the patriarchal notion "that women and children without a man are fundamentally damaged goods."

Bray cites a new study of single mothers (low-wage workers and [20] welfare recipients) by Rutgers University Professor Kathryn Edin, which demonstrates that "women, particularly unskilled women with children, get the worst jobs available, with the least amount of health care, and are the most frequently laid off." Bray observes, "the writers and scholars and politicians who wax most rhapsodic about the need to replace welfare with work make their harsh judgments from the comfortable and supportive environs of offices and libraries and think tanks. If they need to go to the bathroom midsentence, there is no one timing their absence. If they take longer than a half-hour for lunch, there is no one waiting to dock their pay. If their baby sitter gets sick, there is no risk of someone having taken their place at work by the next morning. Yet these are conditions that low-wage women routinely face, which inevitably lead to the cyclical nature of their welfare histories."

In 1990, there were about 3.4 million women, 374,000 men, and 7.7 [21] million children under 18 receiving AFDC. The number of AFDC child recipients as a percent of children in poverty fell from 80.5 percent in 1973 to 59.9 percent in 1990. About 38 percent of AFDC families are white, 40 percent are Black, 17 percent are Latino, 3 percent are Asian, and 1 percent are Native American. There are disproportionately more people of color on welfare because disproportionately more people of color are poor and, as discussed below, they have disproportionately less access to other government benefits such as Social Security and Unemployment Insurance.

Contrary to image, most daughters in families who received wel-   22 fare do not become welfare recipients as adults. And, women receiving welfare don't have more children than others. Most families on AFDC have one child (42 percent) or two children (30 percent); only 10 percent have more than three children.

Abramovitz notes in *Regulating the Lives of Women,* "the percentage   23 of children in female-headed households has risen steadily since 1959, but the percentage of children receiving AFDC has remained constant at about 12 percent. Among black children, the divergence is even greater. Between 1972 and 1980, the number of black children living with just their mothers rose 20 percent while the number of black children receiving AFDC fell by 5 percent." Since 1970, the birth rates of unmarried Black women have fallen—while the birth rates of unmarried white women have risen—but the proportion of Black children born to unmarried mothers is growing because the birth rates of married Black women have fallen much more. (Some unmarried women, of course, are not single parents because they are raising children with male or female partners.)

The welfare system minimizes help and maximizes humiliation.   24 When Barbara Sobel, head of the New York City Human Resources administration, posed as a welfare applicant to experience the system firsthand, she was misdirected, mistreated, and so "depersonalized," she says, "I ceased to be." She remained on welfare, with a mandatory part-time job as a clerk in a city office, despite repeated pleas for full-time work, and learned that most recipients desperately want work (*New York Times,* February 5, 1993).

AFDC benefits have been chopped repeatedly as if, once you have   25 too little money, it doesn't matter how little you have. Since 1972, inflation-adjusted AFDC benefits have plummeted 43 percent. The average monthly benefit for a family of three in 1991 was $367, which at $4,404 a year, is much less than half the official poverty threshold for a family of three that year, $10,973. And the official poverty threshold completely underestimates what it actually costs to feed, house, clothe, etc. Today just two necessities, food and especially housing, take 85 percent of a typical poor family's budget. Less than one out of four AFDC families live in public housing or receive any rent subsidies.

Below-subsistence welfare payments are governmental child   26 abuse. The child-abusing budget cutters hide behind budget deficits (in 1991, AFDC accounted for less than 1 percent of federal outlays and states spent 2.2 percent of their revenues on AFDC) and their stereotypes of cheating "welfare queens." When California reduced its monthly AFDC payment for a mother and two children in 1991 from $694 (which was $2,645 below the annual poverty line) to $663, Governor Pete Wilson said it meant "one less six-pack per week" (*Equal Means,* Spring 1992).

Women turn to AFDC to support them and their children after di- 27 vorce (when their incomes plummet because of no or low wages and no or low child support), after losing a job, after childbirth outside marriage, or while completing their education or job training. While most families receiving AFDC do so for two years or less, a minority of families become long-term recipients. As the 1992 House Committee on Ways and Means *Green Book* noted, "the typical recipient is a short-term user."

Long-term recipients have greater obstacles to getting off welfare 28 such as lacking prior work experience, a high school degree or child care, or having poor health. Many women leave welfare—though often not poverty—after finding jobs and/or marrying men. Black women have a harder time doing either than white women, not because of a self-perpetuating "cycle of dependency," but a cycle of discrimination and demographics. It's fashionable to point to a "dearth of marriageable Black men," i.e. employed men earning above-poverty wages, without mentioning the dearth of Black men, period, as racism-fueled mortality takes its toll. The Black female-male ratio between the ages of 25 and 44, for example, was 100 to 87 in 1989, while it was 100 to 101 for whites.

Being married is neither necessary nor sufficient to avoid poverty. 29 The 1991 poverty rates for married-couple families with children were 7.7 percent for whites, 14.3 percent for Blacks, and 23.5 percent for Latinos.

A new wave of policies is being enacted to address the "behavioral 30 roots of poverty" and reinforce an old patriarchy with a "new paternalism." They punish unmarried women who have additional children—and punish those children—by denying women any increased benefits for new dependents and they reward women who marry. In the 1960s, the federal courts outlawed states' efforts to deny welfare benefits to "illegitimate" children and ended "midnight raids" to kick women off the rolls for having relationships with men. It remains to be seen how much the courts have changed as poor women and their legal advocates fight back.

Although two-thirds of AFDC recipients are children, critics make 31 it sound like most recipients should be employed (then again, child labor is on the rise). Many women work or seek work outside the home while receiving welfare in spite of the near dollar-for-dollar reductions in benefits for wages and insufficient allowance for child care and other work expenses. In recent years, state and federal policy has imposed mandatory work and training programs. In 1990, nearly two-thirds of adult recipients were exempt from registration in work programs, most commonly because they had very young children to care for. Nearly 40 percent of AFDC families had at least one child two years old or younger. In a discriminatory, dangerous move to expand day care for AFDC recipients many states are exempting child care providers from health and safety regulations or loosening them. And prevailing "workfare" programs by whatever name do not help women transcend the growing ranks of the working poor.

Whose "Culture of Poverty"?

The myth of a "culture of poverty" masks the reality of an econ- 32 omy of impoverishment. A lot of single mother families are broke, but they aren't broken.

In 1991, 47.1 percent of all female-headed families with children 33 under 18 were below the official poverty line as were 19.6 percent of male-headed families with children and no wives present. The respective rates were 39.6 and 16.5 percent for whites, 60.5 and 31.7 percent for Blacks, and 60.1 and 29.4 percent for Latinos. In other words, single father families have very high rates of poverty, but single mother families have even higher rates.

It's not surprising that many single parent households are poor 34 since the U.S. government neither assures affordable child care nor provides the universal child supports common in Western Europe. France, Britain, Denmark, and Sweden, for example, have similar or higher proportions of births to unmarried women without U.S. proportions of poverty.

It shouldn't be surprising that Black and Latino single parent fam- 35 ilies have higher rates of poverty than white families since the earnings and job opportunities of people of color reflect continued educational and employment discrimination. The overall poverty rates of Black (28.5 percent) and Latino (26.2 percent) males are much closer to the poverty rate of all female-headed households with and without children, of any race, 35.6 percent, than of white males (9.8 percent). And, it shouldn't be surprising that single mother families are the poorest of all since women are the lowest paid and women of color are doubly discriminated against. The fact that many female-headed households are poorer because women earn less than men is taken as a given in much welfare reform discussion, as if pay equity was a pipe dream not even worth mentioning.

A 1977 Department of Labor study found that if working women 36
were paid what similarly qualified men earn, the number of poor families would decrease by half. In 1977, women working year-round,
full-time earned 59 cents for every dollar earned by men. In 1991, they
earned 70 cents. In 1991, the inflation-adjusted median income for full-
time, year-round workers was $16,244 for Latina women; $18,720 for
Black women; $19,771 for Latino men; $20,794 for white women;
$22,075 for Black men; and $30,266 for white men. Half the full-time
workers in those categories made less than those amounts.

Two out of three workers who earn the minimum wage are 37
women. Full-time work at minimum wage ($4.25 an hour) earns below
the poverty line for a family of two. Discrimination is pervasive from
the bottom to the top of the payscale and it's not because women are
on the "mommy track." *Fortune* magazine (September 21, 1992) reports
"that at the same level of management, the typical woman's pay is
lower than her male colleague's—even when she has the exact same
qualifications, works just as many years, relocates just as often,
provides the main financial support for her family, takes no time off
for personal reasons, and wins the same number of promotions to
comparable jobs."

Nearly two out of three women with children under age six work 38
outside the home. Most working mothers work full-time. Cutting child
care is one of the ways states have balanced the budget on the backs of
children and low-income families. According to a 1992 child care
study commissioned by the Boston Foundation, after food, housing
and taxes, child care is the biggest expense for working parents of all
incomes. Boston's child care costs are among the nation's highest. In a
1988 survey of Boston-area employees, families reported spending an
average of $130 a week for child care (nationally that year child care
teaching staff, mostly women, had average earnings of only $9,363,
while sanitation workers earned $19,163 and workers in cigarette fac-
tories earned $30,590). Because of decreased state-funded child care
subsidies, only one-third of the 10,000 Boston children eligible for such
subsidies will find them.

Under the Upperclass

Terms like "underclass" and "persistent poverty" imply that 39
poverty persists in spite of society's commitment to eliminate it. In reality, the socioeconomic system reproduces poverty no matter how
persistently people are trying to get out or stay out of poverty.

As Adolph Reed Jr. writes in *Radical America* (January 1992) in a 40
critique of various underclass theories, "behavioral tendencies supposedly characterizing the underclass exist generally throughout the

society. Drug use, divorce, educational underattainment, laziness, and empty consumerism exist no less in upper status suburbs than in inner-city bantustans. The difference lies not in the behavior but in the social position of those exhibiting it" and in their access to safety nets. And in their imprisonment rates.

A 1990 study in the *New England Journal of Medicine* found that   41 substance abuse rates are slightly higher for white women than nonwhite women, but nonwhite women are ten times more likely to be reported to authorities. And, while mothers are increasingly prosecuted for drug use during pregnancy, the doors of most drug treatment centers remain closed to pregnant women. Similarly, Black kids are less likely to use drugs than white kids (according to government studies), but much more likely to be stigmatized and jailed for it. If the irrational drug laws were applied equally, we'd see a lot more handcuffed white movie stars, rich teenagers, politicians, doctors, stockbrokers, and CIA officers on the TV news, trying to hide their faces.

Low-income people and communities, like middle- and upper-   42 class people and communities, have a mix of strengths and weaknesses, needs and capacities. But poor communities are uniquely portrayed as the negative sum of their needs and "risks." All people and communities need services. In higher-income communities, people needing doctors or psychologists, lawyers or drug treatment, birth control or abortion, tutors or child care, can afford pricey private practitioners and avoid the stigma that often accompanies stingy public social services. In lower-income communities they cannot. This problem is especially bad in the United States because it lags far behind all other industrialized democracies in assuring the basic human needs of its people.

When health care is a privilege, not a right, children die. But it's   43 cheaper to blame their mothers than provide real universal health care (not Clinton's "managed competition"). Seventy countries provide prenatal care to *all* pregnant women and many have policies requiring *paid* maternity leave. The United States does not. An Ohio study found that a woman on pregnancy leave is 10 times more likely to lose her job than one on medical leave for other reasons (*New York Times*, January 12, 1993.) More children die before their first birthday in the United States per capita than in 21 other countries. Nationally, the infant mortality rate for Black babies is more than twice as high as for whites—the widest gap since 1940, when race specific data were first collected. In Boston, it is three times higher.

The *Boston Globe* (September 10, 1990) investigated "birth in the   44 'death zones,' " illuminating the link between racism, poverty, inadequate health care, and infant mortality. A later *Globe* editorial contrasted the response to that article with reaction to news that a dolphin was going to be dispatched from Boston's aquarium to the U.S. Navy: "Urgent appeals to save the dolphin are pouring in. The dolphin's innocence and dependency upon human kindness are noted. Money is no object to assuring it tender, loving care." For "the babies, most of them black and Hispanic," the common reaction was it's their mothers' fault and the babies deserve what they get. The majority of letters and phone calls concerning the babies, the *Globe* noted, "are ugly and racist. The mothers are termed 'moral-less' and 'irresponsible pigs.' The babies are described as 'inferior' and 'leeches.' They are degraded as 'trash that begets trash.' "

One out of four children is born into poverty in the United   45 States—the highest official rate of any industrialized nation. The official 1991 child poverty rate was 21.8 percent (25.5 percent for children under age three). For white children, it was 16.8 percent; for Latino children, 40.4 percent; and for Black children, 45.9 percent. Poverty rates would be even higher if they counted families whose incomes fell below the poverty line after taxes, and if the poverty threshold was adjusted upward to reflect, not just an inflation-multiplied out of date standard, but the real cost of living. The last time the Department of Labor compiled a "lower family budget," in 1981, it was 65 percent above that year's official poverty line for the same size family. In their book on the working poor, *The Forgotten Americans,* John Schwarz and Thomas Volgy show that based on a stringent economy budget a family of four in 1990 needed an income of about $20,700, or 155 percent of the 1990 official poverty line of $13,360.

Many countries provide a children's allowance or other universal   46 public benefit for families raising children. The United States does not. Throughout the 1980s, the U.S. government preached family values without valuing families. "Under our tax laws," Colorado Congresswoman Pat Schroeder was quoted in a *Time* feature on children (October 8, 1990), "the deduction for a Thoroughbred horse is greater than that for children."

Everything from prenatal care to college is rationed by money in a   47 country where income inequality has grown so much that the top 4 percent of Americans earned as much in wages and salaries in 1989 as the bottom 51 percent; in 1959, the top 4 percent earned as much as the bottom 35 percent. The average chief executive officer (CEO) of a large corporation earned as much in salary as 42 factory workers in 1980 and 104 factory workers in 1991 (Japan's CEOs earn about as much as 18 factory workers).

The top 1 percent of families now have a net worth much greater   48 than that of the bottom 90 percent. In 1989, reports the Economic Policy Institute, the top 1 percent of families had 37.7 percent of total net worth (assets minus debt) and the bottom 90 percent had 29.2 percent;

the bottom 95 percent had 40.7 percent. The top fifth of families had 83.6 percent of net worth; the upper middle fifth, 12.3 percent; the middle fifth, 4.9 percent; the lower middle fifth, 0.8 percent; and the bottom fifth, -1.7 percent. Looking at family income, the top fifth (families with pretax incomes of $61,490 and above in 1990) had 55.5 percent; the upper middle fifth, 20.7 percent; the middle fifth, 13.3 percent; the lower middle fifth, 7.6 percent; and the bottom fifth, 3.1 percent.

U.S. wealth concentration is now more extreme than any time 49 since 1929, and getting worse. For many Americans there's an endless economic depression. The shrinking middle class is misled into thinking those below them on the economic ladder are pulling them down, when in reality those at the top of the ladder are pushing everyone down.

The stereotype of deadbeat poor people masks the growing reality 50 of dead-end jobs. It is fashionable to point to the so-called breakdown of the family as a cause of poverty and ignore the breakdown in wages. The average inflation-adjusted earnings of nonsupervisory workers crashed 19 percent between 1973 and 1990. Minimum wage is 23 percent below its average value during the 1970s. For more and more Americans and their children, work is not a ticket out of poverty, but a condition of poverty.

Living standards are falling for younger generations, despite the 51 fact that many households have two wage earners. The inflation-adjusted median income for families with children headed by persons younger than 30 plummeted 32 percent between 1973 and 1990. Forty percent of all children in families headed by someone younger than 30 were living in poverty in 1990—including one out of four children in white young families.

The entry-level wage for high school graduates fell 22 percent be- 52 tween 1979 and 1991, a reflection, reports the Economic Policy Institute, of "the shift toward lower-paying industries, the lower value of the minimum wage, less unionization" and other trends. Entry level wages for college graduates fell slightly overall (-0.2 percent) between 1979 and 1991, but Black college graduates lost over 3 percent and Latino college graduates lost nearly 15 percent. Between 1979 and 1990, the proportion of full-time, year-round workers, ages 18 to 24, paid low wages (below $12,195 in 1990) jumped from 23 percent in 1979 to over 43 percent in 1990. Among young women workers, the figure is nearly one in two workers. And low-wage jobs are often dead-end jobs with low or no benefits (e.g. health insurance, paid vacation, pension), round-the-clock shifts, and little prospect of advancement.

During the 1960s and 1970s, Blacks were about twice as likely 53 to be unemployed as whites, according to official, undercounting

statistics. In the 1980s, the gap widened: when white unemployment
was 8.4 percent in 1983, Black unemployment was 19.5 percent. When
white unemployment was 4.1 percent in 1990, Black unemployment
was 2.76 times higher at 11.3 percent. Black college graduates had
a jobless rate 2.24 times that of white college graduates. As the Urban
Institute documented in a 1990 study using carefully matched and
trained pairs of white and Black young men applying for entry-level
jobs, discrimination against Black job seekers is "entrenched and
widespread."

To make matters worse, most unemployed people do not receive   54
unemployment insurance benefits. An average one-third of the offi-
cially-counted unemployed nationwide received benefits from 1984 to
1989; the figure rose to 42 percent in the severe recession year of 1991
(76 percent received benefits during the 1975 recession). Eligibility
varies by state and unemployment insurance typically lasts only a
maximum of 26 weeks whether or not you've found a job.

Low wage workers, disproportionately women and people of   55
color, are less likely than other workers to qualify for unemployment
benefits (they may not earn enough or meet work history requirements) and, when they do qualify, their unemployment payments are
only a portion of their meager wages. When the New Deal-era
Unemployment Insurance and Social Security programs were established, the occupations excluded from coverage—such as private domestic workers, agricultural laborers, government and nonprofit employees—were ones with large numbers of women and people of
color. A recent General Accounting Office study reported in the *New
York Times* (May 11, 1992) found that after accounting for such factors
as age, education, and types of disability, "blacks with serious ailments have been much more likely than whites to be rejected for benefits" under the Social Security Disability Insurance and Supplemental
Security Income programs.

Unlike many other countries, U.S. Social Security penalizes   56
women for work force absences due to pregnancy or care of children
and, until 1976, pregnant women could be denied unemployment benefits. Domestic workers became entitled to Social Security pensions in
1951, but received virtually no Unemployment Insurance protection
until 1978, when federal law required coverage of certain farm workers, most state and local government employees, and some private,
household workers. Workers forced to leave their jobs to care for new-
borns or ill family members have been denied unemployment benefits
because they are "voluntarily" unemployed.

"Recent studies in several states have found that a substantial   57
proportion of new AFDC families are headed by individuals who have

recently lost their jobs," reports the Center on Budget and Policy Priorities. "For unemployed people who do not have children, little or no cash assistance may be available if they fail to receive unemployment benefits. Many states and localities lack any general assistance program or else limit such a program to people who are elderly or have disabilities."

In the unusually blunt words of *Time* magazine (September 28, 58 1992), "Official statistics fail to reveal the extent of the pain. Unemployment stands at 7.6 percent . . . but more people are experiencing distress. A comprehensive tally would include workers who are employed well below their skill level, those who cannot find more than a part-time job, people earning poverty-level wages, workers who have been jobless for more than four weeks at a time and all those who have grown discouraged and quit looking. Last year those distressed workers totaled 36 million, or 40 percent of the American labor force, according to the Washington-based Economic Policy Institute."

"We never meant to quit our jobs. They quit on us," says a former 59 Rath Meatpacking employee from Waterloo, Iowa, quoted by Jacqueline Jones in *The Dispossessed.* Corporations are permanently downsizing their workforces and shifting more operations (including service sector jobs such as data processing) to countries where workers have even lower wages and few or no rights. The newer U.S. jobs not only pay less than disappearing unionized jobs, but employers are replacing full-time workers with part-time and temporary workers with even lower benefits and job security.

Broken Ladders

Education is often portrayed as the great ladder out of poverty. 60 But four decades after Brown v. Board of Education many schools are separate and unequal by race and economic status. Public school budgets are heavily determined by private property taxes. In Massachusetts in 1991, the federal share of school funding was 4.9 percent, the state share 37.1 percent, and the local share 58 percent. "Typically," writes Jonathan Kozol in *Savage Inequalities,* "very poor communities place high priority on education, and they often tax themselves at higher rates than do the very affluent communities," but the higher rates cannot offset the income gaps. And, like the mortgage interest deduction, the property tax deduction on federal taxes subsidizes higher income people the most.

The wide variations in local school funding mean that wealthier 61 districts spend two to four times as much per pupil than poorer ones, making the education system more reflective of apartheid than democracy. Wealthier citizens argue that lack of money isn't the problem in poorer schools—family values are—until proposals are made to make school spending more even. Then money matters for those who already have more.

Despite continued discriminatory school resources and expecta-   62
tions, the percentage of Blacks (ages 25–29) who are high school graduates or more has steadily climbed from 22.3 percent in 1947 to 76.6 percent in 1980 to 81.7 percent in 1991, while whites went from 54.9 percent in 1947 to 86.9 percent in 1980 to 85.8 percent in 1991. The percentage of Blacks with four or more years of college has risen from 2.8 percent in 1947 to 11.6 percent in 1980 to 13.4 percent in 1990, while whites went from 5.9 percent in 1947 to 23.7 percent in 1980 and 24.2 percent in 1990. The percentage of Blacks with college degrees fell to 11 percent in 1991, as skyrocketing tuition (rising faster than health care and housing) and educational cutbacks took their toll at a time when a college degree is increasingly crucial for decent pay. Blacks and Latinos are shortchanged in pay at all levels of educational attainment and routinely steered into lower wage fields.

The cycle of unequal opportunity has been reinforced by tax re-   63
form favoring the wealthy and ballooning the national debt. In 1968, the United States had a progressive personal income tax with a bottom tax rate of 14 percent and a top rate of 75 percent. Now—after the tax cuts advertised to stimulate investment, jobs, and trickle-down wealth—it has three rates: 15, 28, and 31 percent. State and local sales, excise, and property taxes are highly regressive (the poor pay a greater portion of their income than the rich). So is the Social Security payroll tax, which increased 30 percent between 1978 and 1990 and exempts incomes above a cap ($53,400 as of 1991), though even the wealthiest receive Social Security. Making things still worse, state and local governments are rushing to expand lotteries, video poker, and other government-promoted gambling to raise revenues, disproportionately from the poor, which they should be raising from a fair tax system.

In *Putting People First*, Bill Clinton and Al Gore offer a mix of   64
coded and partial policies to address poverty: "To ensure that no one with a family who works full-time has to raise children in poverty, we will increase the Earned Income Tax Credit to make up the difference between a family's earnings and the poverty level." At the same time, they recommend, "Scrap the current welfare system to make welfare a second chance, not a way of life. We will empower people on welfare with the education, retraining, and child care they need for up to two years so they can break the cycle of dependency. After that, those who are able will be required to work, either in the private sector or through community service." President Clinton asserted to

the nation's governors in February, "we will remove the incentive for staying in poverty," people should not "draw a check for doing nothing when they can do something." So far, Clinton has backpedaled fast on plans to cut unemployment and underemployment and assure that college is not an unaffordable privilege.

Welfare reform and other ideas are discussed more fully in *Mandate for Change,* the Progressive Policy Institute/Democratic Leadership Council blueprint for Clinton. It's revealing that in the chapter "Replacing Welfare with Work," the only race repeatedly mentioned is Black and the only age given is the atypical "15-year-old welfare mother with a new baby." The chapter is written as if being poor, Black, being on welfare, and being innercity "underclass" are all synonymous. 65

As Marion Wright Edelman, president of the Children's Defense Fund (the organization chaired formerly by Hillary Clinton and Secretary of Health and Human Services-Designate Donna Shalala) told the Clinton Economic Summit, "Contrary to popular myth, the majority of poor children are not Black, not on welfare and don't live in inner cities, but live in working families and outside inner cities in small town, rural and suburban America. Between 1989 and 1992, nearly one-quarter of the 1.7 million children who fell into poverty lived in two-parent white families, many of whom thought they'd never be out of work, need food stamps or face homelessness or hunger. New Hampshire reported the highest rate of growth in food stamp participation in the nation over the past three years." 66

In the words of the Children's Defense Fund, "The slow, grinding violence of poverty takes an American child's life every 53 minutes. The deadly, quick violence of guns takes an American child's life every three hours." Single mothers do not direct the economy—legal or underground. They don't direct the drug war, the National Rifle Association, the military, or the television and movie industries which teach children violence through entertainment and government action. 67

Pointing fingers at an "underclass culture of poverty" diverts attention and anger from the poverty-reproducing upperclass culture of greed. While subsidizing the luxury lifestyle of corporate kingpins and bailing out wealthy bank speculators, politicians pretend that below-subsistence subsidies for poor women and children are destroying the family and bringing down the American economy. Upperclass white America has been built on centuries of discriminatory subsidy and violence, from slavery to segregated suburbanization, Indian removal to "urban renewal," redbaiting, redlining, and union-busting. It's way past time to break upperclass dependency on the cycle of unequal opportunity. 68

Selected Data Resources

U.S. Bureau of the Census, *Statistical Abstract of the United States 1992; Poverty in the United States: 1991; Money Income of Households, Families, and Persons in the United States: 1991; Workers With Low Earnings: 1964 to 1990.*

U.S. Department of Health and Human Services, *Characteristics and Financial Circumstances of AFDC Recipients: FY 1990.*

U.S. House of Representatives, Committee on Ways and Means, *1992 Green Book: Overview of Entitlement Programs,* May 15, 1992; *Background Material on Family Income and Benefit Changes,* December 19, 1991.

QUESTIONS

1. Discuss the main stereotypes and myths that Sklar says the status quo or "culture of greed" perpetrates about poor people in the United States. Which if any of these beliefs have you shared in the past? In your experience, where and how do these beliefs typically get expressed?

2. Why do you think Sklar might argue that poverty is more of a women's issue than a racial issue?

3. Sklar uses many facts, figures, and statistics to build her argument that stereotypes about poverty "reflect power relations" more than they reflect reality. What effect does this amount of detail have on you? How persuaded are you overall by her reasoning and evidence?

American Horse

LOUISE ERDRICH

The woman sleeping on the cot in the woodshed was Albertine 1
American Horse. The name was left over from her mother's short marriage. The boy was the son of the man she had loved and let go. Buddy
was on the cot too, sitting on the edge because he'd been awake three
hours watching out for his mother and besides, she took up the whole
cot. Her feet hung over the edge, limp and brown as two trout. Her
long arms reached out and slapped at things she saw in her dreams.

Buddy had been knocked awake out of hiding in a washing ma- 2
chine while herds of policemen with dogs searched through a large
building with many tiny rooms. When the arm came down, Buddy
screamed because it had a blue cuff and sharp silver buttons. "Tss," his
mother mumbled, half awake, "wasn't nothing." But Buddy sat up
after her breathing went deep again, and he watched.

There was something coming and he knew it. 3

It was coming from very far off but he had a picture of it in his 4
mind. It was a large thing made of metal with many barbed hooks,
points, and drag chains on it, something like a giant potato peeler that
rolled out of the sky, scraping clouds down with it and jabbing or
crushing everything that lay in its path on the ground.

Buddy watched his mother. If he woke her up, she would know 5
what to do about the thing, but he thought he'd wait until he saw it
for sure before he shook her. She was pretty, sleeping, and he liked
knowing he could look at her as long and close up as he wanted. He
took a strand of her hair and held it in his hands as if it was the rein to

---

Louise Erdrich has published poems and short stories in magazines
and journals such as *The New Yorker, North American Review, Ms.,* and
Redbook. Her novels include *Love Medicine* (1984, winner of the
National Book Critics Circle Award; New and Expanded Version,
1993), *The Beet Queen* (1986), *Tracks* (1988), *The Crown of Columbus*
(1991, a collaborative work with her husband, writer Michael Dorris),
and *The Bingo Palace* (1994). Erdrich is the daughter of a Chippewa
Indian mother and German-American father; in her fiction she
explores the experience of Native Americans in North Dakota and
their relations with white culture, with characters representing both
parts of her heritage. This story first appeared in *Earth Power Coming:
Short Fiction in Native American Literature* (1983), edited by Simon J.
Ortiz, and has been anthologized in other collections and composition readers.

a delicate beast. She was strong enough and could pull him along like the horse their name was.

Buddy had his mother's and his grandmother's name because his   6
father had been a big mistake.

"They're all mistakes, even your father. But *you* are the best thing   7
that ever happened to me."

That was what she said when he asked.   8

Even Kadie, the boyfriend crippled from being in a car wreck,   9
was not as good a thing that had happened to his mother as Buddy was. "He was a medium-sized mistake," she said. "He's hurt and I shouldn't even say that, but it's the truth." At the moment, Buddy knew that being the best thing in his mother's life, he was also the reason they were hiding from the cops.

He wanted to touch the satin roses sewed on her pink tee shirt, but   10
he knew he shouldn't do that even in her sleep. If she woke up and found him touching the roses, she would say, "Quit that, Buddy." Sometimes she told him to stop hugging her like a gorilla. She never said that in the mean voice she used when he oppressed her, but when she said that he loosened up anyway.

There were times he felt like hugging her so hard and in such   11
a special way that she would say to him, "Let's get married." There were also times he closed his eyes and wished that she would die, only a few times, but still it haunted him that his wish might come true. He and Uncle Lawrence would be left alone. Buddy wasn't worried, though, about his mother getting married to somebody else. She had said to her friend, Madonna, "All men suck," when she thought Buddy wasn't listening. He had made an uncertain sound, and when they heard him they took him in their arms.

"Except for you, Buddy," his mother said. "All except for you and   12
maybe Uncle Lawrence, although he's pushing it."

"The cops suck the worst, though," Buddy whispered to his moth-   13
er's sleeping face, "because they're after us." He felt tired again, slumped down, and put his legs beneath the blanket. He closed his eyes and got the feeling that the cot was lifting up beneath him, that it was arching its canvas back and then traveling, traveling very fast and in the wrong direction for when he looked up he saw the three of them were advancing to meet the great metal thing with hooks and barbs and all sorts of sharp equipment to catch their bodies and draw their blood. He heard its insides as it rushed toward them, purring softly like a powerful motor and then they were right in its shadow. He pulled the reins as hard as he could and the beast reared, lifting him. His mother clapped her hand across his mouth.

"Okay," she said. "Lay low. They're outside and they're gonna   14
hunt."

She touched his shoulder and Buddy leaned over with her to look 15 through a crack in the boards.

They were out there all right, Albertine saw them. Two officers 16 and that social worker woman. Vicki Koob. There had been no whistle, no dream, no voice to warn her that they were coming. There was only the crunching sound of cinders in the yard, the engine purring, the dust sifting off their car in a fine light brownish cloud and settling around them.

The three people came to a halt in their husk of metal—the car em- 17 blazoned with the North Dakota State Highway Patrol emblem which is the glowing profile of the Sioux policeman, Red Tomahawk, the one who killed Sitting Bull. Albertine gave Buddy the blanket and told him that he might have to wrap it around him and hide underneath the cot.

"We're gonna wait and see what they do." She took him in her lap 18 and hunched her arms around him. "Don't you worry," she whispered against his ear. "Lawrence knows how to fool them."

Buddy didn't want to look at the car and the people. He felt his 19 mother's heart beating beneath his ear so fast it seemed to push the satin roses in and out. He put his face to them carefully and breathed the deep, soft powdery woman smell of her. That smell was also in her little face cream bottles, in her brushes, and around the washbowl after she used it. The satin felt so unbearably smooth against his cheek that he had to press closer. She didn't push him away, like he expected, but hugged him still tighter until he felt as close as he had ever been to back inside her again where she said he came from. Within the smells of her things, her soft skin, and the satin of her roses, he closed his eyes then, and took his breaths softly and quickly with her heart.

They were out there, but they didn't dare get out of the car yet be- 20 cause of Lawrence's big, ragged dogs. Three of these dogs had loped up the dirt driveway with the car. They were rangy, alert, and bounced up and down on their cushioned paws like wolves. They didn't waste their energy barking, but positioned themselves quietly, one at either car door and the third in front of the bellied-out screen door to Uncle Lawrence's house. It was six in the morning but the wind was up already, blowing dust, ruffling their short moth-eaten coats. The big brown one on Vicki Koob's side had unusual black and white markings, stripes almost, like a hyena and he grinned at her, tongue out and teeth showing.

"Shoo!" Miss Koob opened her door with a quick jerk. 21

The brown dog sidestepped the door and jumped before her, tip- 22 toeing. Its dirty white muzzle curled and its eyes crossed suddenly as if it was zeroing its cross-hair sights in on the exact place it would bite her. She ducked back and slammed the door.

"It's mean," she told Officer Brackett. He was printing out some   23
type of form. The other officer, Harmony, a slow man, had not yet re-acted to the car's halt. He had been sitting quietly in the back seat, but now he rolled down his window and with no change in expression un-snapped his holster and drew his pistol out and pointed it at the dog on his side. The dog smacked down on its belly, wiggled under the car and was out and around the back of the house before Harmony drew his gun back. The other dogs vanished with him. From wherever they had disappeared to they began to yap and howl, and the door to the low shoebox-style house fell open.

"Heya, what's going on?"   24

Uncle Lawrence put his head out the door and opened wide the   25
one eye he had in working order. The eye bulged impossibly wider in outrage when he saw the police car. But the eyes of the two officers and Miss Vicki Koob were wide open too because they had never seen Uncle Lawrence in his sleeping get up or, indeed, witnessed anything like it. For his ribs, which were cracked from a bad fall and still mend-ing, Uncle Lawrence wore a thick white corset laced up the front with a striped sneakers' lace. His glass eye and his set of dentures were still out for the night so his face puckered here and there, around its ab-sences and scars, like a damaged but fierce little cake. Although he had a few gray streaks now, Uncle Lawrence's hair was still thick, and be-cause he wore a special contraption of elastic straps around his head every night, two oiled waves always crested on either side of his mid-dle part. All of this would have been sufficient to astonish, even with-out the most striking part of his outfit—the smoking jacket. It was made of black satin and hung open around his corset, dragging a tas-seled belt. Gold thread dragons struggled up the lapels and blasted their furry red breath around his neck. As Lawrence walked down the steps, he put his arms up in surrender and the gold tassels in the inner seams of his sleeves dropped into view.

"My heavens, what a sight." Vicki Koob was impressed.   26

"A character," apologized Officer Harmony.   27

As a tribal police officer who could be counted on to help out the   28
State Patrol, Harmony thought he always had to explain about Indians or get twice as tough to show he did not favor them. He was slow-moving and shy but two jumps ahead of other people all the same, and now, as he watched Uncle Lawrence's splendid approach, he gazed speculatively at the torn and bulging pocket of the smoking jacket. Harmony had been inside Uncle Lawrence's house before and knew that above his draped orange-crate shelf of war medals a blue-black

German luger was hung carefully in a net of flat-headed nails and fishing line. Thinking of this deadly exhibition, he got out of the car and shambled toward Lawrence with a dreamy little smile of welcome on his face. But when he searched Lawrence, he found that the bulging pocket held only the lonesome-looking dentures from Lawrence's empty jaw. They were still dripping denture polish.

"I had been cleaning them when you arrived," Uncle Lawrence 29 explained with acid dignity.

He took the toothbrush from his other pocket and aimed it like 30 a rifle.

"Quit that, you old idiot." Harmony tossed the toothbrush away. 31 "For once you ain't done nothing. We came for your nephew."

Lawrence looked at Harmony with a faint air of puzzlement. 32

"Ma Frere, listen," threatened Harmony amiably, "those two 33 white people in the car came to get him for the welfare. They got papers on your nephew that give them the right to take him."

"Papers?" Uncle Lawrence puffed out his deeply pitted cheeks. 34 "Let me see them papers."

The two of them walked over to Vicki's side of the car and she 35 pulled a copy of the court order from her purse. Lawrence put his teeth back in and adjusted them with busy workings of his jaw.

"Just a minute," he reached into his breast pocket as he bent close 36 to Miss Vicki Koob. "I can't read these without I have in my eye."

He took the eye from his breast pocket delicately, and as he 37 popped it into his face the social worker's mouth fell open in a consternated O.

"What is this," she cried in a little voice. 38

Uncle Lawrence looked at her mildly. The white glass of the eye 39 was cold as lard. The black iris was strangely charged and menacing.

"He's nuts," Brackett huffed along the side of Vicki's neck. "Never 40 mind him."

Vicki's hair had sweated down her nape in tiny corkscrews and 41 some of the hairs were so long and dangly now that they disappeared into the zippered back of her dress. Brackett noticed this as he spoke into her ear. His face grew red and the backs of his hands prickled. He slid under the steering wheel and got out of the car. He walked around the hood to stand with Leo Harmony.

"We could take you in too," said Brackett roughly. Lawrence eyed 42 the officers in what was taken as defiance. "If you don't cooperate, we'll get out the handcuffs," they warned.

One of Lawrence's arms was stiff and would not move until he'd 43 rubbed it with witch hazel in the morning. His other arm worked fine though, and he stuck it out in front of Brackett.

"Get them handcuffs," he urged them. "Put me in a welfare home."   44

Bracket snapped one side of the handcuffs on Lawrence's good   45
arm and the other to the handle of the police car.

"That's to hold you," he said. "We're wasting our time. Harmony,   46
you search that little shed over by the tall grass and Miss Koob and
myself will search the house."

"My rights is violated!" Lawrence shrieked suddenly. They ig-   47
nored him. He tugged at the handcuff and thought of the good heavy
file he kept in his tool box and the German luger oiled and ready but
never loaded, because of Buddy, over his shelf. He should have used
it on these bad ones, even Harmony in his big-time white man job. He
wouldn't last long in that job anyway before somebody gave him
what for.

"It's a damn scheme," said Uncle Lawrence, rattling his chains   48
against the car. He looked over at the shed and thought maybe
Albertine and Buddy had sneaked away before the car pulled into the
yard. But he sagged, seeing Albertine move like a shadow within the
boards. "Oh, it's all a damn scheme," he muttered again.

"I want to find that boy and salvage him," Vicki Koob explained   49
to Officer Brackett as they walked into the house. "Look at his family
life—the old man crazy as a bedbug, the mother intoxicated somewhere."

Brackett nodded, energetic, eager. He was a short hopeful red-   50
head who failed consistently to win the hearts of women. Vicki Koob
intrigued him. Now, as he watched, she pulled a tiny pen out of an or-
namental clip on her blouse. It was attached to a retractable line that
would suck the pen back, like a child eating one strand of spaghetti.
Something about the pen on its line excited Brackett to the point of
discomfort. His hand shook as he opened the screen-door and
stepped in, beckoning Miss Koob to follow.

They could see the house was empty at first glance. It was only one   51
rectangular room with whitewashed walls and a little gas stove in the
middle. They had already come through the cooking lean-to with the
other stove and washstand and rusty old refrigerator. That refrigerator had nothing in it but some wrinkled potatoes and a package of
turkey necks. Vicki Koob noted in her perfect-bound notebook. The
beds along the walls of the big room were covered with quilts that
Albertine's mother, Sophie, had made from bits of old wool coats and
pants that the Sisters sold in bundles at the mission. There was no one
hiding beneath the beds. No one was under the little aluminum dinette
table covered with a green oilcloth, or the soft brown wood chairs
tucked up to it. One wall of the big room was filled with neatly stacked
crates of things—old tools and springs and small half-dismantled

appliances. Five or six television sets were stacked against the wall. Their control panels spewed colored wires and at least one was cracked all the way across. Only the topmost set, with coathanger antenna angled sensitively to catch the bounding signals around Little Shell, looked like it could possibly work.

Not one thing escaped Vicki Koob's trained and cataloguing gaze. 52 She made note of the cupboard that held only commodity flour and coffee. The unsanitary tin oil drum beneath the kitchen window, full of empty surplus pork cans and beer bottles, caught her eye as did Uncle Lawrence's physical and mental deteriorations. She quickly described these "benchmarks of alcoholic dependency within the extended family of Woodrow (Buddy) American Horse" as she walked around the room with the little notebook open, pushed against her belly to steady it. Although Vicki had been there before, Albertine's presence had always made it difficult for her to take notes.

"Twice the maximum allowable space between door and thresh- 53 old," she wrote now. "Probably no insulation. Two three-inch cracks in walls inadequately sealed with white-washed mud." She made a mental note but could see no point in describing Lawrence's stuffed reclining chair that only reclined, the shadeless lamp with its plastic orchid in the bubble glass base, or the three-dimensional picture of Jesus that Lawrence had once demonstrated to her. When plugged in, lights rolled behind the water the Lord stood on so that he seemed to be strolling although he never actually went forward, of course, but only pushed the glowing waves behind him forever like a poor tame rat in a treadmill.

Brackett cleared his throat with a nervous rasp and touched 54 Vicki's shoulder.

"What are you writing?" 55

She moved away and continued to scribble as if thoroughly ab- 56 sorbed in her work. "Officer Brackett displays an undue amount of interest in my person," she wrote. "Perhaps?"

He snatched playfully at the book, but she hugged it to her chest 57 and moved off smiling. More curls had fallen, wetted to the base of her neck. Looking out the window, she sighed long and loud.

"All night on brush rollers for this. What a joke." 58

Brackett shoved his hands in his pockets. His mouth opened 59 slightly, then shut with a small throttled cluck.

When Albertine saw Harmony ambling across the yard with his 60 big brown thumbs in his belt, his placid smile, and his tiny black eyes moving back and forth, she put Buddy under the cot. Harmony stopped at the shed and stood quietly. He spread his arms to show her he hadn't drawn his big police gun.

"Ma Cousin," he said in the Michif dialect that people used if they were relatives or sometimes if they needed gas or a couple of dollars, "why don't you come out here and stop this foolishness?"   61

"I ain't your cousin," Albertine said. Anger boiled up in her suddenly. "I ain't related to no pigs."   62

She bit her lip and watched him through the cracks, circling, a big tan punching dummy with his boots full of sand so he never stayed down once he fell. He was empty inside, all stale air. But he knew how to get to her so much better than a white cop could. And now he was circling because he wasn't sure she didn't have a weapon, maybe a knife or the German luger that was the only thing that her father, Albert American Horse, had left his wife and daughter besides his name. Harmony knew that Albertine was a tall strong woman who took two big men to subdue when she didn't want to go in the drunk tank. She had hard hips, broad shoulders, and stood tall like her Sioux father, the American Horse who was killed threshing in Belle Prairie.   63

"I feel bad to have to do this," Harmony said to Albertine. "But for godsakes, let's nobody get hurt. Come on out with the boy, why don't you? I know you got him in there."   64

Albertine did not give herself away this time. She let him wonder. Slowly and quietly she pulled her belt through its loops and wrapped it around and around her hand until only the big oval buckle with turquoise chunks shaped into a butterfly stuck out over her knuckles. Harmony was talking but she wasn't listening to what he said. She was listening to the pitch of his voice, the tone of it that would tighten or tremble at a certain moment when he decided to rush the shed. He kept talking slowly and reasonably, flexing the dialect from time to time, even mentioning her father.   65

"He was a damn good man. I don't care what they say, Albertine, I knew him."   66

Albertine looked at the stone butterfly that spread its wings across her fist. The wings looked light and cool, not heavy. It almost looked like it was ready to fly. Harmony wanted to get to Albertine through her father but she would not think about American Horse. She concentrated on the sky blue stone.   67

Yet the shape of the stone, the color, betrayed her.   68

She saw her father suddenly, bending at the grille of their old gray car. She was small then. The memory came from so long ago it seemed like a dream—narrowly focused, snapshot-clear. He was bending by the grille in the sun. It was hot summer. Wings of sweat, dark blue, spread across the back of his work shirt. He always wore soft blue shirts, the color of shade cloudier than this stone. His stiff hair had grown out of its short haircut and flopped over his forehead.   69

When he stood up and turned away from the car, Albertine saw that he had a butterfly.

"It's dead," he told her. "Broke its wings and died on the grille."   70

She must have been five, maybe six, wearing one of the boy's tee   71 shirts Mama bleached in Hilex-water. American Horse took the butterfly, a black and yellow one, and rubbed it on Albertine's collarbone and chest and arms until the color and the powder of it were blended into her skin.

"For grace," he said.   72

And Albertine had felt a strange lightening in her arms, in her   73 chest, when he did this and said, "For grace." The way he said it, grace meant everything the butterfly was. The sharp delicate wings. The way it floated over grass. The way its wings seemed to breathe fanning in the sun. The wisdom of the way it blended into flowers or changed into a leaf. In herself she felt the same kind of possibilities and closed her eyes almost in shock or pain, she felt so light and powerful at that moment.

Then her father had caught her and thrown her high into the air.   74 She could not remember landing in his arms or landing at all. She only remembered the sun filling her eyes and the world tipping crazily behind her, out of sight.

"He was a damn good man," Harmony said again.   75

Albertine heard his starched uniform gathering before his boots   76 hit the ground. Once, twice, three times. It took him four solid jumps to get right where she wanted him. She kicked the plank door open when he reached for the handle and the corner caught him on the jaw. He faltered, and Albertine hit him flat on the chin with the butterfly. She hit him so hard the shock of it went up her arm like a string pulled taut. Her fist opened, numb, and she let the belt unloop before she closed her hand on the tip end of it and sent the stone butterfly swooping out in a wide circle around her as if it was on the end of a leash. Harmony reeled backward as she walked toward him swinging the belt. She expected him to fall but he just stumbled. And then he took the gun from his hip.

Albertine let the belt go limp. She and Harmony stood within feet   77 of each other, breathing. Each heard the human sound of air going in and out of the other person's lungs. Each read the face of the other as if deciphering letters carved into softly eroding veins of stone. Albertine saw the pattern of tiny arteries that age, drink, and hard living had blown to the surface of the man's face. She saw the spoked wheels of his iris and the arteries like tangled threads that sewed him up. She saw the living net of springs and tissue that held him together, and trapped him. She saw the random, intimate plan of his person.

She took a quick shallow breath and her face went strange and   78
tight. She saw the black veins in the wings of the butterfly, roads burnt
into a map, and then she was located somewhere in the net of veins
and sinew that was the tragic complexity of the world so she did not
see Officer Brackett and Vicki Koob rushing toward her, but felt them
instead like flies caught in the same web, rocking it.

"Albertine!" Vicki Koob had stopped in the grass. Her voice was   79
shrill and tight. "It's better this way, Albertine. We're going to help
you."

Albertine straightened, threw her shoulders back. Her father's   80
hand was on her chest and shoulders lightening her wonderfully.
Then on wings of her father's hands, on dead butterfly wings,
Albertine lifted into the air and flew toward the others. The light powerful feeling swept her up the way she had floated higher, seeing the
grass below. It was her father throwing her up into the air and out of
danger. Her arms opened for bullets but no bullets came. Harmony
did not shoot. Instead, he raised his fist and brought it down hard on
her head.

Albertine did not fall immediately, but stood in his arms a mo-   81
ment. Perhaps she gazed still farther back behind the covering of his
face. Perhaps she was completely stunned and did not think as she
sagged and fell. Her face rolled forward and hair covered her features,
so it was impossible for Harmony to see with just what particular expression she gazed into the head-splitting wheel of light, or blackness,
that overcame her.

Harmony turned the vehicle onto the gravel road that led back to   82
town. He had convinced the other two that Albertine was more trouble than she was worth, and so they left her behind, and Lawrence too.
He stood swearing in his cinder driveway as the car rolled out of sight.
Buddy sat between the social worker and Officer Brackett. Vicki tried
to hold Buddy fast and keep her arm down at the same time, for the
words she'd screamed at Albertine had broken the seal of antiperspi-
rant beneath her arms. She was sweating now as though she'd stored
an ocean up inside of her. Sweat rolled down her back in a shallow
river and pooled at her waist and between her breasts. A thin sheen of
water came out on her forearms, her face. Vicki gave an irritated moan
but Brackett seemed not to take notice, or take offense at least. Air-con-
ditioned breezes were sweeping over the seat anyway, and very soon
they would be comfortable. She smiled at Brackett over Buddy's head.
The man grinned back. Buddy stirred. Vicki remembered the emergency chocolate bar she kept in her purse, fished it out, and offered it
to Buddy. He did not react, so she closed his fingers over the package
and peeled the paper off one end.

The car accelerated. Buddy felt the road and wheels pummeling 83 each other and the rush of the heavy motor purring in high gear. Buddy knew that what he'd seen in his mind that morning, the thing coming out of the sky with barbs and chains, had hooked him. Somehow he was caught and held in the sour tin smell of the pale woman's armpit. Somehow he was pinned between their pounds of breathless flesh. He looked at the chocolate in his hand. He was squeezing the bar so hard that a thin brown trickle had melted down his arm. Automatically he put the bar in his mouth.

As he bit down he saw his mother very clearly, just as she had 84 been when she carried him from the shed. She was stretched flat on the ground, on her stomach, and her arms were curled around her head as if in sleep. One leg was drawn up and it looked for all the world like she was running full tilt into the ground, as though she had been trying to pass into the earth, to bury herself, but at the last moment something had stopped her.

There was no blood on Albertine, but Buddy tasted blood now at 85 the sight of her, for he bit down hard and cut his own lip. He ate the chocolate, every bit of it, tasting his mother's blood. And when he had the chocolate down inside him and all licked off his hands, he opened his mouth to say thank you to the woman, as his mother had taught him. But instead of a thank you coming out he was astonished to hear a great rattling scream, and then another, rip out of him like pieces of his own body and whirl onto the sharp things all around him.

QUESTIONS

1. From the information given in the story, what do you think best serves the interests of Buddy—going with the social worker (Vicki Koob) or staying with his mother (Albertine)? Why?

2. Discuss how Vicki Koob, Officer Brackett, and Officer Harmony are portrayed by Erdrich. What kind of people are they? How do they seem to view their jobs as representatives of the social welfare system and law enforcement? Through these characterizations, what do you think Erdrich is trying to say about the social institutions they represent?

3. Rewrite this story as you think it might be reported in your city or local newspaper, in about 500 to 750 words. Compare newspaper accounts with classmates, and discuss how people decided what information to include and what to leave out and how to present that information. How might you answer question 1 (above) differently if you had only read the newspaper accounts? Why?

THINKING ABOUT PRIVILEGE, POVERTY, AND MAINSTREAM VALUES

1. Of McGinley's suburbanites or Gilden's warehouse people, who do you think more closely embodies "the Western Code" described by Ehrlich?

2. Gilden says that the warehouse tribes seek "the antithesis of the American Dream" (paragraph 16). Imagine a dialogue about a current social issue, such as homelessness, between one of McGinley's suburbanites from "Spruce Manor"—which might seem to embody the American Dream—and one of Gilden's "garbage people." How would each challenge the other's assumptions and basic values? Try playing both roles with a partner or small group, then write an essay in the form of a dialogue between these characters.

3. How much might Baldwin change his "Letter from Harlem" in order to address it to McGinley or the residents of "Spruce Manor"? Try rewriting a section of Baldwin's essay specifically to this audience; then write a reply to Baldwin from McGinley with the subtitle "A Letter from Spruce Manor."

4. Based on Steele's views about being black in the 1960s, to what extent do you think he would portray Baldwin as "a priest from a church I'd grown disenchanted with" (paragraph 3)? Support your response with evidence from both essays.

5. Steele admits that the imaginary character Sam "looked very much like the white racist stereotype of blacks" (paragraph 16) but defends his family's use of Sam as a vehicle for encouraging "identification with [middle-class] values and patterns of responsibility" (paragraph 17). Steele goes on to argue that he and other middle-class people are "conditioned by these values from birth" (paragraph 18). How do you think Baldwin and Sklar might respond to these arguments? With whose views are you most sympathetic, and why?

6. What misguided beliefs about poverty or poor people, as discussed by Sklar, do you think are held by the characters Koob, Brackett, and Harmony in Erdrich's short story? To what extent do you think that Erdrich's story as a whole encourages or discourages stereotypes about poverty in America?

7. From your reading of Ehrlich, McGinley, and Steele, define a set of values that you associate with the American mainstream, then evaluate these values with help from Gilden, Baldwin, Sklar, and/or

Erdrich. Using these sources together with your own experience, write an essay that asserts your views about mainstream American values.

Exploring Additional Sources

8. The values of the American mainstream are also explored thoughtfully in "The Girl Who Wouldn't Sing" by Kit Yuen Quan (page 118), "The Trip Back" by Robert Olen Butler (page 214), and "Family Values" by Richard Rodriguez (page 340). Choose one of these selections to analyze in conjunction with one or more of the selections in this chapter. For example, contrast the versions of the "American dream family" offered by McGinley and Rodriguez.

9. In the introduction to *The Province of the Heart* (1959), McGinley writes that "Suburbia, of Thee I Sing" was considered very controversial when it first appeared in *Harper's* in 1949, but "now, in a day when Suburbia has pretty well lost its stigma. . . . the heresy has become orthodoxy." And Sklar writes that the "homemaker mom/breadwinner dad marriage—which, though rare for most American history, was enshrined as traditional with the help of postwar television." Test out one or both of these claims by studying a selection of general-interest magazines, television reruns, and/or movies from the 1950s.

10. Conduct research about two current or historical nonmainstream movements that advocated or represented social change in ways similar to the "warehouse tribes," such as the punk movement, the Green Party, the beat subculture of the '50s and '60s, or the hippie counterculture of the '60s and '70s. Analyze a particular aspect of the two groups that interests you, such as the function of music or the prevalent lifestyle habits within the movement.

11. Find the 1960 issue of *Esquire* in which Baldwin first published his "Letter from Harlem." Read other articles in this and other general-circulation magazines from the same time period to get a feel for the way that social conditions, especially U.S. racial tensions, were being represented in the media. Analyze Baldwin's rhetoric—his tone, his language, his style of argumentation—in comparison to the rhetoric of other articles you find addressing the same issues.

12. Steele writes that his father "achieved middle-class standing" for his family partly by a belief in "education for his children (all four of whom have advanced degrees)," while Sklar claims that, although "education is often portrayed as the great ladder out of poverty," that ladder is broken. Evaluate the current reality of educational achievement and opportunity for African Americans at a particular grade level, such as college doctoral programs.

13. Perform volunteer work for a community service agency that works with poor people in your community (your school or college may have a clearinghouse or liaison office for community service). Integrate interviews with the agency's staff and clients into a research paper evaluating the effectiveness of efforts to combat poverty in your community or a nearby community.

14. Research the current social conditions for a particular Native American tribe or reservation community. If possible, interview members of the tribe, teachers, and social workers. If you have a Native American student group on your campus, talk to members about their backgrounds and ask them to suggest books or other sources. You might make a proposal—or evaluate an existing proposal or proposed law—that addresses one or more of the social conditions you discover (for example, some Indian tribes have recently, and controversially, opened gambling casinos as a way to generate revenue).

8

SEXUAL ORIENTATION AND DIVERSITY

Definition of Womanist

ALICE WALKER

Womanist   From *womanish*. (Opp. of "girlish," i.e., frivolous, irresponsible, not serious.) A black feminist or feminist of color. From the black folk expression of mothers to female children, "You acting womanish," i.e., like a woman. Usually referring to outrageous, audacious, courageous, or *willful* behavior. Wanting to know more and in greater depth than is considered "good" for one. Interested in grown-up doings. Acting grown up. Being grown up. Interchangeable with another black folk expression: "You trying to be grown." Responsible. In charge. *Serious.*

2.   *Also:* A woman who loves other women, sexually and/or nonsexually. Appreciates and prefers women's culture, women's emotional flexibility (values tears as a natural counterbalance of laughter), and women's strength. Sometimes loves individual men, sexually and/or nonsexually. Committed to survival and wholeness of entire people, male *and* female. Not a separatist, except periodically, for health. Traditionally universalist, as in: "Mama, why are we brown, pink, and yellow, and our cousins are white, beige, and black?" Ans.: "Well, you know the colored race is just like a flower garden, with every color flower represented." Traditionally capable, as in: "Mama, I'm walking to Canada and I'm taking you and a bunch of other slaves with me." Reply: "It wouldn't be the first time."

3.   Loves music. Loves dance. Loves the moon. *Loves* the Spirit. Loves love and food and roundness. Loves struggle. *Loves* the Folk. Loves herself. *Regardless.*

4.   Womanist is to feminist as purple is to lavender.

—FROM IN SEARCH OF OUR MOTHERS' GARDENS, 1983

Femininity

SUSAN BROWNMILLER

Femininity, in essence, is a romantic sentiment, a nostalgic tradition of imposed limitations. Even as it hurries forward in the 1980s, putting on lipstick and high heels to appear well dressed, it trips on the ruffled petticoats and hoopskirts of an era gone by. Invariably and necessarily, femininity is something that women had more of in the past, not only in the historic past of prior generations, but in each woman's personal past as well—in the virginal innocence that is replaced by knowledge, in the dewy cheek that is coarsened by age, in the "inherent nature" that a woman seems to misplace so forgetfully whenever she steps out of bounds. Why should this be so? The XX chromosomal message has not been scrambled, the estrogen-dominated hormonal balance is generally as biology intended, the reproductive organs, whatever use one has made of them, are usually in place, the breasts of whatever size are most often where they should be. But clearly, biological femaleness is not enough.

Femininity always demands more. It must constantly reassure its audience by a willing demonstration of difference, even when one does not exist in nature, or it must seize and embrace a natural variation and compose a rhapsodic symphony upon the notes. Suppose one doesn't care to, has other things on her mind, is clumsy or tone-deaf despite the best instruction and training? To fail at the feminine difference is to appear not to care about men, and to risk the loss of their attention and approval. To be insufficiently feminine is viewed as a failure in core sexual identity, or as a failure to care sufficiently about oneself, for a woman found wanting will be appraised (and will appraise herself) as mannish or neutered or simply unattractive, as men have defined these terms.

It is fashionable in some quarters to describe the feminine and masculine principles as polar ends of the human continuum, and to sagely profess that both polarities exist in all people. Sun and moon, yin and yang, soft and hard, active and passive, etcetera, may indeed be opposites, but a linear continuum does not illuminate the problem. (Femininity, in all its contrivances, is a very active endeavor.) What, then, is the basic distinction? The masculine principle is better understood as a driving ethos of superiority designed to inspire straightforward, confident success, while the feminine principle is composed of vulnerability, the need for protection, the formalities of compliance and the avoidance of conflict—in short, an appeal of dependence and good will that gives the masculine principle its romantic validity and its admiring applause.

—From *Femininity*, 1984

The Soft Male

ROBERT BLY

In the seventies I began to see all over the country a phenomenon that we might call the "soft male." Sometimes even today when I look out at an audience, perhaps half the young males are what I'd call soft. They're lovely, valuable people—I like them—they're not interested in harming the earth or starting wars. There's a gentle attitude toward life in their whole being and style of living.

But many of these men are not happy. You quickly notice the lack of energy in them. They are life-preserving but not exactly life-giving. Ironically, you often see these men with strong women who positively radiate energy.

Here we have a finely tuned young man, ecologically superior to his father, sympathetic to the whole harmony of the universe, yet he himself has little vitality to offer.

The strong or life-giving women who graduated from the sixties, so to speak, or who have inherited an older spirit, played an important part in producing this life-preserving, but not life-giving, man. . . .

Some energetic women, at that time and now in the nineties, chose and still choose soft men to be their lovers and, in a way, perhaps, to be their sons. The new distribution of "yang" energy among couples didn't happen by accident. Young men for various reasons wanted their harder women, and women began to desire softer men. It seemed like a nice arrangement for a while, but we've lived with it long enough now to see that it isn't working out. . . .

In every relationship something *fierce* is needed once in a while: both the man and the woman need to have it. But at the point when it was needed, often the young man came up short. He was nurturing, but something else was required—for his relationship, and for his life.

The "soft" male was able to say, "I can feel your pain, and I consider your life as important as mine, and I will take care of you and comfort you." But he could not say what he wanted, and stick by it.

—FROM *IRON JOHN: A BOOK ABOUT MEN*, 1990

Masculinity and the Men's Movement

GARY KINSMAN

The limits of "acceptable" masculinity are in part defined by comments like "What are you, a fag?"[1] As boys and men we have heard

---

[1] See G. K. Lehne, "Homophobia Among Men," in Deborah David and Robert Brannon, *The Forty Nine Per Cent Majority* (Reading, Mass.: Addison-Wesley, 1976), 78.

such expressions and the words "queer," "faggot," and "sissy" all our lives. These words encourage certain types of male behavior and serve to define, regulate, and limit our lives, whether we consider ourselves straight or gay. Depending on who is speaking and who is listening, they incite fear or hatred.

Even among many heterosexual men who have been influenced by feminism, the taboo against loving the same sex remains unchallenged. Lines like "I may be anti-sexist, but I am certainly not gay" can still be heard. These men may be questioning some aspects of male privilege, but in attempting to remake masculinity they have not questioned the institution of heterosexuality.[2] As a result their challenge to male privilege is partial and inadequate.

Gay men have often found much support in the "men's movement" or in groups of men against sexism. At the same time we have also seen our concerns as gay men marginalized and pushed aside and have often felt like outsiders. Joe Interrante expresses some of the reservations of gay men about the "men's movement" and its literature:

> As a gay man . . . I had suspicions about the heterocentrist bias of this work. It told me that my gayness existed "in addition to" my masculinity, whereas I found that it colored my entire experience of manhood. I distrusted a literature which claimed that gay men were just like heterosexual men except for what they did in bed.[3]

The literature of the men's movement has tended to produce an image of men that is white, middle-class, and heterosexual. As Ned Lyttleton has pointed out, "an analysis of masculinity that does not deal with the contradictions of power imbalances that exist between men themselves will be limited and biased, and its limits and biases will be concealed under the blanket of shared male privilege."[4] A series of masculinities becomes subsumed under one form of masculinity that becomes "masculinity." As a result, socially organized power relations among and between men based on sexuality, race, class, or age have been neglected. These power relations are major dividing lines between men that have to be addressed if progressive organizing among men is to encompass the needs and experiences of

---

[2]On the notion of institutionalized heterosexuality see Charlotte Bunch, "Not For Lesbians Only," *Quest* 11, no. 2 (Fall 1975). Also see Adrienne Rich, "Compulsory Heterosexuality and Lesbian Existence," in Snitow, Stansell and Thompson, eds., *Powers of Desire: The Politics of Sexuality* (New York: Monthly Review Press, 1983): 177–205.

[3]Joe Interrante, "Dancing Along the Precipice: The Men's Movement in the '80s," *Radical America* 15, no. 5 (September–October 1981): 54.

[4]Ned Lyttelton, "Men's Liberation, Men Against Sexism and Major Dividing Lines," *Resources for Feminist Research* 12, no. 4 (December/January 1983/1984): 33. Several discussions with Ned Lyttelton were very useful in clarifying my ideas in this section and throughout this paper.

all men. The men's movement has reached a turning point.[5] It has to choose whether it is simply a movement for men's rights—defending men's rights to be human too—or whether it will deepen the challenge to an interlocked web of oppression: sexism, heterosexism, racism, and class exploitation. We have to choose between a vision of a world in which men are more sensitive and human but are still "real" men at the top of the social order, and a radically new vision that entails the transformation of masculinity and sexuality and the challenging of other forms of domination.

—FROM "MEN LOVING MEN: THE CHALLENGE OF GAY LIBERATION,"

IN *BEYOND PATRIARCHY*, 1987

---

[5]Interrante, op. cit., 54.

Family Values

RICHARD RODRIGUEZ

I am sitting alone in my car, in front of my parents' house—a 1
middle-aged man with a boy's secret to tell. What words will I use to
tell them? I hate the word *gay,* find its little affirming sparkle more pathetic than assertive. I am happier with the less polite *queer.* But to my
parents I would say *homosexual,* avoiding the Mexican slang *joto* (I had
always heard it said in our house with hints of condescension), though
joto is less mocking than the sissy-boy *maricon.*

The buzz on everyone's lips now: Family values. The other night 2
on TV, the vice president of the United States, his arm around his wife,
smiled into the camera and described homosexuality as "mostly a
choice." But how would he know? Homosexuality never felt like a
choice to me.

A few minutes ago Rush Limbaugh, the radio guy with a voice that 3
reminds me, for some reason, of a butcher's arms, was banging his console and booming a near-reasonable polemic about family values.
Limbaugh was not very clear about which values exactly he considers
to be family values. A divorced man who lives alone in New York?

My parents live on a gray, treeless street in San Francisco not far 4
from the ocean. Probably more than half of the neighborhood is immigrant. India lives next door to Greece, who lives next door to Russia. I
wonder what the Chinese lady next door to my parents makes of the
politicians' phrase *family values.*

What immigrants know, what my parents certainly know, is that 5
when you come to this country, you risk losing your children. The assurance of family—continuity, inevitability—is precisely what
America encourages its children to overturn. *Become your own man.* We
who are native to this country know this too, of course, though we are
likely to deny it. Only a society so guilty about its betrayal of family
would tolerate the pieties of politicians regarding family values.

Richard Rodriguez is a writer, editor for Pacific News Service in
San Francisco, and a contributing editor for *Harper's* magazine and
the Sunday "Opinion" section of the *Los Angeles Times,* where this
essay appeared in 1992. Selections from his memoir *Hunger of
Memory: The Education of Richard Rodriguez* (1982) have been widely
anthologized in composition readers (see, for example, his "Public
and Private Language" beginning on page 142). In 1992 Rodriguez
published the collection of essays *Days of Obligation: An Argument with
My Mexican Father.*

On the same summer day that Republicans were swarming in 6
Houston (buzzing about family values), a friend of mine who escaped
family values awhile back and who now wears earrings resembling in-
trauterine devices, was complaining to me over coffee about the
Chinese. The Chinese will never take over San Francisco, my friend
said, because the Chinese do not want to take over San Francisco. The
Chinese do not even *see* San Francisco! All they care about is their
damn families. All they care about is double-parking smack in front of
the restaurant on Clement Street and pulling granny out of the car—
and damn anyone who happens to be in the car behind them or the
next or the next.

Politicians would be horrified by such an American opinion, of 7
course. But then, what do politicians, Republicans or Democrats, really
know of our family life? Or what are they willing to admit? Even in
that area where they could reasonably be expected to have something
to say—regarding the relationship of family life to our economic system—the politicians say nothing. Republicans celebrate American economic freedom, but Republicans don't seem to connect that economic
freedom to the social breakdown they find appalling. Democrats, on
the other hand, if more tolerant of the drift from familial tradition, are
suspicious of the very capitalism that creates social freedom.

How you become free in America: Consider the immigrant. He 8
gets a job. Soon he is earning more money than his father ever made
(his father's authority is thereby subtly undermined). The immigrant
begins living a life his father never knew. The immigrant moves from
one job to another, changes houses. His economic choices determine
his home address—not the other way around. The immigrant is on his
way to becoming his own man.

When I was broke a few years ago and trying to finish a book, I 9
lived with my parents. What a thing to do! A major theme of America
is leaving home. We trust the child who forsakes family connections to
make it on his own. We call that the making of a man.

Let's talk about this man stuff for a minute. America's ethos is 10
anti-domestic. We may be intrigued by blood that runs through
wealth—the Kennedys or the Rockefellers—but they seem European
to us. Which is to say, they are movies. They are Corleones. Our real
pledge of allegiance: We say in America that nothing about your family—your class, your race, your pedigree—should be as important as
what you yourself achieve. We end up in 1992 introducing ourselves
by first names.

What authority can Papa have in a country that formed its identity 11
in an act of Oedipal rebellion against a mad British king? Papa is a joke
in America, a stock sitcom figure—Archie Bunker or Homer Simpson.
But my Mexican father went to work every morning, and he stood in

a white smock, making false teeth, oblivious of the shelves of grinning false teeth mocking his devotion.

The nuns in grammar school—my wonderful Irish nuns—used to 12 push Mark Twain on me. I distrusted Huck Finn, he seemed like a gringo kid I would steer clear of in the schoolyard. (He was too confident.) I realize now, of course, that Huck is the closest we have to a national hero. We trust the story of a boy who has no home and is restless for the river. (Huck's Pap is drunk.) Americans are more forgiving of Huck's wildness than of the sweetness of the Chinese boy who walks to school with his mama or grandma. (There is no worse thing in America than to be a mama's boy, nothing better than to be a real boy—all boy—like Huck, who eludes Aunt Sally, and is eager for the world of men.)

There's a bent old woman coming up the street. She glances 13 nervously as she passes my car. What would you tell us, old lady, of family values in America?

America is an immigrant country, we say. Motherhood—parent- 14 hood—is less our point than adoption. If I had to assign gender to America, I would note the consensus of the rest of the world. When America is burned in effigy, a male is burned. Americans themselves speak of Uncle Sam.

Like the Goddess of Liberty, Uncle Sam has no children of his 15 own. He steals children to make men of them, mocks all reticence, all modesty, all memory. Uncle Sam is a hectoring Yankee, a skinflint uncle, gaunt, uncouth, unloved. He is the American Savonarola— hater of moonshine, destroyer of stills, burner of cocaine. Sam has no patience with mamas' boys.

You betray Uncle Sam by favoring private over public life, by 16 seeking to exempt yourself, by cheating on your income taxes, by avoiding jury duty, by trying to keep your boy on the farm.

Mothers are traditionally the guardians of the family—against 17 America—though even Mom may side with America against queers and deserters, at least when the Old Man is around. Premature gray hair. Arthritis in her shoulders. Bowlegged with time, red hands. In their fiercely flowered housedresses, mothers are always smarter than fathers in America. But in reality they are betrayed by their children who leave. In a thousand ways. They end up alone.

We kind of like the daughter who was a tomboy. Remember her? 18 It was always easier to be a tomboy in America than a sissy. Americans admired Annie Oakley more than they admired Liberace (who, nevertheless, always remembered his mother). But today we do not admire Annie Oakley when we see Mom becoming Annie Oakley.

The American household now needs two incomes, everyone says. 19 Meaning: Mom is *forced* to leave home out of economic necessity. But lots of us know lots of moms who are sick and tired of being mom, or only mom. It's like the nuns getting fed up, teaching kids for all those years and having those kids grow up telling stories of how awful Catholic school was! Not every woman in America wants her life's work to be forgiveness. Today there are moms who don't want their husbands' names. And the most disturbing possibility: What happens when Mom doesn't want to be Mom at all? Refuses pregnancy?

Mom is only becoming an American like the rest of us. Certainly, 20 people all over the world are going to describe the influence of feminism on women (all over the world) as their "Americanization." And rightly so.

Nothing of this, of course, will the politician's wife tell you. The 21 politician's wife is careful to follow her husband's sentimental reassurances that nothing has changed about America except perhaps for the sinister influence of deviants. Like myself.

I contain within myself an anomaly at least as interesting as 22 the Republican Party's version of family values. I am a homosexual Catholic, a communicant in a tradition that rejects even as it upholds me.

I do not count myself among those Christians who proclaim them- 23 selves protectors of family values. They regard me as no less an enemy of the family than the "radical feminists." But the joke about families that all homosexuals know is that we are the ones who stick around and make families possible. Call on us. I can think of 20 or 30 examples. A gay son or daughter is the only one who is "free" (married brothers and sisters are too busy). And, indeed, because we have admitted the inadmissible about ourselves (that we are queer)—we are adepts at imagination—we can even imagine those who refuse to imagine us. We can imagine Mom's loneliness, for example. If Mom needs to be taken to church or to the doctor or ferried between Christmas dinners, depend on the gay son or lesbian daughter.

I won't deny that the so-called gay liberation movement, along 24 with feminism, undermined the heterosexual household, if that's what politicians mean when they say family values. Against churchly reminders that sex was for procreation, the gay bar as much as the birth-control pill taught Americans not to fear sexual pleasure. In the past two decades—and, not coincidentally, parallel to the feminist movement—the gay liberation movement moved a generation of Americans toward the idea of a childless adulthood. If the women's movement was ultimately more concerned about getting out of the house and into the workplace, the gay movement was in its way more subversive to Puritan America because it stressed the importance of play.

Several months ago, the society editor of the morning paper in San 25 Francisco suggested (on a list of "must haves") that every society dame must have at least one gay male friend. A ballet companion.

A lunch date. The remark was glib and incorrect enough to beg complaints from homosexual readers, but there was a truth about it as well. Homosexual men have provided women with an alternate model of masculinity. And the truth: The Old Man, God bless him, is a bore. Thus are we seen as preserving marriages? Even Republican marriages?

For myself, homosexuality is a deep brotherhood but does not in- 26 volve domestic life. Which is why, my married sisters will tell you, I can afford the time to be a writer. And why are so many homosexuals such wonderful teachers and priests and favorite aunts, if not because we are freed from the house? On the other hand, I know lots of homosexual couples (male and female) who model their lives on the traditional heterosexual version of domesticity and marriage. Republican politicians mock the notion of a homosexual marriage, but ironically such marriages honor the heterosexual marriage by imitating it.

"The only loving couples I know," a friend of mine recently re- 27 marked, "are all gay couples."

This woman was not saying that she does not love her children or 28 that she is planning a divorce. But she was saying something about the sadness of American domestic life: the fact that there is so little joy in family intimacy. Which is perhaps why gossip (public intrusion into the private) has become a national industry. All day long, in forlorn houses, the television lights up a freakish parade of husbands and mothers-in-law and children upon the stage of Sally or Oprah or Phil. They tell on each other. The audience ooohhhs. Then a psychiatrist-shaman appears at the end to dispense prescriptions—the importance of family members granting one another more "space."

The question I desperately need to ask you is whether we 29 Americans have ever truly valued the family. We are famous, or our immigrant ancestors were famous, for the willingness to leave home. And it is ironic that a crusade under the banner of family values has been taken up by those who would otherwise pass themselves off as patriots. For they seem not to understand America, nor do I think they love the freedoms America grants. Do they understand why, in a country that prizes individuality and is suspicious of authority, children are disinclined to submit to their parents? You cannot celebrate American values in the public realm without expecting them to touch our private lives. As Barbara Bush remarked recently, family values are also neighborhood values. It may be harmless enough for Barbara Bush to recall a sweeter America—Midland, Texas, in the 1950s. But the question left begging is why we chose to leave Midland, Texas. Americans like to say that we can't go home again. The truth is that we don't want to go home again, don't want to be known, recognized. Don't want to respond in the same old ways. (And you know you will if you go back there.)

Little 10-year-old girls know that there are reasons for getting away 30
from the family. They learn to keep their secrets—under lock and key—
addressed to Dear Diary. Growing up queer, you learn to keep secrets
as well. In no place are those secrets more firmly held than within the
family house. You learn to live in closets. I know a Chinese man who
arrived in America about 10 years ago. He got a job and made some
money. And during that time he came to confront his homosexuality.
And then his family arrived. I do not yet know the end of this story.

The genius of America is that it permits children to leave home, it 31
permits us to become different from our parents. But the sadness, the
loneliness of America, is clear too.

Listen to the way Americans talk about immigrants. If, on the one 32
hand, there is impatience when today's immigrants do not seem to
give up their family, there is also a fascination with this reluctance. In
Los Angeles, Hispanics are considered people of family. Hispanic
women are hired to be at the center of the American family—to baby-
sit and diaper, to cook and to clean and to ease the dying. Hispanic attachment to family is seen by many Americans, I think, as the reason
why Hispanics don't get ahead. But if Asians privately annoy us for
being so family oriented, they are also stereotypically celebrated as the
new "whiz kids" in school. Don't Asians go to college, after all, to
honor their parents?

More important still is the technological and economic ascendancy 33
of Asia, particularly Japan, on the American imagination. Americans
are starting to wonder whether perhaps the family values of Asia put
the United States at a disadvantage. The old platitude had it that ours
is a vibrant, robust society for being a society of individuals. Now we
look to Asia and see team effort paying off.

In this time of national homesickness, of nostalgia, for how we 34
imagine America used to be, there are obvious dangers. We are going
to start blaming each other for the loss. Since we are inclined, as
Americans, to think of ourselves individually, we are disinclined to
think of ourselves as creating one another or influencing one another.

But it is not the politician or any political debate about family val- 35
ues that has brought me here on a gray morning to my parents' house.
It is some payment I owe to my youth and to my parents' youth. I
imagine us sitting in the living room, amid my mother's sentimental
doilies and the family photographs, trying to take the measure of the
people we have turned out to be in America.

A San Francisco poet, when he was in the hospital and dying, 36
called a priest to his bedside. The old poet wanted to make his peace
with Mother Church. He wanted baptism. The priest asked why.
"Because the Catholic Church has to accept me," said the poet.
"Because I am a sinner."

Isn't willy-nilly inclusiveness the point, the only possible point to 37 be derived from the concept of family? Curiously, both President Bush and Vice President Quayle got in trouble with their constituents recently for expressing a real family value. Both men said that they would try to dissuade a daughter or granddaughter from having an abortion. But, finally, they said they would support her decision, continue to love her, never abandon her.

There are families that do not accept. There are children who are 38 forced to leave home because of abortions or homosexuality. There are family secrets that Papa never hears. Which is to say there are families that never learn the point of families.

But there she is at the window. My mother has seen me and she 39 waves me in. Her face asks: Why am I sitting outside? (Have they, after all, known my secret for years and kept it, out of embarrassment, not knowing what to say?) Families accept, often by silence. My father opens the door to welcome me in.

QUESTIONS

1. Why does Rodriguez think that the recent popular discussion of "family values" is misleading? How would you compare Rodriguez's views of the American family with your own?

2. According to Rodriguez, how do gay and lesbian people fit in with traditional American "family values"?

Sexual Culture

EDMUND WHITE

"Do gay men have friends—I mean," she said, "are they friends 1
with each other?" Since the woman asking was a New Yorker, the
owner of one of the city's simplest and priciest restaurants, someone
who's known gays all her life, I found the question honest, shocking,
and revealing of a narrow but bottomless abyss between us.

Of course New York is a city of total, even absolute strangers rub- 2
bing shoulders: the Hasidim in their yellow school bus being conveyed back to Brooklyn from the jewelry district, beards and black
hats glimpsed through mud-splattered windows in a sundimmed da-
guerreotype; the junkie pushing the baby carriage and telling his wife,
the prostitute, as he points to his tattooed biceps, "I haven't partied in
this vein for years"; Moonies doing calisthenics at midnight in their
Eighth Avenue center high above empty Thirty-fourth Street. . . . But
this alienation wasn't religious or ethnic. The woman and I spoke the
same language, knew the same people; we both considered Marcella
Hazan fun but no substitute for Simone Beck. How odd that she, as
lower-upper-middle-class as I, shouldn't know whether gay men befriended one another.

It was then that I saw how mysterious gay culture is—not homo- 3
sexuality, which is merely an erotic tropism, but modern American
gay culture, which is a special way of laughing, spending money, or-
dering priorities, encoding everything from song lyrics to mirror-
shiny military shoes. None of the usual modes for a subculture will do,
for gay men are brought up by heterosexuals to be straight, they seek
other men through what feels very much like a compulsion though
they enter the ghetto by choice, yet once they make that choice it re-
shapes their lives, even their bodies, certainly their wardrobes. Many

Edmund White is a novelist and writer from New York; he has
taught creative writing at Columbia, Yale, New York University, and
George Mason University. His novels include *Forgetting Elena* (1973)
and *Caracole* (1985). *A Boy's Own Story* (1982) and its sequel, *The
Beautiful Room is Empty* (1988), are autobiographical novels about
growing up gay. White is also co-author (with Charles Silverstein) of
*The Joy of Gay Sex: An Intimate Guide for Gay Men to the Pleasures of a
Gay Lifestyle* (1977), editor of *The Faber Book of Gay Short Fiction* (1991),
and author of *States of Desire: Travels in Gay America* (1980), a nonfiction documentary about homosexual life in fifteen U.S. cities. This
essay first appeared in 1983 in the magazine *Vanity Fair,* where White
has been a contributing editor.

347

gay men live among straights as Marranos, those Spanish Jews who pretended during the Inquisition to convert to Christianity but continued to observe the old rites in cellars, when alone, in the greatest secrecy. Gays aren't *like* blacks or Jews since they often *are* black or Jewish, and their affectional preference isn't a color or a religion though it has spawned a culture not unlike an ethnic minority's. Few Jews have Christian siblings, but most gays have straight brothers and sisters or at least straight parents. Many American Jews have been raised to feel they belong to the Chosen People, at once superior and inferior to gentiles, but every gay discovers his sexual nature with a combination of pain and relief, regret at being excluded from the tribe but elation at discovering the solution to the puzzle.

Gays aren't a nationality. They aren't Chicanos or Italo-Americans 4 or Irish-Americans, but they do constitute one of the most potent political forces in big cities such as New York, Philadelphia, Washington (where gays and blacks elected Marion Barry mayor), Houston, Los Angeles, and San Francisco (where gays are so numerous they've splintered into countless factions, including the lesbian S/M group Samois and the Sisters of Perpetual Indulgence, a group of drag nuns, one of whose members ran in a cowl and wimple as a candidate in the last citywide election). Not ethnic but a minority, not a polis but political, not a nationality but possessed of a costume, customs, and a patois, not a class but an economic force (not only as a market for records, films, vacations, and clothes but also as an army of worker ants who, for better or worse, have gentrified the center cities, thereby creating a better tomorrow for single young white heterosexual professionals).

Imagine a religion one enters against one's parents' will—and 5 against one's own. Imagine a race one joins at sixteen or sixty without changing one's hue or hair texture (unless at the tanning or beauty salon). Imagine a sterile nation without descendants but with a long, misty regress of ancestors, without an articulated self-definition but with a venerable history. Imagine an exclusive club that includes a P.R. (Puerto Rican) boy of sixteen wearing ankle-high black-and-white Converse basketball shoes and a petrol green shirt sawed off to reveal a Praxitelean stomach—and also includes a P.R. (Public Relations) WASP executive of forty in his Prince of Wales plaids and Cole-Haan tasseled loafers.

If one is gay, one is always in a crucial relationship to gayness as 6 such, a defining category that is so full it is nearly empty (Renaud Camus writes: "Homosexuality is always elsewhere because it is everywhere"). No straight man stands in rapt contemplation of his straightness unless he's an ass. To be sure, heterosexuals may wonder over the significance of their homosexual fantasies, though even that morbid exercise is less popular now than formerly; as Barbara Ehrenreich acutely observes in her new study of the heterosexual male revolt, *The Hearts of Men,* the emergence of gay liberation ended the period in which everyone suspected everyone else of being "latently" homosexual. Now there are open homosexuals, and heterosexual men are exempt from the automatic suspicion of deviance.

No homosexual can take his homosexuality for granted. He must 7 sound it, palpate it, auscultate it as though it were the dead limb of a tree or the living but tricky limb of a body; for that reason all homosexuals are "gay philosophers" in that they must invent themselves. At a certain point one undergoes a violent conversion into a new state, the unknown, which one then sets about knowing as one will. Surely everyone experiences his or her life as an artifact, as molten glass being twirled and pinched into a shape to cool, or as a novel at once capacious and suspenseful, but no one is more a *Homo faber* (in the sense of both "fabricator" and "fabulist") than a homo. It would be vain, of course, to suggest that this creativity is praiseworthy, an ambition rather than a response.

Sometimes I try to imagine how straights—not fundamentalist 8 know-nothings, not rural innocents, not Freudian bigots, but educated urban heterosexuals—look at gay men (do they even see lesbians?). When they see gay men, what do they see? A mustache, a pumped-up body in black jeans and a tank top, an eye-catching tattoo (braided rope around the biceps)? And what do they think ("they," in this case, *hypocrite lecteur,* being *you*)? Do you see something at once ludicrous and mildly enviable in the still youthful but overexercised body of this forty-year-old clone with the aggressive stare and soft voice? If you're a woman, do you find so much preening over appearance in a grown man . . . well, if not offensive, at least unappetizing; energy better spent on a career, on a family—on you? If you're a man, does it incense you that this jerk is out of harness, too loose, too free, has so lightly made a mockery of manhood? Once, on a radio call-in show a cop called in to tell me he had to admire the old-style queens back when it was rough being queer but that now, jeez, these guys swapping spit wit' a goil one week, wit' a guy the next, they're too lazy, they just don't know the fine art of being a man, it's all just too easy.

Your sentiments, perhaps? 9

Do you see gays as menacing satyrs, sex fiends around whom it's 10 dangerous to drop your soap, *and* as feeble sissies, frail wood nymphs locked within massive trunks and limbs? Or, more positively if just as narrowly, are you a sybaritic het who greets the sight of gays with cries of glee, convinced you've stumbled on liberty hall, where sexual license of every sort—including your sort—is bound to reign? In fact, such sybarites often do regard gay men as comrades in arms, fellow libertines, and fellow victims in a country phobic to pleasure.

Or do gays just irk you? Do you regard them as a tinselly distrac- 11 tion in your peripheral vision? As errant, obstinate atoms that can't be drawn into any of the usual social molecules, men who if they insist on their gayness won't really do at any of the solemnities, from dinner parties to debutante balls, all of which depend on strict gender dimor- phism for a rational seating plan? Since any proper gathering requires the threat of adultery for excitement and the prospect of marriage as a justification, of what earthly use are gays? Even the few fearless straight guys who've invaded my gay gym drift toward one another, not out of soap-dropping panic but because otherwise their dirty jokes fall on deaf or prettily blushing ears and their taunting, butt-slapping mix of rivalry and camaraderie provokes a weird hostility or a still weirder thrill.

And how do gays look at straights? In Andrew Holleran's superb 12 new novel, *Nights in Aruba,* the narrator wonders "what it would be like to be the head of a family, as if with that all my problems would drop away, when in fact they would have merely been replaced by an- other set. I would not have worried about the size of my penis, the re- strictions of age, the difficulty of finding love; I would have worried about mortgages, tuition, my youngest daughter's asthma, my compe- tition at Shearson Loeb Rhoades." What makes this speculation so characteristically gay is that it is so focused on the family man, for if the nineteenth-century tart required, even invented the convent-bred vir- gin to contemplate, in the same way the homosexual man today must insult and revere, mock and envy this purely imaginary bourgeois pa- terfamilias, a creature extinct except in gay fantasies. Meanwhile, of course, the family man devotes his time to scream therapy and tai chi, ticking off Personals in the *Village Voice* and wriggling out of visits from his kids, two punked-out teens who live in a feminist compound with his divorced wife, now a lesbian potter of great sensitivity and verve if low energy.

So much for how the two sexes (straight and gay) regard each 13 other. If the camera were to pull back and frame both worlds in the lens, how would the two systems compare?

The most obvious difference is that whereas heterosexuality does 14 include two sexes, since homosexuality does not it must improvise a new polarity moment by moment. Such a polarity seems necessary to sexual desire, at least as it is constructed in our culture. No wonder that some gay men search out the most extreme opposites (someone of a distant race, a remote language, another class or age); no wonder that even that convinced heterosexual Flaubert was finally able to unbend with a boy prostitute in Egypt, an exotic who provided him with all the difference desire might demand. Other gay men seek out their twins—so that the beloved, I suppose, can stand in for oneself as one bows down to this false god and plays in turn his father, teacher, son, godfather, or god. Still others institutionalize the polarity in that next-best thing to heterosexuality: sadomasochism, the only vice that anthologizes all family and romantic relationships.

Because every gay man loves men, he comes to learn at first hand   15 how to soothe the savage breast of the male ego. No matter how passive or girlish or shy the new beau might be in the boudoir, he will become the autocrat of the dinner table. Women's magazines are always planning articles on gay men and straight women; I'd say what they have most in common, aside from a few shared sexual techniques, is a body of folk wisdom about that hardhead, that bully, that maddeningly self-involved creature, the human male. As studies have surprisingly shown, men talk more than women, interrupt them more often, and determine the topics of conversation and object to women's assertions with more authority and frequency. When two gay men get together, especially after the first romantic urge to oblige the other wanes, a struggle for conversational dominance ensues, a conflict only symptomatic of larger arguments over every issue from where to live to how and whom to entertain.

To be sure, in this way the gay couple resembles the straight duo   16 that includes an assertive, liberated woman. But while most of the young straight liberated women I know, at least, may protect their real long-range interests (career, mode of life, emotional needs) with vigilance, they're still willing to accommodate *him* in little social ways essential to harmony.

One benign side of straight life is that women conceive of men as   17 "characters," as full-bodied, multifaceted beings who are first social, second familial, third amorous or amicable, and only finally physical. I'm trying politely to say that women are lousy judges of male beauty; they're easily taken in by such superficial traits as loyalty, dependability, charm, a sense of humor. Women don't, or at least didn't, judge men as so much beefcake. But men, both straight and gay, start with looks, the most obvious currency of value, worth, price. Let's say that women see men as characters in a long family novel in which the men are introduced complete with phrenology, genealogy, and one annoying and two endearing traits, whereas men see their partners (whether male or female) as cars, makes to be instantly spotted, appraised, envied, made. A woman wants to be envied for her husband's goodness, his character, whereas a man wants to be envied for his wife's beauty, rarity, status—her drivability. Straight life combines the warmth and *Gemütlichkeit* of the nineteenth-century bourgeois (the woman) with the steely corporate ethos of the twentieth-century functionary (the man). If gay male life, freed of this dialectic, has become supremely efficient (the trapdoor beside the bed) and only momentarily intimate (a whole life cycle compressed into the one-night stand), then the gain is dubious, albeit an extreme expression of one trend in our cultural economy.

But of course most morality, that is, popular morality—not real 18 morals, which are unaffected by consensus, but mores, which are a form of fashion—is nothing but a species of nostalgia, a cover-up for pleasurable and profitable but not yet admissible innovations. If so many people condemn promiscuity, they do so at least partly because there is no available rhetoric that could condone, much less glamorize, impermanence in love. Nevertheless, it strikes me that homosexuals, masters of improvisation fully at home with the arbitrary and equipped with an internal compass that orients them instantly to any social novelty, are perhaps the most sensitive indicators of the future.

The birthrate declines, the divorce rate climbs, and popular culture 19 (movies, television, song lyrics, advertising, fashions, journalism) is so completely and irrevocably secularized that the so-called religious revival is of no more lasting importance than the fad for Kabuki in a transistorized Japan—a temporary throwback, a slight brake on the wheel. In such a world the rate of change is so rapid that children, once they are in school, can learn little from their parents but must assimilate new forms of behavior from their peers and new information from specialized instructors. As a result, parental authority declines, and the demarcations between the generations become ever more formidable. Nor do the parents regret their loss of control, since they're devoting all their energy to cultivating the inner self in the wholesale transition of our society from an ethic of self-sacrifice to one of self-indulgence, the so-called aristocraticization of middle-class life that has dominated the peaceful parts of this century in the industrialized West.

In the contemporary world the nineteenth-century experiment of 20 companionate marriage, never very workable, has collapsed utterly. The exact nature of the collapse isn't very clear yet because of our distracting, probably irrelevant habit of psychologizing every crisis (thus the endless speculations in the lowbrow press on the Irresponsible Male and the Defeminized Female or the paradoxical and cruelly impracticable advice to women readers to "go for it all—family, career, marriage, romance, *and* the reveries of solitude"). We treat the failure of marriage as though it were the failure of individuals to achieve it— a decline in grit or maturity or commitment or stamina rather than the unraveling of a poorly tied knot. Bourgeois marriage was meant to concentrate friendship, romance, and sex into an institution at once familial and economic. Only the most intense surveillance could keep such a bulky, ill-assorted load from bursting at the seams. Once the hedonism of the '60s relaxed that tension, people began to admit that friendship tranquilizes sexual desires (when mates become siblings, the incest taboo sets in) and that romance is by its very nature evanescent though indefinitely renewable given an endless supply of fresh partners. Neither sexual nor romantic attraction, so capricious, so passionate, so unstable, could ever serve as the basis for an enduring relationship, which can be balanced only on the plinth of esteem, that easy, undramatic, intimate kind of love one would say resembled family love if families were more loving.

It is this love that so many gay couples know about, aim for, and 21 sometimes even express. If all goes well, two gay men will meet through sex, become lovers, weather the storms of jealousy and the diminution of lust, develop shared interests (a hobby, a business, a house, a circle), and end up with a long-term, probably sexless camaraderie that is not as disinterested as friendship or as seismic as passion or as charged with contradiction as fraternity. Younger gay couples feel that this sort of relationship, when it happens to them, is incomplete, a compromise, and they break up in order to find total fulfillment (i.e., tireless passion) elsewhere. But older gay couples stay together, cultivate their mild, reasonable love, and defend it against the ever-present danger of the sexual allure exercised by a newcomer. For the weak point of such marriages is the eternally recurring fantasy, first in one partner and then the other, of "total fulfillment." Needless to say, such couples can wreak havoc on the newcomer who fails to grasp that Bob and Fred are not just roommates. They may have separate bedrooms and regular extracurricular sex partners or even beaux, but Bob monitors Fred's infatuations with an eye attuned to nuance, and at a certain point will intervene to banish a potential rival.

I think most straight people would find these arrangements more 22 scandalous than the infamous sexual high jinks of gays. Because these arrangements have no name, no mythology, no public or private acknowledgment, they're almost invisible even to the participants. Thus if you asked Bob in a survey what he wanted, he might say he wanted a "real" lover. He might also say Fred was "just a roommate, my best friend, we used to be lovers." So much for explicit analysis, but over the years Bob has cannily steered his affair with Fred between the Scylla of excessive fidelity (which is finally so dull no two imaginative gay men could endure it) and the Charybdis of excessive tolerance (which could leave both men feeling so neglected they'd seek love elsewhere for sure).

There are, of course, countless variants to this pattern. The men   23
live together or they don't. If they don't, they can maintain the civilized fiction of romance for years. They plan dates, honeymoons, take
turns sleeping over at each other's house, and avoid conflicts about domestic details. They keep their extracurricular sex lives separate, they
agree not to snoop—or they have three-ways. Or one of the pair has an
active sex life and the other has abandoned the erotic arena.

Are gay men friends with each other? the woman asked me.   24

The question may assume that gays are only sexual, and that a   25
man eternally on the prowl can never pause for mere affection—that a
gay Don Juan is lonely. Or perhaps the question reveals a confusion
about a society of one gender. Since a straight woman has other
women for friends and men for lovers, my questioner might have
wondered how the same sex could serve in both capacities.

The first supposition—that gay men are only sexual—is an ancient   26
prejudice, and like all prejudices mostly untrue but in one sense occasionally accurate. If politically conscious homosexuals prefer the word
gay to *homosexual*, they do so because they want to make the world regard attraction to members of the same gender as an affectional preference as well as a sexual orientation.

For instance, there are some gay men who prefer the feel of wom-   27
en's bodies to men's, who are even more comfortable sexually with
women, but whose emotions crave contact with other men. Gay men
have unfinished emotional business with other men—scary, promising, troubling, absorbing business—whereas their sentiments toward
women (at least women not in their family) are much simpler, more
stable, less fraught. Affection, passionate affection, is never simple; it
is built out of equal parts of yearning, fear, and appetite. For that reason the friendship of one gay man fiercely drawn to another is as tense
as any heterosexual passion, whereas a sexless, more disinterested gay
friendship is as relaxed, as good-tempered as a friendship, say, between two straight men.

Gay men, then, do divide other gays into two camps—those who   28
are potential partners (lovers) and those who are not (friends). But
where gay life is more ambiguous than the world at large (and possibly for that reason more baffling to outsiders) is that the members of
the two camps, lovers and friends, are always switching places or hovering somewhere in the margin between. It is these unconfessed feelings that have always intrigued me the most as a novelist—the unspoken love between two gay men, say, who pretend they are just friends,
cruising buddies, merely filling in until Mr. Right comes along (merci-
fully, he never does).

In one sense, the public's prejudice about a gay obsession with sex   29
is valid. The right to have sex, even to look for it, has been so stringently

denied to gays for so many centuries that the drive toward sexual freedom remains a bright, throbbing banner in the fierce winds whipping
over the ghetto. Laws against sex have always created the biggest
problems for homosexuals; they helped to define the very category of
homosexuality. For that reason, the gay community, despite its invention of a culture no more eroticized than any other, still cannot give up
its origin in sexual desire and its suppression.

But what about the "excessive" promiscuity of gay men, the infa-   30
mous quickies, a phenomenon only temporarily held in check by the
AIDS crisis? Don't the quickies prove that gay men are essentially
bizarre, fundamentally lacking in judgment—*oversexed?* Of course,
gay men behave as all men would were they free of the strictures of female tastes, needs, prohibitions, and expectations. There is nothing in
gay male life that cannot be attributed either to its minority status or
to its all-male population. All men want quick, uncomplicated sexual
adventure (as well as sustained romantic passion); in a world of all
men, that desire is granted.

The very universality of sexual opportunity within the modern   31
gay ghetto has, paradoxically, increased the importance of friendship.
In a society not based on the measured denial or canalization of sexual
desire, there is more energy left over for friendship. Relationships are
less loaded in gay life (hence the celebrated gay irony, a levity equivalent to seeing through conventions). In so many ways gays are still
prisoners of the dominant society, but in this one regard gays are freer
than their jailers: because gay relationships are not disciplined by religious, legal, economic, and political ceremonies but only by the dic-
tates of conscience and the impulses of the heart, they don't stand for
anything larger. They aren't symbols but realities, not laws but entities
sufficient unto themselves, not consequential but ecstatic.

QUESTIONS

1.   In paragraphs 8 to 12, White asks his readers a series of questions
about "how the two sexes (straight and gay) regard each other."
Discuss your responses to those questions. Have any of these responses changed after reading White's entire essay? Why or why not?

2.   How do gay male couples differ from heterosexual married couples, according to White?

3.   Whether or not traditional marriage, "never very workable, has
collapsed entirely" (paragraph 20), how does White suggest that gay
relationships offer a critique of and alternative to mainstream values?
How well do you think this alternative model can work for heterosexual relationships?

Ten Good Reasons to Be a Lesbian

AMANDA KOVATTANA

President Clinton's attempt to lift the ban on gays in the military 1
has made the gay lifestyle—my lifestyle—a front-page issue. The national debate that followed has offered me many opportunities to discuss, educate and listen to the opinions of straight people.

Many were surprised to hear that I did not choose to be gay. 2
Growing up a gay adolescent is a suffocating experience I wouldn't
wish on anybody. By the time I reached college, I was convinced that
my sexuality was an ironic curse, since men pursued me at the drop of
a hat and women found me intimidating.

Still, I have heard from my socialist/feminist friends that there are 3
women who choose to be lesbian. Today I wouldn't trade my lesbian
life for a minute. So, let's say it is in part a choice. Is it necessarily a bad
one? I would like to offer (to the women among you) 10 good reasons
to be a lesbian.

1. Beginning with the practical, you can save up to $300 a year in 4
    birth control pills. Your chances of having to consider an abortion
    are lowered considerably. You become a member of the group
    with the least occurrence of HIV infection and other sexually
    transmitted diseases.

2. Your lover understands you in a fundamental way. Not to men- 5
    tion the sex—and as this is a family newspaper, I won't. And she
    never leaves the toilet seat up.

3. In most big cities you will find gay parades, film festivals, and lit- 6
    erary events celebrating your sexuality. These cultural events
    often herald trends that show up later in mainstream culture.

4. Your social position as an outsider gives you a unique perspec- 7
    tive on social mores, prejudice and gender stereotypes.

5. You acquire both an identity and a community. Lesbians travel in 8
    packs. At any given queer event you will see all your lesbian
    friends and they will have saved you a seat.

Amanda Kovattana is a writer and graphic designer who came to the
United States from Thailand in 1968. She is currently finishing an
autobiographical novel. Kovattana is a former member of the Board
of Contributors (local people who contribute regular columns of topical interest) for the *Palo Alto Weekly*, a community newspaper in
California, where she published this essay in 1993. It was also reprinted in *Entré Nous*, a South Bay Area gay and lesbian journal.

6. Women's basketball games take on a whole new dimension. See   9
    hundreds of lesbians rubbing elbows with their straight neigh-
    bors and their children. Since lesbians support women's sports,
    home games are big dyke events in any college town.

7. You have friends in high and low places. The lesbian community   10
    opens doors. That intimidating supervisor/doctor/lawyer in the
    suit becomes a peer. The woman who drives the UPS truck stops
    to chat as a comrade.

8. To commit a daring feat of political activism you need only   11
    "come out."

9. You have a lifelong family that is not biologically determined and   12
    more often includes people of color. According to a survey given
    by *Ms.* magazine on women and race, lesbians are much more
    likely to date, work and live with people of other races and con-
    sider it important to belong to groups that are racially mixed.

10. You don't have to worry about men—getting them, keeping   13
    them, taking care of them. This last reason, given to me by a
    straight woman friend, is really the crux of it. When the object of
    your love is a woman, you spend your time pursuing the con-
    cerns of women, which are also your concerns. This focus on
    women has taken me to the outer limits of women's issues in the
    arena of politics, spirituality, and identity. The support I have re-
    ceived from all these women's communities has added immea-
    surably to my strength as a woman.

    The straight community has often accused gay people of recruit-   14
ing. Have I tempted anyone? Has your wife/daughter/mother gone
AWOL? Who ya gonna call? Dykebusters! (Otherwise known as the
Traditional Values Coalition.)

QUESTIONS

1. Kovattana acknowledges that she is addressing readers of a "family newspaper" (paragraph 5); from other references and clues in the
opening and final paragraphs of the essay, what else can you tell about
her intended audience?

2. From Kovattana's list, how would you describe the major features
of the lesbian community or subculture?

3. What social and political values does Kovattana reveal by her
choice of "good reasons"? Which of these values do you share?

My Interesting Condition

JAN CLAUSEN

Scene: a Brooklyn back yard steeped in humid summer dusk. Four women are sprawled comfortably in lawn chairs, cold liquids in hand.

—*Has she gone off the deep end, or what?*

—*She's got plenty of company, from the stories I'm hearing.*

—*Yeah, it's the in thing this year. The heterodyke.*

—*She's lost it.*

—*So? It happens. Like my grandma used to say—many are called, few are chosen.*

—*It pisses the hell out of me. I mean, who the hell tells these women they can make their name off of us, set themselves up as "spokeswomen" and "leaders" and shit, and then . . .*

—*What goes through my mind when I hear a story like this is, do you suppose she was really straight all along?*

—*She and what's-her-name had been together for ages. I can't believe she was faking all that time.*

—*You think she's faking now? Which is worse?*

—*Don't forget, she comes from a pretty privileged background. I guess when you've grown up white and middle-class, it's a big temptation to just sort of fade back into that cozy old patriarchy.*

—*White, middle-class, and fem!*

—*Who's knocking fems?*

—*Relax, Isis, nobody's knocking fems. But I do think carrying a purse is going a little far.*

—*She carries a purse now?*

—*I saw her in a dress.*

Jan Clausen teaches writing at the Eugene Lang College of the New School for Social Research in New York and in the Goddard College M.F.A. program in Creative Writing. She was a cofounder of *Conditions*, one of the earliest literary journals with a lesbian and multicultural focus. Her books of poems, stories, and novels include *After Touch* (1975), *Mother, Sister, Daughter, Lover: Stories* (1980), *Sinking/ Stealing: A Novel* (1985), and *The Prosperine Papers* (1988). Her essays and feminist book reviews are collected in *A Movement of Poets: Thoughts on Poetry and Feminism* (1982) and *Books and Life* (1989). When "My Interesting Condition" appeared in 1990 in *Out/Look* (a magazine "produced by and for lesbians and gay men," as Clausen explains in her Afterword here), it sparked a good deal of controversy among her lesbian and feminist readers.

—Does she shave her legs, too?

—Hey, I shave my legs.

—Chill, Dido, as long as you continue your time-honored custom of wearing at least three articles of men's apparel at all times, you'll remain above suspicion.

—Very, very funny.

—So what's the boyfriend's story? What's he like?

—Who gives a flying fuck?

—So to speak.

—Nobody seems to know much about him. I think she's sort of been keeping him in the background.

—Well, wouldn't you? In her position?

—Honey, you won't find me in that position.

—Oh yeah? Then how come I find the latest issue of On Our Backs *in the john, every time I come over?*

—Touché, Artemis. Pass the Doritos, will you? And just remember, everybody likes a little ass but nobody likes a smartass.

—Look, everybody, I never mentioned this, but I almost slept with a guy, last year when Lilith dumped me.

An awkward pause. Then, all at once:

—Well, that isn't the same thing at all!

—Temporary insanity. You weren't responsible.

—Anyway, you didn't go through with it.

People talk. It's human nature. I've done plenty of it myself. I 1 remember, for instance, ages ago, regaling friends with the scandalous news that Jill Johnston had gotten married. I remember our sarcasm at the expense of a black feminist poet who was partial to women but insisted on calling herself "bisexual" instead of "lesbian." I remember indignant gossip about Holly Near's rumored backsliding. I do not blame myself or anyone else too much for this behavior. Gossip is one of life's staple pleasures, small reward for all the pains. Besides, it's so useful, helping as it does to delimit the boundaries of peer groups, enforce community standards, strengthen self-definition in a blurred, ambiguous, often hostile world. In lesbian-feminist communities, where identity has been constructed virtually from the ground up over the past twenty years, these functions help to make it an irresistible form of entertainment.

For many if not all of the years I spent as a technically irreproach- 2 able lesbian, I was perfectly well aware that I hadn't shed my potential for physical attraction to men when I came out officially in 1974. I remember at least one mid-eighties conversation about sexuality and roles in which I told a lesbian friend that, strictly speaking, I should probably be considered bisexual. I mentioned this casually, without anxiety, partly because I had no reason to expect a judgmental response, but also because I assumed that my own sexual potential was no different from that of many other lesbians who at some time in their lives had enjoyed sex with men. It never seriously occurred to me that I would shortly find myself in a situation where this theoretical capacity would have practical implications.

Though I probably wouldn't have expressed it quite so crudely, 3 I believed, along with most of my friends, that our lesbian way of life was superior to even the best of heterosexual arrangements. Although I'd never been a separatist, and had long been critical of essentialist thinking, I also harbored what I would have admitted to be the rationally untenable conviction that lesbians themselves were politically and even morally superior to other people—more "evolved," if you will. Besides, I assumed that being a dyke was more fun and less socially constraining than being straight, homophobia notwithstanding. Why, then, would I ever choose a man, when the world is full of women?

"Slipping is crash's law," said Emily Dickinson. In retrospect I can 4 trace a certain amount of slippage in my commitment to the classic lesbian-feminist ideal of woman-identification when I review some of the stresses and disappointments of my own lesbian-feminist life, a point I'll come back to later. Following a painful experience with a group of women writers—one of those situations in which politics and personalities combine in virulent negative synergy—I began to work with a largely heterosexual Central America solidarity organization. For years I'd watched my short list of male friends dwindle toward extinction; now I added several new ones.

Yet the crash seemed sudden indeed when, in 1987, after a period 5 of time during which my crushes on unavailable women had created turmoil in my hitherto monogamous relationship, I became passionately involved with a man I met on a trip to Nicaragua. That event naturally hastened (I don't believe it caused) the end of my dozen years' partnership with a woman in whose company I had participated in the building of a world, the new feminist world of multi-issue activism all mixed up with ideas and books.

From day one of my newly "fallen" state, I resisted considerable 6 pressure, both external and internal, to explain myself. "I don't want to take a position on my body before I know what position my body's in," I insisted to a friend. I was in several kinds of shock, most notably that of the sudden separation from my long-time companion, which by her choice was absolute. I was hardly in shape to make immediate, articulate sense of what I was going through. I knew I needed privacy and time to let meanings emerge, but these suddenly seemed to be terribly scarce commodities in a social universe in which "the personal is political"—and in which, I now understood, my own lesbian family had attained the status of a semipublic institution.

My gut reaction was rebellion against the personal/political equa- 7 tion itself, for it now seemed to me that in the name of creating a theory responsive to the subjective experience of private life, we feminists had perhaps ended up prematurely abolishing private life altogether. I felt the need of a zone of experience off limits to instant political critique.

In this, I knew I had something in common with participants in the 8 feminist sexuality debate who have talked about the complexity and intractability of desire. But though the connection helped support my determination to say yes to what I wanted rather than to what I or anybody else thought I should want, it didn't do much to diminish my sense of isolation. My favorite "sexperts" talked about *lesbian* desire; Joan Nestle, for instance, might have written a sex-positive essay called "My Mother Liked to Fuck," but I didn't assume she meant it was okay for me to like it.

I knew that some (many?) dykes would assume I had become rad- 9 ically Other through the deceptively simple act of taking a male lover. I knew they would come up with a range of patronizing or condemnatory explanations for my behavior, explanations of a different order than would have been invoked by any but my ex-lover's closest friends were my new lover a woman. I also knew, viscerally, that I was not all that different, that my life before and after the "crash" was on a continuum. I felt that if some lesbians did not like the Jan Clausen who manifested the capacity to love a man, then they had never really liked Jan Clausen, for we were not two separate women. I bitterly resented the double standard which dictated that dykes should embrace a Virginia Woolf, an Eleanor Roosevelt, a Muriel Rukeyser as long-lost lesbian sisters given their sometime love for women, but would cast me into the outer darkness because of my refusal to pledge eternal allegiance to the cunt.

Paradoxically, while I was able to draw strength from this intuition 10 of ultimate wholeness, I was simultaneously plunged into an experience of profound discontinuity, my basic sense of who I was called into question. This experience, I believe, casts a novel and potentially valuable light on lesbian identity as it has been constructed by lesbian-feminists over the past two decades, since that identity has usually been discussed either from the perspective of women bidding a relieved goodbye to heterosexual life or from that of those securely ensconced within a lesbian world. Besides, it makes a good human-interest story, full of dramatic irony. It is also some version of the story of more and more lesbians who are rethinking the exclusivity of their sexual orientation.

For all these reasons, I want to set down some of the contradictory   11
feelings, startling juxtapositions, and no-win situations I've confronted
since becoming involved with a man. This is difficult to do without di-
vulging details about my past and current relationships which are nobody's business, but I'm going to try anyway, with the understanding
that the account will have to be partial.

To begin with the literal level, the physical: I feel like Tiresias, in   12
the weird position of being able to make a direct comparison between
two very different forms of sexual pleasure. After all those years of
joining in on the casual putdowns of heterosex that are a lesbian version of locker-room talk, it's startling to discover how much I enjoy the
specific things that two diversely sexed bodies can do together. I also
enjoy a new feeling of specialness which hints at a hidden rivalry I
hadn't suspected in lesbian lovemaking: my two small breasts suddenly without competition, my softness the softest. At the same time,
I feel newly vulnerable in my body, not because of what my lover says
or does but just because we don't share the physical being around
which a damning mythology of female impurity has been constructed.
I no longer casually complain of premenstrual symptoms, announce as
part of the day's news that I got my period. I don't shave my hairy
legs, but I feel defensive about them.

I mentally compare the two kinds of lovemaking to two literary   13
genres, poetry and fiction (lesbian sex is, of course, poetry), or to chore-
ographic styles. Sex with my male lover astonishes me by its physical
directness. So far (and how can I tell to what extent this might be attributable to something about heterosexuality, rather than something
about our two personalities?), it seems much less dependent on some
delicate emotional balance than what I've experienced with women.
It's intense, inventive, very much what I want, yet that doesn't mean
that I don't privately apply some version of the standard lesbian critique of heterosexual practice: why must everything have a beginning,
middle, and end, in that order? For months it makes me uneasy to be
touched or gone down on, since those things remind me of being with
a woman; oddly, "intercourse" at first feels like less of a betrayal.

It's a shock to find myself once again facing problems I dimly re-   14
call from my heterosexual youth, built-in inequities I thought I'd cleverly sidestepped by choosing my own kind. Suddenly, out of two people in a bed, *I'm* the one elected to run the risk of unwanted pregnancy.
Out of a pair drawn together by deliciously mutual lust, *I'm* the one
who, by physiological law, will occasionally be left dangling at the
moment of someone else's climax.

The emotional disparities are equally unsettling. To judge from 15
my recent experience, that old saw about men not sharing feelings has
a lot of truth in it. Or rather, their assumptions about when and how
and how much to share are so wildly divergent from women's that the
two sexes might have been socialized on different planets. At times
this comes as a clear relief to me, after years of analyzing to death
every slightest stirring of affect. I am learning other ways to be close.
But at times it just feels lonely.

I know that I love my lover as a man; to claim that I love him as a 16
"person" would be a transparent evasion, and to say that I'd like him
to be who he is only female would be both nonsensical and a lie. Yet
at times when we make love, I feel so close to his pleasure that I have
the illusion of experiencing his feelings, and when that happens I say
to myself that it's as though I were making love with a woman, and I
am very happy. I want my separation and my fusion, too.

I miss my ex-lover's body, but that missing is inseparable from all 17
my missing of her. I no longer feel, as I did in my early twenties when
I lived with a man following a first brief lesbian affair, that it would be
terrible to die without touching a woman again. Sometimes I wonder
where that urgency went. For the time being, I take casual erotic interest in members of my sex. I notice myself noticing femmes much more,
after years of liking butches, and wonder whether indulging my own
femininity to the hilt has freed some latent butch impulse. I wonder
also about the astonishing malleability of my sexual inclinations: am
I some sort of weirdo, or is it just that most people are a lot more
complicated than the common wisdom of either gay or straight society
encourages us to think?

Increasingly, I recognize myself as the creature not merely of two 18
sexual worlds, but of two cultures. Sometimes this is a fairly superficial matter of style: imagine my dismay the first time I found myself
on the IRT express the morning after a night with my new lover, and
noticed that I was reading *The Guardian* while he was buried in
Monthly Review—I thought the Male Left I'd always been warned
about had me in its toils for sure!

On the other hand, my increasing contacts with straight people 19
(mostly in politically radical, feminist-influenced circles where I was
known as a lesbian before my current relationship) often bring to my
attention subtle and not-so-subtle ways in which my experience and
that of "my" lesbian and gay community are neither seen nor understood, despite good intentions. This is sad and frustrating, and makes
me glad to spend time in lesbian and gay settings where I'm very
much at home—except that I'm on the lookout for criticism. I also have
a tendency to poke and prod my consciousness to make sure I'm still

sufficiently gay-identified to react appropriately to issues that no longer affect me so directly as they would have when I was with a woman.

The truth is that I don't quite belong in either place. And though the boundaries between the two worlds seem to have blurred somewhat in the last five or ten years, I still too often have to choose to be in one setting *or* the other. 20

I experience the usual horrors of dissolving a very long-term lesbian relationship, in the particular form that falls to the lot of she-who-leaves. But the anger, the guilt, the worry over consequences to family members—above all, the pain of losing a piece of one's life—all are complicated by "the man issue." Stunned by the emotional dissonance produced by starting a new relationship before finishing the old one, I'm only partly able to trust my instinctive sense that it's "infidelity," not my new lover's maleness, that underlies my feeling of being in the wrong. 21

I do feel wrong; bad; a bad person. One day when I finally take in how strong these negative judgments are, I am able to name them accurately. I realize that my feelings of guilt amount to a form of self-hatred. 22

I remind myself that *I am still a woman*. As the song says, "They can't take that away from me." Startled, I perceive how crazily tangled my identities had become, so that being my (woman) lover's lover was synonymous with being a lesbian was synonymous with being female. My sense of vertigo comes partly from the fear of losing all at once. 23

My new relationship affords an exhilarating sensation of risk-taking only partially attributable to the fact that it involves physical acts which lesbian-feminism has placed beyond the bounds of its revisionist norm of healthy womanhood. At this moment in the dialectic, heterosex ironically represents for me the anarchic power of the erotic, in contrast to the bourgeois respectability of a stable lesbian family unit. Without denying that I chose to live in that unit, and that there are aspects of it which I now miss profoundly, I come to see that it was to an extent I found oppressive a unit of *production*. As such, it was heavily organized around the care and feeding of feminist institutions, the needs of a growing child, the manufacture and distribution of an unending stream of feminist theory, criticism, poetry, and fiction. It mirrored in form what it seemed to negate in content: the middle-class nuclear family I grew up in. 24

By contrast, my love affair with a man is "without issue," utterly useless to the world at large: just what gay relationships are so often accused of being. It upsets the established order, and therefore initially pleases almost no one except the two of us. It belongs unequivocally in the realm of private life, an exquisite relief to me after years of feeling like a walking revolutionary project. 25

Reactions from other lesbians run the gamut from a curiosity that   26
seems to border on mild envy of my daring ("Maybe I ought to try it—
no man could hurt me worse than X and Y and Z did," is typical here)
to the rigid rejections of my nightmares. Mostly, my friends are helpful. Both they and more remote acquaintances are quite eager to discuss their own experiences with men. Overnight, I seem to have become the repository of heterosexual confessions, the occasion for
articulating thoughts about areas of their lives that lesbians don't frequently discuss with one another.

On the other hand, the venerable tradition of shunning and   27
excommunication is alive and well. It's true that nobody but my ex-
lover chooses to rub my nose in the classic ideological critique of my
behavior. However, two friends of hers who had also been my friends
express their support for her by cutting me off cold, an extreme of
conduct I have to assume they justify on the basis of my new lover's
sex. And I hear the secondhand stories. "I've defended you," a friend
reassures me. "Defended me from what?" "Oh, I was at this party.
Some women you don't know were talking about you, saying you'd
left your lover and run off with a man." *But I'm still living right here on
11th Street,* I thought.

One of my favorite responses came from a close friend who re-   28
marked, after meeting said man, "I realize I'd somehow imagined he'd
be *tall*—I guess I must have exaggerated the stereotypical male qualities." In other words, she'd pictured me with a Generic Member of the
Opposite Sex, which is pretty much how I suspect most lesbians are inclined to view the relationship. I find it striking that I'm rarely asked
what it means to me that my lover is black, though I often feel the
racial difference is at least as charged with tension, fascination,
promise, and difficulty as is the sexual one. In addition, there's the fact
that he's from another country, which contributes to the quality of fa-
miliarity-within-otherness that for me is a special power of our connection: hello, stranger, don't I know you from someplace? The dynamics of this love affair are so much more complicated than the
technically accurate bulletin "lesbian gets involved with straight man"
would suggest.

As vastly different (and incommensurable) as our experiences are,   29
there's a kind of symmetry in our identities: both of us are people who
have known oppression and privilege in the world, in ways that enter
the relationship. If it's going to work, both of us have to keep trying to
understand new things; each of us has to stand behind the other's liberation. My own efforts to do this are shaped in crucial ways by
lessons I learned in lesbian-feminist circles, through struggles with my
own and others' racism, through friendships with women of color,
through reading Third World feminist writing.

Meanwhile, back on the sexual identity front, the dilemma of ter- 30
minology takes up a ridiculous amount of energy, both my own and
other people's. "But what do you *call* yourself?" dykes keep anxiously
prodding, until the lack of a label seems like more of an embarrassment than the actual behavior. (I'm reminded of stories I've read about
the disgrace and discomfiture associated with being "kiki"—neither
butch nor femme—in lesbian circles in the 1950s.) I feel put on the spot
when a lesbian organizer solicits my endorsement of her group's
demonstration, then insists I identify myself as a lesbian on the leaflet;
I end up telling her the story of my life over the telephone. I feel put
on the spot again when a lesbian editor solicits a coming-out poem of
mine for inclusion in an anthology of gay and lesbian poetry. It's clear
to me, however, that the poem in question *is* a lesbian poem, and I'm
furious when another lesbian passionately denounces me for "lack of
ethics" because I agree to the inclusion.

I discover that I have to keep on coming out to straight people— 31
not in so many words, perhaps, but the method hardly matters. When
I describe the plots of my novels, when I challenge heterosexist assumptions, when I explain how it is I have a daughter without having
been a biological mother, naturally I'm viewed as a dyke. Currently,
I'm fast becoming the semi-official lesbian at the institution where I
teach: there are other women on the faculty who have female lovers in
the here and now, but I've got the rep. Of course I sometimes feel like
an impostor. Yet when I tell straight people I have a male lover, I feel
doubly exposed, my sexuality open to prurient speculation not only
because I've done unspeakable things with women, but because I apparently couldn't live without the almighty penis.

I decide that this difficulty in devising appropriate labels is merely 32
the most obvious symptom of an underlying process marked by many
layers of ambiguity, which might aptly be termed *identity loss.* I amuse
myself by inventing ironic self-descriptions, metaphors for my non-
identity: Stateless Person of the Sexual World. Tragic Mulatto of the
Sexual World. Lesbian-feminist Emeritus. Twilight Girl. In conversations with myself, I make reference to "my interesting condition"—
that old-fashioned euphemism for pregnancy which seems to me to
convey not only the thinly veiled, at times intrusive, curiosity with
which others regard me, but my own hopes for extracting meaning
from the mess.

There's an obvious solution to my dilemma over labels, and per- 33
haps to the deeper questions as well. Why don't I simply accept my bisexuality, proclaim it to the world, and perhaps become active in some
sort of group?

Throughout much of my adult life, the insights of identity politics 34 have shaped my world view, informing my activism, my writing, and in many respects the conduct of my most intimate relationships. I've been privileged to know many brilliant, principled women who've used the precept that "the most profound and potentially the most radical politics come directly out of our own identity, as opposed to working to end somebody else's oppression"[1] as though it were a surgeon's scalpel with which to dissect experience in the interests of healing. Given this, it may seem peculiar that I would willingly remain in identity limbo.

On the other hand, I've often felt uneasy about the intensity of the 35 lesbian-feminist focus on identity. It sometimes leads to an obsessive narrowing of perspective. Stress on the potential for change in individuals and social structures is too often abandoned in favor of an essentialist preoccupation with what one "is," as defined by an ever-growing list of measures. At the worst, I've seen paranoid opportunists wield simplistic political theory—and their own identities—as though these were blunt instruments with which to discipline adversaries.

I now experience a foreboding of exhaustion at the prospect of dig- 36 ging out, dusting off, "dealing with," polishing up, inhabiting, and promoting yet another identity. I do not want to become an identity junkie, hooked on the rush that comes with pinning down the essential characteristic that, for the moment, seems to offer the ultimate definition of the self, the quintessence of oppression, the locus of personal value—only to be superseded by the next revelation.

I have a second problem with "identifying" as bisexual, even as I 37 accept the term as a technical description of my sexuality. I do not know what "bisexual" desire would be, since my desire is always for a specifically sexed and general individual. When I am with a woman, I love as a woman loves a woman, and when I am with a man, I love as a woman loves a man. So bisexuality is not a sexual identity at all, but a sort of anti-identity, a refusal (not, of course, conscious) to be limited to one object of desire, one way of loving.

British feminist Jacqueline Rose has argued for recognition of a 38 "*resistance to identity*" which lies at the very heart of psychic life." Basing her discussion on elements of Freudian and subsequent psychoanalytic theory, she paints a picture of identity as a deceptively smooth facade hiding an endless turmoil of contradictory impulses and desires. Socially powerful groups have a stake in promoting the

---

[1]See "The Combahee River Collective Statement" in Barbara Smith, ed., *Home Girls: A Black Feminist Anthology* (Latham, NY: Kitchen Table: Women of Color Press, 1983).

illusion of unconflicted identity because the maintenance of their power depends on keeping in place a constellation of apparently fixed, "natural," immutable social relationships and psychological postures. She spots an irony in the feminist tendency to view psychic conflict as "either an accident or an obstacle on the path to psychic and sexual continuity—a continuity which we, as feminists, recognize as a myth of our culture only to reinscribe it in a different form on the agenda. . . ."[2]

I suggest that when we assume lesbian identity to be unambigu- 39 ous, when we are dismayed to discover attractions to men co-existing with woman-loving, we reinscribe in a different form a prevailing cultural myth about sexuality—one which the early gay liberation movement, with its emphasis on exploration and human variety, attempted to debunk. Rose's argument did help me understand my suspicion that in choosing to love a man, it was, on some level, chaos itself I needed to invoke. It confirms my reluctance to hurriedly replace my lost identity. It also encourages me to inquire how that identity functioned in my life. What benefits made it worth my while to ignore contradiction and conflict? (It's worth reemphasizing that I'm focusing on what it meant to me to be a lesbian-feminist, as opposed to what it meant to be lovers with a woman.)

One answer to the question is suggested by my nagging feeling 40 that in getting involved with a man, as I put it to myself, I stopped being golden. I cannot explain this feeling in rational terms, since I always cast a jaundiced eye on theories of the natural superiority of women, ridiculed separatism, and was vocal about the flaws in lesbian politics and culture. Nevertheless, being a lesbian-feminist apparently provided me with a sense of special worth which is palpable in its absence, and which I don't believe I will ever get back, no matter the future course of my love life. Apparently I bought into the superstitious notion that oppression is destiny, and the more oppressed the more politically valuable and morally admirable the person. My identity was both a membership in an elite sorority and a lavender badge of courage which partially compensated for a lot of things I disliked about myself, like class background and skin color.

I see this quite clearly when I think about my writing: when I felt 41 that my work was *only* that of a woman who is white and middle-class, and consequently doubted what of any real and lasting interest I might have to say to the world about its predicament and its glory, I could take comfort in the fact that it was also the work of a lesbian, someone on the cutting edge. If I now say that my identity was part of

---

[2]Jacqueline Rose, "Femininity and Its Discontents," *Feminist Review*, No. 14 (June 1983). Italics added.

an elaborate guilt management system, I don't mean to dismiss very real questions about the relationship of artistic insight to various forms of privilege, but rather to remind myself how damaging I've found this reductive approach to be. It makes me too cautious, leads me to veil my feelings, smothers whatever fire I may have in me to share, which is fueled by a subtle, infinitely nuanced combination of early experience and adult learning.

My lesbian identity also bestowed, I thought, a basic dignity that 42 my gender had denied me. This was partly a practical matter—as a lesbian, I interacted less frequently with men, thereby avoiding a certain amount of sexism—but the symbolism was just as important to me. I was still a female in a patriarchal system, of course, subject to rape, unequal pay, and the tender mercies of the military-industrial complex. But I *felt* emancipated, felt I'd declared my independence and was therefore less compromised by my second-class status. When I contemplated the possibility of no longer being able to call myself a lesbian, what came to mind was the sense of humiliation I associated with being a straight woman.

My symbolic autonomy had its advantages, but now I actually feel 43 far less helpless as a woman-in-relation-to-men than I'd anticipated. I believe this evolution has its parallels in the experience of many lesbians who have become reinvolved in friendships and working situations with men, following a period of de facto separatism.

If I'm to begin to account for where I've ended up, I need to touch 44 on another dimension of my experience. This is difficult, because it involves my intense anger at women, an anger I would like to neutralize with reasoned analysis, and of course am unable to. The truth is that the lesbian-feminist way of life I knew was very hard on women, yet we were not supposed to notice or complain about that fact. We were supposed to content ourselves with our elect status and the glory of our exhausting service.

I got trashed. I watched friends get trashed. I watched feminist in- 45 stitutions consume staggering quantities of energy and time and go under anyway. I saw a lot of people I loved leave town, which would have been more bearable if so many of them hadn't stopped speaking or writing to each other and to me, for one or another political/personal reason. I saw the destructive pressure on lesbian couples that comes from treating people as political symbols. (A ludicrous but believable example of this: a friend was urged to stay in a difficult relationship in order to provide a positive example of an interracial couple.) Of course all of this happened in a context of oppression; I'm not saying we simply did it to ourselves. Yet I wish we could have been gentler with one another, and more honest about how hard and sometimes disillusioning it was.

This essay is not "The Goddess That Failed." I'm in no way argu- 46
ing that you can't live a really good life in a community of women—
only that my own experience in a particular community of women
convinces me that all human connections are risky, fragile, and non-
ideal. Do what you feel like doing—to hell with living by theory!

But isn't that just a convenient excuse for beating a retreat into 47
heterosexual privilege and generally wishy-washiness (as my old self
might have argued)? I doubt it, at least in my case. Anybody who
thinks relationships between black men and white women enjoy a lot
of societal approval should study the recent murder of Yusuf
Hawkins, a black youth gunned down several miles from my apartment by a gang of whites upset by what the papers refer to as "interracial dating."

It seems to me, however, that there's a much deeper and more 48
painful issue buried here, that of the division between women who
can "pass" and those who can't, between women who love women
but *appear* less threatening to the straight world and women who from
an early age fit the stereotype of the butch lesbian and are brutally
punished for it.

Because my core sexuality is fluid, I never experienced the child- 49
hood terror of being a queer in a heterosexual universe (I felt different,
all right, but not because of my sexuality). As a result, loving women
seemed like an adventure, not something to be hidden or agonized
over. And once I came out, I rarely got hassled on the street the way
my lover did, no matter how short my hair was. I believe it's this sort
of disparity in lesbian experience that gets encoded in a lot of the
angry discussions about "dykes who sleep with men," in a way that's
reminiscent of the very painful tensions among people of color
involving skin tone, class, and access to the dominant culture.

A close friend who's been a great support to me since I became 50
involved with a man gave voice to a poignant moment of insecurity
which perhaps crystallizes the terror behind this issue: "You get the
feeling maybe pretty soon you'll be the only one left." I think I will remember that remark long after I've dismissed all the punitive, judgmental "don't you dare's"; I record it here precisely because it is a feeling, and, as such, is in some absolute sense unanswerable, except by
a social transformation which could remove the need for anyone to
experience dread or loneliness because of sexual choices.

I find that my own loneliness lessens as I continue to insist on 51
being all the parts of who I am. I recently attended New York's
Lesbian and Gay Pride March—an event I'd avoided in Year One of
my interesting condition—and found to my great pleasure that I felt
very much at home. Here, surging down Fifth Avenue, was a grand
celebration of human diversity, an infinite shading of inclination—the

diametric opposite of narrow correctness. Who could resist this, I thought, who wouldn't want to be a part of this? But I know full well how many are itching to destroy it.

Several weeks later, I participated in an abortion rights demon- 52 stration held in the aftermath of the Supreme Court's Webster decision. At the rally in Foley Square and on the march uptown, I saw people I knew from many different lives: old comrades, lesbian and straight, from my days in the Committee for Abortion Rights and Against Sterilization Abuse (CARASA); new friends from the Central America solidarity movement; a gay man who'd briefly been my roommate, and who had helped calm my fears of being an outcast from gay civilization; co-workers from the patchwork of jobs that support my writing habit. I marched part way with a black feminist film critic I'd met recently, talking about teaching, writing, and Spike Lee's *Do the Right Thing*.

As we neared Foley Square, a young, tall, white gay man with a 53 round, pleasant face came up to me and said he'd just finished reading my novel. His enthusiasm produced the confused rush of pleasure strangers' praise for my writing usually generates, mixed with the relief I experience these days in knowing that no matter how shaky my sense of self, my lesbian books are out there in the world, speaking their piece.

Suddenly, the crowd sat down in the street. I thought of my first 54 civil disobedience arrest many years ago, when I was still in college. The mood seemed similar now—spontaneously militant in a way that felt downright old-fashioned. A lot of things could happen. In the next block, an ACT UP contingent was exercising its First Amendment rights, burning a small flag. The gay man turned to me. "What would they do if they knew we were all dykes and faggots?" he grinned. I smiled back, wondering for a moment what my fan would do if he realized this dyke was sleeping with a man. Then I let the worry go. All of us came from such incredibly different places, and here we were together. I knew I was exactly where I wanted to be.

Afterword

Dear Reader,

The first time an editor asked to reprint the foregoing essay in a col- 55 lege composition text, I hesitated to grant permission. A collection of essays for writing students would, I thought, provide such a different context from that of the original publication in *OUT/LOOK*, a now-defunct quarterly produced by and for lesbians and gay men, that the piece might be misunderstood. In that magazine, it seemed perfectly normal to be queer (in fact, it was considered downright boring to be straight). So while "My Interesting Condition" might have ruffled a few feathers, nobody reading it there would be tempted to think for a minute that women loving women had become obsolete. In a textbook that might at best present a handful of essays with openly gay content, on the other hand, would my reflections appear to reconfirm our society's strong bias against same-sex sex and romance?

I was about to say no to the reprint request when I was offered space   56
to add an explanatory note. I jumped at the chance to speak directly
to readers much like the students I encounter each semester in my
own undergraduate writing classes.

I know that many of you are dealing with the relief and novel pres-   57
sures of being newly on your own. You may be confronting with a
new urgency some basic questions about your sexuality. Or perhaps
you've known for a while who you are and what you want to do, but
are just beginning to act freely on that knowledge. Possibly you have
both known and acted for a long time, but in situations where you
had to hide your behavior.

Almost surely you have been subjected to some unwanted sexual   58
pressure—whether it was the pressure to be sexually active when
you weren't ready or interested; to "just say no" when you wanted
to say yes; to sleep with a partner who didn't appeal to you, to prove
your "normality" (when you thought you might be gay); or to "just
make up your mind" (when you thought you might be bi). Perhaps,
like my own daughter, you grew up in an openly gay family—there
are more and more, these days; if so, like her at one point in her teen
years, you may have feared peers' ridicule. More likely, no matter
your sexual orientation, you come from an atmosphere like that
recalled by a college freshman in my class who wrote about attending high school in a small town where he constantly had to hide his
attraction to other males from both friends and family. Perhaps you
are like another student who remembered how he'd used homophobic remarks and heterosexual male bonding to help him overcome
his outsider status as an Asian in Caucasian Middle America—only
to feel sharply ashamed of his prejudice when he learned that his
closest male friend was gay.

Whoever you are, you should know that you are reading this in an   59
era when it is *still* not physically safe to be lesbian or gay in much of
America (as gay bashing statistics attest). In other places and situations, the standard remains that it's semi-okay as long as you keep it
quiet—the cruel charade of the Clinton Administration's "don't ask,
don't tell" approach to gays in the military. As I write this in the
summer of 1994, it's legal to fire someone for being homosexual in
42 states. Anti-gay ballot initiatives—thus far blocked from becoming law by court decisions in Ohio and Colorado—are expected to be
put before voters this fall in up to 9 states.

You should also know how far we've come. There are laws in many   60
locales that *forbid* discrimination on the basis of sexual preference.
There are grassroots street patrols in cities from Seattle to Houston
that counter gay bashing. There are campus support groups and
community centers where gay people can gather, and enormous gay

pride marches every year across the country. There are large national organizations to respond to gay and lesbian social issues, health problems, and legal concerns. There is the Center for Lesbian and Gay Studies (CLAGS) at the City University of New York Graduate Center. There are lesbian-run publishers like Kitchen Table: Women of Color Press and Firebrand Books that publish fiction and poetry and nonfiction prose by lesbian and straight feminists. There are anthologies like Assotto Saint's *The Road Before Us: 100 Black Gay Poets* that counter the myth that "gay" only refers to well-to-do white men. These resources do not exist because of government beneficence or private sector bounty or advanced technology, but because ordinary people have worked hard to create them. In an era when the country is clamoring for "change," they constitute one of the most hopeful signs to all of us that far-reaching, constructive change is indeed possible.

Whoever you are, the history of lesbian and gay agitation for change has meaning for your future. Even if you lack a single ambiguous molecule in your heterosexual makeup (I believe there really are such people!) you must be concerned with the atmosphere that encourages either support or persecution for your lesbian and gay relatives and friends. (They do exist, whether or not you know who they are.) Lesbian and gay liberation also ultimately means that you will be freer to experience your own sexual and affectional choices as just that—*choices*, not a set of rigidly prescribed roles.   61

And the ideal of choice, that feminist buzzword, is what I hope you will take away from this essay—not choice in the weak sense of social permissiveness ("everybody should be free to do their own thing") but in the strong sense of attentive and flexible engagement with feelings, experiences, and knowledge. The point is that "identity" is not one permanent, solid object—however much we might wish it were so. "Identity is a river," as Chicana lesbian writer Gloria Anzaldúa has said. Each of us must run some rapids from time to time. The habit of mind required for this task is, by lucky coincidence, the same one required of the writer, comprising an openness to world and self, an eye for detail, a tolerance for process, and an addiction to revision.   62

Take good care,
Jan Clausen

QUESTIONS

1.   With classmates or other readers, perform a dramatic reading of the playlet-dialogue with which Clausen opens her essay. Discuss your reactions. How do you think the dialogue would change if the woman they're discussing were "coming out" as a lesbian among straight friends, instead of as a bisexual among lesbian friends? What kinds of similar "locker room" dialogues would you create for (a) four straight men discussing a gay friend?; (b) four gay men discussing a straight friend?

2.   Why does Clausen reject the "obvious solution to my dilemma over labels" (paragraph 33) of simply accepting and proclaiming her bisexuality?

3.   Write an open letter back to Clausen in response to her Afterword addressed to writing students. Respond to specific points she raises that have personal meaning or relevance for you.

Territory

DAVID LEAVITT

Neil's mother, Mrs. Campbell, sits on her lawn chair behind a card 1
table outside the food co-op. Every few minutes, as the sun shifts, she
moves the chair and table several inches back so as to remain in the
shade. It is a hundred degrees outside, and bright white. Each time
someone goes in or out of the co-op a gust of air-conditioning flies out
of the automatic doors, raising dust from the cement.

Neil stands just inside, poised over a water fountain, and watches 2
her. She has on a sun hat, and a sweatshirt over her tennis dress; her
legs are bare, and shiny with cocoa butter. In front of her, propped
against the table, a sign proclaims: MOTHERS, FIGHT FOR YOUR CHILDREN'S
RIGHTS—SUPPORT A NON-NUCLEAR FUTURE. Women dressed exactly like
her pass by, notice the sign, listen to her brief spiel, finger pamphlets,
sign petitions or don't sign petitions, never give money. Her weary
eyes are masked by dark glasses. In the age of Reagan, she has declared, keeping up the causes of peace and justice is a futile, tiresome,
and unrewarding effort; it is therefore an effort fit only for mothers to
keep up. The sun bounces off the window glass through which Neil
watches her. His own reflection lines up with her profile.

Later that afternoon, Neil spreads himself out alongside the pool 3
and imagines he is being watched by the shirtless Chicano gardener.
But the gardener, concentrating on his pruning, is neither seductive
nor seducible. On the lawn, his mother's large Airedales—Abigail,
Lucille, Fern—amble, sniff, urinate. Occasionally, they accost the gardener, who yells at them in Spanish.

After two years' absence, Neil reasons, he should feel nostalgia, re- 4
gret, gladness upon returning home. He closes his eyes and tries to
muster the proper background music for the cinematic scene of return.
His rhapsody, however, is interrupted by the noises of his mother's

David Leavitt lives in New York and is author of *Family Dancing:
Stories* (1984) and the novels *The Lost Language of Cranes* (1986), *Equal
Affections* (1989), and *While England Sleeps* (1993). He is also co-editor,
with Mark Mitchell, of *The Penguin Book of Gay Short Stories* (1994).
"Territory" won the Willets Prize for fiction at Yale University, and
Leavitt was 21 and still a student at Yale when *The New Yorker* published the story in 1982. Controversially for its more conservative
readers, this was the first time that the prestigious magazine had published fiction explicitly addressing homosexuality.

trio—the scratchy cello, whining violin, stumbling piano—as she and Lillian Havalard and Charlotte Feder plunge through Mozart. The tune is cheery, in a Germanic sort of way, and utterly inappropriate to what Neil is trying to feel. Yet it *is* the music of his adolescence; they have played it for years, bent over the notes, their heads bobbing in silent time to the metronome.

It is getting darker. Every few minutes, he must move his towel so 5 as to remain within the narrowing patch of sunlight. In four hours, Wayne, his lover of ten months and the only person he has ever imagined he could spend his life with, will be in this house, where no lover of his has ever set foot. The thought fills him with a sense of grand terror and curiosity. He stretches, tries to feel seductive, desirable. The gardener's shears whack at the ferns; the music above him rushes to a loud, premature conclusion. The women laugh and applaud themselves as they give up for the day. He hears Charlotte Feder's full nasal twang, the voice of a fat woman in a pink pants suit—odd, since she is a scrawny, arthritic old bird, rarely clad in anything other than tennis shorts and a blouse. Lillian is the fat woman in the pink pants suit; her voice is thin and warped by too much crying. Drink in hand, she calls out from the porch, "Hot enough!" and waves. He lifts himself up and nods to her.

The women sit on the porch and chatter; their voices blend with 6 the clink of ice in glasses. They belong to a small circle of ladies all of whom, with the exception of Neil's mother, are widows and divorcées. Lillian's husband left her twenty-two years ago, and sends her a check every month to live on; Charlotte has been divorced twice as long as she was married, and has a daughter serving a long sentence for terrorist acts committed when she was nineteen. Only Neil's mother has a husband, a distant sort of husband, away often on business. He is away on business now. All of them feel betrayed—by husbands, by children, by history.

Neil closes his eyes, tries to hear the words only as sounds. Soon, 7 a new noise accosts him: his mother arguing with the gardener in Spanish. He leans on his elbows and watches them; the syllables are loud, heated, and compressed, and seem on the verge of explosion. But the argument ends happily; they shake hands. The gardener collects his check and walks out the gate without so much as looking at Neil.

He does not know the gardener's name; as his mother has re- 8 minded him, he does not know most of what has gone on since he moved away. Her life has gone on, unaffected by his absence. He flinches at his own egoism, the egoism of sons.

"Neil! Did you call the airport to make sure the plane's coming in 9 on time?"

"Yes," he shouts to her. "It is." 10

"Good. Well, I'll have dinner ready when you get back."   11

"Mom—"   12

"What?" The word comes out in a weary wail that is more of an   13
answer than a question.

"What's wrong?" he says, forgetting his original question.   14

"Nothing's wrong," she declares in a tone that indicates that   15
everything is wrong. "The dogs have to be fed, dinner has to be made,
and I've got people here. Nothing's wrong."

"I hope things will be as comfortable as possible when Wayne gets   16
here."

"Is that a request or a threat?"   17

"Mom—"   18

Behind her sunglasses, her eyes are inscrutable. "I'm tired," she   19
says. "It's been a long day. I . . . I'm anxious to meet Wayne. I'm sure
he'll be wonderful, and we'll all have a wonderful, wonderful time.
I'm sorry. I'm just tired."

She heads up the stairs. He suddenly feels an urge to cover him-   20
self; his body embarrasses him, as it has in her presence since the day
she saw him shirtless and said with delight, "Neil! You're growing
hair under your arms!"

Before he can get up, the dogs gather round him and begin to sniff   21
and lick at him. He wriggles to get away from them, but Abigail, the
largest and stupidest, straddles his stomach and nuzzles his mouth.
He splutters and, laughing, throws her off. "Get away from me, you
goddamn dogs," he shouts, and swats at them. They are new dogs, not
the dog of his childhood, not dogs he trusts.

He stands, and the dogs circle him, looking up at his face expec-   22
tantly. He feels renewed terror at the thought that Wayne will be here
so soon: Will they sleep in the same room? Will they make love? He
has never had sex in his parents' house. How can he be expected to be
a lover here, in this place of his childhood, of his earliest shame, in this
household of mothers and dogs?

"Dinnertime! Abbylucyferny, Abbylucyferny, dinnertime!" His   23
mother's litany disperses the dogs, and they run for the door.

"Do you realize," he shouts to her, "that no matter how much   24
those dogs love you they'd probably kill you for the leg of lamb in the
freezer?"

Neil was twelve the first time he recognized in himself something   25
like sexuality. He was lying outside, on the grass, when Rasputin—the
dog, long dead, of his childhood—began licking his face. He felt a tingle he did not recognize, pulled off his shirt to give the dog access to
more of him. Rasputin's tongue tickled coolly. A wet nose started to
sniff down his body, toward his bathing suit. What he felt frightened

him, but he couldn't bring himself to push the dog away. Then his mother called out, "Dinner," and Rasputin was gone, more interested in food than in him.

It was the day after Rasputin was put to sleep, years later, that Neil 26 finally stood in the kitchen, his back turned to his parents, and said, with unexpected ease, "I'm a homosexual." The words seemed insufficient, reductive. For years, he had believed his sexuality to be detachable from the essential him, but now he realized that it was part of him. He had the sudden, despairing sensation that though the words had been easy to say, the fact of their having been aired was incurably damning. Only then, for the first time, did he admit that they were true, and he shook and wept in regret for what he would not be for his mother, for having failed her. His father hung back, silent; he was absent for that moment as he was mostly absent—a strong absence. Neil always thought of him sitting on the edge of the bed in his underwear, captivated by something on television. He said, "It's O.K., Neil." But his mother was resolute; her lower lip didn't quaver. She had enormous reserves of strength to which she only gained access at moments like this one. She hugged him from behind, wrapped him in the childhood smells of perfume and brownies, and whispered, "It's O.K., honey." For once, her words seemed as inadequate as his. Neil felt himself shrunk to an embarrassed adolescent, hating her sympathy, not wanting her to touch him. It was the way he would feel from then on whenever he was in her presence—even now, at twenty-three, bringing home his lover to meet her.

All through his childhood, she had packed only the most nutri- 27 tious lunches, had served on the PTA, had volunteered at the children's library and at his school, had organized a successful campaign to ban a racist history textbook. The day after he told her, she located and got in touch with an organization called the Coalition of Parents of Lesbians and Gays. Within a year, she was president of it. On weekends, she and the other mothers drove their station wagons to San Francisco, set up their card tables in front of the Bulldog Baths, the Liberty Baths, passed out literature to men in leather and denim who were loath to admit they even had mothers. These men, who would habitually do violence to each other, were strangely cowed by the suburban ladies with their informational booklets, and bent their heads. Neil was a sophomore in college then, and lived in San Francisco. She brought him pamphlets detailing the dangers of bathhouses and back rooms, enemas and poppers, wordless sex in alleyways. His excursion into that world had been brief and lamentable, and was over. He winced at the thought that she knew all his sexual secrets, and vowed to move to the East Coast to escape her. It was not very different from the days when she had campaigned for a better playground, or tutored the Hispanic children in the audiovisual room. Those days, as well, he had run away from her concern. Even today, perched in front of the co-op, collecting signatures for nuclear disarmament, she was quintessentially a mother. And if the lot of mothers was to expect nothing in return, was the lot of sons to return nothing?

Driving across the Dumbarton Bridge on his way to the airport, 28 Neil thinks, I have returned nothing; I have simply returned. He wonders if she would have given birth to him had she known what he would grow up to be.

Then he berates himself: Why should he assume himself to be the 29 cause of her sorrow? She has told him that her life is full of secrets. She has changed since he left home—grown thinner, more rigid, harder to hug. She has given up baking, taken up tennis; her skin has browned and tightened. She is no longer the woman who hugged him and kissed him, who said, "As long as you're happy, that's all that's important to us."

The flats spread out around him; the bridge floats on purple and 30 green silt, and spongy bay fill, not water at all. Only ten miles north, a whole city has been built on gunk dredged up from the bay.

He arrives at the airport ten minutes early, to discover that the 31 plane has landed twenty minutes early. His first view of Wayne is from behind, by the baggage belt. Wayne looks as he always looks—slightly windblown—and is wearing the ratty leather jacket he was wearing the night they met. Neil sneaks up on him and puts his hands on his shoulders; when Wayne turns around, he looks relieved to see him. 32

They hug like brothers; only in the safety of Neil's mother's car do they dare to kiss. They recognize each other's smells, and grow comfortable again. "I never imagined I'd actually see you out here," Neil says, "but you're exactly the same here as there."

"It's only been a week." 33

They kiss again. Neil wants to go to a motel, but Wayne insists on 34 being pragmatic. "We'll be there soon. Don't worry."

"We could go to one of the bathhouses in the city and take a room 35 for a couple of aeons," Neil says. "Christ, I'm hard up. I don't even know if we're going to be in the same bedroom."

"Well, if we're not," Wayne says, "we'll sneak around. It'll be 36 romantic."

They cling to each other for a few more minutes, until they realize 37 that people are looking in the car window. Reluctantly, they pull apart. Neil reminds himself that he loves this man, that there is a reason for him to bring this man home.

He takes the scenic route on the way back. The car careers over 38 foothills, through forests, along white four-lane highways high in the mountains. Wayne tells Neil that he sat next to a woman on the plane who was once Marilyn Monroe's psychiatrist's nurse. He slips his foot out of his shoe and nudges Neil's ankle, pulling Neil's sock down with his toe.

"I have to drive," Neil says. "I'm very glad you're here." 39

There is a comfort in the privacy of the car. They have a common 40 fear of walking hand in hand, of publicly showing physical affection, even in the permissive West Seventies of New York—a fear that they have admitted only to one another. They slip through a pass between two hills, and are suddenly in residential Northern California, the land of expensive ranch-style houses.

As they pull into Neil's mother's driveway, the dogs run barking 41 toward the car. When Wayne opens the door, they jump and lap at him, and he tries to close it again. "Don't worry. Abbylucyferny? Get in the house, damn it!"

His mother descends from the porch. She has changed into a blue 42 flower-print dress, which Neil doesn't recognize. He gets out of the car and halfheartedly chastises the dogs. Crickets chirp in the trees. His mother looks radiant, even beautiful, illuminated by the headlights, surrounded by the now quiet dogs, like a Circe with her slaves. When she walks over to Wayne, offering her hand, and says, "Wayne, I'm Barbara," Neil forgets that she is his mother.

"Good to meet you, Barbara," Wayne says, and reaches out his 43 hand. Craftier than she, he whirls her around to kiss her cheek.

Barbara! He is calling his mother Barbara! Then he remembers that 44 Wayne is five years older than he is. They chat by the open car door, and Neil shrinks back—the embarrassed adolescent, uncomfortable, unwanted.

So the dreaded moment passes and he might as well not have been 45 there. At dinner, Wayne keeps the conversation smooth, like a captivated courtier seeking Neil's mother's hand. A faggot son's sodomist—such words spit into Neil's head. She has prepared tiny meatballs with fresh coriander, fettucine with pesto. Wayne talks about the street people in New York; El Salvador is a tragedy; if only Sadat had lived; Phyllis Schlafly—what can you do?

"It's a losing battle," she tells him. "Every day I'm out there with 46 my card table, me and the other mothers, but I tell you, Wayne, it's a losing battle. Sometimes I think us old ladies are the only ones with enough patience to fight."

Occasionally, Neil says something, but his comments seem stupid 47 and clumsy. Wayne continues to call her Barbara. No one under forty has ever called her Barbara as long as Neil can remember. They drink wine; he does not.

Now is the time for drastic action. He contemplates taking 48
Wayne's hand, then checks himself. He has never done anything in her
presence to indicate that the sexuality he confessed to five years ago
was a reality and not an invention. Even now, he and Wayne might as
well be friends, college roommates. Then Wayne, his savior, with a single, sweeping gesture, reaches for his hand, and clasps it, in the midst
of a joke he is telling about Saudi Arabians. By the time he is laughing,
their hands are joined. Neil's throat contracts; his heart begins to beat
violently. He notices his mother's eyes flicker, glance downward; she
never breaks the stride of her sentence. The dinner goes on, and every
taboo nurtured since childhood falls quietly away.

She removes the dishes. Their hands grow sticky; he cannot tell 49
which fingers are his and which Wayne's. She clears the rest of the
table and rounds up the dogs.

"Well, boys, I'm very tired, and I've got a long day ahead of me to- 50
morrow, so I think I'll hit the sack. There are extra towels for you in
Neil's bathroom, Wayne. Sleep well."

"Good night, Barbara," Wayne calls out. "It's been wonderful 51
meeting you."

They are alone. Now they can disentangle their hands. 52

"No problem about where we sleep, is there?" 53

"No," Neil says. "I just can't imagine sleeping with someone in 54
this house."

His leg shakes violently. Wayne takes Neil's hand in a firm grasp 55
and hauls him up.

Later that night, they lie outside, under redwood trees, listening to 56
the hysteria of the crickets, the hum of the pool cleaning itself.
Redwood leaves prick their skin. They fell in love in bars and apartments, and this is the first time that they have made love outdoors.
Neil is not sure he has enjoyed the experience. He kept sensing eyes,
imagined that the neighborhood cats were staring at them from behind a fence of brambles. He remembers he once hid in this spot when
he and some of the children from the neighborhood were playing sardines, remembers the intoxication of small bodies packed together, the
warm breath of suppressed laughter on his neck. "The loser had to go
through the spanking machine," he tells Wayne.

"Did you lose often?" 57

"Most of the time. The spanking machine never really hurt—just a 58
whirl of hands. If you moved fast enough, no one could actually get
you. Sometimes, though, late in the afternoon, we'd get naughty. We'd
chase each other and pull each other's pants down. That was all. Boys
and girls together!"

"Listen to the insects," Wayne says, and closes his eyes. 59

Neil turns to examine Wayne's face, notices a single, small pimple. 60
Their lovemaking usually begins in a wrestle, a struggle for dominance, and ends with a somewhat confusing loss of identity—as now,
when Neil sees a foot on the grass, resting against his leg, and tries to
determine if it is his own or Wayne's.

From inside the house, the dogs begin to bark. Their yelps grow 61
into alarmed falsettos. Neil lifts himself up. "I wonder if they smell
something," he says.

"Probably just us," says Wayne. 62

"My mother will wake up. She hates getting waked up." 63

Lights go on in the house; the door to the porch opens. 64

"What's wrong, Abby? What's wrong?" his mother's voice calls 65
softly.

Wayne clamps his hand over Neil's mouth. "Don't say anything," 66
he whispers.

"I can't just—" Neil begins to say, but Wayne's hand closes over 67
his mouth again. He bites it, and Wayne starts laughing.

"What was that?" Her voice projects into the garden. "Hello?" she 68
says.

The dogs yelp louder. "Abbylucyferny, it's O.K., it's O.K." Her 69
voice is soft and panicked. "Is anyone there?" she asks loudly.

The brambles shake. She takes a flashlight, shines it around the 70
garden. Wayne and Neil duck down; the light lands on them and hovers for a few seconds. Then it clicks off and they are in the dark—a new
dark, a darker dark, which their eyes must readjust to.

"Let's go to bed, Abbylucyferny," she says gently. Neil and Wayne 71
hear her pad into the house. The dogs whimper as they follow her, and
the lights go off.

Once before, Neil and his mother had stared at each other in the 72
glare of bright lights. Four years ago, they stood in the arena created
by the headlights of her car, waiting for the train. He was on his way
back to San Francisco, where he was marching in a Gay Pride Parade
the next day. The train station was next door to the food co-op and
shared its parking lot. The co-op, familiar and boring by day, took on
a certain mystery in the night. Neil recognized the spot where he had
skidded on his bicycle and broken his leg. Through the glass doors, the
brightly lit interior of the store glowed, its rows and rows of cans and
boxes forming their own horizon, each can illuminated so that even
from outside Neil could read the labels. All that was missing was the
ladies in tennis dresses and sweatshirts pushing their carts past bins of
nuts and dried fruits.

"Your train is late," his mother said. Her hair fell loosely on her 73
shoulders, and her legs were tanned. Neil looked at her and tried to

imagine her in labor with him—bucking and struggling with his birth. He felt then the strange, sexless love for women which through his whole adolescence he had mistaken for heterosexual desire.

A single bright light approached them; it preceded the low, haunt- 74 ing sound of the whistle. Neil kissed his mother, and waved goodbye as he ran to meet the train. It was an old train, with windows tinted a sort of horrible lemon-lime. It stopped only long enough for him to hoist himself on board, and then it was moving again. He hurried to a window, hoping to see her drive off, but the tint of the window made it possible for him to make out only vague patches of light—street lamps, cars, the co-op.

He sank into the hard, green seat. The train was almost entirely 75 empty; the only other passenger was a dark-skinned man wearing bluejeans and a leather jacket. He sat directly across the aisle from Neil, next to the window. He had rough skin and a thick mustache. Neil discovered that by pretending to look out the window he could study the man's reflection in the lemon-lime glass. It was only slightly hazy—the quality of a bad photograph. Neil felt his mouth open, felt sleep closing in on him. Hazy red and gold flashes through the glass pulsed in the face of the man in the window, giving the curious impression of muscle spasms. It took Neil a few minutes to realize that the man was staring at him, or, rather, staring at the back of his head— staring at his staring. The man smiled as though to say, I know exactly what you're staring at, and Neil felt the sickening sensation of desire rise in his throat.

Right before they reached the city, the man stood up and sat down 76 in the seat next to Neil's. The man's thigh brushed deliberately against his own. Neil's eyes were watering; he felt sick to his stomach. Taking Neil's hand, the man said, "Why so nervous, honey? Relax."

Neil woke up the next morning with the taste of ashes in his 77 mouth. He was lying on the floor, without blankets or sheets or pillows. Instinctively, he reached for his pants, and as he pulled them on came face to face with the man from the train. His name was Luis; he turned out to be a dog groomer. His apartment smelled of dog.

"Why such a hurry?" Luis said. 78

"The parade. The Gay Pride Parade. I'm meeting some friends to 79 march."

"I'll come with you," Luis said. "I think I'm too old for these 80 things, but why not?"

Neil did not want Luis to come with him, but he found it impossi- 81 ble to say so. Luis looked older by day, more likely to carry diseases. He dressed again in a torn T-shirt, leather jacket, bluejeans. "It's my everyday apparel," he said, and laughed. Neil buttoned his pants, aware that they had been washed by his mother the day before. Luis possessed the peculiar combination of hypermasculinity and effeminacy which exemplifies faggotry. Neil wanted to be rid of him, but Luis's mark was on him, he could see that much. They would become lovers whether Neil liked it or not.

They joined the parade midway. Neil hoped he wouldn't meet 82 anyone he knew; he did not want to have to explain Luis, who clung to him. The parade was full of shirtless men with oiled, muscular shoulders. Neil's back ached. There were floats carrying garishly dressed prom queens and cheerleaders, some with beards, some actually looking like women. Luis said, "It makes me proud, makes me glad to be what I am." Neil supposed that by darting into the crowd ahead of him he might be able to lose Luis forever, but he found it difficult to let him go; the prospect of being alone seemed unbearable.

Neil was startled to see his mother watching the parade, holding 83 up a sign. She was with the Coalition of Parents of Lesbians and Gays; they had posted a huge banner on the wall behind them proclaiming: OUR SONS AND DAUGHTERS, WE ARE PROUD OF YOU. She spotted him; she waved, and jumped up and down.

"Who's that woman?" Luis asked. 84

"My mother. I should go say hello to her." 85

"O.K.," Luis said. He followed Neil to the side of the parade. Neil 86 kissed his mother. Luis took off his shirt, wiped his face with it, smiled.

"I'm glad you came," Neil said. 87

"I wouldn't have missed it, Neil. I wanted to show you I cared." 88

He smiled, and kissed her again. He showed no intention of intro- 89 ducing Luis, so Luis introduced himself.

"Hello, Luis," Mrs. Campbell said. Neil looked away. Luis shook 90 her hand, and Neil wanted to warn his mother to wash it, warned himself to check with a V.D. clinic first thing Monday.

"Neil, this is Carmen Bologna, another one of the mothers," Mrs. 91 Campbell said. She introduced him to a fat Italian woman with flushed cheeks, and hair arranged in the shape of a clamshell.

"Good to meet you, Neil, good to meet you," said Carmen 92 Bologna. "You know my son, Michael? I'm so proud of Michael! He's doing so well now. I'm proud of him, proud to be his mother I am, and your mother's proud, too!"

The woman smiled at him, and Neil could think of nothing to say 93 but "Thank you." He looked uncomfortably toward his mother, who stood listening to Luis. It occurred to him that the worst period of his life was probably about to begin and he had no way to stop it.

A group of drag queens ambled over to where the mothers were 94 standing. "Michael! Michael!" shouted Carmen Bologna, and embraced a sticklike man wrapped in green satin. Michael's eyes were heavily dosed with green eyeshadow, and his lips were painted pink.

Neil turned and saw his mother staring, her mouth open. He 95 marched over to where Luis was standing, and they moved back into the parade. He turned and waved to her. She waved back; he saw pain in her face, and then, briefly, regret. That day, he felt she would have traded him for any other son. Later, she said to him, "Carmen Bologna really was proud, and, speaking as a mother, let me tell you, you have to be brave to feel such pride."

Neil was never proud. It took him a year to dump Luis, another 96 year to leave California. The sick taste of ashes was still in his mouth. On the plane, he envisioned his mother sitting alone in the dark, smoking. She did not leave his mind until he was circling New York, staring down at the dawn rising over Queens. The song playing in his earphones would remain hovering on the edges of his memory, always associated with her absence. After collecting his baggage, he took a bus into the city. Boys were selling newspapers in the middle of highways, through the windows of stopped cars. It was seven in the morning when he reached Manhattan. He stood for ten minutes on East Thirty-fourth Street, breathed the cold air, and felt bubbles rising in his blood.

Neil got a job as a paralegal—a temporary job, he told himself. 97 When he met Wayne a year later, the sensations of that first morning returned to him. They'd been up all night, and at six they walked across the park to Wayne's apartment with the nervous, deliberate gait of people aching to make love for the first time. Joggers ran by with their dogs. None of them knew what Wayne and he were about to do, and the secrecy excited him. His mother came to mind, and the song, and the whirling vision of Queens coming alive below him. His breath solidified into clouds, and he felt happier than he had ever felt before in his life.

The second day of Wayne's visit, he and Neil go with Mrs. 98 Campbell to pick up the dogs at the dog parlor. The grooming establishment is decorated with pink ribbons and photographs of the owner's champion pit bulls. A fat, middle-aged woman appears from the back, leading the newly trimmed and fluffed Abigail, Lucille, and Fern by three leashes. The dogs struggle frantically when they see Neil's mother, tangling the woman up in their leashes. "Ladies, behave!" Mrs. Campbell commands, and collects the dogs. She gives Fern to Neil and Abigail to Wayne. In the car on the way back, Abigail begins pawing to get on Wayne's lap.

"Just push her off," Mrs. Campbell says. "She knows she's not 99 supposed to do that."

"You never groomed Rasputin," Neil complains. 100

"Rasputin was a mutt." 101

"Rasputin was a beautiful dog, even if he did smell." 102

"Do you remember when you were a little kid, Neil, you used to 103
make Rasputin dance with you? Once you tried to dress him up in one
of my blouses."

"I don't remember that," Neil says. 104

"Yes. I remember," says Mrs. Campbell. "Then you tried to orga- 105
nize a dog beauty contest in the neighborhood. You wanted to have
runners-up—everything."

"A dog beauty contest?" Wayne says. 106

"Mother, do we have to—" 107

"I think it's a mother's privilege to embarrass her son," Mrs. 108
Campbell says, and smiles.

When they are about to pull into the driveway, Wayne starts 109
screaming, and pushes Abigail off his lap. "Oh, my God!" he says.
"The dog just pissed all over me."

Neil turns around and sees a puddle seeping into Wayne's slacks. 110
He suppresses his laughter, and Mrs. Campbell hands him a rag.

"I'm sorry, Wayne," she says. "It goes with the territory." 111

"This is really disgusting," Wayne says, swatting at himself with 112
the rag.

Neil keeps his eyes on his own reflection in the rearview mirror 113
and smiles.

At home, while Wayne cleans himself in the bathroom, Neil 114
watches his mother cook lunch—Japanese noodles in soup. "When
you went off to college," she says, "I went to the grocery store. I was
going to buy you ramen noodles, and I suddenly realized you weren't
going to be around to eat them. I started crying right then, blubbering
like an idiot."

Neil clenches his fists inside his pockets. She has a way of telling 115
him little sad stories when he doesn't want to hear them—stories of
dolls broken by her brothers, lunches stolen by neighborhood boys on
the way to school. Now he has joined the ranks of male children who
have made her cry.

"Mama, I'm sorry," he says. 116

She is bent over the noodles, which steam in her face. "I didn't 117
want to say anything in front of Wayne, but I wish you had answered
me last night. I was very frightened—and worried."

"I'm sorry," he says, but it's not convincing. His fingers prickle. 118
He senses a great sorrow about to be born.

"I lead a quiet life," she says. "I don't want to be a disciplinarian. 119
I just don't have the energy for these—shenanigans. Please don't
frighten me that way again."

"If you were so upset, why didn't you say something?" 120

"I'd rather not discuss it. I lead a quiet life. I'm not used to getting 121
woken up late at night. I'm not used—"

"To my having a lover?"   122

"No, I'm not used to having other people around, that's all. Wayne   123
is charming. A wonderful young man."

"He likes you, too."   124

"I'm sure we'll get along fine."   125

She scoops the steaming noodles into ceramic bowls. Wayne re-   126
turns, wearing shorts. His white, hairy legs are a shocking contrast to
hers, which are brown and sleek.

"I'll wash those pants, Wayne," Mrs. Campbell says. "I have a spe-   127
cial detergent that'll take out the stain."

She gives Neil a look to indicate that the subject should be   128
dropped. He looks at Wayne, looks at his mother; his initial embarrassment gives way to a fierce pride—the arrogance of mastery. He is
glad his mother knows that he is desired, glad it makes her flinch.

Later, he steps into the back yard; the gardener is back, whacking   129
at the bushes with his shears. Neil walks by him in his bathing suit,
imagining he is on parade.

That afternoon, he finds his mother's daily list on the kitchen table: 130

TUESDAY

7:00—breakfast
Take dogs to groomer

Groceries (?)

Campaign against Draft—4–7

Buy underwear
Trios—2:00
Spaghetti
Fruit
Asparagus if sale
Peanuts

Milk

Doctor's Appointment (make)
Write Cranston/Hayakawa

re disarmament

Handi-Wraps
Mozart
Abigail
Top Ramen
Pedro

Her desk and trash can are full of such lists; he remembers them from
the earliest days of his childhood. He had learned to read from them.

In his own life, too, there have been endless lists—covered with check marks and arrows, at least one item always spilling over onto the next day's agenda. From September to November, "Buy plane ticket for Christmas" floated from list to list to list.

The last item puzzles him: Pedro. Pedro must be the gardener. He 131 observes the accretion of names, the arbitrary specifics that give a sense of his mother's life. He could make a list of his own selves: the child, the adolescent, the promiscuous faggot son, and finally the good son, settled, relatively successful. But the divisions wouldn't work; he is today and will always be the child being licked by the dog, the boy on the floor with Luis; he will still be everything he is ashamed of. The other lists—the lists of things done and undone—tell their own truth: that his life is measured more properly in objects than in stages. He knows himself as "jump rope," "book," "sunglasses," "underwear."

"Tell me about your family, Wayne," Mrs. Campbell says that 132 night, as they drive toward town. They are going to see an Esther Williams movie at the local revival house: an underwater musical, populated by mermaids, underwater Rockettes.

"My father was a lawyer," Wayne says. "He had an office in 133 Queens, with a neon sign. I think he's probably the only lawyer in the world who had a neon sign. Anyway, he died when I was ten. My mother never remarried. She lives in Queens. Her great claim to fame is that when she was twenty-two she went on 'The $64,000 Question.' Her category was mystery novels. She made it to sixteen thousand before she got tripped up."

"When I was about ten, I wanted you to go on 'Jeopardy,' " Neil 134 says to his mother. "You really should have, you know. You would have won."

"You certainly loved 'Jeopardy,' " Mrs. Campbell says. "You used 135 to watch it during dinner. Wayne, does your mother work?"

"No," he says. "She lives off investments." 136

"You're both only children," Mrs. Campbell says. Neil wonders if 137 she is ruminating on the possible connection between that coincidence and their "alternative life style."

The movie theater is nearly empty. Neil sits between Wayne and 138 his mother. There are pillows on the floor at the front of the theater, and a cat is prowling over them. It casts a monstrous shadow every now and then on the screen, disturbing the sedative effect of water ballet. Like a teen-ager, Neil cautiously reaches his arm around Wayne's shoulder. Wayne takes his hand immediately. Next to them, Neil's mother breathes in, out, in, out. Neil timorously moves his other arm and lifts it behind his mother's neck. He does not look at her, but he can tell from her breathing that she senses what he is doing. Slowly, carefully, he lets his hand drop on her shoulder; it twitches spasmodically, and he jumps, as if he had received an electric shock. His mother's quiet breathing is broken by a gasp; even Wayne notices. A sudden brightness on the screen illuminates the panic in her eyes, Neil's arm frozen above her, about to fall again. Slowly, he lowers his arm until his fingertips touch her skin, the fabric of her dress. He has gone too far to go back now; they are all too far.

Wayne and Mrs. Campbell sink into their seats, but Neil remains 139 stiff, holding up his arms, which rest on nothing. The movie ends, and they go on sitting just like that.

"I'm old," Mrs. Campbell says later, as they drive back home. "I 140 remember when those films were new. Your father and I went to one on our first date. I loved them, because I could pretend that those women underwater were flying—they were so graceful. They really took advantage of Technicolor in those days. Color was something to appreciate. You can't know what it was like to see a color movie for the first time, after years of black-and-white. It's like trying to explain the surprise of snow to an East coaster. Very little is new anymore, I fear."

Neil would like to tell her about his own nostalgia, but how can he 141 explain that all of it revolves around her? The idea of her life before he was born pleases him. "Tell Wayne how you used to look like Esther Williams," he asks her.

She blushes. "I was told I looked like Esther Williams, but really 142 more like Gene Tierney," she says. "Not beautiful, but interesting. I like to think I had a certain magnetism."

"You still do," Wayne says, and instantly recognizes the wrong- 143 ness of his comment. Silence and a nervous laugh indicate that he has not yet mastered the family vocabulary.

When they get home, the night is once again full of the sound of 144 crickets. Mrs. Campbell picks up a flashlight and calls the dogs. "Abbylucyferny, Abbylucyferny," she shouts, and the dogs amble from their various corners. She pushes them out the door to the back yard and follows them. Neil follows her. Wayne follows Neil, but hovers on the porch. Neil walks behind her as she tramps through the garden. She holds out her flashlight, and snails slide from behind bushes, from under rocks, to where she stands. When the snails become visible, she crushes them underfoot. They make a wet, cracking noise, like eggs being broken.

"Nights like this," she says, "I think of children without pants on, 145 in hot South American countries. I have nightmares about tanks rolling down our street."

"The weather's never like this in New York," Neil says. "When it's 146 hot, it's humid and sticky. You don't want to go outdoors."

"I could never live anywhere else but here. I think I'd die. I'm too 147 used to the climate."

"Don't be silly." 148

"No, I mean it," she says. "I have adjusted too well to the 149 weather."

The dogs bark and howl by the fence. "A cat, I suspect," she says. 150 She aims her flashlight at a rock, and more snails emerge—uncountable numbers, too stupid to have learned not to trust light.

"I know what you were doing at the movie," she says. 151

"What?" 152

"I know what you were doing." 153

"What? I put my arm around you." 154

"I'm sorry, Neil," she says. "I can only take so much. Just so 155 much."

"What do you mean?" he says. "I was only trying to show affec- 156 tion."

"Oh, affection—I know about affection." 157

He looks up at the porch, sees Wayne moving toward the door, 158 trying not to listen.

"What do you mean?" Neil says to her. 159

She puts down the flashlight and wraps her arms around herself. 160 "I remember when you were a little boy," she says. "I remember, and I have to stop remembering. I wanted you to grow up happy. And I'm very tolerant, very understanding. But I can only take so much."

His heart seems to have risen into his throat. "Mother," he says, "I 161 think you know my life isn't your fault. But for God's sake, don't say that your life is my fault."

"It's not a question of fault," she says. She extracts a Kleenex from 162 her pocket and blows her nose. "I'm sorry, Neil. I guess I'm just an old woman with too much on her mind and not enough to do." She laughs halfheartedly. "Don't worry. Don't say anything," she says. "Abbylucyferny, Abbylucyferny, time for bed!"

He watches her as she walks toward the porch, silent and regal. 163 There is the pad of feet, the clinking of dog tags as the dogs run for the house.

He was twelve the first time she saw him march in a parade. He 164 played the tuba, and as his elementary-school band lumbered down the streets of their then small town she stood on the sidelines and waved. Afterward, she had taken him out for ice cream. He spilled some on his red uniform, and she swiped at it with a napkin. She had been there for him that day, as well as years later, at that more memorable parade; she had been there for him every day.

Somewhere over Iowa, a week later, Neil remembers this scene, 165 remembers other days, when he would find her sitting in the dark, crying. She had to take time out of her own private sorrow to appease his anxiety. "It was part of it," she told him later. "Part of being a mother."

"The scariest thing in the world is the thought that you could un- 166
knowingly ruin someone's life," Neil tells Wayne. "Or even change
someone's life. I hate the thought of having such control. I'd make a
rotten mother."

"You're crazy," Wayne says. "You have this great mother, and all 167
you do is complain. I know people whose mothers have disowned
them."

"Guilt goes with the territory," Neil says.   168

"Why?" Wayne asks, perfectly seriously.   169

Neil doesn't answer. He lies back in his seat, closes his eyes, imag- 170
ines he grew up in a house in the mountains of Colorado, surrounded
by snow—endless white snow on hills. No flat places, and no trees;
just white hills. Every time he has flown away, she has come into his
mind, usually sitting alone in the dark, smoking. Today she is outside
at dusk, skimming leaves from the pool.

"I want to get a dog," Neil says.   171

Wayne laughs. "In the city? It'd suffocate."   172

The hum of the airplane is druglike, dazing, "I want to stay with 173
you a long time," Neil says.

"I know." Imperceptibly, Wayne takes his hand.   174

"It's very hot there in the summer, too. You know, I'm not think- 175
ing about my mother now."

"It's O.K."   176

For a moment, Neil wonders what the stewardess or the old 177
woman on the way to the bathroom will think, but then he laughs and
relaxes.

Later, the plane makes a slow circle over New York City, and on it 178
two men hold hands, eyes closed, and breathe in unison.

QUESTIONS

1.   After the scene in the movie theater with Neil and Wayne, Mrs.
Campbell says, "I can only take so much" (paragraphs 155 and 160);
what is it that she objects to, and why? Discuss Leavitt's portrayal of
Mrs. Campbell's complex attitude towards her son's homosexuality.

2.   Neil says to Wayne on their way back to New York that "guilt goes
with the territory" (paragraph 168). What does Neil still feel guilty
about? How do you think that Neil's attitude towards his own homosexuality changes in the story?

3.   Compare Neil's experience bringing Wayne home to meet his
mother with your own experience introducing a boyfriend or girlfriend to your family. To what extent do you think that the tension in
the Campbell household is independent of Neil's homosexuality?

THINKING ABOUT SEXUAL ORIENTATION AND DIVERSITY

1. Discuss similarities and differences between (a) Walker's definition of "womanist" and Brownmiller's definition of femininity, and (b) Bly's and Kinsman's concepts of masculinity.

2. Compare and contrast the ways that Rodriguez and White view the relationship of gay men to the traditional heterosexual American family. Do you think that White would dispute Rodriguez's view that "homosexuality is a deep brotherhood but does not involve domestic life" (paragraph 26)? To what extent might White and Rodriguez agree about the subversive nature of gay sexuality?

3. In response to former Vice President Dan Quayle's view that homosexuality is "mostly a choice," Rodriguez says that it "never felt like a choice to me" (paragraph 2). Compare the views of White, Kovattana, and Clausen on the issue of whether homosexuality is more a choice ("sexual preference") or a compulsion ("sexual orientation").

4. Using Kovattana's format and with specific references to the other selections, write (a) "Five Good Reasons to Be a Gay Male" from the viewpoint of Rodriguez; (b) "Five Good Reasons to Be a Gay Male" from the viewpoint of White; (c) "Five Good Reasons to Be a Bisexual" from the viewpoint of Clausen; or (d) "Five Good Reasons to Be a Straight Male [or Female]." You might divide these perspectives among your group or class and then compare your essays.

5. Clausen explores in some depth the issue of sexual and personal identity through "the dilemma of terminology" (paragraph 30) or how to label herself. What do Rodriguez and White say or imply about the labels "gay" and "homosexual"? How do you think Clausen would respond to their attitudes towards these labels?

6. How might Rodriguez analyze Leavitt's story as a test case for his views about the relationship of homosexuality to American "family values"? Based on your interpretation of his intentions in the story, how might Leavitt respond to this analysis?

7. How might White analyze Leavitt's story as a test case for his views about gay relationships and gay sexuality? Based on your interpretation of his intentions in the story, how might Leavitt respond to this analysis?

Exploring Additional Sources

8. Based on their essays, imagine Jan Clausen or Kit Yuen Quan ("The Girl Who Wouldn't Sing," page 118) on the planet Whileaway, the setting for the story "When It Changed" by Joanna Russ (page 38). Rewrite one of Russ's scenes, or create a new scene, integrating one of these characters. How might the other women and the men react to her, and how might she respond in this context?

9. Starting with books and references by Susan Brownmiller or Robert Bly, research and write about changing conceptions of femininity or masculinity in the last decade.

10. Test out a particular claim made by Rodriguez, White, Kovattana, or Clausen about gay relationships or gay sexuality in studies by social scientists published in books and in journals such as *The Journal of Homosexuality* or *GLQ (Gay Lesbian Quarterly): A Journal of Lesbian and Gay Studies.*

11. Several writers in this chapter mention the way that gay or lesbian culture cuts across ethnic and/or class distinctions, yet we hear little in the mainstream media about homosexuality in ethnic minority groups. Explore gay and lesbian issues in one such group. Interview members of this group if possible, and look for relevant articles in magazines and journals. How do this group's concerns compare with those of white, middle- or upper-class gay and lesbian people?

12. As you probably know, some people oppose homosexuality on moral or religious grounds, and several conservative political organizations and religious groups—such as the Traditional Values Coalition referred to by Kovattana—have mobilized around this issue. Write a research-based essay in which you (a) explore moral or religious arguments against homosexuality; (b) examine the history, purpose, and political agenda of a conservative group like the Traditional Values Coalition; or (c) take a position on a current or historical policy proposal involving gay rights in your city, county, or state.

13. Research the background and application of the Clinton Administration's new policy, instituted in 1993, about gays and lesbians serving in the U.S. military, and argue your own position on the controversy.

14. Interview members and leaders of a gay or lesbian student group at your school or a nearby college or university; find out what their concerns are about gays and lesbians on campus or in your community. If possible, attend some meetings of gay organizations or events sponsored by them. Choose a controversial issue, such as the creation of a Gay and Lesbian Studies program or the use of student fees to increase gay and lesbian support services, and write an opinion piece for a campus publication. Follow this up with a specific policy or school legislative proposal addressed to the appropriate administrators or student leaders.

15. Write a literary research paper about the fiction of David Leavitt, Edmund White, Jan Clausen, or another gay or lesbian writer. Study several works by the writer and find an analytical angle, thematic or stylistic, that interests you. Test your analysis against some critical secondary sources.

PART THREE

ENCOUNTERING GLOBAL DIVERSITY

Emphasizing the world's increasing economic interdependence and electronic interconnectedness, the "global economy" and the international "information highway" have become media catch-phrases of the 1990s. The athletic shoes you buy today, made by a multinational company, are likely the product of design, materials, assembly, and marketing across several continents. Financial markets in the United States are affected by stock prices in Japan and interest rates in Germany. Transnational companies and the world's financial markets now exchange information globally at lightning speed. Academic researchers consult databases and collaborate with far-flung colleagues on the Internet, a web of international computer networks; they are being joined by millions of new subscribers to electronic discussion groups and other network resources, hooked into the Internet by telephone modems. Anyone with a television set can watch distant events unfold in his or her own living room, thanks to satellite links and "minicams." Among such events, the 1991 Gulf War will be remembered as the first war to be telecast from beginning to end.

All this cutting-edge communication and interactivity—the so-called "Global Village" effect—has brought new importance and resonance to some very old problems: How well can we understand and get along with our neighbors? What can we learn from other people about ourselves or about how to make our lives better? How should the resources of the "Village" be used, shared, or divided?

We cannot understand fully the rapidly increasing cultural diversity in the United States that is explored in Chapters 1 through 8 of *Encountering Cultures* without placing this diversity in a global context. All Americans know that they live in a wealthy and powerful country, even if many Americans don't share in that wealth or power. It's a truism that people come here from other places seeking opportunity, seeking to live "the American way of life." This country wields unprecedented military power—and with only 5 percent of the world's population, routinely consumes 25 percent or more of the world's resources. Does preserving that way of life complement or conflict with the global responsibilities that such power carries? When individual Americans travel abroad—for business, pleasure, service, or study—to what extent does the personal and cultural baggage they carry color the quality of their experience?

To think clearly and critically about cross-cultural and international relations, we must explore these connections between who "we" are and what happens in the U.S. and who "they" are and what happens in the rest of the world. The essays and stories in these chapters follow American travelers, writers, expatriates, social scientists, and social critics across national borders and overseas to every continent.

"The journey promised by the [travel] posters and brochures is a trip into everyone's imaginary past," writes Alice Bloom in Chapter 9; the natives in the posters are "costumed as attractions" and "character dolls." Walker Percy contends that preconceptions such as these, gleaned from the brochures and the "experts," can rob us of our ability to experience new places authentically. The other travelers in Chapter 9, such as Chitra Divakaruni's fictional tourists in Italy and John Updike's nameless visitor to Venezuela, carry various kinds and amounts of baggage from home.

When we encounter international cultures, the lines between preconceptions, stereotypes, and prejudices may be fuzzy. The dictionary defines stereotypes as "conventional, formulaic, and oversimplified conceptions or images" and prejudices as "adverse judgments or opinions formed beforehand or without knowledge or examination of the facts." For example, according to Margaret K. Nydell, "Arabs feel that they are often portrayed in the Western media as excessively wealthy, irrational, sensuous, and violent." Other writers in Chapter 10 test the boundaries of stereotyping in interpersonal encounters, like that between the daughter of a CIA agent in Chile and her Marxist teacher in Lucia Berlin's story "Good and Bad."

When Americans encounter Third World countries, where most of the world's people live in relative poverty, the gaps in understanding may be the widest, and bridging those gaps may be the most momentous challenge. In Chapter 11, Sarah Streed writes about how she volunteered for the Peace Corps in Morocco intending "to help . . . to change things . . . to participate in a cross-cultural interaction that wasn't tainted by idealism or colonialism" but soon became disillusioned by a reality for which she felt unprepared. Nothing could have prepared the Professor, in Paul Bowles' nightmarish tale "A Distant Episode," for the fate he meets with a nomadic Saharan tribe. Maya Angelou, on the contrary, seems to feel that she successfully transcends cultural boundaries to become "accepted as an African" in a Ghanaian village.

"If the First World is not invariably corrupting the Third," writes Pico Iyer in Chapter 12, "we are sometimes apt to leap to the opposite conclusion: that the Third World, in fact, is hustling the First." With the end of the Cold War that dominated international relations since World War II, the United States and other Western industrial powers would seem to be uniquely positioned to influence global affairs. The extent and quality of that influence is, however, highly controversial. Is the U.S., as Patrick Glynn suggests, engaged "in the effort to posit a new world order based on common democratic values"? Or is the "new world order," as Noam Chomsky suggests, merely "part of the rhetorical background" for what is actually "persistent U.S. opposition to democracy"?

How people living in the U.S. and other wealthy countries respond to the questions raised in these chapters may largely determine the course of global events in the 21st century. If you consider thoughtfully your own attitudes about these difficult issues before you read the essays and stories that follow, you can create a framework in which to approach, evaluate, and write about these selections. For example:

Leaving Home (Chapter 9). Write about your own experience going to an unfamiliar place or encountering an unfamiliar way of life, whether abroad or close to home. Talk to classmates about the relationship between your expectations and preconceptions and the reality that you experienced.

Encountering Stereotypes (Chapter 10). Make lists of stereotypes you hold about people of other nationalities or ethnicities; list stereotypes that you hold, or that you believe other people hold, about Americans. Discuss your lists with a partner, small group, or entire class. What sources can you identify for these beliefs?

Meeting the Third World (Chapter 11). If you have traveled to or come from one of the developing nations of Africa, Asia, or Latin America, how would you describe the attitudes you encountered towards Americans and other "Westerners"? If you have no direct experience with the Third World, what are your perceptions of these attitudes from your reading or exposure to popular media like television or movies? What do you think Americans can bring to the Third World?

Americans in the New World Order (Chapter 12). What does the phrase "new world order" mean to you? How influential—politically, culturally, economically—do you think the United States is in the world? What roles are appropriate for individual Americans to play in other cultures? What roles are appropriate for the United States as a nation to play in the affairs of other countries?

9

LEAVING HOME

The Natives in the Posters

ALICE BLOOM

A study of travel posters and brochures, which in the process of setting dates and buying tickets always precedes a trip, shows us, by projection into these pictured, toothy, tourist bodies, having some gorgeous piece of ingestion: the yellow beach, the mossy blue ruin, a dinner table laden with food and red wine of the region, dancing, skiing, golfing, shopping, waving to roadside natives as our rented car sails by, as though we only go to play, as though all we do here at home is work, as though, for two or four weeks abroad, we seek regression.

Also in the posters, but as part of the landscape, there are the natives—whether Spanish, Greek, Irish, etc.—costumed as attractions, performing in bouzouki or bag-pipe bands, or doing some picturesque and nonindustrial piece of work such as fishing, weaving, selling colorful cheap goods in open-air markets, herding sheep or goats. The journey promised by the posters and brochures is a trip into everyone's imaginary past: one's own, drained of the normal childhood content of fear, death, space, hurt, abandonment, perplexity, and so forth, now presented as the salesmen think we think it should have been: one in which we only ate, slept, and played in the eternal sun under the doting care of benevolent elders. . . .

The natives in the posters (are they Swiss, Mexican, Chilean, Turkish models?) are happy parent figures, or character dolls, and their faces, like the faces of the good parents we are supposed to have dreamed, show them pleased with their own lot, busy but not too busy with a job that they obviously like, content with each other, and warmly indulgent of our need to play, to be fed good, clean food on time, and to be tucked into a nice bed at the end of our little day. They are the childhood people that also existed in early grammar-school readers, and nowhere else: adults in your neighborhood, in the identifiable costumes of their humble tasks, transitional-object people, smiling milkman, friendly aproned store-owner in his small friendly store,

399

happy mailman happy to bring your happy mail, happy mommy, icons who make up a six-year-old's school-enforced dream town, who enjoy doing their nonindustrial, unmysterious tasks: mail, milk, red apple, cooky, just for you, so you can learn to decipher: See, Jip, see.

—FROM "ON A GREEK HOLIDAY," IN *THE HUDSON REVIEW*, 1983

The Traveler's Dilemma

CLAUDE LÉVI-STRAUSS

I should have liked to live in the age of *real* travel, when the spectacle on offer had not yet been blemished, contaminated, and confounded; then I could have seen Lahore not as I saw it, but as it appeared to Bernier, Tavernier, Manucci. . . . There's no end, of course, to such conjectures. When was the right moment to see India? At what period would the study of the Brazilian savage have yielded the purest satisfaction and the savage himself been at his peak? Would it have been better to have arrived at Rio in the eighteenth century, with Bougainville, or in the sixteenth, with Léry and Thevet? With every decade that we traveled further back in time, I could have saved another costume, witnessed another festivity, and come to understand another system of belief. But I'm too familiar with the texts not to know that this backward movement would also deprive me of much information, many curious facts and objects, that would enrich my meditations. The paradox is irresoluble: the less one culture communicates with another, the less likely they are to be corrupted, one by the other; but, on the other hand, the less likely it is, in such conditions, that the respective emissaries of these cultures will be able to seize the richness and significance of their diversity. The alternative is inescapable: either I am a traveler in ancient times, and faced with a prodigious spectacle which would be almost entirely unintelligible to me and might, indeed, provoke me to mockery or disgust; or I am a traveler of our own day, hastening in search of a vanished reality. In either case I am the loser—and more heavily than one might suppose; for today, as I go groaning among the shadows, I miss, inevitably, the spectacle that is now taking shape. My eyes, or perhaps my degree of humanity, do not equip me to witness that spectacle; and in the centuries to come, when another traveler revisits this same place, he too may groan aloud at the disappearance of much that I should have set down, but cannot. I am the victim of a double infirmity: what I see is an affliction to me; and what I do not see, a reproach.

—FROM *TRISTES TROPIQUES*, 1955

Fifteen Types of Travelers

PHILIP L. PEARCE

Traveler Category	The Five Clearest Role-Related Behaviors (in order of relative importance)
Tourist	Takes photos, buys souvenirs, goes to famous places, stays briefly in one place, does not understand the local people
Traveler	Stays briefly in one place, experiments with local food, goes to famous places, takes photos, explores places privately
Holidaymaker	Takes photos, goes to famous places, is alienated from the local society, buys souvenirs, contributes to the visited economy
Jet-setter	Lives a life of luxury, concerned with social status, seeks sensual pleasures, prefers interacting with people of his/her own kind, goes to famous places
Businessperson	Concerned with social status, contributes to the economy, does not take photos, prefers interacting with people of his/her own kind, lives a life of luxury
Migrant	Has language problems, prefers interacting with people of his/her own kind, does not understand the local people, does not live a life of luxury, does not exploit the local people
Conservationist	Interested in the environment, does not buy souvenirs, does not exploit the local people, explores places privately, takes photos
Explorer	Explores places privately, interested in the environment, takes physical risks, does not buy souvenirs, keenly observes the visited society
Missionary	Does not buy souvenirs, searches for the meaning of life, does not live in luxury, does not seek sensual pleasures, keenly observes the visited society
Overseas student	Experiments with local food, does not exploit the people, takes photos, keenly observes the visited society, takes physical risks
Anthropologist	Keenly observes the visited society, explores places privately, interested in the environment, does not buy souvenirs, takes photos
Hippie	Does not buy souvenirs, does not live a life of luxury, is not concerned with social status, does not take photos, does not contribute to the economy
International athlete	Is not alienated from own society, does not exploit the local people, does not understand the local people, explores places privately, searches for the meaning of life
Overseas journalist	Takes photos, keenly observes the visited society, goes to famous places, takes physical risks, explores places privately
Religious pilgrim	Searches for the meaning of life, does not live a life of luxury, is not concerned with social status, does not exploit the local people, does not buy souvenirs

—FROM *THE SOCIAL PSYCHOLOGY OF TOURIST BEHAVIOR*, 1982

Tourists

CHITRA DIVAKARUNI

The heat is like a fist between the eyes. The man and woman wan- 1
der down a narrow street of flies and stray cats looking for the
Caracalla Baths. The woman wears a cotton dress embroidered
Mexican style with bright flowers. The man wears Rayban glasses and
knee-length shorts. They wipe at the sweat with white handkerchiefs
because they have used up all the Kleenex they brought.

The woman is afraid they are lost. She holds on tightly to the man's 2
elbow and presses her purse into her body. The purse is red leather,
very new, bought by him outside the Uffizi museum after a half-hour
of earnest bargaining. She wonders what they are doing in this airless
alley with the odor of stale urine rising all around them, what they are
doing in Rome, what they are doing in Europe. The man tries to walk
tall and confident, shoulders lifted, but she can tell he is nervous about
the youths in tight levis lounging against the fountain, eyeing, he
thinks, their Leica. In his halting guidebook Italian he asks the passersby—there aren't many because of the heat—*Dov'e terme di Caracalla?*
and then, *Dov'e la stazione?* But they stare at him and do not seem to understand.

The woman is tired. It distresses her to not know where she is, to 3
have to trust herself to the truth of strangers, their indecipherable
mouths, their quick eyes, their fingers each pointing in a different direction, *eccolo, il treno per Milano, la torre pendente, la cattedrale, il palazzo
ducale.*[1] She wants to go to the bathroom, to get a drink, to find a taxi.
She asks if it is O.K. to wash her face in the fountain, but he shakes his
head. It's not hygienic, and besides, a man with a pock-marked face

---

[1]*Eccolo, il treno per Milano, la torre pendente, la cattedrale, il palazzo ducale:* Here it is, the train to
Milan, the Leaning Tower, the cathedral, the duke's palace. (Ed.)

Originally from India, **Chitra Divakaruni** is a poet and teacher of
composition and creative writing at Foothill Community College in
Los Altos, California. She is the author of *Black Candle: Poems about
Women from India, Pakistan, and Bangladesh* (1991) and editor of
Multitude: Cross-Cultural Readings for Writers (1993), a composition
anthology similar to *Encountering Cultures*. This story—of a length
often called a "short-short story" or "prose poem"—first appeared in
The House on Via Gombito: Writing by North American Women Abroad
(1991), edited by Madelon Sprengnether and C.W. Truesdale.

and black teeth has been watching them from a doorway, and he wants to get out of the alley as soon as he can.

The woman sighs, gets out a crumpled tour brochure from her 4 purse and fans herself and then him with it. They are walking faster now, she stumbling a bit in her sandals. She wishes they were back in the hotel or better still in her own cool garden. She is sure that in her absence the Niles Lilies are dying in spite of the automatic sprinkler system, and the gophers have taken over the lawn. Is it worth it, even for the colors in the Sistine Chapel, the curve of Venus' throat as she rises from the sea? The green statue of the boy with the goose among the rosemary in a Pompeii courtyard? She makes a mental note to pick up some gopher poison on the way back from the airport.

They turn a corner onto a broader street. Surely this is the one that 5 will lead them back to the Circo Massimo and the subway. The man lets out a deep breath, starts to smile. Then suddenly, footsteps, a quick clattering on the cobbles behind. They both stiffen, remembering. Yesterday one of the tourists in their hotel was mugged outside the Villa Borghesi. Maybe they should have taken the bus tour after all. He tightens his hands into fists, his face into a scowl. Turns. But it is only a dog, its pink tongue hanging, its ribs sticking out of its scabby coat. It stops and observes them, wary, ready for flight. Then the woman touches his hand. *Look, look.* From where they are standing they can see into someone's backyard. Sheets and pillowcases drying whitely in the sun, a palm scattering shade over blocks of marble from a broken column, a big bougainvillea that covers the crumbling wall. A breeze comes up, lifting their hair. Sudden smell of rain. They stand there, man and woman and dog, watching the bright purple flowers tumble over the broken bricks.

QUESTIONS

1. Describe the effect for you of the tourists being referred to only as "the woman" and "the man." Whose perspective is the story told from? From clues in the story, what do you infer about where the woman and man are from and what their relationship is like?

2. Identify the sources of the couple's anxiety. What similar experiences have you had when you've visited an unfamiliar place? What seems to change at the end, when they "see into someone's backyard"?

The Errand

NORA REZA

Lara looked up from the *Time* magazine she was reading. She was 1
in a part of Teheran that was new to her. The modern glass buildings,
wide boulevards, and the view of the mountains had disappeared.
Everything was a dusty clay color. Busses streaming black diesel
smoke screeched around a circle. "Where are we?" she asked, but Mr.
Ali, who was going very fast, did not answer except to mutter under
his breath. Most likely he had planned to have the morning to himself,
and was disgruntled about having to deliver Lara to her aunt.
"Madame Leila?" she reminded him.

"Yes, yes," he nodded. "Soon." He turned the car into a cobbled 2
street, one with a *jube* of dirty water running right down the middle.
"Five minutes," he said, holding up spread fingers. Lara watched him
slip into an alley decorated with the droppings of donkeys and half-
starved dogs. Mr. Ali was so skinny and bent, he resembled his
shadow as it crept along the wall, wavered and disappeared.

Instantly the Mercedes was surrounded by a band of children, who 3
touched the windows, fenders and antenna, regarding Lara with filmy
eyes and faces caulked with dust. Five minutes passed. The car grew
hot. She fanned herself with the magazine, smiled at the children,
looked for Mr. Ali to return at any moment and grew impatient when
he did not. Some women clad in black veils sat in doorways and
watched her. She grew uncomfortable under their gaze. The children
clamored. She tried to read her *Time,* which contained a short article
about the Shah's "White Revolution," how he was giving his land
away to the poor. The children, dressed in tattered rags, stretched out
their hands for change. Soon she was shrugging and saying she had no
more. One boy wanted to wash the windshield and she said no, fear-
ing Mr. Ali's wrath. A couple of older boys came down the street and
looked her over. They made lewd smacking sounds with their lips.
Lara ignored them and they went away.

Nora Reza studied painting and psychology at Stanford University
and now lives in Minnesota, where she is writing an autobiographical
novel. In both her painting and her writing she explores her Persian-
Irish cultural background. This story (like the previous one by
Divakaruni) appeared in *The House on Via Gombito: Writing by North
American Women Abroad* (1991), edited by Madelon Sprengnether and
C.W. Truesdale.

She was, it appeared, in one of the slums of south Teheran, far 4
from her aunt's house. She looked at her watch. An hour had passed.
Her thin dress was wet with perspiration. The children stepped back
when she opened the door. The boys whistled. One threw a small
stone near her foot. She glared at him. He covered his face laughing.
The other children began laughing too. They danced around her. Lara
suppressed a smile. She wanted to remain as irate as possible for Mr.
Ali. He had no right to bring her here and leave her to swelter in the
hot car. She planned to scold him in the same way she had heard Mrs.
Aram scold him. She saw herself standing imperiously before him.
"Take me to my aunt's house this instant!" she would say.

There was a cistern nearby where women were washing clothes. 5
As she passed them they stopped their chatter and stared at her bare
arms and legs. The children followed her. Their tiny sticklike shadows
criss-crossed her own. She felt more and more angry with Mr. Ali.
Facing the twisting alleyways she didn't know which way to turn. She
walked confidently ahead, thinking to fool the children. She knew
where she was going. All of the windows and doors were now shut
against the noon sun. She turned a corner. The alley looked the same.
Where was he? The stupid man! Soon she was lost in a maze of alleyways. The children followed her, laughing and pointing, "Miss, go
down here. Miss, try this one." She refused their directions, knowing
they were trying to trick her. The sun was unbearable and she longed
to be back in Shemiran, beneath the mountains, on the Arams' cool,
flower-strewn patio. She wanted a glass of water or coke. She turned
into a dead end street and came back without seeing Mr. Ali.

The little boy who had thrown the stone at her stopped before a 6
door. Shyly he pointed at it. Lara knocked. The door was opened by a
girl, about twelve, with a checkered scarf wrapped around her head.
She stepped aside to let Lara in. Lara peered into the dark. She was relieved to see Mr. Ali's scullcap, in a backroom, among a crowd of others. His heavy pinstripe suit, which had once belonged to Mr. Aram,
hung ludicrously on his scarecrow body. She entered. On her left,
against a wall, two boys were stretched out asleep on a wooden bed,
made up of rough boards. To her right a table was piled with dry clay
figures and pots. On the floor was a naked child. Among the child's
bare legs and the folds of a dirty blanket some slimy furred creatures
moved. Lara pulled back. Then she saw that the animals were kittens,
recently-born. The child, his nose running, smiled up at her.

She stood there, wondering what to do. She looked at the figures 7
and pots on the table more closely. The figures depicted couples in intercourse. The freestanding ones were phalluses and vulvas. She
looked away, amazed that there were such things in Iran.

Mr. Ali saw her and called, "I've come," which meant "I'm com- 8
ing."

The girl with the checkered head scarf said, "Please enter, Miss." 9
She led Lara to Mr. Ali. Several people stood up and bowed, clearing
a path for her. Lara nodded to them, and made little bowing gestures
as she stepped through the small crowded room. "You're welcome,
Miss," they murmured. "Please . . ." Mr. Ali was near a bed, where a
girl was lying. The girl's hennaed hair was tangled, a scarf had fallen
down around her neck. Her skin was pale and streaked. There were
deep blue shadows under her eyes. The cloth that covered her was
spattered in blood. Oh, God, Lara thought. She's sick. She's dying.
Near the bed was a pan filled with more flesh and blood. When Lara
saw this she felt scared. There was a heavy sick odor in the room. It
was hot and flies were everywhere. An old woman was on her knees
cleaning up. She called, "Miss, dear, come here," and gestured for Lara
to come closer. Obediently Lara stepped forward, averting her eyes
from the bowl of flesh and blood and the bed. The woman lifted up a
cardboard box, which Lara recognized as one of Mr. Aram's wine car-
tons. Lara looked into it. "This hour," the old woman said, smiling.

"Beautiful," Lara answered, although the baby, born while she sat 10
out in the car, looked not much different from the wet rags in the bowl.
The others closed around Lara, regarding her with expectant eyes. She
had no idea what to do. Then the girl who had let her into the room
appeared with a glass of tea. "Thank you," said Lara, and accepted the
tea, which was so hot she could barely hold it. Lara turned her eyes
again to the new mother, a girl who looked not much older than herself. "Boy?" Lara asked, pointing to the box. The mother regarded Lara
dully, and made no answer.

"*Na, dauktar,*" the old midwife said. "Next time, boy." 11

"Congratulations," Lara said. The midwife lifted the ugly wet 12
creature out of the box. For a moment Lara feared that she would be
asked to take it. Instead the midwife put the baby at the mother's
breast. The mother turned her head away and moaned, "*Na . . .*" The
baby made a few miserable sounds. The midwife grinned, as though
all was going well.

Lara took a step back. She turned to Mr. Ali. "Yours?" she asked, 13
indicating the mother and the baby.

He shook his head, but the midwife understood. "*Pedare buzurg,*" 14
she said. Mr. Ali was the grandfather, but of the girl or the baby Lara
wasn't sure. The mother was Lara's age, sixteen. This was her first
child. Her labor had ended with the birth of a daughter, which perhaps accounted for the subdued atmosphere.

Lara said goodbye and walked through the path they had cleared 15
for her. In the front room she followed Mr. Ali past the table of clay ob-

jects, which, in the yellow light of the open door, looked grotesque and lifeless. The little boy still lay on the blanket, squeezing a kitten that desperately sought to get away. In the car, Mr. Ali did not speak. Lara wanted to convey to him that she would not get him in trouble, she would not tell anyone where he had taken her.

"Your daughter is pretty. The baby is pretty," she said after 16 awhile. Mr. Ali grunted and wiped the sweat from his face, and continued to speed and curse his way through traffic. Perhaps he thought that by delivering Lara to her aunt instantly she would forget the little errand he had kept her waiting for.

QUESTIONS

1.   Describe Lara's cultural status or position in Iran. Where do you think she's from? Where does she live, and under what conditions, at the time the story takes place? How is she treated by the people attending the birth?

2.   How would you characterize Lara's relationship with Mr. Ali, and how does this relationship change? Why do you think she decides "that she would not get him in trouble, she would not tell anyone where he had taken her" (paragraph 15)?

Traveling Alone in Mexico

MARY MORRIS

Women who travel as I travel are dreamers. Our lives seem to be 1
lives of endless possibility. Like readers of romances we think that anything can happen to us at any time. We forget that this is not our real
life—our life of domestic details, work pressures, attempts and failures
at human relations. We keep moving. From anecdote to anecdote, from
hope to hope. Around the next bend something new will befall us.
Nostalgia has no place for the woman traveling alone. Our motion
is forward, whether by train or daydream. Our sights are on the horizon, across strange terrain, vast desert, unfordable rivers, impenetrable
ice peaks.

I wanted to keep going forever, to never stop, that morning when 2
the truck picked me up at five a.m. It was like a drug in me. As a traveler I can achieve a kind of high, a somewhat altered state of consciousness. I think it must be what athletes feel. I am transported out of
myself, into another dimension in time and space. While the journey is
on buses and across land, I begin another journey inside my head, a
journey of memory and sensation, of past merging with present, of
time growing insignificant.

My journey was now filled with dreams of other journeys to cool, 3
breezy places. The plateaus of Tibet, the altiplano of Bolivia, cold
places, barren, without tropical splendor. I did not dream of Africa and
its encompassing heat. I longed for white Siberia, for Tierra del Fuego,
the Arctic tundra, vast desolate plains. I longed for what came next.
Whatever the next stop, the next love, the next story might be.

Josh was sitting in the back of the truck when it pulled up to my 4
pension. "I thought you were going to Guatemala City," I said.

Mary Morris is a novelist, short story writer, and travel writer. Her
fiction includes *Vanishing Animals and Other Stories* (1979), *The Bus of
Dreams: Stories* (1985), and *The Waiting Room* (1989). Her most recent
travel memoir is *Wall to Wall: From Beijing to Berlin by Rail* (1991) and
she is editor of *Maiden Voyages: Writings of Women Travelers* (1993).
This selection is from *Nothing to Declare: Memoirs of a Woman Traveling
Alone* (1988), an account of her travels in Mexico and Central America.
"I had grown weary of life in New York and had some money from a
grant," Morris writes about the purpose of her trip. "I went in search
of a place where the land and the people and the time in which they
lived were somehow connected."

"Well," he said, smiling, "there are other ways to get to Panama." 5
He grabbed my duffel and pulled me on. Then we sat across from each
other as we set out through a lush pass in the mountains, bouncing in
the back through a very misty morning, past charging rivers, herds of
cattle and goats, toward the border of Honduras.

At about five-thirty the driver stopped to pick up two women. 6
They were teachers who worked in one-room schoolhouses in the
hills. One of them told us she walked an hour from where the truck
would drop her to her school and she did this twice a day every day.

"You must be exhausted every day," I said. 7

She had a bright smile, sleek black hair, and dark eyes. "Oh, no." 8
She laughed. "The walk is beautiful and I always arrive feeling refreshed."

"You never get tired of it?" I asked, incredulous. 9

"There is always something to see," she said, smiling. At six-thirty, 10
she got off, heading toward the mountains, waving, then disappeared
along a trail.

At seven we reached the frontier and found it closed. We took our 11
bags, waved good-bye to our pickup, and waited for the border to
open and for some other vehicle, which we assumed would material-
ize, to appear. For an hour or so we clomped around, taking pictures
of an enormous cow that was nearby. At last the border opened. "You
want to go into Honduras?" the guard said with a bit of a sneer.

"Yes, we're going to the ruins." I have no idea why I felt the need 12
to say that, but I did.

"Well, if you want to go into Honduras, that's your problem." He 13
stamped our passports just as another minibus arrived, heading for
Copán.

We spent the day at the ruins. We had no plan, really, no sense of 14
whether we would stay there or try to get out of the jungle and to some
city by night. The ruins were fairly deserted and we spent the day
climbing around. We had not gone far when we startled an enormous
blue-black snake that had been asleep. The snake rose up on its side,
then chased us along the path for several feet. I had never been chased
by a snake before and was amazed at how fast it could move. Josh
hurled a stone at it and the snake disappeared into the jungle.

We walked deeper into the jungle and a wasp stung me twice on 15
the knee. Josh scooped wet mud and packed it around the bites. My
knee became very stiff and I thought I couldn't go on, but he coaxed
me and I did.

We came to a pyramid. It was hardly excavated. The steps were 16
broken, stones were covered with moss, but we climbed. My knee

hurt, but I didn't care. We climbed and climbed. It was a very high pyramid and when we reached the top, we were silent. We sat still on the top of this unexcavated pyramid, looking at the tremendous jungle that stretched before us.

I liked Josh. What more can I say. I liked him. I wanted to go with   17 him to Panama. I had only just met him and I hadn't thought it through, but I wanted to go. Thinking about it now, I'm not sure what it was that I liked about him so much—he was, in fact, rather ordinary—but I think it had something to do with the fact that he was an American. He was an intelligent American male and he represented for me all those things that were now missing in my life. He could have dinner with my parents at my father's club. The men would wear suits and ties and discuss the market over Scotch and soda. My mother would wink at me across the table. Later she'd take me aside and say what a nice man he was and how they hoped they'd be seeing more of him.

I thought about Alejandro, sitting in that dark apartment, waiting   18 for my return, telegram in hand, but all I could think about was going on with Josh to Panama. That afternoon as we walked, we spoke of more personal things. I told him I had a boyfriend in Mexico City. He said he had just broken up with a woman in Berkeley.

We checked into the Mayan Copán and had dinner on the patio.   19 Sitting there with Josh in the steam of the jungle brought back to me what until now had seemed farthest away—the hot summer days and nights of Manhattan. Suddenly I found myself longing for a dripping ice cream cone while the plaintive song of a saxophonist echoed up the avenue. I longed for the heat of the pavement, cheap wine during a concert in the park, and black children jumping double-Dutch while illegal aliens sold assorted ices—pineapple, anise, coconut. I wanted to be transplanted, to feel the pace of the city in summer—an afternoon spent at the matinee, a weekend flight to Jones Beach. I even longed for what repulsed me—the garbage, the stench of urine, the homeless, the yellow smogged sky. All the things I swore I'd never miss.

After dinner we sat on the porch of the hotel, drinking rum and   20 Cokes and speaking of our travels. Josh told me about trekking through Afghanistan and hiking across the Khyber Pass, about wanting to walk to Turkistan and getting captured by rebels somewhere along the way. He said that he had talked his way into and out of every situation you could imagine. "But if I were a woman," he said, "I don't know if I'd do it alone."

"It has its ups and downs," I said.   21

"Have you ever had anything bad happen to you?"   22

I shrugged. "Some near-misses, that's all."   23

He sipped his rum contemplatively. "I've heard terrible stories."   24

"Like what?"   25

He leaned over and kissed me on the lips. "I don't want to ruin   26
your evening."

"You may as well tell me now."   27

He pulled his chair closer. "Well, this happened to a friend of a   28
friend of mine. Not someone I really know. I met him once, that's all.
I'm not even sure it happened the way my friend said. This man went
to Turkey with his wife. To Istanbul. He never talks about it, but they
went to Istanbul. It was a kind of second honeymoon. They wanted to
start a family, so anyway, they went on this second honeymoon—"

I reached across, touching his hand. "Just tell me the story." He   29
held onto my fingers and did not let go until he was done.

"All right. So they went. They were at the bazaar one day and his   30
wife wanted to buy a dress. She was a pretty woman, blond. So they
went into a store and after a while he got bored and said he wanted to
take a walk. He said he'd go have a cigarette and be back in half an
hour. They had a little fight about this, but he went anyway. When he
came back, the dress shop was closed and no one was there. So he
thought they'd closed early and he went to the hotel and waited for his
wife to meet him there. But she never went back to the hotel. He
waited and waited, but she never came back. He talked to the police
and the next day they went to the shop, but the people, people he recognized from the day before, said they had never seen the woman and
she'd never been there. He stayed in Istanbul for weeks, but they never
found his wife."

"And he thinks she was kidnapped by the people who owned the   31
dress shop?"

Josh nodded. "Kidnapped. And sold."   32

"Sold?"   33

"That's right. Sold."   34

We sat in silence for a long time, listening to the jungle noises.   35
After a while, Josh pulled me by my hand. "Come on," he said. "Let's
go to sleep."

In the morning we boarded the minibus. The women who got on   36
all had holes cut in their dresses where their nipples hung out and
small children suckled. The men carried machetes, which they checked
with the bus driver by tucking them under his seat. Many of the men
had slash marks on their arms or faces and many were missing fingers
and limbs, so it appeared that this precaution was a necessary one. I
was reminded of the movies about the Wild West, where the gun-
slingers check their guns at the saloon door.

Several hours later we reached La Entrada. Everyone there carried   37
a machete. We went to a bar to have a beer and a man walked in. Both

his hands had been chopped off above the wrist and his nose was missing. "A machete did that," Josh said.

Suddenly I could not bear the thought of spending a moment 38 alone. The story he had told me of the woman in Istanbul stayed in my mind and I knew that having heard it, I'd never be quite the same.

Josh was undecided about which direction he would take and I 39 was undecided as to whether or not I would go with him. I wanted him to ask me. I thought that if he asked me, I'd go. From La Entrada there were buses to either coast and points east and west. The choices were infinite. But Josh had taken a liking to inland Honduras and the guidebook said there were some things to see in a neighboring town called Florida. "Look," Josh said. "How often are you going to be in this part of Honduras?"

"Not often," I said. And we hitched a ride with a farmer in the 40 back of his pickup truck.

Josh had heard about a gas station attendant in Florida who knew 41 everything there was to know about the Mayan ruins in the vicinity.

"I thought you were tired of ruins." 42

"Well, we're here. We may as well make the most of it." 43

We found the gas station attendant and he sent us in the direction 44 of some ruins not far from the border. We crawled around in the heat of the day while Josh tried to decide what kind of people lived in this place. A dog that was skin and bones followed us. I threw him scraps of sandwich, but Josh kept trying to chase the dog away.

Later that night while a tropical breeze blew in through the win- 45 dows of our small room, Josh told me he was going to go to Salvador. I thought to myself how, having lost all sense of proportion, I'd follow this man anywhere, and after about thirty seconds I said, "Mind if I come with you?"

"Not at all," he said. "But what about your boyfriend in Mexico?" 46

"What about him?" 47

"Well, won't he be upset?" 48

"Do you want me to go with you or not?" I asked, pressing the 49 point.

"I want you to do whatever makes you happy," he said. 50

"Well, then I'm going with you." 51

He drifted right to sleep, but I stayed awake. I could not stop 52 thinking about that woman he'd told me about the night before, a captive in some harem, a woman used and tossed aside, trying endlessly to plan her escape. A blonde among dark people. A woman who could not speak their tongue. Perhaps she had been ingenious, learning their ways, and had made a life for herself wherever her prison was. Perhaps she had fallen into the hands of a benevolent sheik who took pity on her, and though his pride would not permit him to release her, he would not abuse her, either.

But I think the scenario is much darker than this. That woman 53 would never be free. She would never return. If it were me, when I realized that rescue wouldn't come, that I would not be found, that I would never go home and would always be a prisoner of men, I would lose my mind. I would die of grief or by my own hand.

In the morning we stood at the crossroads at La Entrada, waiting 54 for the bus for Salvador. Until the bus arrived, I wasn't sure what I was going to do, but as soon as I saw it, kicking up dust, puffing in the distance, I knew what lay before me. When the driver stopped and opened the ancient door, I kissed Josh. "Have a safe journey," I said.

"What? Aren't you coming?" 55

"I'm going to Tegucigalpa." If he begs me, I told myself, I'll go. 56

"Well, whatever suits you." 57

He wasn't begging. He wasn't even asking. "Yes, I guess this suits 58 me." I waved good-bye. Sitting on my duffel in the sun—though dreaming of the way I could have gone with him—I felt sure I was on the right road. About an hour later the bus for Tegucigalpa approached. The bus driver asked me if I was a *gente de la sandía*, a watermelon person. A joke on the Sandinistas, and I said no, I was a tourist from the United States. He nodded and I took a seat in the rear.

It was a big bus this time, heading for the capital. Not long after I 59 boarded a young girl and her father got on, and they sat near the front. After about an hour the bus stopped and the father got off. He kissed his daughter good-bye and waved as the bus drove away. The girl was perhaps thirteen or fourteen and after a few moments she began to cry. She cried uncontrollably and the driver stopped. Women rushed to her, then came away shaking their heads. She was an idiot, one of the women told me. Her father had abandoned her here on this bus. "Too expensive to feed," the man behind me muttered. "Too expensive to keep."

QUESTIONS

1. What attitudes or motivations for travel does Morris reveal in the opening paragraphs? How do you think her experience in this selection measures up to these motivations?

2. Recount Morris's interactions with native people and local culture in Mexico and Honduras. To what extent are men and women portrayed differently in these interactions?

3. Why do you think Josh tells Morris the "white slavery" story? How does she respond? The next day, she changes her mind and decides not to go with Josh to Salvador; how sympathetic are you with her decision?

Venezuela for Visitors

JOHN UPDIKE

All Venezuela, except for the negligible middle class, is divided be- 1
tween the Indians (*los indios*) and the rich (*los ricos*). The Indians are
mostly to be found in the south, amid the muddy tributaries of the
Orinoco and the god-haunted *tepuys* (mesas) that rear their fearsome
mile-high crowns above the surrounding jungle, whereas the rich tend
to congregate in the north, along the sunny littoral, in the burgeoning
metropolis of Caracas, and on the semicircular shores of Lake
Maracaibo, from which their sumptuous black wealth is drawn. The
negligible middle class occupies a strip of arid savanna in the center of
the nation and a few shunned enclaves on the suburban slopes of
Monte Avila.

The Indians, who range in color from mocha to Dentyne, are gen- 2
erally under five feet tall. Their hair style runs to pageboys and severe
bangs, with some tonsures in deference to lice. Neither sex is quite
naked: the males wear around their waists a thong to which their fore-
skins are tied, pulling their penises taut upright; the females, once out
of infancy, suffer such adornments as three pale sticks symmetrically
thrust into their lower faces. The gazes of both sexes are melting,
brown, alert, canny. The visitor, standing among them with his Nikon
FE and L. L. Bean fannypack, is shy at first, but warms to their inquis-
itive touches, which patter and rub across his person with a soft, sandy
insistence unlike both the fumblings of children and the caresses one
Caucasian adult will give another. There is an infectious, wordless ec-
stasy in their touches, and a blank eagerness with yet some parameters
of tact and irony. *These are human presences,* the visitor comes to realize.

John Updike is the author of novels, stories, poetry, essays, and criticism. He is probably best known for his novels exploring middle-
class suburban life in the United States, including *Rabbit, Run* (1960),
A Month of Sundays (1975), and *The Witches of Eastwick* (1984, also
made into a feature film). His fiction has won the Pulitzer Prize, the
National Book Award, and the American Book Award. His nonfiction
has been collected in four books, including, most recently, *Odd Jobs*
(1991). After its publication in *The New Yorker*, "Venezuela for
Visitors" was collected in *Hugging the Shore*, which won the 1984
National Book Critics Circle Award for criticism. "This original piece
of travel writing first appeared in pages of *The New Yorker* normally
reserved for fiction," writes Keath Fraser in *Bad Trips* (Vintage,
1991)—indicating that this essay, in the form of nonfiction, also has
elements of fiction.

The rich, who range in color from porcelain to mocha, are gener- 3
ally under six feet tall. Their hair style runs to chignons and blow-
dried trims. Either sex is elegantly clad: the males favor dark suits of
medium weight (nights in Caracas can be cool), their close English
cut enhanced by a slight Latin flare, and shirts with striped bodies
but stark-white collars and French cuffs held by agates and gold; the
females appear in a variety of gowns and mock-military pants suits,
Dior and de la Renta originals flown in from Paris and New York.
The gazes of both sexes are melting, brown, alert, canny. The visitor,
standing among them in his funky Brooks Brothers suit and rumpled
blue button-down, is shy at first, but warms to their excellent English,
acquired at colleges in London or "the States," and to their impecca-
ble manners, which conceal, as their fine clothes conceal their skins,
rippling depths of Spanish and those dark thoughts that the mind
phrases to itself in its native language. They tell anecdotes culled
from their rich international lives; they offer, as the evening deepens,
confidences, feelers, troubles. These, too, are human presences.

The Indians live in *shabonos*—roughly circular lean-tos woven 4
beautifully of palm thatch in clearings hacked and burned out of the
circumambient rain forest. A *shabono* usually rots and is abandoned
within three years. The interiors are smoky, from cooking fires, and
eye diseases are common among the Indians. They sleep, rest, and die
in hammocks (*cinchorros*) hung as close together as pea pods on a
vine. Their technology, involving in its pure state neither iron nor the
wheel, is yet highly sophisticated: the chemical intricacies of curare
have never been completely plumbed, and with their blow-pipes of
up to sixteen feet in length the Indians can bring down prey at dis-
tances of over thirty meters. They fish without hooks, by employing
nets and thrashing the water with poisonous lianas. All this sounds
cheerier than it is. It is depressing to stand in the gloom of a *shabono*,
the palm thatch overhead infested with giant insects, the Indians
drooping in their hammocks, their eyes diseased, their bellies protu-
berant, their faces and limbs besmirched with the same gray-brown
dirt that composes the floor, their possessions a few brown baskets
and monkey skins. Their lives are not paradise but full of anxiety—
their religion a matter of fear, their statecraft a matter of constant,
nagging war. To themselves, they are "the people" (*Yanomami*); to
others, they are "the killers" (*Waikás*).

The rich dwell in *haciendas*—airy long ranch houses whose roofs 5
are of curved tile and, surprisingly, dried sugar-cane stalks. Some *haciendas* surviving in Caracas date from the sixteenth century, when the
great valley was all but empty. The interiors are smoky, from candlelit
dinners, and contact lenses are common among the rich. The furniture
is solid, black, polished by generations of servants. Large paintings by

Diebenkorn, Stella, Baziotes, and Botero adorn the white plaster walls, along with lurid religious pictures in the colonial Spanish style. The appliances are all modern and paid for; even if the oil in Lake Maracaibo were to give out, vast deposits of heavy crude have been discovered in the state of Bolívar. All this sounds cheerier than it is. The rich wish they were in Paris, London, New York. Many have condominiums in Miami. *Haute couture* and abstract painting may not prove bulwark enough. Constitutional democracy in Venezuela, though the last dictator fled in 1958, is not so assured as may appear. Turbulence and tyranny are traditional. Che Guevara is still idealized among students. To themselves, the rich are good, decent, amusing people; to others, they are "*reaccionarios.*"

Missionaries, many of them United States citizens, move among the Indians. They claim that since Western civilization, with all its diseases and detritus, must come, it had best come through them. Nevertheless, Marxist anthropologists inveigh against them. Foreign experts, many of them United States citizens, move among the rich. They claim they are just helping out, and that anyway the oil industry was nationalized five years ago. Nevertheless, Marxist anthropologists are not mollified. The feet of the Indians are very broad in front, their toes spread wide for climbing avocado trees. The feet of the rich are very narrow in front, their toes compressed by pointed Italian shoes. The Indians seek relief from tension in the use of *ebene,* or *yopo,* a mind-altering drug distilled from the bark of the *ebene* tree and blown into the user's nose through a hollow cane by a colleague. The rich take cocaine through the nose, and frequent mind-altering discotheques, but more customarily imbibe cognac, *vino blanco,* and Scotch, in association with colleagues.

These and other contrasts and comparisons between the Indians and the rich can perhaps be made more meaningful by the following anecdote: A visitor, after some weeks in Venezuela, was invited to fly to the top of a *tepuy* in a helicopter, which crashed. As stated, the *tepuys* are supposed by the Indians to be the forbidden haunts of the gods; and, indeed, they present an exotic, attenuated vegetation and a craggy geology to the rare intruder. The crash was a minor one, breaking neither bones nor bottles (a lavish picnic, including *mucho vino blanco,* had been packed). The bottles were consumed, the exotic vegetation was photographed, and a rescue helicopter arrived. In the Cessna back to Caracas, the survivors couldn't get enough of discussing the incident and their survival, and the red-haired woman opposite the visitor said, "I *love* the way you pronounce 'tepuy.'" She imitated him: *tupooey.* "Real zingy," she said. The visitor slowly realized that he was being flirted with, and that therefore *this woman was middle-class.* In Venezuela, only the negligible middle class flirts. The

Indians kidnap or are raped; the rich commandeer, or languorously give themselves in imperious surrender.

The Indians tend to know only three words of Spanish: "¿Cómo se llama?" ("What is your name?"). In Indian belief, to give one's name is to place oneself in the other's power. And the rich, when one is introduced, narrow their eyes and file one's name away in their mysterious depths. Power among them flows along lines of kinship and intimacy. After an imperious surrender, a rich female gazes at her visitor with new interest out of her narrowed, brown, melting, kohl-ringed eyes. He has become someone to be reckoned with, if only as a potential source of financial embarrassment. "Again, what is your name?" she asks. 8

Los indios and los ricos rarely achieve contact. When they do, mestizos result, and the exploitation of natural resources. In such lies the future of Venezuela. 9

QUESTIONS

1. Review and draw inferences from the information Updike gives about "the visitor." Where do you think the visitor is from? What is his class background? What is the purpose of his visit? Toward whom does the visitor seem most sympathetic?

2. Describe Updike's tone, the attitude the writer expresses towards his subjects—the Indians, the rich, the "negligible middle class," and the visitor. Why do you think Updike chooses to write about the visitor in the third person viewpoint? What overall point do you think Updike is trying to make in this piece?

3. Imitate Updike's comparison and contrast form with your own guide for visitors to the United States, your home town, your college, or another place you're familiar with.

Sightseer[1]

WALKER PERCY

Every explorer names his island Formosa, beautiful. To him it is 1
beautiful because, being first, he has access to it and can see it for what
it is. But to no one else is it ever as beautiful—except the rare man who
manages to recover it, who knows that it has to be recovered.

Garcia López de Cárdenas discovered the Grand Canyon and was 2
amazed at the sight. It can be imagined: One crosses miles of desert,
breaks through the mesquite, and there it is at one's feet. Later the government set the place aside as a national park, hoping to pass along to
millions the experience of Cárdenas. Does not one see the same sight
from the Bright Angel Lodge that Cárdenas saw?

The assumption is that the Grand Canyon is a remarkably interest- 3
ing and beautiful place and that if it had a certain value P for Cárdenas,
the same value P may be transmitted to any number of sightseers—just
as Banting's discovery of insulin can be transmitted to any number of
diabetics. A counterinfluence is at work, however, and it would be
nearer the truth to say that if the place is seen by a million sightseers, a
single sightseer does not receive value P but a millionth part of value P.

It is assumed that since the Grand Canyon has the fixed interest 4
value P, tours can be organized for any number of people. A man in
Boston decides to spend his vacation at the Grand Canyon. He visits
his travel bureau, looks at the folder, signs up for a two-week tour. He
and his family take the tour, see the Grand Canyon, and return to
Boston. May we say that this man has seen the Grand Canyon?

---

[1]This is a retitling of the first section of "The Loss of the Creature." (Ed.)

Walker Percy (1916–1990) was a novelist and essayist who began his
career as a medical doctor. His first novel, *The Moviegoer* (1961), won
the National Book Award, and was followed by five other novels
including *The Last Gentleman* (1966), *Love in the Ruins: The Adventures
of a Bad Catholic at a Time near the End of the World* (1971), and *The
Thanatos Syndrome* (1987). His essays about language and human
understanding were originally published in academic journals beginning in the 1950s and later collected in *The Message in the Bottle: How
Queer Man Is, How Queer Language Is, and What One Has to Do with the
Other* (1975), *Lost in the Cosmos: The Last Self-Help Book* (1983), and,
posthumously, *Signposts in a Strange Land* (1991, edited by Patrick
Samway). "Sightseer" is the first half of a longer essay called "The
Loss of the Creature," collected in *The Message in the Bottle*.

Possibly he has. But it is more likely that what he has done is the one sure way not to see the canyon.

Why is it almost impossible to gaze directly at the Grand Canyon 5 under these circumstances and see it for what it is—as one picks up a strange object from one's back yard and gazes directly at it? It is almost impossible because the Grand Canyon, the thing as it is, has been appropriated by the symbolic complex which has already been formed in the sightseer's mind. Seeing the canyon under approved circumstances is seeing the symbolic complex head on. The thing is no longer the thing as it confronted the Spaniard; it is rather that which has already been formulated—by picture postcard, geography book, tourist folders, and the words *Grand Canyon*. As a result of this preformulation, the source of the sightseer's pleasure undergoes a shift. Where the wonder and delight of the Spaniard arose from his penetration of the thing itself, from a progressive discovery of depths, patterns, colors, shadows, etc., now the sightseer measures his satisfaction *by the degree to which the canyon conforms to the preformed complex.* If it does so, if it looks just like the postcard, he is pleased; he might even say, "Why it is every bit as beautiful as a picture postcard!" He feels he has not been cheated. But if it does not conform, if the colors are somber, he will not be able to see it directly; he will only be conscious of the disparity between what it is and what it is supposed to be. He will say later that he was unlucky in not being there at the right time. The highest point, the term of the sightseer's satisfaction, is not the sovereign discovery of the thing before him; it is rather the measuring up of the thing to the criterion of the preformed symbolic complex.

Seeing the canyon is made even more difficult by what the sight- 6 seer does when the moment arrives, when sovereign knower confronts the thing to be known. Instead of looking at it, he photographs it. There is no confrontation at all. At the end of forty years of preformulation and with the Grand Canyon yawning at his feet, what does he do? He waives his right of seeing and knowing and records symbols for the next forty years. For him there is no present; there is only the past of what has been formulated and seen and the future of what has been formulated and not seen. The present is surrendered to the past and the future.

The sightseer may be aware that something is wrong. He may 7 simply be bored; or he may be conscious of the difficulty: that the great thing yawning at his feet somehow eludes him. The harder he looks at it, the less he can see. It eludes everybody. The tourist cannot see it; the bellboy at the Angel Lodge cannot see it: for him it is only one side of the space he lives in, like one wall of a room; to the ranger it is a tissue of everyday signs relevant to his own prospects—the blue haze down there means that he will probably get rained on during the donkey ride.

How can the sightseer recover the Grand Canyon? He can recover 8
it in any number of ways, all sharing in common the stratagem of
avoiding the approved confrontation of the tour and the Park Service.

It may be recovered by leaving the beaten track. The tourist leaves 9
the tour, camps in the back country. He arises before dawn and approaches the South Rim through a wild terrain where there are no
trails and no railed-in lookout points. In other words, he sees the
canyon by avoiding all the facilities for seeing the canyon. If the benevolent Park Service hears about this fellow and thinks he has a good
idea and places the following notice in the Bright Angel Lodge: *Consult
ranger for information on getting off the beaten track*—the end result will
only be the closing of another access to the canyon.

It may be recovered by a dialectical movement which brings one 10
back to the beaten track but at a level above it. For example, after a lifetime of avoiding the beaten track and guided tours, a man may deliberately seek out the most beaten track of all, the most commonplace
tour imaginable: he may visit the canyon by a Greyhound tour in the
company of a party from Terre Haute—just as a man who has lived in
New York all his life may visit the Statue of Liberty. (Such dialectical
savorings of the familiar as the familiar are, of course, a favorite stratagem of *The New Yorker* magazine.) The thing is recovered from familiarity by means of an exercise in familiarity. Our complex friend
stands behind the fellow tourists at the Bright Angel Lodge and sees
the canyon through them and their predicament, their picture taking
and busy disregard. In a sense, he exploits his fellow tourists; he
stands on their shoulders to see the canyon.

Such a man is far more advanced in the dialectic than the sightseer 11
who is trying to get off the beaten track—getting up at dawn and approaching the canyon through the mesquite. This strategem is, in fact,
for our complex man the weariest, most beaten track of all.

It may be recovered as a consequence of a breakdown of the sym- 12
bolic machinery by which the experts present the experience to the
consumer. A family visits the canyon in the usual way. But shortly
after their arrival, the park is closed by an outbreak of typhus in the
south. They have the canyon to themselves. What do they mean when
they tell the home folks of their good luck: "We had the whole place to
ourselves"? How does one see the thing better when the others are absent? Is looking like sucking: the more lookers, the less there is to see?
They could hardly answer, but by saying this they testify to a state of
affairs which is considerably more complex than the simple statement
of the schoolbook about the Spaniard and the millions who followed
him. It is a state in which there is a complex distribution of sovereignty, of zoning.

It may be recovered in a time of national disaster. The Bright 13
Angel Lodge is converted into a rest home, a function that has noth-

ing to do with the canyon a few yards away. A wounded man is brought in. He regains consciousness; there outside his window is the canyon.

The most extreme case of access by privilege conferred by disas- 14 ter is the Huxleyan novel of the adventures of the surviving remnant after the great wars of the twentieth century. An expedition from Australia lands in Southern California and heads east. They stumble across the Bright Angel Lodge, now fallen into ruins. The trails are grown over, the guard rails fallen away, the dime telescope at Battleship Point rusted. But there is the canyon, exposed at last. Exposed by what? By the decay of those facilities which were designed to help the sightseer.

This dialectic of sightseeing cannot be taken into account by plan- 15 ners, for the object of the dialectic is nothing other than the subversion of the efforts of the planners.

The dialectic is not known to objective theorists, psychologists, 16 and the like. Yet it is quite well known in the fantasy-consciousness of the popular arts. The devices by which the museum exhibit, the Grand Canyon, the ordinary thing, is recovered have long since been stumbled upon. A movie shows a man visiting the Grand Canyon. But the moviemaker knows something the planner does not know. He knows that one cannot take the sight frontally. The canyon must be approached by the stratagems we have mentioned: the Inside Track, the Familiar Revisited, the Accidental Encounter. Who is the stranger at the Bright Angel Lodge? Is he the ordinary tourist from Terre Haute that he makes himself out to be? He is not. He has another objective in mind, to revenge his wronged brother, counter-espionage, etc. By virtue of the fact that he has other fish to fry, he may take a stroll along the rim after supper and then we can see the canyon through him. The movie accomplishes its purpose by concealing it. Overtly the characters (the American family marooned by typhus) and we the onlookers experience pity for the sufferers, and the family experience anxiety for themselves; covertly and in truth they are the happiest of people and we are happy through them, for we have the canyon to ourselves. The movie cashes in on the recovery of sovereignty through disaster. Not only is the canyon now accessible to the remnant: the members of the remnant are now accessible to each other; a whole new ensemble of relations becomes possible—friendship, love, hatred, clandestine sexual adventures. In a movie when a man sits next to a woman on a bus, it is necessary either that the bus break down or that the woman lose her memory. (The question occurs to one: Do you imagine there are sightseers who see sights just as they are supposed to? a family who live in Terre Haute, who decide to take the canyon tour, who go there, see it, enjoy it immensely, and go home content? a family who are entirely innocent of all the barriers, zones, losses of sovereignty I have been talking about? Wouldn't most people be sorry if Battleship Point fell into the canyon, carrying all one's fellow passengers to their death, leaving one alone on the South Rim? I cannot answer this. Perhaps there are such people. Certainly a great many American families would swear they had no such problems, that they came, saw, and went away happy. Yet it is just these families who would be happiest if they had gotten the Inside Track and been among the surviving remnant.)

It is now apparent that as between the many measures which may   17
be taken to overcome the opacity, the boredom, of the direct confrontation of the thing or creature in its citadel of symbolic investiture, some are less authentic than others. That is to say, some stratagems obviously serve other purposes than that of providing access to being—for example, various unconscious motivations which it is not necessary to go into here.

Let us take an example in which the recovery of being is ambigu-   18
ous, where it may under the same circumstances contain both authentic and unauthentic components. An American couple, we will say, drives down into Mexico. They see the usual sights and have a fair time of it. Yet they are never without the sense of missing something. Although Taxco and Cuernavaca are interesting and picturesque as advertised, they fall short of "it." What do the couple have in mind by "it"? What do they really hope for? What sort of experience could they have in Mexico so that upon their return, they would feel that "it" had happened? We have a clue: Their hope has something to do with their own role as tourists in a foreign country and the way in which they conceive this role. It has something to do with other American tourists. Certainly they feel that they are very far from "it" when, after traveling five thousand miles, they arrive at the plaza in Guanajuato only to find themselves surrounded by a dozen other couples from the Midwest.

Already we may distinguish authentic and unauthentic elements.   19
First, we see the problem the couple faces and we understand their efforts to surmount it. The problem is to find an "unspoiled" place. "Unspoiled" does not mean only that a place is left physically intact; it means also that it is not encrusted by renown and by the familiar (as in Taxco), that it has not been discovered by others. We understand that the couple really want to get at the place and enjoy it. Yet at the same time we wonder if there is not something wrong in their dislike of their compatriots. Does access to the place require the exclusion of others?

Let us see what happens.   20

The couple decide to drive from Guanajuato to Mexico City. On   21
the way they get lost. After hours on a rocky mountain road, they find

themselves in a tiny valley not even marked on the map. There they discover an Indian village. Some sort of religious festival is going on. It is apparently a corn dance in supplication of the rain god.

The couple know at once that this is "it." They are entranced. They 22 spend several days in the village, observing the Indians and being themselves observed with friendly curiosity.

Now may we not say that the sightseers have at last come face to 23 face with an authentic sight, a sight which is charming, quaint, picturesque, unspoiled, and that they see the sight and come away rewarded? Possibly this may occur. Yet it is more likely that what happens is a far cry indeed from an immediate encounter with being, that the experience, while masquerading as such, is in truth a rather desperate impersonation. I use the word *desperate* advisedly to signify an actual loss of hope.

The clue to the spuriousness of their enjoyment of the village and 24 the festival is a certain restiveness in the sightseers themselves. It is given expression by their repeated exclamations that "this is too good to be true," and by their anxiety that it may not prove to be so perfect, and finally by their downright relief at leaving the valley and having the experience in the bag, so to speak—that is, safely embalmed in memory and movie film.

What is the source of their anxiety during the visit? Does it not 25 mean that the couple are looking at the place with a certain standard of performance in mind? Are they like Fabre, who gazed at the world about him with wonder, letting it be what it is; or are they not like the overanxious mother who sees her child as one performing, now doing badly, now doing well? The village is their child and their love for it is an anxious love because they are afraid that at any moment it might fail them.

We have another clue in their subsequent remark to an ethnologist 26 friend. "How we wished you had been there with us! What a perfect goldmine of folkways! Every minute we would say to each other, if only you were here! You must return with us." This surely testifies to a generosity of spirit, a willingness to share their experience with others, not at all like their feelings toward their fellow Iowans on the plaza at Guanajuato!

I am afraid this is not the case at all. It is true that they longed for 27 their ethnologist friend, but it was for an entirely different reason. They wanted him, not to share their experience, but to certify their experience as genuine.

"This is it" and "Now we are really living" do not necessarily 28 refer to the sovereign encounter of the person with the sight that enlivens the mind and gladdens the heart. It means that now at last we are having the acceptable experience. The present experience is always measured by a prototype, the "it" of their dreams. "Now I am really living" means that now I am filling the role of sightseer and the sight is living up to the prototype of sights. This quaint and picturesque village is measured by a Platonic ideal of the Quaint and the Picturesque.

Hence their anxiety during the encounter. For at any minute something could go wrong. A fellow Iowan might emerge from a 'dobe hut; the chief might show them his Sears catalogue. (If the failures are "wrong" enough, as these are, they might still be turned to account as rueful conversation pieces: "There we were expecting the chief to bring us a churinga and he shows up with a Sears catalogue!") They have snatched victory from disaster, but their experience always runs the danger of failure. 29

They need the ethnologist to certify their experience as genuine. This is borne out by their behavior when the three of them return for the next corn dance. During the dance, the couple do not watch the goings-on; instead they watch the ethnologist! Their highest hope is that their friend should find the dance interesting. And if he should show signs of true absorption, an interest in the goings-on so powerful that he becomes oblivious of his friends—then their cup is full. "Didn't we tell you?" they say at last. What they want from him is not ethnological explanations; all they want is his approval. 30

What has taken place is a radical loss of sovereignty over that which is as much theirs as it is the ethnologist's. The fault does not lie with the ethnologist. He has no wish to stake a claim to the village; in fact, he desires the opposite: he will bore his friends to death by telling them about the village and the meaning of the folkways. A degree of sovereignty has been surrendered by the couple. It is the nature of the loss, moreover, that they are not aware of the loss, beyond a certain uneasiness. (Even if they read this and admitted it, it would be very difficult for them to bridge the gap in their confrontation of the world. Their consciousness of the corn dance cannot escape their consciousness of their consciousness, so that with the onset of the first direct enjoyment, their higher consciousness pounces and certifies: "Now you are doing it! Now you are really living!" and, in certifying the experience, sets it at nought.) 31

Their basic placement in the world is such that they recognize a priority of title of the expert over his particular department of being. The whole horizon of being is staked out by "them," the experts. The highest satisfaction of the sightseer (not merely the tourist but any layman seer of sights) is that his sight should be certified as genuine. The worst of this impoverishment is that there is no sense of impoverishment. The surrender of title is so complete that it never even occurs to one to reassert title. A poor man may envy the rich man, but the sight- 32 seer does not envy the expert. When a caste system becomes absolute, envy disappears. Yet the caste of layman-expert is not the fault of the expert. It is due altogether to the eager surrender of sovereignty by the layman so that he may take up the role not of the person but of the consumer.

I do not refer only to the special relation of layman to theorist. I refer to the general situation in which sovereignty is surrendered to a class of privileged knowers, whether these be theorists or artists. A reader may surrender sovereignty over that which has been written about, just as a consumer may surrender sovereignty over a thing which has been theorized about. The consumer is content to receive an experience just as it has been presented to him by theorists and planners. The reader may also be content to judge life by whether it has or has not been formulated by those who know and write about life. A young man goes to France. He too has a fair time of it, sees the sights, enjoys the food. On his last day, in fact as he sits in a restaurant in Le Havre waiting for his boat, something happens. A group of French students in the restaurant get into an impassioned argument over a recent play. A riot takes place. Madame la concierge joins in, swinging her mop at the rioters. Our young American is transported. This is "it." And he had almost left France without seeing "it"! 33

But the young man's delight is ambiguous. On the one hand, it is a pleasure for him to encounter the same Gallic temperament he had heard about from Puccini and Rolland. But on the other hand, the source of his pleasure testifies to a certain alienation. For the young man is actually barred from a direct encounter with anything French excepting only that which has been set forth, authenticated by Puccini and Rolland—those who know. If he had encountered the restaurant scene without reading Hemingway, without knowing that the performance was so typically, charmingly French, he would not have been delighted. He would only have been anxious at seeing things get out of hand. The source of his delight is the sanction of those who know. 34

This loss of sovereignty is not a marginal process, as might appear from my example of estranged sightseers. It is a generalized surrender of the horizon to those experts within whose competence a particular segment of the horizon is thought to lie. Kwakiutls are surrendered to Franz Boas; decaying Southern mansions are surrendered to Faulkner and Tennessee Williams. So that, although it is by no means the intention of the expert to expropriate sovereignty—in fact he would not even know what sovereignty meant in this context—the danger of theory and consumption is a seduction and deprivation of the consumer. 35

In the New Mexican desert, natives occasionally come across strange-looking artifacts which have fallen from the skies and which are stenciled: *Return to U.S. Experimental Project, Alamogordo. Reward.* 36

The finder returns the object and is rewarded. He knows nothing of the nature of the object he has found and does not care to know. The sole role of the native, the highest role he can play, is that of finder and returner of the mysterious equipment.

The same is true of the layman's relation to *natural* objects in a 37 modern technical society. No matter what the object or event is, whether it is a star, a swallow, a Kwakiutl, a "psychological phenomenon," the layman who confronts it does not confront it as a sovereign person, as Crusoe confronts a seashell he finds on the beach. The highest role he can conceive himself as playing is to be able to recognize the title of the object, to return it to the appropriate expert and have it certified as a genuine find. He does not even permit himself to see the thing—as Gerard Hopkins could see a rock or a cloud or a field. If anyone asks him why he doesn't look, he may reply that he didn't take that subject in college (or he hasn't read Faulkner).

This loss of sovereignty extends even to oneself. There is the neu- 38 rotic who asks nothing more of his doctor than that his symptoms should prove interesting. When all else fails, the poor fellow has nothing to offer but his own neurosis. But even this is sufficient if only the doctor will show interest when he says, "Last night I had a curious sort of dream; perhaps it will be significant to one who knows about such things. It seems I was standing in a sort of alley—" (I have nothing else to offer you but my own unhappiness. Please say that it, at least, measures up, that it is a *proper* sort of unhappiness.)

QUESTIONS

1. Discuss your own experiences as a "sightseer" at a tourist destination (like the Grand Canyon), on the road, or simply visiting a new place close to where you live. What role did your expectations, or what Percy calls the "preformed symbolic complex," play in your enjoyment of the experience? How were those expectations formed? If you took pictures, how did the act of photographing change your experience of the place? Have you ever approached a place by one of the strategies Percy calls the Inside Track ("leaving the beaten track"), the Familiar Revisited, or the Accidental Encounter (paragraphs 9 to 16)?

2. Notice how, as Percy's hypothetical examples move from domestic to international travel, they also become more complex. For the American couple traveling in Mexico and for the young man visiting France, why, according to Percy, is their recovery of authenticity not clear-cut but "ambiguous"?

3. Percy says he is addressing not just the sightseer but also "the consumer" and "the general situation in which sovereignty is surrendered to a class of privileged knowers, whether these be theorists or artists" (paragraphs 32, 33). In what aspects of your life do you defer to "experts"? To what extent do you agree with Percy that this reliance on experts is a danger?

THINKING ABOUT LEAVING HOME

1.   Which of Pearce's "Fifteen Types of Travelers" best describes the travelers in the selections by Divakaruni, Reza, Morris, and Updike? Based on your own experience and reading in this chapter, what other traveler types and "role-related behaviors" would you propose?

2.   Both the tourist couple in Divakaruni's story and Lara, in Reza's story, encounter in the place they visit the threat of violence and then a vivid domestic scene from ordinary life. Compare these encounters and their effects on the characters. If you have had a similar encounter when you visited an unfamiliar place, recount your experience in a narrative anecdote and consider to what extent were you affected in similar and different ways than these other characters.

3.   "While the journey is on buses and across land," writes Morris, "I begin another journey inside my head, a journey of memory and sensation, of past merging with present, of time growing insignificant" (paragraph 2). Apply this statement to your own experience, if relevant, and to Morris's memoir. To what extent you think the couple in "Tourists," Lara in "The Errand," or the visitor in "Venezuela for Visitors" take such internal journeys along with their external journeys?

4.   In the pieces by Reza, Morris, and Updike, to what extent do you think travelers encounter Bloom's "natives in the posters"?

5.   Compare the writing styles of Morris and Updike. In addition to the different points of view (first person and third person), what other differences do you notice in regard to sentence structures, rhythms, and word choices? Try "translating" Updike's helicopter incident (paragraph 7) or another passage into the style of Morris; then "translate" a characteristic passage from Morris, such as her paragraph 17, into the style of Updike. Discuss the results and what you learned about each writer's style.

6.   In the selections by Morris and Updike, to what extent do you think that the travelers overcome or transcend the "irresoluble" paradox proposed by Lévi-Strauss?

7.   Compare how Percy's "preformed symbolic complex" operates in the stories by Divakaruni and Reza and the memoir by Morris. How successfully, and by what means, do you think the travelers in these selections achieve "it" or the authentic travel experience? To what extent have they lost their sovereignty, in Percy's terms, and how aware are they of the loss?

8.   Do you think we should see the visitor to Venezuela in Updike's essay as more like Percy's "estranged sightseers" in Mexico or more like their ethnologist friend, whose expertise they depend upon in order to validate their own experience? How so?

9.   Use your responses to questions 7 and 8 above, and your own experience, if relevant, to evaluate some aspect of Percy's argument, such as his three suggested strategies for "recovery"—the Inside Track, the Familiar Revisited, and the Accidental Encounter. How might you use the experiences of these other travelers to extend, modify, or re-interpret Percy's hypothetical examples?

Exploring Additional Sources

10.   Test some aspect of Percy's argument about loss of sovereignty with the experiences of travelers from other chapters, in selections such as "All God's Children Need Traveling Shoes" by Maya Angelou (page 469), "A Moroccan Memoir" by Sarah Streed (page 486), "A Distant Episode" by Paul Bowles (page 517), or "God and the Cobbler" by R. K. Narayan (page 569). You may also find Bloom's "poster natives" helpful in analyzing one or more of these selections.

11.   Many of the essays and stories in Chapters 11 and 12 describe experiences that test the paradoxical "double infirmity" proposed by Lévi-Strauss. In two or more of these selections, compare the success with which travelers overcome Lévi-Strauss's paradox.

12.   Analyze the experiences of American women traveling abroad with reference to the selections by Divakaruni, Morris, Maya Angelou ("All God's Children Need Traveling Shoes," page 469), Sarah Streed ("A Moroccan Memoir," page 486), and your own travels, if relevant. Test your analysis in the context of (a) any available statistics about the relative safety of international travel for women, and (b) social science studies of cultural adjustment patterns, cross-cultural communication, or culture shock.

13.   In addition to the (former) Shah's "White Revolution" mentioned in Reza's story, Iran has undergone several other major social upheavals this century—including the CIA-assisted coup that installed Shah Mohammed Reza Pahlavi (1919–1980) in power and the Islamic Revolution of 1979 that replaced him with the Ayatollah Ruholla Khomeini (1900–1989). Research one of these historical incidents and take a position about the involvement of western nations or U.S. foreign policy.

14. Test Updike's generalizations about *los indios* in Venezuela with anthropological studies focusing on a particular indigenous tribe. Brazilian native tribes, some all but extinct, have also been studied by anthropologists, including Lévi-Strauss in his book *Tristes Tropiques.*

15. Follow your interest in the writing style or ideas of Morris, Updike, or Percy by reading other books by the author and writing a literary research paper about some aspect of his or her work.

10

ENCOUNTERING STEREOTYPES

Stereotypes about Americans

GARY ALTHEN

One of the main misconceptions TV and movies convey abroad is that American women are nearly all readily available for sexual activity. Other misconceptions films and TV convey (again, not deliberately) include these:

The United States is composed of New York City, Chicago, Disneyland, Las Vegas, Hollywood, San Francisco, and Texas (at least Dallas).

Most American women are beautiful (according to contemporary Western standards) and most American men are handsome (according to the same standards). Those who are not beautiful or handsome are criminals, deceitful people, and members of the lower class.

Violent crime is an ever-present threat in all parts of the country.

Average Americans are rich and usually do not have to work to get money.

Average Americans live in large, modern, shiny houses or apartments.

Most things in America are large, modern, and shiny.

There is a stratum of American society in which most people are non-white, physically ugly, uneducated, and dedicated to violence.

High-speed automobile chases are frequently seen on American streets.

Non-white people are inferior to white people.

—FROM *AMERICAN WAYS: A GUIDE FOR FOREIGNERS IN THE UNITED STATES*, 1988

Over the Fence in Canada

MARGARET ATWOOD

The noses of a great many Canadians resemble Porky Pig's. This comes from spending so much time pressing them against the longest undefended one-way mirror in the world. The Canadians looking through this mirror behave the way people on the hidden side of such mirrors usually do: They observe, analyze, ponder, snoop and wonder what all the activity on the other side means in decipherable human terms.

The Americans, bless their innocent little hearts, are rarely aware that they are even being watched, much less by the Canadians. They just go on doing body language, playing in the sandbox of the world, bashing one another on the head and planning how to blow things up, same as always. If they think about Canada at all, it's only when things get a bit snowy, or the water goes off, or the Canadians start fussing over some piddly detail, such as fish. Then they regard them as unpatriotic; for Americans don't really see Canadians as foreigners, not like the Mexicans, unless they do something weird like speak French or beat the New York Yankees at baseball. Really, think the Americans, the Canadians are just like us, or would be if they could.

Or we could switch metaphors and call the border the longest undefended backyard fence in the world. The Canadians are the folks in the neat little bungalow with the tidy little garden and the duck pond. The Americans are the other folks, the ones in the sprawly mansion with the bad-taste statues on the lawn. There's a perpetual party, or something, going on there—loud music, raucous laughter, smoke billowing from the barbecue. Beer bottles and Coke cans land among the peonies. The Canadians have their own beer bottles and barbecue smoke, but they tend to overlook it. Your own mess is always more forgivable than the mess someone else makes on your patio.

The Canadians can't exactly call the police—they suspect that the Americans are the police—and part of their distress, which seems permanent, comes from their uncertainty as to whether or not they've been invited. Sometimes they do drop by next door, and find it exciting but scary. Sometimes the Americans drop by their house and find it clean. This worries the Canadians. They worry a lot. Maybe that Americans want to buy up their duck pond, with all the money they seem to have, and turn it into a cesspool or a water-skiing emporium.

FROM "THE VIEW FROM THE BACKYARD," IN *THE NATION*, 1986

Stereotypes in Orbit

JUDITH STONE

Japanese astronauts worry that the Americans aboard space station Freedom will make ill-considered, split-second decisions. The Americans fear that the Japanese preference for protracted group deliberation could prove fatal in an emergency. The Italians are anxious about whether their privacy will be respected. And I'm terrified the French will make everyone watch Jerry Lewis movies.

Anthropologist Mary Lozano is chronicling the concerns of international partners in the space station, scheduled to be built from modules assembled on the ground, launched on the space shuttle, then linked by space crews on 17 flights beginning in November 1995. . . .

"The non-Americans expect the Americans to be arrogant," she reports. "The Americans expect the French to be arrogant. And they consider the Italians emotional, the Germans strict and pompous and the Japanese clannish." . . .

Both Japanese and Americans are interested in understanding each other's decision-making styles, Lozano says.

"The Japanese like to make decisions by consensus. If they're asked how they feel about something, they need time to come up with a decision. When the Japanese say yes, it doesn't always mean yes; they try to avoid conflict and maintain group harmony.

"Americans, on the other hand, debate the issues and come up with a decision right at the table. The rapidity appears irrational to the Japanese; the slowness seems dangerous to the Americans."

—FROM "IT'S A SMALL WORLD AFTER ALL," IN *DISCOVER* MAGAZINE, 1992

Are the French Really Rude?

STANLEY MEISLER

After five years in France, an American still has a puzzling time 1
figuring out the French. Are they really rude? Does their school system
stifle many of them? Do they posture foolishly on the world stage?

There are short answers to each of these questions: no; maybe; yes; 2
no. But there are long, complex, and contradictory answers as well,
for a myriad of ambiguities befuddle any American trying to make out
the French.

To many foreigners, for example, it is not surprising that the pa- 3
tron saint of Paris is St. Genevieve, a nun who fasted and prayed in the
6th century to keep Paris safe from foreigners. She fits an image that
France cannot shake off. All studies show that outsiders look on the
French as the coldest and least welcoming people of Europe.

Yet there are few countries in the world that have welcomed and 4
embraced so many foreigners, from the Italian Renaissance genius
Leonardo Da Vinci to the Spanish painter Pablo Picasso to the Irish
writer James Joyce to the black American singer Josephine Baker. Some
of the most celebrated French of the 20th century, such as Nobel Prize
physicist Marie Curie, actor-singer Yves Montand and novelist Romain
Gary, were born outside France.

Contradictions like these seem even more puzzling because the 5
French at heart ought not to be so puzzling. To an American, the
French are not really exotic like Australian bushmen or the Maya or
even the Japanese. French culture seems familiar. French Champagne
and perfume and cheese and ballads and movies conjure up old and
warm images. Yet, although Americans sometimes feel they have
France in their reach, they rarely can grasp it. No other people so close
seem so far.

A mood, a spirit set the French apart, and moods and spirits are 6
difficult to fathom. Take the French concern for language and ideas.
The French respect for intellect is breathtaking, far beyond the experience of any American.

Politicians and civil servants speak and write with unequaled 7
style, sophistication, flair for literature and grounding in history. Daily

---

As a staff writer for the *Los Angeles Times,* **Stanley Meisler** has written extensively about international affairs. Currently the newspaper's
United Nations correspondent, he has been a foreign correspondent
and served as chief of its Paris Bureau. This article appeared in the *Los
Angeles Times* in 1988.

newspapers devote far more space to philosophy and sociology than sports. The French first came up with the term *intellectuel* at the turn of the century to describe writers, artists and philosophers with influence. Intellectuals still have influence and still matter.

Throughout this year, for example, a controversy has raged over 8 the late German philosopher Martin Heidegger, a controversy set off by a Chilean professor who wrote a book accusing Heidegger of unswerving loyalty to Hitler's Nazi party from 1933 to 1945.

Heidegger is regarded as one of the most influential philosophers 9 of the 20th century, but it is hard to conceive of the same fuss taking place anywhere else. Heidegger has a special place in France because his views influenced those of the great French writer Jean-Paul Sartre. But that does not really explain why the French media have devoted so much attention to him. Heidegger, after all, is unintelligible to the average reader in any language, even French. But the average French reader, whether he reads Heidegger or not, knows that philosophers are important and therefore worth fussing about.

Intellectual achievement is so prized that the smartest secondary 10 students are treated like celebrities. *Le Monde*, France's most influential newspaper, published the full text in July of the student essay that won the annual prize of the Ministry of Education for the best composition in French. These annual prizes, which began in 1747, are major events. The news weekly *Le Point*, in a cover story a few weeks ago, profiled nine of this year's winners in various subjects, revealing their family backgrounds, study habits, heroes and favorite dishes.

The best graduates of the French educational system have a preci- 11 sion of mind, command of language and store of memory that would make the heart of most American educators ache with envy. It is doubtful that any school system in the world teaches more logic and grammar or offers more courses.

But a sobering price is paid. Precision in thought and beauty of 12 language are the products of an elite French school system that is repressive, frightening and stifling to many pupils who cannot keep up. There is no tolerance or time for spontaneity or weakness.

An elite few do well and uphold the glory and grandeur of 13 French culture. But many other students are shunted aside by the system. Almost two-thirds of French pupils who enter secondary school fail to win the baccalaureate degree that is the crowning achievement of their secondary education. Some feel that failure for the rest of their lives.

Dr. Philippe Guran, director of pediatrics at the Richaud Hospital 14 in Versailles, once described the school system as "hazardous to children's health and well-being." The children, he said, are motivated by "the fear of failure rather than the pursuit of success."

Although some French educators question the rigidity and elitism 15
of the school system, most politicians and parents do not. These kinds
of schools, after all, have produced a dozen winners of the Nobel Prize
in literature this century, far more than any other country, including
the United States, with all its emphasis on creativity.

Parents, concerned that their children may fail the national bac- 16
calaureate examinations, complain that a school's standards are not
tough enough. Politicians denounce principals for offering too many
frills. President François Mitterrand insists that teachers should force
pupils to memorize more dates in French history.

No one seems to think of the school system when the French 17
government launches one of its periodic campaigns to persuade the
French to show more hospitality to tourists. Yet the schools, in many
ways, must be blamed for the hoary tourist cliché that the French
are rude.

French education fosters a defensive attitude in those fearful of 18
failure. It is not surprising that foreigners sometimes run into a defensive waiter or store clerk or lower-level bureaucrat. After years of trying to avoid the strictures of their teachers, people like this handle
every hint of a complaint by blaming someone else.

French education also makes it very difficult for the French to un- 19
derstand foreigners who do not speak French well. It has been drilled
into the French for years that they must not mispronounce words
or mangle grammar. Their minds cannot make much of an adjustment
for a foreigner who misses the mark; many French simply do not
understand.

In English, linguists, trying to assess how well a foreigner speaks, 20
measure the level at which he or she will be understood by "a sympathetic native speaker." The concept of such a speaker simply does not
exist in French.

"The cultural capital of the world is a provincial place," a Bolivian 21
writer said in Paris recently. "Nowhere else in the world do people
treat you like the French do if you cannot speak their language. It
would not happen in New York or even London. Paris is a city suspicious of foreigners; it is like the Middle Ages."

The problem is compounded because the French, especially in 22
Paris, are not an open, gregarious people like Americans or Latins.
They are inward and undemonstrative. They do not like to commit
themselves quickly; they do not like to show their feelings openly.

The truth is that the cliché about French rudeness, like most 23
clichés, is exaggerated, sometimes in a spiteful way. Most French are
not defensive, intolerant and insensitive. Most are not rude.

It is true that most French do not open up quickly to people they 24
do not know, whether foreign or French. But, once contact is made and

renewed, they are as kind and loyal as any other people. They show their friendship and emotion, however, with simple civil gestures—a small gift or favor or act of kindness—but not in any extravagant way.

There is another puzzle. The French, in the eyes of many foreign- 25 ers, refuse to accept their role as a middling power. On an official and diplomatic level, many Americans grow irritated with French leaders for what the Americans look on as posturing on the world stage.

France was once a great power. Even as late as the eve of World 26 War II, many analysts thought that the French army was the most powerful in the world. But such notions died in the defeat and disgrace of World War II.

Now, France is a European country of moderate strength, with 27 enough nuclear weapons to count in some councils of war and peace but hardly enough to qualify as a superpower. Yet its leaders, unlike the leaders of Britain, never seem to accept this. The French sometimes sound as if World War II had never come to dash the pretensions of France.

At economic summit conferences, for example, President 28 Mitterrand is one of the few foreign leaders who stands up to the United States and refuses to bow to its power and influence. French officials act not as if they were trying to pose as more than they are but as if past French grandeur and the potential for future French leadership in Europe entitles them to more of a voice than a middling power might expect. The past and future ought to count for something.

The concept is novel, but it may make a lot of sense. It certainly 29 enhances a sense of nationalism and makes the French, as ever, somewhat larger than life.

QUESTIONS

1. Trace the web of causes that Meisler offers to explain why "outsiders look on the French as the coldest and least welcoming people of Europe" (paragraph 3). Which causes are the most immediate, and which are deeper or more remote? Which does Meisler seem to feel are the most important?

2. Choose a commonly held stereotypical belief about a cultural group with which you're familiar and explore the causes of this belief in an essay like Meisler's titled "Are the _____ Really _____?"

Land without Jews

HERBERT GOLD

As a student in the mid-'50s, I spent two years in the Republic of 1
Haiti—a land without Jews except in myth and memory. There was no
Jewish community, no Jewish life. Even that most final sign of Jewish
history, as of all histories, was lacking—no Jewish cemetery, no Jewish
place in a cemetery. A Jew might run and hide—history is full of that—
but the cemetery remains, or the place where the cemetery once stood,
or the memory of this place. None. No graveyard, no place, no memory of the place that never was.

And yet, as it happened, even here, in this lovely, forsaken corner 2
of the world, Jews had come. Since my student days, I have been returning for the past 35 years as a writer enchanted by this place of the
best nightmares on earth.

Before I found the vivid traces of Jews, I found the anti-Semites, 3
refugees from their crimes. The Gestapo informer from Paris who became my friend and companion ("Get me into the States, can't you?
Surely *you* can!"), and the Petainist colonel who had left France for
a Haitian exile after collaborating with the Nazi occupation. Odd
to meet the evidence of my history first in the form of its enemy,
the exiles biting their nails, biding their time in a backwater. And I
found Haitians like Jean Weiner, as handsome and lofty as a Watusi,
who cackled hysterically as he described the origins of his distinguished Roman Catholic family: "A Jew from Vienna came here to
trade in coffee!"

Through Jean, I met a morose accountant with a degree from a 4
school of business in Philadelphia and a mania for recounting the days
of his persecution. Restaurants, doormen, professors, women had all

---

Herbert Gold is a novelist and writer of short stories, essays, and
memoirs. His novels include *Birth of a Hero* (1951), *The Great American
Jackpot* (1969), *A Girl of Forty* (1986), and *Dreaming* (1988). "Land without Jews" appeared in the *San Francisco Chronicle* and makes up, in
slightly different form, a chapter in Gold's 1991 memoir *Best
Nightmare on Earth: A Life in Haiti*. Haiti—"the first independent black
nation of modern times, winning its freedom from France with a slave
revolt against Napoleon at the height of his power," as Gold writes in
the preface to his memoir—is a culturally mixed and poverty-strick-
en Caribbean island nation with a turbulent political history.

treated him like a *Negro*—"*Moi qui est Haitien!*"[1] he cried. Remembering the purgatory of Philadelphia, he despised Haiti, the peasantry and the Jews, and his name was Cohen.

When he confided one evening that the Jews are at the root of all   5
the trouble in Haiti and the world, I said to him, "I'm a Jew." He peered at me blankly through his red-rimmed eyes as if he had never seen one before. "And you, with your name," I said.

"My grandfather came from Jamaica."   6

"You must have had a Jewish grandfather in there someplace."   7

"You're making that up! . . . How did you know?"   8

"Cohen."   9

"*Cohen?*" he asked. To him Cohen was the name of a Mass-going   10
Haitian accountant. I explained that the Cohanim were priests and he was descended from priests and princes.

"Priests don't have children," he said irritably.   11

"Do you really think Jews caused all the trouble in Haiti?"   12

"No, not all," he said, "but the wars, the world wars they started,   13
all the wars hurt us, too."

There was a double ledger for his secret Jewish grandfather and   14
his need to find an explanation for trouble and sin. I could nag at him with facts, scandalize him with my own history, but I could never change his accounting and put Cohen, the Haitian accountant, in touch with Cohen, the man with an ancestor who did not begin the line of Cohens in Jamaica. He was horn-rimmed glasses, owlish eyes with reddened conjunctiva, pockmarked black skin, and a Jew-hating heart that was outraged by the information—which he knew already—that his name meant something drastic in his past. He was not descended from an infinite line of Jamaican mulattos.

"If you knew more about the troubles of the world," I told him,   15
"you'd be safer from them."

"I've had them, *des difficultés.*"   16

I was only confusing the black Roman Catholic Cohen in search of   17
clear definitions.

There were others like him, of course, good Mass-going Haitians   18
with names like Goldenberg or Levi, or with Sephardic names like Mendes or Silvera. In Jacmel, a tiny town on the sea with an unpaved Grand Rue, perhaps once a week a police jeep scattered the traffic jams of black Haitian pigs, flailing dust—the *cochons noirs* as skinny and speedy as dogs. There was a *pension*, telephones and electricity that

---

[1]*Moi qui est Haitien!:* I who am Haitian! (Ed.)

rarely worked, the mud huts of an African village—and in this place, Jacmel, I found a Jewish tailor.

A few elegantly carpentered Haitian dream houses floated above 19 reality like candy visions—slats and shutters, parapets and magic cages filled with lizards or birds—but Monsieur Schneider lived in a dwelling separated only by a few boards and nails from *caille-paille,* the country shelter of mud and straw.

He did his work at a hand-treadled machine in the dusty street, his 20 head tilted to one side to favor his good eye, his joints swollen and his body twisted by arthritis. He was old and wore rags, like many Haitians, but the rags were sewn into the blurred shape of a European shirt and suit. It was too hot for such formality. He was one of three white people in the town. In the air around him, like the insects and the animals, eddied the members of his extended family—the mixed African and Semitic—some dark and some light, children and adults, wives and grandchildren.

"Mister Schneider," I began, first in English. No English, but he 21 understood what I was asking. Was *I?* Yes. *Oui.* A flood of Yiddish poured out of his head. I spoke no Yiddish.

He looked at me as if to doubt my sanity. A Jew, he said, and 22 spoke no Yiddish? He tried Creole. We settled on French, which he spoke in a Yiddish accent, with Creole words and phrases. He believed I was what I said I was, for otherwise what gain for either of us? Who needed to tell lies here, so far from the Czar's police? He kicked amiably at the grandchildren—children?—playing about the treadles of his Singer machine. The treadle was cast with ironwork scrolls and Art Nouveau symbols polished by his bare feet.

He did not have the look of a person who asked deep questions, 23 but he stared at me from his one good eye. "What's a Jew doing in Jacmel?" he asked.

His face was shriveled against sunlight, shrunken by age, blotched 24 and deeply freckled. It looked like a dog's muzzle. "Why is a Jew *living* here?" I asked him in return.

"My home," he said. "You call this a life? My wife is dead. I have 25 another wife. My children and grandchildren are here."

"Would you forgive the question? How did you happen to settle 26 in Jacmel?"

He pumped furiously at the machine. He was fixing a seam, a sim- 27 ple matter, but he gave it all his concentration. Then he squinted around at me. I had moved so he wouldn't be staring into the sun. He winked, Jew to Jew.

"And where else?" 28

Jeremie, St.-Marc, Cap Haitian, Port-au-Prince, Port-de-Paix— 29 that's all. So he settled in Jacmel.

"Were you Polish?"   30

"Russian."   31

"So were my parents. Why didn't you go to the United States?"   32

"Ah," he said. "Because I wished to learn the French and Creole   33
languages, *c'est vrai?*"

"*Non.*"   34

"Because"—and he spread wide his arms—"I had adventure in   35
my heart?"

"No."   36

He put down his cloth and stood up.   37

He put his face close to mine, pulled at the lid of the dead eye as if   38
he were stretching a piece of cloth, and said, "I went to Ellis Isle,
maybe your father did too. But he didn't have a sick eye. It was in-
fected from the filth. They sent me away. And then I wandered, no
place left. So instead of killing myself I came to Haiti."

"I'm sorry," I said, although it seemed foolish to be oppressed by   39
a sick eye from a generation before I was born.

He started to laugh. It was not the dry, old man's laughter of my   40
uncles in Cleveland. It was a rich, abandoned, Haitian old man's
laughter. He clutched at his crotch for luck. "You see these children?
You see all the brown Schneider children in Jacmel? Many died—my
wives often die—but look what I have done. I have proved God is not
malevolent. He let me live. He let some of these children live. God is
indifferent, but I have shown, not proved, of course, but *demonstrated*
that he is not malevolent."

"If you believe, God is not evil, merely all-powerful."   41

He put his face down. He reached for a packet of sugar and held   42
it up to my face. "If he were all-powerful, then he would be evil.
He could not allow what he allows. You like good Haitian coffee,
Monsieur? Martie!" he shouted into the *caille-paille.* "*Blanc v'le café—
poté.*"

I drank coffee with the tailor and his new wife, who said not a   43
word as she sat with us. He sucked at sugar and sipped his coffee
through it.

"I have a few books," he said. "A scholar I was not. My uncle was   44
a rabbi. I think my brother was going to be a rabbi, but"—he
shrugged—"I never found out what he became. You're not a rabbi?"

"No."   45

"It's not so stupid to ask. I heard of rabbis now who don't speak   46
Yiddish."

"I don't speak Hebrew, either."   47

"Then you couldn't be a rabbi, could you?"   48

I wanted to give him answers and ask questions, but we made   49
mere conversation. We were two Jews speaking a peculiar polyglot in

the town of Jacmel. At that time there was no paved road from Port-au-Prince, and when it rained, even jeeps couldn't pass the streams. Jacmel was a port at the end of the world.

His wife watched us with mournful eyes, as if I might take him 50 away from her, but time was taking him away faster than I could. We had little to say across the years and history between us except to give each other greetings.

When I said good-by, dizzy with coffee, he stood up painfully, a 51 small thin bent brown man, a creature neither Russian nor Jewish nor Haitian, something molded in time's hands like a clay doll. He put out his hand and said in a cracked voice, laughing at the peculiar word he must have pronounced for the first time in years: *"Shalom!"*

QUESTIONS

1. Contrast Gold's encounters with Cohen and Schneider. In what ways are all three men guilty of, or victims of, stereotyping? To what extent do they overcome this stereotyping?

2. Do you agree with Gold's interpretation of his meeting with Schneider, as stated in paragraph 50: "We had little to say across the years and history between us except to give each other greetings"? Why or why not?

Beliefs and Values in the Arab World

MARGARET K. NYDELL

Beliefs and Values

When we set ourselves the task of coming to a better understand- 1
ing of groups of people and their culture, it is useful to begin by identifying their most basic beliefs and values. It is these beliefs and values
which determine their outlook on life and govern their social behavior.

Westerners tend to believe, for instance, that the individual is the 2
focal point of social existence, that laws apply equally to everyone, that
people have a right to certain kinds of privacy, and that the environment can be controlled by humans through technological means.
These beliefs have a strong influence on what Westerners think about
the world around them and how they behave toward each other.

Arabs characteristically believe that many if not most things in life 3
are controlled, ultimately, by fate rather than by humans, that everyone loves children, that wisdom increases with age, and that the inherent personalities of men and women are vastly different. As with
Westerners, these beliefs play a powerful role in determining the nature of Arab culture.

One might wonder whether there is in fact such a thing as "Arab 4
culture," given the diversity and geographic disparateness of the Arab
World. Looking at a map, one realizes how much is encompassed by
the phrase "the Arab World." The twenty Arab countries cover considerable territory, much of which is desert or wilderness. Sudan is
larger than all of Western Europe, yet its population is less than that of
France; Saudi Arabia is larger than Texas and Alaska combined, yet

---

Margaret K. Nydell, who holds a Ph.D. in linguistics from
Georgetown University, is a former director of Arabic language train-
ing at the Foreign Service Institute of the U.S. State Department as
well as the School of Arabic Language and Area Studies in Tunis,
Tunisia. She is author of *Understanding Arabs: A Guide for Westerners*
(1987), from which this piece is taken, and co-author of *Update: Saudi
Arabia* (1990). Nydell writes in the preface to *Understanding Arabs* that
her purpose "is to provide a cross-cultural guide for foreigners
[North Americans and Europeans in particular] who are living in an
Arab country, who encounter Arabs frequently, or who are interested in the behavior of Arabs, whether encountered in the media or
personally."

has fewer people than New York City. Egypt, with forty-two million people, is 95 percent desert. One writer has stated: "A true map of the Arab World would show it as an archipelago: a scattering of fertile islands through a void of sand and sea. The Arabic word for desert is 'sahara' and it both divides and joins."[1] The political diversity among the Arab countries is notable; governmental systems include monarchies, military governments, and socialist republics.

But despite these differences, the Arabs are more homogeneous   5 than Westerners in their outlook on life. All Arabs share basic beliefs and values which cross national or social class boundaries. Social attitudes have remained relatively constant because Arab society is conservative and demands conformity from its members. Their beliefs are influenced by Islam even if they are not Moslems, child-rearing practices are nearly identical, and the family structure is essentially the same. Arabs are not as mobile as people in the West, and they have a high regard for tradition.

Initially foreigners may feel that Arabs are difficult to understand,   6 that their behavior patterns are not logical. In fact their behavior is quite comprehensible, even predictable. For the most part it conforms to certain patterns which make Arabs consistent in their reactions to other people.

It is important for the foreigner to be able to identify these cultural pat-   7 *terns and to distinguish them from individual traits.* By becoming aware of patterns, one can achieve a better understanding of what to expect and thereby cope more easily. The following lists of Arab values, religious attitudes and self-perceptions are central to the fundamental patterns of Arab culture. . . .

Basic Arab Values

- A person's dignity, honor, and reputation are of paramount importance and no effort should be spared to protect them, especially one's honor.
- It is important to behave at all times in a way which will create a good impression on others.
- Loyalty to one's family takes precedence over personal needs.
- Social class and family background are the major determining factors of personal status, followed by individual character and achievement.

---

[1]Stewart, Desmond, *The Arab World*, pp. 9–10.

Basic Arab Religious Attitudes

- Everyone believes in God, acknowledges His power and has a religious affiliation.
- Humans cannot control all events; some things depend on God (i.e., "fate").
- Piety is one of the most admirable characteristics in a person.
- There should be no separation between "church and state"; religion should be taught in schools and promoted by governments.
- Religious tenets should not be subjected to "liberal" interpretations or modifications which can threaten established beliefs and practices.

Basic Arab Self-perceptions

- Arabs are generous, humanitarian, polite, and loyal. Several studies have demonstrated that Arabs see these traits as characteristic of themselves and as distinguishing them from other groups.[2]
- Arabs have a rich cultural heritage. This is illustrated by their contributions to religion, philosophy, literature, medicine, architecture, art, mathematics, and the natural sciences.[3]
- Although there are many differences among Arab countries, the Arabs are a clearly defined cultural group, members of the "Arab nation" (al-umma al-'arabiyya).
- The Arab peoples have been victimized and exploited by the West. For them, the experience of the Palestinians represents the most painful and obvious example.
- Indiscriminate imitation of Western culture, by weakening traditional family ties and social and religious values, will have a corrupting influence on Arab society.
- Arabs are misunderstood and wrongly characterized by most Westerners.

Arabs feel that they are often portrayed in the Western media as excessively wealthy, irrational, sensuous, and violent, and there is little   8

---

[2]Dr. Levon H. Melikian (see bibliography) has studied the modal personality of some Arab students, searching for traits to define "national character."

The author administered a word-association test to a group of Lebanese university students in 1972. The most common responses associated with the word "Arabs" were "generous," "brave," "honorable," and "loyal." About half of the forty-three respondents added the word "misunderstood."

[3]This subject is very thoroughly discussed by Abdel-Rahim Omran in his book, *Population in the Arab World*, in the chapter, "The Contribution of the Arabs to World Culture and Science," pp. 13–41.

counterbalancing information about ordinary people who live family-and work-centered lives on a modest scale. One observer has remarked, "The Arabs remain one of the few ethnic groups who can still be slandered with impunity in America."[4] Another has stated, "In general, the image of the Arabs in British popular culture seems to be characterized by prejudice, hostility, and resentment. The mass media in Britain have failed to provide an adequate representation of points of view for the consumer to judge a real world of the Arabs."[5]

Emotion and Logic

How people deal with emotion or what value they place on objective vs. subjective behavior is culturally conditioned. *While objectivity is given considerable emphasis in Western culture, the opposite is true in Arab culture.*   9

Objectivity and Subjectivity

Westerners are taught that objectivity, the examination of facts in a logical way without the intrusion of emotional bias, is the mature and constructive approach to human affairs. One of the results of this belief is that in Western culture, subjectivity, a willingness to allow personal feelings and emotions to influence one's view of events, represents immaturity. Arabs believe differently. They place a higher value on the display of emotion, sometimes to the embarrassment or discomfort of foreigners. It is not uncommon to hear Westerners label this behavior as "immature," imposing their own values on what they have observed.   10

A British office manager in Saudi Arabia once described to me his problems with a Palestinian employee. "He is too sensitive, too emotional about everything," he said. "The first thing he should do is *grow up.*" While Westerners label Arabs as "too emotional," Arabs find Westerners "cold" and inscrutable.   11

Arabs consciously reserve the right to look at the world in a subjective way, particularly if a more objective assessment of a situation would bring to mind a too-painful truth. There is nothing to gain, for example, by pointing out Israel's brilliant achievements in land reclamation or in comparing the quality of Arab-made consumer items with im-   12

[4]Slade, Shelley, "The Image of the Arab in America: Analysis of a Poll of American Attitudes," *Middle East Journal*, p. 143. Many of the stereotypes about the Middle East which are taught in schools or depicted in American media are discussed in *The Middle East, The Image and Reality*, edited by Jonathan Friedlander (see bibliography).

[5]Nasir, Sari J., *The Arabs and the English*, p. 171.

ported ones. Such comments will generally not lead to a substantive discussion of how Arabs could benefit by imitating others; more likely, Arab listeners will become angry and defensive, insisting that the situation is not as you describe it and bringing up issues such as Israeli occupation of Arab lands or the moral deterioration of technological societies.

Fatalism

Fatalism, or a belief that people are helpless to control events, is 13 part of traditional Arab culture. It has been much over-emphasized by Westerners, however, and is far more prevalent among traditional, uneducated Arabs than it is among the educated elite today. It nevertheless still needs to be considered, since it will usually be encountered in one form or another by the Western visitor.

For Arabs, fatalism is based on the religious belief that God has 14 direct and ultimate control of all that happens. If something goes wrong, a person can absolve himself of blame or justify doing nothing to make improvements or changes by assigning the cause to God's will. Indeed, too much self-confidence about controlling events is considered a sign of arrogance tinged with blasphemy. The legacy of fatalism in Arab thought is most apparent in the oft heard and more or less ritual phrase "Inshallah" (if God wills).

Western thought has essentially rejected fatalism. Though God is 15 believed by many Westerners to intervene in human affairs, Greek logic, the humanism of the Enlightenment and cause-and-effect empiricism have inclined the West to view humans as having the ability to control their environment and destinies.

What Is Reality?

Reality is what you perceive—if you believe something exists, it 16 is real to you. If you select or rearrange facts, and repeat these to yourself often enough, they eventually become reality.

The cultural difference between Westerners and Arabs arises not 17 from the fact that this selection takes place, but from how each makes the selection. *Arabs are more likely to allow subjective perceptions to direct their actions.* This is a common source of frustration for Westerners, who often fail to understand why people in the Middle East act as they do.

If an Arab feels that something threatens his personal dignity, he 18 may be obliged to deny it, even in the face of facts to the contrary. A Westerner can point out flaws in his argument, but that is not the point. If he does not want to accept the facts, he will reject them and proceed according to his own view of the situation. An Arab will rarely admit to an error openly if it will cause him to lose face. *To Arabs, honor is more important than facts.*

An American woman in Tunis realized, when she was packing to leave, that some of her clothes and a suitcase were missing. She confronted the maid, who insisted that she had no idea where they could be. When the American found some of her clothes under a mattress, she called the company's Tunisian security officer. They went to the maid's house and found more missing items. The maid was adamant that she could not account for the items being in her home. The security officer said that he felt the matter should not be reported to the police—the maid's humiliation in front of her neighbors was sufficient punishment. 19

In 1974 an Israeli entered a small Arab-owned cafe in Jerusalem and asked for some watermelon, pointing at it and using the Hebrew word. The Arab proprietor responded that it should be called by the Arabic name, but the Israeli insisted on the Hebrew name. The Arab took offense at this point. He paused, shrugged, and instead of serving his customer, said, "There isn't any!" 20

At a conference held to discuss Arab and American cultures, Dr. Laura Nader related this incident: 21

> The mistake people in one culture often make in dealing with another culture is to transfer their functions to the other culture's functions. A political scientist, for example, went to the Middle East to do some research one summer and to analyze Egyptian newspapers. When he came back, he said to me, "But they are all just full of emotions. There is no data in these newspapers." I said, "What makes you think there should be?"[6]

Another way of influencing the perception of reality is by the choice of descriptive words and names. The Arabs are very careful in naming or referring to places, people, and events; slogans and labels are popular and provide an insight into how things are viewed. The Arabs realize that *names have a powerful effect on perception.* 22

There is a big psychological gap between opposing labels like "Palestine/Israel," "The West Bank/Judea and Samaria," and "freedom fighters ('hero martyrs' if they are killed)/terrorists." The 1967 Arab-Israeli War is called "The War of the Setback" in Arabic—in other words, it was *not* a "defeat." The 1973 War is called "The War of Ramadan" or "The Sixth of October War," *not* "The Yom Kippur War." 23

Be conscious of names and labels—they matter a great deal to the Arabs. If you attend carefully to what you hear in conversations with 24

---

[6]Atiyeh, George N., ed., *Arab and American Cultures*, p. 179.

Arabs and what is written in their newspapers, you will note how precisely they select descriptive words and phrases. You may find yourself being corrected by Arab acquaintances, and you will soon learn which terms are acceptable and which are not.

The Human Dimension

Arabs look at life in a personalized way. They are concerned about 25 people and feelings and place emphasis on "human factors" when they make decisions or analyze events. They feel that Westerners are too prone to look at events in an abstract or theoretical way, and that most Westerners lack sensitivity toward people.

In the Arab World, a manager or official is always willing to re- 26 consider a decision, regulation, or problem in view of someone's personal situation. Any regulation can be modified or avoided by someone with enough persuasive influence, particularly if the request is justified on the grounds of unusual personal need. This is unlike most Western societies, which emphasize the equal application of laws to all citizens. *In the Arab culture, people are more important than rules.*

T. E. Lawrence stated it succinctly: "Arabs believe in persons, not 27 in institutions."[7] They have a long tradition of personal appeal to authorities for exceptions to rules. This is commonly seen when they attempt to obtain special permits, exemptions from fees, acceptance into a school when preconditions are not met, or employment when qualifications are inadequate. They do not accept predetermined standards if these standards are a personal inconvenience.

Arabs place great value on personal interviews and on giving peo- 28 ple the opportunity to state their case. They are not comfortable filling out forms or dealing with an organization impersonally. They want to know the name of the top person who makes the final decision and are always confident that the rejection of a request may be reversed if top-level personal contact can be made. Frequently, that is exactly what happens.

Persuasion

Arabs and Westerners place a different value on certain types of 29 statements, which may lead to decreased effectiveness on both sides when they negotiate with each other. Arabs respond much more readily to personalized arguments than to attempts to impose "logical" conclusions. When you are trying to make a persuasive case in your discussions with Arabs, you will find it helpful to supplement your

---

[7]Lawrence, T. E. *Seven Pillars of Wisdom*, p. 24.

arguments with personal comments. You can refer to your mutual friendship, or emphasize the effect which approval or disapproval of the action will have on other people.

In the Middle East negotiation and persuasion have been devel- 30 oped into a fine art. Participants in negotiations enjoy long, spirited discussions and are usually not in any hurry to conclude them. Speakers feel free to add to their points of argument by demonstrating their verbal cleverness, using their personal charm, applying personal pressure, and engaging in personal appeals for consideration of their point of view.

The display of emotion also plays its part; indeed, one of the most 31 commonly misunderstood aspects of Arab communication involves their "display" of anger. Arabs are not usually as angry as they appear to Westerners. Raising the voice, repeating points, even pounding the table for emphasis may sound angry but, in the speaker's mind, indicate sincerity. A Westerner overhearing such a conversation (especially if it is in Arabic) may wrongly conclude that an argument is taking place. *Emotion connotes deep and sincere concern for the outcome of the discussion.*

Foreigners often miss the emotional dimension in their cross- 32 cultural transactions with Arabs. A British businessman once found that he and his wife were denied reservations on an airplane because the Arab ticketing official took offense at the manner in which he was addressed. The fact that seats were available was *not* an effective counter-argument. But when the Arab official noticed that the businessman's wife had begun to cry, he gave way and provided them with seats.

Arabs usually include human elements in their arguments. In ar- 33 guing the Palestine issue, for instance, they have always placed emphasis on the suffering of individuals rather than on points of law or a recital of historical events.

Bibliography

Atiyeh, George N., ed., *Arab and American Cultures*. Washington, D.C.: American Enterprise Institute for Public Policy Research, 1977.

Friedlander, Jonathan, ed., *The Middle East: The Image and the Reality*. Los Angeles: University of California (Curriculum Inquiry Center) Press, 1981.

Lawrence, T. E., *Seven Pillars of Wisdom*. New York: Doubleday & Co., Inc., 1926.

Melikian, Levon H., *Jassim: A Study in the Psychological Development of a Young Man in Qatar*. London: Longman Group Ltd., 1981.

_____"The Modal Personality of Saudi College Students: A Study in National Character," in *Psychological Dimensions of Near Eastern Studies,* edited by L. Carl Brown and Norman Itzkowitz. Princeton: The Darwin Press, 1977, pp. 166–209.

Nasir, Sari J., *The Arabs and the English,* Second edition. London: Longman Group Ltd., 1979.

Omran, Abdel-Rahim, *Population in the Arab World*. London: Croom Helm Ltd., 1980.

Stewart, Desmond, *The Arab World*. New York: Time-Life Books, 1972.

Slade, Shelley, "The Image of the Arab in America: Analysis of a Poll of American Attitudes," *Middle East Journal,* Vol. 35, No. 2, Spring 1981, pp. 143–162.

QUESTIONS

1. In the preface to *Understanding Arabs,* Nydell admits that "any attempt to describe the motives and values of an entire people is risky." What do you think the risks are in such an attempt? How well do you think Nydell overcomes or justifies these risks?

2. Also in the preface to *Understanding Arabs,* Nydell says that her generalized description of Arabs "focuses on the socially elite — businessmen, bureaucrats, managers, scientists, professors, and intellectuals" because these are the people with whom most Westerners will interact. What evidence do you find of an emphasis on social class in her analysis? How, specifically, would you describe the social class of the Westerners that Nydell seems to be addressing?

3. Discuss the various generalizations that Nydell makes about Westerners. How would you qualify these generalizations, or what would you add, in order to make lists (like Nydell's) of "Basic Western (or American) Values, Religious Attitudes, and Self-perceptions"? Try making such lists with a partner or small group, then sharing your results.

Good and Bad

LUCIA BERLIN

Nuns tried hard to teach me to be good. In high school it was Miss 1
Dawson. Santiago College, 1952. Six of us in the school were going on
to American colleges; we had to take American History and Civics
from the new teacher, Ethel Dawson. She was the only American
teacher, the others were Chilean or European.

We were all bad to her. I was the worst. If there was to be a test and 2
none of us had studied I could distract her with questions about the
Gadsden Purchase for the whole period, or get her started on segregation or American imperialism if we were really in trouble.

We mocked her, imitated her nasal Boston whine. She had a tall lift 3
on one shoe because of polio, wore thick wire-rimmed glasses. Splayed
gap teeth, a horrible voice. It seemed she deliberately made herself look
worse by wearing mannish, mismatched colors, wrinkled, soup-spot-
ted slacks, garish scarves on her badly-cut hair. She got very red-faced
when she lectured and she smelled of sweat. It was not simply that she
flaunted poverty ... Madame Tournier wore the same shabby black
skirt and blouse day after day, but the skirt was cut on the bias, the
black blouse, green and frayed with age, was of fine silk. Style, cachet
were all-important to us then.

She showed us movies and slides about the condition of the 4
Chilean miners and dock workers, all of it the U.S.A.'s fault. The am-
bassador's daughter was in the class, a few admirals' daughters. My
father was a mining engineer, worked with the CIA. I knew he truly
believed Chile needed the United States. Miss Dawson thought that she
was reaching impressionable young minds, whereas she was talking to
spoiled American brats. Each one of us had a rich, handsome, powerful American daddy. Girls feel about their fathers at that age like they
do about horses. It is a passion. She implied that they were villains.

Because I did most of the talking I was the one she zeroed in on, 5
keeping me after class, and one day even walked with me in the rose

Lucia Berlin's collections of short fiction include *Angels Laundromat: Stories* (1981), *Phantom Pain: Sixteen Stories* (1984), *Safe and Sound* (1988), *Homesick: New and Selected Stories* (1990; American Book Award, 1991), and *So Long: Stories 1987–1992*, where this story appears. Berlin, now from California, was born in Alaska and partly raised in Idaho, Montana, and Arizona mining camps; she spent most of her childhood in Chile, the setting for this story.

garden, complaining about the elitism of the school. I lost patience with her.

"What are you doing here then? Why don't you go teach the poor 6 if you're so worried about them? Why have anything to do with us snobs at all?"

She told me that this was where she was given work, because she 7 taught American History. She didn't speak Spanish yet, but all her spare time was spent working with the poor and volunteering in revolutionary groups. She said it wasn't a waste of time working with us . . . if she could change the thinking of one mind it would be worthwhile.

"Perhaps you are that one mind," she said. We sat on a stone 8 bench. Recess was almost over. Scent of roses and the mildew of her sweater.

"Tell me, what do you do with your weekends?" she asked. 9

It wasn't hard to sound utterly frivolous, but I exaggerated it any- 10 way. Hairdresser, manicurist, dressmaker. Lunch at the Charles. Polo, rugby or cricket, *thés dansants*, dinners, parties until dawn. Mass at El Bosque at seven on Sunday morning, still wearing evening clothes. The country club then for breakfast, golf or swimming, or maybe the day in Algarrobo at the sea, skiing in winter. Movies of course, but mostly we danced all night.

"And this life is satisfying to you?" she asked. 11

"Yes. It is." 12

"What if I asked you to give me your Saturdays, for one month, 13 would you do it? See a part of Santiago that you don't know."

"Why do you want me?" 14

"Because, basically, I think you are a good person. I think you 15 could learn from it." She clasped both my hands. "Give it a try."

Good person. But she had caught me earlier, with the word 16 Revolutionary. I did want to meet revolutionaries, because they were bad.

Everyone seemed a lot more upset than necessary about my 17 Saturdays with Miss Dawson, which then made me really want to do it. I told my mother I was going to help the poor. She was disgusted, afraid of disease, toilet seats. I even knew that the poor in Chile had no toilet seats. My friends were shocked that I was going with Miss Dawson at all. They said she was a loony, a fanatic, and a lesbian, was I crazy or what?

The first day I spent with her was ghastly, but I stuck with it out 18 of bravado.

Every Saturday morning we went to the city dump, in a pickup 19 truck filled with huge pots of food. Beans, porridge, biscuits, milk.

We set up a big table in a field next to miles of shacks made from flat-tened tin cans. A bent water faucet about three blocks away served the entire shack community. There were open fires in front of the squalid lean-tos, burning scraps of wood, cardboard, shoes, to cook on.

At first the place seemed to be deserted, miles and miles of 20 dunes. Dunes of stinking, smouldering garbage. After a while, through the dust and smoke, you could see that there were people all over the dunes. But they were the color of the dung, their rags just like the refuse they crawled in. No one stood up, they scurried on all fours like wet rats, tossing things into burlap bags that gave them humped animal backs, circling on, darting, meeting each other, touching noses, slithering away, disappearing like iguanas over the ridges of the dunes. But once the food was set up scores of women and children appeared, sooty and wet, smelling of decay and rotted food. They were glad for the breakfast, squatted, eating with bony elbows out like preying mantis on the garbage hills. After they had eaten, the children crowded around me; still crawling or sprawled in the dirt, they patted my shoes, ran their hands up and down my stockings.

"See, they like you," Miss Dawson said. "Doesn't that make you 21 feel good?"

I knew that they liked my shoes and stockings, my red Chanel 22 jacket.

Miss Dawson and her friends were exhilarated as we drove away, 23 chatting happily. I was sickened and depressed.

"What good does it do to feed them once a week. It doesn't make 24 a dent in their lives. They need more than biscuits once a week, for lord's sake."

Right. But until the revolution came and everything was shared 25 you had to do whatever helped at all.

"They need to know somebody realizes they live out here. We tell 26 them that soon things will change. Hope. It's about hope," Miss Dawson said.

We had lunch in a tenement in the south of the city, Six flights up. 27 One window that looked on to an airshaft. A hot plate, no running water. Any water they used had to be carried up those stairs. The table was set with four bowls and four spoons, a pile of bread in the center. There were many people, talking in small groups. I spoke Spanish, but they spoke in a heavy *caló* with almost no consonants, and were hard for me to understand. They ignored us, looked at us with amused tolerance or complete disdain. I didn't hear revolution-ary talk, but talk about work, money, filthy jokes. We all took turns eating lentils, drinking *chicha,* a raw wine, using the same bowls and glass as the person before.

"Nice you don't seem to mind about dirt," beamed Miss Dawson.   28

"I grew up in mining towns. Lots of dirt." But the cabins of   29
Finnish and Basque miners were pretty, with flowers and candles,
sweet-faced Virgins. This was an ugly, filthy place with misspelled
slogans on the walls, communist pamphlets stuck up with chewing
gum. There was a newspaper photograph of my father and the minister of mines, splattered with blood.

"Hey!" I said. Miss Dawson took my hand, stroked it. "Sh," she   30
said in English. "We're on first name basis here. Don't for heaven's
sake say who you are. Now, Adele, don't be uncomfortable. To grow
up you need to face all the realities of your father's personae."

"Not with blood on them."   31

"Precisely that way. It is a strong possibility and you should be   32
aware of it." She squeezed both my hands then.

After lunch she took me to "El Niño Perdido," an orphanage in an   33
old stone ivy-covered building in the foothills of the Andes. It was
run by French nuns, lovely old nuns, with fleur-de-lis coifs and blue-
grey habits. They floated through the dark rooms, above the stone
floors, flew down the passages by the flowered courtyard, popped
open wooden shutters, calling out in bird-like voices. They brushed
away insane children who were biting their legs, dragging them by
their little feet. They washed ten faces in a row, all the eyes blind.
They fed six mongoloid giants, reaching up with spoons of oatmeal.

These orphans all had something the matter. Some were insane,   34
others had no legs or were mute, some had been burned over their entire bodies. No noses or ears. Syphilitic babies and mongoloids in
their teens. The assorted afflictions spilled together from room to
room, out into the courtyard into the lovely unkempt garden.

"There are many things needed to do," Miss Dawson said. "I like   35
feeding and changing babies. You might read to the blind children . . .
they all seem particularly intelligent and bored."

There were few books. La Fontaine in Spanish. They sat in a cir-   36
cle, staring at me, really blankly. Nervous, I began a game, a clapping
and stomping kind of game like musical chairs. They liked that and
so did some other children.

I hated the dump on Saturdays but I liked going to the orphanage.   37
I even liked Miss Dawson when we were there. She spent her time
bathing and rocking babies and singing to them, while I made up
games for the older children. Some things worked and others didn't.
Relay races didn't because nobody would let go of the stick. Jump
rope was great because two boys with Down's syndrome would
turn the rope for hours on end without stopping, while everybody,
especially the blind girls, took turns. Even nuns jumped, jump jump
they hovered blue in the air. Farmer in the Dell. Button Button.

Hide-and-go-seek didn't work because nobody came home. The orphans were glad to see me; I loved going there, not because I was good, but because I liked to play.

Saturday nights we went to revolutionary theatre or poetry readings. We heard the greatest Latin American poets of our century. These were poets whose work I would later love, whom I would study and teach. But then I did not listen. I suffered an agony of self-consciousness and confusion. We were the only Americans there; all I heard were the attacks against the United States. Many people asked questions about American policy that I couldn't answer; I referred them to Miss Dawson and translated her answers, ashamed and baffled by what I told them, about segregation, Anaconda. She didn't realize how much the people scorned us, how they mocked her banal communist clichés about their reality. They laughed at me with my Josef haircut and nails, my expensive casual clothes. At one theatre group they put me on stage and the director hollered, "OK *Gringa*, tell me why you are in my country!" I froze and sat down, to hooting and laughter. Finally I told Miss Dawson I couldn't go out on Saturday nights anymore. 38

Dinner and dancing at Marcelo Errazuriz's. Martinis, consommé in little cups on the terrace, fragrant gardens beyond us. A six course dinner that began at eleven. Everyone teased me about my days with Miss Dawson, begged me to tell them where I went. I couldn't talk about it, not with my friends nor my parents. I remember someone making a joke about me and my *rotos*, "broken" meant poor people then. I felt ashamed, aware that there were almost as many servants in the room as guests. 39

I joined Miss Dawson in a worker's protest outside the United States Embassy. I had only walked about a block when a friend of my father's, Frank Wise, grabbed me out of the crowd, took me to the Crillon Hotel. 40

He was furious. "What in God's name do you think you are doing?" He soon understood what Miss Dawson didn't . . . that I had not the faintest idea of politics, of what any of this was about. He told me that it would be terrible for my father if the press found out what I was doing. I understood that. 41

On another Saturday afternoon I agreed to stand downtown and collect money for the orphanage. I stood on one corner and Miss Dawson on another. In only a few minutes dozens of people had insulted and cursed me. I didn't understand, shifted my sign for "Give to El Niño Perdido," and rattled the cup. Tito and Pepe, two friends, were on their way to the Waldorf for coffee. They whisked me away, forced me to go with them to coffee. 42

"This is *not* done here. Poor people beg. You are insulting the poor.   43
For a woman to solicit anything gives a shocking image. You will destroy your reputation. Also no one would believe you are not keeping
the money. A girl simply can't stand on the street unescorted. You can
go to charity balls or luncheons, but physical contact with other classes
is simply vulgar, and patronizing to them. Also you absolutely cannot
afford to be seen with someone of her sexual persuasion in public. My
dear, you are too young, you don't understand. . . ."

We drank Jamaican coffee and I listened to them. I told them I saw   44
what they were saying but I couldn't just leave Miss Dawson alone on
the corner. They said they would speak to her. The three of us went
down Ahumada to where she stood, proudly, while passersby muttered "*Gringa loca*" or "*puta coja*," crippled whore, at her.

"It is not appropriate, in Santiago, for a young girl to do this, and   45
we are taking her home," was all Tito said to her. She looked at
him with disdain, and later that week, in the hallway at school she
told me it was wrong to let men dictate my actions. I told her that
I felt everybody dictated my actions, that I had gone with her on
Saturdays a month longer than I had first promised. That I wasn't
going any more.

"It is wrong for you to return to a totally selfish existence. To   46
fight for a better world is the only reason for living. Have you learned
nothing?"

"I learned a lot. I see that many things need to change. But it's   47
their struggle, not mine."

"I can't believe you can say that. Don't you see, that's what is   48
wrong with the world, that attitude."

She limped crying to the bathroom, was late to class, where she   49
told us there would be no class that day. The six of us went out and
lay on the grass in the gardens, away from the windows so no one
could see that we weren't in class. The girls teased me, said that I was
breaking Miss Dawson's heart. She was obviously in love with me.
Did she try to kiss me? This really made me confused and mad. In
spite of everything I was beginning to like her, her dogged naive commitment, her hopefulness. She was like a little kid, like one of the
blind children when they gasped with pleasure, playing in the water
sprinkler. Miss Dawson never flirted with me or tried to touch me all
the time like boys did. But she wanted me to do things I didn't want
to do and I felt like a bad person for not wanting to, for not caring
more about the injustice in the world. The girls got mad at me because
I wouldn't talk about her. They called me Miss Dawson's mistress.
There was nobody I could talk to about any of this, nobody to ask
what was right or wrong, so I just felt wrong.

It was windy my last day at the dump. Sand sifted into the por- 50
ridge in glistening waves. When the figures rose on the hills it was
with a swirl of dirt so they looked like silver ghosts, dervishes. None
of them had shoes and their feet crept silently over the soggy mounds.
They didn't speak, or shout to each other, like most people do who
work together, and they never spoke to us. Beyond the steaming dung
hills was the city and above us all the white Andes. They ate. Miss
Dawson didn't say a word, gathering up the pots and utensils in the
sigh of wind.

We had agreed to go to a farm workers' rally outside of town that 51
afternoon. We ate *churrascos* on the street, stopped by her apartment
for her to change.

Her apartment was dingy and airless. The fact that her hot plate 52
for cooking was on the toilet tank made me feel ill, as did the odor of
old wool and sweat and hair. She changed in front of me, which I
found shocking and frightening, her naked, distorted blue-white
body. She put on a sleeveless sundress with no brassiere.

"Miss Dawson, that would be all right at night, in someone's 53
home, or at the beach, but you just can't go around bare like that in
Chile."

"I pity you. All your life you are going to be paralyzed by What Is 54
Done, by what people tell you you should think or do. I do not dress to
please others. It is a very hot day, and I feel comfortable in this dress."

"Well . . . it makes me not comfortable. People will say rude things 55
to us. It is different here, from the United States . . ."

"The best thing that could happen to you would be for you to be 56
uncomfortable once in a while."

We took several crowded busses to get to the *fundo* where the rally 57
was, waiting in the hot sun and standing on the busses. We got down
and walked down a beautiful lane lined with eucalyptus, stopped to
cool off in the stream by the lane.

We had arrived too late for the speeches. There was an empty 58
platform, a banner with "Land Back to the People" hanging askew
behind the mike. There was a small group of men in suits, obviously
the organizers, but most of the people were farm laborers. Guitars
were playing and there was a crowd around a couple dancing *La
Cueca* in a desultory fashion, languidly waving handkerchiefs as they
circled one another. People were pouring wine from huge vats or
standing in line for spit-roasted beef and beans. Miss Dawson told me
to find us a place at one of the tables, that she would bring our food.

I squeezed into a spot at the end of a table crowded with families. 59
Nobody was talking politics, it seemed that these were just country
people who had come to a free barbeque. Everyone was very, very
drunk. I could see Miss Dawson, chattering away in line, she was

drinking wine too, gesticulating and talking very loud so people would understand her.

"Isn't this great?" she asked, bringing two huge plates of food. "Let's introduce ourselves. Try to talk to the people more, that's how you learn, and help." 60

The two farm workers we sat by decided with gales of laughter that we were from another planet. As I had feared, they were amazed by her bare shoulders and visible nipples, couldn't figure out what she was. I realized that not only did she not speak Spanish, she was nearly blind. She would squint through her inch-thick glasses, smiling, but she couldn't see that these men were laughing at us, didn't like us, whatever we were. What were we doing here? She tried to explain that she was in the communist party, but instead of *partido* she kept toasting the *"Fiesta,"* which is a festive party, so they kept toasting her back, *"La Fiesta!"* 61

"We've got to leave," I said, but she only looked at me, slack-jawed and drunk. The man next to me was half-heartedly flirting with me, but I was more worried about the big drunk man next to Miss Dawson. He was stroking her shoulders with one hand while he ate a rib with the other. She was laughing away until he started grabbing her and kissing her, then she began to scream. 62

Miss Dawson ended up on the ground, sobbing uncontrollably. Everyone had rushed over at first, but they soon left, muttering "Nothing but some drunken *gringa*." The men we had sat by now ignored us totally. She got up and began to run toward the road; I followed her. When she got to the stream she tried to wash herself off, her mouth and her chest. She just got muddy and wet. She sat on the bank, crying, her nose running. I gave her my handkerchief. 63

"Miss Perfect! An ironed linen handkerchief!" she sneered. 64

"Yes," I said, fed up with her and only concerned now with getting home. Still crying, she staggered down the path toward the main road, where she started to hail down cars. I pulled her back into the trees. 65

"Look, Miss Dawson. You can't hitchhike here. They don't understand . . . it could get us in trouble, two women hitchhiking. Listen to me!" 66

But a farmer in an old truck had stopped, the engine ticking on the dusty road. I offered him money to take us to the outskirts of town. He was going all the way to downtown, could take us all the way to her house easy for 20 pesos. We climbed into the bed of the truck. 67

She put her arms around me in the wind. I could feel her wet dress, her sticky armpit hairs as she clung to me. 68

"You can't go back to your frivolous life! Don't leave! Don't leave me," she kept saying until at last we got to her block. 69

"Goodbye," I said. "Thanks for everything," or something dumb   70
like that. I left her on the curb, blinking at my cab until it turned the
corner.

The maids were leaning on the gate talking to the neighborhood   71
carabinero, so I didn't think anyone was home. But my father was there,
changing to go play golf.

"You're back early. Where have you been?" he asked.   72

"To a picnic, with my history teacher."   73

"Oh, yes. What is she like?"   74

"OK. She's a communist."   75

I just blurted that out. It had been a miserable day; I was fed up   76
with Miss Dawson. But that's all it took. Three words to my father. She
was fired sometime that weekend and we never saw her again.

No one else knew what had happened. The other girls were happy   77
she was gone. We had a free period now, even though we would have
to make up American history when we got to college. There was
nobody to speak to. To say I was sorry.

QUESTIONS

1.   Contrast the versions of Chilean poor and working class people
presented by Adele (the narrator) and Miss Dawson. "If she could
change the thinking of one mind it would be worthwhile" (paragraph
7), Adele says about Miss Dawson. To what extent do you think Miss
Dawson succeeds in changing Adele's mind?

2.   In what ways is Miss Dawson, like the Chileans, a victim of
stereotyping in this story? Who are the agents of this stereotyping,
and what do they have at stake in perpetrating or perpetuating such
stereotypes?

3.   "Nuns tried to teach me to be good," says Adele in the opening
paragraphs, but "We were all bad to her [Miss Dawson]. I was the
worst." Trace Adele's feelings about Miss Dawson and how they
change. If one purpose of the story is "To say I was sorry" (paragraph
77), how successfully do you think the narrator has done so?

THINKING ABOUT
ENCOUNTERING STEREOTYPES

1. Put together a composite stereotypical view of Americans from the selections by Althen, Atwood, and Stone. How accurate do you find this view? To what extent do you think these stereotypes are based in reality?

2. Compare how Meisler responds to a common stereotype about the French with how Gold responds to the anti-Semitism he encounters in Haiti. Think about a time you have encountered a stereotype, prejudice, or racist belief and how you responded; write about that response, combining a narrative recreating the encounter (like Gold's) with an analysis of causes (like Meisler's).

3. How might Meisler rewrite his essay, following Nydell, as "Beliefs and Values in the French World"? To what extent do you think the French, according to Meisler's analysis, embody the generalizations that Nydell makes about Westerners?

4. According to Nydell, "the Arabs are more homogeneous than Westerners in their outlook on life" and their basic values, religious attitudes, and self-perceptions "cross national or social class boundaries" (paragraph 5). In your view, how homogenous in their outlook are the Jews portrayed by Gold? To what extent do they seem to share—with each other, and with the Arabs—any basic beliefs or values?

5. What basic personal and political "beliefs and values" (like those Nydell describes for Arabs) of Americans and Chileans come into conflict in Berlin's story?

6. Imagine Miss Dawson, from Berlin's story, in one of this unit's other contexts—Meisler's France, Gold's Haiti, or Nydell's Arab cultures. Write a scene with dialogue in which Miss Dawson and another character (a first-person narrator like Adele, Gold, Nydell or one of the people from her examples, etc.) interact with people in this other culture.

7. Compare the extent to which Berlin's characters Miss Dawson and Adele (the narrator) embody the stereotypes of Americans described by Althen, Atwood, and Stone.

Exploring Additional Sources

8. In conjunction with one or more of the selections in this chapter, analyze the way ethnic stereotypes are encountered or encouraged in

"The Errand" by Nora Reza (page 404), "Venezuela for Visitors" by John Updike (page 415), "Return to the Land of *Roots*" by Alex Haley (page 476), "Assembly Line" by B. Traven (page 557), or "God and the Cobbler" by R. K. Narayan (page 569).

9. Apply Nydell's analysis of Arab beliefs and values to the experiences of Sarah Streed in "A Moroccan Memoir" (page 486) and the Professor in Paul Bowles's story "A Distant Episode" (page 517). How might Streed and the Professor have benefitted from Nydell's advice? In light of their experiences, how would you recommend qualifying, extending, or modifying Nydell's analysis?

10. Based on studies conducted by social scientists and other research, evaluate a particular claim in the selections by Stone, Meisler, or Nydell about the Japanese, French, Arabs, or another group. For example, test the extent to which "the Japanese like to make decisions by consensus" (Stone) or test the claim that Arabs "are often portrayed in the Western media as excessively wealthy, irrational, sensuous, and violent, and there is little counterbalancing information about ordinary people" (Nydell).

11. Research conditions of poverty in Haiti or Chile or U.S. relations with one of these countries during a recent historical period. For example, analyze the relationship between Haiti's complex ethnic composition and its endemic poverty, or argue a position about the recent U.S. military occupation of Haiti.

11

MEETING THE THIRD WORLD

Native[1]

RAYMOND WILLIAMS

Native is one of those interesting words which, while retaining a substantial unity of meaning, are applied in particular contexts in ways which produce radically different and even opposite senses and tones. **Native** came into English as an adjective from C14 and as a noun from C15, from fw *natif,* F, which had earlier taken the form *naif* (giving English *naive* in the sense of artless and simple), from *nativus,* L—an adjective meaning innate or natural, and *nativus,* mL—a noun formed from this. The root was the past participle of *nasci,* L—to be born.

Most of the early uses of **native** as an adjective were of a kind we would still recognize: innate, natural, or of a place in which one is born (cf. the related *nation*). A positive social and political sense, as in **native land, native country,** was strong from C16 onwards. But political conquest and domination had already produced the other and negative sense of **native,** in both noun and adjective, where it was generally equivalent to bondman or villein, born in bondage. Though the particular social usage became obsolete, the negative use of **native** to describe the inferior inhabitants of a place subjected to alien political power or conquest, or even of a place visited and observed from some supposedly superior standpoint, became general. It was particularly common as a term for "non-Europeans" in the period of colonialism and imperialism, but it was also used of the inhabitants of various countries and regions of Britain and North America, and (in a sense synonymous with the disparaging use of *locals*) of the inhabitants of a place in which some superior person had settled. Yet all the time, alongside this use, **native** remained a very positive word when applied to one's own place or person.

The negative use, especially for "non-Europeans," can still be found, even in writing which apparently rejects its ideological implications. *Indigenous* has served both as a euphemism and as a more

---

[1]See page 86 for a key to the abbreviations used in this selection. (Ed.)

neutral term. In English it is more difficult to use in the sense which converts all others to inferiors (*to go indigenous* is obviously less plausible than **to go native**). In French, however, *indigènes* went through the same development as English **natives**, and is now often replaced by *autochtones*.

—FROM *KEYWORDS: A VOCABULARY OF CULTURE AND SOCIETY*, REVISED EDITION, 1985

Natives of Tierra del Fuego

CHARLES DARWIN

While going one day on shore near Wollaston Island, we pulled alongside a canoe with six Fuegians. These were the most abject and miserable creatures I anywhere beheld. On the east coast the natives, as we have seen, have guanaco cloaks, and on the west, they possess seal-skins. Amongst these central tribes the men generally have an otter-skin, or some small scrap about as large as a pocket-handkerchief, which is barely sufficient to cover their backs as low down as their loins. It is laced across the breast by strings, and according as the wind blows, it is shifted from side to side. But these Fuegians in the canoe were quite naked, and even one full-grown woman was absolutely so. It was raining heavily, and the fresh water, together with the spray, trickled down her body. In another harbor not far distant, a woman, who was suckling a recently born child, came one day alongside the vessel, and remained there out of mere curiosity, whilst the sleet fell and thawed on her naked bosom, and on the skin of her naked baby! These poor wretches were stunted in their growth, their hideous faces bedaubed with white paint, their skins filthy and greasy, their hair entangled, their voices discordant, and their gestures violent. Viewing such men, one can hardly make oneself believe that they are fellow-creatures, and inhabitants of the same world. It is a common subject of conjecture what pleasure in life some of the lower animals can enjoy: how much more reasonably the same question may be asked with respect to these barbarians! At night, five or six human beings, naked and scarcely protected from the wind and rain of this tempestuous climate, sleep on the wet ground coiled up like animals. Whenever it is low water, winter or summer, night or day, they must rise to pick shellfish from the rocks; and the women either dive to collect sea-eggs, or sit patiently in their canoes, and with a baited hair-line without any hook, jerk out little fish. If a seal is killed, or the floating carcass of a putrid whale discovered, it is a feast; and such miserable food is assisted by a few tasteless berries and fungi.

—FROM *VOYAGE OF THE BEAGLE*, 1839

The Lone Ethnographer

RENATO ROSALDO

Once upon a time, the Lone Ethnographer rode off into the sunset in search of "his native." After undergoing a series of trials, he encountered the object of his quest in a distant land. There, he underwent his rite of passage by enduring the ultimate ordeal of "fieldwork." After collecting "the data," the Lone Ethnographer returned home and wrote a "true" account of "the culture."

Whether he hated, tolerated, respected, befriended, or fell in love with "his native," the Lone Ethnographer was willy-nilly complicit with the imperialist domination of his epoch. The Lone Ethnographer's mask of innocence (or, as he put it, his "detached impartiality") barely concealed his ideological role in perpetuating the colonial control of "distant" peoples and places. His writings represented the human objects of the civilizing mission's global enterprise as if they were ideal recipients of the white man's burden.

The Lone Ethnographer depicted the colonized as members of a harmonious, internally homogeneous, unchanging culture. When so described, the culture appeared to "need" progress, or economic and moral uplifting. In addition, the "timeless traditional culture" served as a self-congratulatory reference point against which Western civilization could measure its own progressive historical evolution. The civilizing journey was conceived more as a rise than a fall, a process more of elevation than degradation (a long, arduous journey upward, culminating in "us").

After returning to the metropolitan center where he was schooled, the Lone Ethnographer wrote his definitive work.

—From *Culture and Truth: The Remaking of Social Analysis*, 1989

Five Stages of Culture Shock

PETER S. ADLER

Stage	Perception	Emotional Range	Behavior	Interpretation
Contact	Differences are intriguing Perceptions are screened and selected	Excitement Stimulation Euphoria Playfulness Discovery	Curiosity Interest Assured Impressionistic	The individual is insulated by his or her own culture. Differences as well as similarities provide rationalization for continuing confirmation of status, role, and identity.
Disintegration	Differences are impactful Contrasted cultural reality cannot be screened out	Confusion Disorientation Loss Apathy Isolation Loneliness Inadequacy	Depression Withdrawal	Cultural differences begin to intrude. Growing awareness of being different leads to loss of self-esteem. Individual experiences loss of cultural support ties and misreads new cultural cues.
Reintegration	Differences are rejected	Anger Rage Nervousness Anxiety Frustration	Rebellion Suspicion Rejection Hostility Exclusive Opinionated	Rejection of second culture causes preoccupation with likes and dislikes; differences are projected. Negative behavior, however, is a form of self-assertion and growing self-esteem.
Autonomy	Differences and similarities are legitimized	Self-assured Relaxed Warm Empathic	Assured Controlled Independent "Old hand" Confident	The individual is socially and linguistically capable of negotiating most new and different situations; he or she is assured of ability to survive new experiences.
Independence	Differences and similarities are valued and significant	Trust Humour Love Full range of previous emotions	Expressive Creative Actualizing	Social, psychological and cultural differences are accepted and enjoyed. The individual is capable of exercising choice and responsibility and able to *create* meaning for situations.

—From "The Transitional Experience: An Alternative View of Culture Shock," in the *Journal of Humanistic Psychology*, 1975

All God's Children Need Traveling Shoes

MAYA ANGELOU

Each morning Ghana's seven-and-one-half million people seemed   1
to crowd at once into the capital city where the broad avenues as well
as the unpaved rutted lanes became gorgeous with moving pageantry:
bicycles, battered lorries, hand carts, American and European cars,
chauffeur-driven limousines. People on foot struggled for right-of-
way, white-collar workers wearing white knee-high socks brushed
against market women balancing large baskets on their heads as they
proudly swung their wide hips. Children, bright faces shining with
palm oil, picked openings in the throng, and pretty young women in
western clothes affected not to notice the attention they caused as they
laughed together talking in the musical Twi language. Old men sat or
stooped beside the road smoking homemade pipes and looking wise
as old men have done eternally.

The too sweet aromas of flowers, the odors of freshly fried fish and   2
stench from open sewers hung in my clothes and lay on my skin. Car
horns blew, drums thumped. Loud radio music and the muddle of
many languages shouted or murmured. I needed country quiet.

The Fiat was dependable, and I had a long weekend, money in my   3
purse, and a working command of Fanti, so I decided to travel into the
bush. I bought roasted plaintain stuffed with boiled peanuts, a quart
of Club beer and headed my little car west. The stretch was a highway
from Accra to Cape Coast, filled with trucks and private cars passing
from lane to lane with abandon. People hung out of windows of the
crowded mammie lorries, and I could hear singing and shouting when

---

Maya Angelou is a poet, playwright, and memoirist and has also performed in plays and films, written musical scores, and produced a TV
series on African American traditions. Her poetry books include *And
Still I Rise* (1978), *Shaker, Why Don't You Sing?* (1983), *Poems* (1986),
and *On the Pulse of Morning* (1993), the Inaugural Poem commissioned
by President Clinton for his inauguration. The first volume of
Angelou's autobiography, *I Know Why the Caged Bird Sings* (1970),
focuses on her childhood in rural, racially segregated Arkansas and
has been frequently excerpted for anthologies used in writing courses. Her other memoirs include *Gather Together in My Name* (1974), *The
Heart of a Woman* (1981), and *All God's Children Need Traveling Shoes*
(1986), from which this selection comes.

the drivers careened those antique vehicles up and down hills as if each was a little train out to prove it could.

I stopped in Cape Coast only for gas. Although many Black 4 Americans had headed for the town as soon as they touched ground in Ghana, I successfully avoided it for a year. Cape Coast Castle and the nearby Elmina Castle had been holding forts for captured slaves. The captives had been imprisoned in dungeons beneath the massive buildings and friends of mine who had felt called upon to make the trek reported that they felt the thick stone walls still echoed with old cries.

The palm tree-lined streets and fine white stone buildings did not 5 tempt me to remain any longer than necessary. Once out of the town and again onto the tarred roads, I knew I had not made a clean escape. Despite my hurry, history had invaded my little car. Pangs of self-pity and a sorrow for my unknown relatives suffused me. Tears made the highway waver, and were salty on my tongue.

What did they think and feel, my grandfathers, caught on those 6 green Savannahs, under the baobab trees? How long did their families search for them? Did the dungeon wall feel chilly and its slickness strange to my grandmothers who were used to the rush of air against bamboo huts and the sound of birds rattling their grass roofs?

I had to pull off the road. Just passing near Cape Coast Castle had 7 plunged me back into the eternal melodrama.

There would be no purging, I knew, unless I asked all the ques- 8 tions. Only then would the spirits understand that I was feeding them. It was a crumb, but it was all I had.

I allowed the shapes to come to my imagination: children passed 9 tied together by ropes and chains, tears abashed, stumbling in dull exhaustion, then women, hair uncombed, bodies gritted with sand, and sagging in defeat. Men, muscles without memory, minds dimmed, plodding, leaving bloodied footprints in the dirt. The quiet was awful. None of them cried, or yelled, or bellowed. No moans came from them. They lived in a mute territory, dead to feeling and protest. These were the legions, sold by sisters, stolen by brothers, bought by strangers, enslaved by the greedy and betrayed by history.

For a long time, I sat as in an open-air auditorium watching a troop 10 of tragic players enter and exit the stage.

The visions faded as my tears ceased. Light returned and I started 11 the car, turned off the main road, and headed for the interior. Using rutted track roads, and lanes a little larger than foot paths, I found the River Pra. The black water moving quietly, ringed with the tall trees, seemed enchanted. A fear of snakes kept me in the car, but I parked and watched the bright sun turn the water surface into a rippling cloth of lamé. I passed through villages which were little more than collections of thatch huts with goats and small children wandering in the lanes. The noise of my car brought smiling adults out to wave at me.

In the late afternoon, I reached the thriving town that was my des- 12
tination. A student whom I had met at Legon had spoken to me often
of the gold-mining area, of Dunkwa, his birthplace. His reports had so
glowed with the town's virtues, and I had chosen that spot for my first
journey.

My skin color, features and the Ghana cloth I wore made me look 13
like any young Ghanaian woman. I could pass if I didn't talk too
much.

As usual, in the towns of Ghana, the streets were filled with ven- 14
dors selling their wares of tinned pat milk, hot spicy Killi Willis (fried,
ripe plaintain chips), Pond's Cold Cream and anti-mosquito incense
rings. Farmers were returning home, children returning from school.
Young boys grinned at mincing girls and always there were the market women, huge and impervious. I searched for a hotel sign in vain
and as the day lengthened, I started to worry. I didn't have enough
gas to get to Koforidua, a large town northeast of Dunkwa, where
there would certainly be hotels, and I didn't have the address of my
student's family. I parked the car a little out of the town center and
stopped a woman carrying a bucket of water on her head and a baby
on her back.

"Good day." I spoke in Fanti, and she responded. I continued, "I 15
beg you, I am a stranger looking for a place to stay."

She repeated, "Stranger?" and laughed. "You are a stranger? No. 16
No."

To many Africans only Whites could be strangers. All Africans be- 17
longed somewhere, to some clan. All Akan-speaking people belong to
one of eight blood lines (Abosua) and one of eight spirit lines (Ntoro).

I said, "I am not from here." 18

For a second fear darted in her eyes. There was the possibility that 19
I was a witch or some unhappy ghost from the country of the dead. I
quickly said, "I am from Accra." She gave me a good smile. "Oh, one
Accra. Without a home." She laughed. The Fanti word *Nkran*, for
which the capitol was named, means the large ant that builds ten-foot-
high domes of red clay and lives with millions of other ants.

"Come with me." She turned quickly, steadying the bucket on 20
her head, and led me between two corrugated tin shacks. The baby
bounced and slept on her back, secured by the large piece of cloth
wrapped around her body. We passed a compound where women
were pounding the dinner foo foo in wooden bowls.

The woman shouted, "Look what I have found. One Nkran has no 21
place to sleep tonight." The women laughed and asked, "One Nkran?
I don't believe it."

"Are you taking it to the old man?" 22

"Of course." 23

"Sleep well, alone, Nkran, if you can." My guide stopped before a 24 small house. She put the water on the ground and told me to wait while she entered the house. She returned immediately followed by a man who rubbed his eyes as if he had just been awakened.

He walked close and peered hard at my face. "This is the Nkran?" 25 The woman was adjusting the bucket on her head.

"Yes, Uncle. I have brought her." She looked at me, "Good-bye, 26 Nkran. Sleep in peace. Uncle, I am going." The man said, "Go and come, child," and resumed studying my face. "You are not Ga." He was reading my features.

A few small children had collected around his knees. They could 27 barely hold back their giggles as he interrogated me.

"Aflao?" 28

I said, "No." 29

"Brong-ahafo?" 30

I said, "No. I am—." I meant to tell him the truth, but he said, 31 "Don't tell me. I will soon know." He continued staring at me. "Speak more. I will know from your Fanti."

"Well, I have come from Accra and I need to rent a room for the 32 night. I told that woman that I was a stranger . . ."

He laughed. "And you are. Now, I know. You are Bambara from 33 Liberia. It is clear you are Bambara." He laughed again. "I always can tell. I am not easily fooled." He shook my hand. "Yes, we will find you a place for the night. Come." He touched a boy at his right. "Find Patience Aduah, and bring her to me."

The children laughed and all ran away as the man led me into the 34 house. He pointed me to a seat in the neat little parlor and shouted, "Foriwa, we have a guest. Bring beer." A small Black woman with an imperial air entered the room. Her knowing face told me that she had witnessed the scene in her front yard.

She spoke to her husband. "And, Kobina, did you find who the 35 stranger was?" She walked to me. I stood and shook her hand. "Welcome, stranger." We both laughed. "Now don't tell me, Kobina, I have ears, also. Sit down, Sister, beer is coming. Let me hear you speak."

We sat facing each other while her husband stood over us smiling. 36 "You, Foriwa, you will never get it."

I told her my story, adding a few more words I had recently 37 learned. She laughed grandly. "She is Bambara. I could have told you when Abaa first brought her. See how tall she is? See her head? See her color? Men, huh. They only look at a woman's shape."

Two children brought beer and glasses to the man who poured 38 and handed the glasses around. "Sister, I am Kobina Artey; this is my wife Foriwa and some of my children."

I introduced myself, but because they had taken such relish in de- 39 tecting my tribal origin I couldn't tell them that they were wrong. Or,

less admirably, at that moment I didn't want to remember that I was
an American. For the first time since my arrival, I was very nearly
home. Not a Ghanaian, but at least accepted as an African. The sensation was worth a lie.

Voices came to the house from the yard.   40

"Brother Kobina," "Uncle," "Auntie."   41

Foriwa opened the door to a group of people who entered speak-   42
ing fast and looking at me.

"So this is the Bambara woman? The stranger?" They looked me   43
over and talked with my hosts. I understood some of their conversation.
They said that I was nice looking and old enough to have a little wisdom.
They announced that my car was parked a few blocks away. Kobina told
them that I would spend the night with the newlyweds, Patience and
Kwame Duodu. Yes, they could see clearly that I was a Bambara.

"Give us the keys to your car, Sister; someone will bring your bag."   44

I gave up the keys and all resistance. I was either at home with   45
friends, or I would die wishing that to be so.

Later, Patience, her husband, Kwame, and I sat out in the yard   46
around a cooking fire near to their thatched house which was much
smaller than the Artey bungalow. They explained that Kobina Artey
was not a chief, but a member of the village council, and all small matters in that area of Dunkwa were taken to him. As Patience stirred the
stew in the pot, which was balanced over the fire, children and women
appeared sporadically out of the darkness carrying covered plates.
Each time Patience thanked the bearers and directed them to the
house, I felt the distance narrow between my past and present.

In the United States, during segregation, Black American travelers,   47
unable to stay in hotels restricted to White patrons, stopped at
churches and told the Black ministers or deacons of their predica-
ments. Church officials would select a home and then inform the un-
expecting hosts of the decision. There was never a protest, but the new
hosts relied on the generosity of their neighbors to help feed and even
entertain their guests. After the travelers were settled, surreptitious
knocks would sound on the back door.

In Stamps, Arkansas, I heard so often, "Sister Henderson, I know   48
you've got guests. Here's a pan of biscuits."

"Sister Henderson, Mama sent a half a cake for your visitors."   49

"Sister Henderson, I made a lot of macaroni and cheese. Maybe   50
this will help with your visitors."

My grandmother would whisper her thanks and finally, when the   51
family and guests sat down at the table, the offerings were so different
and plentiful it appeared that days had been spent preparing the meal.

Patience invited me inside, and when I saw the table I was con-   52
firmed in my earlier impression. Ground nut stew, garden egg stew,

hot pepper soup, kenke, kotomre, fried plantain, dukuno, shrimp, fish cakes, and more, all crowded together on variously patterned plates.

In Arkansas, the guests would never suggest, although they knew 53 better, that the host had not prepared every scrap of food, especially for them.

I said to Patience, "Oh, Sister, you went to such trouble." 54

She laughed, "It is nothing, Sister. We don't want our Bambara rel- 55 ative to think herself a stranger anymore. Come, let us wash and eat."

After dinner I followed Patience to the outdoor toilet, then they 56 gave me a cot in a very small room.

In the morning I wrapped my cloth under my arms, sarong fash- 57 ion, and walked with Patience to the bath house. We joined about twenty women in a walled enclosure that had no ceiling. The greetings were loud and cheerful as we soaped ourselves and poured buckets of water over our shoulders.

Patience introduced me. "This is our Bambara sister." 58

"She's a tall one all right. Welcome, Sister." 59

"I like her color." 60

"How many children, Sister?" The woman was looking at my 61 breasts.

I apologized, "I only have one." 62

"One?" 63

"One?" 64

"One!" Shouts reverberated over the splashing water. I said, "One, 65 but I'm trying."

They laughed. "Try hard, sister. Keep trying." 66

We ate leftovers from the last night feast and I said a sad good-bye 67 to my hosts. The children walked me back to my car with the oldest boy carrying my bag. I couldn't offer money to my hosts, Arkansas had taught me that, but I gave change to the children. They bobbed and jumped and grinned.

"Good-bye, Bambara Auntie." 68

"Go and come, Auntie." 69

"Go and come." 70

I drove into Cape Coast before I thought of the gruesome castle 71 and out of its environs before the ghosts of slavery caught me. Perhaps their attempts had been half-hearted. After all, in Dunkwa, although I let a lie speak for me, I had proved that one of their descendants, at least one, could just briefly return to Africa, and that despite cruel betrayals, bitter ocean voyages and hurtful centuries, we were still recognizable.

QUESTIONS

1. Based on Angelou's narrative, describe the local customs in Dunkwa, Ghana, for the arrival of a stranger in the village. What similar customs does Angelou recognize from her African American experience in Arkansas?

2. How, according to her memoir, is Angelou able to "pass" as an African? Have you ever "passed" or been mistakenly identified with a group to which you do not belong? If so, compare your experience with Angelou's and classmates' experiences.

3. "The sensation" of being taken for a native Ghanaian, says Angelou, "was worth a lie" (paragraph 39). Discuss this morally ambiguous position. To what extent do you think Angelou's fooling of Kobina, Foriwa, and the other villagers is selfish or harmless? How does she justify the lie? Is it worthwhile, and for whom?

Return to the Land of Roots

ALEX HALEY

"Alex! It's Alex!," shouted some of Juffure Village's children, run- 1
ning toward us. They had just recognized me as one of the three men
unloading our car's back seat and trunk of four 100 pound bags of
sugar and rice and the traditional visitor's gift packets of kola nuts
wrapped in big dark-green palm leaves. *Geo* photographer Guido
Mangold and I had been driven from Banjul, the capital of The
Gambia, by the dark, good-looking, fiftyish Kebba Saidy, who would
also be our interpreter. I had purposely sent the Juffure Village folk no
advance word of my coming. I knew they would have put themselves
to much trouble to give me an extravagant welcome, as they'd done on
my previous visits.

I just wanted this to be a quiet arrival on a non-tourist, normal day 2
for the villagers—or, anyhow, whatever had become normal for them
since the world-wide reception given my book *Roots* and its accompanying television film. In part because of the publicity, the previously
little-known Republic of The Gambia suddenly began receiving more
than 20,000 tourists annually. Hot, dusty, back-country Juffure Village
(population 75) simultaneously found itself the country's principal
tourist attraction, because *Roots* had described it as the circa-1750s
home of a Mandinka youth named Kunta Kinte. The book told of
Kunta's capture and abduction on a slave ship to the United States,
where on a Virginia plantation he began a family—and in the process
became my maternal great-great-great-great-grandfather.

The children's noisy commotion roused the elders, who had been 3
escaping the sun within their small mud-walled, thatch-roofed homes.
They came popping through their doorways; then they, too, rushed toward us, waving their arms and exclaiming that I'd returned again.
Gratitude toward them engulfed me, and I felt guilty that nearly two
years had passed since my last visit. I wished I knew a way to convey

---

Alex Haley (1921–1992) was the slain civil rights leader Malcolm X's
collaborator for *The Autobiography of Malcolm X* (1965) and the author
of *Roots: The Saga of an American Family* (1976), which traces Haley's
family history from the slave trade of the mid-18th century. *Roots* was
made into a widely viewed six-part television movie in 1977. *Alex
Haley's Queen* (1993), a sequel to *Roots* based on a television screen-
play, was completed by David Stevens after Haley's death in 1992.
This essay originally appeared in the travel magazine *Geo* in 1981,
with pictures by German photographer Guido Mangold.

to them the irony that when a writer is lucky enough to achieve a major success, then his previous life-style, which in my case would have permitted more visits, is radically changed. That had happened to me since the publication of *Roots*. Then it occurred to me that I probably could not fully understand to what degree the once quiet lives of Juffure's people had also been changed.

Hurrying toward us among the villagers were two tall uniformed 4 policemen. I remembered hearing in the United States how Juffure's swiftly increasing tourism had required the Gambian government to assign a permanent police force there. Even so, daily tourism so disturbed the people's normal way of living that finally tourism within the village as well as its environs was officially permitted only three days a week.

Someone hallooed loudly and repetitively to signal the women and 5 younger men, who were tilling their food crops in the nearby fields. Soon Guido, Kebba and I were the center of an animated crowd of people. Conspicuous among them was a short, brusque, middle-aged man of determined look and manner who was wearing a blue knit cap under the hot sun. He pushed and shoved ahead of the others until he had posted himself directly in front of us. Looking anxious that we acknowledge his mission, he pumped up and down before us what seemed to be a gray metal tool case with a thick steel lock. Cut through the top of the case was a finger-size slot.

Pointing at the slot, the man spoke rapid Mandinka to Kebba 6 Saidy. Kebba translated the message, which was that visitors were expected to drop donations of money into the case: each month the case was unlocked and opened with all observing, and the villagers shared its contents.

It was so different from the Juffure I had first visited. The portable 7 cashbox and its bearer's manner—and the way both appeared to be taken for granted—were at odds with the utter dignity and reserve of the Juffure Village I had known.

Across the intervening thirteen years, I had learned only too well— 8 from considerable travel and some brief periods of residence in underdeveloped countries—that in spending or displaying relative wealth, tourists and other visitors only heighten local perception of relative poverty. I knew that the process had inevitably evolved in so many other places, but I felt no less badly that now it had also happened in Juffure. And where Juffure was concerned, it was harder yet for me to face the fact that I had played the undeniable role of catalyst in the process.

Bursting through my thoughts, the squealing, rail-thin Mrs. Binta 9 Kinte rushed to embrace me, her head and shoulders bound up in one of her trademarked brightly iridescent scarves. Just behind her was the very old, very black *alcala* (village headman), Mr. Bakaryding Taal, a tall, spare man clad in a white pillbox hat and long black robe. I knew the nature of the rivalry between them. Traditionally, nobody ever dares to challenge an alcala's position in the village, but the natural flair and charisma of Mrs. Binta Kinte had long since made her such a tourist favorite that her photograph adorned many thousands of postcards on sale all over The Gambia. Moreover, in 1967 it had been her late husband, the *griot* (oral historian) of Juffure Village, who had told me the ancestral Kinte clan history, of which I had written in *Roots*. And Mrs. Binta Kinte, most aware of all these assets, employs her own subtle ways to require the somber, aged Mr. Bakaryding Taal to compete for such recognition as he can get. It was no accident that the alcala's only alternative was to stand and wait, leaning sourly on his cane, as I sought physically to disengage myself from the practically adhesive arms of Mrs. Binta Kinte before I could grasp and shake his gnarled, wrinkled hands.

Behind Mr. Bakaryding Taal were the village's two policemen. 10 "You are Mr. Alex Haley?" asked the taller one, who spoke with a precise formality. He was Constable Ebrima Jammeh, 23, a six-footer of the Jola tribe from Bulock Village. Affirming that I was, I introduced Guido Mangold as my photographer friend and guest from Germany, and Kebba Saidy as the driver having been kind enough to bring us that morning from Banjul. The policemen exchanged glances and appeared briefly to consider the situation. Then Constable Jammeh said, "Well, this is not a permitted visiting day, but as it is you, sir, I believe exception can be made." He paused, handing me a printed card, and added, "However, these are the rules."

As I scanned the card, my sense of concern was only refueled. Had 11 my book helped or hurt this village? There could be no question that *Roots* had accomplished many desirable things. It had replaced black Africa's long, onerous "Tarzan and Jane" image with the far more accurate and certainly much more appropriate images of Kunta Kinte of Juffure and his people. It was generally conceded that among some 27 million black Americans, *Roots* had generated a new sense of ethnic and ancestral pride. In addition, from black Africa itself there had come praise from heads of state, and the Educational Federation of West Africa had even requested a special primary-school edition spanning only Kunta Kinte's growing-up years. The teachers felt that this part of *Roots* would convey to contemporary African students a greater knowledge and appreciation of the old African culture.

There was all this and much more, yet inescapably, it was also a 12 fact that on the card Constable Jammeh had handed me, each of those printed rules for visitors sought to cope with real dilemmas that now threatened the quality of life in Juffure.

Rule number one directed that tourists give no money or gifts to   13
anyone but the village headman, whose courier bore the portable cashbox. I'd heard about the background for this in America. The initial
waves of tourists into Juffure had set the villagers vying with one another for gifts, until each night brought heated discussions and resid-
ual bad feelings. All this when the amiable, caring and sharing characteristics of rural Gambians are well-known (even city-dwelling
Gambians are noted throughout West Africa for their peacefulness).

Another rule printed on the card prohibited any TV or movie cam-   14
eras: Juffure had been visited by unscrupulous filmmakers encouraging bared breasts or anything else they could photograph to strike a
prurient note. A third rule stipulated a maximum of 25 visitors at any
one time, with each person required to have spent at least one night in
the Gambian capital of Banjul. I knew this rule was intended to foil
shrewd Senegalese speedboat operators who took large tourist parties
directly up the wide Gambia River, first to visit Juffure Village and
then to circle the ancient Fort James Island slave headquarters; they
would then whisk their clients back to Senegal, leaving The Gambia
without a single cent reaped from its visitors.

I thanked Constable Jammeh for the card, assuring him that we'd   15
respect the rules. I was again embraced by Mrs. Binta Kinte, who told
me something in Mandinka; the gathered people nodded vigorously.
Kebba Saidy translated: they were filled with embarrassment because,
not knowing I was coming, they had prepared no suitable welcome.
For the umpteenth time, I felt like kicking myself for never having
learned to communicate even a little in my ancestral tongue so that I
wouldn't always be utterly dependent on an interpreter. Now I was
again asking Kebba Saidy if he'd please relay that I deeply respected
their welcoming custom and that I hoped my not sending advance
word had in no way offended them but that I would never need further assurance of their welcome than that which they had given me
when I returned soon after *Roots* was published.

And indeed I never could forget that welcome. I had brought sev-   16
eral American family members and friends with me, and even before
we reached The Gambia, on arrival in neighboring Senegal, we had received the red-carpet treatment and a special audience with Léopold
Senghor, who was then the president. In The Gambia, President
Dawda Jawara had ordered that his yacht sail all of us upriver to
Juffure.

The village adjacent to Juffure, Albreda, joined in the celebration   17
as our party disembarked at the mooring pier. I remember being physically buffeted between leaping, shouting, dancing celebrants as the
ragged, dusty parade wended its way back toward Juffure. At the entrance to the village, some men sprang from roadside bushes and fired

off ancient-looking muskets that set masked *kankurang* dancers, their bodies covered with leafy green branches, into frenzied motion.

Now, lacking advance notice, some younger men appeared spon- 18
taneously, playing drums, *koras*[1] and balaphons; women and children were singing, dancing and beating dried gourds with sticks. Some women, sweating profusely because they'd just hurried in from the fields, joined in with abrupt bursts of short, stomping steps. Mr. Bakaryding Taal took commanding lead of the procession, punctuating each of his labored steps with his stafflike cane, whose middle was shiny from long use. Mrs. Binta Kinte clung tightly to my left arm.

We reached the village clearing. Mr. Bakaryding Taal, turning, 19
raised his robed arm until all the voices became silent. Brusquely, he issued an order. I knew without translation that it was for the chairs and benches to be brought out and positioned beneath the big tree, the village meeting place.

Mr. Bakaryding Taal, pointing, indicated my seat of honor. Mrs. 20
Binta Kinte had so intertwined her arm with mine that wherever I went, *we* went. Together, we shared the chair.

Guido was moving deftly, photographing the assembly from all an- 21
gles. Young men had brought up the bags of sugar and rice and the packets of kola nuts. The ceremonial acceptance was brief and formal. Mr. Bakaryding Taal sat facing me. As is usual when a group is involved in a translation, he would speak as the alcala, then dramatically lean back in his chair as the villagers chorused an explosive "Hah!" in agreement.

Kebba Saidy translated for me: Allah had blessed us to gather here 22
once again. Some whom I had previously seen as members of the village family were no longer present to the eyes. But their spirits were no less present.

I asked Kebba to say for me that I indeed felt blessed to be among 23
them again, and that I distinctly felt the spirits of those others among us.

The alcala cleared his throat. He sat arrow-straight in his chair. A 24
sense of expectancy hung in the air. He spoke more crisply this time: since I was a son of the village and Allah had blessed me to find great wealth in faraway America, they were certain I would not want to forget that but for the evil known as slavery, I would have been born and christened into my family compound there in Juffure.

"Hah!" 25

I sat for a moment, studying my shoes against the hard-packed 26
brown African earth. I turned to Kebba Saidy to translate for me.

I said that I felt I understood what they had said to me. Yes, but for 27
slavery, I might have been born in Africa rather than in America. I said that my book actually told the general history of all black Americans.

---

[1]*koras:* West African stringed instruments, similar to a harp. (Ed.)

We all descend from some African forefather who was born and reared in some African village like Juffure and was later kidnapped onto some slave ship bound for America or the Caribbean, where by now that original African's family has lived for many generations. My own ancestor, Kunta Kinte of Juffure, lived seven generations ago, I said, and I felt great pride in returning as a son of Juffure Village.

It seemed to me that this was the perfect setting in which to tell the villagers why I had returned again. 28

I said that I had come to ask their approval for building a new mosque in Juffure Village. It would replace the old patched and weathered one in which they had long worshiped. I said that though I was Protestant, a Methodist, I deeply respected every human being's personal faith. They were Muslim, as was my ancestor Kunta Kinte. I said that if they approved, I would like this mosque to be dedicated to Kunta Kinte's memory. 29

Again, I watched their faces closely. Every expression I saw reminded me, hopefully, of something I'd read somewhere: native black Africans, if deeply moved, will try hard not to show it. 30

Mr. Bakaryding Taal briefly addressed his fellow villagers. There was a short, agitated discussion. He turned, his deep-set eyes squarely meeting mine. Yes, the Juffure people would be most happy to have a new mosque dedicated to Kunta Kinte. 31

The sound of the people's "Hah!" was delightful to hear, but then almost immediately I was confused by the ensuing restlessness and murmuring, which seemed to convey that they still awaited something else. Then the alcala spoke again: 32

They were all sure I would want to be told that the farming had been especially poor that year, so that the village people's needs were many. And the people were sure that as a son of the village whom Allah had blessed with wealth, I would not knowingly permit my family in Juffure to continue in want and need— 33

"Hah!" 34

I felt a sense of helplessness. The radical changes that had already affected Juffure within the relatively short span since the first tourists had come there bearing gifts made it clear that the most damaging thing I could do would be to give a sum of money to every person in the village. That, at best, could only apply a temporary balm to a far deeper problem. As I saw it, Juffure's ancient tradition of self-reliance and self-pride was in danger of giving way to a new sense of communal dependency—upon tourists, upon me, upon things beyond the villagers' own resources. 35

My mind searched again for the way I could best express my earnest desire to be as genuinely helpful to them and to all Gambians as I possibly knew how. 36

I asked them to understand that I personally thought that the ben-   37
efits of education were matchless. Hoping that my feelings would thus
be more clearly illustrated, I told them of the number of Gambian
young people whom I was helping to educate in the United States.

Watching the expressions of the Juffure villagers, I could tell that   38
it really held little meaning for them that several Gambian young men
would return trained as teachers or agriculturists; or that Sonha Sallah,
from Banjul, was pursuing her master's degree in communications; or
that Seni Sise, from a village not much bigger than Juffure, was achieving honors in pharmacology, determined to become The Gambia's first
woman pharmacist.

Perhaps, I thought, if any of those students had come from Juffure,   39
then my efforts to help might have been better conveyed to the people.
But it was clear that as things stood, the Juffure people wanted something they could look at and feel in their hands, something tangible;
this made me very sad, for I had really tried to do what I felt was the
best thing.

Soon, I told them through Kebba's translations, we would have to   40
be leaving. I explained that we had to visit Fort James Island, just off-
shore in the Gambia River, and following that, we'd have to hasten
along the roads if we were to make the last night ferryboat at Barra and
reach Banjul and our hotel.

Now the Juffure villagers were perplexed and disappointed.   41
Kebba began to translate as one after another of them abruptly thrust
himself forward and spoke to me in rapid, intense Mandinka.

The first one, a stout, middle-aged man, said I'd returned so dra-   42
matically to them years before, but afterward I'd never seemed to have
much time for them. Why was that?

Asked another: why must I always leave so quickly? In fact, why   43
couldn't I spend at least a few weeks in the village among them?

"After all, we are your family," wailed Mrs. Binta Kinte. "Your   44
cousins are here! This is your home."

I thought of my schedule book, with its blur of business appoint-   45
ments and lectures awaiting in Los Angeles, New York, Chicago,
Detroit, Miami and other cities. Even if this could be explained to
them, how could I possibly ask them to understand that though my
schedule always saw me quickly "leaving them," I loved the village,
the people and Africa; and that an anticipation of "coming home" was
something I always carried with me.

But aloud, via the translator, I only apologized and expressed to the   46
Juffure villagers my sincere desire to try to make my visits more frequent.

Then we all trooped for perhaps an eighth of a mile to the village   47
of Albreda, on the bank of the Gambia River. Protocol demanded that
we reassemble under Albreda's big tree, where their alcala presided.

He stressed how the two villages had always been close neighbors, which meant that our ancestors had surely played together as childhood friends.

Albreda's welcome included a small itinerant troupe of Senegalese 48 entertainers, featuring a plump young woman of about 25. She danced with her whole body, sinuously responding to every nuance of the drums' rhythms. Some people threw her money, which she gracefully retrieved, continuing to dance with the money pressed between her extended fingers.

Mostly, I sat there staring out across the river at Fort James Island: 49 it held the silhouetted ruins of the fort from which so many slave ships had sailed during the trade in human beings that lasted two centuries.

Kebba Saidy was arguing loudly with some boatmen. Their ex- 50 changes grew more heated, and I knew that both they and he were engaging in a traditional bargaining ritual. Finally, an agreement having been reached, Kebba indignantly stalked away as if he had just been robbed. Now our little party moved out to the boats that were moored to the timbers of the long planked pier extending into the river.

We sailed out, the outboard puttering smoothly, and I recalled the 51 first day I had ever seen the Gambia River. En route to The Gambia from Dakar, Senegal, I was flying over the wide, brown river in a small Nigeria Airways plane. My face was pressed against the window, and it seemed that I could see the slave ships sailing those waters I had read so much about. It seemed that I could hear the moans and wails within their holds, and I became so angry up there in the air that I felt like fighting somebody.

But I didn't feel that way now, not anymore. Working for years with 52 slavery records had taught me that in order to be emotionally able to continue, I would do best to deal clinically and abstractly with slavery, adopting something like a surgeon's approach at the operating table.

We landed on Fort James Island. Walking among the familiar 53 ruins of the fort, which had once been a bastion of iron, stone, and concrete, I found myself studying the comparative sizes of the underground slave pens and the far larger, above-ground rooms that had housed the European soldiers who had guarded the fort against enemy fleets trying to take over the lucrative trade in flesh.

The keeper of Fort James Island was Mr. Kebba Jabang, a short 54 man wearing a dark robe; he carried like a Bible a book in which all visitors were required to enter their names and addresses. He said that many of the name-filled books were now stored in the Banjul offices of Mr. Bakari Sidibe, The Gambia's chief archivist.

"Many black people from your country who come here cry as if 55 their hearts will break," Mr. Jabang said. I said that I knew. I had cried there, too.

* * *

We were back in Kebba Saidy's black Ford sedan, returning to-   56
ward Banjul, when Guido Mangold said, "Alex, I am a German, a
white man. I don't have to question why I'm an outsider here. But you,
in a different way, you're also an outsider. You're no longer the true
black color of these people you claim as ancestors."

Guido's observation brought flashing back to me the experience of   57
my first visit to The Gambia, when I had rented a small motor launch
to take a party of 15 from Banjul to Juffure. We had not gone too far
along the river when for some reason I began glancing around at all
the others. Suddenly the realization hit me that I was the only person
on board with a brown complexion, that the skin color of every other
person there was really black. I had felt alien and confused; I had even
felt, among them, that I was impure. I told no one, of course, but it took
me quite some time to cope with that unpleasant, queasy feeling.

And I knew that many other American black people had been   58
affected in later years by some variation of my experience when they
had gone to Africa in fulfillment of a driving desire to visit the motherland. Some blacks of light complexion had even been shocked when
Africans, especially children, innocently referred to them as *toubob*,
the Mandinka word meaning "white man." And indeed, I remembered my father's tales of *his* grandparents, who had been Irish on
the paternal side and black slaves on the maternal side. It was impossible for me to be less than honest—I am, after all, a born-and-reared,
acculturated product of the United States.

Guido's comment had hung in the air as I thought of these things,   59
and I finally said, "Guido, I understand what you mean, but just let
yourself imagine. Across two centuries of slavery, nobody can ever
know the countless times that white males impregnated black slave
women." I thought for a moment. "But we all began from pure
Africans. Guido, being brown doesn't make me any less black. I could
never be an outsider to what I am."

Guido was thoughtful. After a while he said, "I can understand   60
what you say."

Kebba Saidy was pushing the Ford pretty hard. We had to make   61
the ferry at Barra, the site of one of the most bitter pills of my entire
nine years of research before writing *Roots*. For as thousands of whites
had played roles in the taking of Africans into slavery, so had an
infamous few Africans—among them the black king of Barra. He
tricked, trapped, imprisoned, then sold—as "punishment"—many of
his own people. I remember how bitterly I'd hated the man, who had
been dead for more than 200 years. He coated his treachery, cruelty,
and avarice with an egomaniacal pomp that saw him demand 17- and

21-gun salutes from every slave ship entering the river in pursuit of black human cargo. I wished hard that some slaver captain had got the chance—which all of them would have gleefully seized—to grab the king of Barra and sail out with *him* in chains, as just one more item of cargo.

After a night's sleep back in Banjul's brand-new Atlantic Hotel, I 62
took a taxicab to the Gloucester Street home of Alhaji Malik Manga. The Manga family, of the Wolof tribe, have been my close friends since early 1967, when I met the student Ebou Manga at Hamilton College in Clinton, New York. Ebou had accompanied me to The Gambia and had introduced me to his father, Alhaji Manga, who became my mentor in matters Gambian. Ebou's younger brother, Joe, was then about 14 years old. Joe is now 29, a Gambian district engineer who knows the village of Juffure very well. Now once again I talked in Banjul with the Mangas, and with his father's approval, I asked Joe to take over both the architectural design and the physical building of the new mosque for Juffure. After he queried my basic ideas, Joe made some rough first sketches. I liked them and thought the Juffure villagers would, too. Alhaji Manga, Joe and I discussed the probable cost, and I wrote Joe a check with which to get started.

Since my return to the United States, Joe Manga has sent me beau- 63
tifully detailed blueprints of the Juffure mosque, with which, he writes, the villagers are "very happy." Exactly on the site of the old mosque, the somewhat larger new one will service the worshipers from Juffure, Albreda and elsewhere.

I am anxious to return to Juffure as soon as the mosque is finished 64
and ready for dedication to the memory of my ancestor Kunta Kinte. I feel deeply that he would approve.

QUESTIONS

1.   How, according to Haley, has Juffure Village changed since he first visited?

2.   How successfully do you think Haley answers his rhetorical question, "Had my book helped or hurt this village?" (paragraph 11).

3.   Do you think Haley does the best thing in refusing to contribute to the Juffure Village money box? Why or why not? How satisfactory do you find his alternative contribution—the building of the new mosque?

A Moroccan Memoir

SARAH STREED

Settling-in

The eleven week training period was held in Morocco. With the 1
other Peace Corp volunteers, I studied Classical Arabic, the spoken dialect, Teaching Methodology and Cultural Adaptation. At the end, almost all of the fifty that had arrived as a group were invited to the
Swearing-In.

We rode by bus to the resort/hotel poised on the edge of the 2
Mediterranean Sea. It seemed lavish after the summer's hardihood; I
was in a celebratory mood and swam in both the pool and the sea.
Cocktails were served, followed by dinner and speeches. We signed
pledges to uphold the Constitution of the United States of America. I
stood in line—my turn came—I was sworn in as an official Peace
Corps Volunteer.

In a corner, I opened the sealed envelope containing the name of 3
my post—the spot in Morocco where I was going to live and serve for
the next two years. I looked; the name meant nothing. Later, I looked
it up on a map and found it was a large village—actually a town—on
the train line between Casablanca and Marrakesh. Because it was the
only education for miles around, there were two high schools: one
of "Letters" or Humanities, and the other "Science." I was relieved
that I had been assigned to the School of Letters; the students would
probably be receptive to English teachers.

A few weeks later, the train ejected me at my town in the evening. 4
I halted on the platform, checked for the equivalent of $400 in my
pocket (settling-in allowance), gripped my straw basket and travel
bag, then looked around. Everything was dry dust. The dark spread
from the train station, swallowing the yellow flatness of the desert.

Sarah Streed studied literature at Wheaton College and has an
M.F.A. in fiction writing from the University of Arizona. In addition
to the Peace Corps experience she describes in this memoir, she has
spent time overseas as a student in Oxford, England, a governess in
Switzerland, and an employee of the American Legation Museum in
Tangiers, Morocco. Her essay was published in *The House on Via
Gombito: Writing by North American Women Abroad* (1991), edited by
Madelon Sprengnether and C.W. Truesdale.

Men, all around me, alone or in groups, were walking toward a 5
paved road with a landscaped median of palm trees. I didn't move,
just shook my head when the men called to me, until I saw a pretty,
modern woman flanked by two men. I stopped this group and asked
the way to the hotel in town. They were friendly—one of the men took
my travel bag—and we set forth.

We walked down the paved road that stretched off into the night. 6
I didn't see any cars. At one point, a street light lit up a billboard with
the King's portrait and a few yards of sand beyond. Then two uniformed *gendarmes* appeared. They barked fast words in the Arabic dialect and my companions scattered, leaving my travel bag on the road.

The *gendarmes* switched to French to ask for my passport and pa- 7
pers. I was angry and handed them over with a lot of rustling. They
examined them, then one asked, still in French, "So what are you
doing in our town?"

"I'm the new English teacher," I said, "at the High School of Letters." 8

"Do you want to come to dinner sometime?" the same *gendarme* 9
continued.

"Sometime would be fine," I said, lying. 10

They handed back my passport and left, disappearing into the 11
night as fast as my companions had previously. I was alone on a dark
road, and cursed them, but picked up my travel bag and continued
walking. After a few yards, the man who had carried my bag popped
out from the night. In French, he explained the couple had thought it
best to go on but he had waited for me.

We walked together. After a long time I could see the town—a 12
clump of yellow stucco buildings behind a red sign advertising Coca-
Cola in Arabic.

"What are you here for?" he asked me. 13

I told him. 14

"I teach biology at that same school," he said, "I live with the other 15
man you saw—he's an engineer here—and that was his girlfriend. We
were picking her up at the train station."

We arrived in the town proper, but there weren't any streetlights, 16
so I felt, rather than saw, the shadow of buildings. The dense blackness
was eating the town. We stopped at a two-story building with a neon
sign at the top spelling "OTEL" with the "H" missing. I thanked my
companion and walked inside—safe for the night. It was a few days
until school began, so I decided to stay in "OTEL" until I could find a
place to live.

The next morning my companion came back to "OTEL." He intro- 17
duced himself as Najib and offered to help me find a real estate agent.
I worried that perhaps he was helping me because he wanted an

American girlfriend, but I hadn't detected any signs of this in his body language; he was very stiff and distant. I also knew that I couldn't find a real estate agent by myself.

So we left to seek the *simsar.* Daylight images of the town banged   18
at my eyes: a robed woman shrieking at a man behind a cart, a ragged boy swatting at a hunk of meat hanging in flies.

We entered a narrow alley flanked by adobe mounds. Each   19
mound was a cave with an entrance hole. Najib stooped at one, stuck his head in and called. He motioned me to follow with his hand.

The room was four feet by six feet. A large man wearing a white   20
cotton robe and pointed yellow slippers sat on a ripped vinyl chair. I heard Najib explaining that I was the new American schoolteacher and needed a place to live. The man heaved to his feet, belly shaking, and we followed.

The first stop was the traditional Moroccan landowner's house: 21
large, spacious, even a tiled courtyard with a fountain that was presently turned off. I gasped. The *simsar* assured me that the fountain could be turned on at any time.

"It's very nice," I said, "but it's too much." (I waved my arms   22
around). "Much too much. I wish to live like most Moroccans. Even though I'm American, I don't have enough money for this house."

The *simsar* looked at me with something like disgust, then turned   23
on his leather slippers and slapped out. Najib and I again followed.

For such a large old man, he could walk very fast, and we didn't   24
stop until we were on the other side of town. Then he halted before a house that was in the process of being built; some young boys were sawing wood, an older man was pouring cement, and only a frame-work stood.

"So," the *simsar* said to me, "you don't like an old house. Here is a   25
brand new house."

"Yes, I see that," I said, "but it isn't finished."   26

The *simsar* turned and talked with the man pouring cement.   27

"They can finish it in a month," he said.   28

"I need a house NOW," I said.   29

The *simsar* shrugged his shoulders. He took off again, white robe   30
flying.

He next stopped before a pretty second floor apartment with a bal-   31
cony. It was clean and the rent was in the category of what I had been thinking.

"Yes, yes," I said to the *simsar,* "this is perfect."   32

He smiled.   33

Najib pulled me aside.   34

"I don't think you should take this house," he said to me.   35

"Why?" I asked, "It's clean. It's small but pretty. . . ."   36

Najib leaned close to whisper, "This is a street where all the pros- 37
titutes live. I don't think it would be good to have the new American
teacher living on the street with all the prostitutes."

"Yes," I said, "I see what you mean."   38

I turned to the *simsar*. "I'm sorry," I said, "I don't think I'll take this 39
apartment after all."

He threw out his hands in a gesture of exasperation, shook our 40
hands abruptly, and left. Najib and I walked towards the center of
town. I was discouraged.

"There is one thing," said Najib. "There is a top floor apartment 41
available in the building we live in."

I looked at him, considering.   42

"You don't have to worry," he said stiffly, "my roommate and I 43
are moving to another building in a month."

I felt a little sad—but relieved. Just past the *Marche,* we turned off 44
the main road onto a dirt alley. Two little boys were winding thread—
loops of green and blue went back and forth—and Najib bent under
these and ducked into a tiled doorway. I did the same. We climbed
two flights of stairs and waited. One of the little "winding" boys must
have gone to fetch the landlord, for soon a thin man with glasses came
up panting. He explained that he owned the building, including the
shop on the first floor where he sold appliances, and I should drop off
my rent there each month.

He pulled out a key and let me in. It was small—two rooms con- 45
nected by a closet-like kitchen and a chamber with a squat toilet—but
it was clean and cheap, about $50 a month.

"Great," I said to him, "I'll take it."   46

Najib had slipped out. The landlord and I began discussing the 47
terms of the agreement. I gave him two months' rent on the spot, one
month to reserve the room, and one month to rent. He handed me the
key and left.

I walked back to the hotel, paid my bill, then carried my travel bag 48
and straw basket the few blocks back.

Inside my new apartment it was getting dark, so I examined the 49
rooms, taking stock: the smaller room could be the bedroom, next to
that was a cubicle with two footpads on either side of a hole—the
"squat" as we affectionately called it. There was a sink in the entry-
way, but I suspected there was water only in the morning and evening.
There was a tiny kitchen with another sink, and a small tile counter—
I could buy a small gas burner. The larger room I would use as the living room, or a sort of salon.

I opened the shutters of this room. By then it was fully dark. The 50
street below had emptied with the night, but I could hear noise everywhere, murmurs, snatches of music, men talking. Dust drifted in and

settled on my skin. I lit a candle and laid out my sleeping bag on some plastic heaped in the corner.

I took off my sandals and got in the bag. I began to read part of a travel book by candlelight, but then it seemed absurd. I was living in North Africa! This thought was so vigorous and vibrant compared to the typed words on the page, that I grew agitated and blew out the candle. 51

I lay in the dark listening to the noises and after awhile, fell asleep that first night in my new apartment. 52

The Baths

The next day I met my neighbors: Amina, wife and mother, her son Karim, the maid, Halima, and a few hours later, the husband, Hassan. That first day I learned that they were a progressive Moroccan family because, although Hassan's family lived a few blocks away, they had their own place. 53

Amina took me shopping for a Butagaz burner and pointed out the women's public bath, or *hemem,* just down the street from our building. At one stop, she bought a *kis*—a washcloth mitt—for me to take along with my bucket and soap. 54

A day later—the day before school was to start—I went to take my first public bath. 55

The outer room of the *hemem* was a sort of antechamber where all the women were stripping down to their panties and leaving their clothes in a basket. I did the same, feeling uncomfortable with my breasts exposed. I followed the woman in front of me who grabbed her bucket and approached the front of the chamber where a lady with gold teeth and earrings guarded the door. The woman then set down a coin and went through a door. I stepped up. 56

The *"hemem* lady" held out a coin. 57

"*Dirham,*" she said to me in Arabic. "It costs a *dirham.*" 58

I went back to my basket and fetched the right coin. When I returned and gave it to her, she pocketed it. Just as I was about to slip past, she reached out and tweaked my right nipple. 59

"I can see you don't have any children," she said, laughing. 60

Stunned, I walked through the door and into the first empty saunalike cubicle I could find. I filled my bucket with steaming hot water from the spigot, added some cold, and bathed. I washed my hair with another bucketful, rinsed it, and was finished in fifteen minutes, similar to what I would spend taking a shower in the States. 61

The *"hemem* lady" regarded me with surprise as I walked back into the antechamber. As I was dressing, a young woman came up and asked, "Why don't Americans have the little things?" and pinched a black roll of skin off her arm. I shrugged, but when I got home I asked 62

Amina if the next time I could go to the *hemem* with her, which I did three days later.

The *hemem* lady nodded when she saw me with a Moroccan 63 woman. Amina and I stripped, paid, and found an empty cubicle. Then we washed our hair, combed it through and washed it again. Then we scrubbed every inch of our bodies with the *kis* and homemade soap. We repeated this three times, and on the third time the little rolls of black skin came off my body. We cleaned our ears, pumiced our feet, rinsed off completely and finished it all by eating an orange in our own steam.

The thought of going through this process more than once a week 64 exhausted me, so I began attending only on Fridays. The *hemem* lady knew when to expect me and we became friends.

After a few weeks, I noticed another lady hanging about the an- 65 techamber. She was old, without teeth, dressed in a skirt pulled up about her waist. When she ran about the room, her thin breasts hit against her protruding stomach. Once, she came up to me and garbled something in Arabic. I backed off, afraid. The *hemem* lady explained that she was the "scrubber" and would scrub me for a small fee.

"No thanks," I said. The scrubber looked disappointed, but then 66 led me to a cubicle, swinging the door open with a flourish. I laughed and gave her a coin.

As the year wore on, I learned more and more of the Arabic dialect, 67 and began to understand the conversations around me as the women dressed and undressed in the antechamber.

"Yes, teacher of English in our school." 68

"Oh yes, very nice. Speaks Arabic and lives near here, by herself." 69

"Wears the traditional *djellaba* robe, but a bright red one! Can you 70 imagine?"

Slowly, as my *hemem* day—Friday—became known in the town, 71 students and their families began to use this fact to their advantage.

One afternoon, as I was walking to my cubicle, a girl student came 72 quickly out of hers and greeted me with a kiss on both cheeks. I felt that it was inappropriate to chat with a student in my panties, and broke off after the greeting. Later I heard her bragging to a friend that she had seen me in the *hemem* and talked with me.

Another afternoon, just after the first semester grades had gone 73 out, an older woman rushed at me. She grabbed at my free hand—the one that wasn't holding the bucket—with her two hands and clutched.

"Please, please," she implored, bending her face to kiss my hand 74 again and again. I was completely confused.

"Please," I said back to her, pulling my hand away, "what is it?" 75

Grabbing my hand again: "My daughter is failing in your English 76 class. Please give her a passing grade."

I took my hand away for the second time and left her weeping.   77

During summer vacation, I traveled, and thus bathed elsewhere.   78
But with my return in the fall, I resumed my regular *hemem* days. On
the first *hemem* of my new school year, the *hemem* lady gave a cry and
kissed me on both cheeks. From then on, I greeted her in this manner
first thing when I came in the door, just as the other women did. It
made me think of the previous year when I had stalked in—oblivious—taken my bath, and gone home without a word to anyone.

The *hemem* lady began bantering with me in Arabic. She asked if I   79
knew how to make Moroccan tea—a sweet mint drink involving a ritual preparation.

"Of course I do," I said, "I've been living in Morocco for over a   80
year."

"Well then," she said, "why don't you make some and bring it   81
here for me."

I had a vision of transporting the pots of boiling water and sugar   82
in cones and fresh mint leaves and tiny glasses on the proper silver
tray, and I said, "Oh no, that would be much too difficult."

Her face fell.   83

"But," I added, "I'll bring you a Coca." (Coke was sold in bottles   84
and used only on special occasions.)

The *hemem* lady laughed, showing her front gold teeth, and told   85
the scrubber what I had promised.

After that bath, when I was home, I sent Amina's live-in-maid—a   86
nine year old girl from a poor family—to buy bottles of Coke for all of
us. Then I added some money and told her to buy two extra bottles
and deliver them to the *hemem* lady and the scrubber. The girl returned
after a while and told me she had done as instructed.

The following Friday, the *hemem* lady laughed when she saw me   87
and thanked me for the Coca. I started undressing and as I folded up
my clothes I could hear her chatting to the other women in Arabic.

"That's Sarah, she's the teacher. Yes, you'll never believe what she   88
did. I told her to bring me some tea from her house, and she said that
was too difficult but that she would give me Coca instead. . . ."

The Abuse of Women

Whenever out in the streets of my new town—shopping at the   89
market, walking to and from school, going to the post office—I noticed
an aggressive disdain in the manner of the Moroccan male toward all
women. The Moroccan women responded to this by scuttling; eyes
cast down, veils covering three-quarters of the face, *djellaba* hoods
pulled up to cover most of the hair and neck, they crept around outside until they were safely back home.

I also noticed that men continuously lined the streets; they lounged 90 in doorways shaded by the sun, smoked at outdoor cafes facing the *marche,* chatted with friends at the entrance to the baths. And while standing and watching, they softly, almost absent-mindedly, poured out a stream of abuse.

One time I asked a very Westernized Moroccan male why Arabic 91 men treated women in such a degrading fashion. He replied, quite seriously, that according to the Muslim religion men can't speak directly to women so they must resort to oblique harassment and insults to get attention. Whatever the reason, I was an easy target: female, white, single and blond.

On a certain morning I was walking to school, dressed to teach in 92 skirt, pumps, and lipstick. I went my usual route, past the old man stuffing pallets with straw, past the bread man selling fresh round loaves, past the little boy who sat on a mat in the doorway of his father's store and sold drums—big bongos to baby drums the size of a saltshaker.

As I reached the last block where the boys and men loitered in 93 order to watch girl students approach, I saw three or four men gather in a huddle. I walked faster. A few yards past the group, I distinctly heard my name chanted in accompaniment to an intricate rhythm of clapping: Sarah, Sar-ah. Clap, clap-clap.

It couldn't be. I turned to look and the men smiled widely and 94 chanted louder. People turned their heads to watch; I felt a hundred eyes waiting for my reaction. So, deliberately, I grimaced and flicked my outspread hand back and forth by my ear in the Moroccan gesture of being crazy. The crowd laughed, the men laughed—and then stopped.

During my term I had many conversations with Moroccan women 95 about their status—or lack thereof. One of these took place in a compartment of a train. I was travelling to Rabat when suddenly, without any preliminaries, an older Moroccan woman sitting directly across me began speaking.

"In all Arabic countries, we women are the slaves of men," she said. 96

I glanced at the only other occupant of the compartment—male— 97 sitting in the corner.

"Yes, I know there are ears," she continued, "but I must say it. Not 98 just in Morocco but in all Arabic countries, women are slaves. Look at my case." (Her voice was rising.) "I was married to my husband for thirty years when he left me for a young girl of twenty-nine. Now I am fifty-two and what have I got? Nothing. So I am going to try and find work in a foreign country because of what he did to me."

The man rose to his feet and left the compartment. The woman 99 looked at him with a blank face. My stop came shortly after.

"Good luck," I said.   100
"Good luck to you too," she replied.   101

Once, when I had a long weekend off, I went to stay with my friend   102
Rachida and her family in the country. On the first night, just before the
horn from the local mosque rang out to signal the evening meal,
Rachida and I went for a walk in the dusty fields with her older brother.
"Rachida is happy tonight," said the brother. "Because you are   103
here as a guest, she does not need to help with the cooking, but can
walk with us."
"Why must Rachida usually help with the cooking?" I asked.   104
"Because it is the custom, especially for the eldest girl," her   105
brother said. "I think it is different here from America."
"Yes," I said, "there are women in America who, if their husbands   106
tell them to go make a cup of tea, they say 'Go make it yourself.' "
The brother laughed. Rachida put her hand to her face in a gesture   107
of dismay.
"Well," I said, "why should a woman work all day for no pay just   108
because she is a woman? For example, why does Rachida do everything for her brothers, while her brothers spend all their time at the
cafe or the cinema?"
The brother thought.   109
"When I go away to University in Marrakesh," he said, "I wash   110
my own clothes and my roommate and I share the cooking."
"There you are," I said. "Why must women cook just because   111
they're women? Why do men not cook just because they're men?"
The horn blew for dinner so we returned to their home. The par-   112
ents and four children lived in an enlarged hut made of stones, dirt
and mortar. At night, the children grabbed blankets and slept on the
sponge cushions in the main room, while the parents took the only bed
in the other room.
For dinner, Rachida's parents joined us, and we knelt around the   113
table and ate with our fingers from a common bowl. As we ate,
Rachida's brother began to relate how I had said things were different
in America. The mother listened, nodding. After we had finished the
meal, she called to the youngest son, about ten years old, "Hey, you,
clear off the table tonight. Didn't you hear how things are in
America?"
This boy grew red in the face and ungraciously slammed a few   114
wooden bowls around.
Rachida said to me, "If my mother makes my father do anything   115
like that, you'll cause a divorce."
Rachida's eldest brother lay back on the couch.   116
"I have started the Revolution here in Morocco," he crowed.   117
"From now on, wherever, I will plant the seed of this new thought."

A more sobering scenario occurred one day when I was at the local 118
police station renewing my "green card" that allowed me to work in
Morocco.

I sat in the lobby while the paperwork was going through—a 119
process that went on indefinitely, with or without a bribe. After I had
waited about an hour, a weeping, distraught peasant woman dragged
in a cowering girl. They went straight to the reception desk and the
woman—whom I assumed was the mother—raged and screamed at
the man behind it. Occasionally she shoved the girl toward him as if
to say, "See. Look at her." The girl stood silent, her face removed and
vacant, her eyes blank.

The man spoke platitudes—yes, we will look, I will report—and 120
soothed the mother to the point where he could lead both of them to
the bench where I was sitting. The girl crouched down while the
mother put her head in her hands and wept.

The man at the reception desk left to talk to some police officers in 121
the corner. One of the officers nodded, then came over to the mother.
He spoke in a low voice. Jerking her head up, she listened, and then
grabbed the girl's arm. As she pushed up one sleeve of the dirty and
ripped dress, I could see huge purplish bruises, three or four, leading
from the wrist to the shoulder. The policeman nodded and left.

A servant brought my green card up to the desk. The man behind 122
it called my name. I went up, troubled, and glanced back at the woman
and the girl.

"Do you know what this is?" he said in French to me, bobbing his 123
head in the direction of the mother and the daughter.

"No," I said. 124

"C'est un viole," he said, and grinned. ("It's a rape.") 125

Then, continuing in harsh French, "Do you know what a viole is?" 126

"Yes I know what it is," I said, enraged at his horrible grin. 127

"Oh yes," he said. "They're peasants and work in the fields out- 128
side of town. This morning the girl was on her way to a field and a
man attacked her. Because he is married already and has children, he
denies it, and refuses to marry her. That is the usual punishment in our
society: if a man rapes a virgin he must marry her because he is the
first man to sleep with her."

I turned away in disgust, but he hadn't finished and reached for 129
my arm to keep me listening. I drew it away before he could touch it.
He perceived the insult and grew loud.

"You saw the bruises," he sneered. "Everyone knows she was held 130
down by force, that she had nothing to do with it, but because they are
poor, no one can accuse the man, who is rich. That is why the mother
is carrying on so—she knows that it will all end with her daughter
marked for life as a whore, defiled and never being able to marry, because she is not a virgin."

Suddenly he was finished. 131

"You like that story?" He grinned and handed me my green card. 132

I walked out. 133

A List

I began to write down the comments shouted at me in the streets: 134

—We don't want you foreigners.
—You speak the Arabic.
—Ah, you walk back and forth seeing people. You are making a tour?
—I'm going to come to your house. Will you open the door for me?
—Ah my gazelle, you please me.
—Money!
—Lucky, lucky, you American. You have everything.
—Shame on you—you won't give your books away.
—Whore!
—One can sleep with you?
—My blond!
—You have blue eyes, Madame.
—Oh you English speakers. You never say the truth; all is twisted and lies.
—Hey nice teacher, give me English lesson?
—Beauty of America; welcome to Morocco.
—CIA. Are you a spy?
—We know you—you aren't a tourist; you live here.
—I don't like girls.
—A fine day.
—I love you.
—Fish-and-chips. Fish-and-chips. Fish-and-chips.
—Good Morning, America.
—You think you're doing well in Morocco, don't you. Well, watch out!

Sex and Relationships

As my stay in Morocco continued, the exotic sheen wore thin and 135 disclosed dark stains of anger, poverty and ignorance on the underlying fabric.

Earlier in the year, Amina had approached me about hiring her 136 friend as a maid. This woman, a widow supporting two children in a hut outside of town, badly needed the money. After thinking it over I had agreed and Hajiba began cooking my meals, cleaning, and washing for me.

One night after dinner, I was correcting lessons while Hajiba 137
washed up in the kitchen. Suddenly there was a loud smashing sound
in the apartment next door followed by cries and screams. I went out
on the stairwell where the landlord's apprentice joined me. We rang the
doorbell and, as we waited, we heard thumps, then more screaming.

Finally my neighbor Hassan stuck out his head. I could hear 138
Amina sobbing in the background.

"Nothing is the matter," he said vaguely, and shut the door in our 139
faces.

The apprentice muttered, "Drunk, drunk" and went back down- 140
stairs. I went back to my correcting.

Ten minutes later there were louder screams and thumps that 141
seemed to go right through the wall. I went over and knocked on the
door again.

This time Amina opened the door—crying hysterically—and 142
grabbed my wrist to try and pull me inside. Hassan appeared and
tried to shut the door to keep me out, while still keeping his wife in.
Amina wouldn't release my wrist. I called to Hajiba to come help, and
she came out of my apartment. All four of us wrestled together for a
few minutes, and then we were all inside.

Hajiba put her arm around Amina and tried to soothe her as a 143
mother would; I couldn't see their little boy. I approached Hassan who
was pacing around the room.

"Hassan," I said, "please sit down. Just sit down so we can all talk 144
about this."

"It will be fine now, Sarah," he said. "I'm fine. It's all right now. 145
You can leave."

He stopped pacing and went to stand by his wife. I motioned for 146
Hajiba to leave with me. Just as I was closing the door, I looked back,
and Hassan was hitting Amina on the cheek with a closed fist. I pulled
Hajiba back in.

This time I pulled Hassan into another room, and pushed him 147
down on a couch. Amina peered in.

Hassan stood up. 148

"I'm going to my mother," he said, pulling on his jacket over his 149
pajamas, "I've got to get to my mother."

I stopped him before he reached the door. 150

"Hassan," I said, "you're not a little boy; why do you want your 151
mother? You're acting silly. Just calm down."

He sat down again and took off the jacket. I sat down at the other 152
end of the couch.

Hassan leaned forward and said to me, suddenly sober, "Sarah, 153
you don't understand the Moroccans. They are . . ." (He made a circle
with his forefinger and thumb.) "They are zero."

Hajiba and I stayed five hours longer, until Amina tucked Hassan 154 into bed. Then I returned to the correcting, Hajiba to the supper dishes.

Sometimes Najib, his roommate and I would spend Saturday af- 155 ternoons together, drinking mint tea and talking about Morocco. One afternoon, Najib was trying to explain the sexual tension between Moroccan men and women.

"You see, every Moroccan man needs to have sex at least twice a 156 week," he said. "When a man isn't rich enough to get married and support a household, he has to settle for something else. Prostitution is expensive, so sometimes men from the poorer quarters of the city—like where I grew up—get together in a pack and go out to find a younger boy to have intercourse with."

"But that's rape," I said. 157

Najib paused. 158

"Well, it is quite brutal," he admitted. "That's why I never partic- 159 ipated. But it's not considered wrong. It's only the younger boy who has done wrong."

"How so?" I asked. 160

"Because he is the one on the bottom," Najib said. "It's only 161 shameful if a boy, or a man, takes the female role."

His roommate nodded. 162

"But you foreigners are responsible for a lot of it," Najib added. 163

"Responsible for what?" I asked. 164

"For this kind of activity," Najib said. "The rich foreigners come to 165 Morocco interested in the cheap and available young boys. I myself have seen cars drive in from Casablanca and Americans dressed in fur, wearing gold chains. They drive right to the middle of our town and offer the young boys a pencil for sex. I have seen them hold out a pencil to a young boy, in order that he get in the car with them."

At the end of the school year, Nadia invited me to be a guest at her 166 cousin's wedding. It was to be a traditional celebration of an arranged match—and it was an honor for a foreigner to be invited. I accepted with pleasure.

Nine o'clock on Friday evening, we began dressing at Nadia's 167 house. She put on a heavy brocade robe edged in gold braid and gave me a white chiffon gown with silver sequins. After applying heavy make-up, we walked over to a big garage designated for the women guests. The men were in a similar structure down the street.

The room had been whitewashed, then hung with huge banners. 168 It was crammed with women—maybe fifty or more—all dressed in their finery. We chatted together quietly.

After an hour, two sisters carried the bride in on a huge silver plat- 169 ter. All but her face and hands was hidden under a heavy robe, and they were painted with make-up and gold dust. Only her eyes moved—looking about fearfully. A gold necklace, spanning chin to chest, hung below the headdress of jewels. Nadia whispered to me that the outfit had been rented for the occasion.

The women sang and danced as she was held aloft, songs about 170 the bride leaving her parents and going to a new home. Then the bridegroom and his brothers entered. The crowd of women, growing festive, shouted for him to dance. The bride was taken off the platter and the groom put in place. He attempted to dance on the platter as his brothers pushed him in the air. Afterwards, he and the bride were led to thrones at the front of the room where they sat and held court, talking to the various women who approached, before the brothers took the groom back to the men's place.

Four plump women wearing long, loose hair came in. They sang 171 songs about the more ribald aspects of marriage and gyrated seductively. Nadia whispered that these were the *shirets*—singing prostitutes imported from another town to provide wedding entertainment.

The *shirets* alternated between the male and female buildings all 172 night long, because they were the only women who would dance in front of the men. I asked Nadia why they were called prostitutes if they were only dancing. She said that the *shirets* wrote their addresses on small slips of paper to give to men who tucked money into their gold belts, and the men made contact at a later date.

Nadia tied a scarf around her hips—low down—and got up to 173 dance using the pelvic undulation that every woman in the room knew. The *shirets* began to sing a song with my name in it, so I got up and tried to imitate Nadia, but couldn't. Instead, I put a ten *dirham* note in the leader's belt and sat down again.

A few hours later, the *shirets* sang a song with a different, pene- 174 trating, rhythm. The sister of the bride—who was wearing a filmy, siren-red dress—fell down on the floor in a fit, jerking and crying. Her mother and aunts surrounded her so she wouldn't hurt herself, but let her continue the thrashing. When the song ended the girl fell exhausted into a deep sleep and the older women carried her off to a side room.

"What happened to her?" I asked Nadia.

Nadia was excited. "You saw how she had on a red dress? Well, 175 that last song contained the name of a *Gnouoa* spirit in the lyrics and 176 the *Gnouoa* like red. So when their song was sung, one of the spirits entered her and she had the fit." (The *Genouoa* are spirits in an ancient Muslim cult.)

Refreshments were passed; we ate cookies and drank Coke while 177 watching the dancing. A while later Nadia poked me: the sister in red was coming out of the side room, refreshed and smiling. Nadia told me that her mother and aunts had asked her about the fit but she had no memory of what had happened.

During the early morning hours the guests began to grow sub- 178
dued.

"You realize what happens at the end," Nadia said. "They con- 179
summate the marriage and exhibit the blood."

"But what if there isn't any blood?" I asked. 180

"But she's a virgin," Nadia said. 181

I thought of the bride's frightened eyes and the potential disaster. 182

"But what if the hymen is already broken—even if she's a virgin— 183
say if she fell on a bicycle when she was little?"

Nadia disappeared. She reappeared a few minutes later. 184

"I asked the bride," she told me, relieved, "and she has never rid- 185
den a bicycle."

Around ten o'clock a.m.—thirteen hours after the festivities had 186
begun—the guests formed a parade and escorted the bride and groom
to their new home. We wove through the streets banging tin pans,
singing, clapping and shouting their names.

Only the relatives—and myself—entered the house; the other 187
guests went on home. The bride and groom entered the bedroom and
we waited in the salon. The mother stood post by the bedroom door.
Once she looked in and then told us how things were going.

Twenty minutes later, the youngest sister was sent into the bed- 188
room. She came out bearing something white on a silver platter. She
danced and sang around the room. Then she lowered the platter to
show us: a pair of bloodstained white bloomers. All the relatives
around me clapped and cheered. Later the bride came out in her robe
to have breakfast with us. We congratulated her and she smiled—
happy that everything had gone well.

For weeks afterward, I remembered the bride's frightened eyes. 189
I thought of her passive acceptance of the wedding ritual. When I
spoke of it to Nadia, she said that some modern couples—usually the
ones that had chosen their own mate—dispensed with the elaborate
ceremony and got quietly married in order to save money.

"It's nothing," Nadia said. "My cousin and her husband are good 190
together. Sometimes things don't work out so well."

Religion

While living in Morocco, I observed that Muslim believers seemed 191
to fall into two groups. One group, the nominal Muslims, didn't pay the
least attention to religious requirements, like the shopkeeper who, one
day when I was buying some shampoo, pulled out a bottle of vodka
from beneath the counter. "But," I said, knowing that alcohol was forbidden, "aren't you a Muslim?" "Oh," he answered, "just a little."

The devout ones took literally the name of "Islam," which means 192
"The Submission." They rigorously followed the five pillars of the

faith: Profession of Faith, Prayer, Almsgiving, Fasting and Pilgrimage to Mecca, if possible. In my mind, I thought of this group as "extremists," the believers who accounted for every happening by saying, "It's the Will of Allah."

One day a cluster of my more religious students cornered me after 193 class and said, "Please, Miss, just repeat after us that Allah is God and Mohammed is his prophet."

"I can't do that," I said to them. 194

One girl took my hand and looked at me with imploring eyes. 195 "Please Miss, or you'll go to hell," she said.

I said, "Don't you realize that all over the world, people of all 196 different religions feel only they are going to heaven. Think of where I came from—it's a whole nation of Christians—*Nazzerani*—who believe they won't see any non-Christians in heaven."

I could tell she didn't believe me. Muslims in my village had no 197 conception of a world past Tangiers, much less of different religions, each with its zealous converts.

"Just do it for me, Miss," said the girl. She was so sincere. 198

"I'm sorry," I said to her, gently, "I can't." 199

In my school, the faculty referred to these students and others like 200 them as future "fanatics"—that is, political Muslims who refuse to follow the King's edicts because they obey the higher Law of Allah, represented by his Prophet Mohammed.

There was a fanatical Muslim on the faculty. He scared the other 201 teachers because he had power. It was whispered that he had been in jail for a couple of years and hadn't repented under torture, so now he was free to teach whatever he pleased in his classes. I saw him occasionally, dressed in the simplest of robes and a white turban, silently moving about the halls.

The townspeople referred to me as "The *Nazzerani*" or "The 202 Christian." Usually I managed to avoid clashes about religion, but sometimes I couldn't—or wouldn't.

Take, for example, the time that Nadia and Asma and I decided 203 to travel to Fes, the traditional Holy City of Morocco and the current religious center. There was a *moussem* scheduled—a fantasia of lights and music and shooting horsemen.

We crammed into the cross-country bus with everyone else going 204 to Fes, luggage and sheep strapped on top. As soon as we arrived, we reserved a hotel room, left our bags, and then walked to the dusty field on the outskirts of Fes where the fantasia was taking place.

Forty men in full dress—turbans, pointed slippers, robes, bro- 205 caded vests and guns—lined up on horseback at the end of the field. At the sound of the horn they raced, full gallop, guns held in the air. Halfway across the field, they shot in the air without slacking the speed and then reined sharply into the finish.

After watching the performances for an hour or so, Nadia, Asma 206
and I wandered toward the tents set up around the perimeter.
Everywhere there were lesser shows: snake charmers, acrobats, dancing ladies with tambourines, even sellers of *kif,* the Moroccan hashish.

We arrived at a huge tent encircled by a crowd. Maneuvering our 207
way past open-mouthed gazers, we reached the front. I heard frenzied
music. Nadia and Asma were staring at the scene intently. I slipped in
front of a large man and saw—all at once—the sawdust ring, little boys
playing drums, and a man with a lolling head making an incision in
his bare stomach with a knife. It bled and then he made another one.
After the fourth incision, he fell to the floor in a swoon. Another man
with glazed eyes and matted hair danced in to take his place.

A row of bleeding men were lined up off to the side in various 208
stages of exhaustion. One had ten to twelve cuts up and down his arm,
the freshest just beginning to clot. Another sat humped forward so that
the crowd could see the huge gashes on his bare back.

After several minutes I grew sick. I muttered something to Nadia 209
and Asma and they followed without a word. Once outside, we agreed
that it was too much mutilation. We left the *moussem* and walked back
to the hotel.

Perhaps because of what we had seen we didn't walk around the 210
city that night. Instead we stayed in our hotel room. We were lounging in pajamas on the beds, chatting, when the subject of religion came
up—the bizarre sect of flagellation in the back of our minds.

Nadia asked me, "What is it exactly that Christians believe?" 211

"Well," I said, "I guess mainly that Christ is the Son of God and 212
that He died on the cross for our sins and then rose again from the
dead." I was being careful because I knew that in Islam, Jesus was just
another prophet superseded by Mohammed.

Nadia jumped up from the bed. "Oh no Sarah," she cried out, 213
"that's a trick. Jesus never rose; that's not right."

I said, "We're just discussing our religions. You have explained to 214
me what it is that Muslims believe; I'm explaining what it is that
Christians believe."

But she was disturbed by the thought of God having a son. She 215
knelt on the small hard bed in her yellow pajamas—body bowed
in submission—and began to reel off long clumps of the Koran in
classical Arabic. As the minutes passed, her voice got more and more
sing-song and she rocked back and forth.

When I glanced at Asma out of the corner of my eye, I could see 216
that she was moved by this exhibition of faith. I thought of the small
boys I had seen in the Koranic schools in the village, chanting and
rocking for hours. Suddenly, I was angry. What right did Nadia have
to quote me verses from her holy book in a language I couldn't even

understand? Did she think that just the act of saying them would make me aware of the error of my ways and come to see the light of the true Islamic religion?

This anger made me rash. I began to recite—loudly and in 217 English—all the Bible verses I could dredge up from Sunday School Memory Contests. For several minutes Nadia and I refused to stop. We knelt on our beds yelling out verses from the Koran and the Bible.

Soon Asma had had enough. 218

"Stop, stop," she said. 219

Nadia and I paused for breath. 220

"We can't resolve this," Asma said. "We are all devout believers 221 and can't convince each other because we believe too strongly."

Nadia and I both nodded. 222

"Now Sarah," Asma said, "even in your religion you agree that 223 God is never wrong."

"That's true," I said. 224

"So," she continued, "that means either you are wrong, or we are 225 wrong."

I shrugged; as far as I could tell, there was no way Christ could be 226 the son of God and *not* be the son of God at the same time.

"So," Asma said, "we won't know until after death and the 227 Judgment who has been wrong all this time."

And that's where we left it; each of us confident that the other 228 would eventually see the unreasonableness of her position.

While living in Morocco, I was the underdog—a Christian living 229 in an Islamic country, an infidel heathen residing in the land of the true believers. Part of the fault of that night lay in my desire for Nadia and Asma—two intelligent, talented, Moroccan women—to view their religion from a global perspective, one religion among the many of the world. But this was impossible; they had never been out of the country, had never lived away from their families, had never had a chance to view their life from another perspective.

The three of us never discussed religion again. Whenever Nadia 230 stayed overnight, she continued to wash herself in my squat and then kneel on a shawl facing east to pray. I ignored this, just as she ignored my Messiah tapes at Christmas, after I once translated some of the words.

The Cheating

While in Morooco, I considered myself first a schoolteacher, and 231 secondly a Peace Corps Volunteer. Most of my waking time—just as it would be in the States—was spent on the job. I taught two junior classes and one senior class of English five days a week—Tuesdays and Sundays off—at the town High School of Letters.

In the beginning, when I wasn't accustomed to classes of fifty   232 students with barely a book between them, or blackboards without chalk or erasers to go with them, I made many mistakes. They were insignificant errors that were humorous to all. As the months wore on, however, and I persisted in taking my job seriously, mistakes were made—both by me and the students—that had larger, more encompassing consequences. Let me illustrate by recounting four incidents, two that happened at the beginning of my first year, and two that happened well into my term.

During my first year I found it difficult to pronounce the students'   233 names correctly in Arabic, so there was general snickering every time I took roll. This snickering extended into class time, and I didn't get very far in the lesson.

To counteract the problem, I arranged a seating chart that split up   234 the loudest snickerers. On a chosen day, I walked into class, took roll (in order to establish who was actually present) and walked around the classroom tapping each desk and pronouncing the name of the student supposed to be there.

"Now," I said, "move to your correct seat."   235

Wails and complaints assaulted me. I stood firm.   236

"Move," I repeated. "From now on you will sit according to the   237 seating chart."

A few of the girl students timidly went to stand by their new desks   238 but the boys—men really—already sitting there wouldn't move. I recognized one of them, a boy with dark curly hair and a sullen face called Hamid.

The class teetered on the edge of chaos. I knew that if just one of   239 the difficult boys moved, everyone would move and I would be able to get through a lesson. I looked at Hamid and he stared back at me, arrogant, scowling, defiant.

Suddenly a rage filled me: I was their teacher, trained, qualified,   240 smart. How dare a bunch of schoolchildren refuse to do what I, their teacher, had asked?

"Get up!" I screamed at them in English, not caring that they couldn't   241 understand such a furious torrent of foreign words. "Move immediately. I won't have it. I'm the teacher and you do as I say or you are out."

I slapped at the desk nearest me. "Right now—fast. Get to your   242 correct seat. I'm sick of you defying me and not doing as I ask. Hamid, get out of that seat and move to your desk, NOW!" and I pointed at him, finger shaking.

There was a stunned silence as the class took in my anger and the   243 screaming of English words. Then, perhaps in admiration of my fine show of authority, or perhaps simply in admiration of a fine performance, they all raised their hands high in the air and clapped, whistling and cheering. And then, cheerfully, with a rustling of robes and papers, they found their new seats, not one student out of place.

This class was more productive after the new seating chart, but 244 there were still problems. They didn't learn fast and couldn't keep up with the assignments. After a few weeks I noticed that even though I had assigned the textbook in the beginning, there were only a few copies around the classroom. When I referred to a certain page, most of the students got up and clustered around the student nearest them who had the book.

"What does this mean?" I asked one day. "I assigned you the 245 textbook." (I held up my copy that I had purchased at 12 *dirhams*, or approximately $1.50.) "Why haven't you bought the book?"

There was a low growl from all sides of the room. 246

"What is it?" I asked again. "How come most of you haven't 247 bought the book?"

The muttering increased, and then one student, one of the poorer 248 ones in a wooly brown peasant robe, stood up.

"Miss," he said, trying his best in English, "you understand the 249 book is too expensive."

"Oh," I said. Then I thought. "But some of you spend more money 250 on other things. You buy cigarettes." (I made the motion of smoking.) "A packet of black-market Marlboros is as much as two-thirds of this book. Or if you didn't go to the cinema for three weeks you could buy the book."

There was open arguing back and forth. Then one of the wealthier 251 students—a stylish young man who sat in the back wearing store-bought shirts, narrow trousers and leather shoes—stood up.

"You are right, Miss," he said. "It's not too expensive." 252

All over the room students leaped to their feet. Screaming, shout- 253 ing, pointing at him, they forced him back down into his seat with their obvious resentment of his wealth. Two boys began fighting off to the side; a girl's desk was pushed and she fell onto the floor. The roar grew louder and out of the corner of my eye I could see a boy throwing the textbook at the wall.

"Stop it," I shouted. "Sit down all of you." 254

I waded into the middle of it all, slamming my teacher's manual 255 against desks to make loud CRACKING sounds, and trying to push boys back into their seats.

"Now," I said, as I walked back up to the front, "this is what we 256 will do. Two students share each desk. One of these students must have a book. Some of you have books already, some of you must buy one. But tomorrow, I want every desk to have a book."

They nodded their heads, understanding and approving. This was 257 reasonable.

Things were serene for months afterward. Then I began to be 258 aware of larger, less-easily solved problems beneath the surface.

For one, no matter what threats I uttered, or what vigilance I gave 259 to catching the offenders, the majority of the students cheated on tests, exams, and homework assignments. I understood that the Moroccan school system fostered this temptation, because only an educated person could hope to get one of the few available jobs, even with some palm-greasing. But I also felt that if I couldn't give each student an accurate grade, I might as well not teach. For the sake of academic integrity alone, I had to grade according to knowledge and merit, rather than according to which student was the most cunning in his efforts to avoid an accurate grade.

At the end of the semester, I gave the final exam, graded it and 260 then averaged out semester grades. During class, I called each student up to my desk to show the final grade. Grades were calculated on a scale of one to twenty. A Moroccan saying has it that twenty is for the Prophet Mohammed, nineteen for the King, eighteen for the best student and so on, all the way down to zero, with the *moyenne*—or average passing grade—being ten.

I called Hamid—the well-dressed one—up to my desk. His final 261 grade was a number eight. He was extremely upset.

"But look." I showed him the line of figures in my gradebook. 262 "These are all your scores, and they average out to an eight."

"You can't give me a below-average grade," he said to me, gen- 263 uinely shocked. "My father is the richest man in this town."

"This will be your grade," I said. "It's the grade you deserve. Now 264 leave."

After school, he and a friend were waiting. They followed me back 265 to my apartment chanting, "Miss, Miss, please change the grade, just to a ten, just to the average, please." I never said a word, just shut the door in their faces.

The next morning I was organizing my materials in the classroom, 266 waiting for the bell, when I noticed another teacher of English—a young Moroccan man I had seen at teacher's meetings—beckoning to me from the hall.

"Sarah," he said, "I understand you are going to give Hamid a 267 below-passing grade."

"It's an accurate grade," I said. 268

"Oh, I'm sure it is," he said. "It's just that his father is the wealthiest 269 man in our town, and his father doesn't want him to get low marks."

"I don't care what his father wants," I said. 270

"There's just one more thing," the teacher said, visibly embar- 271
rassed. "I share a house with Hamid's brother. I've been sent by the
family, to you as a fellow teacher, to change his grade."

Suddenly, I understood. I had passed his house. It was a nice little 272
bungalow with a yard—much more than a teacher could afford.

"Please," he said, appealing to me directly, "will you change his 273
grade?"

"No," I said, and walked back in the classroom. 274

I ignored the whispering and walked up to the blackboard. I was 275
very angry, but determined not to show it to the students, all of whom
by now knew what was happening.

"Turn in your books to page 23," I said. 276

After school Nadia came to my apartment. Her family lived in a 277
village a one-hour bus ride away, so on the days when she had classes
back to back she spent the nights with me. I told her about the incident.
She wasn't surprised.

"It's very difficult Sarah," she said, "to fight against the corrup- 278
tion. I try to, but am not always successful. Just be sure to mark down
his grade in the gradebook as '08' instead of plain '8' because he might
try to sneak in and put a '1' in front of your '8' and change it that way."

"Thanks for the warning," I said. 279

The next morning instead of going to my classroom, I went to the 280
teacher's salon to record my grades. Each student had one gradebook,
and the teacher marked down the grade in the space next to the proper
subject. When I came to Hamid's English slot, I carefully penned in "08."
As I left, I nodded good-bye to the *shaoush* guarding the door; his sole
responsibility was to let only the teachers in and keep the students out.

Nadia came over about suppertime. 281

"Sarah," she said as I let her in, "you'll never believe what hap- 282
pened with Hamid's grade." Her voice was shaking with anger.
"Sometimes I cannot stand it. I was in the salon marking my grades,
when the History teacher came in—you know her, she's very wealthy
and is friends with the *moudir*. Well, she began marking her grades
and she came to Hamid's name, who is a student of hers in history. She
told us that she had been instructed to add five points onto his History
grade to make up for his English grade. So she gave him a '17' in
History, instead of the '12' he was supposed to get."

It was hopeless. 283

"Oh Nadia," I said, "don't you be upset. It's too bad but it's my 284
problem."

"But that's just it," Nadia said. "I told her she shouldn't change the 285
grade—that it was too corrupt, even here in Morocco—and another
teacher who was listening, sneered at me and said, 'Do you think you
are in the United States or something?' "

We ate our dinner in silence and listened to the street noises com-   286
ing through the open window. All I could think was that Hamid had
won; when his grades were averaged together, he would do fine, because his History grade would make up for the English one. He had
swerved around me and was speeding down the path of academic success without obstacle.

The school year wore on. The cheating abated somewhat, but I   287
suspected that the worst students had been told to stay out of my
classes, because I wouldn't be bribed. Toward the end of the year,
when the tension was at its highest because only a small percentage
of students were allowed to pass, and those who failed would have to
drop out of school forever, something happened that made the
"Hamid Incident" seem trivial.

I was collecting my books and materials after class—including the   288
sponge I carried to erase the board—when I realized my gradebook
was missing. I searched underneath the desk, looked around the
room, even went through my bag, although I knew immediately that
it had been stolen. There was nothing to do but report it to the *moudir*.

"Are you sure?" The *moudir* was skeptical. He was an intimidat-   289
ing man who had achieved his powerful position by means I sensed
rather than actually knew; he emanated an air of corrupt ambition
and cruelty.

"Of course, I'm sure," I answered, keeping my words precise and   290
clear in French, the second language for both of us.

"Well, why do you bring your gradebook to class in the first   291
place?" asked the *moudir* and looked at me angrily.

I stared blankly for a moment.   292

"Because I have to write down attendance and grades and extra-   293
credit assignments."

"Well, you shouldn't, you know. The temptation is too much for   294
these students. If the gradebook is there in front of them . . ." He let
the sentence trail off.

"Anyway, you go teach your next class," he said, "and leave the   295
problem to us."

By "us" I knew he meant the three Moroccan bodyguards he sur-   296
rounded himself with. In my mind, I had referred to them as the
"Goon Squad" ever since they had come into the classroom one day
to push around some troublemakers. I had watched as they had lifted
students out of desks and threw them against the wall. I had cringed
as one had raised his huge boot and literally kicked a student out of
the seat. I didn't want to think about the "Goon Squad" and its methods of finding my gradebook, so I nodded and left.

At the end of the day, I was called back into the *moudir's* office. 297
Cowering in the corner was one of my poorest, slowest, and generally, weakest students.

"Here," said the *moudir*, handing me my gradebook. "This one 298
took it."

I flipped through until I got to the right page. Sure enough, about 299
eight students had changed their grades. They had used the same
color of pen, so it was hard to tell at first glance, but looking closely,
I saw that a consistently "6" and "7" student now had "16's" and
"17's" and that some had even changed "0's" to "8's" by putting a line
through the circle, and a few had blatantly crossed out old grades and
written in new ones.

"Listen," I said to the *moudir*, "this boy is just a scapegoat. The 300
more assured, smarter students got him to change the grades so they
couldn't be traced."

I showed him the changes. 301

"All right," he said, "I'll take care of these students." He wrote 302
down some names. I noticed that he didn't write down the names of
the daughter of the Police Commissioner or the son of the man who
hosted the national soccer team.

I knew that he was going to punish the boy and have done with it. 303

"Fine," I said. "And I'll put a zero in place of every grade that has 304
been changed."

"And I'll expel this boy for good," said the *moudir*. 305

"Don't do that," I said. 306

"Why not?" asked the *moudir*. "I thought you'd be happy with 307
that punishment."

"For the right person, yes," I said. "But this boy is just stupid. 308
He's not mean or malicious like the other, smarter students who
talked him into stealing the gradebook. They're the ones who should
be expelled."

"Tell you what," said the *moudir*, irritated that I wasn't going 309
along with his plan, "I won't expel him, just suspend him for a few
days. But then, you don't change the grades to zeros—that's too hard
on the others."

I wondered how it was that I had gotten into the position of 310
bargaining.

"All right," I gave in. 311

As I left, a ragged woman with a dark scarf covering her face ran 312
up to me. She grabbed my hand and kissed it, then got down on her
knees and garbled out some plea.

"She doesn't want you to expel her son," the *moudir*, watching, 313
called.

I pulled my hand away and went back to my apartment where 314
I was safe, where I didn't have to face another Moroccan student or
administrator until the next day.

Peace Corps Aftershock

Six months before my two-year term was due to end, I was med- 315
ically evacuated back to the States. The evacuation came suddenly. I
had been sick with a variety of intestinal ailments for a long time, but
then, it seemed as if all the volunteers were sick. On the Paris-New
York plane flight everything became bigger, whiter and brighter. The
business of living—for the first time in months—seemed manageable
and desirable.

After landing in New York, I flew on to Washington, D.C., where 316
I underwent a three-week battery of physical and psychological exams.
Once again, I was living in the U.S. I began to try and re-assimilate into
the culture to which I had once belonged. I quickly found that I had
underestimated the changes that had taken place, changes that were a
result of my experience as a Peace Corps Volunteer.

First, and most obviously, my behavior toward men in public 317
places had become extreme. Whether walking to an appointment
in the streets of Georgetown or at a restaurant, I reacted to the presence of strange males by cowering and shrinking back in fear of being
harassed. My sensitivity was made clear one Sunday morning when I
was touring the sights of the Capital alone. As I walked past the White
House gate, a guard said, "hello" and I fled back to my hotel room, certain that he thought I was a whore and was propositioning me.

Then, the abundance of material things—especially food— 318
shocked me. Every trip to the grocery store was pure confusion at
having to choose between so many options or seeing a steak looking
obscene in its redness and blood. To celebrate my return, a cousin
took me out to dinner. While perusing the menu, she remarked on an
item containing cheese. Startled, I blurted, "Cheese? You can get
cheese here?" As she looked at me blankly, I froze—completely lost in
distance and perspective.

Things that might have seemed a pleasure upon returning from a 319
more ordinary kind of trip became a kind of torture for me. For example,
taking a hot shower every day if I wished. I had gone to the *hemem*
once a week for so long that I only felt bewildered, and had a kind of
disgust when I turned on the "H" spigot in the bathroom. Somehow it
was all too easy and convenient. Every time I put on shoes, I stared at
the henna dye Amina had put on my feet for a celebration preceding
my departure. For months, my rust-colored toenails stayed a reminder
of my past life when what I wanted was to wipe out all traces of a
disturbing experience.

After the three weeks of testing were completed, it was recom- 320
mended that I not return to Morocco. The reasons for this were partly
physical: several nodules (probably stress-related) had been discovered
on my small intestine. More important, however, was that I was diag-
nosed as suffering from acute psychological distress. I flew back to my
parents' home in Minnesota, and, during the months of alienation that followed, I tried to sort out what had happened. It was during this time that
I had to acknowledge some drastic changes: my personality presented as
confused and defensive; my mind was disoriented, and conflicting emotions kept me a shattered wreck. In short, I wasn't functioning.

A few months later, I received a letter from one of my students, 321
sent on to my parents' address. It read:

> Dear Miss:
> I was sorry, with all affliction and despair to hear of your leavetak-
> ing. The administration told us you are ill with "SIDA." Please write
> and assure me that this is not true, as you are the best teacher of
> English of all.
>
> Sincerely,
> Your student.

SIDA is the French acronym for AIDS. I understood that someone—
possibly even the *moudir* himself—had started the rumor flying that I
had gone back to the States because I was dying of AIDS. I didn't feel
angry, only a bitter amusement, that this was the Moroccan interpretation of the ending of my career as a Peace Corps Volunteer.

I sat down to answer my former student's letter. First, I wrote that 322
I appreciated being called the "best teacher of English of all." Then I
told him that he was a very good student and should be sure to continue his studies. Finally, I wrote that I did not have "SIDA" and that
I was in no danger of dying. At this point I faltered; how could I explain my sudden departure? I thought and then wrote: "I'm sorry I left
so suddenly, but it was necessary for personal reasons."

A few months before leaving, an old friend had visited me in 323
Morocco. During his visit we had become engaged to be married.
Certain that my former student would read "personal reasons" to
mean "fiancé" and, although not accurate, satisfied with this interpretation, I signed my name and sealed the letter. As I dropped it in the
airmail box, I knew this information would be relayed to anyone in
Morocco who truly cared about my whereabouts.

The post-traumatic stress seemed to center around one particular 324
incident that had happened a few months before I had been evacuated.
I could remember it vividly:

Nadia and I were on our way to the market to buy eggs and veg- 325
etables for supper. It was the dusky time of day, when the robed

women bustled around the stalls, purchasing food and screaming for better bargains. The children played without clothes in the dirt while the men leaned against the buildings and smoked. Everyone was moving fast to get business done before the dark deepened into another black, airless, desert night.

I had slipped my *djellaba* over my jeans and T-shirt and was carry- 326 ing the straw basket to hold the food. Nadia and I wove around the boys spinning thread in the alley. We reached the main street. Nadia took hold of the basket to propel us through the crowd; I was on the outside, Nadia was further in toward the wall of shops.

Some stones thudded behind me; I felt grit and dust swirl around 327 my bare ankles. I didn't look back, not wanting to react in case the stones weren't meant for me—it was so crowded they could have been meant for someone else. Then a bigger stone—it felt about the size of a ripe olive—hit me square on the back of the calf. Another followed, going slightly wide of the mark, and just brushing my waist. I cried out and stopped.

My calf stung viciously (I was to have a bruise that lasted for a 328 week) but mostly I was scared—and angry. The crowd jostled against me. No one gave the slightest sign of noticing the incident, other than stepping around me as I stood, not moving.

"Sarah, let's go," Nadia was tugging at my arm. "Don't stop in the 329 middle of the street."

She was speaking in French, a sign that she didn't want the people 330 around to catch what we were saying.

"Do you know what they did?" I said. "They threw stones at me. One 331 hit me—what if it had been my head?—I could have been badly hurt."

"It's nothing, Sarah," she said. "Just keep walking; don't stop." 332

"What do you mean it's nothing?" I asked. "They're throwing 333 stones at me for God's sake. It's not nothing."

People flowed by. I tried to catch someone's eye. Had no one seen 334 the stone or heard my cry—or was even wondering why I was stopped in the middle of the street arguing with Nadia?

"Please Sarah," Nadia was begging now, "you've got to keep 335 walking. You can't do anything."

Suddenly, I sagged inside. I knew she was right. Even if I had seen 336 who had thrown the stone. . . . I raised my head and by some instinct looked straight across the street. In a gap in the crowd I could see a group of young men, well-dressed, exuding strength. They were looking at me and laughing.

I recognized one—he had been my student once, a serious, 337 respectful student. As I was looking he slapped another on the back, as if saying, "Well done." He looked up, met my eyes for the barest of instants, then turned away. The group huddled, arms around each other's shoulders. The crowd closed in, I couldn't see them anymore, and Nadia led me away.

I completed the shopping trip in a daze. My mind convoluted on the possibilities: Had the stones been meant for me? Why? Why my student!? Nadia selected peas and tomatos for our omelette. I automatically held the basket as she dumped in the packages wrapped in newspaper. I followed her back to my apartment.

In my living room, I slumped down. Now Nadia was willing to talk.

"Forget about it, Sarah," she said, sitting down across from me. "It's different here. It's no good to think about it because you can't do anything."

"Has it ever happened to you?" I asked.

"Well, no," she admitted, "but I have heard of stonings. It used to be a punishment—it was an old Arab custom to stone bad women—but that has changed."

"Not so very much," I said.

"Sarah, you are not a bad woman," she said to me.

"But everyone thinks I am a bad woman," I said, "because I have blond hair and am American, and live by myself without a brother or a cousin or an uncle to take care of me."

"Yes . . . ," Nadia's voice weakened; she didn't want to agree with me, but couldn't think of anything else to say.

"I hate them," I said to her.

"Shh, Sarah," she said, getting up to cook our meal. "Just forget about it."

But I hadn't been able to forget about it. Originally, I had blamed myself: I shouldn't have been walking in the street/maybe it had happened because I had previously caught one of the boys cheating on an exam/I had always been conspicuous with my blond hair so I should have been more aware of the danger. Then the blame had shifted to the boys—after all, I had seen the congratulatory-slap-on-the-back—and lastly, it veered over to the Peace Corps Organization, and there it stayed.

The fault, I felt, lay in the lack of preparation for volunteers. Peace Corps officials had never acknowledged the enormous difference in lifestyle and esteem any American woman would have to face in an Arabic/Muslim country. They had not accounted for the Koranic system of learning—memorizing and recitation—that confronted teachers trained in the Western, Socratic system of question and answer. And they had not emphasized the sacrifices (beyond time and money) required of volunteers to Morocco: health, well-being, and safety.

Reeling from the violence I had encountered, I felt the Peace Corps   351 hadn't prepared volunteers for the risk and the danger. Sure, they admitted a risk—even to the point of glorifying it in their slogan: "Peace Corps—the toughest job you'll ever love." But this risk was never defined. It was left vague—perhaps contracting hepatitis? Having to evacuate your post in case of political turmoil? Never was it specified that—especially in the case of white American women in Arabic countries—the risk might come in the form of personal violence.

I began to compile a list of volunteer casualties in Morocco during   352 my term alone:

>—A volunteer couple living in a small town were forced against the wall of their house by a mob throwing stones. The man stood in front of the woman who covered her head with her hands and crouched against the house. When the mob ran out of stones, the man had a deep cut below one eye and the woman's hands were bruised and cut.
>
>—One woman volunteer was assaulted during daylight—while at her post—and raped.
>
>—A volunteer was walking in his city one night when a Moroccan man he didn't know accosted him with a razor and cut him across the cheek before he could fend him off.
>
>—Another volunteer confiscated the exams of several students he had caught blatantly cheating. The next day he received death threats. When they continued, he changed locations.
>
>—A volunteer posted in a big city was riding his bicycle home from a party one night when a group of men—apparently waiting for him—stepped out and forced him off the bicycle, then attacked him with broken bottles, leaving him cut-up and bruised.
>
>—One volunteer was driving when he had a fatal car accident. There were rumors of suicide, although no one knew for certain. A Peace Corps "official"—the only one I had ever met who seemed to know what went on outside of Washington, D.C.—escorted the body back to the States. Later I found out this person was leaving. I asked why. He said to me, "There are a lot of reasons. One is that this is not the first time my job has included accompanying a body back to the family. I fly with the casket on the plane. Then I meet the parents. And you know, it's just getting to be too hard to do."

And every year a new batch of volunteers is sent to Morocco.   353

I asked someone in Peace Corps Washington why at least the   354 women weren't warned before being posted in Morocco?

"Well, the Peace Corps doesn't want to be sexist," was the answer.   355 "If they admitted a certain country was unsafe for women volunteers, in order to avoid being sexist, they would have to stop sending the men too. Then there wouldn't be any volunteers in Morocco, and that, of course, wouldn't be acceptable."

I knew why "of course" it wouldn't be acceptable. The U.S. cur- 356 rently enjoys a friendly relationship with King Hassan of Morocco. In official language: "The U.S. cannot turn a blind eye to the fact that Morocco has historically been a good friend and indeed, in a practical sense, an ally. . . .we need to nurture our relations as never before with all Islamic and non-aligned states, but we particularly need to stand up for and support our avowed friends and supporters."[1]

Translated, this means that the U.S. cannot afford to offend a politi- 357 cally sensitive country by the cessation of peace offerings, i.e., volunteers.

Questions filled my mind. Had I asked to be used as a peace of- 358 fering? I recalled a conversation I had once had with a Belgian who was in Morocco for his two years of civil service.

"You realize why we're all here," he had said to me. "All of us, the 359 Americans, French, those of us from Belgium, even the British. We're all here for the attention. As foreigners, we're given attention in Morocco whether it's good or bad. Even if the natives stare at you and make nasty remarks in a language you can't understand and spit as you walk by, you are at least noticed. Your existence matters, even if it is acknowledged in a negative way. Whereas if you work in a big city—let's say New York—and travel with a mass of humanity on the subways each day, you are given no indication of your existence whatsoever. If you dropped dead, people would step around you to catch the right line for their suburb. It's addictive to stay here; it's addicting to be given attention all day long, every day, in a thousand little ways. And it's devastating to return to a society where you are completely ignored. No wonder we tolerate anything, take any kind of job in order to keep on."

His words, to some extent, were true. But that hadn't been the 360 whole reason for my wanting to be a volunteer in Morocco. I had wanted to help. I had wanted to change things. I had wanted to participate in a cross-cultural interaction that wasn't tainted by idealism or colonialism. And so I taught English, in a village, on the train line between Casablanca and Marrakesh.

---

[1]Harold J. Saunders, testifying as U.S. Assistant Secretary of State for Near Eastern and South Asian affairs before the Africa subcommittee of the House of Representatives Foreign Affairs Committee.

QUESTIONS

1. According to Streed, what constitutes "the abuse of women" in Morocco? For the incidents she relates—such as the harassment she experiences on her way to school (paragraphs 92 to 94), or her visit with Rachida and her family (paragraphs 102 to 117)—how appropriate do you find Streed's various reactions to this abuse?

2. About the cheating incidents, Streed writes that "mistakes were made—both by me and the students" (paragraph 232). Review these "mistakes" on both sides, and discuss the relative fairness of the solutions proposed by Streed, the *moudir,* and the compromise they reach regarding the stolen gradebook incident. Do you share Streed's moral objections to the cheating and corruption? To the extent that the Moroccans don't share these moral objections, do you think that Streed is imposing a Western or American value system in a cultural context where it doesn't apply? Why or why not?

3. After the stoning incident (described in paragraphs 325 to 348)—which is evidently the precipitating cause of Streed's post-traumatic stress—she blames herself, the boys who threw the rocks, and the Peace Corps. To what extent do you agree with Streed's analysis of the blame? Do you think the Peace Corps might be justified in withholding information from volunteers about sexism in other cultures (as alleged by Streed)?

4. In the last paragraph Streed states her personal goals for her Peace Corps experience. Based on her memoir, how successfully do you think she achieved these goals?

A Distant Episode

PAUL BOWLES

The September sunsets were at their reddest the week the Professor 1
decided to visit Aïn Tadouirt, which is in the warm country. He came
down out of the high, flat region in the evening by bus, with two small
overnight bags full of maps, sun lotions and medicines. Ten years ago
he had been in the village for three days; long enough, however, to establish a fairly firm friendship with a café-keeper, who had written him
several times during the first year after his visit, if never since. "Hassan
Ramani," the Professor said over and over, as the bus bumped downward through ever warmer layers of air. Now facing the flaming sky in
the west, and now facing the sharp mountains, the car followed the
dusty trail down the canyons into air which began to smell of other
things besides the endless ozone of the heights: orange blossoms, pepper, sun-baked excrement, burning olive oil, rotten fruit. He closed his
eyes happily and lived for an instant in a purely olfactory world. The
distant past returned—what part of it, he could not decide.

The chauffeur, whose seat the Professor shared, spoke to him with- 2
out taking his eyes from the road. *"Vous êtes géologue?"*

"A geologist? Ah, no! I'm a linguist." 3

"There are no languages here. Only dialects." 4

"Exactly. I'm making a survey of variations on Moghrebi." 5

The chauffeur was scornful. "Keep on going south," he said. 6
"You'll find some languages you never heard of before."

As they drove through the town gate, the usual swarm of urchins 7
rose up out of the dust and ran screaming beside the bus. The Professor
folded his dark glasses, put them in his pocket; and as soon as the vehicle had come to a standstill he jumped out, pushing his way through

---

Paul Bowles, music composer and writer, was born in the U.S. but has
lived most of his life in Tangiers, Morocco. His fiction is often set in
Morocco or other international locations and deals with the attempts
of Westerners to understand North African and other cultures. His
best-known novel, *The Sheltering Sky* (1949), was made into a feature
film of the same name (directed by Bernardo Bertolucci, 1990).
Bowles's volumes of stories include *A Hundred Camels in the Courtyard*
(1962), *Collected Stories 1939–1976* (1979), and *Points in Time* (1982). In
recent years he has dedicated himself to translating and collaborating
with Mohammed Mrabet and other Moroccan writers. "A Distant
Episode" first appeared in the *Partisan Review* in 1947 and was included in *The Delicate Prey and Other Stories* (1950) and *A Distant Episode:
The Selected Stories* (1988).

the indignant boys who clutched at his luggage in vain, and walked
quickly into the Grand Hotel Saharien. Out of its eight rooms there
were two available—one facing the market and the other, a smaller
and cheaper one, giving onto a tiny yard full of refuse and barrels,
where two gazelles wandered about. He took the smaller room, and
pouring the entire pitcher of water into the tin basin, began to wash the
grit from his face and ears. The afterglow was nearly gone from the
sky, and the pinkness in objects was disappearing, almost as he
watched. He lit the carbide lamp and winced at its odor.

After dinner the Professor walked slowly through the streets to   8
Hassan Ramani's café, whose back room hung hazardously out above
the river. The entrance was very low, and he had to bend down
slightly to get in. A man was tending the fire. There was one guest sip-
ping tea. The *qaouaji*[1] tried to make him take a seat at the other table in
the front room, but the Professor walked airily ahead into the back
room and sat down. The moon was shining through the reed lattice-
work and there was not a sound outside but the occasional distant
bark of a dog. He changed tables so he could see the river. It was dry,
but there was a pool here and there that reflected the bright night sky.
The *qaouaji* came in and wiped off the table.

"Does this café still belong to Hassan Ramani?" he asked him in   9
the Moghrebi he had taken four years to learn.

The man replied in bad French: "He is deceased."   10

"Deceased?" repeated the Professor, without noticing the absur-   11
dity of the word. "Really? When?"

"I don't know," said the *qaouaji*. "One tea?"   12

"Yes. but I don't understand . . ."   13

The man was already out of the room, fanning the fire. The   14
Professor sat still, feeling lonely, and arguing with himself that to do
so was ridiculous. Soon the *qaouaji* returned with the tea. He paid him
and gave him an enormous tip, for which he received a grave bow.

"Tell me," he said, as the other started away. "Can one still get   15
those little boxes made from camel udders?"

The man looked angry. "Sometimes the Reguibat bring in those   16
things. We do not buy them here." Then insolently, in Arabic: "And
why a camel-udder box?"

"Because I like them," retorted the Professor. And then because he   17
was feeling a little exalted, he added, "I like them so much I want to
make a collection of them, and I will pay you ten francs for every one
you can get me."

"*Khamstache*," said the *qaouaji*, opening his left hand rapidly three   18
times in succession.

---

[1]*qaouaji:* café manager. (Ed.)

"Never. Ten."   19

"Not possible. But wait until later and come with me. You can give   20
me what you like. And you will get camel-udder boxes if there are any."

He went out into the front room, leaving the Professor to drink his   21
tea and listen to the growing chorus of dogs that barked and howled
as the moon rose higher into the sky. A group of customers came into
the front room and sat talking for an hour or so. When they had left,
the *qaouaji* put out the fire and stood in the doorway putting on his
burnous. "Come," he said.

Outside in the street there was very little movement. The booths   22
were all closed and the only light came from the moon. An occasional
pedestrian passed, and grunted a brief greeting to the *qaouaji*.

"Everyone knows you," said the Professor, to cut the silence be-   23
tween them.

"Yes."   24

"I wish everyone knew me," said the Professor, before he realized   25
how infantile such a remark must sound.

"*No* one knows you," said his companion gruffly.   26

They had come to the other side of the town, on the promontory   27
above the desert, and through a great rift in the wall the Professor saw
the white endlessness, broken in the foreground by dark spots of oasis.
They walked through the opening and followed a winding road between rocks, downward toward the nearest small forest of palms. The
Professor thought: "He may cut my throat. But his café—he would
surely be found out."

"Is it far?" he asked, casually.   28

"Are you tired?" countered the *qaouaji*.   29

"They are expecting me back at the Hotel Saharien," he lied.   30

"You can't be there and here," said the *qaiouaji*.   31

The Professor laughed. He wondered if it sounded uneasy to the   32
other.

"Have you owned Ramani's café long?"   33

"I work there for a friend." The reply made the Professor more un-   34
happy than he had imagined it would.

"Oh. Will you work tomorrow?"   35

"That is impossible to say."   36

The Professor stumbled on a stone, and fell, scraping his hand. The   37
qaouaji said: "Be careful."

The sweet black odor of rotten meat hung in the air suddenly.   38

"Agh!" said the Professor, choking. "What is it?"   39

The *qaouaji* had covered his face with his burnous and did not an-   40
swer. Soon the stench had been left behind. They were on flat ground.
Ahead the path was bordered on each side by a high mud wall. There
was no breeze and the palms were quite still, but behind the walls was

the sound of running water. Also, the odor of human excrement was almost constant as they walked between the walls.

The Professor waited until he thought it seemed logical for him to 41 ask with a certain degree of annoyance: "But where are we going?"

"Soon," said the guide, pausing to gather some stones in the ditch. 42

"Pick up some stones," he advised. "Here are bad dogs." 43

"Where?" asked the Professor, but he stooped and got three large 44 ones with pointed edges.

They continued very quietly. The walls came to an end and the 45 bright desert lay ahead. Nearby was a ruined marabout, with its tiny dome only half standing, and the front wall entirely destroyed. Behind it were clumps of stunted, useless palms. A dog came running crazily toward them on three legs. Not until it got quite close did the Professor hear its steady low growl. The *qaouaji* let fly a large stone at it, striking it square in the muzzle. There was a strange snapping of jaws and the dog ran sideways in another direction, falling blindly against rocks and scrambling haphazardly about like an injured insect.

Turning off the road, they walked across the earth strewn with 46 sharp stones, past the little ruin, through the trees, until they came to a place where the ground dropped abruptly away in front of them.

"It looks like a quarry," said the Professor, resorting to French for 47 the word "quarry," whose Arabic equivalent he could not call to mind at the moment. The *qaouaji* did not answer. Instead he stood still and turned his head, as if listening. And indeed, from somewhere down below, but very far below, came the faint sound of a low flute. The *qaouaji* nodded his head slowly several times. Then he said: "The path begins here. You can see it well all the way. The rock is white and the moon is strong. So you can see well. I am going back now and sleep. It is late. You can give me what you like."

Standing there at the edge of the abyss which at each moment 48 looked deeper, with the dark face of the *qaouaji* framed in its moonlit burnous close to his own face, the Professor asked himself exactly what he felt. Indignation, curiosity, fear, perhaps, but most of all relief and the hope that this was not a trick, the hope that the *qaouaji* would really leave him alone and turn back without him.

He stepped back a little from the edge, and fumbled in his pocket 49 for a loose note, because he did not want to show his wallet. Fortunately there was a fifty-franc bill there, which he took out and handed to the man. He knew the *qaouaji* was pleased, and so he paid no attention when he heard him saying: "It is not enough. I have to walk a long way home and there are dogs. . . ."

"Thank you and good night," said the Professor, sitting down 50 with his legs drawn up under him, and lighting a cigarette. He felt almost happy.

"Give me only one cigarette," pleaded the man.   51

"Of course," he said, a bit curtly, and he held up the pack.   52

The *qaouaji* squatted close beside him. His face was not pleasant to   53
see. "What is it?" thought the Professor, terrified again, as he held out
his lighted cigarette toward him.

The man's eyes were almost closed. It was the most obvious regis-   54
tering of concentrated scheming the Professor had ever seen. When the
second cigarette was burning, he ventured to say to the still-squatting
Arab: "What are you thinking about?"

The other drew on his cigarette deliberately, and seemed about to   55
speak. Then his expression changed to one of satisfaction, but he did
not speak. A cool wind had risen in the air, and the Professor shivered.
The sound of the flute came up from the depths below at intervals,
sometimes mingled with the scraping of nearby palm fronds one
against the other. "These people are not primitives," the Professor
found himself saying in his mind.

"Good," said the *qaouaji*, rising slowly. "Keep your money. Fifty   56
francs is enough. It is an honor." Then he went back into French: *"Ti
n'as qu'à discendre, to' droit."*[2] He spat, chuckled (or was the Professor
hysterical?), and strode away quickly.

The Professor was in a state of nerves. He lit another cigarette, and   57
found his lips moving automatically. They were saying: "Is this a situation or a predicament? This is ridiculous." He sat very still for several
minutes, waiting for a sense of reality to come to him. He stretched out
on the hard, cold ground and looked up at the moon. It was almost like
looking straight at the sun. If he shifted his gaze a little at a time, he
could make a string of weaker moons across the sky. "Incredible," he
whispered. Then he sat up quickly and looked about. There was no
guarantee that the *qaouaji* really had gone back to town. He got to his
feet and looked over the edge of the precipice. In the moonlight the
bottom seemed miles away. And there was nothing to give it scale; not
a tree, not a house, not a person. . . . He listened for the flute, and heard
only the wind going by his ears. A sudden violent desire to run back
to the road seized him, and he turned and looked in the direction the
qaouaji had taken. At the same time he felt softly of his wallet in his
breast pocket. Then he spat over the edge of the cliff. Then he made
water over it, and listened intently, like a child. This gave him the impetus to start down the path into the abyss. Curiously enough, he was
not dizzy. But prudently he kept from peering to his right, over the
edge. It was a steady and steep downward climb. The monotony of it
put him into a frame of mind not unlike that which had been induced
by the bus ride. He was murmuring "Hassan Ramani" again, repeatedly

---

[2]*Ti n'as qu'à discendre, to' droit:* You only have to go down. (Ed.)

and in rhythm. He stopped, furious with himself for the sinister over-tones the name now suggested to him. He decided he was exhausted from the trip. "And the walk," he added.

He was now well down the gigantic cliff, but the moon, being di-rectly overhead, gave as much light as ever. Only the wind was left be-hind, above, to wander among the trees, to blow through the dusty street of Aïn Tadouirt, into the hall of the Grand Hotel Saharien, and under the door of his little room.   58

It occurred to him that he ought to ask himself why he was doing this irrational thing, but he was intelligent enough to know that since he was doing it, it was not so important to probe for explanations at that moment.   59

Suddenly the earth was flat beneath his feet. He had reached the bottom sooner than he expected. He stepped ahead distrustfully still, as if he expected another treacherous drop. It was so hard to know in this uniform, dim brightness. Before he knew what had happened the dog was upon him, a heavy mass of fur trying to push him backwards, a sharp nail rubbing down his chest, a straining of muscles against him to get the teeth into his neck. The Professor thought: "I refuse to die this way." The dog fell back; it looked like an Eskimo dog. As it sprang again, he called out, very loud: "Ay!" It fell against him, there was a confusion of sensations and a pain somewhere. There was also the sound of voices very near to him, and he could not understand what they were saying. Something cold and metallic was pushed brutally against his spine as the dog still hung for a second by his teeth from a mass of clothing and perhaps flesh. The Professor knew it was a gun, and he raised his hands, shouting in Moghrebi: "Take away the dog!" But the gun merely pushed him forward, and since the dog, once it was back on the ground, did not leap again, he took a step ahead. The gun kept pushing; he kept taking steps. Again he heard voices, but the per-son directly behind him said nothing. People seemed to be running about; it sounded that way, at least. For his eyes, he discovered, were still shut tight against the dog's attack. He opened them. A group of men was advancing toward him. They were dressed in the black clothes of the Reguibat. "The Reguiba is a cloud across the face of the sun." "When the Reguiba appears the righteous man turns away." In how many shops and market-places he had heard these maxims ut-tered banteringly among friends. Never to a Reguiba, to be sure, for these men do not frequent towns. They send a representative in dis-guise, to arrange with shady elements there for the disposal of captured goods. "An opportunity," he thought quickly, "of testing the accuracy of such statements." He did not doubt for a moment that the adventure would prove to be a kind of warning against such foolishness on his part—a warning which in retrospect would be half sinister, half farcical.   60

Two snarling dogs came running from behind the oncoming men   61
and threw themselves at his legs. He was scandalized to note that no
one paid any attention to this breach of etiquette. The gun pushed him
harder as he tried to sidestep the animals' noisy assault. Again he
cried: "The dogs! Take them away!" The gun shoved him forward with
great force and he fell, almost at the feet of the crowd of men facing
him. The dogs were wrenching at his hands and arms. A boot kicked
them aside, yelping, and then with increased vigor it kicked the
Professor in the hip. Then came a chorus of kicks from different sides,
and he was rolled violently about on the earth for a while. During this
time he was conscious of hands reaching into his pockets and remov-
ing everything from them. He tried to say: "You have all my money;
stop kicking me!" But his bruised facial muscles would not work; he
felt himself pouting, and that was all. Someone dealt him a terrific
blow on the head, and he thought: "Now at least I shall lose con-
scaousness, thank Heaven." Still he went on being aware of the guttural voices he could not understand, and of being bound tightly about
the ankles and chest. Then there was black silence that opened like a
wound from time to time, to let in the soft, deep notes of the flute playing the same succession of notes again and again. Suddenly he felt ex-
cruciating pain everywhere—pain and cold. "So I have been unconscious, after all," he thought. In spite of that, the present seemed only
like a direct continuation of what had gone before.

It was growing faintly light. There were camels near where he was   62
lying; he could hear their gurgling and their heavy breathing. He
could not bring himself to attempt opening his eyes, just in case it
should turn out to be impossible. However, when he heard someone
approaching, he found that he had no difficulty in seeing.

The man looked at him dispassionately in the gray morning light.   63
With one hand he pinched together the Professor's nostrils. When the
Professor opened his mouth to breathe, the man swiftly seized his
tongue and pulled on it with all his might. The Professor was gagging
and catching his breath; he did not see what was happening. He could
not distinguish the pain of the brutal yanking from that of the sharp
knife. Then there was an endless choking and spitting that went on automatically, as though he were scarcely a part of it. The word "operation" kept going through his mind; it calmed his terror somewhat as
he sank back into darkness.

The caravan left sometime toward midmorning. The Professor, not   64
unconscious, but in a state of utter stupor, still gagging and drooling
blood, was dumped doubled-up into a sack and tied at one side of a
camel. The lower end of the enormous amphitheater contained a natural gate in the rocks. The camels, swift *mebara*, were lightly laden on
this trip. They passed through single file, and slowly mounted the gentle

slope that led up into the beginning of the desert. That night, at a stop behind some low hills, the men took him out, still in a state which permitted no thought, and over the dusty rags that remained of his clothing they fastened a series of curious belts made of the bottoms of tin cans strung together. One after another of these bright girdles was wired about his torso, his arms and legs, even across his face, until he was entirely within a suit of armor that covered him with its circular metal scales. There was a good deal of merriment during this decking-out of the Professor. One man brought out a flute and a younger one did a not ungraceful caricature of an Ouled Naïl executing a cane dance. The Professor was no longer conscious; to be exact, he existed in the middle of the movements made by these other men. When they had finished dressing him the way they wished him to look, they stuffed some food under the tin bangles hanging over his face. Even though he chewed mechanically, most of it eventually fell out onto the ground. They put him back into the sack and left him there.

Two days later they arrived at one of their own encampments. 65 There were women and children here in the tents, and the men had to drive away the snarling dogs they had left there to guard them. When they emptied the Professor out of his sack, there were screams of fright, and it took several hours to convince the last woman that he was harmless, although there had been no doubt from the start that he was a valuable possession. After a few days they began to move on again, taking everything with them, and traveling only at night as the terrain grew warmer.

Even when all his wounds had healed and he felt no more pain, 66 the Professor did not begin to think again; he ate and defecated, and he danced when he was bidden, a senseless hopping up and down that delighted the children, principally because of the wonderful jangling racket it made. And he generally slept through the heat of the day, in among the camels.

Wending its way southeast, the caravan avoided all stationary civ- 67 ilization. In a few weeks they reached a new plateau, wholly wild and with a sparse vegetation. Here they pitched camp and remained, while the *mehara* were turned loose to graze. Everyone was happy here; the weather was cooler and there was a well only a few hours away on a seldom-frequented trail. It was here they conceived the idea of taking the Professor to Fogara and selling him to the Touareg.

It was a full year before they carried out this project. By this time the 68 Professor was much better trained. He could do a handspring, make a series of fearful growling noises which had, nevertheless, a certain element of humor; and when the Reguibat removed the tin from his face they discovered he could grimace admirably while he danced. They also taught him a few basic obscene gestures which never failed to elicit delighted shrieks from the women. He was now brought forth only after especially abundant meals, when there was music and festivity. He easily fell in with their sense of ritual, and evolved an elementary sort of "program" to present when he was called for: dancing, rolling on the ground, imitating certain animals, and finally rushing toward the group in feigned anger, to see the resultant confusion and hilarity.

When three of the men set out for Fogara with him, they took four 69 *mebara* with them, and he rode astride his quite naturally. No precautions were taken to guard him, save that he was kept among them, one man always staying at the rear of the party. They came within sight of the walls at dawn, and they waited among the rocks all day. At dusk the youngest started out, and in three hours he returned with a friend who carried a stout cane. They tried to put the Professor through his routine then and there, but the man from Fogara was in a hurry to get back to town, so they all set out on the *mebara.*

In the town they went directly to the villager's home, where they 70 had coffee in the courtyard sitting among the camels. Here the Professor went into his act again, and this time there was prolonged merriment and much rubbing together of hands. An agreement was reached, a sum of money paid, and the Reguibat withdrew, leaving the Professor in the house of the man with the cane, who did not delay in locking him into a tiny enclosure off the courtyard.

The next day was an important one in the Professor's life, for it 71 was then that pain began to stir again in his being. A group of men came to the house, among whom was a venerable gentleman, better clothed than those others who spent their time flattering him, setting fervent kisses upon his hands and the edges of his garments. This person made a point of going into classical Arabic from time to time, to impress the others, who had not learned a word of the Koran. Thus his conversation would run more or less as follows: "Perhaps at In Salah. The French there are stupid. Celestial vengeance is approaching. Let us not hasten it. Praise the highest and cast thine anathema against idols. With paint on his face. In case the police wish to look close." The others listened and agreed, nodding their heads slowly and solemnly. And the Professor in his stall beside them listened, too. That is, he was *conscious* of the sound of the old man's Arabic. The words penetrated for the first time in many months. Noises, then: "Celestial vengeance is approaching." Then: "It is an honor. Fifty francs is enough. Keep your money. Good." And the *qaouaji* squatting near him at the edge of the precipice. Then "anathema against idols" and more gibberish. He turned over panting on the sand and forgot about it. But the pain had begun. It operated in a kind of delirium, because he had begun to enter into consciousness again. When the man opened the door and prodded him with his cane, he cried out in a rage, and everyone laughed.

They got him onto his feet, but he would not dance. He stood be- 72
fore them, staring at the ground, stubbornly refusing to move. The
owner was furious, and so annoyed by the laughter of the others that
he felt obliged to send them away, saying that he would await a more
propitious time for exhibiting his property, because he dared not show
his anger before the elder. However, when they had left he dealt the
Professor a violent blow on the shoulder with his cane, called him various obscene things, and went out into the street, slamming the gate
behind him. He walked straight to the street of the Ouled Naïl, because
he was sure of finding the Reguibat there among the girls, spending
the money. And there in a tent he found one of them still abed, while
an Ouled Naïl washed the tea glasses. He walked in and almost de-
capitated the man before the latter had even attempted to sit up. Then
he threw his razor on the bed and ran out.

The Ouled Naïl saw the blood, screamed, ran out of her tent into 73
the next, and soon emerged from that with four girls who rushed together into the coffeehouse and told the *qaouaji* who had killed the
Reguiba. It was only a matter of an hour before the French military police had caught him at a friend's house, and dragged him off to the barracks. That night the Professor had nothing to eat, and the next afternoon, in the slow sharpening of his consciousness caused by
increasing hunger, he walked aimlessly about the courtyard and the
rooms that gave onto it. There was no one. In one room a calendar
hung on the wall. The Professor watched nervously, like a dog watching a fly in front of its nose. On the white paper were black objects that
made sounds in his head. He heard them: "*Grande Epicerie du Sabel.
Juin. Lundi, Mardi, Mercredi. . . .*"[3]

The tiny ink marks of which a symphony consists may have been 74
made long ago, but when they are fulfilled in sound they become im-
minent and mighty. So a kind of music of feeling began to play in the
Professor's head, increasing in volume as he looked at the mud wall,
and he had the feeling that he was performing what had been written
for him long ago. He felt like weeping; he felt like roaring through the
little house, upsetting and smashing the few breakable objects. His
emotion got no further than this one overwhelming desire. So, bellowing as loud as he could, he attacked the house and its belongings.
Then he attacked the door into the street, which resisted for a while
and finally broke. He climbed through the opening made by the
boards he had ripped apart, and still bellowing and shaking his arms
in the air to make as loud a jangling as possible, he began to gallop
along the quiet street toward the gateway of the town. A few people

---

[3]*Grande Epicerie du Sabel. Juin. Lundi, Mardi, Mercredi:* Grand Grocery Store of Sabel. June.
Monday, Tuesday, Wednesday. (Ed.)

looked at him with great curiosity. As he passed the garage, the last building before the high mud archway that framed the desert beyond, a French soldier saw him. *"Tiens,"* he said to himself, "a holy maniac."

Again it was sunset time. The Professor ran beneath the arched 75 gate, turned his face toward the red sky, and began to trot along the Piste d'In Salah, straight into the setting sun. Behind him, from the garage, the soldier took a potshot at him for good luck. The bullet whistled dangerously near the Professor's head, and his yelling rose into an indignant lament as he waved his arms more wildly, and hopped high into the air at every few steps, in an access of terror.

The soldier watched a while, smiling, as the cavorting figure grew 76 smaller in the oncoming evening darkness, and the rattling of the tin became a part of the great silence out there beyond the gate. The wall of the garage as he leaned against it still gave forth heat, left there by the sun, but even then the lunar chill was growing in the air.

QUESTIONS

1. Reread the first paragraph, and discuss the ways in which the movement and events of the story are predicted or foreshadowed from the beginning.

2. What mistakes or misjudgments does the Professor make in his dealings with the local people or culture? How serious do you think these mistakes are? To what extent do you think the Professor himself is responsible for what the Reguibat do to him?

3. "Pain began to stir again in his being" (paragraph 71) when the Professor hears the sounds of classical Arabic and sees the markings on a calendar. Analyze the roles played by language in this story, beginning with the Professor's occupation as a linguist.

Among the Dangs

GEORGE P. ELLIOTT

I graduated from Sansom University in 1937 with honors in his- 1
tory, having intended to study law, but I had no money and nowhere
to get any; by good fortune the anthropology department, which had
just been given a grant for research, decided that I could do a job for
them. In idle curiosity I had taken a course in anthro, to see what I
would have been like had history not catapulted my people a couple of
centuries ago up into civilization, but I had not been inclined to enlarge
on the sketchy knowledge I got from that course; even yet, when I
think about it, I feel like a fraud teaching anthropology. What chiefly
recommended me to the department, aside from a friend, was a combination of three attributes: I was a good mimic, a long-distance runner, and black.

The Dangs live in a forested valley in the eastern foothills of the 2
Andes. The only white man to report on them (and, it was loosely gos-
siped, the only one to return from them alive), Sir Bewley Morehead,
owed his escape in 1910 to the consternation caused by Halley's comet.
Otherwise, he reported, they would certainly have sacrificed him as
they were preparing to do; as it was they killed the priest who was to
have killed him and then burned the temple down. However, Dr.
Sorish, our most distinguished Sansom man, in the early thirties developed an interest in the Dangs which led to my research grant; he
had introduced a tribe of Amazonian headshrinkers to the idea of
planting grain instead of just harvesting it, as a result of which they
had fattened, taken to drinking brew by the tubful, and elevated Sorish
to the rank of new god. The last time he had descended among them—
it is Sansom policy to follow through on any primitives we "do"—he
had found his worshipers holding a couple of young Dang men captive

George P. Elliott (1918–1980) was a professor of English at Syracuse
University and the author of essays, criticism, poetry, and fiction. His
books include the novels *In The World* (1965) and *Muriel* (1972),
Reaching: Poems (1979), *A Piece of Lettuce: Personal Essays on Books,
Beliefs, American Places, and Growing Up in a Strange Country* (1964),
and *Conversations: Literature and the Modernist Deviation* (1971). A
posthumous collection, *A George P. Elliott Reader: Selected Poetry and
Prose*, was published in 1992. "Among the Dangs," probably Elliott's
best-known story, concerns the experiences of a black American
anthropologist studying a fictional South American Indian tribe; it
was collected in *Among the Dangs: Ten Short Stories* (1961).

and preparing them for ceremonies which would end only with the processing of their heads; his godhood gave him sufficient power to defer these ceremonies while he made half-a-dozen transcriptions of the men's conversations and learned their language well enough to arouse the curiosity of his colleagues. The Dangs were handy with blowpipes; no one knew what pleased them; Halley's comet wasn't due till 1986. But among the recordings Sorish brought back was a legend strangely chanted by one of these young men, whose very head perhaps you can buy today from a natural science company for $150 to $200, and the same youth had given Sorish a sufficient demonstration of the Dang prophetic trance, previously described by Morehead, to whet his appetite.

I was black, true; but as Sorish pointed out, I looked as though I   3 had been rolled in granite dust and the Dangs as though they had been rolled in brick dust; my hair was short and kinky, theirs long and straight; my lips were thick, theirs thin. It's like dressing a Greek up in reindeer skins, I said, and telling him to go pass himself off as a Lapp in Lapland. Maybe, they countered, but wouldn't he be more likely to get by than a naked Swahili with bones in his nose? I was a long-distance runner, true, but as I pointed out with a good deal of feeling I didn't know the principles of jungle escape and had no desire to learn them in, as they put it, the field. They would teach me to throw the javelin and wield a machete, they would teach me the elements of judo, and as for poisoned darts and sacrifices they would insure my life—that is, my return within three years—for five thousand dollars. I was a good mimic, true; I would be able to reproduce the Dang speech and especially the trance of the Dang prophets for the observation of science—"make a genuine contribution to learning." In the Sansom concept the researcher's experience is an inextricable part of anthropological study, and a good mimic provides the object for others' study as well as for his own. For doing this job I would be given round-trip transportation, an M.S. if I wrote a thesis on the material I gathered, the temporary insurance on my life, and one hundred dollars a month for the year I was expected to be gone. After I'd got them to throw in a fellowship of some sort for the following year I agreed. It would pay for filling the forty cavities in my brothers' and sisters' teeth.

Dr. Sorish and I had to wait at the nearest outstation for a thun-   4 derstorm; when it finally blew up I took off all my clothes, put on a breechcloth and leather apron, put a box of equipment on my head, and trotted after him; his people were holed in from the thunder and we were in their settlement before they saw us. They were taller than I, they no doubt found my white teeth as disagreeable as I found their stained, filed teeth, but when Sorish spoke to me in English (telling me to pretend indifference to them while they sniffed me over) and in the accents of American acquaintances rather than in the harsh tones of divinity their eyes filled with awe of me. Their taboo against touching Sorish extended itself to me; when a baby ran up to me and I lifted him up to play with him, his mother crawled, beating her head on the ground till I freed him.

The next day was devoted chiefly to selecting the man to fulfill 5 Sorish's formidable command to guide me to the edge of the Dang country. As for running—if those characters could be got to the next Olympics, Ecuador would take every long-distance medal on the board. I knew I had reached the brow of my valley only because I discovered that my guide, whom I had been lagging behind by fifty feet, at a turn in the path had disappeared into the brush.

Exhaustion allayed my terror; as I lay in the meager shade recu- 6 perating I remembered to execute the advice I had given myself before coming: to act always as though I were not afraid. What would a brave man do next? Pay no attention to his aching feet, reconnoiter, and cautiously proceed. I climbed a jutting of rock and peered about. It was a wide, scrubby valley; on the banks of the river running down the valley I thought I saw a dozen mounds too regular for stones. I touched the handle of the hunting knife sheathed at my side, and trotted down the trackless hill.

The village was deserted, but the huts, though miserable, were 7 clean and in good repair. This meant, according to the movies I had seen, that hostile eyes were watching my every gesture. I had to keep moving in order to avoid trembling. The river was clear and not deep. The corpse of a man floated by. I felt like going downstream, but my hypothesized courage drove me up.

In half a mile I came upon a toothless old woman squatting by the 8 track. She did not stop munching when I appeared, nor did she scream, or even stand up. I greeted her in Dang according to the formula I had learned, whereupon she cackled and smiled and nodded as gleefully as though I had just passed a test. She reminded me of my grandmother, rolled in brick dust, minus a corncob pipe between her gums. Presently I heard voices ahead of me. I saw five women carrying branches and walking very slowly. I lurked behind them until they came to a small village, and watched from a bush while they set to work. They stripped the leaves off, carefully did something to them with their fingers, and then dropped them in small-throated pots. Children scrabbled around, and once a couple of them ran up and suckled at one of the women. There remained about an hour till sunset. I prowled, undetected. The women stood, like fashion models, with pelvis abnormally rocked forward; they were wiry, without fat even on their breasts; not even their thighs and hips afforded clean sweeping lines undisturbed by bunched muscles. I saw no men.

Before I began to get into a lather about the right tack to take I   9
stepped into the clearing and uttered their word of salutation. If a strange man should walk in your wife's front door and say "How do you do" in an accent she did not recognize, simultaneously poking his middle finger at her, her consternation would be something like that of those Dang women, for unthinkingly I had nodded my head when speaking and turned my palm up as one does in the United States; to them this was a gesture of intimacy, signifying desire. They disappeared into huts, clutching children.

I went to the central clearing and sat with my back to a log, knowing   10
they would scrutinize me. I wondered where the men were. I could think of no excuse for having my knife in my hand except to clean my toenails. So astonishing an act was unknown to the Dangs; the women and children gradually approached in silence, watching; I cleaned my fingernails. I said the word for food; no one reacted, but presently a little girl ran up to me holding a fruit in both hands. I took it, snibbed her nose between my fingers, and with a pat on the bottom sent her back to her mother. Upon this there were hostile glances, audible intakes of breath, and a huddling about the baby who did not understand any more than I did why she was being consoled. While I ate the fruit I determined to leave the next move up to them. I sheathed my knife and squatted on my hunkers, waiting. To disguise my nervousness I fixed my eyes on the ground between my feet, and grasped my ankles from behind in such a way—right ankle with right hand, left with left—as to expose the inner sides of my forearms. Now this was, as I later learned, pretty close to the initial posture taken for the prophetic trance; also I had a blue flower tattooed on my inner right arm and a blue serpent on my left (from the summer I'd gone to sea), the like of which had never been seen in this place.

At sundown I heard the men approach; they were anything but   11
stealthy about it; I had the greatest difficulty in suppressing the shivers. In simple fear of showing my fear I did not look up when the men gathered around, I could understand just enough of what the women were telling the men to realize that they were afraid of me. Even though I was pelted with pebbles and twigs till I was angry I still did not respond, because I could not think what to do. Then something clammy was plopped onto my back from above and I leaped high, howling. Their spears were poised before I landed.

"Strangers!" I cried, my speech composed. "Far kinsmen! I come   12
from the mountains!" I had intended to say *from the river lands,* but the excitement tangled my tongue. Their faces remained expressionless but no spears drove at me, and then to be doing something I shoved the guts under the log with my feet.

And saved my life by doing so. That I seemed to have taken, 13 though awkwardly, the prophetic squat; that I bore visible marvels on my arm; that I was fearless and inwardly absorbed; that I came from the mountains (their enemies lived toward the river lands); that I wore their apron and spoke their language, albeit poorly, all these disposed them to wonder at this mysterious outlander. Even so they might very well have captured me, marvelous though I was, possibly useful to them, dangerous to antagonize, had I not been unblemished, which meant that I was supernaturally guarded. Finally, my scrutinizing the fish guts, daring to smile as I did so, could mean only that I was prophetic; my leap when they had been dropped onto my back was prodigious, "far higher than a man's head," and my howl had been vatic; and my deliberately kicking the guts aside, though an inscrutable act, demonstrated at least that I could touch the entrails of an eel and live.

So I was accepted to the Dangs. The trouble was that they had no 14 ceremony for naturalizing me. For them every act had a significance, and here they were faced with a reverse problem for which nothing had prepared them. They could not possibly just assimilate me without marking the event with an act (that is, a ceremony) signifying my entrance. For them nothing *just happened*, certainly nothing that men did. Meanwhile, I was kept in a sort of quarantine while they deliberated. I did not, to be sure, understand why I was being isolated in a hut by myself, never spoken to except efficiently, watched but not restrained. I swam, slept, scratched, watched, swatted, ate; I was not really alarmed because they had not restrained me forcibly and they gave me food. I began making friends with some of the small children, especially while swimming, and there were two girls of fifteen or so who found me terribly funny. I wished I had some magic, but I knew only card tricks. The sixth day, swimming, I thought I was being enticed around a point in the river by the two girls, but when I began to chase them they threw good-sized stones at me, missing me only because they were such poor shots. A corpse floated by; when they saw it they immediately placed the sole of their right foot on the side of their left knee and stood thus on one leg till the corpse floated out of sight; I followed the girls' example, teetering. I gathered from what they said that some illness was devastating their people; I hoped it was one of the diseases I had been inoculated against. The girls' mothers found them talking with me and cuffed them away.

I did not see them for two days, but the night of my eighth day 15 there the bolder of them hissed me awake at the door of my hut in a way that meant "no danger." I recognized her when she giggled. I was not sure what their customs were in these matters, but while I was deliberating what my course of wisdom should be she crawled into the hut and lay on the mat beside me. She liked me, she was utterly devoid of reticence, I was twenty-one and far from home; even a scabby little knotty-legged fashion model is hard to resist under such circumstances. I learned before falling asleep that there was a three-way debate among the men over what to do with me: initiate me according to the prophet-initiation rites, invent a new ceremony, or sacrifice me as propitiation to the disease among them as was usually done with captives. Each had its advantages and drawbacks; even the news that some of the Dangs wanted to sacrifice me did not excite me as it would have done a week before; now, I half-sympathized with their trouble. I was awakened at dawn by the outraged howl of a man at my door; he was the girl's father. The village men gathered and the girl cowered behind me. They talked for hours outside my hut, men arrived from other villages up and down the valley, and finally they agreed upon a solution to all the problems: they proposed that I should be made one of the tribe by marriage on the same night that I should be initiated into the rites of prophecy.

The new-rite men were satisfied by this arrangement because of 16 the novelty of having a man married and initiated on the same day, but the sacrifice party was visibly unmollified. Noticing this and reflecting that the proposed arrangement would permit me to do all my trance research under optimum conditions and to accumulate a great deal of sexual data as well I agreed to it. I would of course only be going through the forms of marriage, not meaning them; as for the girl, I took this vow to myself (meaning without ceremony): "So long as I am a Dang I shall be formally a correct husband to her." More's a pity.

Fortunately a youth from down the valley already had been cho- 17 sen as a novice (at least a third of the Dang men enter the novitiate at one time or another, though few make the grade), so that I had not only a companion during the four-month preparation for the vatic rites but also a control upon whom I might check my experience of the stages of the novitiate. My mimetic powers stood me in good stead; I was presumed to have a special prophetic gift and my readiness at assuming the proper stances and properly performing the ritual acts confirmed the Dangs' impressions of my gift; but also, since I was required to proceed no faster than the ritual pace in my learning, I had plenty of leisure in which to observe in the smallest detail what I did and how I, and to some extent my fellow novice, felt. If I had not had this self-observing to relieve the tedium I think I should have been unable to get through that mindless holding of the same position hour after hour, that mindless repeating of the same act day after day. The Dangs *appear* to be bored much of the time, and my early experience with them was certainly that of ennui, though never again ennui so acute as during this novitiate. Yet I doubt that it would be accurate to say they actually are bored, and I am sure that the other novice was not, as a fisherman waiting hours for a strike cannot be said to be bored. The Dangs do not sate themselves on food; the experience which they consider most worth seeking, vision, is one which cannot glut either the prophet or his auditors; they cannot imagine an alternative to living as they live or, more instantly, to preparing a novice as I was being prepared. The people endure; the prophets, as I have learned, wait for the time to come again, and though they are bitten and stung by ten thousand fears, about this they have no anxiety—the time will surely come again. Boredom implies either satiety, and they were poor and not interested in enriching themselves, or the frustration of impulse, and they were without alternatives and diversions. The intense boredom which is really a controlled anxiety, they are protected from by never doubting the worth of their vision or their power to achieve it.

I was assisted through these difficult months during which I was 18 supposed to do nothing but train by Redadu, my betrothed. As a novice I was strictly to abstain from sexual intercourse, but as betrothed we were supposed to make sure before marriage that we satisfied one another, for adultery by either husband or wife was punishable by maiming. Naturally the theologians were much exercised by this impasse, but while they were arguing Redadu and I took the obvious course—we met more or less surreptitiously. Since my vatic training could not take place between sunrise and sundown I assumed that we could meet in the afternoon when I woke up, but when I began making plans to this effect I discovered that she did not know what I was talking about. It makes as much sense in Dang to say, "Let's blow poisoned darts at the loss of the moon," as to say, "Let's make love in broad daylight." Redadu dissolved in giggles at the absurdity. What to do? She found us a cave. Everyone must have known what I was up to, but we were respectable (the Dang term for it was harsher, *deed-liar*) so we were never disturbed. Redadu's friends would not believe her stories of my luxurious love ways, especially my biting with lips instead of teeth. At one time or another she sent four of them to the cave for me to demonstrate my prowess upon; I was glad that none of them pleased me as much as she did for I was beginning to be fond of her. My son has told me that lip-biting has become if not a customary at any rate a possible caress.

As the night of the double rite approached, a night of full moon, a 19 new conflict became evident: the marriage must be consummated exactly at sundown, but the initiation must begin at moonrise, less than two hours later. For some reason that was not clear to me preparing for the initiation would incapacitate me for the consummation. I refrained from pointing out that it was only technically that this marriage needed consummating and even from asking why I would not be able to do it. The solution, which displeased everyone, was to defer the rites for three nights, when the moon, though no longer perfectly round, would rise sufficiently late so that I would, by hurrying, be able to perform both of my functions. Redadu's father, who had been of the sacrifice party, waived ahead of time his claim against me; legally he was entitled to annul the marriage if I should leave the marriage hut during the bridal night. And although I in turn could legally annul it if she left the hut I waived my claim as well so that she might attend my initiation.

The wedding consisted chiefly of our being bound back to back by 20 the elbows and being sung to and danced about all day. At sunset we were bound face to face by the elbows (most awkward) and sent into our hut. Outside the two mothers waited—a high prophet's wife took the place of my mother (my Methodist mother!)—until our orgastic cries indicated that the marriage had been consummated, and then came in to sever our bonds and bring us the bridal foods of cold stewed eel and parched seeds. We fed each other bite for bite and gave the scraps to our mothers, who by the formula with which they thanked us pronounced themselves satisfied with us. Then a falsetto voice called to me to hurry to the altar. A man in the mask of a moon slave was standing outside my hut on his left leg with the right foot against his left knee, and he continued to shake his rattle so long as I was within earshot.

The men were masked. Their voices were all disguised. I won- 21 dered whether I was supposed to speak in an altered voice; I knew every stance and gesture I was to make, but nothing of what I was to say; yet surely a prophet must employ words. I had seen some of the masks before—being repaired, being carried from one place to another—but now, faced with them alive in the failing twilight, I was impressed by them in no scientific or aesthetic way—they terrified and exalted me. I wondered if I would be given a mask. I began trying to identify such men as I could by their scars and missing fingers and crooked arms, and noticed to my distress that they too were all standing one-legged in my presence. I had thought that was the stance to be assumed in the presence of the dead! We were at the entrance to The Cleft, a dead-end ravine in one of the cliffs along the valley; my fellow novice and I were each given a gourdful of some vile-tasting drink and were then taken up to the end of The Cleft, instructed to assume the first position, and left alone. We squatted as I had been squatting by the log on my first day, except that my head was cocked in a certain way and my hands clasped my ankles from the front. The excitements of the day seemed to have addled my wits, I could concentrate on nothing and lost my impulse to observe coolly what was going on; I kept humming *St. James Infirmary* to myself, and though at first I had been thinking the words, after awhile I realized that I had nothing but the tune left in my head. At moonrise we were brought another gourd of the liquor to drink, and were then taken to the mouth of The Cleft again. I did, easily, whatever I was told. The last thing I remember seeing before taking the second position was the semicircle of masked men facing us and chanting, and behind them the women and children—all standing on the left leg. I lay on my back with my left ankle on my right and my hands crossed over my navel, rolled my eyeballs up and held the lids open without blinking, and breathed in the necessary rhythm, each breath taking four heartbeats, with an interval of ten heartbeats between each exhalation and the next inspiration. Then the drug took over. At dawn when a called command awakened me, I found myself on an islet in the river dancing with my companion a leaping dance I had not known or even seen before, and brandishing over my head a magnificent red and blue, newmade mask of my own. The shores of the river were lined with the people chanting as we leaped, and all of them were either sitting or else standing on both feet. If we had been dead the night before we were alive now.

After I had slept and returned to myself, Redadu told me that my vision was splendid, but of course she was no more permitted to tell me what I had said than I was able to remember it. The Dangs' sense of rhythm is as subtle as their ear for melody is monotonous, and for weeks I kept hearing rhythmic snatches of *St. James Infirmary* scratched on calabash drums and tapped on blocks. 22

Sorish honored me by rewriting my master's thesis and adding my name as co-author of the resultant essay, which he published in *JAFA (The Journal of American Field Anthropology):* "Techniques of Vatic Hallucinosis among the Dangs." And the twenty-minute movie I made of a streamlined performance of the rites is still widely used as an audio-visual aid. 23

By 1939 when I had been cured of the skin disease I had brought back with me and had finished the work for my M.S. I still had no money. I had been working as the assistant curator of the University's Pre-Columbian Museum and had developed a powerful aversion to devoting my life to cataloguing, displaying, restoring, warehousing. But my chances of getting a research job, slight enough with a Ph.D., were nil with only an M.S. The girl I was going with said (I had not told her about Redadu) that if we married she would work as a nurse to support me while I went through law school; I was tempted by the opportunity to fulfill my original ambition, and probably I would have done it had she not pressed too hard; she wanted me to leave anthropology, she wanted me to become a lawyer, she wanted to support me, but what she did not want was to make my intentions, whatever they 24 might be, her own. So when a new grant gave me the chance to return to the Dangs I gladly seized it; not only would I be asserting myself against Velma, but also I would be paid for doing the research for my Ph.D. thesis; besides, I was curious to see the Congo-Maryland-Dang bastard I had left in Redadu's belly.

My assignment was to make a general cultural survey but espe- 25 cially to discover the *content* of the vatic experience—not just the technique, not even the hallucinations and stories, but the qualities of the experience itself. The former would get me a routine degree, but the latter would, if I did it, make me a name and get me a job. After much consultation I decided against taking with me any form of magic, including medicine; the antibiotics had not been invented yet, and even if there had been a simple way to eradicate the fever endemic among the Dangs, my advisers persuaded me that it would be an error to introduce it since the Dangs were able to procure barely enough food for themselves as it was and since they might worship me for doing it, thereby making it impossible for me to do my research with the proper empathy. I arrived the second time provided only with my knife (which had not seemed to impress these stone-agers), salve to soothe my sores, and the knowledge of how to preserve fish against a lean season, innovation enough but not one likely to divinize me.

I was only slightly worried how I would be received on my return, 26 because of the circumstances under which I had disappeared. I had become a fairly decent hunter—the women gathered grain and fruit— and I had learned to respect the Dangs' tracking abilities enough to have been nervous about getting away safely. While hunting with a companion in the hills south of our valley I had run into a couple of hunters from an enemy tribe which seldom foraged so far north as this. They probably were as surprised as I and probably would have been glad to leave me unmolested; however, outnumbered and not knowing how many more were with them, I whooped for my companion; one of the hunters in turn, not knowing how many were with me, threw his spear at me. I side-stepped it and reached for my darts, and though I was not very accurate with a blowpipe I hit him in the thigh; within a minute he was writhing on the ground, for in my haste I had blown a venomous dart at him, and my comrade took his comrade prisoner by surprise. As soon as the man I had hit was dead I withdrew my dart and cut off his ear for trophy, and we returned with our captive. He told our war chief in sign language that the young man I had killed was the son and heir of their king and that my having mutilated him meant their tribe surely would seek to avenge his death. The next morning a Dang search party was sent out to recover the body so that it might be destroyed and trouble averted, but it had disappeared; war threatened. The day after that I chose to vanish; they would not think of looking for me in the direction of Sorish's tribe, north, but would assume that I had been captured by the southern tribe in retribution for their prince's death. My concern now, two years later, was how to account for not having been maimed or executed; the least I could do was to cut a finger off, but when it came to the point I could not even bring myself to have a surgeon do it, much less do it myself; I had adequate lies prepared for their other questions, but about this I was a bit nervous.

I got there at sundown. Spying, I did not see Redadu about the vil-   27 lage. On the chance, I slipped into our hut when no one was looking; she was there, playing with our child. He was as cute a little preliterate as you ever saw suck a thumb, and it made me chuckle to think he would never be literate either. Redadu's screams when she saw me fetched the women, but when they heard a man's voice they could not intrude. In her joy she lacerated me with her fingernails (the furrows across my shoulder festered for a long time); I could no less than bite her arm till she bled; the primal scene we treated our son to presumably scarred him for life—though I must say the scars haven't shown up yet. I can't deny I was glad to see her too, for, though I felt for her none of the tender, complex emotions I had been feeling for Velma, emotions which I more or less identified as being love, yet I was so secure with her sexually, knew so well what to do and what to expect from her in every important matter that it was an enormous, if cool, comfort to me to be with her. *Comfort* is a dangerous approximation to what I mean; being with her provided, as it were, the condition for doing; in Sansom I did not consider her my wife and here I did not recognize in myself the American emotions of love or marriage, yet it seemed to me right to be with her and our son was no bastard. *Cool*—I cannot guarantee that mine was the usual Dang emotion, for it is hard for the cool to gauge the warmth of others (in my reports I have denied any personal experience of love among the Dangs for this reason). When we emerged from the hut there was amazement and relief among the women: amazement that I had returned and relief that it had not been one of their husbands pleasuring the widow. But the men were more ambiguously pleased to see me. Redadu's scratches were not enough and they doubted my story that the enemy king had made me his personal slave who must be bodily perfect. They wanted to hear me prophesy.

Redadu told me afterward, hiding her face in my arms for fear of   28 being judged insolent, that I surpassed myself that night, that only the three high prophets had ever been so inspired. And it was true that even the men most hostile to me did not oppose my reëntry into the tribe after they had heard me prophesy; they could have swallowed the story I fed them about my two-year absence only because they believed in me the prophet. Dangs make no separation between fact and fantasy, apparent reality and visionary reality, truth and beauty. I once saw a young would-be prophet shudder away from a stick on the ground saying it was a snake, and none of the others except the impressionable was afraid of the stick; it was said of him that he was a beginner. Another time I saw a prophet scatter the whole congregation, myself included, when he screamed at the sight of a beast which he called a cougar; when sober dawn found the speared creature to be a cur it was said of the prophet that he was strong, and he was honored with an epithet, Cougar-Dog. My prophesying the first night of my return must have been of this caliber, though to my disappointment I was given no epithet, not even the nickname I'd sometimes heard before, Bush-Hair.

I knew there was a third kind of prophesying, the highest, per- 29 formed only on the most important occasions in the Cave-Temple where I had never been. No such occasion had presented itself during my stay before, and when I asked one of the other prophets about that ceremony he put me off with the term Wind-Haired Child of the Sun; from another I learned that the name of this sort of prophesying was Stone is Stone. Obviously I was going to have to stay until I could make sense of these mysteries.

There was a war party that wanted my support; my slavery was 30 presumed to have given me knowledge which would make a raid highly successful; because of this as well as because I had instigated the conflict by killing the king's son I would be made chief of the raiding party. I was uneasy about the fever, which had got rather worse among them during the previous two years, without risking my neck against savages who were said always to eat a portion of their slain enemy's liver raw and whose habitat I knew nothing of. I persuaded the Dangs, therefore, that they should not consider attacking before the rains came, because their enemies were now the stronger, having on their side their protector, the sun. They listened to me and waited. Fortunately it was a long dry season, during which I had time to find a salt deposit and to teach a few women the rudiments of drying and salting fish; and during the first week of the rains every night there were showers of falling stars to be seen in the sky; to defend against them absorbed all energies for weeks, including the warriors'. Even so, even though I was a prophet, a journeyman prophet as it were, I was never in on these rites in the Cave-Temple. I dared not ask many questions. Sir Bewley Morehead had described a temple surrounded by seventy-six poles, each topped by a human head; he could hardly have failed to mention that it was in a cave, yet he made no such mention, and I knew of no temple like the one he had described. At a time of rains and peace in the sky the war party would importune me. I did not know what to do but wait.

The rains became violent, swamping the villages in the lower val- 31
ley and destroying a number of huts, yet the rainy season ended
abruptly two months before its usual time. Preparations for war had
already begun, and day by day as the sun's strength increased and the
earth dried the war party became more impatient. The preparations in
themselves lulled my objections to the raid, even to my leading the
raid, and stimulated my desire to make war. But the whole project was
canceled a couple of days before we were to attack because of the sudden fever of one of the high prophets; the day after he came down five
others of the tribe fell sick, among them Redadu. There was nothing I
could do but sit by her, fanning her and sponging her till she died. Her
next older sister took our son to rear. I would allow no one to prepare
her body but myself, though her mother was supposed to help; I
washed it with the proper infusions of herbs, and at dawn, in the presence of her clan, I laid her body on the river. Thank heaven it floated
or I should have had to spend another night preparing it further. I felt
like killing someone now; I recklessly called for war now, even though
the high prophet had not yet died; I was restrained, not without admiration. I went up into the eastern hills by myself and returned after
a week bearing the hide of a cougar; I had left the head and claws on
my trophy in a way the Dangs had never seen; when I put the skin on
in play by daylight and bounded and snarled only the bravest did not
run in terror. They called me Cougar-Man. Redadu's younger sister
came to sleep with me; I did not want her, but she so stubbornly refused to be expelled that I kept her for the night, for the next night, for
the next; it was not improper.

The high prophet did not die, but lay comatose most of the time. 32
The Dangs have ten master prophets, of whom the specially gifted,
whether one or all ten, usually two or three, are high prophets. Fifteen
days after Redadu had died, well into the abnormal dry spell, nearly
all the large fish seemed to disappear from the river. A sacrifice was
necessary. It was only because the old man was so sick that a high
prophet was used for this occasion, otherwise a captive or a woman
would have served the purpose. A new master prophet must replace
him, to keep the complement up to ten. I was chosen.

The exultation I felt when I learned that the master prophets had 33
co-opted me among them was by no means cool and anthropological,
for now that I had got what I had come to get I no longer wanted it for
Sansom reasons. *If the conditions of my being elevated,* I said to myself, *are
the suffering of the people, Redadu's death, and the sacrifice of an old man,
then I must make myself worthy of the great price. Worthy*—a value word,
not a scientific one. Of course, my emotions were not the simple pride
and fear of a Dang. I can't say what sort they were, but they were
fierce.

At sundown all the Dangs of all the clans were assembled about 34 the entrance to The Cleft. All the prophets, masked, emerged from The Cleft and began the dance in a great wheel. Within this wheel, rotating against it, was the smaller wheel of the nine able-bodied master prophets. At the center, facing the point at which the full moon would rise, I hopped on one leg, then the other. I had been given none of the vatic liquor, that brew which the women, when I had first come among the Dangs, had been preparing in the small-throated pots, and I hoped I should be able to remain conscious throughout the rites. However, at moonrise a moon slave brought me a gourdful to drink without ceasing to dance. I managed to allow a good deal of it to spill unnoticed down with the sweat streaming off me, so that later I was able to remember what had happened, right up to the prophesying itself. The dance continued for at least two more hours, then the drums suddenly stopped and the prophets began to file up The Cleft with me last dancing after the high prophets. We danced into an opening in the cliff from which a disguising stone had been rolled away. The people were not allowed to follow us. We entered a great cavern illuminated by ten smoking torches and circled a palisade of stakes; the only sound was the shuffle of our feet and the snorts of our breathing. There were seventy-six stakes, as Morehead had seen, but only on twenty-eight of them were heads impaled, the last few with flesh on them still, not yet skulls cleaned of all but hair. In the center was a huge stone under the middle of which a now dry stream had tunneled a narrow passage; on one side of the stone, above the passage, were two breastlike protuberances, one of which had a recognizable nipple in the suitable place. Presently the dancing file reversed so that I was the leader. I had not been taught what to do; I wove the file through the round of stakes, and spiraled inward till we were three deep about The Stone; I straddled the channel, raised my hands till they were touching the breasts, and gave a great cry. I was, for reasons I do not understand, shuddering all over; though I was conscious and though I had not been instructed, I was not worried that I might do the wrong thing next. When I touched The Stone a dread shook me without affecting my exaltation. Two moon slaves seized my arms, took off my mask, and wrapped and bound me—arms at my side and legs pressed together in a deer hide—and then laid me on my back in the channel under The Stone with my head only half out, so that I was staring up the sheer side of rock. The dancers continued, though the master prophets had disappeared. My excitement, the new unused position, being mummied tightly, the weakness of the drug, my will to observe, all kept me conscious for a long time. Gradually, however, my eyes began to roll up into my head, I strained less powerfully against the thongs that bound me, and I felt my breathing approach the vatic rhythm. At this point I seemed to break out in a new sweat, on my forehead, my throat, in my hair; I could hear a splash, groggily I licked my chin—an odd taste—I wondered if I was bleeding. Of course, it was the blood of the sick old high prophet, who had just been sacrificed on The Stone above me; well, his blood would give me strength. Wondering remotely whether his fever could be transmitted by drinking his blood I entered the trance. At dawn I emerged into consciousness while I was still prophesying; I was on a ledge in the valley above all the people, in my mask again. I listened to myself finish the story I was telling. "He was afraid. A third time a man said to him: 'You are a friend of the most high prophet.' He answered: 'Not me. I do not know that man they are sacrificing.' Then he went into a dark corner, he put his hands over his face all day." When I came to the Resurrection a sigh blew across the people. It was the best story they had ever heard. Of course. But I was not really a Christian. For several weeks I fretted over my confusion, this new, unsuspected confusion.

I was miserable without Redadu; I let her sister substitute only 35 until I had been elevated, and then I cast her off, promising her however that she and only she might wear an anklet made of my teeth when I should die. Now that I was a master prophet I could not be a warrior; I had enough of hunting and fishing and tedious ceremonies. Hunger from the shortage of fish drove the hunters high into the foothills; there was not enough; they ate my preserved fish, suspiciously, but they ate them. When I left it was not famine that I was escaping but my confusion; I was fleeing to the classrooms and the cool museums where I should be neither a leftover Christian nor a mimic of a Dang.

My academic peace lasted for just two years, during which time I 36 wrote five articles on my researches, publishing them this time under my name only, did some of the work for my doctorate, and married Velma. Then came World War II, in which my right hand was severed above the wrist; I was provided with an artificial hand and given enough money so that I could afford to finish my degree in style. We had two daughters and I was given a job at Sansom. There was no longer a question of my returning to the Dangs. I would become a settled anthropologist, teach, and quarrel with my colleagues in the learned journals. But by the time the Korean War came along and robbed us of a lot of our students, my situation at the university had changed considerably. Few of my theoretical and disputatious articles were printed in the journals, and I hated writing them; I was not given tenure and there were some hints to the effect that I was considered a one-shot man, a flash-in-the-pan; Velma nagged for more money and higher rank. My only recourse was further research, and when I thought of starting all over again with some other tribe—in northern Australia, along the Zambesi, on an African island—my heart sank. The gossip was not far from the mark—I was not a one hundred per cent scientist and never would be. I had just enough reputation and influential recommendations to be awarded a Guggenheim Fellowship; supplemented by a travel grant from the university this made it possible for me to leave my family comfortably provided for and to return to the Dangs.

A former student now in Standard Oil in Venezuela arranged to have me parachuted among them from an SO plane. There was the real danger that they would kill me before they recognized me, but if I arrived in a less spectacular fashion I was pretty sure they would sacrifice me for their safety's sake. This time, being middle-aged, I left my hunting knife and brought instead at my belt a pouch filled with penicillin and salves. I had a hard time identifying the valley from the air; it took me so long that it was sunset before I jumped. I knew how the Dangs were enraged by airplanes, especially by the winking lights of night fliers, and I knew they would come for me if they saw me billowing down. Fortunately I landed in the river, for though I was nearly drowned before I disentangled my parachute harness I was also out of range of the blowpipes. I finally identified myself to the warriors brandishing their spears along the shore; they had not quite dared to swim out after so prodigious a being; even after they knew who I said I was and allowed me to swim to shore they saw me less as myself than as a supernatural being. I was recognized by newcomers who had not seen me so closely swinging from the parachute (the cloud); on the spot my epithet became, and remained, Sky-Cougar. Even so no one dared touch me till the high prophet—there was only one now—had arrived and talked with me; my artificial hand seemed to him an extension of the snake tattooed onto my skin, he would not touch it; I suddenly struck him with it and pinched his arm. "Pinchers," I said using the word for a crayfish claw, and he laughed. He said there was no way of telling whether I was what I seemed to be until he had heard me prophesy; if I prophesied as I had done before I had disappeared I must be what I seemed to be; meanwhile, for the three weeks till full moon I was to be kept in the hut for captives.

At first I was furious at being imprisoned, and when mothers brought children from miles about to peek through the stakes at the man with the snake hand I snarled or sulked like a caged wolf. But I became conscious that one youth, squatting in a quiet place, had been watching me for hours. I demanded of him who he was. He said, "I am your son," but he did not treat me as his father. To be sure, he could not have remembered what I looked like; my very identity was doubted; even if I were myself, I was legendary, a stranger who had

become a Dang and had been held by an enemy as captive slave for
two years and had then become a master prophet with the most wonderful vision anyone knew. Yet he came to me every day and answered all the questions I put to him. It was, I believe, my artificial
hand that finally kept him aloof from me; no amount of acquaintance
could accustom him to that. By the end of the first week it was clear to
me that if I wanted to survive—not to be accepted as I once had been,
just to survive—I would have to prophesy the Passion again. And how
could I determine what I would say when under the vatic drug? I
imagined a dozen schemes for substituting colored water for the drug,
but I would need an accomplice for that and I knew that not even my
own son would serve me in so forbidden an act.

I called for the high prophet. I announced to him in tones all the   39
more arrogant because of my trepidations that I would prophesy without the vatic liquor. His response to my announcement astonished me:
he fell upon his knees, bowed his head, and rubbed dust into his hair.
He was the most powerful man among the Dangs, except in time of
war when the war chief took over, and furthermore he was an old man
of personal dignity, yet here he was abasing himself before me and,
worse, rubbing dust into his hair as was proper in the presence of the
very sick to help them in their dying. He told me why: prophesying
successfully from a voluntary trance was the test which I must pass to
become a high prophet; normally a master prophet was forced to this,
for the penalty for failing it was death. I dismissed him with a wave of
my claw.

I had five days to wait until full moon. The thought of the risk I   40
was running was more than I could handle consciously; to avoid the
jitters I performed over and over all the techniques of preparing for the
trance, though I carefully avoided entering it. I was not sure I would
be able to enter it alone, but whether I could or not I knew I wanted to
conserve my forces for the great test. At first during those five days I
would remind myself once in a while of my scientific purpose in going
into the trance consciously; at other times I would assure myself that
it was for the good of the Dangs that I was doing it, since it was not
wise or safe for them to have only one high prophet. Both of these reasons were true enough, but not very important. As scientist I should
tell them some new myth, say the story of Abraham and Isaac or of
Oedipus, so that I could compare its effect on them with that of the
Passion; as master prophet I should ennoble my people if I could.
However, thinking these matters over as I held my vatic squat hour
after hour, visited and poked at by prying eyes, I could find no myth
to satisfy me; either, as in the case of Abraham, it involved a concept
of God which the Dangs could not reach, or else, as with Oedipus, it
necessitated more drastic changes than I trusted myself to keep

straight while prophesying—that Oedipus should mutilate himself was unthinkable to the Dangs and that the gods should be represented as able to forgive him for it was impious. Furthermore, I did not think, basically, that any story I could tell them would in fact ennoble them. I was out to save my own skin.

The story of Christ I knew by heart; it had worked for me once, per- 41 haps more than once; it would work again. I rehearsed it over and over, from the Immaculate Conception to the Ascension. But such was the force of that story on me that by the fifth day my cynicism had disappeared along with my scientism, and I believed, not that the myth itself was true, but that relating it to my people was the best thing it was possible for me to do for them. I remember telling myself that this story would help raise them toward monotheism, a necessary stage in the evolution toward freedom. I felt a certain satisfaction in the thought that some of the skulls on the stakes in the Cave-Temple were very likely those of missionaries who had failed to convert these heathen.

At sundown of the fifth day I was taken by moon slaves to a cave 42 near The Cleft, where I was left in peace. I fell into a troubled sleep from which I awoke in a sweat. "Where am I? What am I about to do?" It seemed to me dreadfully wrong that I should be telling these, my people, a myth in whose power, but not in whose truth, I believed. Why should I want to free them from superstition into monotheism and then into my total freedom, when I myself was half-returning, voluntarily, down the layers again? The energy for these sweating questions came, no doubt, from my anxiety about how I was going to perform that night, but I did not recognize this fact at the time. Then I thought it was my conscience speaking, and that I had no right to open to the Dangs a freedom I myself was rejecting. It was too late to alter my course; honesty required me, and I resolved courageously, not to prophesy at all.

When I was fetched out the people were in assembly at The Cleft 43 and the wheel of master prophets was revolving against the greater wheel of dancers. I was given my cougar skin. Hung from a stake, in the center where I was to hop, was a huge, terrific mask I had never seen before. As the moon rose her slaves hung this mask on me; the thong cut into the back of my neck cruelly, and at the bottom the mask came to a point that pressed my belly; it was so wide my arms could only move laterally. It had no eye holes; I broke into a sweat wondering how I should be able to follow the prophets into the Cave-Temple. It turned out to be no problem; the two moon slaves, one on each side, guided me by prodding spears in my ribs. Once in the cave they guided me to the back side of The Stone and drove me to climb it, my feet groping for steps I could not see; once, when I lost my balance, the spears' pressure kept me from falling backward. By the time I reached the top of The Stone I was bleeding and dizzy. With one arm I kept the mask from gouging my belly while with the other I helped my aching neck support the mask. I did not know what to do next. Tears of pain and anger poured from my eyes. I began hopping. I should have been moving my arms in counterpoint to the rhythm of my hop, but I could not bear the thought of letting the mask cut into me more. I kept hopping in the same place for fear of falling off; I had not been noticing the sounds of the other prophets, but suddenly I was aware they were making no sounds at all. In my alarm I lurched to the side and cut my foot on a sharp break in the rock. Pain converted my panic to rage.

I lifted the mask and held it flat above my head. I threw my head 44 back and howled as I had never howled in my life, through a constricted, gradually opening throat, until at the end I was roaring; when I gasped in my breath I made a barking noise. I leaped and leaped, relieved of pain, confident. I punched my knee desecratingly through the brittle hide of the mask, and threw it behind me off The Stone. I tore off my cougar skin, and holding it with my claw by the tip of its tail I whirled it around my head. The prophets, massed below me, fell onto their knees. I felt their fear. Howling, I soared the skin out over them; one of those on whom it landed screamed hideously. A commotion started; I could not see very well what was happening. I barked and they turned toward me again. I leaped three times and then, howling, jumped wide-armed off The Stone. The twelve-foot drop hurt severely my already cut foot. I rolled exhausted into the channel in the cave floor.

Moon slaves with trembling hands mummied me in the deerskin 45 and shoved me under The Stone with only my head sticking out. They brought two spears with darts tied to the points; rolling my head to watch them do this I saw that the prophets were kneeling over and rubbing dirt into their hair. Then the slaves laid the spears alongside the base of the Stone with the poisoned pricks pointed at my temples; exactly how close they were I could not be sure, but close enough so that I dared not move my head. In all my preparations I had, as I had been trained to do, rocked and weaved at least my head; now, rigidity, live rigidity. A movement would scratch me and a scratch would kill me.

I pressed my hook into my thigh, curled my toes, and pressed my 46 tongue against my teeth till my throat ached. I did not dare relieve myself even with a howl, for I might toss my head fatally. I strained against my thongs to the verge of apoplexy. For a while I was unable to see, for sheer rage. Fatigue collapsed me. Yet I dared not relax my vigilance over my movements. My consciousness sealed me off. Those stone protuberances up between which I had to stare in the flickering light were merely chance processes on a boulder, similes to breasts. The one thing I might not become unconscious of was the pair of darts waiting for me to err. For a long time I thought of piercing my head against them, for relief, for spite. Hours passed. I was carefully watched.

I do not know what wild scheme I had had in mind when I had   47
earlier resolved not to prophesy, what confrontation or escape; it had
had the pure magnificence of a fantasy resolution. But the reality,
which I had not seriously tried to evade, was that I must prophesy or
die. I kept lapsing from English into a delirium of Dang. By the greatest effort of will I looked about me rationally. I wondered whether the
return of Halley's comet, at which time all the stakes should be
mounted by skulls, would make the Dangs destroy the Cave-Temple
and erect a new one. I observed the straight, indented seam of sand-
stone running slantwise up the boulder over me and wondered how
many eons this rotting piece of granite had been tumbled about by
water. I reflected that I was unworthy both as a Christian and as a
Dang to prophesy the life of Jesus. But I convinced myself that it was
a trivial matter, since to the Christians it was the telling more than the
teller that counted and to the Dangs this myth would serve as a civilizing force they needed. Surely, I thought, my hypocrisy could be forgiven me, especially since I resolved to punish myself for it by leaving
the Dangs forever as soon as I could. Having reached this rational solution I smiled and gestured to the high prophet with my eyes; he did
not move a muscle. When I realized that nothing to do with hypocrisy
would unbind me desperation swarmed in my guts and mounted toward my brain; with this question it took me over: *How can I make myself believe it is true?* I needed to catch hold of myself again. I dug my
hook so hard into my leg—it was the only action I was able to take—
that I gasped with pain; the pain I wanted. I did not speculate on the
consequences of gouging my leg, tearing a furrow in my thigh muscle,
hurting by the same act the stump of my arm to which the hook was
attached; just as I knew that the prophets, the torches, the poisoned
darts were there in the cave, so also I knew that far far back in my
mind I had good enough reasons to be hurting myself, reasons which
I could find out if I wanted to, but which it was not worth my trouble
to discover; I even allowed the knowledge that I myself was causing
the pain to drift back in my mind. The pain itself, only the pain, became my consciousness, purging all else. Then, as the pain subsided
leaving me free and equipoised, awareness of the stone arched over
me flooded my mind. Because it had been invested by the people with
great mystery, it was an incarnation; the power of their faith made it
the moon, who was female; at the same time it was only a boulder. I
understood Stone is Stone, and that became my consciousness.

My muscles ceased straining against the bonds, nor did they   48
slump; they ceased aching, they were at ease, they were ready. I said
nothing, I did not change the upward direction of my glance, I did not
smile, yet at this moment the high prophet removed the spears and
had the moon slaves unbind me. I did not feel stiff nor did my wounds
bother me, and when I put on my cougar skin and leaped, pulled the

head over my face and roared, all the prophets fell onto their faces before me. I began chanting and I knew I was doing it all the better for knowing what I was about; I led them back out to the waiting people, and until dawn I chanted the story of the birth, prophesying, betrayal, sacrifice, and victory of the most high prophet. I am a good mimic, I was thoroughly trained, the story is the best; what I gave them was, for them, as good as a vision. I did not know the difference myself.

But the next evening I knew the difference. While I performed my 49 ablutions and the routine ceremonies to the full moon I thought with increasing horror of my state of mind during my conscious trance. What my state of mind actually had been I cannot with confidence now represent, for what I know of it is colored by my reaction against it the next day. I had remained conscious, in that I could recall what happened, yet that observer and commentator in myself of whose existence I had scarcely been aware, but whom I had always taken for my consciousness, had vanished. I no longer had been thinking, but had lost control so that my consciousness had become what I was doing; almost worse, when I had told the story of Christ I had done it not because I had wanted to or believed in it but because, in some obscure sense, I had had to. Thinking about it afterward I did not understand or want to understand what I was drifting toward, but I knew it was something that I feared. And I got out of there as soon as I was physically able.

Here in Sansom what I have learned has provided me with mate- 50 rial for an honorable contribution to knowledge, has given me a tenure to a professorship—thereby pleasing my wife—whereas if I had stayed there among the Dangs much longer I would have reverted until I had become one of them, might not have minded when the time came to die under the sacrificial knife, would have taken in all ways the risk of prophecy—as my Dang son intends to do—until I had lost myself utterly.

QUESTIONS

1.   What hints are there early on that this is a work of fiction in the guise of autobiography? How do you suppose a real anthropologist would react to the narrator's methods of studying the Dang tribe?

2.   Review the narrator's reasons for going on each of his three trips to study the Dangs. How would you describe his attitude towards academia? How does he seem to feel about other aspects of his home culture? Why do you think Elliott chose to make the narrator black, aside from the fact that his ethnicity allows the narrator to "blend in" with the Dangs?

3.   Discuss the Dangs' changing view of the narrator and his role in their society as his name evolves from "Bush Hair" to "Cougar Man" and "Sky Cougar."

4.   When the narrator leaves the Dangs after his second trip, he says "it was not famine that I was escaping but my confusion," his wish to "be neither a leftover Christian nor a mimic of a Dang" (paragraph 35). How would you describe his religious or spiritual dilemma as it develops during his third and final trip? How successfully do you think the narrator solves his religious and cross-cultural dilemmas?

THINKING ABOUT MEETING THE THIRD WORLD

1. In what senses of "native," as discussed by Williams, is the word used in the selections by Rosaldo and Darwin? Based on their selections, do you think Rosaldo would describe Darwin as a "Lone Ethnographer"?

2. Compare Angelou's and Haley's experiences as African Americans in Africa. How do they react to the old slave forts? Why is Angelou able to "pass" as African, while Haley is not? To what extent do you think that they successfully transcend their "American-ness" to experience the culture of their ancestors?

3. What similar and different American values do you think Haley and Streed bring to their encounters with Third World cultures? Compare how and to what extent their encounters are affected by these values.

4. Although the Saharan nomads who abduct the Professor in Bowles's story are presumably more "primitive" than the villagers that Streed describes in her memoir, both Western protagonists suffer physical and emotional harm as a result of their Moroccan encounters. They both get pelted by stones, for example, and they undergo extreme psychological stress or culture shock. Despite such similarities, how do you think Streed's and Bowles's purposes differ in these texts? How does each want us to feel about her or his protagonist? About the Moroccan culture that they encounter?

5. The narrator of "Among the Dangs" and Angelou, in her travel memoir, both pass more or less successfully as "mysterious outlanders" or "local strangers" who are welcomed into a native tribe. Compare the ways they accomplish this and how the tests performed by the natives reveal features of the local culture.

6. Western academics come to study a Third World culture in both Bowles's and Elliott's stories, with dramatically different results. What positive and negative effects does each of these social science professors have on the culture he comes to study? To what extent might each be described as Rosaldo's "Lone Ethnographer"? How much is each man changed by his experience?

7. Since they voluntarily live for an extended time in the culture they're visiting, Streed and the narrator in Elliott's story would seem to have the most in-depth cross-cultural experiences recounted in this chapter, although Angelou appears to have been the most successful in integrating herself smoothly into another culture. Use criteria from Adler's "Five Stages of Culture Shock" to help you compare the extent to which two of the visitors in this chapter become assimilated into and make compromises with their new culture, and what price they pay in the process.

Exploring Additional Sources

8. Cross-cultural misjudgments, insensitivity, or miscommunication figure prominently in three short stories in adjacent chapters, "Good and Bad" by Lucia Berlin (page 454), "Assembly Line" by B. Traven (page 557), and "God and the Cobbler" by R. K. Narayan (page 569). Analyze some aspect of cross-cultural communication in one or more of these stories in conjunction with one or more selections from this chapter. For example, you might analyze Streed's responses to the treatment of women in Morocco by comparison to Miss Dawson's (in Berlin's story) responses to the sexism she encounters in Chile.

9. Think about your own experience, either as a traveler or as a member of an immigrant culture, with culture shock. Follow your interests to explore a particular aspect of psychological or sociological research in culture shock or cross-cultural adaptation.

10. With the latest research available, update Haley's report on the impact of tourism in The Gambia, or explore the positive and negative effects of tourism in another African or Third World nation. If possible, recommend concrete solutions to problems you uncover.

11. Evaluate Streed's indictment of the Peace Corps by researching its training practices and documenting its alleged casualties. As part of your research, try to interview a Peace Corps official, recruiters, or former volunteers. Alternatively, or additionally, construct an argument supporting your view of the political justifications for Peace Corps policies in regard to North Africa or another part of the world.

12. Identify some organizations in your community that work with Third World people, immigrants, or social and political issues, such as Catholic Charities or Amnesty International. Arrange interviews with people at one or more such agency, and consider performing volunteer work there (if the agency needs some research or writing done, perhaps you can receive college or writing class credit for this work). For a selected issue related to the agency's work, write an argumentative essay combining library research with the results of your interviews or volunteer work.

13. Write a literary research paper addressing some aspect of the work of Angelou, Bowles, or Elliott. For example: (a) after reading several books of Angelou's poetry and memoirs, analyze autobiographical aspects of her poetry or poetic aspects of her autobiographical writing; or (b) analyze Bowles's pessimism about cross-cultural relations as expressed in a number of his short stories and/or the novel *The Sheltering Sky* (you might include in your research the 1990 Bernardo Bertolucci film version of the novel).

12

AMERICANS IN THE "NEW WORLD ORDER"

Western[1]

RAYMOND WILLIAMS

There are now some interesting uses of **Western** and **the West,** in international political description. In some cases the term has so far lost its geographical reference as to allow description of, for example, Japan as a **Western** or **Western-type** society. Moreover **the West** (to be defended) is notoriously subject to variable geographical and social specifications. Meanwhile I have seen a reference to a German Marxist as having an *Eastern* ideology.

The **West-East** contrast, geographical into social, is very old. Its earliest European form comes from the *West-East* division of the Roman Empire, from mC3. There is a very strong and persistent cultural contrast in the division of the Christian church into **Western** and *Eastern,* from C11. These internal divisions, within relatively limited known worlds, were succeeded by definitions of the *West* as Christian or Graeco-Roman (not always the same things) by contrast with an *East* defined as Islam or, more generally, as the lands stretching from the Mediterranean to India and China. **Western** and *Eastern* (or *Oriental*) worlds were thus defined from C16 and C17. The development of systematic geography, in Europe, then defined a *Near* (Mediterranean to Mesopotamia), *Middle* (Persia to Ceylon) and *Far* (India to China) *East,* evidently in a European perspective. A British military command designation before World War II overrode this old designation, making the *Near* into the *Middle East,* as now commonly. Yet meanwhile in Europe there were attempted **West-East** divisions, with the Slav peoples as *Eastern.* There was a different but connecting usage in World War I, when Britain and France were the **Western** powers against Germany, with Russia on the *Eastern* front. In World War II the **Western** Allies, now including USA, were of course related to their

---

[1]See page 86 for a key to the abbreviations used in this selection. (Ed.)

Eastern ally, the USSR. It was then really not until the postwar division of Europe, and the subsequent cold war between these former allies, that *West* and *East* took on their contemporary political configurations, of course building on some obvious geography and on some (but different) earlier cultural configurations. The nature of this definition then permitted the extension of **Western** or **the West** to *free-enterprise* or *capitalist* societies, and especially to their political and military alliances (which then sometimes complicated the geography), and of *Eastern*, though less commonly, to *socialist* or *communist* societies. (Hence the curious description of *Marxism*, which began in what is by any definition **Western** Europe, as an *Eastern* ideology.) The more obvious geographical difficulties which result from these increasingly political definitions are sometimes recognized by such phrases as **Western-style** or **Western-type.**

After this complex history, the problem of defining **Western civilization,** a key concept from C18 and especially C19, is considerably more difficult than it is often made to appear. It is interesting that the appropriation of its cultural usage (Graeco-Roman or Christian) to a contemporary political usage (**the West**) has been complicated by the substitution of *North-South* (rich-poor, *industrial-nonindustrial, developed-underdeveloped* societies and economies) for **West-East** as, in some views, a more significant division of the world. But of course *North-South*, developed from the political and economic form of the **West-East** contrast, has its own geographical complications.

FROM *KEYWORDS: A VOCABULARY OF CULTURE AND SOCIETY*, REVISED EDITION, 1985

American Foreign Aid

AMIRA NOWAIRA

Mr. Rokowski, with clothes studiedly casual, gives me a Jimmy Carter smile especially packaged for export. "Please call me Bill. But before we go on to business I would like to explain why I am here and what I am hoping to achieve." He speaks in Special English, or maybe in E.M.R.—English for the Mentally Retarded—a variety of English which he must have had to master before being sent to exotic lands. "I am here as part of a team of experts on education to help the Ministry in conceptualizing a framework within which the educational task in Egypt may be facilitated and improved."

Hello, America.

"What we are hoping to achieve is to construct a conceptually unified system of education that would take into account the needs of students—educational, moral, aesthetic, etcetera—and would respond to the changes that have taken place over the past few years."

Villages with no fresh water but with bottles of Coca-Cola.

"We will be concentrating a good deal of our attention on rural areas since these have traditionally been deprived, I believe, of their rightful share of interest. And the answer we came up with is this: MUSIC. Our preliminary investigation into the matter showed that a good deal of the failure of the educational system in Egyptian rural areas, and to a lesser extent in urban areas, is a direct result of the unbelievable neglect of such a field of human achievement as music. Music is not only capable of enhancing the quality of life but it is also capable of improving the sense of harmony and mathematical precision which are absolutely essential for the development of the new Egyptian village."

A vision of peasant pupils running barefoot near a stagnant canal to the tune of Beethoven thrills my heart.

"Of course we are conscious of the fact that Western music may be culturally alien to pupils, and we are far from trying to impose it on them. What we will teach them is Egyptian music. We will start off by giving them a good grounding in classical Egyptian music and then will go on to Romantic Egyptian music and from there to modern music, folklore, pop, etcetera. Pupils can then have the option of studying comparative music, which will give them a chance to see their own cultural heritage in relation to other cultures."

—FROM "LOST AND FOUND," IN *EGYPTIAN TALES AND SHORT STORIES OF THE 1970S AND 1980S*, 1987

Alcohol and Cannabis

PAUL BOWLES

If you are going to sit at table with the grown-ups, you have to be willing to give up certain childish habits that the grownups don't like: cannibalism, magic, and "irrational" religious practices in general. You must eat, drink, relax and make love the way the grown-ups do, otherwise your heart won't really be in it; you won't truly be disciplining yourself to become like them. One of the first things you have to agree to when you join the grown-ups' club is the fact that the Judeo-Christians accept only one out of all the substances capable of effecting a quick psychic change in the human organism, and that one is alcohol. The liquid is sacred in the ceremonies of both branches of the Judeo-Christian religion, and therefore all other such substances are taboo. But since you are forsaking your own culture anyway, you won't mind giving up the traditional prescriptions for relaxation it provided for you; enthusiastically you will accept alcohol along with democracy, communism and gadgets, since the sooner you learn to use them all properly, the sooner you can expect to be patted on the head, granted special privileges, and told that you are growing up,— fulfilling your destiny, I think they sometimes call it. This news, presumably, you find particularly exciting.

And so the last strongholds of cultures fashioned around the use of substances other than alcohol are being flushed out. . . .

Cannabis, the only serious worldwide rival to alcohol, reckoned in millions of users, is always described in alcoholic countries as a "social menace." And the grown-ups mean just that. They don't infer that it's detrimental to the health or welfare of the individual who uses it, since for them the individual separated from his social context is an irregularity to be remedied, in any case. No, they mean that the user of cannabis is all too likely to see the truth where it is and to fail to see it where it is not. Obviously few things are potentially more dangerous to those interested in prolonging the status quo of organized society. If people refuse to play the game of society at all, how can they be enticed or threatened, save by the ultimately unsatisfactory device of brute force? No, no, there are no two ways about it: society has got to be held together (and directed), alcohol is the only safe substance to allow the mob, and everything else must go.

—FROM "KIF—PROLOGUE AND COMPENDIUM OF TERMS," IN *KULCHUR 3*, 1961

Assembly Line

B. TRAVEN

Mr. E. L. Winthrop of New York was on vacation in the Republic 1
of Mexico. It wasn't long before he realized that this strange and really
wild country had not yet been fully and satisfactorily explored by
Rotarians and Lions, who are forever conscious of their glorious mission on earth. Therefore, he considered it his duty as a good American
citizen to do his part in correcting this oversight.

In search for opportunities to indulge in his new avocation, he left 2
the beaten track and ventured into regions not especially mentioned,
and hence not recommended, by travel agents to foreign tourists. So it
happened that one day he found himself in a little, quaint Indian village somewhere in the State of Oaxaca.

Walking along the dusty main street of this pueblecito, which knew 3
nothing of pavements, drainage, plumbing, or of any means of artificial
light save candles or pine splinters, he met with an Indian squatting on
the earthen-floor front porch of a palm hut, a so-called jacalito.

The Indian was busy making little baskets from bast and from all 4
kinds of fibers gathered by him in the immense tropical bush which
surrounded the village on all sides. The material used had not only
been well prepared for its purpose but was also richly colored with
dyes that the basket-maker himself extracted from various native
plants, barks, roots and from certain insects by a process known only
to him and the members of his family.

B. Traven was the pseudonym for a reclusive writer who lived most
of his life in Mexico and died there in 1969. Traven may have been
Berick Traven Torsvan, born in Chicago in 1890, or a German actor
and revolutionary named Ret Marut, born in 1882. Although not
widely read in the United States, Traven's books have been translated into thirty languages and sold more than 25 million copies world-
wide. He is best known in the U.S. for *The Treasure of the Sierra Madre*
(Berlin 1927; New York 1935), a novel about the consequences of
human greed, which was made into a popular film (1948) directed by
John Huston and starring Humphrey Bogart. Traven's other novels
include *The Death Ship: The Story of an American Sailor* (Berlin 1926,
New York 1934) and *The Rebellion of the Hanged* (Berlin 1936, New
York, 1952), one of the so-called "jungle novels" which have recently
been reissued in English. His fiction explores the political economy of
exploitation and other working class themes among the oppressed
native Indian peoples of his adopted Mexico. "Assembly Line" was
collected in *The Night Visitor and Other Stories* (1966).

His principal business, however, was not producing baskets. He 5
was a peasant who lived on what the small property he possessed—
less than fifteen acres of not too fertile soil—would yield, after much
sweat and labor and after constantly worrying over the most wanted
and best suited distribution of rain, sunshine, and wind and the changing balance of birds and insects beneficial or harmful to his crops.
Baskets he made when there was nothing else for him to do in the
fields, because he was unable to dawdle. After all, the sale of his baskets, though to a rather limited degree only, added to the small income
he received from his little farm.

In spite of being by profession just a plain peasant, it was clearly 6
seen from the small baskets he made that at heart he was an artist, a
true and accomplished artist. Each basket looked as if covered all over
with the most beautiful sometimes fantastic ornaments, flowers, butterflies, birds, squirrels, antelope, tigers, and a score of other animals
of the wilds. Yet, the most amazing thing was that these decorations,
all of them symphonies of color, were not painted on the baskets but
were instead actually part of the baskets themselves. Bast and fibers
dyed in dozens of different colors were so cleverly—one must actually
say intrinsically—interwoven that those attractive designs appeared
on the inner part of the basket as well as on the outside. Not by painting but by weaving were those highly artistic effects achieved. This
performance he accomplished without ever looking at any sketch or
pattern. While working on a basket these designs came to light as if by
magic, and as long as a basket was not entirely finished one could not
perceive what in this case or that the decoration would be like.

People in the market town who bought these baskets would use 7
them for sewing baskets or to decorate tables with or window sills, or
to hold little things to keep them from lying around. Women put their
jewelry in them or flowers or little dolls. There were in fact a hundred
and two ways they might serve certain purposes in a household or in
a lady's own room.

Whenever the Indian had finished about twenty of the baskets he 8
took them to town on market day. Sometimes he would already be on
his way shortly after midnight because he owned only a burro to ride
on, and if the burro had gone astray the day before, as happened frequently, he would have to walk the whole way to town and back
again.

At the market he had to pay twenty centavos in taxes to sell his 9
wares. Each basket cost him between twenty and thirty hours of constant work, not counting the time spent gathering bast and fibers,
preparing them, making dyes and coloring the bast. All this meant
extra time and work. The price he asked for each basket was fifty centavos, the equivalent of about four cents. It seldom happened, how-

ever, that a buyer paid outright the full fifty centavos asked—or four
reales as the Indian called that money. The prospective buyer started
bargaining, telling the Indian that he ought to be ashamed to ask such
a sinful price. "Why, the whole dirty thing is nothing but ordinary
petate straw which you find in heaps wherever you may look for it; the
jungle is packed full of it," the buyer would argue. "Such a little basket, what's it good for anyhow? If I paid you, you thief, ten centavitos
for it you should be grateful and kiss my hand. Well, it's your lucky
day, I'll be generous this time, I'll pay you twenty, yet not one green
centavo more. Take it or run along."

So he sold finally for twenty-five centavos, but then the buyer 10
would say, "Now, what do you think of that? I've got only twenty centavos change on me. What can we do about that? If you can change me
a twenty-peso bill, all right, you shall have your twenty-five fierros."
Of course, the Indian could not change a twenty-peso bill and so the
basket went for twenty centavos.

He had little if any knowledge of the outside world or he would 11
have known that what happened to him was happening every hour of
every day to every artist all over the world. That knowledge would
perhaps have made him very proud, because he would have realized
that he belonged to the little army which is the salt of the earth and
which keeps culture, urbanity and beauty for their own sake from
passing away.

Often it was not possible for him to sell all the baskets he had 12
brought to market, for people here as elsewhere in the world preferred
things made by the millions and each so much like the other that you
were unable, even with the help of a magnifying glass, to tell which
was which and where was the difference between two of the same
kind.

Yet he, this craftsman, had in his life made several hundreds of 13
those exquisite baskets, but so far no two of them had he ever turned
out alike in design. Each was an individual piece of art and as different from the other as was a Murillo from a Velásquez.

Naturally he did not want to take those baskets which he could 14
not sell at the market place home with him again if he could help it. In
such a case he went peddling his products from door to door where he
was treated partly as a beggar and partly as a vagrant apparently looking for an opportunity to steal, and he frequently had to swallow all
sorts of insults and nasty remarks.

Then, after a long run, perhaps a woman would finally stop him, 15
take one of the baskets and offer him ten centavos, which price through
talks and talks would perhaps go up to fifteen or even to twenty.
Nevertheless, in many instances he would actually get no more than
just ten centavos, and the buyer, usually a woman, would grasp that little

marvel and right before his eyes throw it carelessly upon the nearest table as if to say, "Well, I take that piece of nonsense only for charity's sake. I know my money is wasted. But then, after all, I'm a Christian and I can't see a poor Indian die of hunger since he has come such a long way from his village." This would remind her of something better and she would hold him and say, "Where are you at home anyway, Indito? What's your pueblo? So, from Huehuetonoc? Now, listen here, Indito, can't you bring me next Saturday two or three turkeys from Huehuetonoc? But they must be heavy and fat and very, very cheap or I won't even touch them. If I wish to pay the regular price I don't need you to bring them. Understand? Hop along, now, Indito."

The Indian squatted on the earthen floor in the portico of his hut, 16 attended to his work and showed no special interest in the curiosity of Mr. Winthrop watching him. He acted almost as if he ignored the presence of the American altogether.

"How much that little basket, friend?" Mr. Winthrop asked when 17 he felt that he at least had to say something as not to appear idiotic.

"Fifty centavitos, patroncito, my good little lordy, four reales," the 18 Indian answered politely.

"All right, sold," Mr. Winthrop blurted out in a tone and with a 19 wide gesture as if he had bought a whole railroad. And examining his buy he added, "I know already who I'll give that pretty little thing to. She'll kiss me for it, sure. Wonder what she'll use it for?"

He had expected to hear a price of three or even four pesos. The 20 moment he realized that he had judged the value six times too high, he saw right away what great business possibilities this miserable Indian village might offer to a dynamic promoter like himself. Without further delay he started exploring those possibilities. "Suppose, my good friend, I buy ten of these little baskets of yours which, as I might as well admit right here and now, have practically no real use whatsoever. Well, as I was saying, if I buy ten, how much would you then charge me apiece?"

The Indian hesitated for a few seconds as if making calculations. 21 Finally he said, "If you buy ten I can let you have them for forty-five centavos each, señorito gentleman."

"All right, amigo. And now, let's suppose I buy from you straight 22 away one hundred of these absolutely useless baskets, how much will cost me each?"

The Indian, never fully looking up to the American standing be- 23 fore him and hardly taking his eyes off his work, said politely and without the slightest trace of enthusiasm in his voice, "In such a case I might not be quite unwilling to sell each for forty centavitos."

Mr. Winthrop bought sixteen baskets, which was all the Indian 24 had in stock.

* * *

After three weeks' stay in the Republic, Mr. Winthrop was con- 25
vinced that he knew this country perfectly, that he had seen everything and knew all about the inhabitants, their character and their way
of life, and that there was nothing left for him to explore. So he returned to good old Nooyorg and felt happy to be once more in a civilized country, as he expressed it to himself.

One day going out for lunch he passed a confectioner's and, look- 26
ing at the display in the window, he suddenly remembered the little
baskets he had bought in that faraway Indian village.

He hurried home and took all the baskets he still had left to one of 27
the best-known candy-makers in the city.

"I can offer you here," Mr. Winthrop said to the confectioner, "one 28
of the most artistic and at the same time the most original of boxes, if
you wish to call them that. These little baskets would be just right for
the most expensive chocolates meant for elegant and high-priced gifts.
Just have a good look at them, sir, and let me listen."

The confectioner examined the baskets and found them extraordi- 29
narily well suited for a certain line in his business. Never before had
there been anything like them for originality, prettiness and good
taste. He, however, avoided most carefully showing any sign of enthusiasm, for which there would be time enough once he knew the
price and whether he could get a whole load exclusively.

He shrugged his shoulders and said, "Well, I don't know. If you 30
asked me I'd say it isn't quite what I'm after. However, we might give
it a try. It depends, of course, on the price. In our business the package
mustn't cost more than what's in it."

"Do I hear an offer?" Mr. Winthrop asked. 31

"Why don't you tell me in round figures how much you want for 32
them? I'm not good in guessing."

"Well, I'll tell you, Mr. Kemple: since I'm the smart guy who 33
discovered these baskets and since I'm the only Jack who knows
where to lay his hands on more, I'm selling to the highest bidder, on
an exclusive basis, of course. I'm positive you can see it my way, Mr.
Kemple."

"Quite so, and may the best man win," the confectioner said. "I'll 34
talk the matter over with my partners. See me tomorrow same time,
please, and I'll let you know how far we might be willing to go."

Next day when both gentlemen met again Mr. Kemple said: 35
"Now, to be frank with you, I know art on seeing it, no getting around
that. And these baskets are little works of art, they surely are.
However, we are no art dealers, you realize that of course. We've no
other use for these pretty little things except as fancy packing for our
French pralines made by us. We can't pay for them what we might pay
considering them pieces of art. After all to us they're only wrappings.
Fine wrappings, perhaps, but nevertheless wrappings. You'll see it our

way I hope, Mr.—oh yes, Mr. Winthrop. So, here is our offer, take it or leave it: a dollar and a quarter apiece and not one cent more."

Mr. Winthrop made a gesture as if he had been struck over the head. 36

The confectioner, misunderstanding this involuntary gesture of Mr. 37 Winthrop, added quickly, "All right, all right, no reason to get excited, no reason at all. Perhaps we can do a trifle better. Let's say one-fifty."

"Make it one-seventy-five," Mr. Winthrop snapped, swallowing 38 his breath while wiping his forehead.

"Sold. One-seventy-five apiece free at port of New York. We pay 39 the customs and you pay the shipping. Right?"

"Sold," Mr. Winthrop said also and the deal was closed. 40

"There is, of course, one condition," the confectioner explained 41 just when Mr. Winthrop was to leave. "One or two hundred won't do for us. It wouldn't pay the trouble and the advertising. I won't consider less than ten thousand, or one thousand dozens if that sounds better in your ears. And they must come in no less than twelve different patterns well assorted. How about that?"

"I can make it sixty different patterns or designs." 42

"So much the better. And you're sure you can deliver ten thou- 43 sand let's say early October?"

"Absolutely," Mr. Winthrop avowed and signed the contract. 44

Practically all the way back to Mexico, Mr. Winthrop had a note- 45 book in his left hand and a pencil in his right and he was writing figures, long rows of them, to find out exactly how much richer he would be when this business had been put through.

"Now, let's sum up the whole goddamn thing," he muttered to 46 himself. "Damn it, where is that cursed pencil again? I had it right between my fingers. Ah, there it is. Ten thousand he ordered. Well, well, there we got a clean-cut profit of fifteen thousand four hundred and forty genuine dollars. Sweet smackers. Fifteen grand right into papa's pocket. Come to think of it, that Republic isn't so backward after all."

"Buenas tardes, mi amigo, how are you?" he greeted the Indian 47 whom he found squatting in the porch of his jacalito as if he had never moved from his place since Mr. Winthrop had left for New York.

The Indian rose, took off his hat, bowed politely and said in his 48 soft voice, "Be welcome, patroncito. Thank you, I feel fine, thank you. Muy buenas tardes. This house and all I have is at your kind disposal." He bowed once more, moved his right hand in a gesture of greeting and sat down again. But he excused himself for doing so by saying, "Perdoneme, patroncito, I have to take advantage of the daylight, soon it will be night."

"I've got big business for you, my friend," Mr. Winthrop began. 49

"Good to hear that, señor." 50

Mr. Winthrop said to himself, "Now, he'll jump up and go wild 51
when he learns what I've got for him." And aloud he said: "Do you
think you can make me one thousand of these little baskets?"

"Why not, patroncito? If I can make sixteen, I can make one thou- 52
sand also."

"That's right, my good man. Can you also make five thousand?" 53

"Of course, señor. I can make five thousand if I can make one 54
thousand."

"Good. Now, if I should ask you to make me ten thousand, what 55
would you say? And what would be the price of each? You can make
ten thousand, can't you?"

"Of course, I can, señor. I can make as many as you wish. You see, 56
I am an expert in this sort of work. No one else in the whole state can
make them the way I do."

"That's what I thought and that's exactly why I came to you." 57

"Thank you for the honor, patroncito." 58

"Suppose I order you to make me ten thousand of these baskets, 59
how much time do you think you would need to deliver them?"

The Indian, without interrupting his work, cocked his head to one 60
side and then to the other as if he were counting the days or weeks it
would cost him to make all these baskets.

After a few minutes he said in a slow voice, "It will take a good 61
long time to make so many baskets, patroncito. You see, the bast and
the fibers must be very dry before they can be used properly. Then all
during the time they are slowly drying, they must be worked and handled in a very special way so that while drying they won't lose their
softness and their flexibility and their natural brilliance. Even when
dry they must look fresh. They must never lose their natural proper-
ties or they will look just as lifeless and dull as straw. Then while they
are drying up I got to get the plants and roots and barks and insects
from which I brew the dyes. That takes much time also, believe me.
The plants must be gathered when the moon is just right or they won't
give the right color. The insects I pick from the plants must also be
gathered at the right time and under the right conditions or else they
produce no rich colors and are just like dust. But, of course, jefecito, I
can make as many of these canastitas as you wish, even as many as
three dozens if you want them. Only give me time."

"Three dozens? Three dozens?" Mr. Winthrop yelled, and threw 62
up both arms in desperation. "Three dozens!" he repeated as if he had
to say it many times in his own voice so as to understand the real
meaning of it, because for a while he thought that he was dreaming.
He had expected the Indian to go crazy on hearing that he was to sell
ten thousand of his baskets without having to peddle them from door
to door and be treated like a dog with a skin disease.

So the American took up the question of price again, by which he 63
hoped to activate the Indian's ambition. "You told me that if I take one
hundred baskets you will let me have them for forty centavos apiece.
Is that right, my friend?"

"Quite right, jefecito." 64

"Now," Mr. Winthrop took a deep breath, "now, then, if I ask you 65
to make me one thousand, that is, ten times one hundred baskets, how
much will they cost me, each basket?"

That figure was too high for the Indian to grasp. He became 66
slightly confused and for the first time since Mr. Winthrop had arrived
he interrupted his work and tried to think it out. Several times he
shook his head and looked vaguely around as if for help. Finally he
said, "Excuse me, jefecito, little chief, that is by far too much for me to
count. Tomorrow, if you will do me the honor, come and see me again
and I think I shall have my answer ready for you, patroncito."

When on the next morning Mr. Winthrop came to the hut he found 67
the Indian as usual squatting on the floor under the overhanging palm
roof working at his baskets.

"Have you got the price for ten thousand?" he asked the Indian 68
the very moment he saw him, without taking the trouble to say "Good
Morning!"

"Si, patroncito, I have the price ready. You may believe me when I 69
say it has cost me much labor and worry to find out the exact price, because, you see, I do not wish to cheat you out of your honest money."

"Skip that, amigo. Come out with the salad. What's the price?" Mr. 70
Winthrop asked nervously.

"The price is well calculated now without any mistake on my side. 71
If I got to make one thousand canastitas each will be three pesos. If I
must make five thousand, each will cost nine pesos. And if I have to
make ten thousand, in such a case I can't make them for less than fifteen pesos each." Immediately he returned to his work as if he were
afraid of losing too much time with such idle talk.

Mr. Winthrop thought that perhaps it was his faulty knowledge of 72
this foreign language that had played a trick on him.

"Did I hear you say fifteen pesos each if I eventually would buy 73
ten thousand?"

"That's exactly and without any mistake what I've said, pa- 74
troncito," the Indian answered in his soft courteous voice.

"But now, see here, my good man, you can't do this to me. I'm 75
your friend and I want to help you get on your feet."

"Yes, patroncito, I know this and I don't doubt any of your words." 76

"Now, let's be patient and talk this over quietly as man to man. 77
Didn't you tell me that if I would buy one hundred you would sell
each for forty centavos?"

"Si, jefecito, that's what I said. If you buy one hundred you can 78
have them for forty centavos apiece, provided that I have one hundred, which I don't."

"Yes, yes, I see that." Mr. Winthrop felt as if he would go insane 79
any minute now. "Yes, so you said. Only what I can't comprehend is
why you cannot sell at the same price if you make me ten thousand. I
certainly don't wish to chisel on the price. I am not that kind. Only,
well, let's see now, if you can sell for forty centavos at all, be it for
twenty or fifty or a hundred, I can't quite get the idea why the price
has to jump that high if I buy more than a hundred."

"Bueno, patroncito, what is there so difficult to understand? It's all 80
very simple. One thousand canastitas cost me a hundred times more
work than a dozen. Ten thousand cost me so much time and labor that
I could never finish them, not even in a hundred years. For a thousand
canastitas I need more bast than for a hundred, and I need more little
red beetles and more plants and roots and bark for the dyes. It isn't
that you just can walk into the bush and pick all the things you need
at your heart's desire. One root with the true violet blue may cost me
four or five days until I can find one in the jungle. And have you
thought how much time it costs and how much hard work to prepare
the bast and fibers? What is more, if I must make so many baskets,
who then will look after my corn and my beans and my goats and
chase for me occasionally a rabbit for meat on Sunday? If I have no
corn, then I have no tortillas to eat, and if I grow no beans, where do I
get my frijoles from?"

"But since you'll get so much money from me for your baskets you 81
can buy all the corn and beans in the world and more than you need."

"That's what you think, señorito, little lordy. But you see, it is only 82
the corn I grow myself that I am sure of. Of the corn which others may
or may not grow, I cannot be sure to feast upon."

"Haven't you got some relatives here in this village who might 83
help you to make baskets for me?" Mr. Winthrop asked hopefully.

"Practically the whole village is related to me somehow or other. 84
Fact is, I got lots of close relatives in this here place."

"Why then can't they cultivate your fields and look after your 85
goats while you make baskets for me? Not only this, they might gather
for you the fibers and the colors in the bush and lend you a hand here
and there in preparing the material you need for the baskets."

"They might, patroncito, yes, they might. Possible. But then you 86
see who would take care of their fields and cattle if they work for me?
And if they help me with the baskets it turns out the same. No one
would any longer work his fields properly. In such a case corn and
beans would get up so high in price that none of us could buy any and
we all would starve to death. Besides, as the price of everything would

rise and rise higher still how could I make baskets at forty centavos apiece? A pinch of salt or one green chili would set me back more than I'd collect for one single basket. Now you'll understand, highly estimated caballero and jefecito, why I can't make the baskets any cheaper than fifteen pesos each if I got to make that many."

Mr. Winthrop was hard-boiled, no wonder considering the city he 87 came from. He refused to give up the more than fifteen thousand dollars which at that moment seemed to slip through his fingers like nothing. Being really desperate now, he talked and bargained with the Indian for almost two full hours, trying to make him understand how rich he, the Indian, would become if he would take this greatest opportunity of his life.

The Indian never ceased working on his baskets while he ex- 88 plained his points of view.

"You know, my good man," Mr. Winthrop said, "such a wonder- 89 ful chance might never again knock on your door, do you realize that? Let me explain to you in ice-cold figures what fortune you might miss if you leave me flat on this deal."

He tore out leaf after leaf from his notebook, covered each with 90 figures and still more figures, and while doing so told the peasant he would be the richest man in the whole district.

The Indian without answering watched with a genuine expression 91 of awe as Mr. Winthrop wrote down these long figures, executing complicated multiplications and divisions and subtractions so rapidly that it seemed to him the greatest miracle he had ever seen.

The American, noting this growing interest in the Indian, mis- 92 judged the real significance of it. "There you are, my friend," he said. "That's exactly how rich you're going to be. You'll have a bankroll of exactly four thousand pesos. And to show you that I'm a real friend of yours, I'll throw in a bonus. I'll make it a round five thousand pesos, and all in silver."

The Indian, however, had not for one moment thought of four 93 thousand pesos. Such an amount of money had no meaning to him. He had been interested solely in Mr. Winthrop's ability to write figures so rapidly.

"So, what do you say now? Is it a deal or is it? Say yes and you'll 94 get your advance this very minute."

"As I have explained before, patroncito, the price is fifteen pesos 95 each."

"But, my good man," Mr. Winthrop shouted at the poor Indian in 96 utter despair, "where have you been all this time? On the moon or where? You are still at the same price as before."

"Yes, I know that, jefecito, my little chief," the Indian answered, 97 entirely unconcerned. "It must be the same price because I cannot make any other one. Besides, señor, there's still another thing which perhaps you don't know. You see, my good lordy and caballero, I've to make these canastitas my own way and with my song in them and with bits of my soul woven into them. If I were to make them in great numbers there would no longer be my soul in each, or my songs. Each would look like the other with no difference whatever and such a thing would slowly eat up my heart. Each has to be another song which I hear in the morning when the sun rises and when the birds begin to chirp and the butterflies come and sit down on my baskets so that I may see a new beauty, because, you see, the butterflies like my baskets and the pretty colors on them, that's why they come and sit down, and I can make my canastitas after them. And now, señor jefecito, if you will kindly excuse me, I have wasted much time already, although it was a pleasure and a great honor to hear the talk of such a distinguished caballero like you. But I'm afraid I've to attend to my work now, for day after tomorrow is market day in town and I got to take my baskets there. Thank you, señor, for your visit. Adiós."

And in this way it happened that American garbage cans escaped   98 the fate of being turned into receptacles for empty, torn, and crumpled little multicolored canastitas into which an Indian of Mexico had woven dreams of his soul, throbs of his heart: his unsung poems.

QUESTIONS

1. Contrast the motivations and attitudes of Winthrop and the Indian. How do they view each other? What do they want from each other? From life? How realistic or exaggerated do you find these portrayals of each character?

2. The story portrays bargaining or negotiations between the Indian and people in the market town, between the Indian and Winthrop, and between Winthrop and Mr. Kemple, the confectioner. Describe what's at stake for the bargainers in each circumstance. What rules or etiquette seem to govern the process of bargaining in all these contexts? If you have participated in or observed a similar bargaining process, compare your experience with those of the Indian, Winthrop, and Kemple.

3. The Indian's basket-making process and artistry are detailed in several passages. According to the story, what's the purpose or value of art? What does Traven seem to be suggesting about the compatibility of the global economic order with indigenous art forms?

4. How persuaded are you by the Indian's arguments, in paragraphs 80 to 86, that he should charge higher prices for his baskets the more of them he makes? What does Traven seem to be suggesting about the relationship between international capitalism and local rural economies? What arguments can you add to those offered by Winthrop that suggest a different relationship between these global and local forces, between the world's "developed" and "developing" economies?

God and the Cobbler

R. K. NARAYAN

Nothing seemed to belong to him. He sat on a strip of no-man's- 1
land between the outer wall of the temple and the street. The branch of
a margosa tree peeping over the wall provided shade and shook down
on his head tiny whitish-yellow flowers all day. "Only the gods in
heaven can enjoy the good fortune of a rain of flowers," thought the
hippie, observing him from the temple steps, where he had stationed
himself since the previous evening. No need to explain who the hippie
was, the whole basis of hippieness being the shedding of identity and
all geographical associations. He might be from Berkeley or Outer
Mongolia or anywhere. If you developed an intractable hirsuteness, you
acquired a successful mask; if you lived in the open, roasted by the sun
all day, you attained a universal shade transcending classification or
racial stamps and affording you unquestioned movement across all
frontiers. In addition, if you draped yourself in a knee-length cotton
dhoti and vest, and sat down with ease in the dust anywhere, your
clothes acquired a spontaneous ochre tint worthy of a *sanyasi.* When
you have acquired this degree of universality, it is not relevant to question who or what you are. You have to be taken as you are—a breathing entity, that's all. That was how the wayside cobbler viewed the hippie when he stepped up before him to get the straps of his sandals fixed.

He glanced up and reflected, "With those matted locks falling on 2
his nape, looks like God Shiva, only the cobra coiling around his neck
missing." In order to be on the safe side of one who looked so holy, he
made a deep obeisance. He thought, "This man is tramping down from
the Himalayas, the abode of Shiva, as his tough leather sandals, thick
with patches, indicate." The cobbler pulled them off the other's feet
and scrutinized them. He spread out a sheet of paper, a portion of a
poster torn off the wall behind him, and said, "Please step on this, the

R. K. Narayan is the author of novels, stories, and memoirs about his
native India. This story, which originally appeared in *Playboy,* was
collected in *Malgudi Days* (1982). In the introduction to that book,
Narayan discusses the imaginary village where much of his fiction is
set: "If I explain that Malgudi is a small town in South India I shall
only be expressing a half-truth, for the characteristics of Malgudi
seem to me universal." His other works include *The Guide* (winner of
the 1958 National Prize of the Indian Literary Academy), the memoir
My Days (1974), *The Painter of Signs* (1976), *Talkative Man: A Novel*
(1986), and *A Writer's Nightmare: Selected Essays 1958–1988* (1988).

ground is rather muddy." He had a plentiful supply of posters. The wall behind him was a prominent one, being at a crossing of Ramnagar and Kalidess, leading off to the highway on the east. Continuous traffic passed this corner and poster-stickers raced to cover this space with their notices. They came at night, applied thick glue to a portion of the wall and stuck on posters announcing a new movie, a lecture at the park or a candidate for an election, with his portrait included. Rival claimants to the space on the wall, arriving late at night, pasted their messages over the earlier ones. Whatever the message, it was impartially disposed of by a donkey that stood by and from time to time went over, peeled off the notice with its teeth and chewed it, possibly relishing the tang of glue. The cobbler, arriving for work in the morning, tore off a couple of posters before settling down for the day, finding various uses for them. He used the paper for wrapping food when he got something from the corner food shop under the thatched roof; he spread it like a red carpet for his patrons while they waited to get a shoe repaired and he also slept on it when he felt the sun too hot. The hippie, having watched him, felt an admiration. "He asks for nothing, but everything is available to him." The hippie wished he could be composed and self-contained like the cobbler.

The previous day he had sat with the mendicants holding out their [3] hands for alms on the temple steps. Some of them able-bodied like himself, some maimed, blind or half-witted, but all of them, though looking hungry, had a nonchalant air which he envied. At the evening time, worshippers passing the portals of the temple flung coins into the alms bowls, and it was a matter of luck in whose bowl a particular coin fell. There was a general understanding among the mendicants to leave one another alone to face their respective luck, but to pick a coin up for the blind man if it fell off his bowl. The hippie, having perfected the art of merging with his surroundings, was unnoticed among them. The priest, being in a good mood on this particular evening, had distributed to the mendicants rice sweetened with *jaggery*, remnants of offerings to the gods. It was quite filling, and after a drink of water from the street tap, the hippie had slept at the portal of the temple.

At dawn, he saw the cobbler arrive with a gunny sack over his [4] shoulder and settle down under the branch of the margosa; he was struck by the composition of the green margosa bathed in sunlight looming over the grey temple wall. The hippie enjoyed the sense of peace pervading this spot. No one seemed to mind anything—the dust, the noise and the perils of chaotic traffic as cycles and pedestrians bumped and weaved their way through Moroccans, lorries and scooters, which madly careered along, churning up dust, wheels crunching and horns honking and screaming as if antediluvian monsters were in pursuit of one another. Occasionally a passer-by gurgled and spat out into the air or urinated onto a wall without anyone's noticing or protesting. The hippie was struck by the total acceptance here of life as it came.

With his head bowed, the cobbler went on slicing off leather with an awl or stabbed his bodkin through and drew up a waxed thread, while stitches appeared at the joints as if by a miracle, pale strands flashing into view like miniature lightning. The cobbler had a tiny tin bowl of water in which he soaked any unruly piece of leather to soften it, and then hit it savagely with a cast-iron pestle to make it limp. When at rest, he sat back, watching the passing feet in the street, taking in at a glance the condition of every strap, thong and buckle on the footwear parading before his eyes. His fingers seemed to itch when they did not ply his tools, which he constantly honed on the curbstone. Observing his self-absorption while his hands were busy, the hippie concluded that, apart from the income, the man derived a mystic joy in the very process of handling leather and attacking it with sharpened end. For him, even food seemed to be a secondary business. Beyond beckoning a young urchin at the corner food shop to fetch him a cup of tea or a bun, he never bothered about food. Sometimes, when he had no business for a long stretch, he sat back, looking at the treetop ahead, his mind and attention switched off. He was quite content to accept that situation, too—there was neither longing nor regret in that face. He seldom solicited work vociferously or rejected it when it came. He never haggled when footwear was thrust up to him, but examined it, spread out the poster under the man's feet, attended to the loose strap or the worn-out heel and waited for his wages. He had to be patient; they always took time to open the purse and search for a coin. If the customer was too niggardly, the cobbler just looked up without closing his fingers on the coin, which sometimes induced the other to add a minute tip, or made him just turn and walk off without a word.

While the cobbler was stitching his sandals, the hippie sat down on the sheet of paper provided for him. He was amused to notice that he had lowered himself onto the head of a colorful film star. Not that he needed a paper to sit upon, but that seemed to be the proper thing to do here; otherwise, the cobbler was likely to feel hurt. The hippie was quite used to the bare ground; perhaps in due course he might qualify himself to sit on even a plank of nails with beatitude in his face. It was quite possible that his search for a guru might culminate in that and nothing more. In his wanderings he had seen in Benares yogis sitting on nails in deep meditation. He had seen at Gaya a penitent who had a long needle thrust through his cheeks—only it interfered with his tongue, which he didn't mind, since he was under a vow of silence. The hippie had watched at Allahabad during *Kumbha Mela* millions praying and dipping at the confluence of the rivers Jumna and Ganges. In their midst was a *sadhu* who had a full-grown tiger for company, claiming it to be his long-lost brother in a previous birth; men handled deadly cobras as if they were ropes. There were fire-eaters, swallowers of swords and chewers of glass and cactus. Or the yogis who sat in cremation grounds in a cataleptic state, night and day, without food or movement, unmindful of the corpses burning on the pyres around them. In Nepal, a person produced a silver figure out of thin air with a flourish of his hand and gave it to the hippie; he treasured it in his bag—a little image of a four-armed goddess. In every case, at first he was filled with wonder and he wanted to learn their secret, found the wonder-workers willing to impart their knowledge to him for no higher exchange than a pellet of opium; but eventually he began to ask himself, "What am I to gain by this achievement? It seems to me no more than a moon walk. Only less expensive." He found no answer that satisfied his enquiry. He noticed on the highway, in villages and rice fields, men and women going about their business with complete absorption—faces drawn and serious but never agitated. He felt that they might have a philosophy worth investigating. He travelled by train, trekked on foot, hitchhiked in lorries and bullock carts. Why? He himself could not be very clear about it.

He wished to talk to the cobbler. He took out a *beedi*, the leaf- 7
wrapped tobacco favoured by the masses. (The cigarette was a sophistication and created a distance, while a *beedi*, four for a paisa, established rapport with the masses.) The cobbler hesitated to accept it, but the hippie said, "Go on, you will like it, it's good, the Parrot brand. . . ." The hippie fished matches from his bag. Now they smoked for a while in silence, the leafy-smelling smoke curling up in the air. Auto-rickshaws and cycles swerved around the corner. An ice-cream-seller had pushed his barrow along and was squeaking his little rubber horn to attract customers, the children who would burst out of the school gate presently. By way of opening a conversation, the hippie said, "Flowers rain on you," pointing to the little whitish-yellow flowers whirling down from the tree above. The cobbler looked and flicked them off his coat and then patted them off his turban, which, though faded, protected him from the sun and rain and added a majesty to his person. The hippie repeated, "You must be blessed to have a rain of flowers all day."

The other looked up and retorted, "Can I eat that flower? Can I 8
take it home and give it to the woman to be put into the cooking pot? If the flowers fall on a well-fed stomach, it's different—gods in heaven can afford to have flowers on them, not one like me."

"Do you believe in God?" asked the hippie, a question that sur- 9
prised the cobbler. How could a question of that nature ever arise?

Probably he was being tested by this mysterious customer. Better be careful in answering him. The cobbler gestured towards the temple in front and threw up his arm in puzzlement. "He just does not notice us sometimes. How could He? Must have so much to look after." He brooded for a few minutes at a picture of God, whose attention was distracted hither and thither by a thousand clamouring petitioners praying in all directions. He added, "Take the case of our big officer, our collector—can he be seen by everyone or will he be able to listen to everyone and answer their prayers? When a human officer is so difficult to reach, how much more a god? He has so much to think of. . . ." He lifted his arms and swept them across the dome of heaven from horizon to horizon. It filled the hippie with a sense of immensity of God's program and purpose, and the man added, "And He can't sleep, either. Our pundit in this temple said in his lecture that gods do not wink their eyelids or sleep. How can they? In the winking of an eyelid, so many bad things might happen. The planets might leave their courses and bump into one another, the sky might pour down fire and brimstone or all the demons might be let loose and devour humanity. Oh, the cataclysm!" The hippie shuddered at the vision of disaster that'd overtake us within one eye-winking of God. The cobbler added, "I ask God every day and keep asking every hour. But when He is a little free, He will hear me; till then, I have to bear it."

"What, bear what?" asked the hippie, unable to contain his curiosity. 10

"This existence. I beg Him to take me away. But the time must 11 come. It'll come."

"Why, aren't you happy to be alive?" asked the hippie. 12

"I don't understand you," the cobbler said, and at that moment, 13 noticing a passing foot, he cried, "Hi! That buckle is off. Come, come, stop," to a young student. The feet halted for a second, paused but passed on. The cobbler made a gesture of contempt. "See what is coming over these young fellows! They don't care. Wasteful habits, I tell you. That buckle will come off before he reaches his door; he will just kick the sandals off and buy new ones." He added with a sigh, "Strange are their ways nowadays. For five paise he could have worn it another year." He pointed to a few pairs of sandals arrayed on his gunnysack and said, "All these I picked up here and there, thrown away by youngsters like him. Some days the roadside is full of them near that school; the children have no patience to carry them home, or some of them feel it is a shame to be seen carrying a sandal in hand! Not all these here are of a pair or of the same color, but I cut them and shape them and color them into pairs." He seemed very proud of his ability to match odd shoes. "If I keep them long enough, God always sends me a customer, someone who will appreciate a bargain. Whatever price I can get is good enough."

"Who buys them?"   14

"Oh, anybody, mostly if a building is going up; those who have to   15
stand on cement and work prefer protection for their feet. Somehow I
have to earn at least five rupees every day, enough to buy some corn
or rice before going home. Two mouths waiting to be fed at home.
What the days are coming to! Not enough for two meals. Even betel
leaves are two for a paisa; they used to be twenty, and my wife must
chew even if she has no food to eat. God punishes us in this life. In my
last birth I must have been a moneylender squeezing the life out of the
poor, or a shopkeeper cornering all the rice for profits—till I render all
these accounts, God'll keep me here. I have only to be patient."

"What do you want to be in your next birth?"   16

The cobbler got a sudden feeling again that he might be talking to   17
a god or his agent. He brooded over the question for some time. "I
don't want birth in this world. Who knows, they may decide to send
me to hell, but I don't want to go to hell." He explained his vision of
another world where a mighty accountant sat studying the debits and
credits and drawing up a monumental balance sheet appropriate for
each individual.

"What have you done?" asked the hippie.   18

A suspicion again in the cobbler's mind that he might be talking to   19
a god. "When you drink, you may not remember all that you do," he
said. "Now my limbs are weak, but in one's younger years, one might
even set fire to an enemy's hut at night while his children are asleep.
A quarrel could lead to such things. That man took away my money,
threatened to molest my wife, and she lost an eye in the scuffle when
I beat her up on suspicion. We had more money, and a rupee could
buy three bottles of toddy in those days. I had a son, but after his
death, I changed. It's his child that we have at home now."

"I don't want to ask questions," said the hippie, "but I, too, set fire 20
to villages and, flying over them, blasted people whom I didn't know
or see."

The cobbler looked up in surprise. "When, where, where?"   21

The hippie said, "In another incarnation; in another birth. Can you 22
guess what may be in store for me next?"

The cobbler said, "If you can wait till the priest of the temple   23
comes . . . A wise man, he'll tell us."

The hippie said, "You were at least angry with the man whose hut   24
you burned. I didn't even know whose huts I was destroying. I didn't
even see them."

"Why, why, then?" Seeing that the other was unwilling to speak,   25
the cobbler said, "If it had been those days, we could have drunk and
eaten together."

"Next time," said the hippie, and rose to go. He slipped his feet 26
into the sandals. "I'll come again," he said, though he was not certain
where he was going or stopping next. He gave the cobbler twenty-five
paise, as agreed. He then took the silver figure from his bag and held
it out to the cobbler. "Here is something for you. . . ."

The cobbler examined it and cried, "Oh, this is Durga the goddess; 27
she will protect you. Did you steal it?"

The hippie appreciated the question as indicating perfectly how he 28
had ceased to look respectable. He replied, "Perhaps the man who
gave it to me stole it."

"Keep it, it'll protect you," said the cobbler, returning the silver 29
figure. He reflected, after the hippie was gone, "Even a god steals
when he has a chance."

QUESTIONS

1.   The voice that tells this story shifts among several perspectives, including those of the hippie, the cobbler, and a third-person narrator
observing the characters. Trace how these perspectives alternate and
shift. When do you think the narrative voice is being ironic?

2.   What do you think the hippie is referring to when he says that he,
too, has "set fire to villages and, flying over them, blasted people
whom I didn't know or see" (paragraph 20)? Why does the hippie feel
that the cobbler's burning of a hut was more morally acceptable than
his own? To what extent do you agree with him?

3.   Compare the ways in which the hippie and the cobbler miscon-
strue each other. How does each man's personal and cultural background contribute to his misjudgments?

Tour of the City: Encounters between East and West

PICO IYER

To mention, however faintly, the West's cultural assault on the 1
East is, inevitably, to draw dangerously close to the fashionable belief
that the First World is corrupting the Third. And to accept that AIDS
and Rambo are the two great "Western" exports of 1985 is to encourage some all too easy conclusions: that the West's main contributions
to the rest of the world are sex and violence, a cureless disease and a
killer cure; that America is exporting nothing but a literal kind of in-
fection and a bloody sort of indoctrination. In place of physical imperialism, we often assert a kind of sentimental colonialism that would replace Rambo myths with Sambo myths and conclude that because the
First World feels guilty, the Third World must be innocent—what
Pascal Bruckner refers to as "compassion as contempt."

This, however, I find simplistic—both because corruption often 2
says most about those who detect it and because the developing world
may often have good reason to assent in its own transformation.

This is not to deny that the First World has indeed inflicted much 3
damage on the Third, especially through the inhuman calculations of
geopolitics. If power corrupts, superpowers are super-corrupting, and
the past decade alone has seen each of the major powers destroy a self-
contained Asian culture by dragging it into the cross fire of the Real
World: Tibet was invaded for strategic reasons by the Chinese, and
now the dreamed-of Shangri-La is almost lost forever; Afghanistan
was overrun by Soviet tanks, and now the Michauds' photographic
record of its fugitive beauties must be subtitled, with appropriate
melancholy, "Paradise Lost"; Cambodia, once so gentle a land that
cyclo drivers were said to tip their passengers, fell into the sights of
Washington and is now just a land of corpses.

Pico Iyer, born in England of Indian parents and now living in
California, is a journalist and travel writer. He wrote about world
affairs for *Time Magazine* for four years and continues to write for
other newspapers and magazines such the *Village Voice* and *Times
Literary Supplement.* His latest book is *The Lady and the Monk: Four
Seasons in Kyoto* (1991). This selection is part of the introductory essay,
"Love Match," in his 1988 book, *Video Night in Kathmandu, and Other
Reports from the Not-so-far East.*

On an individual level too, Western tourists invariably visit de- 4
struction on the places they visit, descending in droves on some "authentic Eastern village" until only two things are certain: it is neither
Eastern nor authentic. Each passing season (and each passing tourist)
brings new developments to the forgotten places of the world—and in
a never-never land, every development is a change for the worse. In
search of a lovely simplicity, Westerners saddle the East with complexities; in search of peace, they bring agitation. As soon as Arcadia is
seen as a potential commodity, amenities spring up on every side to
meet outsiders' needs, and paradise is not so much lost as remain-
dered. In Asia alone, Bali, Tahiti, Sri Lanka and Nepal have already
been so taken over by Paradise stores, Paradise hotels and Paradise
cafés that they sometimes seem less like utopias than packaged imita-
tions of utopia; Ladakh, Tibet and Ko Samui may one day follow. No
man, they say, is an island; in the age of international travel, not even
an island can remain an island for long.

Like every tourist, moreover, I found myself spreading corruption 5
even as I decried it. In northern Thailand, I joined a friend in giving hill
tribesmen tutorials in the songs of Sam Cooke until a young Thai girl
was breaking the silence of the jungle with a piercing refrain of "She
was sixteen, too young to love, and I was too young to know." In
China, I gave a local boy eager for some English-language reading
matter a copy of the only novel I had on hand—Gore Vidal's strenu-
ously perverse *Duluth*. And in a faraway hill station in Burma, a group
of cheery black marketeers treated me to tea and I, in return, taught
them the words "lesbian" and "skin flicks," with which they seemed
much pleased.

Yet that in itself betrays some of the paradoxes that haunt our talk 6
of corruption. For often, the denizens of the place we call paradise long
for nothing so much as news of that "real paradise" across the seas—
the concrete metropolis of skyscrapers and burger joints. And often
what we call corruption, they might be inclined to call progress or
profit. As tourists, we have reason to hope that the quaint anachronism we have discovered will always remain "unspoiled," as fixed as
a museum piece for our inspection. It is perilous, however, to assume
that its inhabitants will long for the same. Indeed, a kind of imperial
arrogance underlies the very assumption that the people of the developing world should be happier without the TVs and motorbikes that
we find so indispensable ourselves. If money does not buy happiness,
neither does poverty.

In other ways too, our laments for lost paradises may really have 7
much more to do with our own state of mind than with the state of the
place whose decline we mourn. Whenever we recall the places we

have seen, we tend to observe them in the late afternoon glow of nostalgia, after memory, the mind's great cosmetician, has softened out rough edges, smoothed out imperfections and removed the whole to a lovely abstract distance. Just as a good man, once dead, is remembered as a saint, so a pleasant place, once quit, is recalled as a utopia. Nothing is ever what it used to be.

8

If the First World is not invariably corrupting the Third, we are sometimes apt to leap to the opposite conclusion: that the Third World, in fact, is hustling the First. As tourists, moreover, we are so bombarded with importunities from a variety of locals—girls who live off their bodies and touts who live off their wits, merchants who use friendship to lure us into their stores and "students" who attach themselves to us in order to improve their English—that we begin to regard ourselves as beleaguered innocents and those we meet as shameless predators.

9

To do so, however, is to ignore the great asymmetry that governs every meeting between tourist and local: that we are there by choice and they largely by circumstance; that we are traveling in the spirit of pleasure, adventure and romance, while they are mired in the more urgent business of trying to survive; and that we, often courted by the government, enjoy a kind of unofficial diplomatic immunity, which gives us all the perks of authority and none of the perils of responsibility, while they must stake their hopes on every potential transaction.

10

Descending upon native lands quite literally from the heavens, *dei ex machinae* from an alien world of affluence, we understandably strike many locals in much the same way that movie stars strike us. And just as some of us are wont to accost a celebrity glimpsed by chance at a restaurant, so many people in developing countries may be tempted to do anything and everything possible to come into contact with the free-moving visitors from abroad and their world of distant glamour. They have nothing to lose in approaching a foreigner—at worst, they will merely be insulted or pushed away. And they have everything to gain: a memory, a conversation, an old copy of *Paris Match*, perhaps even a friendship or a job opportunity. Every foreigner is a messenger from a world of dreams.

"Do you know Beverly Hills?" I was once asked by a young Burmese boy who had just spent nine months in jail for trying to escape his closed motherland. "Do you know Hollywood? Las Vegas? The Potomac, I think, is very famous. Am I right? Detroit, Michigan, is where they make cars. Ford. General Motors. Chevrolet. Do you know Howard Hughes? There are many Jewish people in New York. Am I right? And also at *Time* magazine? Am I right?" Tell us about life behind the scenes, we ask the star, and which is the best place in the whole wide world, and what is Liz Taylor really like.

11

The touts that accost us are nearly always, to be sure, worldly prag- 12
matists. But they are also, in many cases, wistful dreamers, whose hopes
are not so different from the ones our culture encourages: to slough off
straitened circumstances and set up a new life and a new self abroad, un-
derwritten by hard work and dedication. American dreams are strongest
in the hearts of those who have seen America only in their dreams.

I first met Maung-Maung as I stumbled off a sixteen-hour third- 13
class overnight train from Rangoon to Mandalay. He was standing
outside the station, waiting to pick up tourists; a scrawny fellow in his
late twenties, with a sailor's cap, a beard, a torn white shirt above his
longyi and an open, rough-hewn face—a typical tout, in short. Beside
him stood his bicycle trishaw. On one side was painted the legend
"My Life"; on the other, "B.Sc. (Maths)."

We haggled for a few minutes. Then Maung-Maung smilingly per- 14
suaded me to part with a somewhat inflated fare—twenty cents—for
the trip across town, and together we began cruising through the wide,
sunny boulevards of the city of kings. As we set off, we began to exchange the usual questions—age, place of birth, marital status and education—and before long we found that our answers often jibed. Soon,
indeed, the conversation was proceeding swimmingly. A little while
into our talk, my driver, while carefully steering his trishaw with one
hand, sank the other into his pocket and handed back to me a piece of
jade. I admired it dutifully, then extended it back in his direction.
"No," he said. "This is present."

Where, I instantly wondered, was the catch—was he framing me, 15
or bribing me, or cunningly putting me in his debt? What was the
small print? What did he want?

"I want you," said Maung-Maung, "to have something so you can 16
always remember me. Also, so you can always have happy memories
of Mandalay." I did not know how to respond. "You see," he went on,
"if I love other people, they will love me. It is like Newton's law, or
Archimedes."

This was not what I had expected. "I think," he added, "it is al- 17
ways good to apply physics to life."

That I did not doubt. But still I was somewhat taken aback. "Did 18
you study physics at school?"

"No, I study physics in college. You see, I am graduate from 19
University of Mandalay—B.Sc. Mathematics." He waved with pride at
the inscription on the side of his trishaw.

"And you completed all your studies?"   20

"Yes. B.Sc. Mathematics."   21

"Then why are you working in this kind of job?"   22

"Other jobs are difficult. You see, here in Burma, a teacher earns 23
only two hundred fifty kyats [$30] in a month. Managing director has

only one thousand kyats [$125]. Even President makes only four thousand kyats [$500]. For me, I do not make much money. But in this job, I can meet tourist and improve my English. Experience, I believe, is the best teacher."

"But surely you could earn much more just by driving a horse cart?"   24

"I am Buddhist," Maung-Maung reminded me gently, as he went   25
pedaling calmly through the streets. "I do not want to inflict harm on any living creature. If I hit horse in this life, in next life I come back as horse."

"So"—I was still skeptical—"you live off tourists instead?"   26

"Yes," he said, turning around to give me a smile. My irony, it   27
seems, was wasted. "Until two years ago, in my village in Shan States, I had never seen a tourist."

"Never?"   28

"Only in movies." Again he smiled back at me.   29

I was still trying to puzzle out why a university graduate would   30
be content with such a humble job when Maung-Maung, as he pedaled, reached into the basket perched in front of his handlebars and pulled out a thick leather book. Looking ahead as he steered, he handed it back to me to read. Reluctantly, I opened it, bracing myself for porno postcards or other illicit souvenirs. Inside, however, was nothing but a series of black-and-white snapshots. Every one of them had been painstakingly annotated in English: "My Headmaster," "My Monk," "My Brothers and Sisters," "My Friend's Girlfriend." And his own girlfriend? "I had picture before. But after she broke my heart, and fall in love with other people, I tear it out."

At the very back of his book, in textbook English, Maung-Maung   31
had carefully inscribed the principles by which he lived.

1. Abstain from violence.
2. Abstain from illicit sexual intercourse.
3. Abstain from intoxicants of all kinds.
4. Always be helpful.
5. Always be kind.

"It must be hard," I said dryly, "to stick to all these rules."   32

"Yes. It is not always easy," he confessed. "But I must try. If peo-   33
ple ask me for food, my monk tell me, I must always give them money. But if they want money for playing cards, I must give them no help. My monk also explain I must always give forgiveness—even to people who hurt me. If you put air into volleyball and throw it against wall, it bounces back. But if you do not put in air, what happens? It collapses against wall."

Faith, in short, was its own vindication.   34

I was now beginning to suspect that I would find no more engag- 35
ing guide to Mandalay than Maung-Maung, so I asked him if he
would agree to show me around. "Yes, thank you very much. But first,
please, I would like you to see my home."

Ah, I thought, here comes the setup. Once I'm in his house, far 36
from the center of a city I don't know, he will drop a drug in my tea or
pull out a knife or even bring in a few accomplices. I will find out too
late that his friendliness is only a means to an end.

Maung-Maung did nothing to dispel these suspicions as he ped- 37
aled the trishaw off the main street and we began to pass through dirty
alleyways, down narrow lanes of run-down shacks. At last we pulled
up before a hut, fronted with weeds. Smiling proudly, he got off and
asked me to enter.

There was not much to see inside his tiny room. There was a cot, 38
on which sat a young man, his head buried in his hands. There was another cot, on which Maung-Maung invited me to sit as he introduced
me to his roommate. The only other piece of furniture was a blackboard in a corner on which my host had written out the statement re-
produced in the epigraph to this book, expressing his lifelong pledge
to be of service to tourists.

I sat down, not sure what was meant to happen next. For a few 39
minutes, we made desultory conversation. His home, Maung-Maung
explained, cost 30 kyats ($4) a month. This other man was also a uni-
versity graduate, but he had no job: every night, he got drunk. Then,
after a few moments of reflection, my host reached down to the floor
next to his bed and picked up what I took to be his two most valuable
belongings.

Solemnly, he handed the first of them to me. It was a sociology 40
textbook from Australia. Its title was *Life in Modern America*. Then, as
gently as if it were his Bible, Maung-Maung passed across the other
volume, a dusty old English-Burmese dictionary, its yellowed pages
falling from their covers. "Every night," he explained, "after I am finished on trishaw, I come here and read this. Also, every word I do not
know I look up." Inside the front cover, he had copied out a few spec-
imen sentences. *If you do this, you may end up in jail. My heart is lacerated
by what you said. What a lark.*

I was touched by his show of trust. But I also felt as uncertain 41
as an actor walking through a play he hasn't read. Perhaps, I said
a little uneasily, we should go now, so we can be sure of seeing all
the sights of Mandalay before sundown. "Do not worry," Maung-
Maung assured me with a quiet smile, "we will see everything. I
know how long the trip will take. But first, please, I would like you
to see this."

Reaching under his bed, he pulled out what was clearly his most 42
precious treasure of all. With a mixture of shyness and pride, he
handed over a thick black notebook. I looked at the cover for markings
and, finding none, opened it up. Inside, placed in alphabetical order,
was every single letter he had ever received from a foreign visitor.
Every one was meticulously dated and annotated; many were accompanied by handwritten testimonials or reminiscences from the tourists
Maung-Maung had met. On some pages, he had affixed wrinkled
passport photos of his foreign visitors by which he could remember
them.

Toward the end of the book, Maung-Maung had composed a two- 43
page essay, laboriously inscribed in neat and grammatical English,
called "Guide to Jewelry." It was followed by two further mono-
graphs, "For You" and "For the Tourists." In them, Maung-Maung
warned visitors against "twisty characters," explained something of
the history and beauty of Mandalay and told his readers not to trust
him until he had proved worthy of their trust.

Made quiet by this labor of love, I looked up. "This must have 44
taken you a long time to write."

"Yes," he replied with a bashful smile. "I have to look many times 45
at dictionary. But it is my pleasure to help tourists."

I went back to flipping through the book. At the very end of the 46
volume, carefully copied out, was a final four-page essay, entitled "My
Life."

He had grown up, Maung-Maung wrote, in a small village, the el- 47
dest of ten children. His mother had never learned to read, and feeling
that her disability made her "blind," she was determined that her children go to school. It was not easy, because his father was a farmer and
earned only 300 kyats a month. Still, Maung-Maung, as the eldest, was
able to complete his education at the local school.

When he finished, he told his parents that he wanted to go to uni- 48
versity. Sorrowfully, they told him that they could not afford it—they
had given him all they had for his schooling. He knew that was true,
but still he was set on continuing his studies. "I have hand. I have
head. I have legs," he told them. "I wish to stand on my own legs."
With that, he left his village and went to Mandalay. Deeply wounded
by his desertion, his parents did not speak to him for a year.

In Mandalay, Maung-Maung's narrative continued, he had begun 49
to finance his studies by digging holes—he got 4 kyats for every hole.
Then he got a job cleaning clothes. Then he went to a monastery and
washed dishes and clothes in exchange for board and lodging. Finally,
he took a night job as a trishaw driver.

When they heard of that, his parents were shocked. "They think I 50
go with prostitutes. Everyone looks down on trishaw driver. Also

other trishaw drivers hate me because I am a student. I do not want to quarrel with them. But I do not like it when they say dirty things or go with prostitutes." Nevertheless, after graduation Maung-Maung decided to pay 7 kyats a day to rent a trishaw full-time. Sometimes, he wrote, he made less than 1 kyat a day, and many nights he slept in his vehicle in the hope of catching the first tourists of the day. He was a poor man, he went on, but he made more money than his father. Most important, he made many friends. And through riding his trishaw he had begun to learn English.

His dream, Maung-Maung's essay concluded, was to buy his own   51 trishaw. But that cost four hundred dollars. And his greatest dream was, one day, to get a "Further Certificate" in mathematics. He had already planned the details of that far-off moment when he could invite his parents to his graduation. "I must hire taxi. I must buy English suit. I must pay for my parents to come to Mandalay. I know that it is expensive, but I want to express my gratitude to my parents. They are my lovers."

When I finished the essay, Maung-Maung smiled back his grati-   52 tude, and gave me a tour of the city as he had promised.

The American empire in the East: that was my grand theme as I   53 set forth. But as soon as I left the realm of abstract labels and generalized forces, and came down to individuals—to myself, Maung-Maung and many others like him—the easy contrasts began to grow confused. If cultures are only individuals writ large, as Salman Rushdie and Gabriel García Márquez have suggested, individuals are small cultures in themselves. Everyone is familiar with the slogan of Kipling's "Oh, East is East, and West is West, and never the twain shall meet." But few recall that the lines that conclude the refrain, just a few syllables later, exclaim, "But there is neither East nor West, border, nor breed, nor birth, / When two strong men stand face to face, though they come from the ends of the earth!"

On a grand collective level, the encounters between East and   54 West might well be interpreted as a battle; but on the human level, the meeting more closely resembled a mating dance (even Rambo, while waging war against the Vietnamese, had fallen in love with a Vietnamese girl). Whenever a Westerner meets an Easterner, each is to some extent confronted with the unknown. And the unknown is at once an enticement and a challenge; it awakens in us both the lover and the would-be conqueror. When Westerner meets Easterner, therefore, each finds himself often drawn to the other, yet mystified; each projects his romantic hopes on the stranger, as well as his designs; and each pursues both his illusions and his vested interests with a curious mix of innocence and calculation that shifts with every step.

Everywhere I went in Asia, I came upon variations on this same 55
uncertain pattern: in the streets of China, where locals half woo, half
recoil from Westerners whose ways remain alien but whose goods are
now irresistible; in the country-and-western bars of Manila, where
former conqueror and former conquest slow-dance cheek to cheek
with an affection, and a guilt, born of longtime familiarity; in the high
places of the Himalayas, where affluent Westerners eager to slough
off their riches in order to find religion meet local wise men so poor
that they have made of riches a religion; and, most vividly of all,
in the darkened bars of Bangkok, where a Western man and a Thai
girl exchange shy questions and tentative glances, neither knowing
whether either is after love or something else. Sometimes, the
romance seemed like a blind date, sometimes like a passionate
attachment; sometimes like a back-street coupling, sometimes like the
rhyme of kindred spirits. Always, though, it made any talk of winners
and losers irrelevant.

Usually, too, the cross-cultural affairs developed with all the con- 56
tradictory twists and turns of any romance in which opposites attract
and then retract and then don't know exactly where they stand. The
Westerner is drawn to the tradition of the Easterner, and almost cov-
ets his knowledge of suffering, but what attracts the Easterner to the
West is exactly the opposite—his future, and his freedom from all
hardship. After a while, each starts to become more like the other, and
somewhat less like the person the other seeks. The New Yorker
disappoints the locals by turning into a barefoot ascetic dressed in
bangles and beads, while the Nepali peasant frustrates his foreign
supplicants by turning out to be a traveling salesman in Levi's and
Madonna T-shirt. Soon, neither is quite the person he was, or the
one the other wanted. The upshot is confusion. "You cannot have
pineapple for breakfast," a Thai waitress once admonished me.
"Why?" I asked. "What do *you* have for breakfast?" "Hot dog."

It is never hard, in such skewed exchanges, to find silliness and 57
self-delusion. "Everybody thought that everybody else was ridicu-
lously exotic," writes Gita Mehta of East-West relations in *Karma Cola*,
"and everybody got it wrong." Yet Mehta's cold-eyed perspective
does justice to only one aspect of this encounter. For the rest, I prefer
to listen to her wise and very different compatriot, R. K. Narayan,
whose typical tale "God and the Cobbler" describes a chance meeting
in a crowded Indian street between a Western hippie and a village cobbler. Each, absurdly, takes the other to be a god. Yet the beauty of their
folly is that each, lifted by the other's faith, surprises himself, and us,
by somehow rising to the challenge and proving worthy of the trust he
has mistakenly inspired: each, taken out of himself, becomes, not a god

perhaps, but something better than a dupe or fraud. Faith becomes its own vindication. And at the story's end, each leaves the other with a kind of benediction, the more valuable because untypical.

Every trip we take deposits us at the same forking of the paths: 58 it can be a shortcut to alienation—removed from our home and distanced from our immediate surroundings, we can afford to be contemptuous of both; or it can be a voyage into renewal, as, leaving our selves and pasts at home and traveling light, we recover our innocence abroad. Abroad, we are all Titanias, so bedazzled by strangeness that we comically mistake asses for beauties; but away from home, we can also be Mirandas, so new to the world that our blind faith can become a kind of higher sight. "After living in Asia," John Krich quotes an old hand as saying, "you trust nobody, but you believe everything." At the same time, as Edmond Taylor wrote, Asia is "the school of doubt in which one learns faith in man." If every journey makes us wiser about the world, it also returns us to a sort of childhood. In alien parts, we speak more simply, in our own or some other language, move more freely, unencumbered by the histories that we carry around at home, and look more excitedly, with eyes of wonder. And if every trip worth taking is both a tragedy and a comedy, rich with melodrama and farce, it is also, at its heart, a love story. The romance with the foreign must certainly be leavened with a spirit of keen and unillusioned realism; but it must also be observed with a measure of faith.

QUESTIONS

1. Discuss to what extent Iyer's experience with Maung-Maung supports some of the generalizations he makes, earlier and later in the essay, about East-West relations. How, for example, does the encounter demonstrate both "unillusioned realism" and "a measure of faith" (paragraph 58), or "some of the paradoxes that haunt our talk of corruption" (paragraph 6)?

2. Iyer says that in his travels "cross-cultural affairs developed with all the contradictory twists and turns of any romance in which opposites attract and then retract and then don't know exactly where they stand" (paragraph 56). Where exactly do you think that Iyer and Maung-Maung stand after their encounter?

3. If you have had a more than superficial encounter with a guide, "tout," street person, or another local while visiting an unfamiliar place—whether close to home or far away—compare your experience to Iyer's. What did each of you have to gain, lose, or learn in the encounter?

The Age of Balkanization

PATRICK GLYNN

Today a fundamental change is under way in the character of global political life. A new era is in the making. Gone or fading are the great bipolar conflicts—between democracy and fascism, between democracy and Communism, and even perhaps between Left and Right—that shaped war and peace in the 20th century. In their place a new political struggle is emerging—more complex, more diffuse, but nonetheless global in character. 1

On every continent, in almost every major nation, and in almost every walk of life the overriding political reality today is that of increasing social separatism and fragmentation—a sometimes violent splintering of humanity by ethnic group, race, religion, and even (to a less dramatic extent) such characteristics as gender or sexual orientation. While the causes of this phenomenon are as yet imperfectly understood, its implications could hardly be more far-reaching. 2

The most dramatic manifestation of the change is found, of course, in the countries that used to be known as Yugoslavia and Czechoslovakia, and it is also showing itself in other parts of the defunct Soviet empire, not to mention the old Soviet Union itself. But the phenomenon is not merely one of Communism giving way to nationalism, nor is it confined to the old Communist world. 3

Indeed, everywhere one sees well-established nation-states threatened with disunion, and even in countries without explicit separatist movements, the unifying themes of political life are increasingly under attack. Canada copes with Quebec's secessionism, the United Kingdom with Scottish separatists, Italy with increasing tensions between its north and its south. In Germany, as well as in France and Britain, ethnically motivated violence has become a major factor in politics, and rebellious youths are inflamed by a puzzling new ideology of ethnic hatred. 4

Even in America—the proverbial melting pot—racial, ethnic, and other varieties of separatism are distinctly on the rise. Blacks assert 5

Patrick Glynn is a resident scholar at the American Enterprise Institute for Public Policy Research in Washington, D.C., a private "think tank" with a reputation for conservative politics. He is the editor of the American Enterprise Institute booklet *Unrest in the Soviet Union* (1989) and the author of *Closing Pandora's Box: Arms Races, Arms Control, and the History of the Cold War* (1992). This essay appeared in *Commentary*, a journal addressing contemporary issues published by the American Jewish Committee, in 1993.

their identity as "African-Americans"; homosexuals discover in their sexual orientation a basis for political action; Christian fundamentalists exert more and more influence as an organized political force.

Nor is this phenomenon merely political. It also finds its reflection 6 in the highest reaches of contemporary culture and intellectual life. The controversial doctrine of "multiculturalist education" and the "postmodernist" philosophy now so current in American universities are both essentially codifications of the new experience of fragmentation.

Side by side with this splintering, paradoxically, has gone a fresh 7 drive for unity. As the cold war was ending, George Bush, then still in the White House, hailed the advent of a Europe "whole and free," and in the lead-up to the Gulf war he spoke hopefully of a "new world order." Since then, European Community leaders have worked to forge a unitary Europe, while Germany's leadership has sought to make one nation out of two. In Russia, Boris Yeltsin fights a parallel battle, desperately trying to hold Russia together while moving toward democracy in the face of radical nationalism and mounting pressures for regional secession.

But these efforts at unification—including the effort to posit a new 8 world order based on common democratic values—have thus far proved unable to stem the powerful counter-currents rooted in separatist identities. For this new cultural struggle is taking place not only within nations, but among them. Attempts to expand the postwar liberal trading order have been frustrated by intensified cultural conflict between America and Japan and, to a lesser extent, between America and Western Europe. Islamic fundamentalism poses a threat to moderate Arab regimes and increases the likelihood of eventual armed conflict between the West and radical Arab states.

Slowly this clash between, on the one hand, ethnic (and other 9 types of) particularism and, on the other hand, what might be called democratic universalism seems to be replacing the old Left-Right and class polarities that have governed political life for nearly a century. It has every appearance of becoming the new bipolarity of global politics, the new dialectic of a new age.

What are the reasons for this great shift? The most obvious cause 10 would seem to lie in the collapse of Soviet Communism. Communism repressed national differences; indeed, Marxist-Leninist ideology, rooted as it was in Enlightenment economic thinking, defined national and ethnic differences as epiphenomenal, stressing instead the primacy of class. Under Communism, nationalism was either disguised or stifled.

What we have seen since the breakdown of Communism— 11 whether in the former Soviet Union, the former Yugoslavia, or the rest of Eastern Europe—is, to borrow a phrase from Sigmund Freud, a "return of the repressed," a resurgence of powerful national and ethnic feelings which had been simmering angrily beneath the surface.

But if Communist regimes ruthlessly imposed unity on their own 12 peoples, they also evoked a more or less united response from the outside world they threatened. The unitary nature of the Communist threat inspired an unprecedented degree of cooperation—under American leadership—among heretofore uncooperative states. European adversaries laid aside age-old grudges to join NATO. New security relationships were forged among the United States and major Asian nations, including Japan.

To be sure, Woodrow Wilson and Franklin Roosevelt had earlier 13 sought on their own initiative to structure a more or less unified world order, to export America's stated principles of ethnic tolerance, and to bring the many nations of the world together on the basis of common interests and goals. But it is far from clear that, absent the Soviet threat, so many disparate nations would have been so successful in achieving collaboration, not just on trade but on a host of diplomatic and security matters, as they were during the cold war. Long ago the sociologist Georg Simmel posited that human societies were cemented together by the need to cope with outside threats. This was clearly true of what we used to call the "free world."

Even within American politics, the anti-Communist imperative 14 had a powerful unifying effect. It produced, albeit intermittently, bipartisanship in foreign policy. It also, at various times, unified each of the two major parties. In the early years of the cold war, the Democrats, and in the later years, the Republicans, found a basis for party solidarity in the anti-Communist cause. So much was this the case that when the Democrats and then the Republicans experienced ruinous internal division, it was owing in part to a perceived or real diminution of the Soviet threat—for the Democrats during the late 1960s and early 1970s, when many believed the cold war to have become obsolete, and for the Republicans in recent years, when it became plain that the cold war was in fact over.

The Republican case is especially interesting, for what else but fear 15 of the Soviet threat could finally have held together the diverse elements of Ronald Reagan's winning electoral coalition: Christian fundamentalists, Jewish neoconservative intellectuals, free-market libertarians, blue-collar Democrats, and traditional Republican voters? Should it surprise us that with the subsidence of the Soviet threat, old party alignments would weaken? Is it illogical that with external dangers reduced we would turn inward as a society and discover social and political differences among one another that we had previously been willing to overlook?

Yet while the collapse of Soviet Communism remains the signal 16
event of our age, many of the trends we are discussing were apparent
before the Berlin Wall came down. Ethnic, national, and racial awareness was already growing, on both sides of the iron curtain. Here in
America, for example, the multiculturalist movement—now so famous
and controversial for its advocacy of heightened ethnic and racial consciousness in schools—was already making inroads into secondary and
higher education. On both sides of the iron curtain, faith in central authority was declining and had been declining for some time. Even before the advent of Mikhail Gorbachev, Western Sovietologists debated
whether Communist leaders still actually believed their ideology.
Ironically, a weakening in the influence of received values—society's
traditional unifying ideas—was apparent in our own culture as well,
observed by intellectuals and documented by opinion polls.

In other words, it is hard to say whether the demise of Soviet 17
Communism is the ultimate cause of the change we are witnessing, or
whether Soviet Communism itself fell victim to some vaster trend,
some grand Hegelian shift in human consciousness.

Certainly the contemporary experience of social and political frag- 18
mentation was foreshadowed by new directions in intellectual life, long
before the social consequences were apparent. One of the major proponents of "postmodernist" thinking, Fredric Jameson of Duke University,
has written of the postmodern idiom in contemporary literature:

> Perhaps the immense fragmentation and privatization of modern lit-
> erature—its explosion into a host of distinct private styles and man-
> nerisms—foreshadow deeper and more general trends in social life
> as a whole. Supposing that modern art and modernism—far from
> being a kind of specialized aesthetic curiosity—actually anticipated
> social developments along these lines; supposing that in the decades
> since the emergence of the great modern styles society has itself
> begun to fragment in this way, each group coming to speak a curious
> private language of its own, each profession developing its own pri-
> vate code or idiolect, and finally each individual coming to be a kind
> of linguistic island, separated from everyone else?

Behind this new experience of cultural and intellectual fragmenta- 19
tion lies a loss of faith in general truths, and even, at its most radical, a
loss of faith in the very possibility of general truths. Notably, the most
sophisticated humanities instructors in our major universities today
will no longer venture to assert that a proposition is "true," merely that
it is "productive" or "intriguing," i.e., a basis for reflection or intellectual play. This premise lends a notable arbitrariness to "postmodern"
modes of expression, robbing contemporary literature, criticism, and
even philosophy of a certain weight, authority, or seriousness.

The same mixture of posturing and pastiche has become evident 20
in our political discourse (think back to Bush's Gulf war speeches).
However glorious the phrases—"freedom," "tyranny," "new world
order"—they are uttered today with a certain self-conscious nostalgia.

We have lived through an era when people attached themselves to 21
grand ideas—whether for good or for evil—and fought and sometimes
died for them. But for some reason these ideas collectively seem to be
losing their force. Such is the defining tendency of our age.

The resulting fragmentation is far from being a propitious devel- 22
opment. At stake, one could argue, is the future of civilization itself.
The struggle for civilization has always been a struggle for unity, universality, ecumenism. The great ages of civilization have been periods
of concord and commonality, when large tracts of the globe were more
or less united by common values, and sometimes even by a common
language and common laws—the Roman empire, the era of
Charlemagne, the Renaissance, the 19th-century Concert of Europe.
These periods have been succeeded in turn by periods of fragmentation, factional strife, and relative barbarism: the Dark Ages, the feudal
era, the Reformation with its religious wars, and of course the long
"civil war" that wrenched Europe between 1914 and 1945. Looking
back, one can see that Western history has been marked by a cyclical
pattern in which unifying ideas triumph, only gradually to lose their
hold on the imagination and to be replaced by factional struggle and
particularism.

It is possible that we are on the threshold of a new such cyclical turn. 23

At the root of the problem lies the very large and very deep question 24
of human identity. In a sense, the master-idea of Western civilization is
the view that the identifying feature of the human being qua human
being is the faculty of reason. When the Greek philosophers hit upon this
notion of man as the rational animal, they made possible the creation of
large political orders on a basis other than that of pure despotism.

Furthermore, as Socrates and his students saw, this conception tran- 25
scended differences of nationality and race: rational man could not be
defined as Athenian or Spartan or even Greek or barbarian. And with
this insight, the philosophers ceased to be good citizens of their cities,
their *poleis*, at least in the terms of those cities: they became citizens of
the rational universe—to use a somewhat later term, cosmopolitans—
and they challenged the laws and gods of their fellow citizens.

It was this cosmopolitan vision, as Hans Jonas pointed out in his 26
famous study of the gnostic religion, that helped define the ambitions
of Alexander the Great. Alexander, a student of Aristotle, created the
first great Western empire—the Hellenic empire—based on universalist
principles. He was the first leader to unify the "West."

The Romans, having imbibed Greek learning, revived and reinsti- 27 tutionalized Greek rationalism as they gradually transformed themselves from a republic into an empire. By the time of the early empire, to be a Roman citizen—a *civis Romanus*—no longer meant to belong to the tribes of the Romans. Now it meant to fulfill certain formal and legal requirements of citizenship, often through military service. Thus Paul, an ethnic Jew who became a Christian, could also be a Roman citizen. By the 3rd century, Roman citizenship was extended to all freemen of the empire.

This unifying idea allowed for the organization of a vast political 28 system that granted a measure of freedom to individuals while protecting the general peace: the *pax Romana*. Systematically, step by step, the Romans replaced local laws rooted in local cults and customs with Roman law, which was rational, universal, and said to be derived from the law of nature, rationally understood. It is from *civis* that our word "civilization" comes.

For more than 1,000 years after the disintegration of the empire, 29 tumultuous Europe looked back on imperial Rome as the lamented Golden Age. Hence the ambition of the greatest statesmen of Europe was to recreate the unity of Rome on whatever scale they could. That was the signal achievement of Charlemagne, or Charles the Great, who unified a large region of Europe stretching from south of the Pyrenees to the Elbe, placed it under more rational administration, and was crowned emperor of the West in his time.

Charlemagne, however, was unable to secure his legacy, and 30 slowly Europe descended into feudalism and the wars of the barons. Yet over time the Church—which had been touched by classical culture from the beginning, and which explicitly assimilated the Greco-Roman idea through the work of Aquinas and others—became a more rational and more catholic institution, providing a measure of unity to European life. This in turn prepared the stage for the full recovery in the Renaissance of the classical idea of rational man.

Periods when this idea of man is in the ascendancy have been the 31 great periods of civilization as we in the West know it. It is during such periods that peace reigns, learning spreads and advances, and the arts flourish. Yet experience shows that this idea does not hold indefinitely.

Perhaps the reason simply has to do with the inherent restless- 32 ness of human beings. When it first appears on the scene, the idea of rational man has a demythologizing force; it is an exploder of myth. Socrates' notion of rational man was subversive of the laws, customs, and gods of Athens—which is why he was condemned to death by his fellow citizens. Roman law, too, was subversive of local traditions and local religions; it was the "modern" idea of its era. The Renaissance was anti-traditional in the same sense—introducing ideas from the classics that raised questions about Christian beliefs.

Perhaps human beings have an overriding need for myth, or per-   33 haps the act of demythologization always contains within it the seeds of its own destruction. At any rate, periods of demythologization tend to be followed by periods of remythologization. Secular, rationalistic Hellenic culture was eventually challenged by the religious intensities and excesses of gnosticism. Roman imperial rationality gradually gave way to Christianity. The rationality of the Renaissance gave way to the religious wars of the Reformation.

Remythologization and reversion to ethnic particularism have   34 tended to go hand in hand. People cease to find satisfactory selfhood in large unities, become alienated from the larger whole, and begin to seek identity in smaller units. Such periods are characterized by diminished will on the part of those who stand for reason to defend reason, by a diminished appeal of reason to the human imagination. Civilization is destroyed by those whose attachment to religious or ethnic identity gives them the zeal which the defenders of reason come to lack. Civilization falls victim to barbarians from without and zealots from within. In such periods, as Yeats famously wrote, "The best lack all conviction, while the worst/ Are full of passionate intensity."

There are hints of all this in the emerging mood of our own time.   35 The ferocious war in the Balkans is but one manifestation of a reemergent barbarism apparent in many corners of the earth. In the Balkans, the voices of the rational and the tolerant—for example, officials of the secular-minded Bosnian government—have been drowned out by the guns of ethnic fanatics. Efforts to secure democracy on the basis of rational Western principles have been crushed by the bloodthirsty exponents of "ethnic cleansing."

The new barbarians differ fundamentally from the old enemies of   36 liberal democracy in feeling no need to justify themselves before the court of reason. The Communists, too, practiced barbarism, but they harbored a powerful imperative to vindicate themselves on the basis of some general truth: hence their elaborate ideology. Paradoxically, it was to prove they had the truth that they fashioned huge tissues of lies. Much the same was true of the Nazis, who invented the technique of the Big Lie.

The new tyrants—such characters as Slobodan Milosevic, Radovan   37 Karadzic, or for that matter Saddam Hussein—feel no such pressures. They offer as justification for their actions the thinnest pretexts. Their explanations are less an appeal to reason than a pure gesture of defiance.

Precisely because these tyrants lack intellectual seriousness, we are   38 likely to discount them. But we forget that the great ideological struggle that characterized most of our century was the exception rather than the rule in history. Usually the enemies of civilization have not been so intellectually well-armed as the Communists (and even, in their way, the Nazis) were; but despite this they have often succeeded in prevailing. The once-mighty Romans, after all, were finally defeated by forces culturally, intellectually, and technologically inferior to them.

Like the Romans, we have been slow to understand the nature of 39 the incipient threat. Indeed, only now are we beginning to see the gravity of the issues at stake when tyrants motivated by nothing more complicated than primitive ethnic fanaticism are allowed to get away with mass murder.

Nor is this problem merely one of foreign policy or regional con- 40 flict. The very idea of rational man—the cardinal concept of our civilization—is, as we have already seen, under explicit attack in our own universities. Our students are today being taught that such categories as "African-American," "female," or "person of color" are in effect more fundamental than the category of American, let alone of rational man, the human being qua human being.

While the motives and consequences may be vastly different in the 41 two cases, the multiculturalist doctrine that is fragmenting our universities as well as our intellectual life, and the "ethnic cleansing" of the Serbs, belong to the same troubling cultural and historical moment.

It is especially disturbing that this should be happening here, for 42 America has always been the most rationally constituted of nations. It is the heir and perfecter of the great Roman idea of the *civis,* a country where nationality has nothing to do with ethnicity, a nation which has fought, through civil war and great domestic turmoil, to realize, however imperfectly, the principle of universality and tolerance.

We are now in an age that will move either toward ever greater 43 fragmentation and violence or toward the ever wider spread of the tolerance and rationality by which we in the West have learned to live and prosper. As was true for most of this century, it is American leadership that will determine the path that history finally takes.

QUESTIONS

1. According to Glynn, what constitutes today's "fundamental change" in global politics? Draw a diagram or web of how Glynn understands the causes of this change, distinguishing between more obvious and immediate causes and deeper, historical causes.

2. Is it your experience, as Glynn claims, that "the very idea of rational man—the cardinal concept of our civilization—is . . . under attack in our universities," or that you are "being taught that such categories as 'African-American,' 'female,' or 'person of color' are in effect more fundamental than the category of American" (paragraph 40)?

3. How persuaded are you by Glynn's argument that multiculturalism at home and "ethnic cleansing" in the Balkans have the same cultural and historical roots?

A View from Below

NOAM CHOMSKY

There have been important changes in the international order in the 1
past several decades, but the continuities are no less significant, particularly with regard to North-South relations. Although U.S. policies toward the Third World were framed within a Cold War context, that was more a matter of doctrinal utility than of fact. The North-South conflicts, with their deep roots in the colonial era, are likely to continue as the policies of the United States and other advanced industrial powers are adapted to changing circumstances, of which the end of the Cold War is only one aspect.

By the 1970s, the United States had lost its post-World War II posi- 2
tion of overwhelming dominance, and there was speculation about competing trading blocs (dollar, yen, European Currency Union). While it remains the leading economic power, the United States faces serious internal problems, exacerbated by policies of the past decade whose social and economic costs cannot be indefinitely deferred. At the same time, Soviet military expenditures were levelling off and internal problems were mounting, with economic stagnation and increasing pressures for an end to tyrannical rule. A few years later, the Soviet system had collapsed. The Cold War ended with the victory of what had always been the far richer and more powerful contestant. The Soviet collapse was part of a much more general economic catastrophe of the 1980s, more severe in the Third World domains of the West than in the Soviet empire.

Noam Chomsky is Institute Professor in linguistics and philosophy at Massachusetts Institute of Technology (MIT). His work in theoretical linguistics has been very influential in the social sciences and in the newly emerging field of cognitive science. Since the 1960s, he has also written many books offering radical critiques of American foreign policy and mainstream media, including *Necessary Illusions: Thought Control in Democratic Societies* (1989), *Deterring Democracy* (1991), *Year 501: The Conquest Continues* (1992), and *Rethinking Camelot: JFK, the Vietnam War, and U.S. Political Culture* (1993). A documentary film about Chomsky, *Manufacturing Consent: Noam Chomsky and the Media,* was released in 1992. The essay that appears here was part of a 1992 symposium on "The End of the Cold War" in *Diplomatic History,* the scholarly journal of the Society for Historians of American Foreign Relations. The editor of *Diplomatic History* asked Chomsky and the other contributors "to write a 'think-piece' on the subject of the symposium, a longer, more historically informed version of the kind of essay that appears on the editorial page of the best newspapers."

As commonly observed, the global system has become economi-   3
cally tripolar but militarily unipolar. The Soviet empire is in disarray,
and in much of the Third World, economic decline and violence, often
conducted or backed by the West, have left a grim and ominous
legacy. These developments have elicited much triumphalism in the
West, but Third World reactions have been different, not surprisingly.

In concluding its report *The Challenge to the South*, the nongovern-   4
mental South Commission called for a "new world order" that will respond to "the South's plea for justice, equity, and democracy in the
global society," though its analysis offers little basis for hope.[1] Some
months later, George Bush appropriated the phrase "new world
order" as part of the rhetorical background for his war in the Gulf. The
Third World did not join in the enthusiastic U.S. welcome for the vision proclaimed by the president. Most shared the interpretation of *Die
Zeit* editor Theo Sommer, who saw "an unabashed exercise in national
self-interest, only thinly veiled by invocations of principle."[2] In a typical Third World reaction, the Jesuit journal *Proceso* (El Salvador)
warned of the "ominous halo of hypocrisy, the seed of new crises and
resentments." "This hypocrisy," it continued, "is extreme in the case of
the United States, the leader of the allied forces and the most war-
mongering of them all, whose recent history includes the invasion of
Grenada and the military occupation of Panama."[3] Cardinal Paulo
Evaristo Arns of São Paulo captured the general mood when he wrote
that in the Arab countries "the rich sided with the U.S. government
while the *millions* of poor condemned this military aggression."
Throughout the Third World, he continued, "there is hatred and fear:
When will they decide to invade us," and on what pretext?[4]

When the president declared that the United States "has a new   5
credibility" and that dictators and tyrants everywhere know that
"what we say goes," few voices in the South celebrated the dawn of
"an era full of promise."[5] Bush's words are more likely to evoke memories of Palmerston declaring that the capture of an Afghan fort would
"cow all Asia and make everything more easy for us."[6] "Credibility"
and "prestige" have always been the watchwords of empire. It is
hardly surprising that the *Times of India* should describe Bush's Gulf

[1]*The Challenge to the South*, Report of the South Commission, Julius K. Nyerere, Chairman (Oxford, 1990), 287.

[2]*Guardian* (London), 13 April 1991.

[3]Editorial, *Proceso*, 23 January 1991.

[4]Foreword, Thomas Fox, *Iraq* (Kansas City, 1991), ix.

[5]Bush, 1 February 1991, quoted in Robert Parry, "The Peace Feeler that Was," *Nation*, 15 April 1991. James Baker, "Why America is in the Gulf," address to the Los Angeles World Affairs Council, 29 October 1990.

[6]Quoted in V. G. Kiernan, *European Empires from Conquest to Collapse, 1815–1960* (London, 1982), 158.

war as an effort to establish a "regional Yalta where the powerful
nations agree among themselves to a share of Arab spoils," a war that
"has revealed the seamiest sides of Western civilisation: its unre-
stricted appetite for dominance, its morbid fascination for hi-tech military might, its insensitivity to 'alien' cultures, its appalling jingoism."[7]
And Third World observers readily understand that Bush's words are
not directed to dictators and tyrants, but to anyone who steps out of
line. The United States and its allies have been happy to support the
most murderous brutes—Saddam Hussein is only the most recent
example—and to destroy democratic forces, as calculations of self-
interest dictate.

In the old world order, the South was assigned a service function: 6
for example, to provide resources, cheap labor, markets, and opportunities for investment and for the export of pollution. The primary
threat to U.S. interests has therefore always been "radical and nation-
alistic regimes" that are responsive to popular pressures for "immediate improvement in the low living standards of the masses" and for
diversification of the economies, tendencies that conflict with the
need to protect sources of raw materials and to encourage "a political
and economic climate conducive to private investment" and to the
repatriation of "a reasonable return" on foreign investment.[8]
Applauding the overthrow of the parliamentary Mossadegh regime,
the *New York Times* editors warned that "underdeveloped countries
with rich resources now have an object lesson in the heavy cost that
must be paid by one of their number which goes berserk with fanatical nationalism."[9] The record is also replete with self-congratulatory
flourishes. As in the case of any state, these are to be evaluated in
terms of the historical record, which conforms well to the harsher
doctrines.

The North-South conflict takes new forms with changing circum-   7
stances, but the basic themes are resilient. After World War I, British
imperial managers realized that it would be more efficient to rule the
Middle East behind an "Arab Facade," with "absorption" of the
colonies "veiled by constitutional fictions as a protectorate, a sphere of
influence, a buffer State, and so on."[10] Today, there are gestures to formal
democracy and diversity, but within strict limits. Summarizing policies conducted "with the best of intentions," Robert Pastor writes that

---

[7]Quoted in William Dalrymple, "Crazy for Saddam," *Spectator* (London), 23 February 1991.

[8]NSC 5432/1, 3 September 1954, U.S. Department of State, *Foreign Relations of the United States, 1952–1954* (Washington, 1984), 4:81ff.

[9]Editorial, *New York Times*, 6 August 1954.

[10]Lord Curzon (and Eastern Committee), 24 April 1918, and Curzon memorandum, 12 December 1917, cited by William Stivers, *Supremacy and Oil: Iraq, Turkey, and the Anglo-American World Order, 1918–1930* (Ithaca, 1982), 28, 34.

"the United States did not want to control Nicaragua or the other nations in the region, but it also did not want to allow developments to
get out of control. It wanted Nicaraguans to act independently, *except*
when doing so would affect U.S. interests adversely."[11] One consequence of this interpretation of freedom of choice is the persistent U.S.
opposition to democracy, unless the rule of reliable business and
landowning interests is assured. Another is the resort to coercive
means: subversion, terror, aggression, economic warfare.

Fear of what is called "communism" is rooted in the same con-   8
cerns. One important study identifies the threat as the economic transformation of the Communist powers "in ways that reduce their willingness and ability to complement the industrial economies of the
West."[12] Unlike us, the "Communists" could "appeal directly to the
masses," Eisenhower complained.[13] The Dulles brothers, in private
conversation, deplored the Communist "ability to get control of mass
movements," "something we have no capacity to duplicate." "The
poor people are the ones they appeal to and they have always wanted
to plunder the rich."[14] The same concerns extended to "the preferential option for the poor" of the Latin American bishops and other
commitments to independent development or democracy in more
than form, and also to such friends as Mussolini, Trujillo, Noriega, and
Saddam Hussein when they "get out of control."

From 1917 to the 1980s, the "Communist threat" provided the ide-   9
ological framework for intervention, including intervention in Russia
itself after the Bolshevik revolution. This was a defensive action, John
Lewis Gaddis argues, "in response to a profound and potentially far-
reaching intervention by the new Soviet government in the internal affairs, not just of the West, but of virtually every country in the world,"
namely, "the Revolution's challenge . . . to the very survival of the
capitalist order."[15] The reasoning applies to a huge country or a speck
in the Caribbean: intervention is entirely warranted in defense against
a change in the social order, interfering with the service function,
and a declaration of revolutionary intentions. The danger is magnified
because "the rot may spread" and the "virus" may "infect" others,
to borrow familiar terms. Although the Sandinista "revolution without borders" was a government-media fabrication, the propaganda

---

[11]Pastor, *Condemned to Repetition* (Princeton, 1987), 32.

[12]William Yandell Elliot, ed., *The Political Economy of American Foreign Policy* (New York, 1955), 42.

[13]Eisenhower to Harriman, quoted in Richard H. Immerman, "Confessions of an Eisenhower Revisionist," *Diplomatic History* 14 (Summer 1990): 319–42.

[14]John Foster Dulles telephone call to Allen Dulles, 19 June 1958, "Minutes of telephone conversations of John Foster Dulles and Christian Herter," Dwight D. Eisenhower Library, Abilene, Kansas.

[15]John Lewis Gaddis, *The Long Peace: Inquiries into the History of the Cold War* (New York, 1987), 10.

images reflected an authentic and traditional concern: from the perspective of a hegemonic power, declaration of an intent to provide a model that will inspire others amounts to aggression.

The Cold War itself had important North-South dimensions. 10 Soviet domains had in part been quasi-colonial dependencies of the West, which were removed from the Third World and pursued an independent path, no longer available "to complement the industrial economies of the West."[16] Furthermore, the Soviet Union offered a model of development that was not without appeal in the Third World, particularly in earlier years. Conventional practice is to contrast Eastern and Western Europe, which have not been similar in historical memory, but more realistic comparisons (for example, to Brazil or Guatemala) have led Third World commentators to rather different conclusions. Soviet power and brutality also offered a ready rationalization, however thin, for Third World intervention; Woodrow Wilson needed different pretexts when he sent marines to Hispaniola, just as Bush needs others today. Finally, the Soviet Union and its satellites interfered with Western exploitation and control over the South by supporting independent nationalist movements, and Soviet power had a deterrent effect, limiting the ability of the United States and its allies to exercise force for fear of confrontation with a dangerous enemy. These have been crucial features of the Cold War era. They help to explain Third World trepidations as the Cold War ends and provide certain guidelines for what may lie ahead.

One consequence of the collapse of the Soviet bloc is that much of 11 it may undergo a kind of "Latin Americanization," reverting to the service role, with the ex-*nomenklatura* perhaps taking on the role of the Third World elites linked to international business and financial interests. A second is that a new ideological framework is needed for intervention. The problem of the vanishing pretext arose through the 1980s, requiring a propaganda shift to international terrorists, Hispanic narcotraffickers, crazed Arabs, and other chimeras. A third consequence is the collapse of the Soviet deterrent, which "makes military power more useful as a United States foreign policy instrument . . . against those who contemplate challenging important American interests,"[17] an insight echoed by Elliott Abrams during the invasion of Panama and by commentators during the Gulf crisis, who noted that the United States could now send armed forces to the region without concern.

There are, however, several factors that are likely to inhibit the 12 resort to force. Among them are the successes of the past years in

---

[16]Elliot, ed., *Political Economy.*
[17]Dimitri K. Simes, "If the Cold War Is Over, Then What?," *New York Times,* 27 December 1988.

crushing popular nationalist and reform tendencies, the elimination of
the "Communist" appeal to those who hope to "plunder the rich," and
the economic catastrophes of the last decade. In the light of these developments, limited forms of diversity and independence can be tolerated with less concern that they will lead to meaningful change.
Control can be exercised by economic measures: structural adjustment, the IMF regimen, selective resort to free trade measures, and so
forth. Needless to say, the successful industrial powers do not accept
these rules for themselves, and never have. But for the purposes of
domination and exploitation, there is great merit in imposing them on
the weak: the Third World and its likely new members in the East.

Another inhibiting factor is that the domestic base for foreign   13
adventures has eroded. A leaked fragment of an early Bush administration national security review observes that "much weaker enemies"
must be defeated "decisively and rapidly"; any other outcome would
be "embarrassing" and might "undercut political support."[18] The
Reagan administration was forced to resort on an unprecedented scale
to clandestine terror and proxy forces because political support for violent intervention was so thin. And it has been necessary to whip up
impressive propaganda campaigns to portray "much weaker enemies" as threats to our very existence, so as to mobilize a frightened
population to at least temporary support for decisive and rapid action.

Still another problem is that German-led Europe and Japan have   14
their own interests, which may not conform to those of the United
States, though there is a shared interest in subduing Third World independence, and the internationalization of capital gives competition
among national states a different cast than in earlier periods.

Yet another impediment is that the United States no longer has the   15
economic base for intervention, a fact that has led to proposals that it
take on "a more explicitly mercenary role than it has played in the
past."[19] We must become "willing mercenaries," financial editor
William Neikirk of the *Chicago Tribune* advises, using our "monopoly
power" in the "security market" to maintain "our control over the
world economic system," selling "protection" to other wealthy powers
who will pay us a "war premium."[20] The profits of Gulf oil production
must also be available to help support the economies of the United
States and its British associate, who will carry out the enforcer role.

[18]Maureen Dowd, "Bush Gamble: More War, Not Inconclusive Diplomacy," *New York Times*,
23 February 1991.
[19]David Hale "How to pay for the global policeman," *Financial Times* (London), 21 November
1990.
[20]William Neikirk, "We are the world's guardian angels," *Chicago Tribune*, 9 September 1990;
"Supercost to be sole superpower," ibid., 27 January 1991.

These developments are foreshadowed in British and American internal documents after the Iraqi military coup of 1958, which emphasize that Kuwaiti oil and investment must remain available to prop up the ailing British economy.[21] By the 1970s, such concerns extended to the United States as well, a significant factor in Middle East policy.

Events of the recent past illustrate the interplay of these factors. As [16] the South Commission observed, there were some gestures to Third World concerns in the 1970s, "undoubtedly spurred" by concern over "the newly found assertiveness of the South after the rise in oil prices in 1973." As the threat abated, the industrial societies lost interest and turned to "a new form of neo-colonialism," monopolizing control over the world economy, undermining the more democratic elements of the United Nations, and in general proceeding to institutionalize "the South's second class status."[22] Japan and the EC recovered from the recession of the early 1980s, though they did not resume earlier growth rates. U.S. recovery involved massive state stimulation of the economy, mainly through the Pentagon-based public subsidy to high technology industry, along with a sharp increase in protectionist measures and a rise in interest rates. This contributed to the crisis of the South, as interest payments on the debt rose while investment and aid declined, and the wealthy classes invested their riches in the West. There was a huge capital flow from South to North, with effects that were generally catastrophic, apart from the NICs[23] of East Asia, where the state is powerful enough to control capital flight and direct the economy efficiently.

The first years of the post-Cold War era reveal how little has [17] changed, tactical adjustments aside. With Gorbachev's "new thinking" (that is, the decline of Soviet support for targets of U.S. attack, and of the Soviet deterrent), overt intervention became a more feasible option, but on condition that it be "decisive and rapid" and accompanied by massive propaganda campaigns of demonization. Immediately after the fall of the Berlin Wall, symbolically ending the Cold War, Bush inaugurated the new era by invading Panama, restoring the rule of the tiny white minority and returning the security forces to U.S. control. The United States vetoed two Security Council condemnations, joined in one case by the United Kingdom and France. All of this is so familiar as barely to merit a footnote in history, but there were some novelties. Even the most fertile imagination could not conjure up a

---

[21]For a review of these see my *Deterring Democracy* (London, 1991), 183f.
[22]*The Challenge to the South*, 216ff., 71f.
[23]Newly industrializing countries. (Ed.)

Soviet threat, so new pretexts were needed. And, as noted, there was 18 no concern over a Soviet response.

Reactions to the invasion north and south of the Rio Grande differed sharply. In the United States, opinion hailed "Operation Just Cause." In contrast, the Group of Eight Latin American democracies, which had suspended Panama because of Noriega's crimes, expelled it permanently as a country under military occupation. In August 1990, a Panamanian presidential commission called for an end to the "occupation of the State and its territory by U.S. troops" and the reestablishment of national sovereignty. A leading Honduran journal denounced the "international totalitarianism" of George Bush "in the guise of 'democracy.' " Bush, it said, has "declared plainly to Latin America that for the North American government, there is no law— only its will—when imposing its designs on the hemisphere." "We live in a climate of aggression and disrespect," "hurt by our poverty, our weakness, our naked dependence, the absolute submission of our feeble nations to the service of an implacable superpower. Latin America 19 is in pain."[24]

The second act of post-Cold War aggression was Iraq's invasion of Kuwait, shifting Saddam Hussein overnight from friend and favored trading partner to reincarnation of Attila the Hun, the familiar pattern when some murderous tyrant steps out of line. The United States and United Kingdom moved quickly to bar the diplomatic track, for fear that peaceful means might "defuse the crisis" with "a few token gains" for their former friend, as the administration position was outlined by *Times* diplomatic correspondent Thomas Friedman.[25] The war policy was strongly opposed by the population in the region. The Iraqi democratic opposition, always rebuffed by Washington, opposed U.S. policy throughout: the pre-August 1990 support for the Iraqi dictator, the resort to war rather than peaceful means, and finally the tacit support for Saddam Hussein as he crushed the Shi'ite and Kurdish rebellions. One leading spokesman, banker Ahmad Chalabi, who described the outcome of the war as "the worst of all possible worlds" for the Iraqi people, attributed the U.S. stand to its traditional policy of "supporting dictatorships to maintain stability." In Egypt, the one Arab ally with a degree of internal freedom, the semiofficial press wrote that the outcome demonstrated that the United States only wanted to cut Iraq down to size and thus to establish its own unchallenged hegemony, in "collusion with Saddam himself" if necessary, agreeing with the

---

[24]Inter Press Service, *Latinamerica press* (Lima), 30 August 1990. *Tiempo* (Honduras), 5 January 1990.

[25]Friedman, "Behind Bush's Hard Line," *New York Times*, 22 August 1991.

"savage beast" on the need to "block any progress and abort all hopes, however dim, for freedom or equality and for progress towards democracy."[26]

The United Nations suffered further blows. Since it fell "out of   20 control" by the 1960s, the United States has been far in the lead in vetoing Security Council resolutions and hampering UN activities generally. The invasion of Kuwait was unusual in that the United States and the United Kingdom opposed an act of international violence, and thus did not block the usual condemnations and efforts to reverse the crime. But under U.S. pressure, the Security Council was compelled to wash its hands of the matter, radically violating the UN Charter by leaving individual states free to respond to the aggression as they chose. Further U.S. pressures prevented the council from responding to the call of member states for meetings, as stipulated by council rules that the United States had vigorously upheld when they served its interests. That Washington has little use for diplomatic means or institutions of world order, unless they can be used as instruments of its own power, has been dramatically illustrated in Southeast Asia, the Middle East, Central America, and elsewhere. Nothing is likely to change in this regard.

Hostility to meaningful democracy also continued without change.   21 As the Berlin Wall fell, elections were held in Honduras in "an inspiring example of the democratic promise that today is spreading throughout the Americas," in George Bush's words.[27] The candidates represented large landowners and wealthy industrialists, with close ties to the military, the effective rulers, under U.S. control. Their political programs were virtually identical, and the campaign was largely restricted to insults and entertainment. Human rights abuses by the security forces escalated before the election. Starvation and misery were rampant, having increased during the "decade of democracy," along with capital flight and the debt burden. But there was no major threat to order, or to investors.

At the same time, the electoral campaign opened in Nicaragua. Its   22 1984 elections do not exist in U.S. commentary, though they were favorably described by a host of observers, including Western government and parliamentary delegations and a study group of the Latin American Studies Association. The elections could not be controlled, and therefore are not an inspiring example of democracy. Taking no chances with the long-scheduled 1990 elections, Bush announced as

---

[26]Ahmad Chalabi, "What the Iraqi Resistance Wants," *Wall Street Journal*, 8 April 1991; *Mideast Mirror* (London), 15 March 1991. Salaheddin Hafez, deputy editor, *al-Ahram*, 9 April 1991, quoted in *Mideast Mirror*, 10 April 1991.

[27]Associated Press, 17 April 1990.

the campaign opened that the embargo would be lifted if his candidate won. The White House and Congress renewed their support for the contra forces in violation of the agreement of the Central American presidents and the judgment of the World Court. Nicaraguans were thus informed that only a vote for the U.S. candidate would end the terror and illegal economic warfare. In Latin America, the electoral results were generally interpreted as a victory for George Bush, even by those who celebrated the outcome. In a typical reaction, a Guatemala City journal attributed the result to "ten years of economic and military aggressions waged by a government with unlimited resources": "It was a vote in search of peace by a people that, inevitably, were fed up with violence, . . . a vote from a hungry people that, more than any idea, need to eat." In the United States, in contrast, the result was hailed as a "Victory for U.S. Fair Play," with "Americans United in Joy," as *New York Times* headlines put it.[28]

Again expressing traditional attitudes, a Latin American Strategy Development Workshop at the Pentagon in September 1990 concludes that current relations with the Mexican dictatorship are "extraordinarily positive," untroubled by stolen elections, death squads, endemic torture, scandalous treatment of workers and peasants, and so forth. But "a 'democracy opening' in Mexico could test the special relationship by bringing into office a government more interested in challenging the U.S. on economic and nationalist grounds," the fundamental concern over many years.[29]

The first post-Cold War National Security Strategy report sent to Congress, in March 1990, recognized that military power must target the Third World, primarily the Middle East, where the "threats to our interests" that have required force "could not be laid at the Kremlin's door," a fact now acknowledged. Furthermore, the Soviet pretext for military spending having disappeared, the threat now becomes "the growing technological sophistication of Third World conflicts." The United States must therefore strengthen its "defense industrial base," with incentives "to invest in new facilities and equipment as well as in research and development," and develop further forward basing and counterinsurgency and low-intensity conflict capacities.[30] In brief, the prime concerns continue to be control of the South and support for high tech industry at home, with the ideological framework adapted to new contingencies.

[28]Guatemala City journal quoted in *Central America Report* (Guatemala City), 2 March 1990. David Shipler, "Nicaragua, Victory for U.S. Fair Play," op-ed, *New York Times,* 1 March 1990. Elaine Sciolino, "Americans United in Joy, But Divided over Policy," ibid., 27 February 1990. For review of Latin American and U.S. reaction see Chomsky, *Deterring Democracy,* chap. 10.

[29]*Latin America Strategy Development Workshop,* 26 and 27 September 1990, minutes, 3. Andrew Reding, "Mexico's Democratic Challenge," *World Policy Journal* (Spring 1991).

[30]*National Security Strategy of the United States,* the White House, March 1990.

The use of force to control the Third World is a last resort. Econo-   25
mic weapons are far more efficient. Some of the newer mechanisms can
be seen in the GATT[31] negotiations. Western powers call for liberalization when it is in their interest, and for enhanced protection when that
is in their interest. One major U.S. concern is the "new themes": guar-
antees for "intellectual property rights," such as patents and software,
that will enable transnational corporations to monopolize new technology; and removal of constraints on services and investment, which will
undermine national development programs in the Third World and effectively place investment decisions in the hands of TNCs and the financial institutions of the North. These are "issues of greater magni-
tude" than the more publicized conflict over agricultural subsidies,
according to William Brock, head of the Multilateral Trade Negotiations Coalition of major U.S. corporations.[32] In general, the wealthy industrial powers advocate a mixture of liberalization and protectionism
(such as the Multifiber Arrangement and its extensions, the U.S.-Japan
semiconductor agreement, Voluntary Export Arrangements, etc.), designed for the interests of dominant domestic forces, and particularly
for the TNCs that are to dominate the world economy. Third World
proposals have been ignored.

The effects would be to reduce Third World governments to a po-   26
lice function, with the task of controlling their own working classes
and superfluous population while TNCs gain free access to their resources and control new technology and global investment—and, of
course, are granted the central planning and management functions
denied to governments, which are unacceptable agents because they
might fall under the influence of popular pressures reflecting domestic needs, what is referred to as "ultranationalism" in the internal planning record.

Meanwhile, the United States is establishing a regional bloc that   27
will enable it to compete more effectively with the Japan-led region
and the EC. Canada's role is to provide resources and some services
and skilled labor, as it is absorbed more fully into the U.S. economy
with the reduction of the welfare system, labor rights, and cultural independence. The Canadian Labour Congress reports the loss of over
225,000 jobs in the first two years of the Free Trade Agreement, along
with a wave of takeovers of Canadian-based companies. Mexico,
Central America, and the Caribbean are to supply cheap labor for
assembly plants, as in the maquiladora industries of northern Mexico,
where horrendous working conditions and wages and the absence of

---

[31]General Agreement on Tariffs and Trade. (Ed.)
[32]Quoted in Martin Khor Kok Peng, *The Uruguay Round and Third World Sovereignty* (Penang, 1990), 10. See also Chakravarthi Raghavan, *Recolonization: GATT, the Uruguay Round & the Third World* (Penang, 1990).

environmental controls offer highly profitable conditions for investors. These regions are also to provide export crops and markets for U.S. agribusiness. Mexico and Venezuela are also to provide oil, with U.S. corporations granted the right to take part in production, reversing efforts at domestic control of natural resources.

Such policies are likely to extend to Latin America generally. And, 28 crucially, the United States will attempt to maintain its dominant influence over Gulf oil production and the profits that derive from it. Other economic powers, of course, have their own ideas, and there are many potential sources of conflict. In general, prospects for the South, or for the domestic poor in an American society taking on certain Third World aspects, are not auspicious.

QUESTIONS

1. How does Chomsky explain the collapse of the Soviet Union, and what does he see as the primary effects of the end of the Cold War?

2. What evidence does Chomsky offer that, contrary to the conventional or mainstream view, the United States is actively and purposefully hostile to "meaningful democracy" in other countries? How persuaded are you by this evidence?

3. Chomsky often mimics, in sardonic or mocking fashion, the reasoning or arguments of the position with which he disagrees; for example, in paragraph 14 he writes, "Still another problem is that German-led Europe and Japan have their own interests" and in paragraph 22 that "The elections [in Nicaragua] could not be controlled, and therefore are not an inspiring example of democracy." How would you rephrase these statements to reflect, directly rather than indirectly, Chomsky's own position? Find other examples of this sardonic strategy and rephrase them as the "real" arguments they seem to represent. To what kind of readers or audience do you think this strategy is most likely to appeal? How effective is this strategy for you?

THINKING ABOUT AMERICANS
IN THE "NEW WORLD ORDER"

1.   To compare the encounters between Americans and native artisans in "Assembly Line" and "God and the Cobbler," imagine the businessman Winthrop (from Traven's story) and the international hippie (from Narayan's story) changing places. How do you think Winthrop would deal with the cobbler in India? How would the cobbler respond? How might the hippie deal with the Mexican Indian basket maker, and how would the Indian respond? Rewrite a scene from one or both stories according to this scenario, and share the results with classmates.

2.   After considering the previous question, compare what you think Traven and Narayan are trying to say about these encounters between Westerners and native cultures. How romanticized or idealized do you find the portrayals of the native characters? To what extent do both the businessman Winthrop and the international hippie impose their own values and expectations on their encounters with a native artisan? How might each be said to be exploiting the culture through his encounter, and which kind of exploitation do you think is preferable?

3.   Iyer, in paragraph 57 of his essay, refers to Narayan's short story and offers a specific interpretation. To what extent do you agree with this interpretation, and what evidence from the story can you supply for your view? How might you apply Iyer's interpretation of the Narayan story to his own narrative about Maung-Maung?

4.   Although he set out to discover "the American empire in the East" (paragraph 53), Iyer finds the reality more complex: neither is the First World "invariably corrupting the Third" nor is the Third World always "hustling the First" (paragraph 8). Analyze one or more of the other selections in this chapter according to some of Iyer's criteria along this range. For example, to what extent do you think Iyer might accuse Traven or Chomsky of the "imperial arrogance" that he discusses in paragraph 6?

5.   Glynn and Chomsky discuss many of the same international issues from radically different viewpoints and sets of assumptions, often using the same language in very different ways. What does each of them say about the "new world order"? How does each see "the Soviet threat"? Find and discuss other examples where Glynn and Chomsky use similar phrases for contrary purposes or else use different language to describe the same phenomenon.

6. To what extent do you think Chomsky's views on international relations embody what Glynn calls "increasing social separatism and fragmentation" (paragraph 2), "balkanization," or the postmodern "loss of faith in general truths" (paragraph 19)? To what extent do you think Glynn's essay embodies what Chomsky calls the "new ideological framework [that] is needed for intervention" (paragraph 11) in other countries by the United States, now that the Cold War is over?

7. Use Williams' definition of "Western" to help you compare the portrayals of Westerners or "Western culture" in two or more selections in this chapter, such as those by Nowaira, Narayan, and Iyer.

Exploring Additional Sources

8. In several selections in other chapters, Americans test their relationships with people in other cultures against a backdrop of global change. Analyze some aspect of these relationships in one or more such selections—especially "Venezuela for Visitors" by John Updike (page 415), "Good and Bad" by Lucia Berlin (page 454), "Return to the Land of *Roots*" by Alex Haley (page 476), or "A Moroccan Memoir" by Sarah Streed (page 486)—in conjunction with an essay or story in this unit.

9. In Traven's story, Winthrop "left the beaten track and ventured into regions not especially mentioned, and hence not recommended, by travel agents," so he would seem to exemplify Walker Percy's "Inside Track" solution to recovering sovereignty, as Percy discusses in his essay "Sightseer" (page 419). How do you think Percy would further analyze Winthrop's experience? Alternatively, apply and test Percy's analysis to the experience of the hippie in Narayan's story or Iyer in his encounter with Maung-Maung.

10. Research both scholarly and popular-press accounts of the maquiladora system of factory employment in Mexico, and evaluate its success. Or research a recent international trade agreement, such as the North American Free Trade Agreement (NAFTA) or the General Agreement on Tariffs and Trade (GATT). Evaluate the provisions and measurable effects of the agreement. How fair is it for all countries concerned? Which people in each country does the agreement primarily benefit?

11. Using Narayan's story or Iyer's essay as a springboard, explore some aspect of Americans' spiritual quests in Asia. You might start with books by Peter Matthiesen, John Krich, or Gary Snyder.

12.   Research some aspect of the Balkan conflict, the Gulf War, or another global conflict mentioned in this chapter in which the United States has played a significant role.

13.   Glynn makes a number of historical claims, often based on assumptions of certain values. For example, he suggests that the Romans were "defeated by forces culturally, intellectually, and technologically inferior to them" and that during such periods as Roman rule, the rule of Charlemagne, and the Renaissance "peace reigns, learning spreads and advances, and the arts flourish." Test one of these ideas with evidence from historians, and take a position on the values implied in his claim.

14.   Chomsky and Glynn offer radically different views of the fall of communism, popular movements of ethnic nationalism, and American commitment to democracy around the world, among other controversial issues. Choose one of the incidents explored by Chomsky—such as the elections in Nicaragua, the invasion of Panama, or the Gulf War—and research the role played by the United States. Look up some of the sources cited by Chomsky and find evidence for alternative views to help you formulate your own argument about the U.S. role in the incident.

15.   Chomsky questions the basis of some of the rhetoric that has accompanied United States foreign policy since World War II, terms such as the "Communist threat," "international terrorism," "free trade," and the "new world order." Follow accounts of a current international situation in which the U.S. is involved by watching television news and reading the mainstream press, such as large-circulation newspapers and news magazines, and compare these accounts with those of some alternative media (such as an independent radio station and journals listed in the *Alternative Press Index* in the library). Evaluate the language used to describe American policies in these different sources.

Acknowledgments

Peter S. Adler, "Five Stages of Culture Shock" from "The Transitional Experience: An Alternative View of Culture Shock" in the *Journal of Humanistic Psychology* 15 (1975). Table 5.4. © 1975 by P. S. Adler. Reprinted by permission of Sage Publications, Inc.

Gary Althen, "Stereotypes of Americans" from *American Ways: A Guide for Foreigners in the United States* by Gary Althen. Reprinted by permission of Intercultural Press, Inc.

Maya Angelou, "All God's Children Need Traveling Shoes" from *All God's Children Need Traveling Shoes* by Maya Angelou. © 1986 by Maya Angelou. Reprinted by permission of Random House, Inc.

Gloria Anzaldúa, "How to Tame a Wild Tongue" from *Borderlands/La Frontera: The New Mestiza.* © 1987 by Gloria Anzaldúa. Reprinted with permission from Aunt Lute Books (415) 826-1300.

Margaret Atwood, "Over the Fence in Canada" from "Canada: Through the One-Way Mirror." Reprinted with permission from *The Nation.* © 1986 The Nation Company, Inc.

Eugene August, "Real Men Don't: Anti-Male Bias in English" from *The University of Dayton Review,* 1987. Reprinted by permission of the author.

Richard W. Bailey, "English in the Next Decade" from "English at Its Twilight" in *The State of the Language* edited by Christopher Ricks and Leonard Michaels. © 1990 by The Regents of the University of California. Reprinted by permission of University of California Press.

James Baldwin, "Fifth Avenue, Uptown: A Letter from Harlem" from *Nobody Knows My Name.* © 1961. Copyright renewed 1989. First published in *Esquire,* July 1960. Reprinted with permission of the James Baldwin Estate.

Lucia Berlin, "Good and Bad." © 1993 by Lucia Berlin. Reprinted from *So Long: Stories 1987–1992* with the permission of Black Sparrow Press.

Charles F. Berlitz, "The Etymology of the International Insult." Reprinted by permission of the author. Mr. Berlitz has not been associated with the Berlitz Language School since 1967.

Alice Bloom, "The Natives in the Posters" from "On a Greek Holiday." Reprinted by permission from *The Hudson Review,* Vol. XXXVI, No. 3, Autumn 1983. © 1983 by Alice Bloom.

Robert Bly, "The Soft Male" from *Iron John* (pp. 2–4). © 1990 by Robert Bly. Reprinted by permission of Addison-Wesley Publishing Company, Inc.

Haig Bosmajian, "The Dehumanization of the Indian" from Haig Bosmajian, *The Language of Oppression.* University Press of America. © 1973. Reprinted by permission of the author and publisher.

Paul Bowles, "Alcohol and Cannabis" from KULCHUR 3 (1961). Reprinted by permission of Lita Hornick. "A Distant Episode." © 1950 by Paul Bowles. Reprinted from *Collected Stories 1939–1976* with the permission of Black Sparrow Press.

Susan Brownmiller, "Femininity" from *Femininity* by Susan Brownmiller. © 1984 by Susan Brownmiller. Reprinted by permission of Simon & Schuster, Inc.

Jose Antonia Burciaga, "Chief *Wachuseh*" from *Drink Cultura: Chicanismo* (1993). Reprinted by permission of Joshua Odell Editions.

Robert Olen Butler, "The Trip Back" from *A Good Scent from a Strange Mountain* by Robert Olen Butler. © 1992 by Robert Olen Butler. Reprinted by permission of Henry Holt and Company, Inc.

Juan Cadena, "It's My Country Too" from *Mexican Voices/American Dreams* by Marilyn P. Davis. © 1990 by Marilyn P. Davis. Reprinted by permission of Henry Holt and Company, Inc.

Art Carey, "White Guys" from *The San Jose Mercury News,* June 15, 1993. Reprinted by permission of Tribune Media Services.

Noam Chomsky, "A View from Below" from *Diplomatic History* 16(1): 85–94. Reprinted by permission of Diplomatic History.

Ward Churchill, "The Indian Chant and the Tomahawk Chop" from *Z Magazine,* March 1993. Reprinted by permission of the author.

Sandra Cisneros, "My Name" from *The House on Mango Street.* © by Sandra Cisneros 1984. Published by Vintage Books, a division of Random House, Inc., New York, and in hardcover by Alfred A. Knopf in 1994. Reprinted by permission of Susan Bergholz Literary Services.

Robert Claiborne, "The WASP Stereotype" from *A WASP Stings Back.* © 1974 by Robert Claiborne. All rights reserved. Reprinted by permission of the Estate of Robert Claiborne.

611

Jan Clausen, "My Interesting Condition" from *Out/Look* (Winter 1990). © 1990 by Jan Clausen. Reprinted by permission of the author.

Michelle Cliff, "No Reggae Spoken Here" from "Journey into Speech" in *The Land of Look Behind* by Michelle Cliff. © 1985 by Michelle Cliff. Reprinted by permission of Firebrand Books, Ithaca, New York.

Alexis de Tocqueville, "The Founding of New England," excerpt from *Democracy in America* by Alexis de Tocqueville. Edited by J. P. Mayer and Max Lerner, translated by George Lawrence. English translation © 1965 by Harper & Row, Publishers, Inc. Copyright renewed. Reprinted by permission of HarperCollins Publishers, Inc.

Chitra Divakaruni, "Tourists" from *The House on Via Gombito: Writing by North American Women Abroad.* Edited by Madelon Sprengnether and C. W. Truesdale. Published by New Rivers Press, 1991. Reprinted by permission of New Rivers Press.

Barbara Ehrenreich, "Cultural Baggage" from *The New York Times Magazine*, April 5, 1992. © 1992 by The New York Times Company. Reprinted by permission.

Gretel Ehrlich, "The Western Code" from *The Solace of Open Spaces* by Gretel Ehrlich. © 1985 by Gretel Ehrlich. Used by permission of Viking Penguin, a division of Penguin Books USA Inc.

George P. Elliott, "Among the Dangs" from *Among the Dangs* by George Elliott. Reprinted by permission of Russell & Volkening as agents for the author. © 1961 by George Elliott, renewed in 1989 by George Elliott.

Louise Erdrich, "American Horse." © 1983 by Louise Erdrich. This story, in altered form, is part of Louise Erdrich's novel, *The Bingo Palace* (published by HarperCollins 1994). Reprinted by permission of the author.

Ernesto Galarza, "Colonia Mexicana" from *Barrio Boy* by Ernesto Galarza. © 1971 by University of Notre Dame Press. Used by permission.

Julia Gilden, "Warehouse Tribes: Living in the Cracks of Civilization" from *This World* (1989). Reprinted by permission of the author.

Hal Glatzer, "What We Can Learn from Hawaii" from the *San Francisco Chronicle*, December 29, 1991. © 1994 by Hal Glatzer. Reprinted by permission of the author.

Patrick Glynn, "The Age of Balkanization," reprinted from *Commentary*, July 1993, by permission; all rights reserved.

Herbert Gold, "Jews in a Land without Jews" from *Best Nightmare on Earth: A Life in Haiti.* Published by Prentice Hall. Reprinted by permission of Herbert Gold.

Paul Greenberg, " 'Redneck' Is Not a Dirty Word." © 1988 by Los Angeles Times Syndicate. Reprinted with permission.

Rose Del Castillo Guilbault, "Huppies," excerpt from "This World" in the *San Francisco Chronicle*, January 7, 1990, reprinted by permission of the author.

Alex Haley, "Return to the Land of *Roots*" from *Geo: The Earth Diary.* © 1981 by Alex Haley. Reprinted by permission of John Hawkins & Associates, Inc.

Arturo Islas, "Thanksgiving Border Crossing" from *Migrant Souls* by Arturo Islas. © 1990 by Arturo Islas. By permission of William Morrow & Company, Inc.

Pico Iyer, "Tour of the City: Encounters between East and West" from *Video Night in Kathmandu* by Pico Iyer. © 1988 by Pico Iyer. Reprinted by permission of Alfred A. Knopf, Inc.

June Jordan, "Nobody Mean More to Me than You and the Future Life of Willie Jordan" from *On Call: Political Essays* by June Jordan. Published by South End Press, 1985. Reprinted by permission of the author.

Maxine Hong Kingston, "The Wild Man of the Green Swamp" from *China Men* by Maxine Hong Kingston. © 1980 by Maxine Hong Kingston. Reprinted by permission of Alfred A. Knopf, Inc.

Gary Kinsman, "Masculinity and the Men's Movement" from "Men Loving Men: The Challenge of Gay Liberation" in *Beyond Patriarchy*. Edited by M. Kaufman. Published by OUP, 1987. Reprinted by permission of the author.

Amanda Kovattana, "Ten Good Reasons to Be a Lesbian" from the *Palo Alto Weekly*, February 24, 1993. Reprinted by permission of the Palo Alto Weekly.

Charles Kuralt, "Different Drummers." Reprinted by permission of The Putnam Publishing Group from *On the Road* with Charles Kuralt by Charles Kuralt. © 1985 by CBS Inc.

Robin Lakoff, "Women's Language and Men's Language" excerpt from *Language and a Woman's Place* by Robin Lakoff. © 1975 by Robin Lakoff. Reprinted by permission of HarperCollins Publishers, Inc.

David Leavitt, "Territory" from *Family Dancing* by David Leavitt. © 1983, 1984 by David Leavitt. Reprinted by permission of Alfred A. Knopf, Inc.

Claude Lévi-Strauss, "The Primary Function of Writing" and "The Traveler's Dilemma" from *Tristes Tropiques* by Claude Lévi-Strauss. English translation © 1961 by Hutchinson & Co. (Publishers) Ltd. Copyright renewed. Reprinted by permission of HarperCollins Publishers, Inc.

Rosalie Maggio, "Sexist Language." Reprinted from *The Dictionary of Bias-Free Usage: A Guide to Nondiscriminatory Language* by Rosalie Maggio. © 1991 by Rosalie Maggio. Published by The Oryx Press. Used by permission of Rosalie Maggio and The Oryx Press, 4041 N. Central at Indian School Rd., Phoenix, AZ 85012, (800) 279-ORYX.

Valerie Matsumoto, "Two Deserts" from *Making Waves* by Asian Women United. © 1989 by Asian Women United. Reprinted by permission of Beacon Press.

Cyra McFadden, "In Defense of Gender" from *The New York Times Magazine*, August 2, 1981. © 1981 by The New York Times Company. Reprinted by permission.

Phyllis McGinley, "Suburbia, of Thee I Sing" from *Province of the Heart* by Phyllis McGinley. © 1959 by Phyllis McGinley, renewed 1987 by Patricia Hayden Blake. Used by permission of Viking Penguin, a division of Penguin Books USA Inc.

Stanley Meisler, "Are the French Really Rude?" © 1988, Los Angeles Times Syndicate. Reprinted with permission.

Barbara Mellix, "From Outside, In" originally in *The Georgia Review*, Volume XLI, No. 2 (Summer 1987). © 1987 by The University of Georgia. © 1987 by Barbara Mellix. Reprinted by permission of Barbara Mellix and *The Georgia Review*.

Jane Miller, "Bilingual Advantages" from "How Do You Spell Gujarati, Sir?" in *The State of the Language*. Edited by Christopher Ricks and Leonard Michaels. © 1990 by The Regents of the University of California. Reprinted by permission of University of California Press.

Nicholasa Mohr, "The English Lesson" by Nicholasa Mohr is reprinted with permission from the publisher of *In Nueva York*, Arte Publico Press-University of Houston, 1988.

Mary Morris, "Traveling Alone in Mexico" from *Nothing to Declare* by Mary Morris. © 1988 by Mary Morris. Reprinted by permission of Houghton Mifflin Company. All rights reserved.

Kevin Mullen, "The Irish Cop" from the *San Francisco Chronicle*, March 17, 1991. Reprinted by permission of the author.

Tahira Naqvi, "Thank God for the Jews" from *Imagining America: Stories from the Promised Land*. Edited by Wesley Brown and Amy Ling. Published by Persea Books, 1991. Reprinted by permission of the author.

R. K. Narayan, "God and the Cobbler," from *Malgudi Days* by R. K. Narayan. © 1972, 1975, 1978, 1980, 1981, 1982 by R. K. Narayan. Used by permission of Viking Penguin, a division of Penguin Books USA Inc.

Malgorzata Niezabitowska, "Melting Pot in Lewellen, Nebraska" from "Discovering America" in *National Geographic*, January 1988. Reprinted by permission of the National Geographic Society.

Alleen Pace Nilsen, "Sexism in English: A 1990s Update." © by Alleen Pace Nilsen. English Department, Arizona State University, Tempe, AZ. Reprinted by permission of the author.

Amira Nowaira, "American Foreign Aid" excerpt from "Lost and Found" by Amira Nowaira in *Egyptian Tales and Short Stories of the 1970s and 1980s*. Edited by W. M. Hutchins. © 1987 by The American University in Cairo Press. Published by arrangement with The American University in Cairo Press.

Margaret K. Nydell, "Beliefs and Values, Emotion and Logic in the Arab World" from *Understanding Arabs: A Guide for Westerners* by Margaret K. Nydell. Reprinted by permission of Intercultural Press, Inc.

Simon J. Ortiz, "Acoma and English" from "The Language We Know." Reprinted from *I Tell You Now: Autobiographical Essays by Native American Writers*. Edited by Brian Swann and Arnold Krupat. By permission of the University of Nebraska Press. © 1987 by the University of Nebraska Press.

Grace Paley, "The Loudest Voice" from *The Little Disturbances of Man* by Grace Paley. © 1956, 1957, 1958, 1959 by Grace Paley. Used by permission of Viking Penguin, a division of Penguin Books USA Inc.

Philip L. Pearce, "Fifteen Types of Travelers" from *The Social Psychology of Tourist Behavior*. Edited by Michael Argyle. Published by Pergamon, 1982. Reprinted by permission of the author.

Walker Percy, "Sightseer" Section 1 from "The Loss of the Creature" in *The Message in the Bottle* by Walker Percy. © 1975 by Walker Percy. Reprinted by permission of Farrar, Straus & Giroux, Inc.

Kit Yuen Quan, "The Girl Who Wouldn't Sing." © 1990 by Kit Yuen Quan. From *Making Face, Making Soul/Haciendo Caras: Creative and Critical Perspectives by Feminists of Color*. © 1990 by Gloria Anzaldúa. Reprinted with permission from Aunt Lute Books (415) 826–1300.

William Raspberry, "Black and White" from "What It Means to Be Black" in *The Washington Post* (1985). © 1985, Washington Post Writers Group. Reprinted with permission.

Ishmael Reed, "America: The Multinational Society." Reprinted with the permission of Atheneum Publishers, an imprint of Macmillan Publishing Company from *Writin' Is Fightin': Thirty-Seven Years of Boxing on Paper* by Ishmael Reed. © 1988 by Ishmael Reed.

Nora Reza, "The Errand" from *The House on Via Gombito: Writing by North American Women Abroad.* Edited by Madelon Sprengnether and C. W. Truesdale. Published by New Rivers Press, 1991. Reprinted by permission of New Rivers Press.

Richard Rodriguez, "Public and Private Language" from *Hunger of Memory* by Richard Rodriguez. © 1981 by Richard Rodriguez. Reprinted by permission of Georges Borchardt, Inc. for the author. "Family Values," originally titled "Huck Finn, Dan Quayle and the Value of Acceptance," from the *Los Angeles Times Magazine.* © 1992 by Richard Rodriguez. Reprinted by permission of Georges Borchardt, Inc. for the author.

Renato Rosaldo, "The Lone Ethnographer" from *Culture and Truth* by Renato Rosaldo. © 1989 by Renato Rosaldo. Reprinted by permission of Beacon Press.

Joanna Russ, "When It Changed" from *Again, Dangerous Visions.* Edited by Harlan Ellison. Reprinted by permission of Joanna Russ. © 1972 by Joanna Russ.

Nancy Masterson Sakamoto, "Conversational Ballgames" from *Polite Fictions: Why Japanese and Americans Seem Rude to Each Other* by Nancy Sakamoto and Reiko Naotsuka. © 1982 by Nancy Sakamoto and Reiko Naotsuka. Reprinted by permission of Nancy Masterson Sakamoto.

Arthur M. Schlesinger, Jr., "The Cult of Ethnicity." © 1991 Time Inc. Reprinted by permission.

John Simon, "Good English" from "Why Good English Is Good for You" in *Paradigms Lost* by John Simon. © 1976, 1977, 1978, 1979, 1980 by John Simon. Used by permission of Clarkson N. Potter, Inc.

Kate Simon, "Workers' Utopia: The Bronx," brief excerpt from *A Wider World: Portraits in an Adolescence* by Kate Simon. © 1986 by Kate Simon. Reprinted by permission of HarperCollins Publishers, Inc.

Holly Sklar, "The Upperclass and Mothers N the Hood" from *Z Magazine,* March 1993. © Holly Sklar. Reprinted by permission of the author.

Gary Snyder, "Turtle Island" from *Turtle Island* by Gary Snyder. © 1975 by Gary Snyder. Reprinted by permission of New Directions Publishing Corp.

Shelby Steele, "On Being Black and Middle Class" from *The Content of Our Character.* © 1990 by Shelby Steele. Reprinted with permission of St. Martin's Press.

Judith Stone, "Stereotypes in Orbit." Judith Stone/© 1992 The Walt Disney Co. Reprinted with permission of *Discover Magazine.*

Sarah Streed, "A Moroccan Memoir" from *The House on Via Gombito: Writing by North American Women Abroad.* Edited by Madelon Sprengnether and C. W. Truesdale. Published by New Rivers Press, 1991. Reprinted by permission of New Rivers Press.

Amy Tan, "The Language of Discretion" from *The State of the Language.* Edited by Christopher Ricks and Leonard Michaels. © 1990 by Amy Tan. Reprinted by permission of the author and the Sandra Dijkstra Literary Agency.

Deborah Tannen, "Sex, Lies and Conversation: Why Is It So Hard for Men and Women to Talk to Each Other?" from the *Washington Sunday Post,* 1990. Reprinted by permission of International Creative Management, Inc. © 1990 by Deborah Tannen.

Alexandra Tantranon-Saur, "What's Behind the 'Asian Mask'?" from *Our Asian Inheritance,* Issue #6, 1986. Rational Island Publishers, 719 2nd Avenue North, Seattle, WA 98109. Reprinted by permission of the publisher.

B. Traven, "Assembly Line" from *The Night Visitor and Other Stories* by B. Traven. © 1966 by B. Traven. Reprinted by permission of Hill and Wang, a division of Farrar, Straus & Giroux, Inc.

John Updike, "Venezuela for Visitors" from *Hugging the Shore* by John Updike. © 1983 by John Updike. Reprinted by permission of Alfred A. Knopf, Inc.

Michael Ventura, "Talkin' America 2." © 1990 by Michael Ventura. This article first appeared as one of the author's "Letters at 3 a.m." in the *L.A. Weekly,* November 16, 1990. Reprinted by permission of the author.

Alice Walker, "Definition of a Womanist" from *In Search of Our Mothers' Gardens: Womanist Prose.* © 1983 by Alice Walker. Reprinted by permission of Harcourt Brace & Company.

Edmund White, "Sexual Culture" from *The Burning Library* by Edmund White. This article was originally published in *Vanity Fair*. © 1994 by Edmund White. Reprinted by permission of Alfred A. Knopf.

Raymond Williams, "Dialect," "Ethnic," "Native," and "Western" from *Keywords: A Vocabulary of Culture and Society*, by Raymond Williams. Revised Edition. © 1976, 1983 by Raymond Williams. Reprinted by permission of Oxford University Press, Inc. and M. Williams.

Rhetorical Index

Cause/Effect Analysis

Classification/Division

Comparison/Contrast

Definition

Process Analysis

INDEX OF AUTHORS AND TITLES